Land Law

CORE TEXT SERIES

Land Law

Fifth Edition

KEVIN GRAY LLD DCL, FBA

Of the Middle Temple, Barrister
Fellow of Trinity College, Cambridge
Professor of Law, University of Cambridge

SUSAN FRANCIS GRAY MA

Solicitor of the Supreme Court
Sometime Assistant Land Registrar, HM Land Registry, and
Senior Lecturer in Law, University of Greenwich

Series editor

NICOLA PADFIELD

Fitzwilliam College, Cambridge

OXFORD
UNIVERSITY PRESS

OXFORD
UNIVERSITY PRESS

Great Clarendon Street, Oxford OX2 6DP

Oxford University Press is a department of the University of Oxford.
It furthers the University's objective of excellence in research, scholarship,
and education by publishing worldwide in

Oxford New York

Auckland Cape Town Dar es Salaam Hong Kong Karachi
Kuala Lumpur Madrid Melbourne Mexico City Nairobi
New Delhi Shanghai Taipei Toronto

With offices in

Argentina Austria Brazil Chile Czech Republic France Greece
Guatemala Hungary Italy Japan Poland Portugal Singapore
South Korea Switzerland Thailand Turkey Ukraine Vietnam

Oxford is a registered trade mark of Oxford University Press
in the UK and in certain other countries

Published in the United States
by Oxford University Press Inc., New York

British Library Cataloguing in Publication Data

Data available

Library of Congress Cataloging in Publication Data

Data available

Typeset by Newgen Imaging Systems (P) Limited, Chennai, India
Printed in Great Britain
on acid-free paper by
Ashford Colour Press Ltd., Gosport, Hampshire

ISBN 978–0–19–921378–8

10 9 8 7 6 5 4 3 2

Preface

This book seeks both to inform and to challenge. We aim to provide not only a succinct introduction to the subject of land law, but also a thoughtful and critical account of the inner dynamic of land and the legal issues which it generates. The book comprises a companion volume to our *Elements of Land Law* (also published by Oxford University Press) and follows, chapter by chapter, the coverage which is contained in that rather longer work.

The importance of land law can scarcely be overestimated, for it has something to say about almost every aspect of our daily lives. Moreover, as Lord Browne-Wilkinson once observed, a fundamental fact about real property is that 'there is a defined and limited supply of the commodity' (*Linden Gardens Trust Ltd v Lenesta Sludge Disposals Ltd* (1994)). Yet land law is, in many ways, a closed system of logic—an odd sort of jigsaw puzzle—and the difficulty for the student is that this particular jigsaw puzzle must be tackled without the benefit of any prior image of the completed task. There is no pictorial guide on the lid of the box. In terms of a different metaphor, the venture facing the student is a journey into *terra incognita*—accompanied by the uncomfortable realisation that it would all be so much easier if one only knew at the beginning what one comes to know by the end. It is also the case that, unlike explorations of, say, the law of contract or tort (which could be begun from almost any starting point and treated in virtually any order), the student's journey through land law can be undertaken only in carefully planned incremental stages, each building upon the experience and expertise acquired in the last.

The nature of the subject is the torment of the teacher. How can one impart knowledge of a subject where truth comes in layered and interdependent increments, but in which genuine understanding of the integrated whole and of the relationship between its component parts often arrives only towards the end of the exercise? In this book we adopt two pedagogic techniques which, it is hoped, will be of aid to the traveller across the terrain of land law. First, we try, at an early stage (in Chapter 2) to provide a 'bird's eye view'—an anticipatory overview in vastly simplified form—of the essential landscape of land law, so that the student has some incipient idea of where the journey is leading. It is important only that the student should, at this stage, acquire some rough sense of orientation: the preliminary overview will be amplified and intensified at many later points in the book.

Second, we have attempted to structure each chapter in the book so as to provide a pathway of sequential steps which lead logically (and, we hope, fairly painlessly) from one concept to another. An extensive cross-referencing system is available to throw the reader back, if necessary, to the location where any particular concept was first met. In these ways, reverting to our earlier metaphor, we trust that—sooner rather than later—most of the pieces of the jigsaw puzzle of land law will fit together to form an integrated picture of the subject's rich and complex expanse.

One other matter bulks large for the traveller in foreign parts—the problem of language. It often seems that, at the beginning of the land law journey, the student walks straight into a very solid feature of the built environment—a brick wall of apparently incomprehensible terminology, where each new concept is explicable only in terms of some other equally unfamiliar concept. Again, we try to ease the reader into some understanding of the conceptual world of the land lawyer, using the frequent and interlinked repetition of ideas and phrases as an aid to transparency of meaning. At the heart of the book is the thesis that law and language are necessarily and insidiously interdependent; and the lawyer's task is always to use language with scrupulous care and integrity. In the context of realty the law embodies both a grammatical structure and an essential vocabulary which the student must master before engaging fluently in the *language* of land. It is our hope that this book will enable the reader to relax into a conversational familiarity with land law which inspires further exploration of the subject.

Today's student confronts the subject of land law, of course, at a momentous point in its historical development. Throughout most of the twentieth century the real property law of England and Wales was dominated by a vast corpus of legislation which emerged from nineteenth-century origins and was finalised in the series of statutes which came into effect on 1 January 1926. Chief amongst these were the Law of Property Act 1925, the Settled Land Act 1925, and the Trustee Act 1925, with the Land Registration Act 1925 tacked on as an ill-drafted piece of legislation relating to a little used form of title registration. It is also worth remembering that the huge majority of the population were unaffected by the advent of the 1925 property legislation. At that time some 90 per cent of all dwellings were privately rented and therefore, so far as their occupiers were concerned, fell almost completely outside the scope of the statutory 'code' relating to property.

How different things are today. Britain has been converted into a 'home-owning democracy' in which 70 per cent of all residential property is now occupied by freehold owners. Many of the structural features of twentieth-century land law have been removed, sidelined or transformed beyond recognition. The 1925 legislation is beginning to look, in many respects, like a curious form of legal history.

Unregistered land law, which formed the core of the 1925 legislation, is virtually a thing of the past. Indeed, the last 10 years of change have fundamentally altered English land law (by which is meant, of course, the law of England *and Wales*). A glance at any recent compilation of property law statutes immediately reveals that, during this period, there has been an explosion of legislation on trusts of land and the responsibilities of trustees, the enforcement of landlord and tenant covenants, the rights of neighbours, the conduct of mortgage business, the proliferation of leasehold enfranchisement, the introduction of commonhold ownership, and the statutory deflection of contractual benefit to new landowners not privy to the contractual bargain. Modern land law is also being reshaped by the impact of the Human Rights Act 1998, European Union law and the law of environmental regulation. Far-reaching reformulations of the law of easements and the codes regulating domestic lettings are now imminent or well within view. Suddenly the land law of the immediately foreseeable future appears markedly different from the law we have known in the past—scarcely the picture of stasis which many associate with the subject.

Above and beyond all this, we have now entered an era of almost universal registration of title and must prepare rapidly for the brave new world of electronic conveyancing. The enactment of the Land Registration Act 2002 has altered the legal landscape in a hugely significant way. The impact on the structure of this book is considerable and, in our treatment, we have distinguished between the *definitional* and *operational* aspects of the various land entitlements with which we are concerned. Chapters 7–10 outline the definitional characteristics of a range of interests in land, leaving their operational (or practical) consequences to be explored in Chapters 11–15. This organisational strategy is intended to mirror the shape of the future as ordained by the Land Registration Act 2002. The central feature of this statute involves the substantive registration of title to certain key estates in land (each under a unique title number), the effect being to confirm these entitlements as *legal* estates. These estates—foremost amongst them the fee simple estate and certain long terms of years—we have therefore identified in some detail in Chapter 7, indicating their essential characteristics and modes of creation. The title to other kinds of estate in land (such as easements and mortgages) can also be registered, not under their own independent title number but by reference to existing substantively registered titles. On registration such estates also rank as *legal* estates and in Chapter 8 we again perform the definitional task of outlining their characteristics and modes of creation. Chapters 9 and 10 then mop up the extensive range of other entitlements in land (such as estate contracts, various charges, restrictive covenants and trust interests), which remain *equitable* only and whose existence is merely *noted* or otherwise flagged up on existing substantively registered titles. The functional dimension of all these entitlements is then described in the remaining chapters of the book, with particular attention being devoted in Chapter 12 to the impact of dealings with substantively registered estates—the primary dynamic of modern land law.

But a study of land law is not merely about gaining a perspective on external legal change. Nor is it just about developing a capacity for the manipulation of complex legal ideas. It is not even simply a matter—important though this is—of generating a lifetime's concern with the utilisation of the vital resource of land. A large part of the objective of the land law teacher is actually to provoke *evaluative reflection* on the part of the student—to keep alive the spirit of sceptical inquiry with which each is deemed to begin the course—to inculcate a collective culture of critical realism about the law. Ultimately the educational focus comes to bear upon those internal, latent, barely conscious assumptions and perceptions which each of us bring to the study of land law. The questions (and the answers) lie not outside, but inside, ourselves. Indeed, we all start our exploration of land law, in one sense, as fully fledged experts on property. We have all spent at least two decades—some of us perhaps many more—engaged in the constant, instinctive classification of the things and opportunities of the external world as owned either by ourselves or by somebody else.

Although the primary emphasis of this book falls on an exposition and analysis of the conceptual structure of English land law, it is inevitable that certain wider questions are prompted by this concentration on realty. These questions relate to a number of subliminal themes in this book which help to open up our understanding of other areas of property law and of the phenomenon of property in general. Cautious and sensitive introspection by the land law student will begin to reveal answers to some of the following issues:

(1) Are you, by nature, a 'property absolutist' or a 'property relativist' (see e.g. *R v Martin (Anthony)* (2003), **3.8**; *Jaggard v Sawyer* (1995), **3.9, 13.19**)? Do you believe, in other words, that ownership of land is unqualified, sacrosanct, and inviolable? Or are you more receptive to the view that property rights in land are constantly redefined by social context and community-oriented obligation?

(2) Should the principal objective of land law be certainty of entitlement or fairness of outcome (see e.g. *Midland Bank Trust Co Ltd v Green* (1981), **12.14, 12.35**)? Is it, in effect, 'more important that the applicable rule of law be settled than that it be settled right' (see *Burnet v Coronado Oil and Gas Co* (1932) per Justice Brandeis)?

(3) Is property in land based on socially constituted fact or on artificially defined jural entitlement (see e.g. *JA Pye (Oxford) Ltd v Graham* (2003), **6.11**)? Does the organic reality of what actually happens on the ground eclipse the dusty record of 'words upon parchment' (**6.1**) or even the digital record of an impersonal register of title?

(4) Should land law reflect a culture of *exclusion* (driven by motivations of fear and insecurity) or a culture of *inclusion* (driven by motivations of social justice and equal opportunity)? The 'exclusion question' mirrors—indeed epitomises—one of the more profound problems of social philosophy with which we have to engage during the foreseeable future (see e.g. *CIN Properties Ltd v Rawlins* (1995), **4.5**).

(5) What is 'property' anyway?

This final question—which encapsulates all the other questions just posed—places an intense spotlight on the precise content of one of our oldest and most significant human institutions. The enduringly tantalising query for property scholars across the world is whether, if the holy grail of property is ever discovered, there will actually be anything in it. For some, the ultimate fact about property is that it does not really exist—it is mere illusion (see *Yanner v Eaton* (1999), **2.1**)—an empty space or mirage containing only thin air. The phenomenon which we conceptualise as 'property' may connote not an objective or indefeasible entitlement of any kind at all, but merely a variable register of the day-to-day outcomes produced by the constant interplay of power-relationships in society.

The student of land law will not necessarily succeed in solving the riddle of property in one short course—it has beguiled thinkers for centuries—but land law throws up a number of fascinating clues in pursuit of the mystery. A major achievement for the student will be the realisation that 'property' is not really quite what he or she had previously been led to believe. Indeed, one of the fortuitous effects of the current transformation of English land law—particularly in view of the pervasive impact of human rights standards—is that the modern student of the subject has arrived just in time to witness an experimental process predicted by Professor CB Macpherson some three decades ago. Macpherson thought it likely, if not inevitable, that the idea of property would gradually be broadened to include a 'right to a kind of society or set of power relations which will enable the individual to live a fully human life' (see Macpherson, 'Capitalism and the Changing Concept of Property', in E Kamenka and RS Neale (eds), *Feudalism, Capitalism and Beyond* (1975), p. 120). The land law students of this generation will, in their own lifetime, have a unique opportunity to observe whether this conceptual evolution is ever carried through to completion.

One index of the ever-changing nature of modern land law is that, even as we write, we await developments which may alter the face of some of the land law that we currently teach. The Grand Chamber of the European Court of Human Rights will soon hand down its decision in *JA Pye (Oxford) Ltd v United Kingdom*, a ruling which will help to clarify the status of the adverse possession principle in English law (**6.5**). The House of Lords has yet to deliver judgment in *Stack v Dowden* (**10.15–10.16**), its first appeal on trusts of the family home in almost two decades. Further afield we are still assimilating the impact of a ruling of the United States Supreme Court (see *Kelo v City of New London* (**13.24**)), which suggested that all property rules tend ultimately to collapse into liability rules (**3.9, 13.19**). If this is so, the effect is to confirm privately owned assets as simply a mush of social and economic resource to be reallocated at will by the state. We shall, of course, try to incorporate some reference to imminent developments if they appear in time,* but the point is amply made that nowadays even land law has a certain global quality. Across a number of jurisdictions the law of realty generates problems of a common nature—and very often throws up similar solutions. Today, as citizens of the world, we must learn our land law not just at home, but also abroad.

In bringing the present edition to completion, we have been helped and encouraged by a number of friends and colleagues. The usual suspects know exactly who they are. We also gratefully acknowledge the help given by the editorial staff of Oxford University Press, not least in sparing us any involvement in the preparation of lists and tables. Our constant thanks are due, of course, to the staff of the Squire Law Library in Cambridge (and in particular Lesley Dingle, David Wills and Peter Zawada) and to Jules Winterton, Librarian of the Institute of Advanced Legal Studies in the University of London. Ultimately, as always, our greatest debt is to those who persevered in teaching *us* land law, Peter Cook, Paul Fairest and Graham Tooke. Together they imparted an enthusiasm for the order and value of land law which is ineradicable and which we have tried to pass on to others.

Kevin Gray
Susan Francis Gray
March 2007

---

* The outcome of the appeal in *Stack v Dowden* emerged on 25 April 2007 ([2007] UKHL 17; [2007] 2 WLR 831) and we have managed to incorporate references to this ruling at proof stage.

Contents

Table of cases

Essential Cases for detailed reading are indicated in **bold**

Table of statutes

Abbreviations

Legislation:

AEA 1925	Administration of Estates Act 1925
AHA 1986	Agricultural Holdings Act 1986
AJA 1970	Administration of Justice Act 1970
AJA 1973	Administration of Justice Act 1973
ANLA 1992	Access to Neighbouring Land Act 1992
ASBA 2003	Anti-social Behaviour Act 2003
CALRA 2002	Commonhold and Leasehold Reform Act 2002
C(RTP)A 1999	Contracts (Rights of Third Parties) Act 1999
CCA 1974	Consumer Credit Act 1974
CCA 1984	County Courts Act 1984
CJAPOA 1994	Criminal Justice and Public Order Act 1994
CLA 1977	Criminal Law Act 1977
CLPA 1852	Common Law Procedure Act 1852
COA 1979	Charging Orders Act 1979
CPR	Civil Procedure Rules 1998 (SI 1998/3132)
CROWA 2000	Countryside and Rights of Way Act 2000
CTA 1987	Channel Tunnel Act 1987
ECHR	European Convention for the Protection of Human Rights and Fundamental Freedoms
EPA 1990	Environmental Protection Act 1990
FLA 1996	Family Law Act 1996
FSAMA 2000	Financial Services and Markets Act 2000
HA 1985	Housing Act 1985
HA 1988	Housing Act 1988
HA 1996	Housing Act 1996
HA 2004	Housing Act 2004
HRA 1998	Human Rights Act 1998

IA 1986	Insolvency Act 1986
L&TA 1927	Landlord and Tenant Act 1927
L&TA 1954	Landlord and Tenant Act 1954
L&TA 1985	Landlord and Tenant Act 1985
L&TA 1987	Landlord and Tenant Act 1987
L&TA 1988	Landlord and Tenant Act 1988
L&T(C)A 1995	Landlord and Tenant (Covenants) Act 1995
LA 1980	Limitation Act 1980
LCA 1925	Land Charges Act 1925
LCA 1972	Land Charges Act 1972
LPA 1925	Law of Property Act 1925
LPA 1969	Law of Property Act 1969
LP(MP)A 1989	Law of Property (Miscellaneous Provisions) Act 1989
LP(R)A 1938	Leasehold Property (Repairs) Act 1938
LRA 1925	Land Registration Act 1925
LRA 1967	Leasehold Reform Act 1967
LRA 2002	Land Registration Act 2002
LRH&UDA 1993	Leasehold Reform, Housing and Urban Development Act 1993
LRR 2003	Land Registration Rules 2003 (SI 2003/1417)
MHA 1983	Matrimonial Homes Act 1983
PA 1832	Prescription Act 1832
PACPA 2004	Planning and Compulsory Purchase Act 2004
PEA 1977	Protection from Eviction Act 1977
RA 1977	Rent Act 1977
SCA 1981	Supreme Court Act 1981
SLA 1925	Settled Land Act 1925
T&CPA 1990	Town and Country Planning Act 1990
TA 1925	Trustee Act 1925
TA 1996	Treasure Act 1996
TA 2000	Trustee Act 2000
TOLATA 1996	Trusts of Land and Appointment of Trustees Act 1996
UCTA 1977	Unfair Contract Terms Act 1977

Law Commission Reports:

Law Com No 127   *Transfer of Land: The Law of Positive and Restrictive Covenants* (January 1984)

Law Com No 142   *Codification of the Law of Landlord and Tenant: Forfeiture of Tenancies* (March 1985)

Law Com No 158   *Property Law: Third Report on Land Registration* (March 1987)

Law Com No 174   *Landlord and Tenant: Privity of Contract and Estate* (November 1988)

Law Com No 188   *Transfer of Land: Overreaching: Beneficiaries in Occupation* (December 1989)

Law Com No 194   *Landlord and Tenant: Distress for Rent* (February 1991)

Law Com No 201   *Transfer of Land: Obsolete Restrictive Covenants* (July 1991)

Law Com No 221   *Landlord and Tenant Law: Termination of Tenancies Bill* (February 1994)

Law Com No 238   *Landlord and Tenant: Responsibility for State and Condition of Property* (March 1996)

Law Com No 254   *Land Registration for the Twenty-First Century: A Consultative Document* (September 1998)

Law Com No 270   *Limitation of Actions* (July 2001)

Law Com No 271   *Land Registration for the Twenty-First Century: A Conveyancing Revolution* (July 2001)

Law Com No 284   *Renting Homes* (November 2003)

Law Com No 297   *Renting Homes: The Final Report* (May 2006)

Law Com No 303   *Termination of Tenancies for Tenant Default* (October 2006)

Other:

Bl Comm   W Blackstone, *Commentaries on the Laws of England* (1st edn, London 1765–1769)

1

Land

SUMMARY

Land is a phenomenon of many dimensions in English law. In this chapter we outline:

- the three-dimensional definition of land as a *physical reality*;

- the fourth, more conceptual, dimension added by the development of the *doctrine of estates*; and

- the extra dimension implicit in the categorisation of land rights as either legal or equitable.

The construction of a legal regime for land

1.1 Since land provides the physical base for all human activity, there is no moment of any day in which we lie beyond the pervasive reach of land law. The law of land has something to say to us, whether we are relaxing in our homes or sitting in a lecture theatre, cooking a meal in a bed-sit or engaging in a spot of D-I-Y, simply walking in the countryside or rushing along a footpath to catch a bus for a shopping expedition to the local mall. Our presence in each of these locations has a distinct significance for the land lawyer, for land law constantly describes our jural status in relation to land and its other users. Largely unnoticed, land law provides a running commentary on every single action of every day. Not only does it supplement or reinforce our instinctive labelling of the things of the external world as *meum* and *tuum*; it also plays a deeply instrumental role in regulating the efficient social and economic use of all land resources.

— *The definition of 'land'* The construction of a coherent legal regime for land has not been a simple or instant process. The evolution of our present system of land law has taken most of a millennium, resulting in the remarkable corpus of legislation found largely in the property statutes of 1925, as now supplemented by the Land Registration Act 2002 and the Commonhold and Leasehold Reform Act 2002. But what precisely is *land*? More relevantly for lawyers within this juris-diction, what exactly constitutes the definition of *land* in England and Wales? Our first footfall upon the terrain of land law inevitably involves a consideration of the nature and scope of the territory which is to be our concern. As will rapidly emerge, the legal concept of land includes several surprising components, together with some features which, even today, remain remarkably pragmatic or uncertain in their operation.

— *The multiple dimensions of land* When you look at landscape, whether urban or rural, what do you see? The common lawyer's understanding of land still hovers ambivalently between a purely material conception of the physical stuff of land and a more cerebral image of land as comprising a coordinated set of abstract entitle-ments (**1.4, 2.16**). This underlying tension between the *physical* and the *con-ceptual* has imparted a multi-dimensional complexity to the term 'land'. The first three dimensions of land—as a solid reality—are perfectly consistent with the pragmatic empiricism which characterises so much of our land law (**1.2–1.13**). To these crudely factual dimensions the common law then added a fourth, more subtle, dimension of *time* in the form of the *doctrine of estates* (**1.15**). A fifth dimension of land emerged later with the recognition that these notional estates in land could be held either *at law* or *in equity*—a quantum leap of imagination which made possible the evolution of the juristic device of the trust (**1.23–1.26**).

The first two dimensions of land

1.2 One attempt at a definition of land might reasonably focus upon the way in which the surface area of England and Wales has been meticulously mapped by the Ordnance Survey, a task which began in 1791 and continues to this day. The mapping tools may have changed from theodolite and chain to digital imaging by satellite, but the product remains the same—a remarkably detailed two-dimensional representation of the defining contours, features, and limits of the jurisdiction, essential to the activities of land registrars, conveyancers, surveyors, and ramblers alike. Yet even this attempt at definition remains, for many reasons, incomplete. The land comprised within England and Wales probably includes territory beyond the low water mark at the coastline. The sea bed underlying an encircling three-mile belt of territorial waters constitutes part of England and Wales. Moreover, in an act of territorial expansion unknown since England occupied Normandy in the 15th century, the Channel Tunnel Act 1987 provides that, even outside the three-mile limit, the space of the Channel Tunnel and its immediately surrounding subsoil extending to the mid-point of the English Channel are 'incorporated into England' and form part of the county of Kent (CTA 1987, s 10(1)). So, all other complications apart, the definition of land in English law must somehow cope with the fact that 'land' includes 'land covered with water' (see e.g. CTA 1987, s 49(1); LRA 2002, s 132(1)).

But this is far from being the only definitional difficulty. We may well speak of leasing 50,000 square feet of office space or of transferring a 10 hectare field, but the truth is, of course, that the physical world is *three-dimensional* in nature. Any elucidation of the concept of land must grapple with the quantification of not merely two, but three, measures of territorial or jurisdictional control.

Statutory definitions of 'land'

1.3 Blackstone warned us more than two centuries ago that 'land' is 'a word of a very extensive signification' (*Commentaries on the Laws of England* (1766), vol II, p 16). Something of its amplitude is captured in a number of statutory definitions which, although far from uniform or consistent, point to the surprisingly multi-faceted understanding of the term 'land' in English law. In the primary statute contained within the corpus of 1925 legislation, 'land' is described as including

> land of any tenure, and mines and minerals, whether or not held apart from the surface, buildings or parts of buildings (whether the division is horizontal, vertical or made in any other way) and other corporeal hereditaments; also a manor, an advowson, and a rent and other incorporeal hereditaments, and an easement, right, privilege, or benefit in, over, or derived from land (Law of Property Act 1925, s 205(1)(ix)).

This cumbersome definition is echoed, with variations, in many other interpretation sections (see e.g. Land Registration Act 2002, s 132(1); Land Charges Act 1972, s 17(1); Trusts of Land and Appointment of Trustees Act 1996, s 23(2)). The statutory formulation, despite its unsatisfactorily circular nature, serves to convey some incipient idea of the breadth of the meaning of land, although it has to be said that the draftsmen of the 1925 legislation were certainly no devotees of a plain language style of prose construction. One of the problems faced early in any land law course is the need to decode the seeming obfuscations—the gobbledegook—of much statute law.

Corporeal hereditaments

1.4 The first thing to unscramble from the common elements in the statutory definitions of 'land' is that 'land' comprises both 'corporeal' and 'incorporeal' components (or 'hereditaments'). In broad terms *corporeal hereditaments* refer to the physical and tangible characteristics of land, whilst *incorporeal hereditaments* refer to certain intangible rights which may be enjoyed over or in respect of land (**1.14**). (Here again we find a deep structural indeterminacy as to whether 'land' is essentially a matter of physical fact or of abstract entitlement.) In essence corporeal hereditaments are constituted by those 'substantial and permanent objects' (*Bl Comm*, vol II, p 17) which are integral to, or closely connected with, immovable property. Corporeal hereditaments thus include not merely the clods of earth which make up the surface layer of land (or *solum*), but also all physical things which are attached to or are inherent in the ground. Subject to a few very specific exceptions, corporeal hereditaments extend to cover such things as buildings, trees, subjacent minerals, and even some portion of the superjacent airspace. Together corporeal and incorporeal hereditaments are sometimes known as 'realty'—to distinguish them from 'personalty' (i.e. *personal* or *movable* property).

The third dimension of land

1.5 A recurring theme in this area is the resort to curious phrases of medieval Latin in the attempt to explain the concept of land. One such phrase recites that *cuius est solum eius est usque ad coelum et ad inferos* (the person who owns the land owns everything reaching up to the very heavens and down to the depths of the earth). This maxim, although it appears to conjure up an image of land as having an almost infinitely three-dimensional quality, has little definitional value and provides only a crude approximation of the truth. The idea that land can ever comprise a virtually limitless cubic domain lacks that certain practical realism which characterises a large part of the common law perspective on property (see *Comr for Railways et al v Valuer-General* (1974) per Lord Wilberforce), and the maxim has been dismissed in recent times as nothing more than a colourful phrase. In any event, the perception that land connotes an indefinitely extended quantum of territorial space would lead to 'the absurdity of a trespass at common law being committed by a satellite every time it passes over a suburban garden' (*Bernstein v Skyviews & General Ltd* (1978) per Griffiths J).

It remains the case, however, that land must have at least *some* three-dimensional significance: a transfer of a mere two-dimensional plot of land would have little meaning and even less utility. So much is already conceded by the standard statutory definitions of 'land' which recognise that land may be 'held apart from the surface' and that it may be subject to horizontal division (**1.3**). In the result, it is quite clear that the land comprised within any specified map coordinates must include at least limited portions of the *subjacent* and *superjacent* domains. It follows moreover that, to this extent, titles to land can be stratified and vested in various owners simultaneously, each holding a different portion or stratum of cubic space either below or above the surface layer of the ground. It is in precisely this way that the occupiers of, say, different floors in a block of flats may each claim a leasehold estate (**7.10**) or freehold title by way of 'commonhold' (**7.41**) in their respective flats.

Subterranean zones

1.6 English law recognises that the land to which a landowner is entitled includes at least some quantum of the underlying soil or void encapsulated within the two-dimensional coordinates of his surface boundaries. The keen gardener is doing no more than explore the third dimension of his estate; the homeowner may install a swimming pool in her own back garden. But beware the neighbour who builds hard up on a mutual boundary, for his foundations may well trespass into the subsoil on the wrong side of that boundary (see e.g. *ER Ives Investment Ltd v High* (1967), **10.21, 12.46**, although compare Party Wall etc Act 1996, s 1(4)–(7), **8.20**).

— *Minerals* Minerals and other inorganic substances present in the ground (e.g. stone, gravel, sand, and china clay) comprise part of the realty and are normally annexed to the estate of the surface landowner.

— *Hidden objects* The person in lawful possession of the land (whether as freeholder or leaseholder) has, in respect of all objects concealed or embedded *within* the ground, a right superior to that of any finder who locates a previously unknown item. The finder's act of excavation is almost inevitably an act of trespass to the soil, the object in question being treated as 'an integral part of the realty as against all but the true owner' (*Parker v British Airways Board* (1982) per Donaldson LJ).

> *Waverley BC v Fletcher* (1996) F, with the aid of a metal detector, discovered a medieval brooch (which was not treasure trove) nine inches below the surface of a public park owned and maintained by WBC. F reported his find, but the Court of Appeal held WBC to have the better title as against a mere finder whose actions in the 'digging and removal of property in the land' were, in the absence of specific authority, those of a trespasser.

Note that in relation to objects found not embedded within, but resting upon, land, the rule is different. For instance, the occupier of a building has rights superior to those of a finder 'if, but only if, before the chattel is found, he has manifested an intention to exercise control over the building and the things which may be upon it or in it' (see *Parker v British Airways Board* (1982), where a gold bracelet was successfully claimed by a passenger who found it on the floor of an executive lounge at Heathrow Airport).

— *Special exceptions to the surface owner's rights* In English law there exist certain exceptions from the scope of the land which may be claimed by the surface owner. The ownership of all unworked coal is vested by statute in the Coal Authority (Coal Industry Act 1994, ss 1(1), 7(3)) and all rights in petroleum (inclusive of mineral oil and natural gas) existing in its natural condition in strata are vested in the crown (Petroleum Act 1998, ss 1(a), 2(1)). The crown has a prerogatival right to mines of gold and silver. The old law of treasure trove was abolished by the Treasure Act 1996, but this statute introduced a new, and wider, definition of 'treasure' which, when found, will normally vest in the crown (Treasure Act 1996, s 4(1)). 'Treasure' comprises objects (other than single coins) at least 300 years old bearing 10 per cent precious metal; finds of ten or more coins of any metal which are at least 300 years old; and other designated objects which are at least 200 years old (TA 1996, s 1(1)). The purpose of the Act is clearly to assist the preservation of a broad category of antiquities as part of the national heritage. It becomes, accordingly, a criminal offence to fail to report a relevant find within 14 days (TA 1996, s 8), although a reward out of public funds is normally paid on an ex gratia basis to those who declare their find.

— *Strata titles* Within the limits of practicality, the landowner can transfer away separate estates in subjacent strata, with the result that others may end up owning a freehold or leasehold estate (**1.18–1.20**) in an underground cavern or cellar or layer of minerals (see *Grigsby v Melville* (1974)). Alternatively, the surface owner may dispose of the surface layer, retaining title to only the subjacent soil, as for instance in the case of land which is taken over by a statutory highway authority and maintained thereafter as a public highway. Here the highway authority normally takes a freehold in the surface of the highway and in so much of the subjacent land and superjacent airspace as is required for the discharge of its statutory duties (Highways Act 1980, s 263).

Superjacent space

1.7 The definition of 'land' must also comprise some sector of the airspace above ground level, since the surface owner would otherwise constitute a trespasser in that airspace as soon as he sets foot on his own land. As Justice William Douglas once said in the Supreme Court of the United States, the landowner must have 'exclusive control of the immediate reaches of the enveloping atmosphere' since otherwise 'buildings could not be erected, trees could not be planted, and even fences could not be run' (*United States v Causby* (1946)). The common law thus draws a pragmatic distinction between two different strata of airspace.

— *The lower stratum* The lower stratum of airspace comprises that portion of the immediately superjacent airspace whose effective control is necessary for the landowner's reasonable enjoyment of his land at ground level. This stratum is unlikely in most cases to extend beyond an altitude of much more than 150 or 200 metres above roof level, this being roughly the minimum permissible distance for normal overflight by any aircraft (see Rules of the Air Regulations 1996 (SI 1996/1393), Sch 1, r 5(2), as amended by SI 2005/1110).

• *Lateral invasion* It follows that any lateral invasion of lower stratum airspace—however trivial—is prima facie actionable in trespass (and possibly in nuisance). Frequent causes of wrongful intrusion include the overhanging branches of a neighbour's tree (*Lemmon v Webb* (1895)), his ever so slightly bulging flank wall (*Cooperative Wholesale Society Ltd v British Railways Board* (1995)), and his projecting eaves or advertising signs (*Kelsen v Imperial Tobacco Co (of Great Britain and Ireland) Ltd* (1957)). Of such stuff is the endless saga of neighbour disputes. Another prime example is provided by that most frequent of urban trespassers, the jib of the sky crane (see e.g. *Anchor Brewhouse Developments Ltd v Berkley House (Docklands Developments) Ltd* (1987)).

• *Transfers of thin air* It also follows that, within the lower stratum of airspace, a three-dimensional quantum of airspace, whether or not separate from the physical solum, can exist as an independent unit of real property, thereby neatly belying any assumption that land is necessarily a tangible resource. Such airspace is capable of transfer or lease (*Reilly v Booth* (1890)) or compulsory purchase (compare *Taylor v North West Water* (1995)). The commerciability of airspace is particularly useful not only for the purpose of down-town developments involving the construction of new buildings or walkways suspended above street level, but also for the lease of motorway bridges as service station cafeterias.

— *The higher stratum* It is clear that the maxim *cuius est solum* ... (**1.5**) has no relevance at all to the higher stratum of airspace which lies beyond any reasonable possibility of purposeful use by the landowner below. Above the limited zone of lower stratum airspace, the skies are alike free for the hang-glider (see *Staden v Tarjanyi* (1980)) and the overflying aircraft engaged in innocent passage (see Civil Aviation Act 1982, s 76(1)).

Bernstein v Skyviews & General Ltd (1978) B claimed trespass by reason of S & G's overflight over B's home for the purpose of commercial aerial photography. Griffiths J rejected the claim on the ground that a landowner's rights in upper stratum airspace are restricted to 'such height as is necessary for the ordinary use and enjoyment of his land and the structures upon it'. Above this height the landowner 'has no greater rights in the air space than any other member of the public'.

Buildings and other constructions

1.8 English law adopts an ancient rule of accession to realty, derived from Roman law, under which buildings and other constructions integrally linked with land merge with, and become part and parcel of, that land (see also LPA 1925, s 205(1)(ix); LRA 2002, s 132(1), **1.3**). This general principle is expressed in yet another Latin maxim: *superficies solo cedit* (a building becomes part of the ground or *solum*). Thus a house or other structure which cannot be removed without demolition or destruction is presumed to have been intended to 'form part of the realty' (*Elitestone Ltd v Morris* (1997) per Lord Lloyd of Berwick), and the same status attaches to such other features as brick-built garages and sheds. Even the top floor of a high-rise block of flats would, on this basis, comprise 'land'. Likewise a dry stone wall inheres in the landscape in such a way as to 'become part of the land' (see *Holland v Hodgson* (1872) per Blackburn J). Whether any particular construction is intended to be annexed to, and thereby become 'part and parcel' of, the realty falls to be determined, not by reference to the subjective intention of the builder, but by the objectively understood purpose of the construction.

> *Elitestone Ltd v Morris* (1997) M's predecessor constructed a wooden bungalow or chalet resting on concrete pillars attached to E's land. The structure could be used only in situ and could not be removed to another location without demolition. The House of Lords held unanimously that the structure was not a 'fixture' as such (**1.9**), but must nevertheless be taken to have been intended to accede to, and become 'part and parcel' of, the realty of the freehold. (Compare *Chelsea Yacht and Boat Co Ltd v Pope* (2000), where a houseboat with easily removable plug-in or snap-on service connections was held *not* to have become part of the land to which it was moored.)

The rule *superficies solo cedit* finds strong confirmation in the important word-saving provisions of section 62 of the Law of Property Act 1925 (**8.20, 8.24**), which stipulate that, in the absence of contrary intention, any 'conveyance of land' is deemed without further verbiage to include all buildings then attached to the land (s 62(1)), together with any outhouses, erections, fixtures, and other features of the built environment which appertain to the land (s 62(2)).

Fixtures

1.9 Section 62 of the Law of Property Act 1925 includes 'fixtures' within the presumptive operation of a 'conveyance of land', thereby confirming a slightly uneasy distinction in English law between a category of *fixtures* (physical objects which are regarded as acceding to the realty) and *chattels* (physical objects which always retain their independent character as personalty).

Fixtures comprise those material objects which, as a matter of law, merge with the freehold *either* by reason of their physical bond with existing land *or* (more rarely) by reason of their highly purposive juxtaposition with such land (*Elitestone Ltd v Morris* (1997) per Lord Clyde). In either case, installation of the object causes its title to vest forthwith in the owner of the freehold. The provider of the object—if he is not the freehold owner—is immediately expropriated, even though he may have attempted to protect himself by means of a retention of title clause (*Aircool Installations v British Telecommunications* (1995)). The object itself is annexed permanently to the realty and normally cannot thereafter be severed from it by any limited owner. The freehold owner alone, by virtue of his comprehensive right of ownership, may of course sever the fixture from the realty, but unless and until this happens any further 'conveyance of land' will presumptively carry the fixture, as an integral part of the undifferentiated freehold, into the hands of the new freehold owner (LPA 1925, s 62(1)). In this way English law gives effect to another Latinate tag, *quicquid plantatur solo, solo cedit* (whatever is attached to the ground becomes a part of it).

By contrast, the category of *chattels* consists of physical objects which retain their status as personalty even though placed in some close relation with realty. Never merging within the realty of the freehold, such chattels do not automatically pass with conveyances of the land. As personal property they may be removed at any time by their owner.

- *The relevance of classification* The elusive distinction between fixtures and chattels used to be primarily relevant at the point when land came to be sold.

- *Implications for the buyer* In the absence of contrary contractual stipulation, the purchaser is entitled to all fixtures attached to the land at the date of exchange of contracts (**12.4**) or even at the earlier point in time when the offer of purchase is invited and the land is inspected by potential buyers (see *Taylor v Hamer* (2003) at [93] per Sedley LJ). However, much of the heat has now been removed from what used to be a vexed aspect of conveyancing. In modern conveyancing practice the widespread use of 'tick lists' of items to be retained by a vendor has tended, in most cases, to clarify the contractual position beyond all doubt.

• *Implications for a mortgagee* If anything, the contemporary spotlight has moved away from transactions of *sale* to those of *mortgage*, where the lender (or *mortgagee* (**8.28, 15.1**)) is only too anxious in circumstances of default to maximise the value of the land over which his security has been taken. This value is effectively inflated by any genuine accretions to the realty paid for by the borrower during the currency of the mortgage loan. And, as a sociological aside, the items so often at stake in today's case law are no longer the statuary, stuffed birds and tapestries of the late Victorian era but rather the sophisticated household appliances and artefacts associated with a more recent culture of aggressive domestic consumption (see e.g. *Botham v TSB Bank plc* (1996)).

• *Other relevant contexts* Further critical contexts in which the fixture/chattel borderline now threatens to become increasingly important involve the precise definition of 'land' for the purposes of taxation (see e.g. *Melluish v BMI (No 3) Ltd* (1996)) and environmental or heritage conservation (see e.g. *R v Secretary of State for Wales, ex parte Kennedy* (1996)).

— *The distinction between fixtures and chattels* The distinction between fixtures and chattels is often described as turning on two separate but related tests. Both tests attempt to assess the intention of the original owner of the object at the time when he brought the object into close association with the realty. These tests (see *Elitestone Ltd v Morris* (1997) per Lord Lloyd of Berwick) refer to

• the *physical degree* of annexation involved, and

• the *deemed purpose* of the annexation as viewed objectively, often many years later.

In reality, however, the differentiation of fixtures and chattels may now depend so heavily upon the circumstances of each individual case that relatively few guidelines remain in the modern law which are capable of unambiguous application.

— *The physical degree of annexation* It is often said, by way of a primitive rule of thumb, that the more permanently, firmly or irreversibly an object is affixed to existing land, the more likely is the object to be classified as a *fixture*. Conversely, a crude sort of 'gravity test' seems to point to a *chattel* classification for those objects which rest on land merely by the force of their own weight. Thus, for instance, the status of fixture has been accorded to spinning looms bolted to the floor of a mill (*Holland v Hodgson* (1872)), but not to heavy printing machinery otherwise unattached to a floor (*Hulme v Brigham* (1943)). Likewise fixtures have been held to include air conditioning equipment cut into, and bolted on to, the walls of a building (*Aircool Installations v British Telecommunications* (1995)), but not fitted and integrated kitchen appliances which, although connected electrically, remained in position by their own weight (*Botham v TSB Bank plc* (1996)). Even slight degrees of physical attachment (as in the case of bathroom cabinets, overhead heaters or extractor fans) can cause the objects in question to become prima facie part of the land.

— *The deemed purpose of the annexation* The presumptions flowing from physical annexation are neither uniform in their application nor entirely conclusive in their effect. Not everything which is screwed or bolted to realty necessarily becomes a fixture (see *Potton Developments Ltd v Thompson* (1998)). The tenor of recent case law strongly suggests that the legal impact of the *degree of annexation* has now been overtaken by more subtle considerations relating to the *objectively understood purpose* which must, by inference, have motivated the annexation. Both sets of factors may frequently lead to the same conclusion, but this is not always the case. The physical circumstances of a particular installation point only to a prima facie classification as a fixture or chattel which is rebuttable by evidence of some contrary purpose or scheme underlying the installation.

— *Objective purpose* This element of purpose must, however, be determined *objectively* by inference from the externally observable circumstances of the case (*Elitestone Ltd v Morris* (1997) per Lords Lloyd and Clyde). No person 'can make his property real or personal by merely thinking it so' (*Dixon v Fisher* (1843) per Lord Cockburn). Ultimately the question is whether the installation of an object would normally have been intended to effect a permanent accretion to, or improvement of, the realty or only a temporary or removable addition to a building or landscape (see *Botham v TSB Bank plc* (1996)). Thus a freestanding garden gnome in a suburban garden mercifully constitutes a mere chattel, whilst a substantial collection of carefully coordinated garden ornaments may well comprise a group of fixtures (see *Hamp v Bygrave* (1983)).

> *D'Eyncourt v Gregory* (1866) Heavy ornamental marble statues of lions resting merely by gravity in strategic locations were held to have been intended to meld permanently with the land as an integral part of a general scheme for the improvement of the realty. The objects thus acquired the status of fixtures rather than retaining the mere chattel character which would have been assigned by the 'gravity test'.

— *Overriding purpose* It is equally clear that the *purpose of annexation* test can override the initial fixture classification which would otherwise follow from the *degree of annexation* of an object. Items which are firmly fixed to the realty may still rank as chattels if the purpose of the annexation was merely to facilitate enjoyment of them as chattels and if the degree of annexation was no more than was necessary for the achieving of that purpose. Much may turn on whether the purpose of attachment was more heavily directed towards promoting increased enjoyment of the object in itself or towards maximising the use which could be made of the land (*Elitestone Ltd v Morris* (1997) per Lord Lloyd). Was the underlying motivation to *enhance the chattel* or to *improve the realty?*

> *Leigh v Taylor* (1902) The House of Lords held that valuable tapestries pinned to a wall constituted mere chattels and did not become part of the freehold. The mode of attachment used indicated no necessary intention that the tapestries should attach indefinitely and gratis to the realty, but afforded the only realistic way in which the objects could be enjoyed in their own right. (The same approach has been adopted in relation to such items as display cases of stuffed birds (*Viscount Hill v Bullock* (1897)) and fitted carpets and curtains (*Botham v TSB Bank plc* (1996)).)

— *Ultimately indeterminate tests* The relative indeterminacy of fixture status may mean that the contemporary borderline between fixtures and chattels has become more case-specific and more context-dependent than was once believed. The ultimate test of fixture character may well rest on informed intuitions as to the likelihood that the annexor, if questioned by some officious bystander, would realistically have reserved the right to remove the disputed object from the realty in the event of a future sale of the land.

— *Common law rights to remove fixtures* The legal differentiation of fixtures and chattels has always been confused by one further dimension of the issue of removability (see *Elitestone Ltd v Morris* (1997) per Lords Lloyd and Clyde). A fixture, once attached to land, is in principle irremovable except by the freehold owner or by another pursuant to agreement with the freehold owner. Yet, outwith these circumstances, the common law has for several centuries permitted a tenant (or *lessee*), at the expiry of his tenancy, to sever from the realty certain kinds of fixture attached during the course of the tenancy. This concession in respect of *tenants' fixtures* owes its existence to the fact that the normal rule of real annexation would operate unduly harshly upon a tenant whose improvements otherwise confer an uncovenanted and uncompensated benefit upon the landlord (or *lessor*) as freehold owner of the realty. Accordingly the tenant's common law privilege to remove tenants' fixtures extends to objects which have been attached or installed for trade, ornamental and domestic, and certain agricultural purposes (the last instance now being reinforced by Agricultural Holdings Act 1986, s 10; Agricultural Tenancies Act 1995, s 8(1)–(2)).

— *Contract-based rights to remove fixtures* Contract sometimes threatens to come into collision with property, as for instance when an object is attached to land in circumstances where the provider of the object has reserved a contractual right to remove the fixture in question. Such circumstances are almost inevitably present where equipment or machinery on hire or hire-purchase from a stranger is affixed to the land of the hirer. Upon annexation the stranger automatically loses title to the equipment or machinery, but usually retains a contractual right to sever the fixture from the land in the event of any default in payment of hire charges or hire-purchase instalments. The conflict between the proprietary and contractual positions becomes even more stark if the land is transferred or mortgaged to a third party during the currency of the hire or hire-purchase. Can a contractual right of recovery prevail against the new owner of proprietary rights in the land? English law partially resolves these conundra by recognising that title to the equipment or machinery has merged in the freehold title, but that its former owner has an equitable interest in the land (often called a *right of entry* (**8.35**)) which entitles him, at least as against the original hirer—and, in certain circumstances, as against third parties—to enter and remove the goods in question.

Trees, plants, and flowers

1.10 'Land' includes for legal purposes all trees, shrubs, hedges, plants and flowers growing thereon, whether cultivated or wild. Such forms of growth attach to the realty and are thus part of the estate owned by the landowner, although the maximum height which may be attained by certain trees or hedges is now controlled by statute (see e.g. the limitations on 'high hedges' imposed by Anti-social Behaviour Act 2003, ss 65–84).

Wild animals

1.11 Whilst alive, wild animals cannot be the subject of absolute ownership. The owner of land inhabited by such animals has only a 'qualified property' in them, entitling him (subject to modern conservationist legislation) to hunt and catch them and thereby reduce them into his possession (*Blades v Higgs* (1865)). Wild animals can become personalty and, accordingly, proper objects of absolute ownership only when killed.

Water

1.12 In English law water is incapable of being owned, with the odd consequence that, although the law can contemplate with equanimity the transfer of an estate in thin air (**1.7**), it has substantially more difficulty in relation to conveyances of water. Inland water (whether a river or lake) is regarded as no more than 'a species of land' or, more accurately, 'land covered with water' (*Bl Comm*, vol II, p 18). Thus a transfer of the land in question carries with it certain rights over the superjacent water, in particular an exclusive right to fish in any non-tidal river which runs through the land. A transfer of riparian land bounded by a non-tidal river carries with it the soil *ad medium filum* (i.e. to the middle point of the river).

Fish

1.13 The landowner's right to fish in superjacent water confers on him no more than a 'qualified property' in fish found within the limits of his fishery. The fish become his absolute property, on an analogy with wild animals, only when he catches and kills them.

Incorporeal hereditaments

1.14 In English law the concept of 'land' includes, within the meaning of this term, the notion of the *incorporeal hereditament* (**1.3**). Incorporeal hereditaments refer to certain intangible rights over or in respect of land (**1.4**) and, not being 'the object of sensation', can neither be seen nor handled, but 'are creatures of the mind, and exist only in contemplation' (*Bl Comm*, vol II, p 17). Under the general heading of incorporeal hereditaments, the most widely applicable statutory definition of 'land' expressly embraces such abstract entitlements as 'an easement, right, privilege, or benefit in, over, or derived from land' (see LPA 1925, s 205(1)(ix)). A typical easement comprises the right of way which one landowner, A, may have over the land of another, B (**8.3**). The statutory definitions of 'land' effectively bring about a remarkable reification of intangible entitlement—a frequent feature of the common law mindset. The abstract benefit of A's right of way over B's land is accordingly conceptualised as an integral component of *A's land*—another example of the intermittent tendency in English land law to conflate property as *fact* with property as *right* (**1.4**). This benefit being notionally affixed to A's land (LPA 1925, s 187(1)), in rather the same manner that fixtures become annexed to realty (**1.9**), it follows that any future transfer of A's 'land' to C will effectively pass to C not merely A's corporeal hereditaments but also the benefit of the right of way (see LPA 1925, s 62(1)–(2); LRA 2002, Sch 2, para 7(2)(b), LRR 2003, r 5(b)(ii), **8.16, 8.24**).

The fourth dimension of land

1.15 The first three dimensions of land in English law relate essentially to physical reality. From the early medieval period onwards, however, the concept of land was taken into a fourth, more cerebral, dimension with the introduction of a theory of notional *estates* in land. The device of the 'estate' in land did not merely articulate the jural relationship between the landholder and his land. The inspired evolution of the *estate* eventually came to provide a functional alternative to those more holistic ideas of *dominium* (or direct ownership of the land itself) which were part of the European heritage derived from Roman law. Indeed, perhaps the single most striking feature of English land law has always been the absence, within its conceptual apparatus, of any overarching notion of *ownership*.

The doctrine of estates

1.16 The doctrine of estates carefully avoided the absolutist dogma that a person could have any direct relation of ownership of physical land. Indeed, there could never be any direct ownership of land outside the *allodium*—or prerogatival ownership—of the crown (*Minister of State for the Army v Dalziel* (1944) per Latham CJ). The doctrine of estates gave expression to the idea that each landholder (or 'tenant') owned not land but *a slice of time in the land*. The object of his ownership was, accordingly, an abstraction called an 'estate', the precise nature of each estate being graded by its temporal duration. All proprietary relationships with land were to be analysed at one remove—through the intermediacy of an *estate*—with the consequence that one had ownership of an intangible right (i.e. an *estate*) rather than ownership of a tangible thing (i.e. the *land* itself). At this point the law of real property became distanced from the physical reality of land and entered a world of conceptual—indeed some would say virtually mathematical—abstraction.

> *Walsingham's Case* (1573) '[T]he land itself is one thing, and the estate in the land is another thing, for an estate in the land is a time in the land, or land for a time, and there are diversities of estates, which are no more than diversities of time.'

Estates as slices of time

1.17 It was left to the doctrine of estates to quantify the abstract entitlement which might be enjoyed by any particular landholder within the tenurial framework (**1.22**). The doctrine spelt out a complex calculus of carefully graded estates in land, each estate representing an artificial proprietary construct interposed between the landholder (or 'tenant') and the physical object of his tenure. Each estate comprised a time-related segment—a temporal slice—of the rights and powers exercisable over land; and the doctrine of estates effectively provided diverse ways in which three-dimensional realty might be carved up in a fourth dimension of time. As Lord Hoffmann declared in *Newlon Housing Trust v Alsulaimen* (1999),

> in English law, rights of property in land are four-dimensional. They are defined not only by reference to the physical boundaries of the property but also by reference to the time for which the interest will endure.

The old freehold estates of the common law

1.18 The rich taxonomy of estates in medieval land law provided for a number of *freehold estates* which together facilitated the fragmentation of ownership and conferred enormous flexibility in the management of landed wealth. The substitution of *abstract estates* in land as the object of proprietary rights enabled grantors to preside over almost endless disaggregations of title through the conferment of successive freehold estates (e.g. where X granted Greenacre to A *for life*, then to B *in tail*, and finally to C *in fee simple*). Each successive interest could enjoy an immediate jural reality as of the date of the original grant; and each was freely commerciable (i.e. saleable or mortgageable) long before the estate in question actually fell *into possession* (**7.4**). The freehold estates, in their most basic form, comprised the following:

— The *estate in fee simple* denoted (and still denotes) tenure of potentially unlimited duration, the amplest estate which a tenant can have in or over land. The fee simple confers 'the widest powers of enjoyment in respect of all the advantages to be derived from the land itself and from anything found on it' (*Wik Peoples v Queensland* (1996) per Gummow J), and constitutes effectively the 'local equivalent of full ownership' (ibid per Kirby J). The tenant of an unencumbered estate in fee simple has, without question, the largest possible 'bundle of rights' exercisable with respect to land (*Minister of State for the Army v Dalziel* (1944) per Rich J).

> *Walsingham's Case* (1573) '[H]e who has a fee-simple in land has a time in the land without end, or the land for time without end.'

The fee simple was (and still is) capable, more or less indefinitely, of transfer inter vivos or of devolution on death. The owners of the fee simple estate may come and go but the estate remains, since it is of potentially infinite duration. Each new owner merely steps into the shoes of his or her predecessor—the modern effect of the Statute *Quia Emptores* 1290 (**1.22**).

— The *fee tail* (or *entailed estate*) represented an interest in land which endured so long as the original grantee or any of his lineal descendants remained alive, thus providing an ideal means of retaining dynastic land within the family.

— The *life estate* was (and still is) coextensive and coterminous with the life of its original grantee. If conveyed to a stranger, it ranks in his hands as an interest *pur autre vie*, still lasting only for the lifetime of the original grantee—not necessarily a good investment for a canny purchaser!

Emergence of the leasehold estate

1.19 During the last three centuries the gradual decline of the lesser freehold estates has been accompanied by the increasing prominence of the *leasehold estate*. This estate— more properly known as a 'term of years absolute'—denotes exclusive possession of land for a term certain. Although the lease was viewed, in the early days of the common law, as conferring rights of a merely personal or contractual nature, the leasehold device later came to be recognised as giving rise to entitlements of a distinctly proprietary character. The 1925 legislation duly confirmed the status of the term of years absolute as an estate in land (LPA 1925, s 1(1)(b)). The leasehold estate, comprising by definition a slice of time of fixed maximum duration (**7.10–7.12**), can be granted either out of the allodium of the crown (by way of crown lease), or by the owner of a fee simple estate, or indeed by a leaseholder by way of sublease (for any period shorter than the duration of his own leasehold estate (**7.17**)).

The modern impact of the doctrine of estates

1.20 The old common law estates were preserved, with modifications and additions, in the property legislation of 1925. Indeed the scheme of title registration now contained in the Land Registration Act 2002 is actually premised on the intellectual construct of the *estate* (see LRA 2002, ss 2(a), 3(1)–(2), 4(1)–(2), 6(1), 132(1); LRR 2003, r 2(2), **1.22**).

— *Decline of the lesser freehold estates* Even by 1925 it had become clear that the fee simple estate was the primary estate in English law and that the grant of the other former freehold estates (necessarily in *equitable* form, **2.29**) had become—for reasons both social and fiscal—really rather rare. Therefore, in the absence of words of limitation which expressly cut back the scope of a grant, all conveyances were, from 1926 onwards, presumed to invest the grantee with a *fee simple* estate (LPA 1925, s 60(1)). Being relegated to equitable status, the old qualified freehold estates (i.e. other than the fee simple) were capable of creation only under some statutorily regulated trust or settlement (**9.43–9.44**).

- As of 1 January 1997 a life interest can be conferred only under a 'trust of land' (TOLATA 1996, s 2(1), **9.42**).
- Any purported grant of an entailed interest now takes effect, not as a grant in tail, but as a declaration that the land is held in trust for the grantee *absolutely* (i.e. in fee simple in equity) (see TOLATA 1996, Sch 1, para 5(1), **9.37**).

— *Rationalisation of the major estates in land* The 1925 legislation further rationalised the modern doctrine of estates by restricting the number of major legal estates to two: the 'fee simple absolute in possession' and the 'term of years absolute' (LPA 1925, s 1(1)). Other simplifying rules were added.

• Neither a fee simple absolute nor a term of years absolute may normally be held at law by more than *four* persons as co-owners (TA 1925, s 34(2); LPA 1925, s 34(2)–(3)).

• Neither a fee simple absolute nor a term of years may be held at law by a *minor* (LPA 1925, ss 1(6), 20, 205(1)(v); TOLATA 1996, Sch 1, para 1(1)(a)). Although it is perfectly possible that the *equitable* version of either estate may be vested in a person under the age of 18 (see e.g. *Kingston upon Thames BC v Prince* (1999) (equitable lease)), any attempt to transfer a *legal* estate to a minor now operates merely as declaration that the land is held in trust for that person (TOLATA 1996, s 2(1), (6), Sch 1, para 1(1)(b)).

The constant intermediacy of estate ownership

1.21 Throughout its history the ingenious compromise of the doctrine of estates has quietly rendered it unnecessary for the common law to develop any comprehensive theory of ownership of land. Even modern property legislation faithfully maintains the ancient theory that land ownership and use are mediated, not by the attribution to individuals of any direct ownership or *dominium* over the land itself, but rather by the distribution of intangible jural entitlements which are interposed *between* persons and land (**1.16**). The perspective embraced by the statutory scheme is, essentially, of property as an *abstract right* rather than as a *physical resource*, precisely on the footing that the only property in land which one can have is necessarily property in the form of a *right* (**2.3**).

The theory of tenure

1.22 It follows from the pre-eminence of the estate concept as the vehicle of modern land ownership that relatively little now remains of the medieval theory of tenure. Under the tenurial system of tiered or hierarchical landholding, all land in England (save unalienated crown land) was held, in pyramidal relationships of reciprocal obligation, either mediately or immediately of the crown. Thus whereas the concept of the estate systematised the relationship between the landholder (or 'tenant') and the physical land, the doctrine of tenures described the relationship between each tenant and his immediate superior within a feudal structure which had the king at its apex. With its complex tariff of services owed to the feudal superior (and of the valuable *incidents* or privileges of tenure), the doctrine of tenures indicated more precisely the nature of the relationship between every occupier of land and his *baron* or lord.

— *The 'radical title' of the crown*   The theory of tenure ultimately identified the 'radical title' at the back of all relationships in respect of land—the sovereign title of the king as paramount lord, achieved by conquest in 1066 and sustained by strong political control thereafter. Unlike the proprietary estates, which could be parcelled out amongst the subjects of the crown, this radical title was, in truth, no proprietary title at all, but merely an expression of the *Realpolitik* which served historically to hold together the theory of tenure. It denoted the political authority of the crown both to grant estates in the land to be held of the crown and also to prescribe the residue of unalienated land as the sovereign's beneficial demesne.

— *The demise of the tenurial structure*   The doctrine of tenures lost most of its practical importance after the dismantling of the feudal system. Already, by the Statute *Quia Emptores* 1290, the tenant had been guaranteed the right to alienate land without the consent of his lord. (It is this statute which still—quite unnoticed—regulates every transfer of land in fee simple in England and Wales today.) The beginning of the end came with the Tenures Abolition Act of 1660, although the process was completed—amazingly—only by the Law of Property Act 1922. All tenure has now been commuted to a uniform 'socage tenure' directly from the crown (LPA 1922, s 128, Sch 12, para 1).

— *Vestiges of tenurial consequence*   Only the most rudimentary traces of tenurial theory remain today. It is still true, however, that no subject can own land *allodially*, i.e. except by tenure from the crown (however unreal this concept may nowadays appear). Moreover, Land Registry is empowered to register title only to 'estates' in 'land', and the latter term is statutorily defined as requiring the existence of 'tenure' (see LRA 2002, s 132(1), incorporating by reference LPA 1925, s 205(1)(ix)–(x)). Otherwise, however, the last lingering implications of tenurial orthodoxy have all but disappeared.

• The age-old theory that the crown could never hold land of itself has been reversed by the LRA 2002, which enables the crown, in respect of 'demesne land', to grant itself a freehold estate which is both registrable and disposable (LRA 2002, ss 79(1), 132(1)).

- The LRA 2002 has also modified the rule that a freeholder's estate reverts automatically—or 'escheats'—to the crown in the event of the freeholder's death without any competent successor (AEA 1925, s 46(1)(vi)) or on a disclaimer of the freehold estate by a company liquidator acting under the Insolvency Act 1986 (see *Scmlla Properties Ltd v Gesso Properties (BVI) Ltd* (1995), **7.9**). Such implosions of the largest common law estate used to revest the land within the allodium of the crown, in rather the same way in which a lease for years falls in for the landlord on the expiration of the term granted (**7.29**). The LRA 2002 now provides for rules which, notwithstanding the destruction of the tenurial relationship (**7.5**), will prevent the automatic closure of registered titles to escheated land (LRA 2002, s 82; LRR 2003, rr 79(3), 173, **7.9**).

The fifth dimension of land

1.23 If land is capable of description in *three* physical dimensions, and of extension into a *fourth* dimension by the component of time, English law soon added one further dimension of analysis. This extra dimension turned on the 'legal' or 'equitable' quality accorded to the various abstract rights which had emerged from the medieval conceptualism of estates. It came to be recognised that each estate could itself be 'the subject of "ownership" both in law and in equity' (*Mabo v Queensland (No 2)* (1992) per Deane and Gaudron JJ). Although for historical reasons 'legal estates and equitable estates have differing incidents', it is truly the case that 'the person owning either type of estate has a right of property' (*Tinsley v Milligan* (1994) per Lord Browne-Wilkinson). Indeed, much of the rich complexity of today's law of property results from the potential *duality* of estate ownership, for amidst other consequences it makes possible that most distinctive of English contributions to jurisprudence, the institution of the *trust* (**1.26, 9.34**).

Legal and equitable rights

1.24 Within the field of proprietary rights in land, English law still draws a fundamental distinction between *legal* and *equitable* rights. Historically this distinction was grounded on the fact that *legal* rights were enforceable only in the common law courts of the king, whereas *equitable* rights fell within the exclusive and conscience-based jurisdiction, initially of the king's Chancellor, and later of the Court of Chancery. Equity was conceived as a corrective system of justice, designed to supplement the common law by responding more flexibly and sensitively to the need for fair dealing and just outcomes. It addressed, on an instance-specific basis, the hard cases for which the generalised dogmas of the common law afforded no adequate remedy. Inevitably the jurisdictions of common law and equity came into conflict, in so far as they frequently recognised different forms of entitlement and provided different forms of remedy for the litigant. After several centuries of fierce competition between the rival jurisdictions, the administration of legal and equitable rules was finally fused within our court system towards the end of the 19th century. It can thus be said today that 'English law has one single law of property made up of legal and equitable interests' (*Tinsley v Milligan* (1994) per Lord Browne-Wilkinson). Rights and remedies, *whether legal or equitable*, are now recognised and enforced in all courts, albeit subject to the overriding principle that in cases of conflict the rules of equity shall prevail (Supreme Court of Judicature Act 1873, s 25(11), now Supreme Court Act 1981, s 49(1)).

— *The distinction between legal and equitable rights* Many important differences nevertheless persist between legal and equitable proprietary rights. It is difficult to summarise these differences here, since they constitute much of the substance of this book. Moreover, the borderline between legal and equitable rights in land has been artificially, and somewhat arbitrarily, redefined by modern legislation (**2.28–2.30**).

— *Differences of origin* Under the statutory categorisation of rights in 1925 some sorts of entitlement may now exist *either* at law or in equity; others may exist *only* in equity. But there remains considerable truth in the idea that legal rights are normally created by compliance with various statutory requirements of documentary formality or registration, whereas equitable rights are often generated, in a more diffuse fashion, by informal transactions, by implications from circumstance, and by obligations of conscience.

— *Differences between form and substance* In some important sense—particularly in the context of the trust—legal rights can often be said to represent *form*, whereas equitable rights represent *substance*. It is frequently the case that legal rights comprise merely a nominal or paper title, as evidenced in some superficial record, and therefore carry more of a connotation of responsibility than of entitlement. Equitable rights, on the other hand, reflect more clearly the *inner reality* (as distinct from the *outer form*) of a transaction and generally locate rather more accurately the substance of intended beneficial enjoyment.

— *Differences of binding impact* At the level of raw common law principle, legal rights are automatically binding upon the world. In practice the enhanced publicity inherent in the formal or documentary derivation of most legal rights has tended to ease the impact of legal rights upon strangers (**2.38**). Equitable rights frequently arise in less formal circumstances, with the consequence that, although the recent extension of title registration has eroded some of the practical distinction between legal and equitable rights, the enforcement of equitable entitlements against strangers often requires the assistance of various mechanisms of bureaucratic recordation (**2.30–2.32, 2.41, 12.35**) or even the application of conscience-based doctrines of equity such as the *doctrine of notice* (**1.26, 2.43, 12.42**).

Differentiation of legal and equitable ownership

1.25 Where the 'whole right of property' is vested in one person, there is 'no need to suppose the separate and concurrent existence of two different kinds of estate or interest, i.e. the legal and the equitable' (*Comr of Stamp Duties (Queensland) v Livingston* (1965) per Viscount Radcliffe). The sole estate owner of Greenacre need not see himself as owning both a *legal* and an *equitable* estate in the land. Merger in one owner of the totality of entitlement renders such a distinction unnecessary and even impossible: the absolute owner has no separate equitable estate since this is absorbed within his legal estate. But the moment this totality of ownership is split between two or more persons, the device of the *trust* becomes virtually unavoidable in English law, ownership of the formal or documentary estate being a phenomenon recognised *at law* and ownership of the beneficial estate being recognised only *in equity*. In this way equity 'calls into existence and protects equitable rights and interests in property only where their recognition has been found to be required in order to give effect to its doctrines' (*Comr of Stamp Duties (Queensland) v Livingston* (1965)).

The institution of the trust

1.26 The institution of the trust provides the classic circumstance where equitable ownership necessarily diverges from legal ownership.

— *The basic structure of the trust* The essence of the trust is the idea that the formal or titular interest in some asset (e.g. the *legal estate* in fee simple) is vested, in a nominal capacity, in one or more persons *as trustee*. The strict duty of such persons is to deflect all beneficial enjoyment of the asset to the *beneficiaries* or *cestuis que trust*, who are together entitled to the equitable interests (e.g. the *equitable estate* in fee simple). It is, in short, the *beneficiaries* who *benefit* under a trust (see *Fig 1*).

— *The enforcement of a moral obligation* In the trust the existence of an equitable estate (and the entitlement of the equitable owner) result from the enforcement of

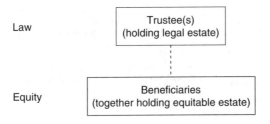

Law	Trustee(s) (holding legal estate)
Equity	Beneficiaries (together holding equitable estate)

Fig 1

the moral obligation which is fastened upon the conscience of the trustee (**9.35**). In an expressly created trust (**9.37**) it is the trustee, after all, who has consented to undertake the function of trusteeship and in conscience he cannot later be heard to disavow his trust. Under the trust, as Maitland pointed out long ago, 'the benefit of an obligation has been so treated that it has come to look rather like a true proprietary right' (*Equity*, p 115). Equitable rights in trust property thus derive from conscientious obligations to deal with an asset or resource in a certain way. Equity answers its primary call of conscience by engrafting a corrective image of entitlement—a species of equitable ownership—upon the legal estate of the trustee (see Gray, 'Equitable Property' (1994) 47(2) *Current Legal Problems* 157 at 163, 207). Nowhere is the duality of estate ownership more plainly demonstrated.

— *The beneficiaries' interests under the trust* The beneficiaries' interests under the trust are usually—although not always—quantifiable as fractional shares in the assets of the trust. Thus, in an example which recurs in many forms throughout land law, the legal estate in a family home may be held by a trustee or by trustees, who hold on trust for two beneficiaries who take equitable shares of, say, 75 per cent and 25 per cent respectively, or 50 per cent each, or indeed any other percentages which add up to a unity (see *Fig* 2).

— *The impact of the trust on third parties* Although the trust relationship was initially based upon an essentially *personal* confidence reposed in the trustee on behalf of his beneficiary, the courts of equity, comprising a jurisdiction of conscience, inevitably extended the ramifications of the trust *beyond* the nexus of trustee and beneficiary. Trusts would have had only limited significance if the moral obligation underlying the trust had remained enforceable merely against the original trustee. The fiduciary responsibility implicit in the trust would have been dislocated by any subsequent change of legal title, whether occurring on the death or bankruptcy of the trustee or on his transfer of the legal estate in the trust property to some third party. Equity accordingly expanded the reach of the beneficiary's rights against third parties under a rule which eventually came to be known as the *bona fide purchaser rule* or the *equitable doctrine of notice* (and which

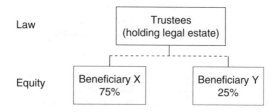

Fig 2

ultimately governed even those equitable rights which arose *outside* the context of a trust (**12.39**)). This extension of trust liability to third parties reinforced, in its turn, the perception that *equitable* rights were akin to *proprietary* rights. In effect, the benefit of the fiduciary obligation of the trust enlarged into a form of *proprietary* title or interest.

The gradual diffusion of trust liability occurred with the transmission of the trustee's legal estate in the trust property to various kinds of third party. Trusts came to be enforced against:

• *persons who succeeded to the legal estate of the trustee* on his death, i.e. his personal representatives, who could not claim to stand in any better position than the trustee himself;

• *creditors of the trustee*, who could not, of course, be allowed to claim the trust property in satisfaction of personal debts owed by the trustee;

• *donees from the trustee*, who, having received a gratuitous transfer of a legal estate to which they had no prior title, could not be heard to disavow the trust attached to that estate ('equity will not assist a volunteer');

• *purchasers from the trustee with actual notice of the trust*, since it would be contrary to conscience—a kind of *fraud*—for a purchaser who bought a legal estate with *actual* knowledge of the existence of a trust subsequently to disclaim that trust; and

• *purchasers from the trustee with constructive notice of the trust*, who were treated *as if* they had actual knowledge of the trust in those circumstances where, had they acted with due diligence in inspecting land and title, notice of the trust would inevitably have come to their attention.

— *The equitable doctrine of notice* Before 1926 all equitable rights, by analogy with this extended operation of trust liability, came to be regarded as enforceable against all persons other than:

> a bona fide purchaser of a legal estate for valuable consideration without notice (whether actual or constructive).

This formula, comprising what is known as the *equitable doctrine of notice* (or *bona fide purchaser rule*), provided immunity from pre-existing equitable rights only in the case of the purchaser whose conscience was wholly unaffected. In his case, however, the plea of purchase for valuable consideration without notice was 'an absolute, unqualified, unanswerable defence' in the eyes of equity (see *Pilcher v Rawlins* (1872) per James LJ). Such a purchaser was sometimes known simply as 'Equity's Darling'—one who had earned the favour of equity. Even nowadays it is still said that '[t]he doctrine of notice lies at the heart of equity. Given that there are two innocent parties, each enjoying rights, the earlier right prevails against the later right if the acquirer of the later right knows of the earlier right (actual notice) or would have discovered it had he taken proper steps (constructive notice)' (*Barclays Bank plc v O'Brien* (1994) per Lord Browne-Wilkinson).

— *Modern displacement of the notice doctrine* During the course of the last century, however, this doctrine of notice, albeit the continuing inspirational force behind much of our land law, was severely cut back in scope. As we shall see, the *bona fide purchaser* rule has no application to land titles registered under the Land Registration Act 2002 (**2.27, 12.14**) and has only a residual relevance in the law of unregistered land (**2.43, 12.42**). In effect, the significant role played by the historic doctrine of notice has been displaced, largely by mechanisms of *registration* under which the publicity secured by the registration of rights now operates as a form of mandatory notice to the world at large (see e.g. LRA 2002, ss 28(1), 29(1)–(2)(a)(i), **2.32, 12.11**; LPA 1925, s 198(1), **12.35**).

— *The express trust as a management device* The expressly created trust is, in effect, a sophisticated form of management device. It depends fundamentally on a functional separation of *administration* and *enjoyment*. The trustee is invested with a purely nominal (or 'legal') title—indeed so nominal that any unauthorised personal benefit derived by him from the trust signifies in itself a grave breach of trust except in so far as the trustee may also happen to be one of the designated beneficiaries. The substance of the practical benefit derived from the land held on trust—whether by way of occupation, rental exploitation or sale—is reserved at all times for the 'equitable' owner, the beneficiary or beneficiaries. Express trusts of land are necessarily marked by a certain degree of documentary formality in their creation. It is one of the venerable rules of trust law that a declaration of trust respecting land must be 'manifested and proved by some writing' signed by the author of the trust (LPA 1925, s 53(1)(b), **9.38**).

— *Implied trusts* Many trusts arise by *express creation*, the author of the trust quite explicitly nominating both the trustees and the desired range of beneficiaries and stipulating the precise terms of the trust. Probably even more trusts are created *by implication* (**9.36**)—particularly in the family context—since it falls within the general remit of any court, in the exercise of its equitable jurisdiction, to recognise or *construct* equitable entitlement on behalf of any claimant who can demonstrate that another has incurred a conscientious obligation to hold a legal title on trust for him or her as beneficiary. In relation to implied trusts, the requirement of formal creation is necessarily abrogated (LPA 1925, s 53(2), **9.39**), although the standard of evidence required in order to make good a claim of implied trust may still be disconcertingly demanding (**10.5, 10.15–10.16**). Implied trusts fall into two broad categories—the *resulting trust* (**10.3**) and the *constructive trust* (**10.6**)—and it is not impossible that circumstances which fail to disclose the existence of an enforceable express trust of land may nevertheless give rise to a valid resulting or constructive trust (**9.39**).

FURTHER READING

Gray and Gray, *Elements of Land Law* (4th edn, OUP, 2005), ch 1.

Relevant sections of this work and other land law textbooks may be supplemented with:

Birks, Peter 'Before We Begin: Five Keys to Land Law', in S. Bright and J.K. Dewar (eds), *Land Law: Themes and Perspectives* (OUP, 1998), p 457.

Bright, Susan 'Of Estates and Interests: A Tale of Ownership and Property Rights', in S. Bright and J.K. Dewar (eds), *op cit*, p 529.

Luther, Peter 'Fixtures and Chattels: A Question of More or Less ...' (2004) 24 *OJLS* 597.

SELF-TEST QUESTIONS

1   The annexation of an object to land brings about a curious form of expropriation. Explain the proprietary effects of annexation and severance of such objects (**1.8–1.9**).

2   Does a television aerial (or a satellite dish) constitute a fixture or a chattel (**1.9**)?

3   How essential is the concept of the 'estate' today (**1.16–1.21**)?

4   How relevant is the notion of 'ownership' in English land law (**1.15, 1.21–1.22**)?

5   How do legal and equitable ownership differ (**1.24–1.26**)?

2

Property

SUMMARY

This chapter explores the meaning of 'property' in land by pointing to key features inherent in the constitution of *proprietary* (as distinct from *personal* or *human*) rights. These characteristics of 'property' in land help to mark out the categories of rights whose relationship is governed by the property legislation of 1925 and 2002. In order to gain a preliminary understanding of this legislation, the chapter also provides a 'bird's-eye view' of the way in which all proprietary rights in land are classified and regulated by the 1925 scheme. This analysis is supplemented by reference to the way in which the Land Registration Act 2002 (and the digital revolution which it facilitates) will eventually allow proprietary rights to be disposable by electronic dealings.

The fragile concept of property

2.1 Few concepts are quite so fragile, so elusive and so often misused as the notion of property. There is a pervasive element of shared deception in our normal property talk: property is not theft, but *fraud* (see Gray, 'Property in Thin Air' [1991] *CLJ* 252). We commonly speak of property as if its meaning were entirely clear and logical. But our daily references to property tend to be a mutual conspiracy of unsophisticated semantic allusions and confusions, which we tolerate—often, indeed, do not notice—largely because our linguistic shorthand has a certain low-level communicative efficiency. Part of our present task is therefore to jolt ourselves out of our conventional, reassuringly three-dimensional, imagery about property. As Bruce Ackerman once said, one of the main purposes of a property course is to disabuse law students of their 'primitive lay notions regarding ownership' (*Private*

Property and the Constitution (1977), p 26). Not the least significant aspect of this process is the abandonment of the 'absolutist' view of property with which most of us begin—the passionate and instinctive belief that ownership is unqualified, sacrosanct and inviolable—and the adoption of a more 'relativist' perception that entitlements of property are constantly defined and redefined by competing user rights, by social context and by community-directed obligation.

— *Limitations of the property reference* It remains painfully true that most of our everyday references to property are naive and moderately meaningless. In our crude way we are seldom concerned to look behind the immediately practical or functional sense in which we employ the term 'property' in relation to land. What does it really mean to say that Greenacre is your 'property' or that you 'own' 88 Mill Road, Sodcaster? It certainly does not mean that you are entitled to exercise an unlimited range of rights over this land. You are not automatically entitled to alter your 'property', build on it or extend it, paint it whatever colour you like, or even destroy it if you should so choose. 'Your' land may well be subject to a multitude of rights vested simultaneously in a number of strangers. 'Your' land remains vulnerable to compulsory purchase by the state, on usually less than satisfactory terms, if such unconsented transfer is ever deemed to serve a higher public or social purpose or even, sometimes, if you fail (or simply cannot afford) to maintain the land to the standard deemed appropriate by some state official. What then of the lofty assertion that this is your 'property'?

— *The mistaken reification of property* The root of the difficulty lies in the fact that non-lawyers (and sometimes even lawyers) tend to speak rather loosely of 'property' as the *thing* which is owned (e.g. 'That book/car/house is my *property*'). Whilst this reification of property is harmless enough in casual conversation, it has the effect of obscuring important features of property as a legal and social institution (see *Yanner v Eaton* (1999) at [18] per Gleeson CJ, Gaudron, Kirby and Hayne JJ). We must therefore begin with some conceptualisation about property. Abstractions are never easy, of course, but bear with them for the moment because they should illuminate some of what follows in this book.

— *Property is not actually a thing but a power relationship* Deep at the heart of the phenomenon of property is the semantic reality that 'property' is not a thing, but rather the condition of being 'proper' to a particular person (e.g. 'That book/ car/house is *proper* to *me*'). Indeed, in archaic English, the word 'proper' served precisely to indicate relationships of proprietary significance. Thus the poor were described as not 'hauyng ony thynge proper'; and a very early 15th-century reference describes someone as having been slain 'with his own propre swerd'. For serious students of property, the beginning of truth is the recognition that property is not a *thing* but a *power relationship*—a power relationship of social and legal legitimacy existing between a person and a valued resource (whether tangible or intangible). Several consequences follow.

All property talk is value-laden

2.2 The etymological links between such terms as 'property', 'proper', 'appropriate', and 'propriety' underscore the value-laden complexity of inter-relating nuances of property talk. Genuine property discourse thinly conceals a subtext of *social propriety*: all property references are, at some level, a statement about the social legitimacy attaching to the claim in question. The limits of property, it was once said, 'are the interfaces between accepted and unaccepted social claims' (*Dorman v Rodgers* (1982) per Murphy J). Indeed the law of property has always said much more than is commonly supposed about the subject of human rights, which is one of the reasons why the English law of realty is now so heavily implicated in the assimilation of European human rights standards brought about by the Human Rights Act 1998 (**2.15**).

— *Property in slaves* Test some of the foregoing propositions by transmuting the sentence, 'That slave is Robert's property', into the more revealing assertions that 'Robert has property in that slave', and then 'That slave is proper to Robert'. It becomes more immediately apparent why the institution of slavery came to be viewed as morally abhorrent and as (eventually) worthy of legal repression. The possibility of having property in other human beings was repudiated when it became socially accepted that human beings could never be described as exhibiting the condition of being 'proper' to other fellow human beings.

— *The modern 'right to roam'* A similar evolution of proprietary morality is to be found in the insistence, on the part of supporters of the statutory 'right to roam' (**5.6**), that no individual may ever claim *exclusive* property in a mountain or any other extensive tract of wild country. (For some, a certain sense of incomprehension is provoked by the recollection that Quinag, an incomparably fine mountain in Sutherland, was once presented as a gift by one member of the landed aristocracy to another.) Today there is, unquestionably, an incipient collective doubt as to the propriety of large vestings of scenic space in relatively small numbers of private and exclusive 'owners'. This is particularly so since '[i]n the case of real property there is a defined and limited supply of the commodity' (*Linden Gardens Trust Ltd v Lenesta Sludge Disposals Ltd* (1994) per Lord Browne-Wilkinson). The modern expansion of rights of recreational access over privately held land articulates one increasingly important component of the liberal democratic ideal, a virtue which some have called 'pedestrian democracy'.

— *The ultimate link between property and human value* Excessive claims of exclusive ownership always threaten, in John Locke's well-known phrase, to bring about a world in which there is not 'enough, and as good left in common for others' (*Two Treatises of Government: The Second Treatise*, s 27). It was Henry George who more darkly imagined that if one claimant could concentrate in himself 'the individual rights to the whole surface of the globe, he alone of all the teeming population of the earth would have the right to live' (*Poverty and Progress* (1981) (first published 1879), p 345). And, as Lord Bingham of Cornhill has more recently declared, 'few things are more central to the enjoyment of human life than having somewhere to live' (*Harrow LBC v Qazi* (2004) at [8]).

Property is a quantum of socially approved control

2.3 Once property is recognised as a relationship of socially approved control, it becomes infinitely more accurate to say that one has property *in* a thing than to declare that something is one's *property*. To claim 'property' in a resource is, in effect, to assert a strategically important degree of control over that resource. 'Property' is simply the word used to describe particular concentrations of *power over* things and resources, and every claim of 'property' comprises the assertion of some *quantum* (or amount) of socially permissible power as exercisable in respect of some socially valued resource. The implications of this perspective are significant.

— *Property is relative* The power relationship implicit in property is not an *absolute* but a *relative* phenomenon. In relation to land, as we shall see later, the common law knows no absolute title; all title remains relative and, even in its statutory form, essentially defeasible (see the law of registered title, **12.28**).

— *Property has gradations* There can be *gradations* of 'property' in a resource; and these gradations may even vary over time (see e.g. the law of adverse possession (**6.4**); the law of proprietary estoppel (**10.26**)). The *quantum* of property which a specified individual may claim in any piece of land can be calibrated as falling somewhere between a *maximum* value and a *minimum* value. A maximal property value is, of course, provided by something like ownership of the fee simple estate (**1.18, 7.2**). But where a property value tends towards zero (as, for instance, in the claim of a bare licensee (**4.2**)), it may become a misuse of language to say that the claimant has any property at all in the land in question. Yet even here it is noticeable that one of the cutting edges of contemporary human rights jurisprudence concerns the degree to which various rather imprecise 'expectations' relating to land can be regarded as 'possessions' capable of protection under the property guarantee of the European Convention on Human Rights (**2.7, 2.15**).

— *Property in land* In the absence of any generalised concept of *dominium* or direct ownership of land (**1.15**), the historic technique of the common law has been to parcel up various degrees of socially approved control over the resource of realty, describing each parcel (or *quantum*) of control in terms of some artificially defined conceptual entitlement in respect of the land (**1.16–1.17**). The precise quantum of control which any individual has over a particular block of land—or, as one might just as easily say, the amount of 'property' which he or she has in that land— is therefore demarcated by the size of the 'estate' or 'interest' (if any) which he or she holds.

• Some abstract bundles of entitlement connote the allocation to the right-holder of a large element of socially permitted control over the use and exploitation of the land in question. For example, those who own a fee simple estate (or even a term of years) in Greenacre can quite accurately assert that they have a lot of 'property' in that land (**3.4**).

• Other bundles of entitlement connote that the right-holder enjoys sig-nificantly less control over—i.e. has only a *limited* quantum of 'property' in—the land concerned. For instance, the person who owns an easement to use another's land as a communal garden can certainly claim to have *some* 'property' in that land, but not to the extent of having a right to dictate that a flower bed be maintained for ever in one particular location in the garden (see *Jackson v Mulvaney* (2003) at [25]). This kind of claim to a much more intense degree of control over the terrain is inconsistent with the 'estate' actually owned (i.e. an easement) and is, instead, an illicit assertion of some rather larger quantum of 'property' in the land such as that denoted by a fee simple estate (see e.g. *Copeland v Greenhalf* (1952), **8.14**).

— *There is a spectrum of 'propertiness'* Most kinds of property claim lie straddled at some intermediate point across a spectrum of 'propertiness'. Far from being a monolithic notion of standard content and invariable intensity, 'property' turns out to have an almost infinitely gradable quality; and it can be quite important to measure the *quantum* of property which someone has in a particular resource at any particular time. Upon this may depend the ability of a specific entitlement to survive onward transfers of an estate in the land concerned (**2.12**) or even to qualify for protection under the European Convention on Human Rights (**2.7**). The element of relativity pervades all rights in realty; land-related claims cover a broad spectrum. Some claims simply lack a sufficient quantum of 'property' to enter the threshold of the land lawyer's concern. But just as some land-related claims lack sufficient gravamen to rank in terms of 'property', so too other claims may be ruled out precisely because they assert over-large powers of control which, if unchecked, threaten to operate in an anti-social manner. In this way the concept of 'property' in land is curtailed at both ends of the spectrum.

Impact of wider rights and responsibilities

2.4 Property is a socially constructed concept; and former perceptions of property as a monopolistic right of control and exploitation have long since been eroded by wider conceptions of the public good. *Maximal* claims of property in land are far from *absolute* entitlements of property. Even the maximal claim asserted by the fee simple owner is nowadays subject to severe restriction in the public interest (**13.3**, **13.22**). The purchase of a 'bundle of rights' in land, it has been aptly said, 'necessarily includes the acquisition of a bundle of limitations' (see *Gazza v New York State Department of Environmental Conservation* (1997)).

— *Impermissible arrogations of proprietary power* Some kinds of claim, as we have already noted (**2.3**), constitute excessive, and therefore impermissible, arrogations of property in the resource of land. The fee simple owner who bars the way to those who would rescue the child from the mad axeman on his premises is doubtless claiming a quantum of property in excess of our collective social tolerances. His assertion, in these circumstances, of an otherwise standard exclusory privilege (**2.8**) takes him well beyond the limits of the property which we nowadays recognise in land.

— *Public interest controls on property in land* The quantum of property which any person may claim in land today is curtailed both by human rights considerations (**2.15**) and by the impact of an extensive range of planning and environmental controls which regulate the development of the urban and rural landscape (**2.19, 13.22**). Parliament has already, for purposes of enhanced recreational access and greater 'social equity', limited the powers of estate owners to exclude the general public from substantial tracts of wild and scenic country (**2.2**). There is also nowadays a large question whether landowners may properly claim a right to exclude the individual citizen for no good reason from various sorts of socially valuable 'quasi-public' space which function as attractive venues for a range of recreational, educational and associational uses (**4.5**).

Multiple claims of 'property' in the same land

2.5 It follows from the gradable quality of 'property' that, even in relation to the same land, the law often oversees a simultaneous distribution to a number of persons of distinct allocations of 'property', each of a different form of intensity. It is almost uniformly the case that one person's claim of 'property' in a particular parcel of land is wholly consistent with the acquisition or retention by *others* of different quantums of 'property' in the same resource. Let us consider, for a moment, a hypothetical block of land, Greenacre, the fee simple estate in which is owned by X.

— *The landlord–tenant relationship* X's ownership of a *fee simple estate* in Greenacre is entirely compatible with Y's assertion of a *term of years* (or *lease*) in the same land (**7.10**): X is simply Y's landlord. Both may quite correctly claim to have 'property' in Greenacre, albeit that the quantum of each property claim is different— X's is larger because unlimited by time—and even though their respective claims are mediated through the language of different estates in the land (**1.16–1.21**).

— *Restrictive covenants* Suppose that one of X's neighbours, N, acquires from X the benefit of some restrictive undertaking respecting the user of Greenacre, e.g. an agreement that no building of more than one storey will be constructed on it. An agreement of this kind confers on N a degree of control over the use and exploitation of Greenacre which, although markedly less extensive than the control implicit in ownership of (say) the fee simple estate, is nevertheless of some significance. For over 150 years English law has recognised that such adjustments of the balance of power in respect of land connote the allocation of a distinct quantum of 'property' to the beneficiary of the arrangement. For this reason N is acknowledged to be the owner of an equitable proprietary interest in Greenacre—an entitlement which is known as a *restrictive covenant* (see *Tulk v Moxhay* (1848), **9.26–9.27**).

— *Easements* Likewise, if another of X's neighbours, Q, acquires a right of way over Greenacre—e.g. shared use of a driveway—this entitlement denotes that a further sliver or quantum of 'property' in Greenacre has been transferred to Q. This particular marginal shift in the balance of control over Greenacre is described as the grant of an *easement* (**2.3**, **8.3**, **9.12**).

— *Other proprietary claims* The taxonomy of claims affecting Greenacre is readily expandable: a bank may hold a *legal charge* (or *mortgage*) over Greenacre (**8.28**, **9.16**), whilst a partner or an ageing parent or a business associate may have rights, based on *co-ownership* or *estoppel*, to share a house or other building constructed on Greenacre (**9.37**, **10.2**, **10.18**, **11.1**). Likewise, the supplier of industrial plant may have a *right of entry*, entitling him (in the event of default) to come and remove machinery which has been hired for use in a factory on Greenacre (**1.9**, **8.35**). Alternatively a property developer may hold an *option* to purchase either the fee simple estate or a long lease in Greenacre, a right of option being considered to confer on the option-holder a substantial form of property in the land (**9.10**).

— *Parasitic (or dependent) forms of property in land* It is already abundantly clear that Greenacre may be the subject of multiple, and wholly reconcilable, claims of property vested in a number of different persons. Each quantum of property is capable of independent allocation, although in some cases (such as the property comprised in the restrictive covenant or easement) the 'property' in question is parasitic (or dependent) upon some larger form of 'property' in *other* land—let us say, *Redacre*—which receives the benefit of the arrangement. This means, in practice, that the benefit of restrictive covenants and easements over *Greenacre* must be 'annexed' or attached to an estate in fee simple or a term of years in *Redacre* (**8.6, 9.29**) and that the person who seeks to enforce the restrictive covenant or easement against *Greenacre* must be the freeholder or leaseholder of *Redacre*. It also follows that the benefit of such a restrictive covenant or easement cannot be transferred to a third party except in conjunction with a disposition of a freehold or leasehold estate in *Redacre* (**8.24, 9.32**).

Irreducible features of property

2.6 Although the definition of proprietary entitlement comprises a notorious con-undrum of the law, it is possible to isolate at least three key features which lie irreducibly at the core of property as a social and semantic phenomenon:

- immunity from summary cancellation or extinguishment (**2.7**);
- presumptive entitlement to exclude others (**2.8**);
- entitlement to prioritise resource values (**2.9**).

Immunity from summary cancellation or extinguishment

2.7 Firmly embedded in the notion of 'property' is the idea that 'property' implies an entitlement which is not arbitrarily terminable at the will of others. Irrevocability is 'an important feature of an estate or interest in land' (*R v Toohey, ex parte Meneling Station Pty Ltd* (1982) per Wilson J). Precarious enjoyment and fragility of tenure are the antithesis of 'property'; and rights which are liable to summary, uncon-sented and uncompensated cancellation—whether by the state or by some other party—cannot comprise 'property' in the generally accepted sense of the term.

- The prohibition on the arbitrary deprivation of property 'expresses an essential idea which is both basic and virtually uniform in civilised legal systems' (*Newcrest Mining (WA) Ltd v Commonwealth of Australia* (1997) per Kirby J). The common law instinct against peremptory dispossession is at least as old as Magna Carta and it is even arguable that the ideal of democratic government developed specifically in Northwestern Europe during the last millennium is derived from some Anglo-Saxon and Norse concept of the importance of 'seisin' or undisturbed possession (**3.3**) (see A. E-S. Tay, 'Law, the citizen and the state', in E. Kamenka, R. Brown, and A. E-S. Tay (eds), *Law and Society: The Crisis in Legal Ideals* (Edward Arnold, London, 1978), p 10).

• Herein lies one of the more important interfaces between 'property' and the modern law of human rights. The human right to protection from arbitrary dispossession is nowadays encapsulated in ECHR Protocol No 1, Art 1 (see Human Rights Act 1998, s 1(1), Sch I, Part II). This pivotal provision proclaims that

> Every natural or legal person is entitled to the peaceful enjoyment of his possessions. No one shall be deprived of his possessions except in the public interest and subject to the conditions provided for by law and by the general principles of international law.
>
> The preceding provisions shall not, however, in any way impair the right of a State to enforce such laws as it deems necessary to control the use of property in accordance with the general interest or to secure the payment of taxes or other contributions or penalties.

• *The 'fair balance' test* Although affording a significant safeguard against capricious expropriation, ECHR Protocol No 1, Art 1 makes it clear that the property guarantee is not *absolute*, but is instead heavily qualified by the 'public' or 'general' interest (see e.g. *R (Clays Lane Housing Co-operative Ltd) v Housing Corporation* (2005) at [12]). Whether an interference with property offends the overarching promise of 'peaceful enjoyment' depends ultimately on whether a 'fair balance' has been struck between 'the demands of the general interest of the community and the requirements of the protection of the individual's fundamental rights' (*Rita Ippoliti v Italy* (2006) at [39]). This kind of adjudication in turn necessitates an investigation of whether there exists 'a reasonable relationship of proportionality between the means employed and the aim sought to be realised' (see *James v United Kingdom* (1986) at [50]; *Allan Jacobsson v Sweden* (1989) at [55]). Accordingly, the 'fair balance' test is failed only where one landowner has been singled out to bear an 'individual and excessive burden' in relation to some community-directed obligation or sacrifice which should have been shared more broadly (*Sporrung and Lönnroth v Sweden* (1982) at [73]; *James v United Kingdom* (1986) at [50]).

• *Distinction between confiscation and regulation* ECHR Protocol No 1, Art 1 distinguishes between *deprivations* of property and the *control of use* of property.

Thus, whilst a 'deprivation' of property (i.e. an outright confiscation of title in the public interest) normally necessitates the payment of compensation to the land-owner (see *James v United Kingdom* (1986)), a mere 'control' of land use (e.g. through the imposition of environmental or planning restrictions) is a presumptively legitimate form of community-directed intervention which carries no 'inherent' right to compensation (see *Banér v Sweden* (1989); *R (Trailer and Marina (Leven) Ltd) v Secretary of State for the Environment, Food and Rural Affairs* (2005) at [57]–[58]). There is nevertheless an increasing inclination in modern European jurisprudence to view the more extreme forms of land use control, if unaccompanied by compensation from public funds, as a violation of the Convention (see e.g. *Matos e Silva, LDA v Portugal* (1997), **13.24**).

Presumptive right to exclude

2.8 In the traditional perception of the common law, one of the irreducible components of proprietary right is a general entitlement to exclude others from enjoyment of, or from interfering with one's own mode of enjoyment of, the resource in which 'property' is claimed.

- The 'propertiness' of property thus depends heavily on some concept of defensible monopoly, i.e. on a right to control the access of strangers to the various benefits inherent in a given resource (see *Yanner v Eaton* (1999) at [18] per Gleeson CJ, Gaudron, Kirby and Hayne JJ). Freeholders, declared Lord Russell of Killowen CJ over a century ago, 'have the right to forbid anybody coming on their land or in any way interfering with it' (*South Staffordshire Water Co v Sharman* (1896)). Were it not for the primacy of this general right of exclusion, property law would dissolve into the chaos of the commons in which all assets are constantly up for grabs and in which the process of trading with assets is neither meaningful nor necessary. It is for reasons such as these that the courts of the common law world have united behind Justice Rehnquist's iconic descriptions of the right to exclude strangers as a 'fundamental element of the property right' (*Kaiser Aetna v United States* (1979)) and as 'one of the essential sticks in the bundle of property rights' (*PruneYard Shopping Center v Robins* (1980)).

- In conventional analysis proprietary entitlement has therefore been widely understood as conferring a prerogative—however arbitrary, selective or capricious—to determine who may enjoy the resource of land and on what terms. In one extreme—and almost certainly untenable—formulation, the proprietary owner may be said to have purchased (or otherwise acquired) the right to be utterly *unreasonable* in shutting his doors against all comers (**4.5**).

Right to prioritise resource values

2.9 Not only does the notion of proprietary entitlement connote some basic exclusionary privilege exercisable against the rest of the world. The concept of property also implies, on behalf of the proprietor, a vital discretion over the priority to be accorded to the various forms of value inherent in a particular asset. The owner is, by definition, entitled to prioritise the relevant values which the land holds for him, that is to determine whether, at any given moment, to devote his interest in the land toward the objective of use, sale, endowment or recreational or cultural enjoyment, and so forth. It is this element of decisional control—of functional discretion in the governance of the resource—which goes far to distinguish proprietary entitlements from other species of right recognised by law.

The rational coordination of property in land

2.10 It falls to the land lawyer to provide a rational coordination of the many claims of property which may arise in relation to land. In separating off land as a subject of especial legal concern, English law merely follows the practice of most developed systems of law in regarding land as having enhanced qualities of utility and indestructibility which justify its differentiation from other, more perishable, forms of resource. Since land provides the physical substratum for all human interaction, the law of land inevitably operates as an instrument of social and economic engineering. In so far as land law impinges upon the orderings and expectations of the entire community, the legal coordination of the diverse species of property in land assumes enormous importance.

— *The versatility of land* We have just seen how it is possible for a number of people to acquire different, but potentially compatible, rights in respect of the same land resource (**2.5**). Somehow land law must coordinate the different property claims which proliferate around the modern freehold estate (or *fee simple*); and indeed the inter-relation of such claims comprises the stuff of much contemporary land law. Land law is made more complex because the physical asset of land is capable of simultaneously supporting an almost infinite variety of purposeful modes of exploitation, social, recreational, commercial, industrial and agricultural. The multiplicity of uses sustained by a particular block of land need not, in itself, generate conflict. It is the task of the law of property to organise a sensible structuring of land-related claims, to regulate the allocation and transfer of such claims amongst a diverse range of potential resource users, and ultimately to determine questions of priority should conflict between these resource users prove inevitable.

— *The importance of commerciability* The complexity of the task facing the land lawyer is accentuated by the significance of land as a commerciable resource. A key premise in our regime of land law has been the perception that it is vital to a functioning economy that land should remain permanently open to efficient processes of sale, lease, mortgage and other disposition. It is important, so to speak, that land should be kept on the move. One of the central truisms of market economics is the idea that the free alienability of property rights 'in practice make[s] it less likely that they will fall into disuse: market forces will tend to bring the rights into the ownership of those who will make best use of them' (*Bettison v Langton* (2000) per Robert Walker LJ). Moreover, the borrowing of money secured by mortgages of land operates as an extremely powerful engine of wealth creation, industrial growth, and commercial investment. English property law is accordingly pervaded by a strong bias in favour of commerciability, as was made clear in Lord Upjohn's memorable observation that '[i]t has been the policy of the law for over a hundred years to simplify and facilitate transactions in real property' (*National Provincial Bank Ltd v Ainsworth* (1965)). Lord Upjohn added, significantly, that it is 'of great importance that persons should be able freely and easily to raise money on the security of their property.' These large policy motivations nevertheless produce an inevitable tension between the promotion of the commerciability of land and the need to afford long-term security to a number of rights which have already been created in or over the land. When the estate owner of Greenacre deals with his estate in favour of a purchaser, what happens to the motley range of subsidiary rights which have already been generated on behalf of partners, parents, tenants, neighbours or business associates? Are their claims of property in the land destroyed by the dealing or do they somehow survive?

— *Wide definitions of the conveyancing process* Land is kept on the move by the processes of 'registered disposition' and 'conveyance', these terms being used to refer to dealings with *registered* and *unregistered* estates respectively (**2.22–2.24**).

• It is important to note that English property legislation defines the terms 'registrable disposition' and 'conveyance' extremely broadly so as to include not merely the outright transfer of an estate in land, but also the creation of any legal charge or mortgage over such an estate, together with the grant of many kinds of leasehold term out of an estate (LRA 2002, ss 27(2), 132(1); LPA 1925, s 205(1) (ii), **11.30**). A 'purchaser' is likewise defined as including 'a lessee, mortgagee or other person who for valuable consideration acquires an interest in land' (see

LPA 1925, s 205(1)(xxi)). In practice, the term 'disponee'—now a statutory term of art (see e.g. LRA 2002, ss 26(3), 52(2))—is accorded a similar ambit except in so far as a 'disponee' can also include a *donee* or a *trustee in bankruptcy*.

• The inclusion of mortgage transactions as a relevant form of disposition dramatically intensifies the practical difficulty of coordinating a myriad of potential property claims in land. As Lord Diplock famously pointed out in *Pettitt v Pettitt* (1970), Britain has evolved into 'a property-owning, particularly a real-property-mortgaged-to-a-building-society-owning, democracy'. Any disadvantage imposed by the rules of land law on large lending institutions such as banks and building societies has the potential to exert a damaging impact both on business life and on the living patterns of millions (**15.12**).

The central problem of conveyancing

2.11 Every working day in England and Wales sees the completion of thousands of transactions falling within the statutory concept of 'registered disposition' or 'conveyance'. There is, quite simply, a lot of land on the move. It has been estimated, for example, that on average one in ten adults in Great Britain moves house in any one year (*Social Trends 29* (1999 edn, London), p 171). Land Registry (the new corporate name of HM Land Registry) claims to process approximately £1 million worth of property every minute, i.e. one property sale every nine seconds (Land Registry Press Notice LRP03/03, issued 4 February 2003). Given both the sheer volume of land transactions and the importance of the policy of commerciability extolled by Lord Upjohn (**2.10**), it is plain that the operation of an efficient conveyancing system calls imperatively for a high degree of clarity in determining the fate of any property claim in land following a disposition of the estate to which it relates. As Peter Gibson LJ said in *State Bank of India v Sood* (1997), a 'principal objective' of the 1925 property legislation was 'to simplify conveyancing and the proof of title to land'. There is even a more general argument that civilised living in market economies is due not simply to greater prosperity, but rather to the order brought about by a system of formalised property rights (see Hernando de Soto, *The Mystery of Capital: Why Capitalism Triumphs in the West and Fails Everywhere Else* (Bantam Press, 2000)).

The *central problem of conveyancing* is therefore the question whether various subsidiary claims relating to land survive dispositions of the major estates (**1.20**), thereby remaining valid and enforceable against that land in the hands of another (see *Fig 3*).

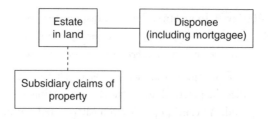

Fig 3

Indeed the fate of such property claims in the context of a disposition of land is a matter of some significance for *both* the disponee *and* the claimant of the subsidiary rights in question. People tend to make the largest investment of their lifetime in realty. It is, for them, a matter of substantial concern that rights for which they have given value should not be taken away, superseded or destroyed without proper compensation—a concern which applies just as much to the claimant of some subsidiary interest in the land as it does to the disponee of one of the major estates. Every purchaser of an estate in land (including a lender or 'mortgagee') has a clear and legitimate interest in knowing precisely which rights will remain binding on him in the aftermath of the transaction. 'In matters relating to the title to land, certainty is of prime importance' (*Ashburn Anstalt v Arnold* (1989) per Fox LJ). Any *uncertainty* over the impact of a land transaction has the effect of inhibiting purchasers and of stultifying dealings in land. No purchaser wants to risk his money if there is any danger that the land purchased may be subject to adverse claims vested in others which prejudice the value of the estate which he has taken. No one really wants to buy a law suit.

Proprietary and non-proprietary rights in land

2.12 For the purpose of determining which kinds of entitlement survive a dealing and remain binding on a new estate owner or purchaser, English land law draws a conventional distinction between 'proprietary' and 'personal' rights in respect of land.

— *Differential effects*   Only those rights classified as *proprietary* have even the potential to bind a purchaser of the land; *personal* rights can never do so, although they may sometimes retain a limited enforceability (usually by way of a remedy in damages) against their grantor, the former owner of the estate now transferred. In effect, those claims or interests which appear low in the calibrated scale of 'property' value described earlier (**2.3**) will simply not make the grade. Even though they relate in some way to the land concerned, they will not rank, in the conveyancing sense, as *proprietary* rights and cannot therefore survive dispositions of the estate to which they refer. Binding impact on a purchaser is therefore made to depend upon a threshold criterion of proprietary quality—which explains why we have invested considerable effort in articulating the theory of property in land.

— *The proprietary threshold* Somewhere across the spectrum of 'propertiness' in land there comes a point at which certain rights gather sufficient gravamen to qualify, for conveyancing purposes, as *proprietary* rights in the land. It is even possible that, in large historic processes of evolutionary development, some kinds of claim affecting land can actually alter their status, moving backwards or forwards across this threshold of proprietary quality, thereby losing or gaining that vital attribute of potential third party impact. The most famous examples of such movement include the *term of years* (**7.10**), which began as a contractual relationship only to emerge as one of our most significant proprietary estates, and the *restrictive covenant* (**2.5, 9.24**), which 150 years ago shifted significantly across the spectrum of propertiness to assume a proprietary (as distinct from purely personal) dimension. A contemporary instance involves *licences* created by *contract* (**4.6**) or *estoppel* (**4.9, 10.18**), the suggestion appearing increasingly frequently (in both statute and judge-made law) that such entitlements have now acquired certain important proprietary characteristics (**4.11, 12.20**).

Some practical illustrations

2.13 Some practical examples may serve to illustrate the way in which certain kinds of claim relating to land are recognised, almost intuitively, as having either *proprietary* or *non-proprietary* quality.

• *The dinner party invitation* Suppose we invite you to a dinner party in our home in Eden Street in three weeks' time but, without giving you any warning, sell up and move house before the appointed date. Are you, on the evening of the projected dinner party, entitled to present yourself before the new owner of our former home and demand to be wined and dined? Quite clearly not. Our original invitation conferred on you no sufficient quantum of property in our Eden Street home. In conventional analysis, you received no *proprietary* rights which could conceivably survive the transfer of our home to a total stranger. The latter would, in any event, be more than a little puzzled if you suddenly turned up and demanded a free meal. The rights which our invitation gave you were entirely *personal* in quality and, having been created gratuitously, attract no remedy even as against us, the original grantors. As we shall see later, your rights are merely those of a *bare licensee* or *invitee* (**4.2**).

• *The sitting tenant* It is really rather different if we vary the above facts by granting you a two-year leasehold term in the self-contained attic flat in our Eden Street home some three weeks before we sell up, again without warning, and transfer the house to a new estate owner. Does the tenancy which you took up now bind the unsuspecting stranger? Almost certainly yes. For reasons which we shall shortly explore (**7.13**), our grant of a *term of years* has conferred on you a sufficient quantum of property to enable you to oppose your rights against the estate taken by the new owner. In conventional analysis, your rights—the *estate* held by a sitting tenant—have crossed that vital threshold of proprietary quality and therefore have acquired the potential to bind all comers.

— *Why the difference?* Whilst the outcome in both of the above instances may seem instinctively correct, a less superficial glance at the factual situations involved may indicate greater uncertainty about the precise distinction between the cases. A purchaser is bound by one set of rights but not by the other. Yet both the dinner party guest and the sitting tenant were, alike, the recipients of the clearest permission to be present on the land in question. Neither would have ranked as a trespasser in the circumstances envisaged by the permission. The rights conferred in either case did not require to be generated in any particularly formal way, by writing or otherwise, but were capable of purely oral creation (**2.30**, **7.18**). The longer duration of the leasehold is irrelevant: a term of years can comprise the merest fragment of a year (**7.10**). It is also irrelevant that the dinner party guest was intended to give no consideration (other than the pleasure of his or her company), whilst the sitting tenant was, presumably, intended to pay a periodic rent. On closer analysis, the distinction between their rights is rather more elusive than might at first appear. The difference turns ultimately on the precise *quantum of property* which each is perceived to have been granted in our Eden Street home (**2.3**). Two further examples may assist.

• *The restaurant patron* Just in case you feel that the presence or absence of money payment was a legitimate ground of distinction between your rights as a dinner party guest and your rights as a sitting tenant, consider a slightly different case. Say that we run a restaurant in Eden Street and that you book a table three weeks ahead. Again, in the meantime and without warning, we move away, selling up to a stranger who converts our former restaurant back into residential accommodation. Are you now entitled to turn up with your fellow diners on the appointed day and insist on claiming your table as planned? Have we, by changing the circumstances, ratcheted up the 'property' component of your rights sufficiently to allow them to become enforceable against the estate taken by the new owner of our former restaurant? Again, clearly not. The restaurant booking could not be said to have conferred on you any significant 'property' in the land, any more than your cinema ticket would give you any significant 'property' in the cinema. Similarly, as the Chief Justice of Australia once tersely remarked, '[f]ifty thousand people who pay to see a football match do not obtain fifty thousand interests in the football ground' (*Cowell v Rosehill Racecourse Co Ltd* (1937) per Latham CJ).

Your rights as an intending restaurant patron, although perhaps a little more substantial than those of the dinner party invitee, are still merely those of a *contractual licensee* (**4.6**). Some claims of 'property' in land simply lack critical mass or gravamen. Thus your rights will have remained on the *personal* rather than *proprietary* side of the divide which separates out those kinds of entitlement which alone can survive transfers of estates in land. But the line of demarcation is now beginning to look just a little less distinct than before. Later we shall observe some measure of judicial uncertainty as to whether various kinds of long-term contractual licence—particularly those which most closely resemble the (indubitably proprietary) term of years—have themselves acquired a sufficient quantum of property to cross the borderline and assume the potential of binding impact upon purchasers of the relevant estate (**12.25, 12.42**).

- *The student lodger* In one final variation of our working example, suppose that, just three weeks before abruptly selling up our home in Eden Street, we took you in as a student lodger in one of our upstairs bedrooms. Under the terms of the deal you contracted to pay rent for this bedroom during the remainder of the academic year and we promised to allow you use of the kitchen and bathroom when not otherwise occupied by us. We also warned you sternly that you were not permitted to play loud music or entertain guests after 11 pm. Would your rights, so described, survive our unexpected transfer of the freehold estate in the house to a new owner? In the aftershock of our departure, are you entitled to continue to occupy your room and enjoy the other domestic facilities offered? Here, again, everything depends on the quantum of property in the land conferred on you by the terms of the original deal. Perhaps disconcertingly, the contracted arrangement in many ways resembles the case of the sitting tenant considered earlier. In conventional analysis, however, the student lodger would almost certainly not be viewed as having rights which are sufficiently proprietary to remain binding upon the new home owner. Your entitlement as our lodger was merely *personal* and *contractual*, thereby raising a money remedy against us for early and wrongful termination, but otherwise comprising no 'property' in the land which could affect a purchaser. Your rights were probably no more than those of a *contractual licensee* (**4.6**) (see e.g. *R v Tao* (1977)), although admittedly we have, once again, entered an area of penumbral uncertainty which we shall have to explore more fully (**4.11, 7.14, 12.25, 12.42**).

The definition of proprietary quality

2.14 Nowhere, perhaps, is the fragile logic of English land law more apparent than in its attempt to delineate *proprietary* rights in land from those rights which are *non-proprietary* (or merely *personal*). Yet this watershed distinction marks out the hugely significant divide between those claims which have the potential to bind third parties after a land transfer and those which never can. Although the way in which English law identifies the categories of *proprietary* right is deeply unsatisfying, there has usually been little doubt, except at the perimeters of the field, as to whether a particular entitlement is or is not *proprietary* in the relevant conveyancing sense.

— *The conventional understanding*   Conventional wisdom dictates that, in order to enjoy a proprietary as distinct from a merely personal character, rights in land must be capable of third party impact (see e.g. *Bruton v London & Quadrant Housing Trust* (1998) per Millett LJ). In other words, their benefit must be inherently transferable to strangers and their burden must also be potentially binding on new owners of the relevant estate in land. These twin indicia of assignability of benefit and enforceability of burden—of commerciability and durability—are deeply embedded in one of the classic statements of English property law. In *National Provincial Bank Ltd v Ainsworth* (1965), Lord Wilberforce declared that before a right or interest can be admitted into the 'category of property, or of a right affecting property', it must be 'definable, identifiable by third parties, capable in its nature of assumption by third parties, and have some degree of permanence or stability.' *Personal* rights in respect of land seldom enjoy any of these characteristics. Thus, for instance, the informal dinner party invitation (**2.13**)—to an occasion of ill-defined content and uncertain duration—is neither transferable to others nor apt to endure through a change of ownership of the freehold estate in the land.

— *The vice of circularity*   The difficulty with this orthodox understanding of proprietary quality is, of course, that it is riddled with circularity; it becomes entirely self-fulfilling. On conventional reasoning, a claim is proprietary if *enforceable against strangers*; and claims are enforceable against strangers provided that they are *proprietary* in character. Such propositions are tautological in so far as proprietary quality is supposedly made to depend on some criterion of 'permanence' or 'stability'; and it is radical and obscurantist nonsense to formulate a test of proprietary character in this way (see Gray [1991] CLJ 252 at 292–3). Quite often, as for instance in the *Ainsworth* case itself (above), the reason for asking whether a particular claim is *proprietary* is precisely in order to determine whether the claim is *capable* of binding purchasers of the land, thereby attaining the relevantly critical qualities of *permanence* and *stability*. Exactly the same applies to the dinner party invitation (**2.13**). Enforceability against third parties cannot serve as a criterion of 'propertiness'. Durability of entitlement cannot be both the *cause* and the *effect* of proprietary quality. Indeed, in some parallel universe (for all we know), dinner party invitations may actually command such social or ritual significance as to obligate or burden unknown third party hosts—in which case, on our conventional analysis, we would immediately ascribe to such invitations an undoubted *proprietary* quality!

— *The snare of market psychology* In present respects English property thinking has become locked into a preoccupation with commerciability which impedes deeper understanding of the third party impact of 'property'. At the core of the property lawyer's instincts is the crude belief that if something is property, you can *buy and sell it in the market*; if you can buy and sell it, it must be *property*. In a lazy confusion of thought we have tended to assume that those *descriptive* qualities of certainty and stability (which serve most usefully to identify the benefits to be traded to others) also operate as *prescriptive* hallmarks of the kinds of claim which, in the context of transfer, ought to bind third parties.

Human property rights

2.15 The fundamental, if philosophically inexact, distinction between *proprietary* and *personal* rights marks out the field of operation of the English law of realty. *Proprietary* rights alone remain the authentic concern of the land lawyer, for only these rights are capable of enduring effect, in one way or another, on all comers to the land concerned. *Personal* rights in respect of land can, on this view, be safely left to the contract lawyer, since most personal rights originate in contract and generally sound only in money damages against the other contracting party. Personal rights thus remain *outside* the realm of real property. However, this relatively simple analysis takes no account of the newly emerging phenomenon—at least in English law—of human rights jurisprudence. Almost by accident, the 'new landscape created by the Human Rights Act 1998' (see *Harrow LBC v Qazi* (2004) at [27], [32] per Lord Steyn) has threatened to transcend the classic functional divide between proprietary and personal rights. In recent years the process has evoked a distinct measure of judicial apprehension lest traditional forms of proprietary entitlement be weakened or even obliterated from the 'new landscape' (see e.g. *R (Gangera) v Hounslow LBC* (2003) per Moses J; *Newham LBC v Kibata* (2003) per Mummery LJ).

— *Human rights as a bridge between personal and proprietary entitlement* The European Convention on Human Rights identifies a number of rights and freedoms, both substantive and procedural, which are considered to be 'most central to the enjoyment of human life in civil society' (*Qazi* at [8] per Lord Bingham of Cornhill). Domestic legislation must now be given effect 'in a way which is compatible with the Convention rights' (HRA 1998, s 3(1)); and it has become unlawful for any public authority to act 'in a way which is incompatible with a Convention right' (HRA 1998, s 6(1)). One of the Convention guarantees is directly concerned to protect the citizen against interference with 'the peaceful enjoyment of his possessions' (see ECHR, Protocol No 1, Art 1, **2.7**) and is therefore a provision of key relevance in the delineation of proprietary entitlements. But other guarantees contained in the ECHR, whilst initially seeming to have a purely *personal* significance, can be seen—in so far as they regulate what can and cannot be done with realty—as creative of new forms of *proprietary* entitlement. With the incorporation of these guarantees in the Human Rights Act 1998 it has become possible to argue that certain *human* rights now bridge the divide between the *personal* and the *proprietary*. Consider the following examples.

• *Respect for private and family life and the home* ECHR Art 8 confirms that everyone 'has the right to respect for his private and family life [and] his home' and that no public authority may interfere with the exercise of this right unless such interference is necessary on specified grounds of public interest or for the 'protection of the rights and freedoms of others.' ECHR Art 8 has been described as underpinning rights of central importance to the individual's 'identity, self-determination, physical and moral integrity . . . and a settled and secure place in the community' (*Connors v United Kingdom* (2004) at [82]). Does this composite entitlement—particularly the requirement of 'respect' for one's 'home'—mean that the citizen has acquired some new form of proprietary protection which, subject only to issues of 'proportionality' (**2.15**), ranks alongside and potentially overrides the proprietary rights of others? Can, for instance, the homeowner assert his Art 8 rights as a defence against a possession claim brought by a bank which alleges that he has defaulted on his mortgage repayments (**15.20**) or by a landlord who seeks to forfeit his lease on grounds of breach of covenant (**14.11**)? Has ECHR Art 8 effectively engrafted a 'new equity' on to the property relationships of citizens? Has ECHR Art 8, as one judge recently put it, created a 'reservoir of entitlement upon which the occupier of a home can draw in order to resist an order for possession when domestic law leaves him defenceless'? (see *Patel v Pirabakaran* (2006) at [41] per Wilson LJ).

• *Rights to freedom of expression, assembly and association* ECHR Arts 10 and 11 guarantee certain rights to freedom of expression, assembly and association.

Do these freedoms indirectly alter the balance of existing proprietary rights in or over land, so as to create new entitlements for the citizen, in appropriate circumstances, to have access to the land of others for the purpose of exercising the guaranteed rights of free speech, assembly and association? It is salutary to remember that democracy remains a futile ideal without assured access to the space or terrain within which to exercise supposed democratic freedoms. Does the ECHR, in relevant respects, generate on behalf of the citizen what American jurists have called 'a kind of First Amendment easement' (see Harry Kalven, 'The Concept of a Public Forum' 1965 *Sup Ct Rev* 1 at 13)?

• *Environmental human rights* A further point of coalescence between personal and proprietary entitlement appears in the emerging concept of civic rights to environmental welfare. The ECHR guarantee of the 'right to life' (see ECHR Art 2(1)), together with the protection afforded to 'family life' and the 'home' (see ECHR Art 8), has generated in the individual a qualified claim to live free of environmental pollution and other environmental hazards (see e.g. *Lopez Ostra v Spain* (1994); *Guerra v Italy* (1998)). The overall effect may be the gradual evolution of certain 'environmental human rights' as a new jurisprudential category which straddles the boundary between personal and proprietary entitlement.

• *'Legitimate expectations' relating to realty* It is even beginning to be suggested that certain hopes or aspirations created by a public body in relation to realty rank as 'legitimate expectations' and therefore, in turn, as 'possessions' in the sense of the property guarantee of ECHR, Protocol No 1, Art 1 (see *Rowland v Environment Agency* (2004) at [85], [92] per Peter Gibson LJ, [104] per May LJ (see the horrified response from P Kenny [2003] Conv 184)). Thus, for instance, the European Court of Human Rights has upheld a claim to protection under Protocol No 1, Art 1 (**2.7**) in respect of a tenant's option to renew his lease—an option long assumed by the parties to be valid—in circumstances where the grant of the option eventually turned out to be null and void as ultra vires the supposed grantor (*Stretch v United Kingdom* (2003)).

— *A sharp division of judicial philosophy* In a series of controversial rulings the House of Lords has recently attempted to foreclose the argument that certain categories of human rights, as confirmed by the HRA 1998, give rise to freestanding proprietary entitlements and protections which compete with, and potentially derogate from, established proprietary rights under English domestic law. At stake has been the issue whether European guarantees have indirectly equipped English courts with an extra layer of discretion, based on the social merits of each individual case, to decline to enforce rights and obligations which, apart from the HRA 1998, are absolutely clear as a matter of domestic law. The question has inevitably generated a profound cleavage of opinion: the debate has ultimately been as much about the proper inter-relation of English and European legal cultures as about the delineation of proprietary entitlements. One case, in particular, was destined to pose in dramatic form the question whether a human rights defence can ever be raised in opposition to an otherwise irresistible claim for the repossession of residential premises.

> *Harrow LBC v Qazi* (2004) H, a local housing authority, claimed possession of a council house from Q, a former joint tenant whose tenancy had been terminated by his wife's unilateral notice to quit the premises (**7.31**). Q, who was left with no legal or equitable right in the house under the municipal law of property, nevertheless continued to live in the house together with his new partner. Q argued that the HRA 1998 had now interposed a requirement that any court hearing the possession claim against him must test the 'proportionality' of his eviction against the Convention guarantee of 'respect' for his 'home' (see ECHR Art 8). In forceful dissents Lord Bingham of Cornhill and Lord Steyn agreed that the potential of such scrutiny was exactly what was envisaged in the 'new landscape' created by the HRA 1998. By contrast, the majority of the House of Lords declared that the European test of 'proportionality' was entirely irrelevant in the context of a claim by a party who, like H, was already fully entitled under domestic law to obtain an automatic possession order against a former tenant. There is, said Lord Millett (at [108]) 'nothing further to investigate' in terms of 'proportionality'. The landlord's existing proprietary entitlements 'under the ordinary law' could not be deflected by some additional exercise of discretionary judgment based on 'the degree of impact on the tenant's home life of the eviction'. To hold otherwise would be to 'engage in social engineering in the housing field' and to effect a significant judicial 'amendment of the domestic social housing legislation' ([123], [146], [151]–[152] per Lord Scott of Foscote). ECHR Art 8, said the majority, is concerned with *privacy* rather than *property*, with the result that this Article can never be invoked to defeat contractual or proprietary rights to possession which are already established under municipal law ([50]–[53], [82]–[84] per Lord Hope of Craighead [89], [109] per Lord Millett, [149] per Lord Scott). Any contrary construction, indicated Lord Scott (at [125]), would 'hold that Article 8 can vest property rights in the tenant and diminish the landlord's contractual and property rights … an effect which [Article 8] was never intended to have'.

• In *Qazi* the House of Lords thus struck the first blow in the battle to determine whether the ECHR alters the force field of existing entitlements under the orthodox law of property. Albeit by a narrow majority, the House affirmed that the enforcement of proprietary rights as already established under municipal law does not necessitate any further scrutiny in terms of a supra-national charter of rights. In particular, the Art 8 guarantee of 'respect' for the citizen's 'home' does not 'vest in the home-occupier any contractual or proprietary right which he would not otherwise have' ([144] per Lord Scott). For the minority in *Qazi*, however, this immensely conservative and non-purposive conclusion exhibited a 'basic fallacy' in that, contrary to 'the general thrust' of the decisions of the European Court of Human Rights, it 'allows domestic notions of title, legal and equitable rights, and interests, to colour'—one might even say to *control*—the interpretation of ECHR Art 8 ([27] per Lord Steyn). To withdraw domestic law procedures from judicial scrutiny for conformity with Art 8 was to cause the ECHR to be 'much more remotely engaged in the fabric of our domestic law' and, thereby, to fail to provide a process which is 'demanded by the fullness of our municipal law of human rights' (see *Sheffield CC v Smart* (2002) at [27] per Laws LJ).

• An opportunity to revisit the issues addressed in *Qazi* soon arose when the European Court of Human Rights, without referring to *Qazi*, seemed to hold that ECHR Art 8 remains applicable notwithstanding the exhaustion of domestic law entitlements (see *Connors v United Kingdom* (2004)). The apparent conflict of approach fell to be resolved in the context of two further cases in which defendants were confronted with claims of possession which, as a matter of domestic law, were absolutely unqualified and irresistible. In the conjoined appeals in *Kay v Lambeth LBC; Leeds CC v Price* (2006) the House of Lords—sitting this time as a panel of seven judges—struggled to reconcile *Qazi* and *Connors*. In the result four law lords effectively reaffirmed, in very large part, the view taken by the majority in *Qazi*, but the partial dissents of three judges serve to indicate that the debate may not yet be concluded. (An invaluable synthesis of the many divergent strands in the seven *Kay/Price* speeches is to be found in the Court of Appeal's ruling in *Doherty v Birmingham CC* (2006) at [22]–[60].)

• In *Kay/Price* all seven law lords accepted that a public authority landowner is not normally required, in each and every instance of repossession, to plead or prove affirmatively that the defendant's eviction is justifiable by reference to the social merits of the case. In other words, it can ordinarily be presumed that the land-owner's proprietary entitlement as landowner automatically supplies the justification required by ECHR Art 8 for interference with the occupier's right to respect for his home. The court may assume that domestic law has already struck the proper balance between the relevant competing interests and is compatible with ECHR Art 8. It is clear that such an approach averts the 'colossal waste of time and money' which would otherwise be inflicted on the processing of possession claims in the courts ([55] per Lord Nicholls of Birkenhead). All seven law lords also accepted that the extreme proposition advanced by some of the judges in *Qazi*— that the enforcement of an unqualified right to possession under domestic law can *never* be incompatible with ECHR Art 8—must now be modified in the light of the *Connors* ruling, although this partial retreat from *Qazi* should be narrowly defined. Notwithstanding this concession, it was agreed by all that none of the defendants involved in *Kay/Price* could succeed in resisting the claims to possession brought against them.

• It was at this point that a divergence of view began to emerge in the speeches in *Kay/Price*. The majority accepted that a successful defence might be raised to summary judgment on otherwise unassailable claims to possession—but only in rare and exceptional cases. These cases would occur only where:

— there is a seriously arguable challenge under ECHR Art 8 to the law (i.e. the legal regime or framework) under which a possession order is sought and only where it is possible (with the interpretative aids of the HRA 1998) to adapt the domestic law to make it more compliant

or

— there is a seriously arguable challenge on conventional judicial review grounds (rather than under the HRA 1998) to the *decision* by the public authority landowner to recover possession.

In the majority view, the *Connors* ruling (which involved the eviction of a family of gipsies) could be rationalised on the first of these bases as a case in which the 'legal framework' under which possession was claimed was itself 'defective' both for want of due procedural safeguards and also because of a lack of 'special consideration' for the vulnerable minority group with which *Connors* was concerned ([67], [97]–[100], [108]–[114] per Lord Hope). But, whilst a human rights challenge might be mounted against the *law* which authorised repossession, the majority strongly denied that a human rights defence to possession proceedings can ever be raised on the sole basis of the defendant's *individual circumstances* (however compassionate or meritorious) or on the basis of the *social impact* which eviction would have on his home life (see e.g. [109]–[110] per Lord Hope). The HRA 1998 simply does not provide an occupier 'with a freestanding defence independent of whatever rights he may have under domestic law' ([198] per Lord Brown of Eaton-under-Heywood).

• It was here that the minority in *Kay/Price* disagreed, adopting a broader view of the kinds of circumstance which might provide a human rights defence to otherwise unqualified claims of possession. Led by Lord Bingham, the minority pointed out that, amongst the 'excepting conditions' to be met under ECHR Art 8 were the requirements that any interference with a home 'must answer a pressing social need and be proportionate to the legitimate aim which it is sought to achieve.' Individual defendants must therefore be 'given a fair opportunity to contend that the excepting conditions … have not been met on the facts of the case.' On this view, the HRA 1998 *entitles* occupiers to raise a ECHR Art 8 challenge, although such a challenge is likely to succeed only in 'rare and exceptional cases' ([28]–[30] per Lord Bingham, [56] per Lord Nicholls). Unlike the majority view (which would restrict the focus of a human rights challenge to cases of *defective law*), the minority was prepared to widen that focus to embrace issues of *social fact*. In other words, the personal circumstances of the defendant could never be ruled wholly irrelevant to the question of repossession, although Lord Bingham thought that 'problems and afflictions of a personal nature' should not avail the occupier where there are 'public services to address and alleviate those problems.'

- It remains to be seen whether the approach taken by the majority of the House of Lords in *Kay/Price* is ultimately approved when, as must some time happen, these issues are canvassed again before the European Court of Human Rights. At the time of the enactment of the HRA 1998, there was some speculation that the 'bringing home' of ECHR rights would facilitate a 'major judicial recasting of much of our social, administrative, housing and landholding law' (see David Hughes and Martin Davis, [2006] *Conv* 526). For the moment—albeit by a slender margin—the preponderant analysis in *Kay/Price* points to a 'triumph of property' (in the orthodox sense) over the broader human and social concerns which animate the ECHR and European jurisprudence in general.

Fluctuating perspectives on proprietary entitlement

2.16 Given the frailty of the conventional definition of proprietary entitlement, our own efforts to distil the essence of property in English land law must now range a little more widely. We shall find that the idea of property in land fluctuates inconsistently between perceptions of property as:

- socially constituted fact (**2.17, 6.1**);
- abstractly defined entitlement (**2.18**); and
- stewardship of a community resource (**2.19**).

In this way land law embraces a strange blend of the *behavioural*, the *conceptual*, and the *obligational* (**1.1**), a mix of overlapping perceptions which we can explore in order to get closer to the meaning of property (see Gray and Gray, 'The Idea of Property in Land', in S. Bright and J. K. Dewar (eds), *Land Law: Themes and Perspectives* (1998), p 15). There are, in effect, competing models of property as a *fact*, property as a *right*, and property as a *responsibility*. Something of the tension between these various images of property in modern land law is already apparent in the way in which ECHR protection focuses, sometimes controversially, on the organic connections surrounding the 'home' (**2.15**) and on the socialised sense of community-oriented duty which is assumed to constrain the use of land (**13.24**). Meanwhile, by contrast, domestic property legislation such as the Land Registration Act 2002 firmly characterises property in land in terms of a series of tightly defined conceptual abstractions (**2.31**).

Property as socially constituted fact

2.17 According to a deeply pragmatic approach which characterises much of the English law of realty, the phenomenon of 'property' in land is simply a product of behavioural reality or socially constituted fact. 'Property' in land is no more and no less than a socially accepted *fait accompli* based on the successful assertion of de facto possessory control. Such a view is entirely consistent with the theory that property denotes a socially endorsed concentration of power over things and resources (**2.3**).

— *The territorial imperative* On this analysis, property derives from the elemental primacy of sustained territorial domination, and the quantum of property which a person has in land is measured by his ability to vindicate his sovereign control over territorial space. 'If we defend the title to our land ... we do it for reasons no different, no less innate, no less eradicable, than do lower animals. The dog barking at you from behind his master's fence acts for a motive indistinguishable from that of his master when the fence was built' (Robert Ardrey, *The Territorial Imperative* (1967), p 16). It is, ultimately, this earthily empirical perception of property which has underpinned the historic law of adverse possession (**6.4**). It also links private law notions of property with international and constitutional law concepts of sovereignty (see *Wik Peoples v Queensland* (1996) per Gummow J). And, again, it is the want of any sense of overall territorial control which alike relegates such persons as the dinner party guest, the restaurant patron and the student lodger to the *personal* rather than *proprietary* end of the spectrum of land-related rights (**2.13**).

— *The propriety of property* At the back of this territorial perception of property is some inner sense, almost inevitably pre-legal in character, of the *propriety* of one's nexus with land.

• To have 'property' in land is not to allege a mere casual physical affinity with a particular piece of land, but rather to stake a claim to the legitimacy of this land area as one's personal space. It is to assert that the land is 'proper' to one; that one has a significant, self-constituting, self-realising, self-identifying connection with it; often that the land is, in some measure, an organic embodiment of one's personality and autonomy. To have 'property' in land connotes, ultimately, a deeply instinctive or gut sense of self-affirmation, belonging and control (see e.g. L. Fox, 'The Meaning of Home: A Chimerical Concept or a Legal Challenge?' (2002) 29 *J Law & Soc* 580). Although property in land is not, of course, confined to residential premises, it was to this same idea of organic connection that Lord Millett once alluded when he defined a 'dwelling' as the place where a person 'lives and to which he returns and which forms the centre of his existence' (*Uratemp Ventures Ltd v Collins* (2002) at [31]). For a similar perception of an owner's home as 'his own portion of the earth', see V. S. Naipaul's *A House for Mr Biswas* (Collins, 1961), p 8.

• It is this psycho-spatial understanding of property which helps to identify the two pre-eminent proprietary estates of modern law, the *fee simple* and the *term of years* (LPA 1925, s 1(1), **7.2, 7.10**). Thus the 'property' enjoyed by the leaseholder, and a fortiori by the freeholder, is indelibly associated with the claim to hold a 'stake' in the premises (see *Marchant v Charters* (1977) per Lord Denning MR). The estate owner, as distinct from the mere licensee, can 'call the place his own' (*Street v Mountford* (1985) per Lord Templeman). As Coke CJ put it so long ago, 'the house of every one is to him as his castle and fortress' (*Semayne's Case* (1604), **3.3**). And it is for these reasons that, no matter how genial the dinner party host, no matter how smooth the *maître d'*, there can be no illusion that either the dinner guest or the restaurant patron can claim any significant quantum of property in the premises in which he hopes to dine.

— *Stakeholder status* Likewise the occupant of the student bed-sit lacks the overall territorial control, the general immunity from supervisory regulation, and the self-validating inner confidence of the stakeholder, which together tend to mark out substantial claims of 'property' in land. The lodger does not feel himself to be quite 'at home' because he is apt to sense that his presence on the land—as distinct, say, from that of the sitting tenant occupying the self-contained attic flat—is somehow crucially dependent on the sufferance of another. His occupancy resonates with a certain permissive quality rather than with the arrogance of right. This deficit of overall control is particularly evident in the absence of two key features of territorial control which are particularly associated with claims of 'property' in land—*transferability of possession* (by assignment or subletting) and *defensibility of territory* (by action in trespass). Can the claimant *deal* or *trade* with his entitlement and can he *resist trespass*?

• For example, without a word having been said on the subject, the student lodger will generally feel that he is inhibited from any unilateral transfer of his room to another person—although the possibility of transfer would normally comprise an incident of 'property' in land. The average student will not assume that it is inherently permissible for him to rent his room out for a few weeks to another student or to an American tourist, even if to do so would enable him to repay his entire student loan. Some instinctive understanding of the balance of power in the lodger-relationship seems to preclude such a possibility.

• Furthermore, if the student returns to his room one day to find that his landlady (or the college housekeeper) has invaded it in her search for a missing kitchen utensil or to inspect his freshly painted walls for Blu-Tack or lurid posters, he is highly unlikely to issue a claim against her in the local county court for damages and an injunction to restrain further trespass. Yet some element of *exclusory capacity* and *quiet enjoyment* epitomises all true claims of property; and, by his supine acquiescence in someone else's overriding territorial control, the lodger has merely demonstrated that he lacks any significant quantum of property in the land (**3.4**).

One of the most critical determinants of 'property' in land is thus the mode of behaviour adopted, consciously or unconsciously, by the occupier. In some elusive way, the occupier is the master of his own destiny: he is accredited with the quantum of property which corresponds most closely to the quality of his own behaviour.

Property as conceptual entitlement

2.18 Over time an almost imperceptible by-product of the notion of 'property' as *fact* is the emergence of 'property' as *entitlement*. It is an intensely human (and largely subconscious) trait to attempt to clothe might with right, to extrapolate from de facto control to de iure entitlement, to move from pragmatic to cerebral analyses of property in land. As soon as some notion surfaces of the 'propriety' of one's territorial control, it is only a short (although important) step to conceptualise one's relationship with land in terms of certain abstract and technically manipulable *rights*. This process involves a number of implications for English law.

— *Sharply defined intellectual constructs*   As abstract perceptions of 'property' in land begin to overshadow the essentially factual, the phenomenon of 'property' in land becomes increasingly subject to stringent demands of definitional rigour. We have already seen how, centuries ago, English law invented an entire intellectual apparatus of artificial constructs in order to explain various dimensions of entitlement to land (**1.16–1.21**). 'Property' in land, in its many forms, thus appears to be constituted by a number of notional blocks of entitlement whose parameters require, at all times, clear and careful delineation. Each discrete block of entitlement—each estate or interest in land—must have cleanly hewn, crystalline edges.

• Given the doctrinal impossibility of any proprietary relationship with land except through the medium of artificial jural abstractions (**1.16**), a premium is immediately placed on the maintenance of sharp boundaries around the various intellectual constructs which form part of the overall scheme. The rights which comprise 'property' must therefore have a hard-edged integrity: 'property' must always come in neat, discrete, pre-packaged conceptual compartments. Claims of 'property' in land must be expressible in clear-cut terms which allow no doubt as to either the substance of the claim or the nature of any infringement.

• This preoccupation with definitional clarity is a consistent theme of English land law, and has served in recent years to draw particularly rigid limits around the species of right which may properly be asserted as tenancies (**7.11**), easements (**8.2, 8.5**), and restrictive covenants (**9.27**). This vigilant approach has tended to stigmatise loose, over-broad, vague or ill-defined claims as failing to exhibit a sufficient quantum of 'property' in land to qualify for enforcement against later purchasers. Victims of this filter process include many forms of mere licence and contract (**12.25**) as well as a range of extravagant or amorphous claims (such as a claim of privacy or a claim to a good view) which, by proliferating long-term burdens or 'clogs upon title', threaten to inhibit the marketability of land (**8.11**). The tendency in favour of discrete definition will doubtless be intensified by the steady inculcation of a culture of registration of rights and by current moves towards a comprehensive regime of electronic transactions in land (**2.23**).

Property as stewardship of a community resource

2.19 The role of government in the regulation of land use (**13.4–13.7, 13.22–13.24**) is now so pervasive that 'property' in land is often said to have taken on the character of a kind of social stewardship. On this analysis 'property' in land simply comprises those privileges of use and enjoyment which the state chooses to dispense to individuals and corporate actors in the implementation of its communal strategies of social and environmental design. 'Property' can therefore be conceptualised as involving—on a vast scale—the distribution by the state of user rights which are heavily conditioned and delimited by the public interest (**13.6**). On this view, 'property' in land comprises not so much a 'bundle of rights', but rather a form of delegated responsibility for land as a valuable community resource.

• Estate ownership is, in effect, nothing other than a bare residuum of socially permitted power over land resources. The precise content of each estate or interest in land is determined by the state-controlled addition or subtraction of isolated elements of 'property' (whether as part of the public planning process or by reason of the delegated bargaining power supplied by the law of easements and covenants).

• Seen from this angle, 'property' incorporates a concept not of *right* but of *restraint*, reflecting a state-regulated responsibility to contribute towards the optimal exploitation of all land resources for communal benefit. In so far as this pervasive connotation of community-directed obligation plays a pivotal role in the advancement of our environmental welfare, many now view 'property' in land in terms of a *stewardship* which resonates with the obligations of a civic or environmental trust (see e.g. Gray, 'Equitable Property' (1994) 47(2) *Current Legal Problems* 157 at 188–206; D. W. McKenzie Skene, J. Rowan-Robinson, R. Paisley, and D. J. Cusine, 'Stewardship: From Rhetoric to Reality' (1999) 3 *Edinburgh L Rev* 151).

The modern taxonomy of entitlements in land

2.20 English law has traditionally placed stringent limits on the kinds of entitlement which are considered 'proprietary' and therefore within the scope of the axiomatic rules of land law (see *Charles v Barzey* (2002) per Lord Hoffmann). The catalogue of proprietary entitlement in land has tended to comprise a closed list—a *numerus clausus*—of recognised estates and interests. In fact, these permissible forms of conceptual entitlement probably total no more than a dozen or so (see Bernard Rudden, 'Economic Theory v Property Law: The *Numerus Clausus* Problem', in J. Eekelaar and J. S. Bell (eds), *Oxford Essays in Jurisprudence (Third Series)* (Clarendon Press, 1987), pp 241–2). Unlike the position in contract, land law has generally allowed the citizen no freedom to customise new species of right. We are all required to construct our proprietary relationships using only the conventional building blocks constituted by the known 'estates' and 'interests'. As Lord Brougham LC observed in *Keppell v Bailey* (1834), 'it must not ... be supposed that incidents of a novel kind can be devised and attached to property at the fancy or caprice of any owner' (see also LPA 1925, s 4(1), proviso).

> *Hill v Tupper* (1863) (**8.7**) 'A new species of incorporeal hereditament cannot be created at the will and pleasure of an individual owner of an estate; he must be content to take the estate and the right to dispose of it subject to the law settled by decisions, or controlled by act of parliament' (Pollock CB).

A strong concern for the schematic order of land law underlies most attempts to explain the *numerus clausus* principle. The restriction on the proliferation of proprietary rights in land has allegedly served to reinforce certainty in matters of ownership and obligation and also to prevent the cluttering of land with long-term burdens of an idiosyncratic or antisocial nature. Thus, it is claimed, the maintenance of the *numerus clausus* facilitates commerce in realty by reducing the transaction costs otherwise incurred in trading with unfamiliar, non-uniform or unorthodox packages of entitlement. However, as will emerge later in this book, the advent of an increasingly comprehensive mechanism of recordation of land rights in a publicly accessible register has, in recent years, dramatically reduced the need to constrict the menu of rights deemed capable of proprietary status. The categories of proprietary entitlement are beginning to loosen up (**4.11, 9.11, 12.20**). It is nevertheless safe to say that the principal species of property right with which readers of this book will be concerned include the following (see LPA 1925, s 1(1)–(3), **2.29**):

- the fee simple absolute in possession (**7.2**);
- terms of years absolute (**7.10**);
- mortgages (**8.28**);
- easements (**8.5**);
- restrictive covenants (**9.24**);
- profits *à prendre* (**8.4**);
- beneficial interests existing under a trust of land (**9.34**);
- estate contracts (including options) (**9.8**);
- unpaid vendors' liens (**9.22**);
- purchasers' liens to secure deposit (**9.23**);
- rights of entry (**8.35**);
- rentcharges (**8.27**).

We shall, in due course, explore each of these kinds of entitlement in their turn.

A bird's-eye view of land law

2.21 Much of the difficulty in mastering land law is connected with the problems of overall structure and perspective. It is not always easy to see the regime of land law as an integrated whole. We shall therefore attempt, at this relatively early stage, to provide a bird's-eye view of the entirety, leaving the detail to be unpacked later as we proceed. (You may wish to keep your own eye trained, from time to time, on *Fig* 4.) It is worthwhile remembering that the grand scheme of English land law, as laid out in the 1925 legislation and streamlined by the Land Registration Act 2002, extends only to those rights which, in the conventional understanding, are

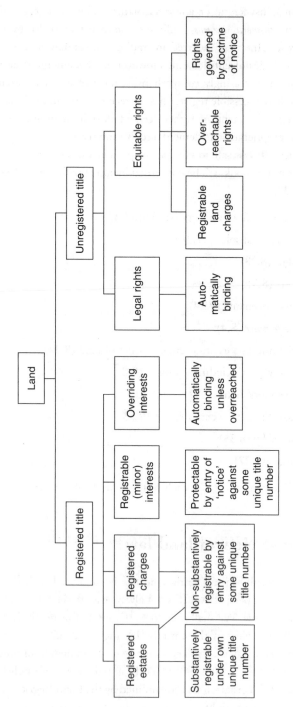

Fig 4

proprietary in nature (**2.12–2.14**). In other words, only those rights which comprise a sufficient or 'threshold' degree of property content are included within the statutory scheme; only such rights can ever bind third parties. All other entitlements in respect of land remain unregulated by the 1925 regime, usually having a mere *personal* or *contractual* significance as between grantor and grantee.

Distinction between registered and unregistered title

2.22 The most fundamental classification of the structure of English land law lies in the distinction between estates whose title has been *registered* (i.e. centrally recorded) at Land Registry and estates whose title has *not yet* been so registered. It is important to recognise that this major dichotomy between the regimes of registered and unregistered title exerts a deep impact upon the systematic organisation of land interests and the way in which these interests are protected on a transfer of title. There are, in effect, 'two systems of land ownership in this country which rest upon wholly different foundations' (Law Commission and Land Registry, *Land Registration for the Twenty-First Century* (Law Com No 254, September 1998), para 10.18). Although unregistered land cannot be ignored, the system of unregistered title 'has had its day' and will be phased out of existence within the foreseeable future (see Law Commission and Land Registry, *Land Registration for the Twenty-First Century: A Conveyancing Revolution* (Law Com No 271, July 2001), para 1.6). Increasing numbers of unregistered estates have already been drawn on to the Land Register maintained by Land Registry (**2.25, 12.33**). *Registered title* is incontestably the primary regime of modern land law and inevitably, therefore, we shall place it in the forefront of our analysis in this book.

The basic structure of title registration

2.23 With effect from 13 October 2003 the law of registered title in England and Wales has been governed by the Land Registration Act 2002 and by its satellite regulatory system, the Land Registration Rules 2003. This new and significantly rationalised legislative scheme replaces the Land Registration Acts 1925–1997 and marks an important advance towards the long-awaited goal of comprehensive registration of electronically transactable titles in land.

— *The key strategy* The linchpin of the LRA 2002 is the general idea that every *fee simple estate* and long *term of years* (i.e. every leasehold term of more than seven years) may, and often must, be recorded as an individual registered title on the Land Register under a unique title number (see LRR 2003, r 4(1))—a process sometimes known as 'independent' or 'substantive' registration (**2.31, 7.7, 7.19–7.22**). Under the statutory scheme most other sorts of proprietary interest affecting either of these registered estates are then entered against the *burdened* title number (and often also entered on the title number of the estate *benefited*) (**12.11**). The estate contained in each substantively registered title therefore functions, in effect, as a kind of *major* interest around which are clustered register entries relating to a range of *minor* interests. (Although the terminology of major and minor interests is not used by today's legislation (**12.6**), this was the way in which Viscount Dilhorne—not a trained exponent of land law principle—found it helpful to express the broad organisational strategy of registered land during argument before the House of Lords in *Williams & Glyn's Bank Ltd v Boland* (1981).)

— *The mirror principle* Individual registers of title at Land Registry are publicly accessible sources of information relating to land, the overwhelming majority of such registers now existing in the form of data recorded on hard disk. The information collated by the Chief Land Registrar at first registration (**12.33**) is held in one or other of the three subdivisions of each individually numbered register of title (i.e. the 'proprietorship register', the 'property register' and the 'charges register' (LRR, 2003, rr 4–9, **6.2**)). A register of title, once created, is updated not only on subsequent registered dealings with the title, but also as further entries are made to protect freshly arising minor interests relating to the land. Thus, in respect of any particular registered estate, the register of title is broadly intended to operate as a *mirror*, reflecting to the potential disponee (and to any other interested person) the totality of the proprietary benefits and burdens which currently affect the land. The register provides, in effect, a pretty accurate snap-shot of title at any given moment. The disponee of a registered estate is, of course, bound by the contents of the relevant register (LRA 2002, s 29(1)–(2), **12.9**) but, as we shall see, the repetitive investigation of paper title which is characteristic of transactions in unregistered conveyancing (**2.24**) is rendered wholly redundant. The definitive record of the register eliminates any need for retrospective documentary investigation *outside* the register. As Lord Oliver of Aylmerton indicated in *Abbey National Building Society v Cann* (1991), the 'governing principle' of land registration is that 'the title to land is to be regulated by and ascertainable from the register alone'. The overall objective is that a prospective purchaser of registered land should always be able to verify, by simple examination of the register, the exact nature of all interests existing in or over the land which he proposes to buy.

— *The 'crack in the mirror'* The LRA 2002—as earlier the LRA 1925—nevertheless allows some kinds of proprietary entitlement to exist 'off the register' (even in certain cases where the rights involved *could* have been protected by entry in the register). These unrecorded rights, which are generally detectable on a physical inspection of the land, are known as interests which 'override' registered titles. The most important comprise short legal leases not exceeding seven years (**7.23, 12.17**) and any proprietary interest belonging to a 'person in actual occupation' of the land (see LRA 2002, ss 11(4)(b), 12(4)(c), Sch 1, s 29(1)–(2)(a)(ii), Sch 3, **2.33, 12.18**). Such entitlements—commonly known as 'overriding interests'—automatically bind any proprietor of a registered title and thereby detract, at least marginally, from the completeness of the mirror image which the Land Register is meant to reflect.

— *The eventual aim of dematerialised conveyancing* As long ago as 1857 it was the fervent hope of the Royal Commissioners on Land Transfer and Registration to enable owners 'to deal with land in as simple and easy a manner ... as they can now deal with moveable chattels or stock'. The aim of the modern Land Registry is effectively the same—to maintain a 'cornerstone for the creation and free movement of interests in land' and to 'provide ready access to up-to-date and guaranteed land information, so enabling confident dealings in property and security of title' (Land Registry, *Annual Report and Accounts 2005/6* (July 2006), p 9). The Registry is 'passionate about making property transactions easier for all ... We want Land Registry to be at the heart of the most efficient property market in the world' (ibid, Appendix 4 (p 112)). In the next few years this vision will become more readily attainable with the advent, under the LRA 2002, of a new system of electronic or dematerialised conveyancing in which the process of transacting with land is generally inseparable from simultaneous entry in, or amendment of, the Land Register (**12.5**). The professed (and indeed the 'fundamental') objective of the Act of 2002 is to render the register a 'complete and accurate reflection of the state of the title to land at any given time, so that it is possible to investigate title on line, with the absolute minimum of additional enquiries and inspections' (Law Com No 271 (2001), para 1.5). Towards this end the new legislation removes many of the deficiencies in the mirror image presented by the register, not least by severely reducing the categories of overriding interest permitted under the registered land scheme (**12.15**).

The basic structure of unregistered title

2.24 The regime of *unregistered* title contrasts markedly with the largely comprehensive and definitive public record of proprietary rights contained in the Land Register.

— *Title deeds* Unregistered titles exist only in the form of chains of documentary records (or 'title deeds') which detail successive transactions with reference to a particular parcel of land (**6.1**). These historic documents of title remain essentially private, under the control of the owner of the estate to which they relate, but must be produced on any conveyance of the land in order to enable a purchaser to verify his vendor's title. By investigating title (i.e. by examining the relevant title deeds stretching back over a period of at least 15 years (LPA 1969, s 23, **12.37**)), the purchaser is generally able to discover most of the proprietary estates, interests and charges impinging upon the land. If this process of exploration enables him to find a 'good root of title' and an unbroken chain of subsequent dealings leading out of the past straight to his vendor, the purchaser can safely complete the transaction by paying over the purchase money and taking a conveyance of the unregistered estate.

— *The deficiencies of unregistered conveyancing* Unregistered conveyancing has always been a cumbersome process, proving self-perpetuating, repetitive, protracted and costly. In *Williams & Glyn's Bank Ltd v Boland* (1981), Lord Scarman spoke of the 'wearisome and intricate task of examining title'. Titles have to be investigated afresh on every successive purchase, obliging each intending purchaser to form his or her own judgement as to the quality of the relevant title and to calculate the likelihood that any defects in that title may prejudice future value or marketability. (This aspect of unregistered conveyancing contrasts unfavourably with the more streamlined proof of title provided by registered conveyancing, where the title to be transacted has already been examined definitively by the Chief Land Registrar prior to first registration, graded and guaranteed by him, and accurately updated since then.) In unregistered conveyancing, moreover, the purchaser's liability to pre-existing entitlements is extended by a scheme of *land charge registration* (**2.41, 12.35**) and by the operation of equitable rules relating to *actual* or *constructive notice* (i.e. real or deemed knowledge on the part of the purchaser) (**1.26, 12.39–12.42**).

The transition to registered title

2.25 For some time the jurisdiction of England and Wales has been moving inexorably towards the comprehensive registration of title. Virtually all forms of disposition of an unregistered estate nowadays 'trigger' a compulsory first registration of title at Land Registry. For example, such registration is now mandatory in the case of most transfers of an unregistered legal freehold (**7.7**) or of an unregistered legal leasehold with more than seven years left to run (**7.21**). Likewise all new grants of a leasehold term of more than seven years, together with most first legal mortgages relating to any unregistered freehold or leasehold estate, require to be completed by registration of title to the relevant lease or charge (LRA 2002, ss 4(1)–(2), 6(1)–(3), **7.7, 7.20–7.21**). The steady extension of the triggers for first registration has ensured that the number of currently unregistered estates is rapidly diminishing as more newly transacted titles are brought on to the Land Register. (It has been estimated that some 85 per cent of all land titles in England and Wales are now registered under the Land Registration Act: see Land Registry, *Annual Report and Accounts 2001–2002* (July 2002), p 52.) One overall objective of this conversion of title to the computerised format of the Land Register has been, quite clearly, the creation of the legal and technological framework for a system of 'paperless' transactions and electronic dealings with interests in land (see Law Com No 271 (2001), paras 1.1, 1.4, 2.1, 2.41), a scheme which is expected to be piloted from 2007 (**12.3**).

A growing 'culture of registration'

2.26 An important motivation underlying the enactment of the LRA 2002 was the vision, jointly entertained by the Law Commission and Land Registry, of a future founded upon a 'culture of registration' (see Law Com No 254 (1998), para 1.14). Against the background of what will soon become a world of electronic commerce and dematerialised conveyancing, both bodies accepted that it was right to 'lay to rest the notion ... that it is somehow unreasonable to expect those who have rights over registered land to register them' (Law Com No 271 (2001), para 8.58).

— *Synchronous registration* The modern aim is a 're-engineering [of] the conveyancing process' (Land Registry, *Annual Report and Accounts 2001–2002* (July 2002), p 20). Accordingly the LRA 2002 not only makes the process of registration very much easier, but also envisages that, in relation to the express creation or transfer of most land rights, 'the execution of the transaction in electronic form and its simultaneous registration will be inextricably linked' (Law Com No 271, para 1.9, **7.8, 12.2, 12.5**). Such synchronous registration of electronic dispositions is 'the single most important technical objective' of the LRA 2002 (ibid, para 2.60); and the 'essential feature' of the new scheme of electronic conveyancing will be the idea that registration itself operates as the sole constitutive source of expressly created rights in registered land (ibid, para 5.3). It will not therefore be possible to generate or dispose of most interests except by means of some contemporaneous entry in the register. The fact that entitlement will be conferred by 'registration and registration alone' will serve dramatically to reinforce the 'fundamental principle of a conclusive register' which underpins the Act of 2002 (ibid, para 1.10). Indeed, one of the most significant effects of the new Act is to consolidate and protect the proprietorship of registered estates in land, making them far less vulnerable to unforeseen or adventitious claims which derogate from the plenary quality of the title conferred by registration (see Gray and Gray, 'The rhetoric of realty', in J. Getzler (ed.), *Rationalizing Property, Equity and Trusts: Essays in Honour of Edward Burn* (Butterworths, 2003), p 244).

— *The residue of unregistered estates* For a relatively brief period a residue of *unregistered* estates will continue to exist in English land (e.g. short leases and estates owned by corporations which have no need to sell or mortgage their land). And it is, in general, the principles of unregistered land law which determine, on first registration of title, the nature and priority of the estates, interests and rights which have accumulated around unregistered titles and which need to be recorded on the Land Register. Nevertheless the Law Commission, immediately prior to the enactment of the LRA 2002, committed itself to the view that 'remaining unregistered land should be phased out as quickly as possible' (Law Com No 271 (2001), para 2.9). The continued existence of two separate systems of conveyancing—the registered and the unregistered—was and is 'absurd' and it is now clear that the unregistered regime 'must be given its quietus' (ibid, para 2.6). It is likely that, at some future point, all surviving unregistered titles will be swept compulsorily on to the Land Register and Land Registry has targeted 2012 as the year in which it expects to have created a 'comprehensive Land Register for England and Wales' (see Land Registry, *Annual Report and Accounts 2005/6* (July 2006), p 11, Appendix 4 (p 112)).

Divergent principles of registered and unregistered land law

2.27 As will soon become apparent, there are often marked differences between the principles governing registered and unregistered estates. Many of the classic concepts of unregistered land (e.g. the equitable doctrine of notice, **1.26, 2.43, 12.39**) are rendered redundant in the scheme of registered title and would, in any event, be wholly incompatible with the successful operation of electronic conveyancing (see Law Com No 271 (2001), paras 5.16 and 5.21). From time to time the divergence of registered and unregistered land principles causes large discrepancies of substantive outcome (see e.g. *Lloyds Bank plc v Carrick* (1996), **9.8**, where the Court of Appeal reached a conclusion in terms of unregistered title which Morritt LJ openly conceded would have been resolved in a diametrically opposite direction if the land had been *registered*). The Law Commission has long acknowledged that 'there are substantive differences between registered and unregistered land', but accepts that there is 'little justification in trying at all costs to keep the two systems in step'. Registered land, said the Commission, 'is after all to be the way forward, the new improving on the old' (Law Com No 158 (1987), para 2.5). The Commission has since observed that there 'seems little point in inhibiting the rational development of the principles of property law by reference to a system which is rapidly disappearing, and in relation to which there is diminishing expertise amongst the legal profession' (Law Com No 254 (1998), para 1.6).

The watershed between legal and equitable rights

2.28 Following the distinction between registered and unregistered titles, the next most important structural classification in English land law is the differentiation of *proprietary* rights into categories of *legal* and *equitable* entitlement. Although historical factors underlie the distinction (**1.24**), the borderline between legal and equitable rights in land is now drawn, definitively and pretty arbitrarily, by the legislation of 1925 and 2002. The ultimate importance of the distinction is being steadily eroded by the extension of title registration, but this historic watershed between various sorts of right in land still provides a vital key to resolving many disputed issues of priority.

The statutory starting-point

2.29 Some realisation of the significance of the distinction between legal and equitable rights may be gained from the fact that the demarcation of these categories appears in the opening section of the primary enactment of 1925, the Law of Property Act 1925, as adapted by the Land Registration Act 2002.

— *Rights authorised to exist 'at law' (i.e. as legal rights)* The range of proprietary entitlements in or over land comprises a relatively limited canon of rights (i.e. a *numerus clausus*, **2.20**). From within this cluster of rights the LPA 1925 isolates a group of estates, interests and charges which are expressly declared to be capable of existing as *legal* rights (LPA 1925, s 1(1)–(2)). The entitlements which, in the words of LPA 1925, s 1(4), are 'authorised to subsist or to be conveyed or created at law' include:

- the fee simple absolute in possession (**7.2**);
- the term of years absolute (**7.10**);
- easements (**8.3**);
- profits *à prendre* (**8.4**);

- rentcharges (**8.27**);
- mortgage charges (**8.28**); and
- rights of entry (**8.35**).

Whether such rights *actually* attain legal quality usually depends on compliance with some requirement of formal creation or transfer or of due registration at Land Registry. But one thing is clear: any proprietary rights *not* included within the above-mentioned group are relegated, automatically and irreversibly, to *equitable* status only (LPA 1925, s 1(3)).

— *Rights which are inherently equitable* Simply by virtue of their categorical exclusion from LPA 1925, s 1(1)–(2), certain proprietary entitlements never have the potential to rank as *legal* rights in or over land. This residue of rights remains *inherently equitable*. Such rights include:

- determinable fee simple estates (**7.3**);
- estate contracts (including options) (**9.8**);
- restrictive covenants (**9.24**); and
- beneficial interests existing under a trust of land (**9.34**).

— *Informal or incomplete entitlements ranking as merely equitable rights* There remains a further category of rights which, by reason of some deficiency of formal creation or transfer or of some failure of completion by registration at Land Registry, survive as merely *equitable* entitlements. These entitlements are, quite simply, the analogue of those rights which, to borrow the terminology of the old LRA 1925, have the capacity to subsist validly at law if properly 'clothed with the legal estate' (see LRA 1925, s 3(xi)), but which, for want of such clothing, are consigned to *equitable* status only. Most important amongst these rights are:

- the fee simple absolute in possession (**7.2**);
- the term of years absolute (**9.9**);
- easements and profits *à prendre* (**9.12**); and
- mortgage charges (**9.16**).

'Legal estates' in land

2.30 Once created or conveyed in compliance with any relevant requirement of formality or due registration, all potentially legal rights become known generically, within the scheme of the property legislation, as 'legal estates' in land (see LPA 1925, ss 1(4), 205(1)(x); LRA 2002, ss 7(1), 132(1)).

— *Estates which 'subsist' at law* A limited class of estates can be said to subsist 'at law' *without* the necessity of compliance with any requirements of form or due registration. The best example is provided by certain kinds of lease granted for a term of not more than three years (LPA 1925, s 54(2)). Such leases may be created either by informal writing or even orally **(7.18)** and rank immediately as 'legal estates' quite irrespective of whether the land to which they relate is the subject of any registration at Land Registry.

— *Estates which must be conveyed or created by formal means* In most other cases the LPA 1925 stipulates a basic minimum requirement of documentary formality before the creation or conveyance of a potentially legal entitlement can generate a 'legal estate' in its recipient. With certain exceptions, all conveyances of land or of any interest in land are declared to be 'void for the purpose of conveying or creating a legal estate' *unless* made by deed (or formal writing) (LPA 1925, s 52(1); LRR 2003, r 58, **7.6, 7.18**). Many 'legal estates' in unregistered land owe their origin precisely to compliance with this statutory requirement of a deed, although, as we shall see immediately below, most new dealings with such estates now also trigger a requirement of first registration at Land Registry as a condition of the continuance of the 'legal estate'. It is clear, moreover, that the technical requirement of a deed will soon have to be modified to take account of the advent of electronic dealings (i.e. 'paperless' transactions) in respect of land **(7.6)**.

— *Estates which require registration at Land Registry* The generic category of 'legal estates' provides a vital bridge into the registration provisions of the LRA 2002. The Chief Land Registrar is empowered to register title to two sorts of interests:

• Certain 'unregistered legal estates' (LRA 2002, s 2(a)), i.e. entitlements in *unregistered* land whose legal quality has already been established through compliance with the formality of conveyance or creation by deed. Registration of title to such estates may be 'voluntary' on the part of the estate owner (LRA 2002, s 3) or 'compulsory' in the case of specified 'events' which trigger a mandatory requirement of first registration at Land Registry (LRA 2002, s 4, **7.7, 7.20–7.21**).

• Certain 'interests capable of subsisting at law' which are created by a disposition of an estate whose title is *already registered* at Land Registry (LRA 2002, s 2(b)). Registration of the disponee's title to such interests is a precondition of the vesting of any 'legal estate' in that disponee **(7.8, 7.22, 8.16)**.

It is, accordingly, a fairly pervasive feature of the LRA 2002 that the *legal* status of any entitlement which is caught by a requirement of compulsory registration crystallises finally and permanently *only* when the disposition of that interest is duly registered at Land Registry. At this point the arrival of the 'legal estate' in the disponee is said, in the self-explanatory parlance of the LRA 2002, to equip the disponee in most cases with a 'registered estate', i.e. a 'legal estate the title to which is entered in the register' (LRA 2002, s 132(1)).

• *Effect of non-registration* For want of appropriate registration, a transaction with a previously 'unregistered legal estate' quickly becomes 'void as regards the transfer, grant or creation of a legal estate' (LRA 2002, s 7(1), **7.7, 7.20–7.21**); and the disposition of an already registered estate, whether freehold or leasehold, 'does not operate at law' until it is appropriately 'completed by registration' (LRA 2002, s 27(1), **7.8, 7.22**), i.e. by entry of the disponee as proprietor of the relevant estate. In this way the withholding of the legal estate until registration provides a healthy incentive for registration and thereby ensures that the Land Register is kept constantly updated.

• *Equitable entitlement in default of due registration* Notwithstanding the failure of any attempted vesting of a 'legal estate', it remains quite possible that the *equitable* version of the same estate may already have vested in the intended disponee—usually by force of some pre-existing and specifically enforceable contract (**2.29, 7.8, 9.8–9.9**).

Registration of estates at Land Registry

2.31 By reason of the inter-connecting provisions of the LPA 1925 and the LRA 2002, the generic category of 'legal estates' includes the fee simple and the term of years, together with easements, profits *à prendre*, rentcharges, mortgage charges and rights of entry (**2.29–2.30**). In the scheme of registered land, title to *any* of these 'estates' may be registered in the name of a particular proprietor, thus in most instances conferring on that proprietor a 'registered estate' in respect of the land concerned. However, only certain categories of 'estate' are 'independently registrable' (see LRA 2002, Sch 2, para 6), i.e. capable of 'substantive registration' in the Land Register in a newly opened register of title identified by its own unique title number (see *UCB Group Ltd v Hedworth* (2002) at [28] per Jonathan Parker LJ). All other 'estates' are eligible for *non-substantive* registration, i.e. registration by some subsidiary form of entry in existing registers of title.

— *Substantively registrable estates* The principal estates capable of *substantive* registration in the Land Register under an independent title number are (see LRR 2003, r 2(2)):

- the fee simple absolute in possession (**7.7**);
- the term of years absolute—subject to the proviso that substantive registration of leasehold estates extends, in general, only to legal terms of more than seven years (**7.19–7.23**);
- a profit *à prendre* in gross (**8.4**); and
- a rentcharge (**8.27**).

It is not, of course, impossible that one parcel of land may be the subject of two or more substantively registered titles under different title numbers, as, for instance, where the freehold title to Greenacre is subject to one or more long leaseholds (**7.19**).

— *Other registrable estates* Other rights falling within the generic category of 'legal estates' are eligible for *non-substantive* registration under the LRA 2002. Formally created easements, mortgage charges, and rights of entry can thus be registered in the name of their respective proprietors, not under independent title numbers, but in the register of the substantively registered estate to which they relate. In some cases an elaborate cross-referencing system links the correlative benefits and burdens associated with various kinds of entitlement.

Example 1: The creation of a legal charge in favour of a bank, building society or other lender is completed by registration of details of the charge in the charges register of the borrower's substantively registered title, immediately followed by the entry of the lender's name in that register as proprietor of the charge in question (LRA 2002, ss 27(2)(f), 59(2), Sch 2, para 8; LRR 2003, r 9(c)–(e), **8.29**). Such registration finally confers on the lender (or 'chargee') a 'legal estate' in the mortgage. At this point the charge becomes known, in statutory terminology, not as a 'registered estate' but, more specifically, as a 'registered charge' (LRA 2002, s 132(1)). In the absence of registration, however, the chargee holds only an equitable charge (**9.18**).

Example 2: The express grant of an easement (e.g. a right of way, **1.14, 8.16**) is completed by registration of the benefit of the easement as appurtenant to the substantively registered estate in the 'dominant' or benefited land (LRA 2002, ss 27(2)(d), 59(1), Sch 2, para 7(2)(b); LRR 2003, r 5(b)(ii)). The registered proprietor of the dominant land thus becomes the registered proprietor of the 'legal estate' in any easement which benefits his land and he can be described as holding a 'registered estate' in that easement (LRA 2002, s 132(1)). The correlative burden of the easement can and should be entered by 'notice' (**2.32, 12.11**) in the substantively registered title of the 'servient' land (LRA 2002, ss 32, 38, Sch 2, para 7(2)(a); LRR 2003, r 9(a)).

— *Non-registrable estates in land* The number of non-registrable estates in land has been significantly diminished by the lowered threshold for leasehold registration introduced by the LRA 2002 (**7.19**). A lease granted for a term not exceeding *seven* years now provides the prime example of an estate which remains at present ineligible for substantive registration at Land Registry. The tenant under such a lease, although unable to apply for first registration as owner of his estate, nevertheless finds that other forms of protection are available.

• *Overriding interest protection* In general, a lease granted for a term of seven years or less constitutes an unregistered interest which 'overrides' any first registration of the superior estate out of which it is carved (LRA 2002, ss 11(4)(b), 12(4)(c), Sch 1, para 1). Even after the superior estate becomes a registered title, such a lease is declared to 'override' any subsequent disposition of that reversionary estate, thereby automatically binding all transferees or chargees of the landlord's title (LRA 2002, s 29(1), (2)(a)(ii), Sch 3, para 1, **2.23, 7.23, 12.17**).

• *Protection by 'notice' on the register* A lease granted for a term of more than *three* years can be noted on the landlord's title, as and when that title is registered (LRA 2002, ss 32, 33(b), **2.32, 7.23**).

'Minor' interests affecting a registered estate

2.32 In keeping with the 'mirror principle' which underlies the entire statutory scheme (**2.23**), the LRA 2002 ensures that a range of entitlements in registered land which are *neither* registered estates *nor* registered charges can still be reflected in the record of the Land Register. These interests can be made the subject of a 'notice' entered in the register of title to the estate which they affect (LRA 2002, ss 32–33, **12.11**) and, if safeguarded in this way, become binding on subsequent disponees of that registered freehold or leasehold estate (LRA 2002, s 29(1), (2)(b)(i), **12.9**). The entitlements which are protectable by 'notice' are sometimes termed *registrable interests* (in order to distinguish them from 'registered estates' and 'registered charges'). However, it may ultimately be easier—and it is certainly very tempting— to borrow the familiar language of the LRA 1925 and describe this category of protectable entitlements as 'minor' interests. Such terminology also has the advantage that it highlights the essential strategy of the LRA 2002, under which the substantively registered estates—Viscount Dilhorne's 'major' interests (**2.23**)— provide a vital point of reference for the entry of a range of 'minor' interests. It is likewise part of the overall statutory strategy that a 'minor' interest, if not protected in the relevant register of a 'major' title, is ineffective against a purchaser for value under any subsequent registered disposition (**12.13**)—unless, of course, the unprotected interest also happens to rank as an 'overriding' interest (**2.33, 12.15**).

'Overriding' interests affecting a registered estate

2.33 Overriding interests, which by definition *never* appear on the register of title (see LRA 2002, s 29(3)), have hitherto played an important role in the scheme of title registration (**2.23**). Registered land is potentially burdened by a fairly extensive list of overriding interests, each of them proprietary in nature, and almost all detailed with some specificity (LRA 2002, Sch 1, Sch 3). The majority are uncontentious, litigation having tended to cluster around the provisions which notoriously protect interests belonging to persons 'in actual occupation' of the land (**12.18**). The LRA 2002 has nevertheless imposed significant restrictions on the range and scope of the interests which are allowed to 'override' (**12.15**).

— *Rights of occupiers* The interests of those 'in actual occupation' of land are statutorily declared to 'override' both the first registration of title at Land Registry and also subsequent registered dispositions of the estate comprised in that title (LRA 2002, ss 11(4)(b), 12(4)(c), Sch 1, para 2, s 29(1), (2)(a)(ii), Sch 3, para 2). This head of protection is rather open-ended, affording shelter to *any* proprietary rights held by occupiers other than the registered proprietor of the land. In practice, the overriding interest offers a lifeline to vulnerable occupiers whose interests in land have arisen unwittingly or have been created casually. Amidst the confusion of dealings with title such persons are protected from 'having [their] rights lost in the welter of registration'. The claimant occupier may simply 'stay there and do nothing', since nobody can 'buy the land over his head and thereby take away or diminish his rights' (*Strand Securities Ltd v Caswell* (1965) per Lord Denning MR). Effectively, therefore, an onus is placed on all transferees or chargees of the land to carry out a physical inspection of the premises and to make inquiry of any person found to be present.

— *Possible overlaps of interest* Interests which 'override' registered dispositions under the LRA 2002 include certain entitlements which could (and ideally should) have been protected by some form of entry against the register of the burdened title. For example, options of purchase and certain leases for a term in excess of three years are protectable by the entry of a 'notice' in the Land Register (**2.32, 7.23, 9.10, 12.11**), but nevertheless qualify—in default of such protection—as overriding interests if held by persons who happen to be in 'actual occupation' of the land (**12.18–12.20**). Some interests may therefore 'override' by force of statute even though they 'might have been protected by alternative means' (*Ferrishurst Ltd v*

Wallcite Ltd (1999) per Robert Walker LJ). The categories of entitlement in registered land are not mutually exclusive. There is, as Lord Wilberforce once said, no 'firm dividing line or … unbridgeable gulf' between registrable interests and those interests which are declared to 'override' (*Williams & Glyn's Bank Ltd v Boland* (1981)). Indeed, rights in registered land may, at various stages in their existence, shift between the categories of registered estate/charge (i.e. 'major' interest), 'minor' interest and 'overriding' interest.

The principle of 'overreaching'

2.34 Much of the 1925 property legislation was directed towards the need to balance the commerciability of freehold and leasehold titles against the concern lest subsidiary interests in the land be prejudiced or destroyed by the process of disposition (**2.11**). At first these competing objectives appear set against each other in irreconcilable opposition. The 1925 Acts (and their successors) nevertheless confirm the operation, in certain defined circumstances, of one very neat means of resolving this tension between the requirement of facility for disponees and the countervailing requirement of protection for lesser interests (often acquired for valuable consideration) which may affect the same land. This convenient solution comprises the device of 'overreaching' (**11.30**).

— *Some equitable interests are 'shifted from the land'* The device of 'overreaching' operates in certain circumstances to enable the owners of a legal estate to make a conveyance of that estate free of beneficial interests which previously bound the estate.

• In the event of certain statutorily specified dispositions of title, overreaching has the effect of equipping the disponee with a legal estate which, by force of statute, enjoys 'an absolute priority' over all beneficial trust interests otherwise existing in the land (*City of London Building Society v Flegg* (1988) per Lord Oliver of Aylmerton). An overreaching disposition of land compulsorily subordinates certain adverse equitable interests to the estate taken by the disponee, thereby sweeping them off the land and presenting the disponee with a clean title. In short, the purchaser simply 'overreaches' many of the obstacles to achieving an unencumbered estate in the land.

• At the same time, the equitable rights swept off the land are *not* extinguished and lost. Instead they are deflected or 'shifted from the land' (explained Lord Oliver in *Flegg*'s case) so as to attach thereafter not to the *land*, but to the *capital money* arising on the disposition. Herein lies the genius of the overreaching device.

The disponee is given an extended immunity from various forms of pre-existing equitable (or *beneficial*) right—'whether or not he has notice' of them (LPA 1925, s 2(1))—while these rights are, in their turn, transmuted into equivalent entitlements against the money proceeds of the transaction. Thus long-term protection for equitable interests is imaginatively coupled with ultimate convenience for the disponee, a combination of effects which remains untouched by the LRA 2002 (see Law Com No 271 (2001), para 6.41).

— *Categories of overreachable right* It must always be remembered that statutory overreaching operates upon only those equitable interests which are 'capable of being overreached' (LPA 1925, s 2(1)). Overreachable interests comprise those *general* (or *non-specific*) burdens on land which, at least in the view of the draftsmen of the 1925 legislation, are readily convertible into a cash equivalent (e.g. beneficial interests under a trust of land (**1.26, 9.34**)). Overreaching cannot apply, however, to other kinds of interest in land which lack this quality of exchangeability and which were always intended to remain, even following a disposition of title, as permanent burdens on the specific land to which they relate. Thus the statutory mechanism of overreaching never catches such equitable rights as options, leases and other estate contracts, easements or restrictive covenants (**11.30**), which cannot 'sensibly shift from the land affected . . . to the proceeds of sale' (*Birmingham Midshires Mortgage Services Ltd v Sabherwal* (2000) per Robert Walker LJ). The latter species of *real* or *specific* burden are left, in the registered land scheme of things, to be protected through the entry of a 'notice' against the relevant registered title (**12.11–12.13**). Some of these rights may, alternatively, qualify for protection as overriding interests (**2.23, 2.33, 12.15**).

— *Overreaching transactions and trusts of land* The most significant category of potentially overreaching transaction specified by the 1925 legislation comprises a disposition of the legal title held by the trustees of a trust of land (LPA 1925, s 2(1)(ii), **9.34–9.36**). Here, provided that the capital money arising under the disposition is paid to all the trustees of the land (of whom there must normally be at least *two*), the beneficial interests under the former trust of land are automatically translated into precisely equivalent interests in the money now held by those trustees as personalty. Thus, for example, a beneficiary's 75 per cent share under a trust of land is preserved, after an overreaching transfer of title, as a 75 per cent share of the trust money.

— *Overreaching transactions and overriding interests* The overreaching effect of a registered disposition made by trustees of land (in the *plural*) displaces any possibility under the LRA 2002 that the equitable rights of trust beneficiaries may rank as the interests of persons 'in actual occupation' and thereby 'override' the title taken by the disponee. The disposition itself acknowledges the trustees' receipt of any capital money due, so that by the time the disposition takes effect the money has *already* reached the hands of the trustees and the overreaching principle has *already* swept the beneficiaries' rights off the land. The stark consequence is that the beneficiaries cannot be said to retain any 'interest affecting the estate immediately before the disposition' which could possible 'override' the entitlement taken by the registered disponee (LRA 2002, s 29(1): see *City of London Building Society v Flegg* (1988), **11.30**). Even if the trust beneficiaries had decided to protect their equitable rights by the entry of a 'restriction' in the relevant register of title (**7.8, 11.29**), this entry would have done no more than ensure that the Land Registry could never subsequently process any dealing with the title other than a disposition effected by at least *two* trustees of land (thus activating, of course, the overreaching device). The outcome is very different if the disposition of a registered title is executed by a *sole* trustee of land (see e.g. *Williams & Glyn's Bank Ltd v Boland* (1981), **12.24**). Here no statutory overreaching can possibly occur—for want of the payment of capital money to land trustees (in the *plural*)—and the possibility remains that a beneficiary under such a trust of land, if 'in actual occupation' of the land, may be able to claim that her interest 'overrides' a registered disposition of the relevant estate to a transferee or chargee.

Priority in registered land

2.35 We are now in a position to make a preliminary stab at the principle of priority which currently governs most dealings with registered estates in land (see LRA 2002, ss 28, 29(1)–(2), **12.9**):

A disponee for value (i.e. a transferee, chargee, or lessee) of a substantively registered estate, on being registered as proprietor of the interest disposed of, takes title *subject to*:

- all registered estates, charges and interests already affecting the land;
- all unregistered interests affecting the land and declared by statute to 'override' the registered disposition (unless, of course, such interests have been overreached); and
- (in the case of leasehold land) certain covenants and obligations arising under the relevant lease (**14.23–14.24**).

Unregistered legal estates

2.36 The law of *unregistered* land, which now governs a diminishing number of titles in England and Wales, recognises broadly the same basic demarcation of potentially legal and equitable rights as prevails in relation to registered land (LPA 1925, s 1(1)–(2)). Thus the rights which are *capable* of existing 'at law' in unregistered land comprise:

- the fee simple absolute in possession (**7.2**);
- the term of years absolute (**7.10**);
- easements (**8.3**);
- profits *à prendre* (**8.4**);
- rentcharges (**8.27**);
- mortgage charges (**8.28**); and
- rights of entry (**8.35**).

These rights, if created or conveyed with appropriate formality, give rise to what is statutorily declared to be a 'legal estate' in land (LPA 1925, ss 1(4), 52(1)), but, as before, all other proprietary rights in land are *equitable only* (LPA 1925, s 1(3)).

Steady encroachment of registration of title

2.37 In those transactions with an unregistered estate which do not trigger a compulsory first registration at Land Registry, the legal status of an entitlement rests solely on due compliance with the appropriate rules of formal creation and conveyance (**1.24, 7.6, 7.18, 7.23**) with no additional necessity of completion by registration. The only requirement is, effectively, that a 'legal estate' must normally be created or transferred by *deed* (LPA 1925, s 52(1), **2.30, 7.6**), although an important exception still relates to the grant of certain leasehold terms not exceeding three years (LPA 1925, s 54(2)).

Over the past decade, however, the steady extension of compulsory first registration of title at Land Registry has, in many cases, superimposed an extra requirement of *completion by registration* as the precondition of the creation or transfer of a legal estate in what was unregistered land (**2.25**). Thus the transfer of a previously unregistered freehold estate now requires to be completed by the substantive registration of the new estate owner as proprietor of a registered title (LRA 2002, s 4(1)(a), Sch 2, para 2(1), **7.7**). Today, in unregistered land, the creation of legal rights outside the mandatory embrace of the LRA 2002 is confined primarily to the grant of a leasehold term for seven years or less (**2.31, 7.23**) and the creation of a second mortgage charge (**7.7, 8.31**). Neither form of disposition at present triggers registration at Land Registry of any title or interest, although power has been reserved for the Lord Chancellor to extend the circumstances which activate the requirement of registration (LRA 2002, ss 5(1), 118(1), **7.19**).

The binding impact of legal rights in unregistered land

2.38 In unregistered land, legal rights (as defined by reference to LPA 1925, ss 1, 52) are automatically binding on and effective against *all* persons *irrespective* of knowledge or 'notice'. Thus purchasers (and, indeed, all others) take land subject to any pre-existing legal rights such as easements and terms of years. This axiomatic rule of priority is part of the deep historic structure of unregistered land law (**12.34**). Legal rights in unregistered land effectively take care of themselves. With a very few exceptions relating to certain kinds of mortgage (**8.31–8.32, 12.36**), legal entitlements require no artificial protection against third parties; their integrity is inviolable. Nor does this outcome often work injustice, since the documentary formality normally required to constitute the legal quality of such rights also ensures their discoverability on a purchaser's investigation of the vendor's title, particularly when investigation is reinforced by a physical inspection of the land.

Equitable rights in unregistered land

2.39 In relation to land of unregistered title, the categories of equitable entitlement include, as in the case of registered land, not merely those rights which are inherently equitable, but also certain rights which would have been legal but for some want of formality (LPA 1925, s 1(3), **2.29**). Together these categories of equitable right comprise principally:

- estate contracts (including options and equitable leases) (**9.8–9.10**);
- equitable easements and profits *à prendre* (**9.12**);
- equitable charges (**9.16**);
- restrictive covenants (**9.24**); and
- beneficial interests under a trust of land (**9.34**).

The binding impact of equitable rights in unregistered land

2.40 The impact of equitable rights on purchasers of unregistered estates was radically reorganised by the 1925 legislation. Here the field of equitable interests was statutorily subdivided into two distinct categories. Some rights were rendered capable of surviving successive transfers of title by means of a limited system of *land charge registration* (**2.41**). Other rights were earmarked as capable of being swept off the land by the process of *statutory overreaching* (**2.42**). Then, more by accident than by design, this subdivision of unregistered land interests threw up a third, residual, category of equitable rights in unregistered land to which the pre-1926 rules of priority (i.e. *notice-based* rules) continue to apply (**2.43**). As and when an unregistered estate is brought on to the Land Register for the first time, it is this complex of priority rules (together with the axiomatic protection given to legal rights) which determines the range of entitlements which require to be reflected on the face of the newly registered estate at Land Registry.

Registration of land charges

2.41 The Land Charges Act 1972 (the modern successor of the Land Charges Act 1925) subjects substantial categories of equitable rights to a limited regime of registration against the *name* of the estate owner whose land they affect (**12.35**). Although, confusingly, a scheme of registration within the domain of 'unregistered' land, this form of registration contrasts markedly with the comprehensive registration of *titles*, under distinct title numbers, found in the wholly separate Land Register maintained by Land Registry (**2.23, 6.2**).

— *Coverage of land charge registration* The land charges scheme applies to important kinds of right which, once created, merit either long- or short-term preservation against purchasers of a legal estate. Such rights include:

- estate contracts (including options and equitable leases) (**9.8–9.10**);
- equitable easements and profits *à prendre* (**9.15**);
- certain equitable charges (**9.18–9.20**); and
- restrictive covenants between freeholders (**9.32**).

— *The effect of land charge registration* The registration of these specified kinds of interest in the Register of Land Charges is 'deemed to constitute actual notice ... to all persons and for all purposes' of the existence of the right in question (LPA 1925, s 198(1)). In a draconian corollary, unregistered land charges are rendered statutorily *void* as against virtually all purchasers (LCA 1972, s 4, **12.35**); and purchasers are declared unaffected by any registrable, but unregistered, right of which they have knowledge from a source *outside* the Register of Land Charges (LPA 1925, s 199(1); *Midland Bank Trust Co Ltd v Green* (1981)). Thus, for relevant forms of right, land charge registration has now become the *only* form of notice which can bind a purchaser of title. The elements of publicity and certainty inherent in registration cause these rights to bind the world, whilst also enabling all intending purchasers, by a simple search of the Register of Land Charges, to discover their existence.

Statutory overreaching of trust beneficial interests

2.42 The device of statutory overreaching (**2.34**) is just as applicable to *unregistered land* as to *registered land*. Thus the equitable interests of beneficiaries under a trust of land may be cleared off the title taken by a purchaser of unregistered land, provided, as always, that there is compliance with the statutory requirements respecting the payment of capital money arising on the transaction (**11.30**). The beneficial interests concerned are simultaneously deflected on to—and preserved in the form of—the capital money in the hands of the trustees. In this way the 1925 legislation aims to guarantee the purchaser immunity from substantial categories of pre-existing equitable entitlement in the land, whilst safeguarding such rights in an alternative medium of money.

The residual application of the 'bona fide purchaser rule'

2.43 A residual category of equitable rights in unregistered land continues to impact on purchasers in accordance with the historic axiom that equitable rights bind all persons other than a *bona fide purchaser of a legal estate for value without notice* (**1.26**). This 'doctrine of notice' or 'bona fide purchaser rule', which *never* applies in relation to titles which have already been registered under the LRA 2002, ensures that purchasers take free of any equitable interests of which they have no knowledge (actual or constructive) at the date of their purchase (**12.39–12.42**).

— *Modern curtailment of the 'bona fide purchaser rule'* The modern scope of this old priority rule has been severely curtailed by land charge registration and statutory overreaching, which effectively render notice to the purchaser either *inescapable* or *irrelevant*. But the 'bona fide purchaser rule' still catches those 'rights, of an equitable character, outside the provisions as to registration [of land charges] ... which are incapable of being overreached' (*Shiloh Spinners Ltd v Harding* (1973) per Lord Wilberforce).

— *Remaining instances of notice-based entitlement* There thus persists a limited, but consistently awkward, category of notice-based equitable rights in unregistered land. Perhaps the most prominent example comprises the equitable interest of a beneficiary under a trust of land where legal title has been conveyed by a sole land trustee (see e.g. *Kingsnorth Finance Ltd v Tizard* (1986), **12.42**). In these circumstances the beneficiary's rights fall outside the major classifications of *over-reachable right* (because capital money has not been paid over to at least two trustees) and *registrable land charge* (because the rights, being inherently over-reachable, were excluded from the LCA 1972). The purchaser of the legal estate from the sole trustee takes free of the beneficiary's rights only if he is a bona fide purchaser for value without notice. Similarly notice-based equitable rights include rights founded on 'proprietary estoppel' (see e.g. *ER Ives Investment Ltd v High* (1967), **10.21, 12.42**) and certain restrictive covenants (**9.32**) and equitable easements created before 1926 (**9.15**).

Priority in unregistered land

2.44 We are now, at last, able to summarise the basic principle of priority as it affects unregistered land:

A purchaser (including a mortgagee) of an unregistered legal estate takes title *subject to*:

- any other pre-existing legal estates or interests;
- any rights registered under the Land Charges Act;
- any unoverreached equitable interests of which he has notice (actual, constructive or imputed); and
- (in the case of leasehold land) certain covenants and obligations arising under the relevant lease (**14.23–14.24**).

FURTHER READING

Gray and Gray, *Elements of Land Law* (4th edn, OUP, 2005), ch 2.

Relevant sections of this work and other land law textbooks may be supplemented with:

Bright, Susan 'Article 8 Again in the House of Lords' [2006] *Conv* 294.

Dixon, Martin 'Proprietary and non-proprietary rights in modern land law', in L. Tee (ed.), *Land Law: Issues, Debates, Policy* (Willan, 2002), p 8.

Goymour, Amy 'Proprietary Claims and Human Rights—A "Reservoir of Entitlement"?' [2006] *CLJ* 696.

Gray, Kevin and Francis Gray, Susan 'The Idea of Property in Land', in S. Bright and J. K. Dewar (eds), *Land Law: Themes and Perspectives* (OUP, 1998), p 15.

Howell, Jean 'Notices to Quit and Human Rights' [2004] *Conv* 406.

Lucy, William and Mitchell, Catherine 'Replacing Private Property: The Case for Stewardship' [1996] *CLJ* 566.

Merrill, Thomas W. and Smith, Henry E. 'Optimal Standardization in the Law of Property: The Numerus Clausus Principle' 110 *Yale LJ* 1 (2000).

Pottage, Alain 'The Originality of Registration' (1995) 15 *OJLS* 371.

Rotherham, Craig 'Conceptions of property in common law discourse' (1998) 18 *Legal Studies* 41.

SELF-TEST QUESTIONS

1   Do you have any claim to 'property' in your current living accommodation (**2.12–2.13, 2.17**)?

2   To what extent do property rights and human rights overlap or coalesce (**2.2–2.4, 2.15**)?

3   To what extent does the Land Register 'mirror' the totality of estates and interests affecting registered land (**2.23, 2.31–2.33**)?

4   What is the role of the 'bona fide purchaser rule' in modern land law (**2.40, 2.43**)?

3

Possession

SUMMARY

Historically the notion of 'possession' has been the single most heavily formative influence behind the development of English land law. In this chapter we explore the nature of possession and examine the way in which possession has traditionally provided not only an authentic root of title but also the basis on which various rights can be vindicated against strangers who enter upon land without consent.

Possession

3.1 The casual lay concept of ownership is a relatively recent intrusion into the thought patterns of the common lawyer, more relevant to the ordering of the personal property generated by the industrial changes of the last two centuries than to the law of real property. In relation to land the common lawyer's operative concept has always been the more subtle, more pragmatic notion of *possession*. As Lord Hoffmann observed in *Hunter v Canary Wharf Ltd* (1997), '[e]xclusive possession de jure or de facto, now or in the future, is the bedrock of English land law.' Historically, the actuality of social or behavioural fact (in the form of sustained assertion of physical possession of land) has long functioned as the authentic root of title. Even today unregistered conveyancing ultimately comprises the handing on from seller to buyer of a title evidenced by undisturbed possession (see LPA 1969, s 23, **2.24**). The social imperative of peaceful possession finds timeless expression from Magna Carta to the European Convention on Human Rights (**2.7**). Yet, as will become apparent in following chapters, the philosophical base of title in English law has shifted significantly in recent years from *possession* to *ownership*. The traditional perception of property as rooted in empirically defined fact is being rapidly displaced by a more modern view of property as the exclusive product of a state-administered system of computerised entitlement.

The nature of 'possession'

3.2 'Possession', in the legal sense, is no simple concept. 'Possession' has been aptly described as 'a conclusion of law defining the nature and status of a particular relationship of control by a person over land' (*Mabo v Queensland (No 2)* (1992) per Toohey J). The emphasis here is upon the word 'control'.

— *Possession is more than mere occupancy*   At common law the term 'possession' does much more than express the idea of a bare physical occupancy of land. Possession is an inherently behavioural phenomenon which incorporates a particular mindset. Far from denoting a mere factual presence upon land, possession comprises a range of inner assumptions as to the power relationships generated by such presence (**6.12**). Possession is necessarily underpinned by a demonstrable state of mind (or *animus*) which encapsulates the possessor's own perception of the permanence and defensibility of his rights in relation to the land. Thus, for instance, no 'possession' can properly be attributed to a mere 'overnight trespasser' or to a friend who has expressly agreed to look after a house during its owner's absence on holiday (see *JA Pye (Oxford) Ltd v Graham* (2003) at [40] per Lord Browne-Wilkinson).

— *Possession is ultimately indivisible and autonomous*   In strict terms the concept of 'possession' is a free-standing notion which admits little descriptive qualification. Possession is the self-evident state of affairs which prevails where one person is in a position to 'control access to [land] by others and, in general, decide how the land will be used' (*Western Australia v Ward* (2002) at [52] (High Court of Australia)). Thus, in the view of the common law, possession is intrinsically indivisible and autonomous. Possession has a recognisable integrity and uniformity and, since exclusivity is 'of the essence of possession' (see *JA Pye (Oxford) Ltd v Graham* (2003) at [70] per Lord Hope of Craighead), even the adjective 'exclusive' adds nothing to an understanding of the phenomenon. '[P]ossession that is not exclusive is a contradiction in terms, for the right of general control and exclusion is central to the concept of legal possession' (*Western Australia v Ward* at [477] per McHugh J). Equally, the qualifier 'adverse' does little to explicate the inherent nature of 'possession' (**6.4**), since it connotes merely that the possessor's presence on land is contrary to the interests of others (see *JA Pye (Oxford) Ltd v Graham* at [69] per Lord Hope).

Historic importance of the 'seisin-possession' concept

3.3 The primacy accorded to pragmatic notions of possession was described in earlier times by reference to 'seisin'. The concept of 'seisin' embodied the common law tradition that proprietary rights in land are based on physical possession rather than on abstract title. As Lord Millett emphasised recently, '[a] person who is in actual possession of land is entitled to remain in peaceful enjoyment of the property without disturbance by anyone except a person with a better right to possession. It does not matter that he has no title' (*Harrow LBC v Qazi* (2004) at [85]). It is this idea, declared Lord Millett, which is 'now enshrined in suitably restrained and less colourful language' in ECHR Art 8 (**2.15**).

— *Seisin as fact not right*   Seisin thus consisted essentially of actual or de facto possession of land—quite irrespective of right. A man had 'seisin' of land 'when he is enjoying it or in a position to enjoy it' (Pollock and Maitland, *The History of English Law*, vol 2, p 34). Seisin was fact not right, but provided heavily presumptive evidence of entitlement within the medieval framework of rights in land. From the 15th century onwards no freehold could be passed without seisin; and a 'feoffment' (or conveyance of freehold land) required a symbolic handing over or 'livery' of seisin. This transmission of seisin had a solemn physical aspect, as captured delightfully in Rudyard Kipling's *Puck of Pook's Hill*:

> 'What's taking seizin?' said Dan, cautiously. 'It's an old custom the people had when they bought and sold land. They used to cut out a clod and hand it over to the buyer, and you weren't lawfully seized of your land—it didn't really belong to you—till the other fellow had actually given you a piece of it—like this.' He held out the turves.

— *Protection for actual occupiers*   The quaint ritual of livery of seisin is no longer necessary for the transfer of an estate in land. All interests in land now 'lie in grant' and may be conveyed 'without actual entry' upon the land (LPA 1925, s 51(1)). The notion of seisin, in its preoccupation with factual possession, has nevertheless left a mark on the way in which modern property lawyers think of land. The protection accorded raw possession expresses a strong sense of respect for what one finds on the ground, thereby providing a link with both the law of adverse possession (**6.4**) and much of the law of human rights and civil liberties (see e.g. *Semayne's Case* (1604), **2.15, 4.5**). The idea of seisin also finds a contemporary echo in the force accorded to certain unregistered interests which are statutorily declared to 'override' first registrations of title and subsequent registered dispositions under the LRA 2002. Such 'overriding interests' include the rights of persons 'in actual occupation' of the land (see LRA 2002, ss 11(2)–(4), 12(2)–(4), Sch 1, para 2, Sch 12, para 7, s 29(1), (2)(a)(ii), Sch 3, para 2, **2.33, 12.18**). The element of 'actual occupation' which triggers this powerful protection of unregistered rights has been described as pre-eminently a matter of 'physical presence, not some entitlement in law' (*Williams & Glyn's Bank Ltd v Boland* (1981) per Lord Wilberforce). A similar deference towards the rights of persons present on land is evident in the rule which, in other than exceptional circumstances, safeguards the title of a registered proprietor from unconsented and prejudicial alteration 'in relation to land in his possession' (LRA 2002, ss 65, 131(1)–(2), Sch 4, paras 3(2), 6(2), **12.29**).

Possession, property, title, and estate

3.4 The law of real property has long exhibited a tension between empirical and conceptual models of entitlement (**2.16**). In terms of *cerebral* analysis, English law recognises only the ownership of abstract 'estates' rather than any direct ownership of land itself: 'property' in land is necessarily articulated through the medium of notional 'estates' or 'interests' in realty (**1.16**). A person may have 'title' to one of these 'estates' in the original common law sense of having an *entitlement* to assert that 'estate' (and the various rights connected with it) against other persons. In terms of *pragmatic* analysis, however, it is the behavioural reality of *possession* which has tended to be regarded, in default of any better methodology, as the ultimate ground of claim to a 'title' to an 'estate' in land. Indeed, in less sophisticated times the derivation of title from visible physical possession performed a valuable function in limiting the information costs associated with the ascertainment of estate ownership. As Kitto J once observed, 'men generally own the property they possess' and the law simply 'recognises the probability which common experience suggests' (*Allen v Roughley* (1955)). The common law theory of relativity of title (**6.1**) therefore predicated that the best 'title' to the largest 'estate' in land was simply that of the person whose claim to 'possession' was superior to that of anyone else. Conversely, a deficit of overall possessory control points towards a claim to some lesser form of 'property' in land or may even indicate that the claimant lacks any 'property' in the land at all.

The 'property' denoted by the major estates in realty has tended, historically, to be a derivative of unqualified possessory control over defined terrain—as amply demonstrated by the two primary estates acknowledged today in English law, the *fee simple* (**7.2**) and the *term of years* (**7.10**) (see LPA 1925, s 1(1)). '[E]xclusive and unrestricted use of a piece of land' generally signifies ownership of a freehold estate (see *Reilly v Booth* (1890) per Lopes LJ). Thus, for example, a water company's exercise of statutory powers to install a sewer in privately owned land invests the company as a freeholder with 'property in ... the whole of the space occupied by the sewer' (*Taylor v North West Water* (1995)). Likewise, as Windeyer J explained in *Radaich v Smith* (1959), exclusive possession for a limited term is 'the proper touchstone' of a lease or tenancy.

• Consistently with this approach, it was an absence of overall possessory control which caused the student lodger, whose legal rights were considered in Chapter 2 (**2.13**), to be relegated to the status of a licensee. His lack of territorial power, embodied in his subordination to the supervisory authority of a freehold owner, deprived him of any credible claim to have *possession*, as distinct from a mere personal *occupancy*, of his living accommodation. In an unlegalistic, but highly indicative, turn of phrase, the student lodger lacked any 'stake' in the land (see Lord Denning MR's use of precisely this instinctive criterion of estate ownership in *Marchant v Charters* (1977), **2.17**). Thus the lodger had neither 'possession' of the land nor any 'property' in it.

• The estate owner generally has 'title' to his 'estate'. It is possible, however, that one can own an 'estate' in land, but have no 'title' to assert it against a particular person (or even at all). In rare circumstances—such as those of *adverse possession* of one's land by another (**6.4**)—'title' and 'estate' may become detached so that the estate owner loses his entitlement to enforce his estate (and its various possessory incidents). Under the Limitation Act 1980, for example, a 12-year period of adverse possession against an estate owner extinguishes that owner's 'title' to his 'estate', but does not extinguish the 'estate' itself (*St Marylebone Property Co Ltd v Fairweather* (1963) per Lord Radcliffe).

• Following chapters of this book will point to an emerging distinction between the *common law* notion of 'title' (as founded essentially on the raw fact of unchallenged possession) and the increasingly pervasive *statutory* perception of 'title' (as based on the state-administered registration of artificially defined legal ownership).

'Property' in land can sometimes arise independently of any claim to 'possession' of land and may, indeed, be inconsistent with such a claim. We have seen, for instance, that the grantee of an easement can be registered in the Land Register as proprietor of the 'estate' of the easement (**2.31**), even though in English law the possessory character of easements is necessarily restricted (*Copeland v Greenhalf* (1952), **2.3, 8.14**). Accordingly an easement comprising a right of way may involve an intermittent and non-exclusive right of passage over another's land, but not a much more extensive right such as to monopolise that way for purposes of (say) parking or construction.

Possession as the root of title

3.5 At the heart of the common law perception of property—although not of the new statutory regime of registered land—is therefore the primacy accorded to possession in fact. For the common lawyer the root of title is not 'words upon parchment' (see *Bl Comm*, vol II, p 2), but rather the raw circumstance of sustained possession. At least historically, ownership of an estate in land has been founded ultimately on the successful assertion of de facto control or the continuity of a de facto exercise of power.

— *Possession generates a common law freehold* In typically pragmatic fashion the common law has long presumed that a person who is in 'possession' of land has a fee simple estate in that land unless and until the contrary is shown. 'Possession is prima facie evidence of seisin in fee simple' (*Peaceable d Uncle v Watson* (1811)). Thus possession, even though tortiously acquired, throws up for the possessor (or 'squatter') a 'common law freehold' which, in the absence of any superior claim to the fee simple estate, is enforceable against the world.

— *Inchoate rights of the possessor* It is also clear that from the inception of his possession the possessor acquires certain important rights in relation to the land possessed. These rights flow in part from the respect accorded by the common law to the fact of his possession and in part from the common law freehold generated by that possession. In the ancient words of Bracton, 'everyone who is in possession, though he has no right, has a greater right [than] one who is out of possession and has no right.'

• Notwithstanding that he is vulnerable to any *superior* claim to possession and may therefore be turned out by legal process, a possessor of land is entitled to vindicate his possession against *other* strangers. The squatter cannot be evicted 'save at the suit of someone with a better right to possession, and even then that person must rely on the strength of his own title and not the weakness of the squatter's' (*Harrow LBC v Qazi* (2004) at [87] per Lord Millett). Indeed, strictly speaking, it is possession which provides the authentic basis of the right to sue in trespass and private nuisance (**3.7**): trespass to land is 'essentially a wrong against possession, not against ownership' (*Simpson v Fergus* (2000) per Robert Walker LJ). And the House of Lords went to some pains in *Hunter v Canary Wharf Ltd* (1997) to confirm that standing in the law of nuisance is confined to those who are linked to the land by some form of possessory claim.

• Even before his possessory title is perfected by the effluxion of a limitation period, the squatter is entitled to sell, devise or otherwise transfer his possessory interest (see *Asher v Whitlock* (1865)). If he dies intestate, his rights devolve upon his next of kin. A squatter's possession may also be 'tacked' on to that of a successor in title as squatter for the purpose of any claim by the latter to a completed possessory title (LRA 2002, Sch 6, para 11(2)(a)).

Recovery of possession

3.6 English law has always applied a visceral rule of priority, namely that 'as between mere possessors prior possession is a better right' (*Mabo v Queensland (No 2)* (1992) per Toohey J). It follows that possession, even if lost, gives rise to a right to recover possession—a principle which, historically, has been subject only to the barring of prior rights of recovery after the effluxion of the statutory limitation period (**6.4**). The possessor of land has access, in effect, to a remedy of recovery in specie which goes far beyond the mere recovery of damages for another's trespass (**3.9**).

— *Remedy by common law action for possession*   For centuries English law has provided a curial means by which a person dispossessed of land can dislodge trespassers, this legal process taking the form of the common law action for possession. By the 1970s, however, this civil remedy was beginning to prove cumbersome and inflexible. It was particularly ineffective where the illicit occupiers of premises were unidentifiable or followed each other in and out of occupation in quick succession.

— *The 'possession claim against trespassers'*   Most of the technical defects of the common law action for possession were alleviated in 1970 with the reformulation of the Supreme Court Rules and County Court Rules to provide a summary procedure for the recovery of possession against clear trespassers.

The expedited remedy of the 'possession claim against trespassers', as now provided by the Civil Procedure Rules 1998 (SI 1998/3132, as amended by SI 2001/256 and SI 2002/2058), lends substantial and speedy assistance against any person who occupies land without consent (see CPR 55.1). Possession may be claimed even against nameless defendants and the court has no discretion to withhold or suspend the order for possession once the case for possession has been established (*McPhail v Persons (Names Unknown)* (1973) per Lord Denning MR). The possession order may extend to a larger area of the owner's property than originally affected by the adverse occupation (see *University of Essex v Djemal* (1980)) and can generally be enforced against any person who subsequently returns to the site or premises (see *Wiltshire CC v Frazer (No 2)* (1986)).

In many cases the removal of trespassers from privately owned land can be justified, in terms of the ECHR Art 8, as 'necessary in a democratic society . . . for the protection of the rights and freedoms of others' (*R (Gangera) v Hounslow LBC* (2003) at [41]). However, the very automaticity of court orders for possession may now fuel the argument that, in certain cases involving the eviction of long-standing residential occupiers, a summary procedure which affords the defendant no opportunity to ventilate the merits of his dispossession before an independent tribunal constitutes a denial of the procedural safeguards which would otherwise ensure that the interference with residential security is 'fair' and such as to accord 'due respect' to the defendant's Convention rights (see *Connors v United Kingdom* (2004) at [94]–[95], [114], **2.15**).

— *Interim possession orders*   Under an even more expeditious procedure introduced in 1995, the county court also has power to make an interim possession order against an alleged trespasser on residential premises, on an application made within 28 days of known entry upon land, which obliges the respondent to vacate the premises within 24 hours of service of the order (CPR 55.20–55.28). The respondent is not entitled, as of right, to appear before the county court at the interim order stage; no oral evidence can be offered; and the court has discretion whether to make the possession order final at some later date when the respondent is already out of possession (CPR 55.25(4), 55.27(3)). It is normally a criminal offence for *any* person to trespass on the land during the currency of a duly served interim possession order (CJAPOA 1994, s 76(2)).

Trespass

3.7   The wrongful assumption of possession inevitably constitutes a trespass to land; but not all infringements of land boundaries constitute an assumption of possession. Some sorts of invasion are merely intermittent or non-exclusive (e.g. that of the individual who takes a short cut across another's land or of the casual intruder whose presence is temporary). In the latter kinds of case the appropriate remedy lies, not in any action for the recovery of possession, but in a civil action for trespass to land. Even in cases of *dispossession* from land, an action for trespass may, in conjunction with the recovery of possession, offer the additional prospect of recovering damages in respect of any loss inflicted by or during the period of dispossession, together with the further possibility of obtaining injunctive relief.

• The person who is currently entitled to possession of land may bring an action in trespass against anyone who enters the land without his consent, with the sole exception of a person who has a better title than himself (see *Hunter v Canary Wharf Ltd* (1997) per Lord Hoffmann).

• In what seems an unprincipled erosion of the historic concept of possession (**3.2**), English courts are nowadays beginning to accord some of the attributes of 'possession' to certain categories of licensee. In the teeth of clear doctrine that a licence connotes only a fragile, non-possessory presence on land (**4.2**), the courts have conceded that 'exclusive possession' of land may sometimes be enjoyed by a licensee (*Hunter v Canary Wharf Ltd* (1997) per Lord Hoffmann) and even by a 'tolerated trespasser' (*Pemberton v Southwark LBC* (2000)). The result has been to extend the availability of trespass remedies to a number of persons otherwise unentitled to sue (see e.g. *Mehta v Royal Bank of Scotland plc* (1999) (contractual licensee)). Contrast, however, *Manchester Airport plc v Dutton* (2000) (**4.11, 6.1**), where Chadwick LJ dissented precisely because he rejected the suggestion that there is 'now a concept of "relative possession"'.

— *An ancient territorial imperative* The idea of trespass and the correlative notion of licensed entry upon land (**4.2**) are ineradicable components of the deep structure of real property. 'Our law holds the property of every man so sacred, that no man can set his foot upon his neighbour's close without his leave' (*Entick v Carrington* (1765) per Lord Camden CJ). At the heart of this absolutist dogma is the notion of trespass. Trespass is the act of unauthorised and unjustifiable entry upon land in another's possession; and the wrong of trespass is actionable regardless of the extent of the incursion and without any necessary showing of injury or damage to the claimant. There is, in English law, a 'fundamental right ... to object to trespass' (*Newbury DC v Russell* (1997) per Rattee J) and in certain restricted circumstances the commission of trespass to land is not merely a tort, but also a crime (**3.10**).

— *Dimensions and varieties of trespass* Trespass can involve not merely an unconsented footfall upon terrain, but also the lateral invasion of one's airspace. It is well known, for instance, that where the branches of a neighbour's tree overhang the land of an adjoining owner, the latter is entitled, without giving prior notice, to lop off the branches which intrude into his airspace (*Lemmon v Webb* (1895)). Trespass is also committed through the projection of overhanging eaves, by protruding scaffolding and advertising signs and—in that most contentious example of urban trespass—by the oversailing jib of the sky crane (see e.g. *Anchor Brewhouse Developments Ltd v Berkley House (Docklands Developments) Ltd* (1987)). No trespass arises, however, merely because some stranger overlooks one's land from a position outside one's boundaries (*Entick v Carrington* (1765) per Lord Camden CJ), although the visual invasion of privately held land may nowadays be actionable under the head of breach of confidence (see *Campbell v MGN Ltd* (2005)) and may even constitute a violation of the right to respect for 'private and family life' and the 'home' (see ECHR Art 8, **2.15**).

— *Justifications for trespass* In the absence of any licence authorising his access or of any statutory right of entry, an intruder upon land is left to show justification for his entry. In general, however, the common law has allowed very few forms of defence or justification to curtail the right to complain of trespass. For example, a mistaken belief by the trespasser (e.g. that he is on his own land) affords no recognisable excuse (*Conway v George Wimpey & Co Ltd* (1951)). In exceptional circumstances trespass may be justified on the ground of necessity, but usually only if there exists no public authority responsible for the protection of the relevant interests of the public. Thus, for instance, in *Monsanto plc v Tilly* (2000) the genuine concern of a protest group over the harmful effects of genetically modified crops did not justify trespass upon land (or the destruction of plants thereon) where responsibility for the safety of such forms of cultivation fell within the purview of the Department of the Environment. Likewise, in the light of the extensive public law obligations now fastened on local authority housing departments, the plight of homelessness cannot comprise, in itself, a form of social necessity justifying unconsented entry upon another's land (see *McPhail v Persons (Names Unknown)* (1973) per Lord Denning MR).

Physical resistance to trespass

3.8 Where strangers have taken over occupation of land, any person in possession of that land may exercise the remedy of self-help at any stage *before* the occupying strangers acquire possession in the sense currently required by the law of adverse possession. Self-help may take the form of peaceable re-entry while the intruders are temporarily absent from the premises. Moreover, the householder who returns home from a short holiday to find his house occupied by squatters is entitled to use reasonable force and throw the intruders out of his house without further cere-mony. In such circumstances the trespassers' occupation has not yet hardened into the elements of *factum* and *animus* which, for relevant purposes, comprise 'pos-session' (**6.10**). The legality of their summary eviction is 'beyond question', although self-help 'is not a course to be recommended because of the disturbance which might follow' (*McPhail v Persons (Names Unknown)* (1973) per Lord Denning MR) and also because of the risk of criminal liability (see Criminal Law Act 1977, s 6, as amended by CJAPOA 1994, s 72 (**15.16**)). The mere fact of trespass does not, of course, justify extreme retaliation or disproportionate force and the use of excessive violence against the trespassers may itself constitute an actionable civil wrong (see e.g. *Revill v Newbery* (1996)) or even a criminal offence (see e.g. *R v Martin (Anthony)* (2003)). In most instances it is preferable to recover the premises by way of a 'possession claim against trespassers' brought in the county court (or, exceptionally, in the High Court) (**3.6**).

Curial remedies for trespass

3.9   In cases of proven trespass the court retains a significant discretion to determine the appropriate remedy, which may range from a simple declaration of rights to an award of money damages and/or various kinds of injunctive relief. Something may depend on whether the trespass was an isolated occurrence or is of a continuing nature.

— *Past acts of trespass*   The primary response to a past act of trespass lies in the common law remedy of damages (*Jaggard v Sawyer* (1996) per Sir Thomas Bingham MR). This remedy provides retrospective compensation in respect of causes of action which are complete at the date of the claim, although if no real injury has been inflicted by a technical trespass upon land—particularly in circumstances of harmless recreational trespass upon scenic terrain—the court may award nothing more than a declaration of rights and/or nominal damages (see e.g. *Behrens v Richards* (1905)). In the event that a court decides to award a substantial money remedy (or 'mesne profits'), the trespass victim must elect before judgment to have his claim calculated on one or other of two bases, the preponderant emphases of which are, respectively, *compensatory* and *restitutionary* in character.

• Where a past trespass has inflicted damage upon the land, the claimant may ask for a *compensatory* award which covers the cost of any works reasonably required in order to restore his enjoyment of the land. If reinstatement of the land is impossible, the relevant measure of compensation is the diminution in the value of the land (see *Burton v Winters* (1993)).

• An alternative method of quantifying a money award involves a calculation of the benefit deemed to have been received by the trespasser by reason of his unauthorised use of the land (see *Attorney-General v Blake* (2001) per Lord Nicholls of Birkenhead). This basis of calculation is sometimes termed the 'user principle', in that it restores to the trespass victim the price which a reasonable person would have been prepared to pay for the user concerned had it been required to be purchased (i.e. very commonly the ordinary letting value of the land on the open market). Unlike the compensatory approach outlined above, this *restitutionary* approach requires no proof of loss on the victim's part. Restitutionary awards may be particularly appropriate in relation to incursions made by commercial developers and utility undertakers who trespass in the furtherance of their business interests (e.g. the operators of sky cranes in downtown sites (**3.7**)). In effect, commercial trespassers are made to 'internalise the externalities' of construction and other projects.

— *Future or continuing acts of trespass* In cases of continuing trespass the common law remedy of damages tends to be inadequate precisely because such damages operate retrospectively and cover only past, and not future, acts of trespass. For this reason equity has long asserted a power to afford the trespass victim a prospective form of relief which goes far beyond the common law remedy of damages for a series of past wrongs. The court has discretion to issue a negative or prohibitory injunction restraining future trespass or even a mandatory injunction to reverse unlawful conduct through the removal of a trespass (see *Jaggard v Sawyer* (1996) per Sir Thomas Bingham MR). Furthermore the court has available a supplementary power, first conferred by the Chancery Amendment Act 1858 ('Lord Cairns's Act'), to award *equitable damages* in respect of future or continuing wrongs either in addition to or in substitution for injunctive relief (see Chancery Amendment Act 1858, s 2).

• Injunctive relief is sometimes said to be a prima facie right of the trespass victim (see *Anchor Brewhouse Developments Ltd v Berkley House (Docklands Developments) Ltd* (1987) per Scott J), but nowadays it is increasingly apparent that the remedy of injunction is no longer an automatic or necessary judicial response to trespass. In cases of relatively minor infringement occurring in a context of close neighbourhood, there are gathering indications that proprietary and possessory rights may not always be capable of such ultimate or unlimited vindication. Under the contemporary equivalent of Lord Cairns's Act (Supreme Court Act 1981, s 50), injunctive relief is frequently withheld in favour of an award of equitable damages in respect of future or continuing acts of trespass.

• Modern imperatives of social accommodation and of 'reasonableness between neighbours' (**13.19**) often point away from the absolutist remedy of the injunction, with the result that the courts increasingly exercise a power to license, on payment of compensation, a broadly acceptable compromise of conflicting interests (see Gray and Gray, 'The rhetoric of realty', in J Getzler (ed.), *Rationalizing Property, Equity and Trusts: Essays in Honour of Edward Burn* (Butterworths, 2003), pp 257–9). 'Property rules' are often commuted into 'liability rules' (Calabresi and Melamed, 'Property Rules and Liability Rules: One View of the Cathedral' 85 *Harv L Rev* 1089 (1971–2)). Or, as Millett LJ observed in *Jaggard v Sawyer* (1995), '[m]any proprietary rights cannot be protected at all by the common law', with the result that the aggrieved owner 'must submit to unlawful interference with his rights and be content with damages'. In the process it becomes steadily more apparent that the ability of proprietors and possessors to dictate what shall or shall not be done on their own land is rather more limited than may be generally thought. But this merely reflects the wider reality that the law of trespass is slowly being modified, in certain contexts, by an overriding proviso of reasonableness (**4.5, 8.20**).

Burton v Winters (1993) W's predecessors in title built a garage along the boundary line separating W's land from that of B. The garage, when constructed, projected some 10 cm over the boundary line. B sued for a mandatory injunction requiring removal of the offending garage wall, but was relegated to a mere damages award in respect of the trespass. Far from being able to insist on the removal of the encroaching wall, B was later sentenced to two years' imprisonment for contempt when she continued to inflict physical damage on the garage by making holes in its roof and attacking its walls with a sledge hammer. The Court of Appeal upheld the sentence, Lloyd LJ observing that B was still entitled to enforce a damages claim in respect of any diminution in the value of her property caused by the encroachment (compare the outraged response of the trespass victim in *Jaggard v Sawyer* (1995), **13.19**).

- The choice between injunctive and monetary relief has long been constrained by the 'good working rule' propounded by A L Smith LJ in *Shelfer v City of London Electric Lighting Co* (1895) (**13.19**). According to this guideline, damages for a continuing trespass may be awarded in lieu of an injunction if the injury to the claimant's rights is small, if the damage can be estimated in money and would be adequately compensated by a small money payment, and if it would be 'oppressive' to the defendant to grant an injunction. In such cases the power to award damages in lieu of an injunction enables the court to 'give an equivalent for what was lost by the refusal of an injunction' (see *Attorney-General v Blake* (2001) per Lord Nicholls of Birkenhead).

- Damages may be calculated, if necessary, on a restitutionary basis by reference to the benefits likely to be obtained or enjoyed in the future by the trespasser. The ultimate award can therefore reflect the 'likely reasonable outcome' of hypothetical negotiations for settlement of the trespass issue between the parties (see *Severn Trent Water Ltd v Barnes* (2004) at [35] per Potter LJ (where a water undertaker had wrongfully inserted a water main through 20 metres of the claimant's land)). The extreme sanction of the injunction tends to be reserved for acts of especially flagrant or repeated trespass and for cases of permanent or continuing annexation of land (see e.g. *Harrow LBC v Donohue* (1995); *Daniells v Mendonca* (1999)). In less significant instances of trespass, damages—usually inclusive of a 'once and for all' award in respect of future wrongs—are often thought to represent the more appropriate remedy even though the withholding of injunctive relief causes the court, in effect, to 'authorise the continuance of an unlawful state of affairs' (*Jaggard v Sawyer* (1995) per Millett LJ). The controversial feature of a damages remedy is undoubtedly the fact that the trespasser is enabled to buy his way out of a wrongful incursion and to purchase immunity from further enforcement of the trespass victim's possessory rights. In effect, the restitutionary measure of damages for trespass represents 'the price payable for the compulsory acquisition of a right' (*Attorney-General v Blake* (2001) per Lord Nicholls).

Criminal liability for trespass

3.10 In the generality of cases the act of trespass on another's land is merely a civil wrong. In certain circumstances, however, trespass constitutes a criminal offence. Indeed the criminalisation of trespass has been significantly extended by modern legislation.

• A criminal offence is committed by any person who, having entered residential premises as a trespasser, fails to leave those premises on being required to do so by or on behalf of either a 'displaced residential occupier' or a 'protected intending occupier' of those premises (Criminal Law Act 1977, s 7(1)). Public order legislation has also strengthened the law against mass occupation and trespass. The Criminal Justice and Public Order Act 1994 confirms a similar criminal offence in the case of those who, in certain kinds of circumstance, fail to vacate land on the direction of a senior police officer who 'reasonably believes' that two or more such persons have entered land as trespassers and 'are present there with the common purpose of residing there for any period' (CJAPOA 1994, s 61). Although eviction in pursuance of the 1994 Act engages the right to respect for 'private and family life' and the integrity of the 'home' (ECHR Art 8(1), **2.15**), interference with this right has been held to be justified by reference to the national economic interest and to the illegality (and temporary nature) of the trespassory presence (*R (Fuller) v Chief Constable of Dorset Police* (2003) at [76]–[78]).

• The 1994 Act also creates an offence of 'aggravated trespass', where trespass on land involves a threatened or actual interference with 'any lawful activity' on that land (CJAPOA 1994, s 68(1), as amended by ASBA 2003, s 59). Originally intended to counteract the conduct of such persons as hunt saboteurs, this criminal offence may extend more widely to catch many other kinds of trespassory presence whether or not on open land. Criminal liability may likewise attach to unauthorised campers who fail to leave when directed by a local authority (CJAPOA 1994, s 77) and to persons involved in certain kinds of trespassory assembly of 20 or more persons (Public Order Act 1986, ss 14A, 14B, as introduced by CJAPOA 1994, s 70; but see *DPP v Jones* (1999)).

• A far-reaching form of trespassory crime arises in the context of anti-social behaviour orders made by a magistrates' court pursuant to the Crime and Disorder Act 1998 (CADA 1998, s 1(4)). An 'ASBO' may prohibit (for an initial period of two years) the entry of any named person aged at least 10 years upon defined premises or parts of a locality. Breach of the order without reasonable excuse renders the subject of the order criminally liable (CADA 1998, s 1(10)).

• The Anti-social Behaviour Act 2003 creates further forms of criminal liability in connection with presence on land. It becomes a criminal offence for any person to remain on or enter, in contravention of a closure order, any premises where drugs have been used unlawfully (ASBA 2003, s 4(1)). It is likewise a criminal offence for any person knowingly to contravene a direction given by a senior police officer for the dispersal of groups of persons reasonably suspected to have been associated with anti-social behaviour in a public place (ASBA 2003, s 32).

FURTHER READING

Gray and Gray, *Elements of Land Law* (4th edn, OUP, 2005), ch 3.

Relevant sections of this work and other land law textbooks may be supplemented with:

Pollock, Frederick and Wright, Robert *Possession in the Common Law* (Clarendon Press, 1888).

Tromans, Stephen and Thomann, Colin 'Environmental Protest and the Law' [2003] *JPL* 1367.

SELF-TEST QUESTIONS

1   What is the difference between 'possession' and mere occupancy of land (**3.1–3.4**)?

2   What rights has English law accorded to the possessor of land (**3.5–3.7**)?

3   Is trespass more appropriately remedied by an award of damages or by an injunction (**3.9**)?

4

Licences

SUMMARY

Licences to enter upon someone else's land play an important role in the organisation of everyday life. This chapter describes the most common forms of licence known to English law. These range from the 'bare' licence or permission to be present on land to more complex variants of the device of the licence such as the contractual licence and the 'licence coupled with an equity'. Hovering above the whole area is the question whether any of these versions of the fundamental concept can properly be said to comprise a *proprietary* interest in the land to which it relates.

Varieties of licence

4.1 In English law the 'licence' to enter upon land falls unmistakably towards the lower end of the calibrated scale of 'property' value which distinguishes entitlements in respect of realty (**2.3**). Licences may assume various forms and perform a multiplicity of purposes. The categories of licence recognised by the law include:

- bare licences (**4.2**);
- contractual licences (**4.6**);
- licences coupled with an equity (**4.9**); and
- licences coupled with the grant of an interest (**4.10**).

Bare licences

4.2 *A bare licence* is a personal permission, given otherwise than for consideration, to enter or be present upon somebody else's land. The grant of a bare licence performs the minimal function of providing a defence against the allegation of trespass—and even then only so long as the licensee does not overstep the ambit of the licence conferred (see e.g. *Tomlinson v Congleton BC* (2004) at [52] per Lord Hutton, [67] per Lord Hobhouse of Woodborough). In the famous phrase of Scrutton LJ, '[w]hen you invite a person into your house to use the staircase, you do not invite him to slide down the bannisters' (*The Carlgarth* (1927)). It is equally clearly established that a licence 'properly passeth no interest nor alters or transfers property in any thing, but only makes an action lawful, which without it had been unlawful' (*Thomas v Sorrell* (1673) per Vaughan CJ). Having neither a *proprietary estate* in the land nor even any *possession* of the land in the strict sense, the bare licensee has no rights which are directly assignable to a stranger and he cannot normally create any proprietary estate in the land such as a term of years. His rights are merely *personal* as against the author of his own fragile rights, his licensor.

Creation of bare licences

4.3 A bare licence can be created purely *orally* and may arise either *expressly* or *impliedly*. Common examples include the dinner party invitation (**2.13**); and even the residential status of a child in the family home probably rests, at least after the age of majority, on nothing more than a bare licence. Bare licences frequently emerge by implication from circumstances or conduct (see *R (Beresford) v Sunderland CC* (2004) at [59] per Lord Rodger of Earlsferry, [75] per Lord Walker of Gestingthorpe). It is even possible that a tolerated trespass can shade into an implied licence, as, for example, where a landowner, with knowledge that others are enjoying access to his land, habitually makes no objection to their presence and is therefore taken to have granted a tacit (albeit revocable) permission (see e.g. *Canadian Pacific Railway Co v The King* (1931) per Lord Russell of Killowen; *R (Beresford) v Sunderland CC*, supra at [76] per Lord Walker).

- The occupier of a dwelling-house is normally taken to issue an *implied* licence to any member of the public to come through his garden gate (if he has one) and up to his front door in order to request admission to the house or to do other legitimate business (*Robson v Hallett* (1967)). Although the scope of this implied invitation extends no further than the householder's front door, it is equally available, in the absence of some contrary warning or notice, to the postman, the milkman, to election canvassers, door-to-door salesmen and even police officers.

- Similarly, business premises are usually the subject of an implied licence permitting entry by members of the public for commercial or consumer purposes (but not, for instance, for the purpose of skateboarding, aggressive investigative journalism or the conduct of an armed robbery). School premises are likewise subject to certain limited rights of access for parents who wish to be informed about the progress or welfare of their children (*Wandsworth LBC v A* (2000)). It is, in general, the existence of such implied licences which helps to 'facilitate the practical functioning of the community' (see *Edwards v Attorney-General* (1986)), without conferring on the licensee any kind of *proprietary* interest in the land which he or she visits.

Revocation of bare licences

4.4 A bare licence can be revoked by the licensor by any words or actions which sufficiently indicate that a permission to be present on land has been withdrawn (but see *Gilham v Breidenbach* (1982), where even the most robust form of request to depart was held ineffective). The licensee is entitled to 'reasonable notice of revocation' (see *Canadian Pacific Railway Co v The King* (1931) per Lord Russell of Killowen), although in many circumstances of casual presence on land the period of notice regarded as 'reasonable' may be minimal to the point of non-existence (see *Winter Garden Theatre (London) Ltd v Millennium Productions Ltd* (1948) per Lord MacDermott). Following the successful revocation of a bare licence, the licensee has a reasonable time within which to vacate the premises (see *Robson v Hallett* (1967)), this period varying in accordance with the circumstances. A licensee who fails to leave the licensor's land within the relevant period of grace reverts to the status of a trespasser and may be evicted from the land by the use of reasonable force.

The correlation of licence and trespass

4.5 The idea of licence and the correlative notion of trespass are ineradicable components of the common law conception of defensible space. Together licence and trespass provide the supportive sanction of the civil law for an ancient territorial imperative: it is in this area that property and privacy concerns most obviously coalesce. As Lord Camden CJ observed in *Entick v Carrington* (1765), '[b]y the laws of England every invasion of land, be it ever so minute, is a trespass. No man can set his foot upon my ground without my licence.' Such statements have long been assumed, not wholly accurately, to confirm the existence of a facility of 'arbitrary exclusion' as the unqualified incident of possession of land.

— *The 'arbitrary exclusion' rule* The licensor's facility of arbitrary exclusion emanates from a widely held belief that, at common law, persons in possession of land enjoy an absolute prerogative to determine—no matter how arbitrarily or unreasonably—who may enter or remain on their land. The peremptory revocability of the bare licence (**4.4**) is often taken to demonstrate that the estate owner (or anyone else in possession) has a virtually unchallengeable discretion to exclude strangers from trespassing on land.

• *An ancient public purpose* Few claims of necessity or public interest have been allowed to constrain the landowner's totalitarian privilege (see e.g. *Monsanto plc v Tilly* (2000), where the Court of Appeal held that a genuine concern relating to the harmful effects of genetically modified crops could not justify trespass upon farm land). In the past this right to control access to one's land—and, in particular, the concept of the home as one's 'castle and fortress' (*Semayne's Case* (1604))—have served as pillars of constitutional liberty in a country which has long had no written constitution.

• *Physical resistance to trespass* The common law has for centuries allowed the occupier of land who is aggrieved by an act of trespass to employ reasonable physical force in order to exclude or evict the trespasser. The mere fact of trespass does not, however, justify extreme retaliation or excessive force (**3.8**). For example, an occupier cannot simply 'treat a burglar as an outlaw' (*Revill v Newbery* (1996) per Neill LJ).

— *Necessary modern modification* We tend to live nowadays in a crowded urban environment where recreational, associational and expressional space is increasingly at a premium. It is beginning to be recognised, in this context, that an estate owner's exercise of arbitrary powers of exclusion and eviction may sometimes *derogate* from certain important civil liberties. The threat is particularly real in relation to many modern downtown venues which are opened up to the public for recreational, educational, general leisure or consumer activities. Such locations, even though privately owned, are so heavily affected with a public interest that they assume a hybrid or 'quasi-public' character (see Gray and Gray, 'Civil Rights, Civil Wrongs and Quasi-Public Space' (1999) 4 *European Human Rights Law Review* 46).

CIN Properties Ltd v Rawlins (1995) After unsubstantiated allegations of misbehaviour on the part of a group of unemployed youths, CIN, the leasehold estate owner of a downtown shopping centre, purported to ban the group indefinitely from the precincts of the shopping mall. The ban, subsequently reinforced by court injunction, effectively excluded the youths for life from a large part of the centre of their own home town. CIN claimed, as estate owner, to be entitled to deny entry to the shopping mall without any showing of good (or indeed any) cause. The Court of Appeal upheld this claim and the European Commission of Human Rights (sub nom *Mark Anderson and Others v United Kingdom* (1998)) was unable to intervene, largely because the United Kingdom had never ratified the guarantee of liberty of movement contained in the European Convention on Human Rights.

— *The limits of 'property'* The ruling in *CIN Properties Ltd v Rawlins* placed a fresh and challenging focus on the parameters of the 'property' comprised in estate ownership in English law—it truly tested the limits of the owner's proprietary sovereignty over land. The outcome in this case contrasts markedly with the greater sensitivity shown in other jurisdictions to the human rights consequences—the threat to 'pedestrian democracy'—implicit in the unfettered exercise of an estate owner's exclusory privilege over areas of quasi-public space (see e.g. *New Jersey Coalition Against War in the Middle East v JMB Realty Corporation* (New Jersey, 1994)). The recent privatisation of much formerly public space—usually in the shape of private sector redevelopment of town centres—has equipped a generation of property developers with an unprecedented power to control the exercise of the citizen's essential freedoms of movement, assembly, association and speech. In the words of one judge in the European Court of Human Rights,

> It cannot be the case that through privatisation the public authorities can divest themselves of any responsibility to protect rights and freedoms other than property rights ... The old traditional rule that the private owner has an unfettered right to eject people from his land and premises without giving any justification and without any test of reasonableness being applied is no longer fully adapted to contemporary conditions and society (*Appleby v United Kingdom* (2003) (partly dissenting opinion of Judge Maruste)).

— *A 'reasonable access' rule* It is likely that the assimilation of European jurisprudence under the Human Rights Act 1998 will gradually curtail the more capricious features of proprietary power over quasi-public areas of land. The view taken by the Court of Appeal in *Porter v Commissioner of Police of the Metropolis* (1999)—in relation to an aggrieved customer's expulsion from an electricity board showroom—already points towards an 'incremental development of the common law' in this direction. The modern trend is towards the displacement of the rule of 'arbitrary exclusion' by a rule of 'reasonable access' under which entry to quasi-public locations can be denied only for 'articulated good reason' (see e.g. the approach of the New Zealand Court of Appeal in *Sky City Auckland Ltd v Wu* (2002)).

• The European Court of Human Rights has indicated that the state may be obligated to 'protect the enjoyment of Convention rights by regulating property rights' where, for example, a bar on access to land has the consequence of 'preventing any effective exercise' of freedoms of expression, assembly and association (see *Appleby v United Kingdom* (2003) at [47]). In a limited range of circumstances such an approach will require that landowners demonstrate that any exclusion from privately owned areas of quasi-public space is justified on *reasonable* grounds which do not contravene the guaranteed liberties of the citizen.

• A similar trend towards rights of reasonable access is evident in recent legislation such as the 'right to roam' provisions of the Countryside and Rights of Way Act 2000 (**5.6**). We live in a time of change and some of our traditional proprietary classifications (and their accompanying mindset) are having to respond to a new social and political ecology of urban and rural space (see Gray and Gray, 'Private Property and Public Propriety', in J. McLean (ed.), *Property and the Constitution* (Hart Publishing, 1999), p 11).

Contractual licences

4.6 A *contractual licence* comprises a contractually created permission to be present on land. It differs from the *bare licence* in that it is founded upon valuable consideration moving from the licensee (see *Horrocks v Forray* (1976) per Megaw LJ). The contract on which the licence is based may be express or implied.

• The contractual licence today ranks as one of the most controversial categories of entitlement in modern land law. Although plainly rooted in *contract*, it hovers ambivalently on the threshold of *property*, often performing much the same role and evincing some of the same characteristics as conventionally recognised proprietary rights. There is little doubt that, in at least some of its manifestations, the contractual licence is slowly undergoing the sort of transformation which in the 19th century converted the *restrictive covenant* into a proprietary interest of an equitable character (**2.12, 9.26**).

• Indeed some contractual licences already shade into the area of the *equitable* or *estoppel-based* licence which, as we shall see, is nowadays accepted as having a clear proprietary dimension (**10.18, 12.25, 12.42**). At present, however, the *contractual* licence has not yet acquired full proprietary status, although some forms of contractual licence are certainly beginning to look like a species of *quasi-proprietary* right in land. Everything turns on the precise quantum of property inherent in various claims of contractual licence and, as has been said before, the notion of 'property' in land is a relative concept expressible across a spectrum of varying degrees of propertiness (**2.3**).

The disparate functions of contractual licences

4.7 The contractual licence is a chameleonic device which performs many different kinds of function ranging from the short to the long term. An ordinary cinema ticket is the visible expression of a contractual licence, just as another form of contractual licence is exemplified in the presence of the football supporter at White Hart Lane. One peculiarly modern emanation of the contractual licence is found in agreements for the remote housing of networked computer equipment under co-location service contracts. Likewise the building contractor on the construction site and the paid-up member of the golf club are recipients of a contractual licence, although none of the instances mentioned so far could necessarily be said to involve the conferment of any *proprietary* interest in land (see *Cowell v Rosehill Racecourse Co Ltd* (1937) per Latham CJ (**2.13**)). It is generally where the contractual licence provides for rights of long-term occupancy that the rights of the contractual licensee begin to resemble those of a conventional estate owner such as a tenant or lessee (compare the case of the student lodger, **2.13**). In such contexts the distinction between the residential contractual licence and a proprietary interest in land often looks pretty blurred (**7.14**), and property rules which are wholly inappropriate for short- or medium-term contractual licences suddenly appear quite plausibly to apply to longer term arrangements (**12.25**). Herein lies much of the modern ambivalence of the contractual licence.

Termination of contractual licences

4.8 A fixed-term contractual licence terminates, without any requirement of notice, on the expiration of the fixed term (see e.g. *Sandhu v Farooqui* (2004) at [20]). Other kinds of contractual licence are terminable only upon the giving of reasonable notice to quit (see e.g. *Parker v Parker* (2003) at [286]) and, in the case of the statutorily defined 'periodic licence', the minimum permissible period of notice is four weeks' notice in writing (Protection from Eviction Act 1977, s 5(1A)). In most cases of licence to occupy a dwelling it is unlawful to enforce any right to recover possession from the resident licensee otherwise than by court proceedings (PEA 1977, s 3(1)–(2), (2B)).

In the middle of the 19th century the paramount quality of the estate owner's territorial control was recognised in the confirmation of a doctrine which enabled a contractual licensor effectively to revoke a contractual licence at any time, notwithstanding that the revocation constituted a breach of contract (see *Wood v Leadbitter* (1845)). Although the unjustified premature termination of the licence gave the disappointed contractual licensee a clear right to recover contractual damages, the breach of the licence gave rise to no further liability (whether in tort or otherwise) if the licensee was forcibly ejected or barred from the land.

• During the last 90 years, however, the case law development of the contractual licence has rather backtracked from this draconian position, the courts preferring in many cases to imply into the contractual licence a *negative contractual term* restraining improper or premature revocation by the licensor (see *Winter Garden Theatre (London) Ltd v Millennium Productions Ltd* (1948)). Thus, where a contractual licence envisages occupation of the licensor's land for a specific purpose or period of time (e.g. for a building construction project), it is often possible to spell out in the contract an implied obligation on the part of the licensor not to revoke the licence before the completion of that purpose or period (see *Hounslow LBC v Twickenham Garden Developments Ltd* (1971)). In cases of premature and wrongful termination threatened by a licensor, this implied obligation can then be enforced by injunction—effectively reversing the doctrine of *Wood v Leadbitter* and restraining wrongful breach of the contractual licence.

• In some instances it is even possible to invoke the remedy of specific performance in order to ensure that the terms of the licence are indeed duly carried out (see e.g. the enforcement of the booking of a public hall for a National Front meeting in *Verrall v Great Yarmouth BC* (1981)). Thus, although not feasible in every case, the use of *equitable* remedies has tended not merely to alter the rules as to the revocability of contractual licences but to impart something approaching *proprietary* character to the rights of the contractual licensee.

In certain circumstances a licensor's failure to ensure the unhindered enjoyment of a contractual licence may now constitute an interference with the licensee's right to peaceful enjoyment of possessions guaranteed by ECHR Protocol No 1, Art 1 (**2.7**) (see *Iatridis v Greece* (1999)).

Licences 'coupled with an equity'

4.9 The equitable development of the contractual licence (and particularly of the remedies available in cases of breach) is closely allied to the modern emergence of the *licence coupled with an equity*. This concept, although of ancient origin (see *Webb v Paternoster* (1619)), has played a significant role in the evolution of the modern *equitable licence*, itself a notion which obscures the precise borderline between *personal* and *proprietary* rights. (Only of true proprietary interests is the distinction between *legal* and *equitable* quality strictly appropriate.)

- The *licence coupled with an equity* or *equitable licence* is regarded as conferring a licence which is not arbitrarily terminable by the licensor. Such kinds of licence arise where the owner of land 'grants a licence to another to go upon land and occupy it for a specific period or a prescribed purpose, and on the faith of that authority the licensee enters into occupation and does work, or in some other way alters his position to his detriment' (*National Provincial Bank Ltd v Hastings Car Mart Ltd* (1964) per Lord Denning MR). In these circumstances, equity will restrain the owner from revoking the licence so as to defeat the period or purpose for which it was granted.

- As we shall see later, this doctrine, which makes legal sense of many messy, ill-defined and informal relationships in respect of land, is closely analogous to the concept of *proprietary estoppel* (**10.18**). The latter term has come to be associated in recent times with the recognition of entitlements in land which certainly bear a strong *proprietary* resonance, not least as measured in terms of binding effect on third parties (see now LRA 2002, s 116(a), **12.8, 12.25**). Together the amalgam of these versions of licence has done much, in the area of family property relationships, to counteract the grievous deficiencies of the law of trusts (**10.15–10.16**) by providing precisely that flexibility of approach which the clumsy and doctrinaire concepts of trust law have so conspicuously lacked. Just how fluid the categories of licence have become may be judged from *Tanner v Tanner* (1975).

Tanner v Tanner (1975) M, a young mother of twins gave up a Rent Act protected tenancy in order to move into a house bought in his own name by T, the father of her children. When he later evicted her from that house, the Court of Appeal awarded M compensation of £2,000 for the loss of a *contractual licence* (consideration having been demonstrated in the detriment involved in her surrender of her protected tenancy). Lord Denning MR construed the situation as being governed by an implied contract by T that the house would be provided for M and the children 'for the foreseeable future', indeed possibly for 'so long as [the children] were of school age and the accommodation was reasonably required'. Since the licence had already been terminated, compensation was now the only remedy available. The Court of Appeal's finding of contractual licence appeared, in many respects, strained and artificial, and it is not insignificant that, in dealing with similar circumstances of family disfunction, subsequent courts tended to resort instead to the terminology of *proprietary estoppel* (see e.g. *Pascoe v Turner* (1979)

(**7.6, 10.24**)) and *equitable licence* (see *Hardwick v Johnson* (1978); *Re Sharpe (A Bankrupt)* (1980) (**10.4**)).

Licences coupled with the grant of an interest

4.10 If licences can be graded across a span of *propertiness*, with the bare licence most lacking in proprietary content, the form of licence which undoubtedly crosses the threshold of recognised proprietary rights in land is the 'licence coupled with the grant of an interest'. This kind of licence is fairly unusual today, but comprises a permission to enter upon another's land for the specific purpose of removing something from that land (e.g. timber, minerals, fish, crops, or game). The licence thus combines the grant of an interest such as a profit *à prendre* (**8.4**) with an ancillary permission to enter the land in order to realise or exploit that interest. The licence coupled with a grant is irrevocable during the subsistence of the proprietary interest to which it pertains (see *Wood v Leadbitter* (1845); *Hounslow LBC v Twickenham Garden Developments Ltd* (1971)). The licence enjoys the perpetually binding effect attributed to the proprietary interest to which it is annexed and is therefore not only binding on the licensor and all his successors in title (*Webb v Paternoster* (1619)) but is itself capable of assignment to third parties (*Muskett v Hill* (1839)).

Just how proprietary is the modern licence?

4.11 There is no entirely clear or complete answer to this controversial question. Some forms of *bare licence* (e.g. the dinner party invitation (**2.13**)) have no true proprietary content and can never bind third parties. Some forms of licence, particularly those coupled with an *equity* (**4.9**) or with the *grant of an interest* (**4.10**), are widely regarded as having substantial proprietary significance (**12.8, 12.25**). It is the *contractual licence* which poses the real dilemma.

• If the 'property' component in the contractual licence is measured by its capacity to *bind a third party* who purchases the licensor's estate, the strong trend in the modern case law is to maintain that 'a contractual licence does not create a property interest' (*Ashburn Anstalt v Arnold* (1989) per Fox LJ; *Lloyd v Dugdale* (2002) at [52(4)] per Sir Christopher Slade (**10.25, 12.25**)). Contractual licences are not nowadays regarded as impacting on purchasers in the generality of cases, this approach being said to depend—although again in a somewhat circular fashion

(**2.14**)—on an historic view of 'an important and intelligible distinction between contractual obligations which gave rise to no estate or interest in the land and proprietary rights which, by definition, did' (*Ashburn Anstalt v Arnold* per Fox LJ).

• If proprietary quality turns, instead, on the *defensibility* of an interest against trespassers (**2.8**), there is now ground for thinking that at least some varieties of licence have gathered a certain proprietary momentum. Thus, for instance, it used to be said that a licensee, having neither a proprietary estate nor exclusive possession of the land (**3.4**), could never sue to recover possession from a stranger (see *Allan v Liverpool Overseers* (1874); *Radaich v Smith* (1959) per Windeyer J; *Street v Mountford* (1985) per Lord Templeman, **7.12, 7.14**). The licensee, it was generally maintained, had no right to take action against a third party in respect of any disturbance of his rights, since his remedy (if any) lay only against his licensor (see *Hill v Tupper* (1863), **8.7**). Now, however, it seems to be accepted that even a licensee may sue in trespass if he has exclusive possession (see *Hounslow LBC v Twickenham Garden Developments Ltd* (1971) per Megarry J) and, even more strangely, that a licensee armed with an as yet unexercised contractual right to 'enter and occupy' land is entitled to recover possession summarily from trespassers under CPR 55.2 (**3.6**).

> *Manchester Airport plc v Dutton* (2000) In order to facilitate the construction of a second runway at Manchester Airport, the National Trust, as owner of neighbouring woodland, licensed the airport company to lop and fell some trees. Before the company could do so, the area was invaded by trespassing protesters, who built a tree camp. The National Trust declined to intervene. The Court of Appeal held, by a majority, that the airport company was entitled to a summary possession order against the trespassers even though the company had neither possession nor occupation of the land (compare the slightly different circumstances present in *Countryside Residential (North Thames) Ltd v (1) A Child; (2) Persons Unknown* (2001)).

If some kinds of contractual licence can nowadays attract this degree of possessory protection, it is far from impossible that the contractual licence may one day be recognised more generally as a species of proprietary interest. There is already a tendency in modern statute law to treat the contractual licence as on a par with proprietary estates in land such as a term of years (see e.g. Housing Act 1985, s 79(3) (*secure tenancy*); Agricultural Holdings Act 1986, s 2(2)(b) (*agricultural holding*)). The law of licences, and especially the law relating to the contractual licence, is undoubtedly passing through a period of steady evolution—with all the uncertainty which this entails. One judge has even declared himself unconvinced 'that, in modern law, there is a bright line difference between a contractual licence and a consensual licence' (*Parker v Parker* (2003) at [276] per Lewison J).

FURTHER READING

Gray and Gray, *Elements of Land Law* (4th edn, OUP, 2005), ch 4.

Relevant sections of this work and other land law textbooks may be supplemented with:

Gray, Kevin and Francis Gray, Susan 'Civil Rights, Civil Wrongs and Quasi-Public Space' (1999) 4 *EHRLR* 46.

Grear, Anna 'A tale of the land, the insider, the outsider and human rights' (2003) 23 *Legal Studies* 33.

Hill, Jonathan 'The Termination of Bare Licences' [2001] *CLJ* 89.

SELF-TEST QUESTIONS

1   In what ways does the device of the licence mark the boundary between lawful and unlawful presence on another's land (**4.2–4.3, 4.6–4.7**)?

2   What constraints limit the termination of modern contractual licences (**4.8**)?

3   On a visit to your local shopping mall, you are asked by the security guard to leave the premises because (i) he thinks (wrongly) that he saw you shoplifting a week earlier, (ii) he thinks (wrongly) that you look like trouble, or (iii) he alleges that he is entitled to throw you out without proffering any justification at all. In each of these alternative circumstances, what rights (if any) do you have to remain on the premises (**4.5**)?

4   Which forms of licence have any claim to be regarded as *proprietary* (**4.11**)?

5

Public rights in land

SUMMARY

Earlier chapters have adverted to the nature of 'property' in land. It now becomes possible to examine some rights relating to land which fall towards the weaker end of the proprietary spectrum. Many of these entitlements comprise rights of a public nature, i.e. rights which are exercisable by *anyone* merely by virtue of the fact that he or she is a member of the public (or of a section of the public).

The nature of public rights in land

5.1 Following the description of the concept of property contained in Chapters 2, 3, and 4, this chapter analyses a number of rights which generally confer only limited degrees of control over or access to land. Although the intensity of the precise stake conferred in the land depends upon the right in question, these entitlements may—for want of a better term—be termed 'quasi-proprietary' in that they exhibit only tentatively or imperfectly the characteristics which are conventionally associated with 'property' in land. Many of the rights falling within this category nevertheless display at least one of the orthodox proprietary attributes: they comprise 'rights in reference to land which have the quality of being capable of enduring through different ownerships of the land' (see *National Provincial Bank Ltd v Hastings Car Mart Ltd* (1964) per Russell LJ). Most of these 'quasi-proprietary' entitlements comprise rights of a public nature, i.e. rights which are exercisable by anyone, whether or not he or she owns land, merely by virtue of being a member of the public (or of a section of the public). Some public rights resemble profits *à prendre* (e.g. the public right of fishing, **5.4**). Other public rights are akin to easements (e.g. the public right in respect of the highway, **5.2**). However, all public rights are distinct from easements, since they do not presuppose the existence of any 'dominant tenement' and are never the subject of a specific grant to any individual (**8.6**).

Public right to use the highway

5.2 Every citizen has a right of reasonable use of any highway over which the public has acquired a right of way either by statute or by reason of dedication and acceptance at common law. For this purpose the highway includes not only a carriageway over which there is a right of way for vehicular traffic, but also the adjoining pavements (where there is merely a public right of way on foot), together with public footpaths, byways and bridleways. Rights over the highway have an obvious importance not only in facilitating transport, but also in promoting recreational access to the countryside and in underpinning vital liberties of movement, expression, association and assembly. Public rights in respect of the highway have at least some proprietary dimension in that they constitute overriding interests pursuant to the Land Registration Act 2002 (LRA 2002, Sch 1, para 5, Sch 3, para 5, **12.15**) and probably cannot be defeated by adverse possession (see *Bromley LBC v Morritt* (1999)).

— *Dedication and acceptance of a public highway* Apart from express statutory provision, a public highway is created not by a process of grant, but in accordance with the common law doctrine of dedication and acceptance (see *DPP v Jones* (1999) per Lord Irvine of Lairg LC). Dedication of a public right of way normally comprises any sufficient indication by the competent landowner, whether express or implied, that the right of the public to use a path or track over his land is intended to be permanent (*R (Beresford) v Sunderland CC* (2004) at [45] per Lord Scott of Foscote). However, a longstanding permissive user which clearly rests only on the landowner's revocable licence or consent cannot raise any inference of dedication. Moreover, the common law doctrine requires proof not merely of dedication but also of the fact that the proffered dedication was accepted by or on behalf of the public (see *Secretary of State for the Environment, Transport and the Regions v Baylis (Gloucester) Ltd and Bennett Construction (UK) Ltd* (2000)). Acceptance, which is normally demonstrated by evidence of actual public use, imports a positive obligation on the part of the local highway authority to maintain the highway.

— *Statutory presumption from long user* There is also nowadays a general (although rebuttable) statutory presumption that a way is deemed to have been dedicated as a public highway where the way has been 'actually enjoyed by the public as of right and without interruption for a full period of 20 years' (Highways Act 1980, s 31(1), although see the prohibition of long user by mechanically propelled vehicles contained in Natural Environment and Rural Communities Act 2006, s 66). The concept of enjoyment 'as of right' does not, however, imply any requirement of actual legal entitlement on the part of those members of the public who avail themselves of the route in question. The phrase 'as of right' means little more than 'as if of right' (*R (Beresford) v Sunderland CC* (2004) at [72] per Lord Walker of Gestingthorpe) with the corollary that a landowner's mere toleration of a continuing user by the public is *not* inconsistent with a claim of user 'as of right' (*R v Oxfordshire CC, ex parte Sunningwell PC* (2000) per Lord Hoffmann). It is clear, however, that user pursuant to an overt communication of a revocable licence cannot found the statutory presumption (see *R (Beresford) v Sunderland CC* (2004) at [73]–[85] per Lord Walker of Gestingthorpe). It has also been emphasised— although controversially—that the statutory presumption can be ousted by an expression of contrary intention on the landowner's part, even though that intention was never brought to the attention of the public (*R (Godmanchester TC) v Secretary of State for the Environment, Food and Rural Affairs* (2005)).

— *Content of the citizen's rights over the highway* The citizen's entitlement to use the public highway is not confined to a minimal privilege of passage and re-passage for purposes of travel, but extends to activities (e.g. the conducting of some assemblies or protests) which are 'reasonable, do not involve the commission of a public or private nuisance, and do not amount to an obstruction of the highway unreasonably impeding the primary right of the general public to pass and re-pass' (*DPP v Jones* (1999) per Lord Irvine of Lairg LC). The confirmation in this context of a 'reasonable user' test is symptomatic of a more general infusion of a criterion of reasonableness in the regulation of access to land (**4.5**).

Public right of passage in navigable waters

5.3 There is, as a basic entitlement of the common law, a public right of passage at will over all navigable tidal waters for the purposes of 'navigation, commerce, trade, and intercourse' (*Blundell v Catterall* (1821)). There is also a public right of passage in respect of non-tidal rivers and lakes, although this right is subject to statutory regulation (see e.g. Water Resources Act 1991, Sch 25) and entitles the citizen to exercise only reasonable rights of user which are incidental to a right of passage and re-passage. The reasonableness of any particular user is measured with reference to the 'capacity and quality' of the river or other waterway (*Wills' Trustees v Cairngorm Canoeing and Sailing School Ltd* (1976) per Lord Wilberforce), but the public right of passage does not extend to any use of the bed or banks of a river other than for anchoring in an emergency or for landing at some place where the person concerned is entitled to do so (*Attorney-General ex rel Yorkshire Derwent Trust Ltd v Brotherton* (1992) per Lord Jauncey of Tullichettle).

Public right of fishing

5.4 From ancient times there has been a common law right, vested in members of the public, to fish in the open sea and in all tidal and salt waters. There is, however, no similar public right in respect of a non-tidal river, even if the river is subject to a public right of navigation. It is also highly unlikely that any public right of fishing exists in relation to inland non-tidal lakes (see *Johnston v O'Neill* (1911)).

Local customary rights

5.5 Certain entitlements in respect of land may be enjoyed by way of local customary right. The entitlements which fall within this category normally have a quaint or archaic quality and their utility as a means of generalising rights of access is severely limited by the requirement that a distinct local dimension should underpin the assertion of customary entitlement. Customary rights are exercisable, not by the public at large, but predominantly by the inhabitants of a particular local community such as a town or a parish or 'district'. 'Custom' is, in effect, a form of 'local common law' specific to a particular place (*Hammerton v Honey* (1876) per Jessel MR), and customary rights have been held to extend to such activities as the use of an access path to the local church, the playing of sports and pastimes on a piece of land, the drying of fishing nets in a certain location, and the holding of an annual fair or wake. Local customary rights can arise at common law only if they are ancient, certain, reasonable and continuous. In theory 'ancient' rights must pre-date 1189, but in practice the requirement of ancient origin is satisfied by evidence of uninterrupted long user for 20 years (or perhaps within living memory), provided always that there is no proof that the user actually originated after 1189 (see *R v Oxfordshire CC, ex parte Sunningwell PC* (2000)).

Rights of recreational access

5.6 Historically English law has conferred on members of the public only extremely limited rights of recreational user in respect of land and water, although substantial de facto access has tended to be enjoyed in a rather ill-defined way. Recreational access has represented, at best, a tolerated user in respect of which the landowner by long tradition—in the generality of cases—has sought no remedy in trespass. Nor does the public have any general right to walk upon the foreshore or to have access to the seashore for the purpose of swimming or other recreation (*Blundell v Catterall* (1821)). Such privileges are normally enjoyed, if at all, only by way of licence (**4.2–4.5**).

— *No general right to wander*   The common law tradition refuses, in all but the most restrictive of contexts (**8.7, 8.11**), to accept that members of the public can ever acquire a *ius spatiandi* (or right to wander at large) over land in the proprietorship of another person (see *Attorney-General v Antrobus* (1905) per Farwell J). Such an unqualified and wide-ranging form of entitlement is exactly the sort of right which denotes ownership of an estate in fee simple or for a term of years, rather than the kind of right which can be claimed by a stranger to the land.

— *Gradual extension of recreational access rights*   In England and Wales it is now increasingly recognised that there is a large public interest in the promotion and protection of general access to open countryside. A gathering array of legal provisions underpins the revitalised concern to diffuse the benefits of personal self-realisation and social hygiene which open-air access is perceived to confer. The national network of public rights of foot and horse way has been preserved and strengthened (see e.g. the power of local authorities to initiate a 'public path creation order' (Highways Act 1980, ss 26–28)). Members of the public also have statutory 'rights of access for air and exercise' to any land which comprises a metropolitan common or a local authority common, an entitlement which now covers much park land in the cities and extensive commons in the Lake District and South Wales (LPA 1925, s 193(1)). It is even tentatively acknowledged that many other areas of municipally owned park land are subject to a species of public trust which not only imposes duties of management and maintenance on the local authority owner, but also confers at least some form of access entitlement upon members of the public (see *R (Beresford) v Sunderland CC* (2004) at [87] per Lord Walker of Gestingthorpe). By contrast, certain activities which are now deemed improper forms of recreational pursuit—such as the hunting of wild mammals with dogs—have been prohibited by the Hunting Act 2004. The courts have so far resisted any attempt to challenge this legislation on the ground of incompatibility with ECHR Arts 8 and 11 (**2.15**) and Protocol No 1, Art 1 (**2.7**) (see e.g. *R (Countryside Alliance) v Attorney General* (2006)).

— *Registration of common land and greens under the Commons Act 2006*   Significant claims of recreational access are indirectly preserved by a process of registration under the Commons Act 2006. With effect from various dates in 2007/2008, this statute will replace the Commons Registration Act 1965. The 1965 Act was introduced in recognition of the public importance of certain privately owned open spaces and in order to protect such spaces from commercial development. The device of registration has recently been used with increasing frequency as a weapon of environmental warfare and, indeed, some doubt has been expressed as to the propriety of such registration as a means of bypassing 'normal development controls' (see *R (Beresford) v Sunderland CC* (2004) at [92] per Lord Walker of Gestingthorpe).

• User 'as of right' by local inhabitants, if continued over the statutory 20-year period, will generate an entitlement to registration under the CA 2006—on similar conditions to those specified by the CRA 1965—unless the landowner has unequivocally indicated to members of the public that their licence to use his land is intended to be merely temporary, entirely permissive and inherently revocable (*R (Beresford) v Sunderland CC* (2004) at [68] per Lord Rodger of Earlsferry, [79] per Lord Walker of Gestingthorpe). To 'suffer in silence' in the face of general recreational resort to one's land is to engage in a form of acquiescence or 'passive inactivity' which is in no way inconsistent with a claim of user 'as of right'. In the absence of an expressly revocable permission, the operation of the CA 2006 will be precluded only by evidence of 'some overt act which is intended to be understood, and is understood, as permission to do something which would otherwise be an act of trespass' (*Beresford* at [75] per Lord Walker). An affected landowner will be unable to frustrate the statute by the simple ploy of obstructing access to the relevant land immediately following an application for registration (see CA 2006, s 15(2), confirming the House of Lords' ruling in relation to the CRA 1965 in *Oxfordshire County Council v Oxford City Council* (2006)).

— *A statutory 'right to roam'* To date the most ambitious extension of recreational access rights in England and Wales is that provided by the Countryside and Rights of Way Act 2000, an enactment which began to take effect on 19 September 2004. The CROWA 2000 gives legislative force to an entitlement which the common law could never recognise, i.e. a generalised right of self-determining pedestrian access to privately owned open land—in effect, a statutory *ius spatiandi*. The CROWA 2000 was rolled out over England and Wales during 2005/2006 and in consequence all persons now enjoy an unprecedented public right 'to enter and remain … for the purposes of open-air recreation' on any 'access land' as defined by the Act (CROWA 2000, s 2(1)).

• 'Access land' automatically includes land more than 600m above sea level, together with other mapped areas of 'open country', registered common land, and land which is irrevocably dedicated by the owner to purposes of public access (CROWA 2000, ss 1(1)–(2), 16). There is also statutory power to extend the right of public access to the foreshore and other coastal land (CROWA 2000, s 3). The statutory right of access is limited to access on foot (although at all hours of day and night) and is conditional on compliance with a code of reasonable and responsible user of the countryside (CROWA 2000, s 2(1)(b), Sch 2). It is estimated that the CROWA 2000 affords a general entitlement to access on foot in respect of something between 8 and 12 per cent of the total land area of England and Wales.

• Even more extensive access legislation has been enacted in Scotland with effect from 9 February 2005, where, subject to limited exceptions, *all* land is made presumptively available for recreational, educational and certain commercial activities (see Land Reform (Scotland) Act 2003, ss 1–3). Access legislation of this kind—both north and south of the border—marks a steady advance towards the realisation of a 'pedestrian democracy' which is founded on a perceived need 'to promote social inclusion by improving people's health and their quality of life' (Scottish Executive, *Draft Land Reform (Scotland) Bill: Consultation Paper* (2001), para 1.5).

FURTHER READING

Gray and Gray, *Elements of Land Law* (4th edn, OUP, 2005), ch 5.

Relevant sections of this work and other land law textbooks may be supplemented with:

Gray, Kevin 'Equitable Property' (1994) 47(2) *CLP* 157, at 188–206.

Rowan Robinson, Jeremy 'Reform of the Law Relating to Access to the Countryside: Realising Expectations?' [2003] *JPL* 1394.

SELF-TEST QUESTIONS

1 Can public rights over land ever comprise proprietary rights in that land **(5.2, 5.6)**?

2 To what extent does modern English law confirm the existence of a 'pedestrian democracy' **(5.6)**?

6

Title

SUMMARY

The notion of 'title' in English law is currently undergoing an important transformation. The changing nature of modern title marks the transition from a world
in which title to an estate in land ultimately derives from physical possession
towards a rather different world in which title to an estate is constituted by the
formal registration of an abstract proprietary entitlement. This evolutionary
process is nowhere better demonstrated than in the recent (and rather fundamental) amendments which have occurred in the law of adverse possession.

The common law perception of title

6.1 Reference has already been made to the difference between the *common law* notion
of title and the increasingly pervasive *statutory* perception of title in English law
(**3.4**). At common law 'title' has always been the term used to denote an owner's
right or *entitlement*—the etymological links are not accidental—to assert his 'estate'
in land (together with its various incidents) against strangers. 'Title' to an estate
also carries other rights to determine or dictate the use, exploitation and disposition
of the land concerned. In the common law analysis, 'title' to an estate proceeds from
the raw fact of physical possession of land and is generally handed on through a
succession of estate owners by documentary transfer, although, as Blackstone
astutely pointed out, 'there is no foundation in nature or in natural law, why a set of
words upon parchment should convey the dominion of land' (*Bl Comm*, vol II, p 2).

— *Relativity of title* Unlike other European systems of property law, the
common law has never had any concept of *absolute* title. Even in respect of land,

ultimately the most durable of assets, all title remains essentially *relative*, the relativity usually turning on the presence or absence of factual possessory control.

— *All possessory claims are gradable*   Deep at the heart of the common law perception of title is the proposition that some claims to possession of land are better than others: land titles are always 'relatively good or relatively bad' (*Shaw v Garbutt* (1996) per Young J). From this flow certain important implications. In typically pragmatic fashion the common law presumes that any person in possession of land has a fee simple estate *unless and until* the contrary is shown (**3.5**). In effect, the 'title' of the present possessor is normally upheld unless and until a better claim is advanced on behalf of somebody else (see *Asher v Whitlock* (1865) per Cockburn CJ). In this strange world of relativity all claims to possession of land are gradable against each other and one claim, however fragile, may be adjudged marginally better than another. As the Court of Appeal indicated in *Manchester Airport plc v Dutton* (2000), even a licensee, if armed with 'effective control' of land or with a contractual right to 'enter and occupy' it, has a better claim to possession than does a 'bare trespasser', a factor of increasing importance in confrontations today between property developers and environmental protesters (**4.11**). In the pre-eminent illustration of relativity of title in English law, even a 'paper' or 'documentary' title can be defeated where a squatter enters land unlawfully and maintains an unchallenged adverse possession of that land during the course of a statutorily specified limitation period (**6.4**). With the effluxion of the limitation period the earlier title has proved vulnerable to the showing of a superior claim to possession.

— *Property as a self-defining fact*   In consequence of the principle of relativity, the common lawyer has always been fundamentally *unable* to make abstract pronouncements as to the ownership of particular plots of land. The common law's crude proprietary technique is restricted to determinations as to which of two claimants of a possessory estate has the *better* claim to possession. In this sense the common lawyer can never say who owns, but only who does *not*, albeit that such a ruling tends in practice to leave the preferred claimant with a fee simple title which is *pro tempore* unchallengeable. In this way—at least historically—English law has given expression to the self-defining quality of 'property' as an empirical fact (**2.17**).

— *Evidence of title*   In England and Wales all land titles are either *registered* (i.e. recorded in the Land Register) or *unregistered*. (The compulsory nature of title registration has already been explained (**2.25**), although it may take some time before all potentially registrable titles are in fact brought on to the Register.) In the case of an estate whose title has *never* been registered, there is no general or centralised public record of ownership. Accordingly, the 'essential indicia of title' are provided by the title deeds, normally retained within the control of individual estate proprietors, which relate to successive transactions with the land over time (see *Sen v Headley* (1991) per Nourse LJ, **10.29**). The documents contained in these 'deeds bundles', when coupled with the fact of undisturbed possession, generally identify the person who currently has the best 'title' to any relevant estate in the land. Title to an estate can also be claimed, however, by one who holds no supporting documentary evidence but relies instead on the sheer fact of his own possession. The possessor's undocumented claim usually exists concurrently with, and in direct competition against, some other person's paper title. In these circumstances extrinsic evidence of the possessor's title to a common law free-hold may be provided by statutory declarations which attest to the sustained possession alleged by the claimant. Declarations of this kind, sworn under the Statutory Declarations Act 1835, generally provide a proof of estate ownership sufficient to satisfy a purchaser of the land (see LRA 2002, ss 9(5), 10(6); LRR 2003, r 27, **7.7, 7.20**).

— *Relevance of possessory concepts at first registration of title* Possession-based notions of title retain a substantial relevance up to and including the point when unregistered estates in land are finally brought on to the Land Register. First registration of title is, so to speak, the terminal event in the lifetime of an unregis-tered estate before it is translated into one of the registered titles governed by the LRA 2002. For this reason the priorities surrounding a previously unregistered estate require to be determined at first registration by reference to *unregistered land* principles which are still overshadowed by the significance traditionally assigned at common law to the fact of possession. Thus, for example, a squatter who is a mere trespasser on unregistered land may voluntarily apply to be entered in the register as a first registered proprietor with 'possessory title' (**7.7**), a status which may be granted if the registrar is 'of opinion that the person is in actual possession of the land' by virtue of his common law estate (LRA 2002, ss 9(5), 10(6)). Furthermore, all first registered proprietors—irrespective of the quality of the title awarded to them by Land Registry—are bound by interests acquired by other persons under the Limitation Act of which they have notice (LRA 2002, ss 11(4)(c), 12(4)(d), **7.7, 7.21**).

The Land Register

6.2 In the common law analysis, 'title' to an 'estate' ultimately derives from the earthy reality of behavioural fact; and the potentially variable nature of human behaviour ensures that all title is ultimately relative. Completely definitive identification of estate ownership is never possible. Yet this is precisely the major objective of the Land Register for England and Wales which is maintained pursuant to the LRA 2002. In relation to those estates whose title is registered under the 2002 Act, the Land Register attempts to provide a decisive attribution of proprietorship. Estate owners are conclusively identified on the face of an authoritative public record; and this statutory regulation of estate ownership has indirectly brought about a significant evolution in the nature of 'title' in English law.

— *Guiding principles of land registration* The concept of formal registration of land titles was first adopted in the Torrens registration schemes introduced in Australia in the 1850s (and based on much earlier Hanseatic systems of mercantile registration). 'Torrens Title' legislation has now spread across most of the common law world and is, in many ways, the inspirational force behind the LRA 2002 (as, indeed, of the earlier LRA 1925). As we noted in Chapter 2, the linchpin of title registration under the 2002 Act is the idea that the title to certain major estates in land—principally the fee simple estate and any leasehold term of more than seven years—is substantively registered under an individual title number in the Land Register (**2.23**). Relevant information about the estate concerned is then entered against the title as appropriate and further transactions with the land are effected with reference to the proprietor's numerically identified estate. A former Chief Land Registrar (T.B.F Ruoff, *An Englishman Looks at the Torrens System* (Law Book Co of Australia (at Sydney), 1957), p 8) once described the common irreducible features of any Torrens scheme as comprising:

- the *mirror principle* under which the register of title reflects the totality of estates and interests affecting the registered land (**2.23**);

- the *curtain principle* under which trust interests are kept off the registered title (**11.29**); and

- the *insurance principle* under which the accuracy of registered titles is guaranteed and an indemnity paid from Land Registry funds in cases of loss (**12.30**).

— *A new 'culture of registration'* The ideals of Torrens may never have been quite fully realised in the LRA 1925 but, as we proceed into the 21st century, it becomes clear that the historic guiding principles of Torrens legislation have stimulated a significant mutation or adaptation of English law. The LRA 2002 incorporates a vision of the future which is firmly based on a 'culture of registration' (see Law Com No 254 (1998), para 1.14, **2.26**). With the advent of electronic conveyancing within the foreseeable future, entry in the register will become the *essential* constitutive source of most expressly created entitlements in land. In other words, entry in the register will be integral to the very process of *creating* interests in registered land. Transfer and registration will become both instant and inseparably linked; and few interests will be capable of express creation except as part of a simultaneous process of register entry (**12.2**, **12.5**). With the realisation of this objective, the *mirror principle* will take on a new and much more comprehensive significance. The register will reflect a 'real time' mirror image of land interests, since most interests will actually have no existence *off* the register.

— *The individual register of title* Throughout this book we have employed the term *substantive registration* (**2.31**) to indicate the registration of title to:

- a freehold estate (**7.7**);
- a leasehold estate granted for a term of more than seven years (**7.19–7.20**);
- a profit *à prendre* in gross (**8.4**); and
- a rentcharge (**8.27**).

On first registration of title to any of these forms of estate, a unique title number is allocated by Land Registry (LRR 2003, r 4(1)) and is used thereafter to identify the estate referred to in the title (i.e. the physical extent of the land and the particular estate held in it). The register created for each title is generally sub-divided into three parts or sub-registers, known respectively as the *property register*, the *proprietorship register*, and the *charges register* (LRR 2003, r 4(2)).

- *Property register* (LRR 2003, rr 5–6) As its name suggests, the *property register* contains a geographical description of the registered estate (e.g. the freehold land known as 88 Mill Road, Sodcaster) and refers also to the *title plan* (or *filed plan*) on which the land in the title is edged in red. The property register records, moreover, the benefit of any legal easements created by deed in favour of the land comprised within the title (**8.16**). The property register of a leasehold estate also provides sufficient particulars of the registered lease to enable that lease to be identified (LRR 2003, r 6(1)).

- *Proprietorship register* (LRR 2003, r 8) At the head of the *proprietorship register* appears the *class of title* awarded in respect of the land (**7.7, 7.20**). This sub-register contains the name and address of the owner of the substantively registered estate, together with the entry of any 'restrictions' (see LRA 2002, ss 40–3, **7.8, 11.29**) which cut back the otherwise plenary powers of disposition enjoyed by the registered proprietor (LRA 2002, s 23(1)).

- *Charges register* (LRR 2003, r 9) Whereas the property register describes the *positive* side of estate ownership, its *negative* aspects (judged from the registered proprietor's viewpoint) are revealed in the *charges register*. This sub-register refers to burdens on the registered title which have been protected by the entry of a 'notice' (LRA 2002, ss 32–4, **12.11**), such as leases (**7.8, 7.20**), easements (**8.16, 8.24, 9.15**), freehold restrictive covenants (**9.32, 13.18**), estate contracts (**9.8**) and home rights (**12.11–12.12**). The charges register is also the location for the registration of any mortgage charge created by the registered proprietor of a freehold or leasehold estate (**2.31, 8.29**).

— *Evidence of title* The LRA 2002 makes outline provision for the issue by Land Registry to newly registered estate proprietors of some form of *land certificate* (comprising, on the historic model, a print-out of the register bound up in a cover with a photocopy of the title plan) (see LRA 2002, Sch 10, para 4). However, such certificates can never in themselves constitute conclusive evidence of title to registered land (see *Freeguard v Royal Bank of Scotland plc* (2000) per Robert Walker LJ). There is, for instance, no guarantee, at any point following the date of its issue, that the print-out contained in a land certificate will remain up-to-date and accurate—a difficulty likely to intensify with the introduction of electronic conveyancing (see Law Com No 271 (2001), paras 9.86–9.88). The only truly reliable evidence of any registered proprietor's title is that contained in a *contemporary* official copy of the register of title supplied, on payment of a fee, by Land Registry (see LRA 2002, s 67; LRR 2003, r 134). This official copy bears a date and time of issue and reveals definitively the state of the register at that precise moment. Accordingly Land Registry has announced that, as a matter of practice, it will automatically issue a 'title information document' whenever a particular register of title is changed. Such documents, incorporating a contemporary official copy of the register and title plan as amended, will serve, in effect, to replace the traditional form of one-off and rapidly outdated land certificates (*Report on Responses to Land Registration Rules 2003—A Land Registry Consultation* (2003), p 11, paras 2.2, 2.18).

— *Administration of the Land Register* Contrary to common supposition, the Land Register is not some vast Domesday Book, but rather a collection of hard disks housed at Land Registry. The administration of the Land Register and the conduct of all Registry business are ultimately the responsibility of the Chief Land Registrar (LRA 2002, s 99). The current 'mission' of Land Registry is avowedly to provide 'the world's best service for guaranteeing ownership of land and facilitating property transactions' (Land Registry, *Annual Report and Accounts 2005/6* (July 2006), p 8). The Land Register contains over 20 million separate registered titles and is used each year to record nearly 5 million registered dealings with the land comprised in these titles. It is, in effect, the world's largest online transaction-processing database. The determination of various categories of dispute arising in the context of registration is now entrusted (see LRA 2002, ss 107–8) to the Adjudicator to Land Registry, the holder of a new office independent of the

Registry, from whose decisions appeal lies to the Chancery Division of the High Court (LRA 2002, s 111).

— *Public access* The Land Register is open to public access in the sense that, on payment of a small fee, any person may obtain a print-out of an individual register of title and a copy of any documents referred to therein (LRA 2002, ss 66–7; LRR 2003, rr 134–5). This means that potentially sensitive information contained in leases and charges referred to in the register can be exposed to public scrutiny unless the registrar has been called on to designate a particular document as an 'exempt information document' (LRR 2003, r 136) and this designation is subsequently upheld by the registrar on a stranger's application for an official copy of the document in question (LRR 2003, r 137). In this way 'prejudicial information' may be withdrawn from the public domain if, but only if, its disclosure would be likely to cause 'substantial unwarranted' damage or distress to the registered proprietor or would be likely to 'prejudice' his 'commercial interests' (LRR 2003, r 131). The registrar is ultimately obligated to disclose even sensitive documents if the balance of 'public interest' so dictates (LRR 2003, r 137(4)).

— *Land information as public information* The access provisions of the LRA 2002 give effect to the view that the contents of the Land Register should no longer be regarded 'as a private matter relevant only to the parties to a conveyancing transaction'. The Law Commission has observed that the general principle of an open register has 'fundamentally changed both the perception and the potential of land registration' as a means of affording on-line access and as a source of public information (see Law Com No 271 (2001), para 9.37). It is indeed the same approach which underlies Land Registry's current provision of on-line viewing and searching services to account holders' office computers ('Land Registry Direct') and its commitment as a key supplier of data to the National Land Information Service (NLIS) as first envisaged in the 'Citizen's Charter' White Paper of 1992.

A new statutory perception of title

6.3 The enactment of the LRA 2002 and the rapidly expanding coverage of the Land Register have together conduced towards an important transformation of the concept of title in English law. Title to an estate in land, once entered in the Land Register, is no longer primarily a function of undisturbed possession, but is constituted instead by the formal record of the register itself.

— *The 'statutory magic' of registration* Titles to estates registered at Land Registry draw their legitimacy from the sheer fact of registration. The bureaucratic act of registration operates a certain 'statutory magic' (**7.7**), conferring an immediate title on the newly registered proprietor irrespective of the provenance of the estate concerned and subject only to the possibility that the register may subsequently be rectified in rare cases of mistake or irregularity. It can therefore be said, with justification, that the LRA 2002 provides 'not a system of registration of title but a system of title by registration' (see *Breskvar v Wall* (1971) per Barwick CJ). The transition is from a *common law* perception of title as rooted in organic fact to a *statutory* perception of title as inherent in a computerised record maintained by the state. Registration is fast becoming, in effect, the exclusive source of title. Indeed, under the LRA 2002 'title' is no more and no less than the register entry which records proprietorship of the relevant estate (see LRR 2003, r 217(1)). The concentrated quality of this new form of register-based title is encapsulated in the way in which the 2002 Act welds concepts of 'title', 'estate', and 'proprietor' into a form of statutory ownership of land which begins to resemble the civilian model of proprietorship. The 'registered proprietor' now holds a 'registered title' which is inseparable from—indeed has no meaning apart from—the 'registered estate' in the 'registered land' to which it relates. With the enactment of the 2002 Act the brightlines of land ownership have been significantly intensified. A new *in rem* quality has been conferred on estate proprietorship (and particularly on ownership of the fee simple estate).

— *A shift in the philosophical base of English land law*   With its definitive record of estate ownership, the LRA 2002 confirms a large shift in the philosophical base of English land law away from the phenomenon of *possession* and towards a new ideology of *ownership*. The messy empiricism of common law title has finally given way to the more crystalline statutory title established by entry in the Land Register. Title to an estate, once recorded in the Register, is no longer primarily a reflection of behavioural fact, but emanates instead from a computerised record of abstract rights of proprietorship and their subsequent registered disposition. As will become steadily apparent throughout this book (**6.7, 12.7, 12.9**), the regime of title registration inaugurated by the LRA 2002 offers a new degree of stability and security for those estates in land which are brought on to the Land Register. An inevitable product of the modern statutory regime is the emergence of a much more robust and deeply stabilised form of state-endorsed title. By virtue of their greatly enhanced protection the titles maintained by Land Registry will inevitably evince a more 'absolute' quality than they have ever previously enjoyed. We are, in effect, moving inexorably towards a continental concept of *dominium* (especially in relation to the freehold estate in land) (see Gray and Gray, 'The rhetoric of realty', in J Getzler (ed.), *Rationalizing Property, Equity and Trusts: Essays in Honour of Edward Burn* (Butterworths, 2003), p 244).

— *The modern demise of adverse possession* The ultimate achievement of the LRA 2002 lies in its ruthless maximisation of rational legal order, an aim which is symbolised by the statutory vision of an electronic register of virtually indefeasible titles, transactable by automated dealings and guaranteed by the state. The LRA 2002 has thus overseen a remarkable transition from title as self-authenticating social fact to title as state-regulated administrative fact. It was inevitable, in the context of this evolutionary process, that the impact of relativity of title, whilst not wholly eliminated from the law of registered land, should be greatly curtailed. Under the tightly organised regime of the LRA 2002, estate ownership, as constituted by the register record, becomes a heavily protected phenomenon, leaving little room for the operation 'off the record' of some ancient and pragmatic principle of adverse possession.

Title by adverse possession

6.4 Nothing so clearly illustrates the changing nature of 'title' as the recent history of the inaptly named law of 'adverse' possession. The principle of adverse possession has played a venerable role in the development of the English law of land. By pressing relativity of title to its limit, the principle has served effectively to uphold estates in land held by persons who have no *formal* ownership. Acquisition of title by adverse possession depends upon the operation of the Limitation Acts— currently the Limitation Act 1980—and differs markedly from any form of acquisition of title by grant, transfer or conveyance.

— *The central feature of adverse possession* The essence of adverse possession is the idea that if an estate owner (usually the 'paper owner' or owner of the 'paper title') fails within a prescribed period to take active steps to secure the eviction of a squatter or trespasser from his land, his own title is in principle extinguished and he is thereafter statutorily barred from recovering possession of the land. Title to land being relative, the intruder thus acquires—as an indirect effect of the Limitation Act—a title which recognises and legitimises his continuing possession.

— *Even wrongful possession generates a fee simple estate* English law presumes that any person in 'possession' of land holds a *fee simple estate* (or common law freehold) which remains valid and effective unless defeated by some better claim (**3.5**). Possession gives an ownership 'good against everyone except a person who has a better, because older, title' (*Newington v Windeyer* (1985) per McHugh JA). Thus, even from the inception of his wrongful entry into possession, an intruder acquires a 'property' in the land which, if unchallenged for the duration of the legally stipulated limitation period, conclusively bars all prior rights of recovery.

And if the assertion of *all* older titles ever becomes statute-barred by the effluxion of time, the current possessor's title becomes, for practical purposes, an unimpeachable fee simple title to the land, resting as it does on the infirmity of all other claims to eject him.

The rationale of adverse possession

6.5 Adverse possession sometimes appears to constitute a primitive taking of land by theft or robbery (see e.g. *Ellis v Lambeth LBC* (2000), where a squatter controversially, but successfully, claimed a council house reportedly worth some £200,000). For many the uncompensated deprivation of title following a statutorily prescribed period of adverse possession seems 'draconian', particularly in a 'climate of increasing awareness of human rights, including the right to enjoy one's own property' (*JA Pye (Oxford) Ltd v Graham* (2000) per Neuberger J). Historically, however, the phenomenon of adverse possession has been supported by powerful arguments based on doctrine and policy. Although adverse possession is unashamedly 'possession as of wrong' (*Buckinghamshire CC v Moran* (1990) per Nourse LJ), the common law premise of relativity of title has tended to ensure that long possession eventually causes that wrong to mature into a right. Land claims, however unmeritorious, come in time to enjoy a certain self-righting quality. As Dean Ames once said, 'English lawyers regard not the merit of the possessor, but the demerit of the one out of possession' ('The Nature of Ownership', in *Lectures on Legal History* (Harvard University Press, Cambridge, Mass. 1913), p 197).

— *Avoidance of protracted uncertainty as to title* The adverse possession rule accords an important recognition to the primal territorial bondings generated by prolonged possession of land. The rule effects a compromise between moral entitlement and social utility, thereby ensuring that land titles eventually conform to lived boundaries rather than the reverse. By endorsing a definitive (albeit uncompensated) shift of economic value to the squatter or interloper, the limitation principle also suppresses the otherwise constant agitation of stale grievances. The rule conduces towards 'the interests of peace' (see *Minister of State for the Army v Dalziel* (1944) per Latham CJ). As Lord Bingham of Cornhill has pointed out, 'in the days before registration became the norm' the law of adverse possession 'could no doubt be justified as avoiding protracted uncertainty where the title to land lay' (*JA Pye (Oxford) Ltd v Graham* (2003) at [2]). In reality, the long possession rule has operated as a controlled trade-off between documentary title and pragmatic fact, this trade-off allegedly serving both to avert costly disputes and to promote the stabilisation of title for the benefit of third parties (such as purchasers and lenders). For all these reasons the application of the limitation principle—at least in relation to *unregistered* land—has generally been thought to be justified, within the terms of ECHR Protocol No 1, Art 1 (**2.7**), as a rule which ultimately operates 'in the public interest', even though it results in a 'deprivation' of possessions (see *Harrow LBC v Qazi* (2004) at [124] per Lord Scott of Foscote). The same rationale may not be so readily available in respect of registered land (see e.g. *Beaulane Properties Ltd v Palmer* (2005) at [140]).

— *Territorial context of adverse possession* It would, in any event, be wrong to suppose that most instances of adverse possession necessarily involve the consciously wrongful seizure of large areas of land. Today adverse possession tends to arise more frequently where someone claims that a minute sliver of land formally titled in his neighbour has been inaccurately fenced in his own favour. Moreover, as every conveyancer is fully aware, the principle of adverse possession has always provided the ultimate cure or longstop remedy for defectively drawn ground plans which erroneously enclose a small portion of a neighbour's land within the claimant's boundary lines. Normally, however, neither ignorance nor mistake will prevent the operation of adverse possession (**6.11**).

— *Diminishing force of the rationale of adverse possession* As already noted, the underlying rationale of adverse possession has become increasingly contentious in modern times. Although the common law principle of relativity of title still operates within the statutory regime of registered land, the LRA 2002 has brought about a dramatic curtailment of the limitation principle within the registered context (**6.7**). The real force of the long possession rule is now effectively confined to unregistered land—a proviso which heavily colours much of what follows.

The operation of the Limitation Act 1980 in unregistered land

6.6 The primacy accorded at common law to factual possession of land would obviously have led to an aggressive free-for-all in land holdings, had it not been for the 'first in time' principle that prior possession generates a legal right to defend possession. Possession, even if lost, gives rise to a right to recover possession (**3.6**), but for almost 400 years this common law right to recover possession has been crucially bounded by statutory limitation periods which penalise those who sleep on their rights.

— *The limitation periods* The general rule is that '[n]o action shall be brought by any person to recover any land after the expiration of twelve years from the date on which the right of action accrued to him' (LA 1980, s 15(1)). There is no requirement that this period of 12 years should immediately precede the bringing of the paper owner's action for recovery. It follows that a current paper owner's rights may have become barred at some point in the long distant past—a clear hazard for strangers who later seek to rely on his apparent documentary title. In respect of *crown actions* for recovery, the relevant limitation period is 30 years (and in respect of the recovery of foreshore, 60 years) (LA 1980, Sch 1, paras 10–11).

— *The aggregation principle* For the purpose of establishing the expiration of any limitation period, immediately consecutive periods of adverse possession may be aggregated (LA 1980, s 15(1); see *Mount Carmel Investments Ltd v Peter Thurlow Ltd* (1988)).

> **Example**: X (the original paper owner) is dispossessed by A, who four years later transfers his rights—such as they are—to B. Thereafter B continues in possession for a further eight years. B is then entitled to add the period of A's adverse possession to his own in defence against any action for recovery brought by X, these two periods together totalling 12 years.

— *Proposals for reform* The Law Commission has proposed that the general limitation period for most actions for the recovery of land (including actions brought by the crown) be reduced to *10* years (see Law Com No 270 (2001), paras 4.126–4.135). Claims in respect of foreshore would continue to be limited by the present period of 60 years (see Draft Limitation Bill 2001, cl 16(1)–(2)).

— *The extinguishment of prior titles* It is always said, in relation to an unregistered estate, that the effluxion of the limitation period does not bring about, in favour of the adverse possessor, any 'parliamentary conveyance' or 'assignment' of the former owner's paper title. Instead, the Limitation Act provides for the *extinguishing* of the title of any person who is statutorily barred from recovery of possession (LA 1980, s 17). All prior rights of recovery now being barred and all prior titles extinguished, the squatter's independent possessory title (as generated by his initial entry into possession) now 'becomes impregnable, giving him a title superior to all others' (*Buckinghamshire CC v Moran* (1990) per Nourse LJ). Thus, in unregistered land, the adverse possessor simply emerges with a new and unchallengeable legal title of his own.

— *Effect of adverse possession of an unregistered freehold* Even though a squatter establishes a freehold title by adverse possession of unregistered land, he takes this title subject to such third party rights (e.g. easements, profits *à prendre* and restrictive covenants) as already affect the land. In effect, the squatter is bound by all valid pre-existing legal and equitable rights over the land, irrespective of whether these rights have been duly registered under the Land Charges Act (**2.41**,

12.35–12.36). Furthermore, having taken title by operation of law, the squatter cannot even establish the defence of the bona fide *purchaser* without notice (**2.43, 12.40**) and is clearly subject to equitable interests such as pre-1926 restrictive covenants (*Re Nisbet and Potts' Contract* (1906)).

— *Effect of first registration of adversely possessed land*   Where a completed period of adverse possession of unregistered land lies buried in the past and the paper owner has since resumed possession, the successful squatter is accorded a certain limited protection in the event that the land is later the subject of some application for first registration of title at Land Registry (**6.7, 7.7**).

Adverse possession under the Land Registration Act 2002

6.7   In recent years it has seemed increasingly strange that adverse possession should play any significant role in a regime where the formal registration of title is supposed to provide a definitive record of ownership (see e.g. *JA Pye (Oxford) Ltd v Graham* (2003) at [2] per Lord Bingham of Cornhill). There also emerged a growing public perception that it is 'too easy for squatters to acquire title', a criticism which attracts added force where difficulties in the effective policing of local authority premises can ultimately lead to substantial losses for the public purse (see Law Com No 271 (2001), paras 2.70–2.71, 14.4). In *JA Pye (Oxford) Ltd v Graham* itself, the House of Lords upheld an adverse possession claim in respect of 25 hectares of prime development land reputedly worth £10 million, a result which the senior law lord, Lord Bingham, professed himself to 'arrive at with no enthusiasm' (see also 'Britain's biggest ever land-grab', *Guardian*, 9 July 2002). If 'property' is indeed a relationship of socially approved control over a valued resource (**2.3**), it is quite clear that, in the Britain of the 21st century, the adverse possession of land has become a form of control which is no longer socially approved. Added to these concerns has been the increasing apprehension that, in relation to registered titles, the operation of adverse possession may be incompatible with ECHR Protocol 1, Art 1 (**2.7**)—a view which was finally endorsed by the European Court of Human Rights in *JA Pye (Oxford) Ltd v United Kingdom* (2005) (**6.11**). Here the Court ruled, by the narrowest of margins (four votes to three) that the law of adverse possession under the LRA 1925 violated the property guarantee of the ECHR. In the Court's view, the required fair balance between an individual owner's 'peaceful enjoyment' of his possessions and the demands of the public interest was irretrievably upset by the absence of any monetary compensation for the affected owner and by the lack of adequate procedural protection in the form of advance notification to the owner of an imminent loss of title. The *Pye* ruling is currently the subject of a reference to the Grand Chamber of the European Court of Human Rights and a final decision is keenly awaited as this book goes to press. The European Court appeared to imply, however, that the reformulated law of adverse possession under the LRA 2002—precisely because it remedies some of the deficiencies of its predecessor—is likely to prove Convention-compliant.

— The LRA 2002, although implicitly recognising that adverse possession may have some continuing importance in unregistered land, has now engineered a very substantial strengthening of the position of *registered* proprietors against the claims of squatters—a feature which must have been intended, in part, as a powerful incentive towards voluntary first registration of titles (**7.7**). In the words of one commentator, the 'much watered-down version of adverse possession' contained in the 2002 Act is 'undoubtedly one of the most fundamental changes to property law in the past century' (Roger Smith, 'The role of registration in modern land law', in L. Tee (ed.), *Land Law: Issues, Debates, Policy* (Willan Publishing, 2002), p 55).

— *Mere lapse of time no longer bars registered titles* The LRA 2002 makes a decisive break away from the historic tradition that estate ownership is rooted in the actuality of behavioural fact. The Act puts in place a 'wholly new system of adverse possession . . . applicable to registered land' (Law Com No 271 (2001), para 14.2). The LRA 2002 introduces, with prospective effect, an unprecedented premise in English law, i.e. that mere lapse of time cannot, in itself, bar the rights of a registered proprietor. Time, in other words, no longer runs in favour of a squatter by reason of his occupation of registered land (see LRA 2002, s 96(1), (3)); and it therefore becomes immaterial whether or not the registered proprietor has commenced legal proceedings to terminate the squatter's possession (LRA 2002, Sch 6, para 11(3)(a)).

— *Requirement of positive application by squatter* The LRA 2002 substitutes a very different order of things in place of the common law notion of title by mere lapse of time. The Act promotes the 'fundamental concept of indefeasibility that is a feature of registered title' (Law Com No 271 (2001), para 14.3), by placing an onus on the squatter, if he wishes to take over an existing registered title, to make a positive application to Land Registry for registration. A person may apply to be registered as proprietor of any relevant registered estate if he has been in 'adverse possession' for the period of 10 years *immediately preceding* the date of his application (LRA 2002, s 97, Sch 6, para 1(1)). The estate in question need not itself have been registered at Land Registry throughout the entirety of this period (LRA 2002, Sch 6, para 1(4)), but for all material purposes 'adverse possession' retains substantially the same meaning as in the law of unregistered land (LRA 2002, Sch 6, para 11(1)–(2), **6.10–6.12**).

— *The squatter's application can normally be defeated by simple objection* The dramatic impact of the LRA 2002 emerges in what next follows. The squatter's application for registration is notified by Land Registry to the relevant estate proprietor and also to other parties such as registered chargees (i.e. mortgagees) and proprietors of any superior leasehold estate. The application will normally be defeated—and defeated conclusively—by *any* objection raised by any of these parties within a period of 65 business days (LRA 2002, Sch 6, paras 2–5; LRR 2003, r 189). It is indeed this process of notification and possible objection which substantially ensures the compatibility of the new provisions with the property guarantee of the ECHR. Only in the absence of objection (or if the squatter, notwithstanding objection, remains in adverse possession for *two further years*) is the squatter entitled to be registered as proprietor of the relevant estate in place of the dispossessed proprietor (LRA 2002, Sch 6, paras 6–7). In effect, existing registered proprietors, if challenged by a squatter, are given a longstop period of two additional years either to evict the squatter or to regularise the squatter's position by the grant of some licence or tenancy.

— *Statutory transfer by registration of the successful adverse possessor* The effect of the LRA 2002 is clearly to 'make it much harder for a squatter who is in possession of registered land to obtain a title to it against the wishes of the proprietor' (*JA Pye (Oxford) Ltd v Graham* (2003) at [73] per Lord Hope of Craighead). However, in the unlikely event that a squatter's inchoate rights survive this process of legal attrition, he is normally entitled to be registered as the new proprietor with absolute title, this registration serving to replace (and thereby extinguish) the common law freehold acquired by the squatter on his initial assumption of possession (LRA 2002, Sch 6, para 9(1)). The overall outcome is therefore the conferment on the successful squatter of a statutory right to be substituted in the Land Register as the current estate proprietor—a process which is 'to all appearances a statutory conveyance' of the relevant registered estate (see *Central London Commercial Estates Ltd v Kato Kagaku Ltd* (1998) per Sedley J).

— *Effect of adverse possession of a registered freehold* Even where a squatter acquires a registered freehold title by adverse possession, he takes this title subject to almost all valid pre-existing legal and equitable rights over the land. His registration as the new proprietor is stipulated by statute to have no impact on 'the priority of any interest affecting the estate' (LRA 2002, Sch 6, para 9(2)). The successful adverse possessor is therefore bound by most third party rights (e.g. easements, profits *à prendre* and restrictive covenants) which already encumber the land and have not yet been extinguished. By way of exception, however, the squatter generally takes free of any registered charge (i.e. mortgage) affecting the registered estate immediately before his own registration, not least because the registered chargee will, by definition, have failed to object to the squatter's application for registration (LRA 2002, Sch 6, para 9(3)–(4)).

— *Exceptions to the right of conclusive objection*   The LRA 2002 allows only a few exceptions to the statutory right of arbitrary rebuttal of a squatter's claims (LRA 2002, Sch 6, para 5). In these exceptional cases the squatter normally acquires an unqualified statutory right to take over the relevant registered title.

Objections to a squatter's application for registration are required to be disregarded in each of the following circumstances:

• where it would be 'unconscionable because of an equity by estoppel' for the registered proprietor to seek to dispossess the applicant and the circumstances are such 'that the applicant ought to be registered as proprietor' of the estate in question (see also LRA 2002, s 110(4));

• where the applicant is entitled 'for some other reason' (e.g. under an uncompleted contract of purchase) to be registered as proprietor;

• where the land in dispute borders upon land belonging to the applicant for registration, the exact boundary line never having been fixed, and was 'reasonably believed' by the applicant over at least the preceding 10-year period to have belonged to himself (LRA 2002, Sch 6, para 5(4)–(5), effective 13 October 2004: see Land Registration Act 2002 (Commencement No 4) Order (SI 2003/1725)).

— *An historic change of emphasis*   The foregoing analysis makes it fairly clear that the LRA 2002 marks an historic change in fundamental features of the English law of realty. Estate ownerhip is no longer regulated by effective possession and the mere lapse of time. Registration has replaced possession as the source of title and with the inexorable movement towards comprehensive registration has come a new conceptualism of ownership. The philosophical base of English land law has shifted from empirically defined fact to state-defined entitlement, from property as a reflection of social actuality to property as a product of state-ordered or political fact. In short, instead of the citizen telling the state who owns land, the state will henceforth tell the citizen.

— *Protection of rights accrued prior to the LRA 2002*   It should be noted that the LRA 2002 preserves, in some degree, the rights of squatters in whose favour time had already successfully run *prior to* the commencement of the 2002 Act.

• *Registered land* A squatter on registered land who had completed the requisite period of adverse possession is automatically entitled to be registered as proprietor of the relevant estate (LRA 2002, Sch 12, para 18(1)). In the absence of such registration, his rights, if he is still in 'actual occupation', will 'override' any subsequent disposition of the registered estate (LRA 2002, s 29(1), (2)(a)(ii), Sch 3, para 2, **12.18**).

• *Unregistered land* The rights accrued prior to the commencement of the LRA 2002 by a successful squatter on unregistered land are deemed to 'override' any first registration of that land if the squatter remains in 'actual occupation'. Even if the successful squatter has since gone out of 'actual occupation' following the completion of his adverse possession, his rights bind any first registered proprietor who has notice of them (LRA 2002, s 11(4)(c)) and are otherwise specially protected for a period of three years from the effective date of LRA 2002, Sch 1 (LRA 2002, Sch 12, para 7), during which period he can apply for first registration himself.

Special rules relating to leases

6.8   Under the Limitation Act 1980 adverse possession in the leasehold context is governed by several special rules.

—   *Adverse possession by a tenant*   No tenant can claim adverse possession *against his landlord* during the subsistence of his lease or tenancy. In respect of the land which is the subject of the lease, time cannot run against the landlord, not least since the tenant's possession is by consent and cannot therefore be considered *adverse* (**6.11**). Nor does mere non-payment of rent during a fixed term render the tenant's continuing possession adverse. In the case of a periodic tenancy in writing, possession adverse to the landlord can occur only after the tenancy has been determined. In other cases of periodic tenancy, the tenant's possession becomes adverse only when the period covered by the last payment of rent has expired (LA 1980, Sch 1, para 5). Moreover, if the tenant should encroach on any land belonging to his landlord which is not subject to the lease, the tenant is viewed as merely extending the potential locus of his tenancy to include the area of his encroachment. Conversely, if the tenant encroaches on adjoining land belonging to a *stranger*, his adverse possession is normally presumed to operate (if at all) for the benefit of his landlord as reversioner (*Smirk v Lyndale Developments Ltd* (1975)).

—   *Adverse possession by a stranger of a freehold subject to a lease*   Where a stranger enters into possession of land which is the subject of a lease, the intruder is immediately deemed to hold a common law freehold estate in that land (**3.5**). During the currency of the lease, however, the squatter's possession can normally be considered 'adverse' only in relation to the dispossessed *leasehold* owner.

It cannot rank as 'adverse' in relation to the *freehold* owner (or landlord), whose entitlement to resume physical possession arises, in principle, only on the determination of the lease. It follows, therefore, that the achievement of an unassailable fee simple title for the squatter on leasehold land requires the extinguishment of *both* the tenant's leasehold interest *and* the landlord's freehold interest.

— *Effect of adverse possession of registered leasehold land* Where throughout the requisite 10-year period a squatter has been in adverse possession of registered freehold land which is subject to a registered lease, the squatter is clearly in a position to apply to be registered as the new proprietor of the registered *leasehold* estate (LRA 2002, Sch 6, para 1(1), **6.7**).

• The squatter's application may well be defeated by objection from the current registered proprietor of the leasehold title (or, indeed, from the proprietor of any superior estate or from any registered chargee). If, however, the application succeeds, the squatter takes over the registered leasehold title, in effect, as an assignee of the leasehold estate and is therefore bound by the covenants and obligations of the lease (see LRA 2002, Sch 6, para 9(2), effectively following *Central London Commercial Estates Ltd v Kato Kagaku Ltd* (1998) per Sedley J).

• In such circumstances the squatter is still some distance from being able to claim that his adverse possession is effective against the registered proprietor of the freehold title (i.e. the landlord). The dispossessed proprietor of the registered leasehold (i.e. the former tenant) is not allowed to accelerate the landlord's right to possession against the squatter by a collusive surrender (**7.33**) of the leasehold term to the landlord (see *Spectrum Investment Co v Holmes* (1981)). It is only at the termination of the lease—which may be a distant point in time if the leasehold term is of long duration (e.g. a lease of 99 years)—that the squatter may begin to mount an assault on the registered *freehold* title. A further 10 years of adverse possession would then entitle the squatter or his successor to apply for registration in place of the existing registered proprietor of the fee simple estate, although this application would, of course, again be subject to arbitrary rebuttal by simple objection (LRA 2002, Sch 6, paras 2–5, **6.7**).

— *Effect of adverse possession of unregistered leasehold land* Matters are both simpler and more complex in unregistered land. Where a tenant of unregistered land is dispossessed during the currency of his lease, the squatter's adverse possession of the leasehold is effective immediately and time begins to run against the tenant (*Chung Ping Kwan v Lam Island Co Ltd* (1997)). Twelve years of such adverse possession will, of course, bar the tenant's right to recover from the squatter. However, precisely because the tenant has never conveyed any leasehold title to the adverse possessor, the latter does not rank as an 'assignee' of the leasehold term (**7.17, 14.20**) and is therefore not directly liable on the tenant's covenants under the lease, although due performance may be indirectly enforced upon him by the threat of re-entry (e.g. forfeiture for non-payment of rent) without any right of relief (**8.35, 14.11–14.15**).

All the while the landlord's unregistered freehold remains unaffected, notwithstanding the squatter's successful adverse possession against the tenant, since it is only on the determination of the lease that the landlord's independent right of action for recovery accrues (LA 1980, Sch 1, para 4). In principle, therefore, the unregistered freehold title cannot be extinguished until, at the earliest, *12 years after* the end of the leasehold term. It seems, however, that in unregistered land the strategy of collusive surrender by the dispossessed tenant may well enable the landlord, as freehold owner, to claim that the lease has been terminated, thereby accelerating his own entitlement to recover possession from the squatter (see the controversial decision of the House of Lords in *St Marylebone Property Co Ltd v Fairweather* (1963)).

The inception of a new (and adverse) possession

6.9 The paper owner of land is generally under no obligation to make use of his land: mere neglect does not cause him to lose his title. The paper owner's rights are at risk only when the land is 'in the possession of some person in whose favour the period of limitation can run' (LA 1980, Sch 1, para 8(1)). Without this element of a *new* possession asserted by an intruder there would, of course, be no right of action in the paper owner to be statute-barred through the effluxion of time (see *Hughes v Cork* (1994) per Beldam LJ). This underlying premise applies equally (albeit somewhat circuitously) to registered land. Although the LRA 2002 prevents any limitation period from running against a registered proprietor (LRA 2002, s 96(1), **6.7**), squatters are treated as being in 'adverse possession' if, but for this statutory prohibition, time would have run in their favour under the Limitation Act (see LRA 2002, Sch 6, para 11(1)). It follows therefore that, in the case of both registered and unregistered land, a claimant of title by long possession must show *either* a 'dispossession' (or 'ouster') of the paper owner *or* a 'discontinuance by the paper owner followed by possession'. As Nourse LJ conceded in *Buckinghamshire CC v Moran* (1990), the distinction between these two kinds of event is 'a very fine one'.

— *Dispossession* occurs where a squatter 'comes in and drives out the true owner from possession' (*Buckinghamshire CC v Moran* (1990) per Nourse LJ). Indeed, in more recent times the notion of 'dispossession' has been applied to cases (other than of 'discontinuance') where a squatter simply 'assumes possession in the ordinary sense of the word', thus covering circumstances in which a squatter remains on land in the face of the clearest evidence that his permission to be present there has expired or been withdrawn (see *JA Pye (Oxford) Ltd v Graham* (2003) at [38] per Lord Browne-Wilkinson, **6.11**). At least in relation to large tracts of land, true cases of dispossession are nowadays somewhat rare. Dispossession typically arises on a smaller scale where, for instance, one neighbour, A, repositions a boundary fence so as to enclose part of the land belonging to his neighbour, B. Here the relevant period of 'adverse possession' runs from the date of B's dispossession (LA 1980, Sch 1, para 1).

— *Discontinuance of possession*   occurs where the true owner 'goes out of possession and is followed in by the squatter' (*Buckinghamshire CC v Moran* (1990) per Nourse LJ). Any claim based on discontinuance (or abandonment) of possession requires the rebuttal of a fairly heavy presumption that the paper owner *continues* in possession. But an example of discontinued possession is provided where B carelessly repositions a boundary fence so as to exclude part of his own land in favour of his neighbour, A, who then begins to use the land as his own (see e.g. *Hounslow LBC v Minchinton* (1997)). In cases of discontinued possession the relevant period of 'adverse possession' runs from the date of the inception of the new possession (LA 1980, Sch 1, para 8(1)).

— *Dormant possession*   It used to be thought that even extensive possessory acts by a squatter on land currently lying dormant could not destroy the continuing possession of the paper owner provided that such acts did not substantially interfere with the paper owner's plans for the future use of the land (the so-called rule in *Leigh v Jack* (1879)). This presumption against the disturbance of possession has now been 'exploded' (see *Hounslow LBC v Minchinton* (1997) per Millett LJ). The most that can now be said is that a squatter's awareness of a 'special purpose for which the paper owner uses or intends to use the land' may, in rare circumstances, provide some support for a finding that the squatter lacked any genuine intention to possess the land (*JA Pye (Oxford) Ltd v Graham* (2003) at [45] per Lord Browne-Wilkinson).

> *Buckinghamshire CC v Moran* (1990) A local authority acquired land for the purpose of a future highway improvement. Over the following 30 years a neighbouring landowner, N, enclosed the land as an annexe to his garden and his successor in title, M, installed a lock and chain which rendered the plot accessible only from his own land. Both N and M were well aware that the local authority had plans for the future use of the land. The Court of Appeal nevertheless upheld M's claim of adverse possession, Slade LJ rejecting the proposition that 'an owner who retains a piece of land with a view to its

utilisation for a specific purpose in the future can never be treated as dispossessed, however firm and obvious the intention to dispossess, and however drastic the acts of dispossession of the person seeking to dispossess him may be'.

The meaning of adverse possession

6.10 The constituent features of adverse possession were exposed to a comprehensive review by the House of Lords in *JA Pye (Oxford) Ltd v Graham* (2003), a decision which now colours much of the law in this area. In the case of both dispossession and discontinuance of possession, it is clear that the element of possessory control which connotes 'adverse possession' bears a heavily specialised meaning. The concept of 'possession' is an amalgam of physical and mental components. 'Possession' can be attributed to the squatter only if he has both factual possession (*factum possessionis*) and the requisite intention to possess (*animus possidendi*) (see *JA Pye (Oxford) Ltd v Graham* at [40] per Lord Browne-Wilkinson, [70] per Lord Hope of Craighead, [74] per Lord Hutton). The elements of *factum* and *animus* interact heavily: the squatter must have a 'subjective intention to possess the land but he must also show by his outward conduct that that was his intention' (*Prudential Assurance Co Ltd v Waterloo Real Estate Inc* (1999) per Peter Gibson LJ). In practice, 'the best evidence of intention is frequently found in the acts which have taken place' (*JA Pye (Oxford) Ltd v Graham* at [70] per Lord Hope).

Factual possession

6.11 Adverse possession 'must be peaceable and open' (*Browne v Perry* (1991) per Lord Templeman). The factual possession (or *factum possessionis*) which underlies the squatter's claim must exhibit certain characteristics which endure throughout the period of the alleged adverse possession.

— *Possession must be exclusive to the claimant* although it is possible that 'there can be a single possession exercised by or on behalf of several persons jointly' (*Powell v McFarlane* (1977) per Slade J).

— *Possession must be 'adverse' to the paper owner* No 'adverse' possession can be claimed where the occupation of land is shared with the paper owner or is enjoyed by virtue of some lease, licence or consent from the paper owner (see *JA Pye (Oxford) Ltd v Graham* (2003) at [37] per Lord Browne-Wilkinson). Any element of permission negates the otherwise adverse quality of the claimant's possession.

But it is no longer to be 'assumed by implication of law' that a squatter's occupation of vacant land is the consequence of some *implied* licence or permission of the paper owner merely because the squatter's occupation is not inconsistent with the paper owner's present or future enjoyment of the land (LA 1980, Sch 1, para 8(4)). Nor does a squatter's possession cease to be 'adverse' merely because it appears that he would, if challenged, have been willing to vacate the land or pay rent for his occupation (*JA Pye (Oxford) Ltd v Graham* (2003) at [46] per Lord Browne-Wilkinson, [78] per Lord Hutton). However, any *written and signed* acknowledgement of the paper owner's title within a period of otherwise 'adverse' possession is fatal to the squatter's claim (LA 1980, ss 29–30; and see *Lambeth LBC v Archangel* (2002)).

— *Adverse possession need not be hostile or confrontational* Adverse possession operates as an essentially objective process of law and may occur through ignorance or mistake, without any knowledge or awareness on the part of *either* the paper owner *or* the adverse possessor (see e.g. *Wilson v Martin's Executors* (1993)). The claimant of adverse possession must harbour an intention to possess (**6.12**), but not necessarily any intention to *dispossess* (*Hughes v Cork* (1994)).

— *Possession must be open* The requirement of open, notorious and unconcealed possession ensures that the paper owner is given every opportunity of challenging the possession before it can ripen into an unimpeachable title. Any element of *fraud* or *concealment* prevents the limitation period from running until the paper owner could with reasonable diligence have discovered the presence of either (LA 1980, s 32(1)).

— *The standard of physical possession required* The *factum* of possession depends ultimately on evidence that the claimant of adverse possession has asserted a 'complete and exclusive physical control' over the land (*Buckinghamshire CC v Moran* (1990) per Slade LJ). Although the intensity of this control will vary with different kinds of terrain, it must be shown that 'the alleged possessor has been dealing with the land in question as an occupying owner might have been expected to deal with it and that no-one else has done so' (*Powell v McFarlane* (1977) per Slade J). The required degree of 'physical custody and control' implies 'a "hands-on" user of the land' (*Brown v Faulkner* (2003) at [30] per Higgins J). The duration of the squatter's occupation, its exclusivity and the acts of user relied upon are usually verifiable by a physical survey of the land.

JA Pye (Oxford) Ltd v Graham (2003) Following the expiration of G's written grazing licence over P's potentially valuable development land, P repeatedly refused a request for renewal of the grazing agreement. G nevertheless continued, for over 12 years, to use the land for agricultural purposes in the self-confessed hope that a formal agreement authorising his use would be forthcoming. During this period the land was accessible only through a gate kept padlocked by G, who effectively farmed the disputed area as a unit with his own adjoining land. The House of Lords upheld G's claim to have taken title by adverse possession, not least because G and his family had 'used the land as their own and in a way normal for an owner to use it' and had acted 'in a way which, to their knowledge, was directly contrary to the wishes of the proprietors' ([59]–[61] per Lord Browne-Wilkinson). G and his family had, in short, done 'everything which an owner of the land would have done' ([75] per Lord Hutton). (P was later able to challenge the operation of the adverse possession principle before the European Court of Human Rights (**6.7**). In *Pye v United Kingdom* (2005) the Court, by a majority, indicated its willingness to order the United Kingdom—in other words the United Kingdom's taxpayers—to compensate P for the compulsory loss of his title under the then current LRA 1925. The Court's ruling is now the subject of a reference to the Grand Chamber.)

— *Relevance of enclosure*   Absolute physical control of open land is normally impracticable 'if only because it is generally impossible to secure every part of a boundary so as to prevent intrusion' (*Powell v McFarlane* (1977) per Slade J). Usually, however, enclosure is the 'strongest possible evidence of adverse possession' (*Seddon v Smith* (1877) per Cockburn CJ). Thus the erection of fencing will normally demonstrate adverse possession (*George Wimpey & Co Ltd v Sohn* (1967) per Russell LJ; but compare *Boosey v Davis* (1988) and *Marsden v Miller* (1992)). In *Buckinghamshire CC v Moran* (**6.9, 6.12**), for instance, it will be remembered that the successful squatter had placed a new lock and chain on the gate to the disputed area.

— *Other sufficient acts of user*   Possession may also be established by a wide variety of other acts of user. Claims of possession cannot be founded on trivial or equivocal conduct (see e.g. *Tennant v Adamczyk* (2005)), but what is trivial varies in accordance with the nature and location of the land being claimed. Acts which are insignificant in relation to large areas of open land may take on a quite different relevance in a suburban garden. In *Hounslow LBC v Minchinton* (1997), Millett LJ observed, with reference to hedge trimming, weeding and the creation of a compost heap, that the conduct relied upon was 'not substantial . . . [b]ut that was the only sensible use of the land. It was rough land at the end of a garden.' In different contexts, sufficient possessory conduct can include the parking of cars (*Burns v Anthony* (1997)); the grazing of animals (*JA Pye (Oxford) Ltd v Graham* (2003)); the erection of 'no trespassing' signs (*Powell v McFarlane* (1977)); the imposition of entry charges for strangers (*Carroll v Manek and Bank of India* (2000)); and the installation of a security camera, security lighting and an entryphone system (*Prudential Assurance Co Ltd v Waterloo Real Estate Inc* (1999)). However, acts of user wholly in accordance with the paper owner's intended purposes in respect of the land have been held to negative any claim of dispossession (see *Pulleyn v Hall Aggregates (Thames Valley) Ltd* (1993)). For adverse possession there must be conduct inconsistent with, and in denial of, the rights of the paper owner as the legal owner of the land concerned.

> *Pollard v Jackson* (1994) J was the tenant of the ground floor of a house whose registered title was owned by P's father. When the father died in 1971 leaving no will and no known relatives, J stopped paying rent, cleared out the upper floors of the house and took over occupation of the whole. In 1983 J claimed title by adverse possession and the Court of Appeal eventually upheld this claim as against P, who was finally traced to Canada, where she had emigrated 40 years earlier.

> *Tecbild Ltd v Chamberlain* (1969) The Court of Appeal disallowed, as involving mere 'trivial acts of trespass', a claim of adverse possession based on assertions that the claimant's children had been accustomed to play on the disputed plots of land as and when they wished and that the family ponies had been tethered and exercised there.

Intention to possess (*animus possidendi*)

6.12 The claimant by adverse possession must show not only factual possession throughout the limitation period, but also a continuing possessory intent (*Railtrack plc v Hutchinson* (1998)). This element—*animus possidendi*—comprises 'the intention, in one's own name and on one's own behalf, to exclude the world at large, including the owner with the paper title ... so far as is reasonably practicable and so far as the processes of the law will allow' (*Powell v McFarlane* (1977) per Slade J). The latter proviso is, of course, necessary in that 'a squatter will normally know that until the full time has run, the paper owner can recover the land from him' (*JA Pye (Oxford) Ltd v Graham* (2003) at [43] per Lord Browne-Wilkinson). During recent years the courts have engaged, somewhat unsatisfactorily, in a progressive curtailment of the content of the possessory intent required of the adverse possessor.

— *Intention to possess, not intention to own*   One matter is the subject of clear consensus: it is widely accepted in the modern law that the adverse possessor need not have entertained any intention to *own* the land or to exclude the owner of the paper title in *all* future circumstances. The required mental state relates to *possession* rather than *ownership* (see *JA Pye (Oxford) Ltd v Graham* at [42] per Lord Browne-Wilkinson), with the result that it is frequently said to be sufficient that the squatter should demonstrate merely 'an intention for the time being to possess the land to the exclusion of all other persons' (*Buckinghamshire CC v Moran* (1990) per Slade LJ). Thus in *Lambeth LBC v Blackburn* (2001), adverse possession of a council house was successfully claimed by a squatter whose modest intention had only been to remain until he was evicted—a fate which, as it happened, never befell him.

> *Buckinghamshire CC v Moran* (1990) M, the adverse occupier, had intended to continue in possession of the disputed plot of land only until such time as the paper owner activated its plans to build a proposed by-pass over it (**6.9**). Notwithstanding that the statutory 12-year period had run its course against the background of this consciously limited or tentative form of intention, the Court of Appeal upheld M's claim of adverse possession largely in view of the combined strength of the evidence of factual possession and *animus*.

— *General irrelevance of bad faith*   There is no requirement in English law that the claimant of adverse possession should believe that the land he occupies is his own. The doctrine of long possession operates even in favour of the opportunist or consciously wilful trespasser (*Prudential Assurance Co Ltd v Waterloo Real Estate Inc* (1999)). There is, however, some authority that the requisite *animus possidendi* is absent if the claimant squatter believes, whether mistakenly or not, that his occupation of the land is by permission of the true owner (*Clowes Developments (UK) Ltd v Walters* (2006)).

— *Shift of emphasis from exclusory intent to conscious furtherance of self-interest*   Contrary to the tenor of earlier case law, the House of Lords has indicated that there is no necessity to 'show that there was a deliberate intention to exclude the paper owner or the registered proprietor' (*JA Pye (Oxford) Ltd v Graham* (2003) at [71] per Lord Hope of Craighead). Instead, the former emphasis on exclusory intent has been commuted, in large degree, into a concern with whether the squatter engaged in a conscious furtherance of his own self-interest. 'The only intention which has to be demonstrated,' declared Lord Hope, is 'an intention to occupy and use the land as one's own.' The identifying characteristic of the successful squatter is the intention to 'stay as long as he can for his own benefit' (at [40] per Lord Browne-Wilkinson). Viewed in this way, *animus* becomes merely the 'intention to exercise . . . custody and control on one's own behalf and for one's own benefit.' Thus, for example, there is no inconsistency between a claim of *animus possidendi* and an evident historic preparedness on the part of an opportunistic squatter, if challenged, to pay a money rent or otherwise negotiate the terms of his occupancy ([46] per Lord Browne-Wilkinson, [78] per Lord Hutton). Mere recognition of someone else's temporarily superior entitlement does not, in itself, derogate from the fact that the squatter is currently in 'possession'.

— *Demonstrations of animus* It has always been said that the adverse claimant's intention must not only be genuine; it must also be made 'clear to the world' (*Powell v McFarlane* (1977) per Slade J). Although the requisite *animus* is not necessarily incompatible with mistake or ignorance as to the true ownership of the land in question, the claimant must consciously act in a manner which is objectively consistent with a claim to exclusive possession on his own behalf (see *Wilson v Martin's Executors* (1993)). His intention must be sufficiently plain that the paper owner, 'if present at the land, would clearly appreciate that the claimant is not merely a persistent trespasser, but is actually seeking to dispossess him' (*Powell v McFarlane*, as endorsed in *Lambeth LBC v Blackburn* (2001) at [18] per Clarke LJ). In some circumstances an even higher threshold of proof can come to govern possessory intention (see e.g. *Stacey v Gardner* (1995)). Where, for example, a squatter knows of some future use intended by the paper owner, this knowledge may 'affect the quality of his own intention, reducing it below that which is required to constitute adverse possession' (*Buckinghamshire CC v Moran* (1990) per Nourse LJ, **6.9**).

— *Intention as inferred from conduct* It has long been acknowledged that relevant evidence of intention must usually—if not always—be inferred from conduct (see *Lambeth LBC v Blackburn* (2001) at [46] per Clarke LJ). Courts attach 'very little evidential value' to retrospective assertions of *animus* because 'they are obviously easily capable of being merely self-serving, while at the same time they may be very difficult for the paper owner positively to refute' (*Powell v McFarlane* (1977) per Slade J). Moreover, where evidence of possessory conduct is equivocal, such evidence must be reinforced by particularly compelling evidence of intention (see *Prudential Assurance Co Ltd v Waterloo Real Estate Inc* (1999) per Peter Gibson LJ). Accordingly, if alleged possessory conduct is open to more than one interpretation and the claimant of adverse possession has not made his intention 'perfectly plain to the world at large', he will be treated as not having had the requisite *animus possidendi* (*Powell v McFarlane* (1977) per Slade J).

> *Powell v McFarlane* (1977) Slade J declined to find the necessary *animus* proved on behalf of a squatter who, at the age of 14, had begun to use land for the purpose of grazing his cow. The conduct of one so young was 'not necessarily referable' to any intention to dispossess the paper owner and to occupy the land 'wholly as his own property'.

— *Intention as implicit in 'possession'* Further evidence of the modern downgrading of the requisite *animus* is to be found in the decision of the House of Lords in *JA Pye (Oxford) Ltd v Graham* (2003). Here Lord Hutton seemed to suggest (at [76]) that a rebuttable presumption of *animus* arises where 'the actions of the occupier make it clear that he is using the land in the way in which a full owner would and in such a way that the owner is excluded'. In such circumstances the squatter 'in the normal case ... will not have to adduce additional evidence to establish that he had the intention to possess'. Instead, an evidential onus shifts to the paper owner to 'adduce other evidence which points to a contrary conclusion'. Ironically, this marked weakening of the requirements of adverse possession emerges at just the point in time when, by virtue of the changes effected by the LRA 2002 (**6.7**), the acquisition of title by long possession appears likely to become a relatively unusual occurrence in English law.

Recovery of possession

6.13 In the new order instituted by the LRA 2002, a dispossessed registered proprietor is generally entitled to bring proceedings for the recovery of his land at any time (irrespective of the duration of the relevant adverse possession). The mere effluxion of time now affords no defence to the squatter. (Under the Limitation Act any action for the recovery of unregistered land must be brought *before* the expiration of the limitation period.) In no circumstances, however, can the squatter plead any ground of necessity or social utility in support of his trespass. Neither homelessness nor destitution provides a defence against the recovery of possession (see *McPhail v Persons (Names Unknown)* (1973); *Southwark LBC v Williams* (1971)). The process of recovery of possession of land was described in Chapter 3 (**3.6**).

FURTHER READING

Gray and Gray, *Elements of Land Law* (4th edn, OUP, 2005), ch 6.

Relevant sections of this work and other land law textbooks may be supplemented with:

Clarke, Alison 'Use, Time, and Entitlement' (2004) 57 *CLP* 239.

Dixon, Martin 'Adverse possession in three jurisdictions' [2006] *Conv* 179.

Dockray, Martin 'Adverse Possession and Intention' [1982] *Conv* 256.

Dockray, Martin 'Why Do We Need Adverse Possession?' [1985] *Conv* 272.

Green, Kate 'Citizens and Squatters: Under the Surfaces of Land Law', in S. Bright and J.K. Dewar (eds), *Land Law: Themes and Perspectives* (OUP, 1998), p 229.

Pottage, Alain 'Evidencing Ownership', ibid, p 129.

Tee, Louise 'A Harsh Twilight' [2003] *CLJ* 36.

Thompson, Mark 'Adverse Possession: The Abolition of Heresies' [2002] *Conv* 480.

SELF-TEST QUESTIONS

1 How can acts which are initially tortious or even criminal give rise to a title to land by reason merely of the passage of time? Is it desirable that they should do so (**6.4–6.5**)?

2 What role remains for adverse possession under a system of registration of title (**6.7**)?

3 Are the component elements of adverse possession construed more sympathetically in relation to possessory claims made by the middle-class homeowner or those made by the homeless traveller or environmental protester (**6.9–6.12**)?

7

Freehold and leasehold estates in land

SUMMARY

The primary *legal estates* in modern land law are:

- the fee simple absolute in possession (the 'freehold' estate); and
- the term of years absolute (the 'leasehold' estate).

Under the scheme of the Land Registration Act 2002 the proprietorship of either of these estates is generally capable of 'substantive registration' in the Land Register under a unique title number. (Certain short leasehold terms, although not substantively registrable, provide an important basis for a range of residential and commercial occupancy.)

This chapter focuses on the *definitional* aspects of freehold and leasehold estates, outlining the way in which they may be created, transferred and terminated, and indicating the pivotal role which each plays in the organisation of proprietary interests in registered (and unregistered) land. The *operational* aspect of leaseholds—the content and enforcement of leasehold obligations—is the subject of more detailed examination in Chapter 14.

The present chapter also outlines the new form of estate ownership—freehold ownership of commonhold land—introduced by the Commonhold and Leasehold Reform Act 2002.

The statutory ground rules

7.1 Chapter 1 pointed to the way in which, in English law, proprietorship of an abstract 'estate' in land serves as our closest approximation to ownership of land itself (**1.16–1.21**). We must now examine estates in greater detail, for it is these estates which comprise the basis of the structural grammar of our land law. In its opening subsection the Law of Property Act 1925 marks out, with particular emphasis, two potential *legal estates* in land—the 'freehold' and 'leasehold' estates respectively (LPA 1925, s 1(1), **2.29**). Such is the significance of these estates that neither can be held *at law* by a minor (LPA 1925, s 1(6)), although a minor may validly hold the *equitable* version of one or other estate, necessarily behind some trust of land (**1.20, 9.34**).

The fee simple absolute in possession

7.2 At common law the primary estate in land is the *freehold*—or *fee simple absolute in possession*—an estate of intrinsically unlimited duration which connotes the virtual reality, if not the rigorous theory, of plenary entitlement to land in England and Wales (**1.18**). Indeed, some 70 per cent of the country's entire housing stock is now occupied by fee simple owners (*Social Trends 34* (2004 edn, London), p 153). The fee simple can assume several forms, but it is only the fee simple *absolute in possession* which is statutorily declared to be 'capable of subsisting or of being conveyed or created' as a legal estate in land (LPA 1925, s 1(1)(a)). Whether this fee simple estate *actually* attains legal status usually depends on compliance with various formalities of transfer or registration (**7.6–7.8**).

Definition of the fee simple 'absolute'

7.3 As a matter of strict definition, the fee simple *absolute* must be distinguished from certain forms of *modified* fee simple estate, all nowadays extremely uncommon.

— *The determinable fee simple* is an estate of potentially perpetual duration which is liable to be cut short automatically by some specified change of circumstance or by the occurrence of some named but unpredictable event (e.g. 'Greenacre to A in fee simple until she ceases to be qualified to practise as a solicitor'). Not being *absolute*, such a fee simple can never be created as a legal estate. As a mere equitable interest it must take effect under a pre-1997 strict settlement (SLA 1925, s 1(1)(ii)(c), **9.43**) or behind a new trust of land (**11.25**).

— *The conditional fee simple* is an estate of potentially perpetual duration which is defeasible on the satisfaction of a 'condition subsequent' (e.g. 'Greenacre to A on condition that she shall not cease to be qualified to practise as a barrister'). The grant of a conditional fee simple is almost invariably accompanied by an express *right of entry* (**8.35**), which entitles the grantor, should he so choose, to terminate the fee simple estate in the event of the fulfilment or breach of the specified condition. Such a fee simple, although not strictly 'absolute', is treated for statutory purposes as if it were a 'fee simple absolute' (see LPA 1925, s 7(1)), and is therefore, and somewhat confusingly, rendered capable of existing as a *legal* estate in land. Ironically, the conditional and determinable forms of fee simple estate often sound very similar and may differ only as a matter of technical wording.

Definition of the fee simple 'in possession'

7.4 The only form of fee simple absolute capable of existing as a legal estate is the fee simple absolute *in possession*. The qualifying phrase 'in possession' connotes that the grantee is immediately entitled to occupation and enjoyment of the land from the effective date of the grant; the grantee is not subject to any interest prior in time to his own. In this context 'possession' does not necessarily mean physical possession. 'Possession' is statutorily defined as including 'receipt of rents and profits or the right to receive the same' (LPA 1925, s 205(1)(xix)). Thus a fee simple absolute does not cease to be an estate *in possession* merely because the owner grants a lease to a tenant: both landlord and tenant have, in the currently relevant sense, estates *in possession*.

Estates 'in possession' differ sharply from estates 'in remainder' and estates 'in reversion', which, according to the inexorable logic of the Law of Property Act 1925 (see LPA 1925, s 1(3)), can take effect only *in equity* under a pre-1997 strict settlement (**9.43**) or behind a new trust of land (**11.25**).

— *Estates in remainder* An interest 'in remainder' confers a *present* right to *future* enjoyment, in the sense that the 'remainderman' is excluded from immediate enjoyment only by reason of the presence of a prior interest or prior interests vested in somebody else.

> **Example**: By his will H leaves the family home to W for life, with remainder to their children in fee simple. W is entitled to a life interest in possession as from the date of H's death; the children hold, at the date of H's death, a fee simple absolute *in remainder*. The children's interest will 'fall into possession' on the termination of W's prior interest (i.e. when W herself dies).

— *Estates in reversion* An estate 'in reversion' is the sum total of the rights retained by a grantor who fails to exhaust the entire interest in the land in the terms of his grant or conveyance to another. A grantor who fails to dispose of the fee simple absolute inevitably retains a fee simple 'in reversion' from the moment of his non-exhaustive grant. This fee simple estate will fall into possession on the expiration of the limited interest or interests which he has granted away.

Example: S, having purchased the fee simple estate in a house, grants his elderly mother, M, a life interest (but makes no other disposition). M clearly takes a life interest *in possession*, but S, since he has not granted away the entire interest in the land, retains the fee simple absolute in reversion.

Creation of the fee simple estate

7.5 The *creation* of a fee simple absolute in possession (as distinct from the *subsequent transfer* of such an estate) is today relatively rare since it involves the formation of a new estate in land out of the allodial 'demesne' comprising the unalienated lands of the crown (**1.16, 1.22**). When, however, the crown does grant an estate in fee simple out of the allodium and the grantee applies for first registration with an absolute title, the Chief Land Registrar does not normally investigate any title prior to that grant. The grantee holds, as indeed all owners of a fee simple today hold, by *socage tenure* from the crown (**1.22**). It used to be that the crown could not hold land of itself—an inevitable implication of the doctrine of tenures—but the LRA 2002 now enables the crown to grant itself a freehold estate in 'demesne land' which is both registrable and disposable (LRA 2002, ss 79(1), 132(1)).

Dealings with the fee simple estate

7.6 While a fee simple estate is in existence, the estate owner enjoys virtually plenary powers of disposition, e.g. by way of gift, sale, lease or mortgage charge (see also LRA 2002, ss 23–4). This policy in favour of marketability reflects the common law's longstanding concern with freedom of alienation as an intrinsic incident of property (see *National Provincial Bank Ltd v Ainsworth* (1965) per Lord Upjohn, **2.10**). The LRA 2002 now reinforces this strong public policy by ensuring that the title taken by the disponee of registered land is unaffected by any non-statutory limitation on the disponor's powers which is not itself reflected on the face of the latter's register of title (LRA 2002, s 26(1)–(2)).

— *General requirement of deed* A valid conveyance of a legal fee simple estate must generally be contained in a *deed*:

All conveyances of land or of any interest therein are void for the purpose of conveying or creating a legal estate unless made by deed (LPA 1925, s 52(1)).

— *Exceptions* To the requirement of freehold conveyance by deed there are a number of exceptions, the most important relating to assents by personal representatives (LPA 1925, s 52(2)(a)) and conveyances which take effect by operation of law (LPA 1925, s 52(2)(g)). Clearly no *oral* conveyance can operate to transfer a legal estate. A parol grant has merely the fragile effect of creating an *interest at will* (LPA 1925, s 54(1), **7.27**), although in rare circumstances an attempted verbal conferment of a fee simple estate may give rise to a *constructive trust* of the legal title for the promisee (**10.7**) or to a court-ordered transfer of the fee simple following proof of a *proprietary estoppel* (see e.g. *Pascoe v Turner* (1979), **10.24**).

> *Pascoe v Turner* (1979) P and T had lived in a de facto relationship in a house owned by P. On the breakdown of the relationship, P moved out, but told T orally that 'the house is yours and everything in it'. Although this formula was clearly ineffective as a conveyance of P's legal estate, the Court of Appeal later ordered P to transfer his fee simple to T on the ground that T's subsequent expenditure on the property had generated in her favour an 'equity' founded on proprietary estoppel.

— *Constituent elements of a deed* The historic purpose of a deed has been to indicate the highest level of formality attendant upon a solemn transaction in the law. For centuries the validity of a deed in English law rested on compliance with the requirements that the deed be *signed, sealed, and delivered*. These requirements have been modified in respect of all deeds executed on or after 31 July 1990, the validity of a deed now depending on its being *signed, attested, and delivered* (Law of Property (Miscellaneous Provisions) Act 1989, s 1). The requirement of sealing—long criticised as 'mumbo-jumbo'—has been abandoned in all cases other than deeds executed by a corporation (see LPA 1925, s 74(1)). Due execution of a deed now requires:

- *Signature* A deed must be contained in some durable form of writing signed by the individual making the deed and must make it clear on its face that it is intended to be a deed (LP(MP)A 1989, s 1(1)–(3)). For this purpose the standard forms of transfer and charge of a registered estate introduced by the LRA 2002 are all expressly drawn as deeds (see LRR 2003, rr 58–9, 103, Sch 1, **7.8**). The mere fact that an instrument is executed under seal is no longer sufficient to indicate its status as a deed (LP(MP)A 1989, s 1(2A), inserted by Regulatory Reform (Execution of Deeds and Documents) Order 2005 (SI 2005/1906)). Signature is, of course, the single fundamental and irreducible feature of a deed (see *Shah v Shah* (2002) at [30] per Pill LJ).

- *Attestation* An instrument is validly executed as a deed only if a witness also signs to attest that the signature of the author of the deed was effected in the witness's presence (LP(MP)A 1989, s 1(3)(a)(i)).

- *Delivery* Delivery of a deed does not necessarily connote any physical transfer of the instrument, but merely that the transaction contained in the deed is *irreversible* by the person making the deed. Delivery comprises any unilateral act or statement by the author which signifies that he adopts the deed irrevocably as his own and operates as a representation that the deed has been duly signed and attested (*Shah v Shah* (2002) at [33] per Pill LJ).

— *Deed becomes a statutory fiction* The regime of electronic conveyancing soon to be instituted under the LRA 2002 (**2.23, 12.3–12.5**) will necessitate profound changes in the modalities of dealings with estates in land. In an age of paperless transactions the deed will become a mere fiction of statute. Although paper-based and electronic systems of transacting will coexist during a transitional period (see Law Com No 271 (2001), paras 1.12, 2.61), the LRA 2002 provides that, on compliance with certain conditions, the electronic disposition of estates and interests in registered land will be deemed to satisfy the existing formality requirements for a written document or deed (see Law Com No 271 (2001), paras 13.11, 13.18). The same facility of electronic disposition will apply to any conveyance of unregistered land which triggers (**7.7**) a requirement of first registration at Land Registry (see LRA 2002, s 91(2)(c)).

• *Electronic signature* In order to be effective, an electronic disposition will have to specify the time and date at which it is to take effect and must contain the *electronic signature* of each person by whom the disposition purports to be authenticated (i.e. the disponor and often, also, the disponee) (see LRA 2002, s 91(1)–(4)). Electronic signatures will probably be effected with the aid of some form of dual key cryptography and must be certified by some certifying authority.

• *Impact on traditional requirements of a deed* Subject to the conditions outlined above, an electronic disposition will be deemed to be a 'deed' (LRA 2002, s 91(5)); the concept of delivery becomes irrelevant (see Law Com No 271, para 13.13); and the process of attestation unnecessary (LRA 2002, s 91(8)).

— *Completion by registration* Nowadays almost all forms of dealing with a fee simple estate require to be completed by registration at Land Registry. A distinction must be drawn between the registration provisions which relate to *first registration* (**7.7**) and those provisions which govern *subsequent transfers* (**7.8**) of an already registered estate.

First registration of an unregistered legal freehold estate

7.7 Substantive registration of title to a previously *unregistered* legal freehold estate is always available under the LRA 2002 as a matter of *voluntary election* on the part of the owner of that estate (LRA 2002, s 3(1)–(2)). In some circumstances, however, first registration of an unregistered legal freehold estate becomes *mandatory*. The LRA 2002 provides that first registration at Land Registry is made compulsory by the occurrence of any of several kinds of statutorily specified 'event' (**2.25**). The principal triggers for obligatory registration of title to a freehold estate (LRA 2002, s 4(1)–(2)) comprise:

• Any *transfer* of an unregistered legal freehold whether by way of sale, gift, assent (i.e. perfection of a gift of land by will or on intestacy) or court order (LRA 2002, s 4(1)(a)). The duty to apply for registration of the estate transferred rests on the transferee (LRA 2002, s 6(1), (3)(b)).

• Any *protected first legal mortgage* of an unregistered legal freehold (LRA 2002, ss 4(1)(g), 6(2)(a)). For this purpose a 'protected' mortgage is, in effect, a first mortgage charge protected by deposit of documents relating to the mortgaged estate (LRA 2002, s 4(8), **8.31**). The duty to apply for registration of the freehold estate charged by mortgage rests on the *mortgagor* (i.e. the owner of the mortgaged estate) (LRA 2002, s 6(1)–(2)(b)), although the mortgagee may also, in the mortgagor's name and irrespective of the mortgagor's consent, apply for such registration (LRA 2002, s 6(6); LRR 2003, r 21). It is, of course, open to the parties to agree that the mortgagee should, as a matter of convenience, apply for registration of the freehold simultaneously with its own application to be registered as legal chargee.

— *Consequence of failure to apply for first registration* Failure to apply for first registration of title to the freehold estate within *two months* of the date of any 'relevant event' renders the triggering disposition 'void' for the purpose of transferring, granting or creating a *legal* estate (LRA 2002, ss 6(4), 7(1), **2.30**). At this point, title to the legal estate reverts to the transferor, who now holds it on a bare trust for the transferee; and the transferee's title, having been a *legal* title during the first two months, is meanwhile relegated to *equitable* status only (LRA 2002, s 7(2)(a)). The two-month period may be extended by order of the registrar (LRA 2002, s 6(5)). Alternatively, the transferee may be forced to arrange (at his own cost) for a retransfer of the intended legal estate, followed this time by somewhat swifter registration (LRA 2002, s 8).

> **Example 1**: V by deed transfers an unregistered freehold estate to P. P immediately acquires the legal fee simple, but if P fails within two months to apply to Land Registry for first registration of the title to this estate, the bare legal estate reverts to V. P is left with the equitable fee simple absolute in possession.
>
> **Example 2**: M borrows £50,000 from the Bank. To secure the loan M executes a deed of legal charge over his unregistered freehold land and deposits his documents of title with the Bank (**8.31**). The Bank immediately acquires a legal charge. If within the next

two months no application is lodged at Land Registry for first registration of M's freehold
title (and of the Bank's charge over the land), M will nevertheless continue to hold a legal
fee simple in what is still unregistered land. The Bank, however, will no longer hold a
legal charge. Instead its deed of charge will take effect only as a contract for value to
create a legal charge (i.e. as a mere equitable charge) (LRA 2002, s 7(2)(b)).

— *Classes of freehold title on first registration* On an application for first registration of title, the applicant's title deeds and other relevant claims are examined by
the registrar, who determines which quality of title to award (LRA 2002, s 9(1),
7.7, 7.20, 12.33). The class of title accorded to the first registered proprietor is then
indicated in the proprietorship register of the newly opened register of title (**6.2**).
In relation to freehold land there are three possible classes of title, each reflecting
a different perception of the strength and reliability of the title offered for
registration:

• *Absolute title*, the most frequently awarded class, is the most reliable and
extensively guaranteed form of title. Absolute title is awarded if the registrar is of
opinion that the applicant's title is 'such as a willing buyer could properly be advised
by a competent professional adviser to accept' (LRA 2002, s 9(2)). Absolute title
connotes a holding which is unlikely to be disturbed (see LRA 2002, s 9(3)).

• *Qualified title* is awarded in rare cases to an applicant who can establish title
only in respect of a limited period or only subject to certain reservations which
cannot be disregarded by the registrar (LRA 2002, s 9(4)).

• *Possessory title* is awarded to an applicant who is in actual possession (or in
receipt of rents and profits) but who cannot produce sufficient documentary
evidence of title (LRA 2002, s 9(5)). The applicant's title deeds may have been lost
or destroyed or he may be relying on a period of adverse possession of the land
concerned (**6.4**).

The registrar has power subsequently to upgrade title 'if satisfied' as to its quality
(LRA 2002, ss 62–3, LRR 2003, r 124), e.g. if convinced that a suspected flaw in
title is no longer material. In particular, a possessory title may be upgraded to an
absolute title after 12 years if the registrar is satisfied that the proprietor is 'in
possession of the land' (LRA 2002, s 62(4)).

— *First registration with absolute freehold title* confers the most ample form of
ownership known in English law, but cannot *enhance* the applicant's existing rights
in relation to the land. Such registration has the effect (see LRA 2002, s 11(2)–(5))
of vesting in the registered proprietor the legal fee simple absolute

• *together with* all interests subsisting for the benefit of the estate (e.g. the
benefit of appurtenant easements)

- *subject* only to
  - — interests entered in the register (by the registrar) in order to reflect pre-existing rights which burden the land (**12.33**);
  - — certain unregistered interests which are statutorily declared to 'override first registration', e.g. legal leases for a term of seven years or less and any proprietary interest belonging to a 'person in actual occupation' (LRA 2002, Sch 1, **12.33**);
  - — interests acquired by squatters under the Limitation Act 1980 of which the proprietor has notice (actual or constructive) (**6.1**); and
  - — (where the proprietor takes land as a trustee) such beneficial interests of which he has notice. (The new proprietor's title is subject, in effect, to any beneficial interest under a trust of land which was not disclosed in his application for registration and of which he is deemed to have notice.)

— *First registration with qualified freehold title* produces a result similar to registration with absolute title, but subject also to any estate, right or interest which was specifically excepted from the effect of the qualified registration (LRA 2002, s 11(6)).

— *First registration with possessory freehold title* invests the applicant with a legal freehold estate (with the same benefits and burdens as in the case of an absolute title), but subject also to any adverse estates, rights and interests which existed at the date of first registration and were not revealed in the application (LRA 2002, s 11(7)).

— *A new statutory estate* Irrespective of the precise class of title awarded, the registered proprietor's title to land is so heavily regulated by statute that it is probably best to say that common law estates, when registered at Land Registry, are replaced by some new and artificial kind of *statutory* estate. Entry of a person in the register as the proprietor of a legal estate has been said to operate a certain 'statutory magic' (*Argyle Building Society v Hammond* (1985) per Slade LJ), in that even if 'the legal estate would not otherwise be vested in him, it shall be deemed to be vested in him as a result of the registration' (LRA 2002, s 58(1)). In the absence of any 'alteration' of the register (**12.27**), registered proprietorship is *pro tempore* definitive and conclusive. In effect, the title afforded by registration is not ultimately historical or derivative, but 'is the title which registration itself has vested in the proprietor' (*Breskvar v Wall* (1971) per Barwick CJ); and the registered proprietor can indeed be regarded as 'a statutory person having a statutory title to a statutory "thing" with a statutory power to dispose of it' (H Potter, (1942) 58 LQR 356 at 367). This perspective helps to make sense of much of the law of land registration and richly confirms that the principles of registered title have evolved into a law of land which is significantly different from the unregistered or 'old system' regime which preceded it (**2.27**).

Subsequent dispositions of a registered freehold estate

7.8 Once title to a fee simple estate has been registered, almost all subsequent dealings with this estate require to be registered at Land Registry as a precondition of their effectiveness at law (LRA 2002, s 27(1)–(2), Sch 2, paras 1–8, **2.30**). There is thus no provision, as with dispositions which necessitate *first* registration (**7.7**), for a reversible vesting of the legal estate during the two months immediately following the disposition.

— *Range of 'registrable dispositions'* The 'registration requirements' of the LRA 2002 are activated by certain specified kinds of 'disposition of a registered estate', a phrase which is broad enough to embrace a number of dealings under which lesser entitlements are *carved out of* the registered estate (see LRA 2002, s 27(2)).

• The range of 'disposition' which must be completed by registration therefore includes not only transfers of the registered freehold estate itself, but also the creation of various kinds of lease (**7.20**), mortgage charge (**8.29**), easement (**8.16**), profit *à prendre* (**8.16**), rentcharge (**8.27**), and right of entry affecting the freehold estate (**8.35**).

• All registrable transfers of the freehold estate normally require to be made using one of the forms prescribed by the LRR 2003 (see LRA 2002, s 25(1); LRR 2003, rr 58–9, 206, 209, Sch 1, **7.6**). A standard form of legal charge of the registered estate is now offered by the LRR 2003 (see LRR 2003, r 103, Sch 1, **8.29**); and, with effect from 19 June 2006, most registrable leases granted out of a registered estate must be prefaced by certain prescribed clauses (see LRR 2003, r 58A, as introduced by SI 2005/1982, **7.20**).

— *Application for registration* All 'registrable dispositions' must be completed by the entry of the disponee in the Land Register as the proprietor of the relevant interest under the disposition (LRA 2002, Sch 2, paras 2–8). Thus, in the case of a freehold transfer, the transferee must apply to be registered as proprietor of the fee simple estate in place of the transferor. The transfer is made final and effective at law only by this act of registration (**12.5**) although, for reasons of administrative convenience, the date of registration of the new proprietorship is deemed retrospectively to be the date on which the application was actually lodged at Land Registry (LRA 2002, s 74). But while an application for registration is the act of the *transferee*, it is clear that the transfer of the legal title is ultimately an act of the *state* (or, more accurately, of the civil servant responsible for updating Land Registry's computer record). In this way the scheme of land registration can be said to provide 'not a system of registration of title but a system of title by registration' (*Breskvar v Wall* (1971) per Barwick CJ).

— *'Restrictions' upon disposition* Although the proprietor of a registered estate enjoys, in principle, plenary powers of disposition over his estate (see LRA 2002, ss 23–4, **7.6**), it is possible that these powers may be limited by the entry of certain kinds of 'restriction' in the proprietorship register pertaining to his title. Such 'restrictions' comprise entries in the register which regulate the circumstances in which a subsequent disposition of the registered estate (whether freehold or, for that matter, leasehold) may be recorded in the Land Register (LRA 2002, s 40(1)). In cases governed by some 'restriction' entered in the register, Land Registry is disabled from processing any application for registration by a disponee of the registered estate *unless and until* there has been compliance with the terms of the relevant 'restriction' (LRA 2002, s 41(1)).

• The proprietor of any registered estate (and, in certain cases, other persons (**11.29**)) may apply for the entry of a 'restriction' in the relevant proprietorship register (LRA 2002, s 43(1); LRR 2003, rr 92–3).

• The most common form of 'restriction' arises in the case of a trust of land (**11.29**) and effectively prohibits the registration of any future dealing with the land by a *sole trustee* which would fail to attract the advantageous effects of statutory overreaching (LRA 2002, s 42(1)(b), **2.34, 11.30**).

• A 'restriction' may also be entered in order to reflect the limited dispositionary powers of an incorporated body (see LRA 2002, s 26(1)–(2), **7.6**) or to ensure that no registered disposition of land can occur without the consent of some named person or persons whose consent has been made requisite (usually by the terms of some trust or settlement (**11.28**)).

• A 'restriction' may be entered on the application of a person who claims some beneficial entitlement to the registered estate by way of resulting or constructive trust (**10.3–10.8**) or who is currently entitled to the benefit of a charging order in respect of an equitable interest under a trust of registered land (**9.21**).

• The court has power, in certain instances, to order the entry of a 'restriction' in the register (LRA 2002, s 46(1)), but no restriction may ever be entered for the purpose of protecting the priority of an interest which is, or could be, the subject of a 'notice' in the register (LRA 2002, s 42(2), **12.11**).

• The LRA 2002 imposes a duty not to apply for the entry of a restriction 'without reasonable cause' (LRA 2002, s 77(1)). In appropriate cases, a restriction, once it has exhausted its protective function, may be cancelled or withdrawn from the register of title (LRA 2002, s 47; LRR 2003, rr 97–9).

— *Effect of completion of disposition by registration* When a disposition of the freehold estate is duly completed by registration, entry of the disponee in the Land Register as proprietor has definitive effect. The legal estate in question is statutorily 'deemed to be vested in him as a result of the registration' (LRA 2002, s 58(1), **7.7**) so that, in the absence of any subsequent 'alteration' of his title (**12.27**), he remains registered proprietor even though the disposition may have been voidable for forgery or other irregularity (see e.g. *Argyle Building Society v Hammond* (1985)). Moreover, the disponee of a registered estate for valuable consideration generally takes that estate free of all pre-existing interests other than registered charges, other interests already noted in the relevant register of title, and those unregistered interests which are statutorily declared to 'override' registered dispositions (LRA 2002, s 29(1)–(2), Sch 3, **2.32–2.33, 12.9, 12.11, 12.15**).

— *Consequence of failure to apply for registration of a 'registrable disposition'* Until the disponee under a 'registrable disposition' is registered as the new proprietor of the estate in question, the disposition does not 'operate at law' (LRA 2002, s 27(1)) and takes effect, at best, merely in equity. In other words the disponee, for want of completion by registration, acquires only an equitable version of the estate which was intended to pass at law (see *ES Schwab & Co Ltd v McCarthy* (1976) per Oliver J).

• *Unregistered transfers of a freehold estate* In the case of an unregistered transfer of a registered freehold, the transferor necessarily remains proprietor of the legal fee simple, holding as a bare trustee for the intended transferee (**2.30, 11.26**). The latter receives only an *equitable* fee simple and any future dealings by him (e.g. by way of transfer, lease or mortgage) inevitably take effect merely in equity (see e.g. *First National Bank plc v Thompson* (1996)).

• *Risk for intended transferee* Statute imposes no time limit on the registration of a transfer of registered land, but for so long as he remains unregistered as proprietor, the transferee is exposed to the risk of adverse dealings by his transferor. In some circumstances, however, as for example where the transferee goes into 'actual occupation' of the land, his unregistered estate (i.e. his equitable interest) may 'override' dispositions made by the transferor in favour of strangers (LRA 2002, s 29(2)(a)(ii), Sch 3, para 2, **2.33, 12.18**).

• *Exempt dispositions* The requirement of completion by registration does not apply to certain dispositions by operation of law, e.g. a transfer on the death or bankruptcy of an individual proprietor (LRA 2002, s 27(5)).

— *Electronic dispositions of registered land* The 'single most important function' of the LRA 2002 is to institute the necessary legal framework for a system of electronic conveyancing which will come into operation in some years' time and which will make land dealings quicker, safer and more efficient (see Law Com No 271 (2001), paras 2.41, 13.1, **12.3–12.5**).

• *The register as a 'real time' mirror image of interests in land* Under a regime of e-conveyancing, most land interests will be incapable of creation or transfer without a simultaneous electronic manipulation of the register record; disposition and registration will coincide exactly in point of time (**2.26**); and the register of title will accurately and definitively record the priority of such rights.

• *Dispositions wholly ineffective unless registered* The system of electronic transfer will simplify matters to the extent that, in accordance with the new principle of synchronous registration of dealings, dispositions of a registered estate will have *no* effect at all—*either* at law *or* in equity—until communicated electronically to the registrar and simultaneously recorded in the Land Register (LRA 2002, s 93(1)–(4), Sch 2).

Termination of the fee simple estate

7.9 All estate owners in fee simple hold directly of the crown as 'tenants in chief'—the last relic of the medieval doctrine of tenures (**1.22**). But if the tenurial relationship, even in its modern vestigial form, comes to an end, the freehold title 'goes back to the Crown on the principle that all freehold estate originally came from the Crown, and that where there is no one entitled to the freehold estate by law it reverts to the Crown' (*Re Mercer and Moore* (1880) per Jessel MR). 'Escheat' describes the process by which a fee simple estate falls in to the crown, the crown's seignory or radical title being thereafter 'no longer encumbered by the freehold interest' (*Scmlla Properties Ltd v Gesso Properties (BVI) Ltd* (1995)).

— *Escheat following disclaimer* The incidence of escheat is nowadays rare, arising in some 500 cases each year and tending to cluster around instances of corporate and personal insolvency. It is open to company liquidators and trustees in bankruptcy to disclaim 'onerous property' held by an insolvent entity or person, usually, in the case of land, where the asset is subject to substantial financial burdens arising by covenant or mortgage (see e.g. Insolvency Act 1986, ss 178(2), 315(1)–(2), **7.34**). The effect of such disclaimer is the termination of the freehold and the automatic escheat of the relevant land to the crown.

— *Preservation of registered titles to escheated estates* The LRA 2002 contains provisions which, despite the destruction of the tenurial relationship (**7.5**), prevent—at least temporarily—the closure of any registered title to escheated freehold land, thereby allowing register entries to remain on the Land Register until the land is disposed of by the crown or by order of the court (see LRA 2002, s 82; LRR 2003, rr 79(3), 173).

The term of years absolute

7.10 The other major 'estate' in land demarcated by the Law of Property Act 1925 is the 'term of years absolute' (LPA 1925, s 1(1)(b), **2.29–2.31**). Here the qualifier 'absolute' has no special significance, and a term of years is commonly known as a 'leasehold estate' and its owner as a *leaseholder* as distinct from a *freeholder*. A term of years is also often called, somewhat loosely or inaccurately, a lease or tenancy, its distinguishing characteristic being the conferment by the *lessor* (or *landlord*) on the *lessee* (or *tenant*) of a right of exclusive possession of land for a period of pre-arranged maximum duration. It matters not whether this period is *fixed* and therefore self-determining (**7.29**) or *periodic* and therefore capable of extension or termination at the will of the parties (**7.31**). The period may be one week or thousands of years: a term of years can exist in either case (LPA 1925, s 205(1)(xxvii)). (The longest term of years on record is a perfectly valid leasehold grant for 10 million years!) Whether it comprises a vast tract of land or a single room, any area can constitute the locus of a tenancy if granted for a determinate period as the 'exclusive domain of a particular individual' (see *AG Securities v Vaughan* (1990) per Lord Oliver of Aylmerton).

— *The political future of the leasehold estate*   In modern Britain the term of years accounts for a large proportion of occupancy in the commercial or business sector and also for some 30 per cent of all household tenure (*Social Trends 34* (2004 edn London), p 153). It is fair to say, however, that there is an increasing level of disenchantment with the fixed-term leasehold estate as a medium of residential ownership. The present Labour Government views the existing residential lease-hold system as 'fundamentally flawed.' The law of leasehold has, accordingly, been condemned as having 'its roots in the feudal system', as being 'heavily weighted in favour of one party (i.e. the landlord)', and as conferring on the tenant, in many cases, an asset of a wasting nature for which he has paid a full market price (see *Commonhold and Leasehold Reform: Draft Bill and Consultation Paper* (Lord Chancellor's Department, Cm 4843, August 2000), Part I, para 2.3.1 (p 85), Part II, para 1.1 (p 107), Annex A, para 7 (p 101)).

— *The hybrid character of the leasehold*   The leasehold is a chameleonic creature and many of its difficulties and uncertainties arise because essentially the same legal concept does service for widely differing sorts of arrangement. Being an estate in land, the term of years provides, of course, a flexible base for other transactions with the land. The term may itself become the subject matter of either an *assignment* (i.e. transfer) or a *subletting* or *underlease* (**7.17**). The term of years is therefore clearly a *proprietary* estate in land, but this should not obscure the fact that at its root lies the *contractual* relationship of landlord and tenant. Indeed the modern law of leases is pervaded by the ambivalence of the leasehold device as both a *proprietary* and a *contractual* phenomenon, these two perspectives being apt to point towards 'diametrically opposite conclusions' in relation to some of the large questions raging in contemporary law (see *Hammersmith and Fulham LBC v Monk* (1992) per Lord Browne-Wilkinson).

— *The 'contractualisation' of the term of years* The tension between the proprietary and the contractual in the leasehold context is rendered all the more palpable by the emergence of the residential lease as a specialised form of consumer contract, under which the tenant bargains for a range of utilities and services to be provided by his landlord. Under the influence of the steady 'contractualisation' of the lease, courts have begun to expose tenancies to a much more comprehensive application of ordinary contract principles. Such principles may have seemed largely irrelevant where the dominant analysis of the lease was that of an *executed demise* under which a proprietary estate in land passed to the tenant. Nowadays, however, leases no longer lie beyond the reach of general contractual doctrines such as those of frustration, repudiatory breach and mitigation of loss (see e.g. *Hussein v Mehlman* (1992), **7.35, 14.6**). Yet the underlying tension remains: the leasehold is no less a form of proprietary control than the freehold. Indeed, the tenant is fully entitled 'to exercise the rights of an owner of land, which is in the real sense his land albeit temporarily and subject to certain restrictions' (*Street v Mountford* (1985) per Lord Templeman). And the role of the leasehold as a medium of proprietary ownership has been accentuated by recent reforms, such as the statutory extension of leasehold enfranchisement and the council tenant's 'right to buy', which underscore the fact that leasehold status frequently provides a gateway to enlarged rights of fee simple ownership (**7.40**).

— *The contractual or non-proprietary lease* A new complexity in the nomenclature surrounding the leasehold estate has been generated by the ruling in *Bruton v London & Quadrant Housing Trust* (2000) (**7.25**). Here the House of Lords drew an important distinction between the 'lease' (or 'tenancy') and the 'term of years' and indirectly confirmed the modern drift towards a contractual characterisation of the landlord-tenant nexus.

• In *Bruton v London & Quadrant Housing Trust* Lord Hoffmann indicated that the creation of a 'lease' (or 'tenancy') in itself implies no necessary conferment of a proprietary estate in the form of a term of years. A 'lease' (or 'tenancy') is, in this most basic sense, a mere agreement for exclusive possession for a term at a rent—a device of intrinsically *contractual* rather than *proprietary* significance. As Lord Hoffmann went on to say, a lease 'may, and usually does, create a proprietary interest called a leasehold estate or, technically, a "term of years absolute" ', but whether in fact it does so 'will depend upon whether the landlord had an interest out of which he could grant it. Nemo dat quod non habet'. The decision in *Bruton* thus controversially confirms the existence in English law of the phenomenon of the contractual or non-proprietary lease, with the result that it is possible (as in *Bruton*'s case itself) for someone to create a 'lease' over land (e.g. a 'tenancy by estoppel') even though he has no proprietary estate out of which he can grant a 'term of years'. Although the possibility of a '*Bruton* tenancy' is, for some, a modern heresy (see e.g. Martin Dixon, 'The Non-Proprietary Lease: The Rise of the Feudal Phoenix' [2000] *CLJ* 25), the House of Lords has reiterated its belief in the existence of 'non-estate' tenancies, whilst insisting that such tenancies have no binding impact on third parties (*Kay v Lambeth LBC* (2006) at [143]–[148] per Lord Scott of Foscote).

• There is an overwhelming suspicion that the new terminological exactitude insisted upon by the House of Lords in *Bruton*'s case was driven by the social need to ensure, by means of a less restrictive identification of landlord–tenant relationships, that a wider range of residential occupiers qualifies for the benefit of the repairing obligations fastened upon 'landlords' by the Landlord and Tenant Act 1985 (**14.5**). It is also likely, in the longer-term perspective, that *Bruton* evidences the slow eclipse of the leasehold relationship as involving the conferment of a proprietary estate, thus foreshadowing the gradual decline of this (nowadays) politically incorrect device into something much more closely resembling the civilian concept of a contract of hire of land.

Essential elements of a lease or tenancy

7.11   In the absence of any particularly helpful statutory definition of the 'term of years' (see LPA 1925, s 205(1)(xxvii)), it has been left to the courts to fashion the parameters of the leasehold device. In *Street v Mountford* (1985) the House of Lords identified three large structural components as inherent in any lease or tenancy. According to Lord Templeman the lessee or tenant must be granted:

   • exclusive possession (**7.13**);

   • for a fixed or periodic term certain (**7.12**);

   • in consideration of a premium (i.e. lump sum) or periodical payments (**7.11**).

The strict necessity for rent or other consideration has since been doubted (see *Ashburn Anstalt v Arnold* (1989)), but probably remains a sine qua non of at least the *periodic* tenancy (**7.24**) (see *Prudential Assurance Co Ltd v London Residuary Body* (1992) per Scott LJ). The other two elements lie, indubitably, at the core of the lease or tenancy of land (as was heavily reinforced by the House of Lords in *Bruton v London & Quadrant Housing Trust* (2000) (**7.10, 7.25**)), and their presence, in conjunction with a proprietary estate vested in the grantor, will ensure the creation of a 'term of years'.

A lease or tenancy must have a fixed maximum duration

7.12 Whereas a leasehold term may relate to any defined period of time long or short, the common law has imposed a centuries-old rule that the *maximum* duration of the term must be ascertainable from the very outset. This concern with discrete temporal definition highlights once again the tension between *proprietary* and *contractual* perspectives on the law of leases. The 'certainty of term' rule embodies a property-oriented perspective which insists that it is simply not competent for landlord and tenant, as a sheer act of contractual volition, to bargain for open-ended or indefinite terms of years. The essence of proprietary entitlement lies in the certain demarcation of borderlines (**2.18**), since otherwise neither the immediate parties nor strangers nor even the court itself can know the extent of the maximum enforceable commitment or identify true cases of breach. Thus, for instance, the courts have classically struck down 'leases' purportedly created for such uncertain periods as 'the duration of the war' (*Lace v Chantler* (1944)), and would have been equally prepared to deny leasehold status to a term supposedly continuing 'until Britain wins the Davis Cup' (see *Prudential Assurance Co Ltd v London Residuary Body* (1992) per Scott LJ). The 'certainty of term' rule does not, however, prevent the use of a 'break clause' which allows for determination of the lease by either party *before* the expiry of the full term granted (**7.30**).

— *Disenchantment with the 'certainty of term' rule* The downside of the 'certainty of term' rule is that it denies efficacy to perfectly sensible arrangements derived from a process of conscious bargain between free-willing parties. After all, why should not a landlord and tenant, if they so wish, agree on an indefinite term which may be brought to an end at any time on, say, the giving of three months' notice by either party? Why should the law frustrate clear contractual intentions for the sake of compliance with some archaic common law dogma which even the House of Lords has declared to have no 'satisfactory rationale' (*Prudential Assurance Co Ltd v*

London Residuary Body (1992) per Lord Browne-Wilkinson)? Quite often the availability of a flexible, open-ended letting makes enormous commercial sense in terms of the efficient short-term exploitation of land which lies temporarily redundant or unused. In the light of such factors the courts were clearly tempted during the 1980s to relax the rigour of the 'certainty of term' rule (see e.g. *Ashburn Anstalt v Arnold* (1989)), not least because it could be so easily evaded by the provision of a lengthy maximum term expressed to be subject to determination on some earlier and uncertain event.

> **Example**: Whereas a lease 'until England wins the World Cup' is, in every sense, hopelessly invalid, no legal objection could ever be raised against a lease for 99 years subject to earlier determination on England actually winning the Cup.

— *Reaffirmation of the 'certainty of term' rule* Such considerations notwith-standing, the House of Lords has strongly reaffirmed the principle that the maximum duration of a lease must be ascertainable at its commencement.

> *Prudential Assurance Co Ltd v London Residuary Body* (1992) LRB's predecessor in title granted a 'tenancy' in 1930 until such time as it required the land for a road improve-ment, a proposal which never materialised. The rent reserved was £30 per annum, but by the 1980s the annual rental value of the premises had become something in excess of £10,000. Unsurprisingly LRB claimed that the occupier held not an indefinite long-term lease pending the road improvement, but only a yearly tenancy arising from entry into possession and the payment of a periodic rent (**7.24**), in which case the tenancy was terminable on the giving of half a year's notice (**7.31**). The House of Lords upheld this periodic tenancy analysis, ruling with brutal simplicity that an agreement for inde-terminate occupation can never, in the absence of much needed legislative reform, constitute a lease.

There is now a compelling argument for enacting a statutory conversion of all uncertain terms (other than those already covered by legislation) into a deter-minable term of, say, 90 years.

— *Statutory modifications of the 'certainty of term' rule* It has long been the case that *leases for life* and *leases until marriage* (if granted at a rent or premium) are statutorily converted into a 90-year term determinable on the death or marriage of the original lessee (LPA 1925, s 149(6)). A lease for life granted in return for the sale of the freehold at a discounted price is also eligible for this statutory conversion (see *Skipton Building Society v Clayton* (1993)), but not a rent-free occupancy for life (see *Binions v Evans* (1972), **12.42**). Similarly, a perpetually renewable lease is converted automatically into a term of 2,000 years determinable only by the lessee (LPA 1922, s 145, Sch 15).

— *Periodic tenancies* It has never been easy to reconcile the 'certainty of term' principle with the phenomenon of the periodic tenancy, which, according to strict classical theory, continues indefinitely as a single, infinitely expandable, term until determined by the appropriate notice to quit given by one or other party (**7.31**). No maximum duration can be predicated at the commencement of the tenancy. Notwithstanding this doctrinal embarrassment, there is no serious doubt as to the leasehold quality of the periodic tenancy (see e.g. LPA 1925, s 205(1)(xxvii)).

• Some courts have simply taken the view that the general requirement of prefixed maximum duration 'cannot ... have direct reference to periodic tenancies' (*Re Midland Railway Co's Agreement* (1971) per Russell LJ).

• More recently courts have emphasised that each prolongation of the periodic tenancy constitutes a positive act of continued endorsement of the leasehold relationship on both sides (see *Hammersmith and Fulham LBC v Monk* (1992), **7.24**), with the consequence that, at any given time, 'the tenancy ... has no greater life than the period up to the time when the next notice can be given and would terminate' (*Crawley BC v Ure* (1996) per Hobhouse LJ). If either party avails himself of the initially agreed facility of termination by notice to quit, the periodic tenancy is simply said to be terminated by the effluxion of time. The tenancy merely reaches 'the end of its natural life' and comes 'to its predetermined end in accordance with the terms of the tenancy agreement' (*Barrett v Morgan* (2000) per Lord Millett). However, even this sophistry may not quite meet the common law dogma that the maximum duration of the term be ascertainable at its commencement. It is ironic, moreover, that, in attempting to deflect an awkward implication of a property-based dogma about 'certainty of term', the courts, in respect of periodic tenancies alone, have unashamedly resorted to a 'contractual approach' (see e.g. *Notting Hill Housing Trust v Brackley* (2002) at [26] per Peter Gibson LJ).

A lease or tenancy must confer a right of exclusive possession

7.13 It is consistent with the proprietary character of leaseholds that 'the proper touchstone' of a lease or tenancy should comprise the legal right to exclusive possession of the land (*Radaich v Smith* (1959) per Windeyer J). A tenant without exclusive possession is a contradiction in terms: no tenancy can exist unless such a right has been conferred on the occupier. Exclusory power is of the essence of proprietary estates in land (**2.8**). As Lord Templeman confirmed in *Street v*

Mountford (1985), the tenant is, in reality, owner pro tempore, and is entitled to 'keep out strangers and keep out the landlord unless the landlord is exercising limited rights reserved to him by the tenancy agreement to enter and view and repair.' (It is instructive at this point to contrast the licensee (**4.2, 4.6**), who has 'no legal title which will permit him to exclude other persons' (*AG Securities v Vaughan* (1990) per Lord Oliver of Aylmerton; but compare *Manchester Airport plc v Dutton* (2000), **4.11**).) Irrespective of its duration or scope, the lease guarantees the tenant a right of territorial control coupled with a general immunity from any detailed supervision of his activities on the demised premises. Correspondingly, the reservation for the freeholder of an unlimited right of access or of overall super-visory control clearly precludes any assertion of tenancy. Any genuine requirement that the occupier should vacate the premises for a defined portion of each day likewise militates against the claim of tenancy (see *Aslan v Murphy (No 1)* (1990), **7.15**). Moreover, mere physical occupancy of land does not necessarily connote the *exclusiveness of possession* which epitomises the status of the tenant (**2.13, 7.13**). Many contractual licensees and lodgers (e.g. students in university halls of resi-dence, residents in a hotel, and persons living in an old people's home) enjoy sole occupation, but equally clearly hold no tenancy or lease (see e.g. *Mehta v Royal Bank of Scotland* (1999)).

> *Westminster CC v Clarke* (1992) C was the occupant of a room in a council-run hostel for homeless persons. Under the hostel's regulations no occupant was entitled to any particular room; each could be required to share with other persons; each was for-bidden to entertain visitors without permission; and hostel staff were entitled to 'enter the accommodation at any time'. The House of Lords concluded that C's claim of tenancy was incompatible with the 'totality, immediacy, and objectives of the powers exercisable by the council and the restrictions imposed on [the occupant].' C could assert no right of exclusive possession since, in reality, it was the council which 'retained possession of all the rooms of the hostel in order to supervise and control the activities of occupiers'.

The distinction between lease and licence

7.14 It is sometimes difficult to distinguish a lease (or tenancy) from a mere *licence*, although the distinction may, in some contexts, be quite significant. A term of years constitutes a transferable and enforceable proprietary estate, whereas even a contractual licence is generally regarded as creating no interest in land at all (see *Ashburn Anstalt v Arnold* (1989), **4.11, 12.25**). Moreover, certain fields of protective legislation (**14.26–14.29**) apply only to the tenant and not to the licensee (see e.g.

Rent Act 1977, s 1 (protected tenancy); Housing Act 1988, s 1 (assured tenancy); and Landlord and Tenant Act 1954, s 23 (business tenancy)). Yet often, particularly in the residential context, a lease looks pretty similar to a mere licence and the courts have been required to demarcate what is, on the ground, quite an elusive boundary.

— *Exclusive possession is necessary but not sufficient* Clearly no arrangement can constitute a lease unless it confers a right of *exclusive possession* (**7.12**). Equally clearly, however, some apparent instances of exclusive possession are attributable to other categories of legal relationship than that of landlord and tenant. In such instances overall territorial control of the land is reserved not for the actual occupier but for the *landowner himself*, although the latter's 'possession' casts a shadow in the form of the exclusive occupation enjoyed by the occupier. Appearances can nevertheless be hugely deceptive, since exclusive occupation at a rent often closely mimics tenancy. Yet in the case of, say, the lodger in a bed-sit (**2.13**) or the occupant of serviced, sheltered or charitable housing or the resident of a hostel, a vital element of territorial dominion is usually retained by somebody else (see e.g. *Gray v Taylor* (1998)). Similarly accommodation underpinned by some motivation of friendship or generosity or by a relationship of a domestic or quasi-familial character is likely to be construed as having failed to confer on the occupant the exclusiveness of possession which is the sine qua non of tenancy (see *Heslop v Burns* (1974)). But where an occupier genuinely enjoys a right of exclusive possession, free of overriding external control of his premises, the relationship is inevitably one of tenancy, even if this classification imposes highly onerous operating conditions upon a social landlord such as a charitable housing trust (see *Bruton v London & Quadrant Housing Trust* (2000), **7.10, 7.25**).

— *The status of the 'lodger'* In particular, an occupier is a mere 'lodger' (as distinct from a tenant) if the owner of premises provides attendance or services 'which require the landlord or his servants to exercise unrestricted access to and use of the premises' (*Street v Mountford* (1985) per Lord Templeman). The lodger lacks a vital territorial stake in the premises which he occupies (**3.4**), being entitled to live there without being able to 'call the place his own' (ibid, per Lord Templeman). The decisive factor in distinguishing lease from licence consists in the absence of any right in the occupier to resist intrusion: it is the *owner* who 'retains possession' precisely in order to supply services or attendance (see *Antoniades v Villiers* (1990) per Lord Templeman).

— *The 'tolerated trespasser'* In certain rather special circumstances there is simply no intention in the relevant parties to create a legal relationship of any sort (whether lease or licence). The House of Lords has held, for instance, that no tenancy or licence arises where a local authority landlord, having obtained a possession order under the Housing Act 1985 against a defaulting council tenant, allows the former tenant to remain in occupation so long as all instalments of rent arrears and future rent are paid. In these circumstances of 'limbo', the former council tenant ranks merely as a 'tolerated trespasser' (*Burrows v Brent LBC* (1996) per Lord Browne-Wilkinson).

— *Ultimate irrelevance of labels* In determining the nature and quality of an occupancy, the subjective intentions of the parties are largely irrelevant. Since the court's task is to ascertain the 'true bargain between the parties' (*Aslan v Murphy* (1990) per Lord Donaldson of Lymington MR), the court retains a jurisdiction to overturn any superficial label which falsely describes the parties' legal relationship (see e.g. *Clore v Theatrical Properties Ltd and Westby & Co Ltd* (1936) (so-called 'lease' held to be licence); *Addiscombe Garden Estates Ltd v Crabbe* (1958) (so-called 'licence' held to be lease)). The definitional intent of the parties is relevant only in so far as it correctly conveys the inner substance—the jural reality—of the transaction. As Bingham LJ graphically pointed out in *Antoniades v Villiers* (1990), '[a] cat does not become a dog because the parties have agreed to call it a dog.'

The parties cannot contract away their true legal status

7.15 There is no freedom to stipulate—even by express contractual provision—for a status at law which does not correspond to the inner reality of the parties' dealing.

> *Street v Mountford* (1985) In return for a weekly 'licence fee', M was given a right of exclusive occupancy of a self-contained flat under a written 'licence agreement' in which she specifically disavowed any intention to take a tenancy. The House of Lords nevertheless decided that M held as a tenant because, irrespective of the parties' subjective intentions, their agreement exhibited all the hallmarks of a lease (**7.11**) and M thus qualified for the protection of the Rent Act 1977. 'If the agreement satisfied all the requirements of a tenancy, then the agreement produced a tenancy and the parties cannot alter the effect of the agreement by insisting that they only created a licence. The manufacture of a five-pronged implement for manual digging results in a fork even if the manufacturer, unfamiliar with the English language, insists that he intended to make and has made a spade' (per Lord Templeman). In consequence, the parties could not, by misdescription, contract out of Rent Act protection. (Exactly parallel reasoning has since been employed to ensure that parties are similarly unable to contract out of the statutory repairing liabilities imposed on landlords (see *Bruton v London & Quadrant Housing Trust* (2000), **7.10, 7.25**).)

— *Identification of shams and pretences*   In view of the temptation for landlords to circumvent protective legislation, courts have become more vigilant in detecting the presence of *sham* or *pretence* terms in occupation agreements whose sole purpose is to exploit the vulnerability of those who desperately seek residential accommodation and will sign almost anything in order to obtain it. Courts are nowadays more astute to strip away from an agreement any contractual term which is blatantly improbable or cynically inconsistent with the reasonably practical circumstances of the envisaged occupancy. The discarding of such terms—as 'pro non scripto' (*Antoniades v Villiers* (1990) per Lord Jauncey of Tullichettle)—enables the court then to determine whether the residue of agreed terms genuinely discloses the presence of a *lease* or *tenancy*.

> *Antoniades v Villiers* (1990) V and his partner each entered into an identical con-temporaneous 'licence' agreement with A, the owner of a small attic flat. A purported to retain rights (never in fact exercised) to use the flat in common with them 'at any time' and also to introduce limitless numbers of other licensees to share the cramped prem-ises with the young couple. The House of Lords held that these 'non-exclusive occu-pation licence' agreements were riddled with 'pretence', but that once the elements of 'pretence' were cut away the documents, when read together, plainly revealed the existence of a lease granted to V and his partner as joint tenants. The physical circumstances of the letting pointed up the 'air of total unreality' surrounding A's crude attempts to deny the young couple the exclusiveness of possession inherent in a tenancy. The disingenuous clauses contained in the agreements had not been 'ser-iously intended' to have any practical effect or to serve any other purpose than to avert 'the ordinary legal consequences attendant upon letting the appellants into possession at a monthly rent'.
>
> *Aslan v Murphy (No 1)* (1990) The Court of Appeal, in upholding a claim of tenancy, took the view that the 'true bargain between the parties' could not sensibly have included a 'wholly unrealistic' provision that a supposed 'licensee' should vacate his rented room every day between 10.30 am and midday.

Although there are today signs of an increased judicial willingness to strike down as unenforceable any improper attempt to evade mandatory schemes of statutory security of tenure for vulnerable renters (see e.g. *Bankway Properties Ltd v Pensfold-Dunsford* (2001) at [55]–[58] per Arden LJ), there are also indications that the courts may be more prepared to take at face value the descriptive labels attached to the transactions of equally balanced and well advised commercial parties. Thus, where such parties frame their relationship expressly in terms of a 'licence', this reference may serve 'as a pointer' and, in the words of the Court of Appeal, it would be 'a strong thing for the law to disregard totally the parties' choice of wording and to do so would be inconsistent with the general principle of freedom of contract' (*National Car Parks Ltd v Trinity Development Co (Banbury) Ltd* (2002) at [28]–[29] per Arden LJ).

Arrangements for multiple occupation

7.16 Where two or more persons jointly share exclusive possession of premises (even under the terms of separate, but contemporaneous, letting documents), it is likely that their unity of possession will be analysed as giving rise to joint tenancy under a lease. Where, however, premises are shared by a shifting population of previously unassociated individuals—as in the classic flat-share arrangement—such persons are highly unlikely to be able to demonstrate the 'four unities' of possession, interest, title and time which are necessarily present in a joint tenancy (**11.5**). The flat-sharers, precisely because they do not hold under contemporaneous agreements and quite often pay different rents, are inevitably disabled from claiming any collective status as joint tenants in respect of the entire flat. They rank as contractual licensees only (see *AG Securities v Vaughan* (1990)).

Creation and disposition of leasehold estates

7.17 By way of contrast with the creation of fee simple estates (**7.5**), the creation of *leasehold* estates is extremely common. Shop leases, business leases, residential long leases and periodic tenancies abound. Because the term of years is an alienable proprietary estate in land, the creation and disposition of leasehold estates provide a highly flexible framework for the distribution of possessory rights in land. Few rules constrain this flexibility, but no *minor* (i.e. a person under the age of 18) may hold a *legal* lease (LPA 1925, s 1(6), **1.20, 7.1**); nor may any person grant to himself a lease out of an estate of which he is himself the owner (*Rye v Rye* (1962)). A lessor who is entitled to a fee simple holds a marketable asset and may, of course, transfer his freehold reversion (**7.6**)—effectively to a new landlord who remains subject to any subsisting rights of lease. Likewise, in the absence of any limiting contractual provision, it is open to the lessee to deal independently with the unexpired term of his lease by either *assignment* or *sublease* (see *Fig 5*).

— *Assignment* (or *transfer*) of a term of years comprises a disposition by the lessee (T1) of his *entire* interest in the leasehold land, the assignee (T2) thenceforth standing in the assignor's shoes as owner of the residue of the term of years (i.e. as the new lessee).

• In the case of a long lease (e.g. a 99-year lease of a flat), the transfer will usually command a cash premium (or lump sum) payable by T2 to T1. T2 may well charge his newly acquired leasehold term in order to raise this sum by mortgage

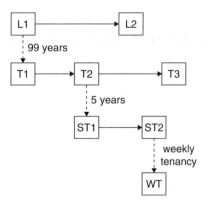

Fig 5

loan (**8.30–8.31**). In most cases of a short lease at an open market rent (e.g. the five-year lease granted by T2 to ST1), a future assignment of the lease to ST2 will simply result in ST2 taking over the payment of the covenanted rent without any payment of a premium to ST1.

• Any assignment of a legal leasehold interest (irrespective of its duration) must, if it is to transfer a *legal* estate to the assignee, be effected by *deed* (see *Crago v Julian* (1992)) and must also, in most cases, be completed by registration at Land Registry (**7.8, 7.21–7.22**).

— *Sublease* comprises the creation of a new leasehold estate in the land out of the lessee's own leasehold term. In this way the relationship of landlord and tenant can be replicated many times over, each leasehold term being carved out of the immediately superior estate. It follows that a sublease can be granted only for some shorter period of time than the term enjoyed by the sublessor, who therefore retains a 'reversion' on the sublease (see e.g. the five-year sublease granted by T2 to ST1 and the weekly tenancy granted by ST2 to WT). The sublessor's relationship with the head lessor continues unaffected. A purported subletting which attempts to carve out a term for the sublessee equal to or in excess of the residue of the sublessor's own term takes effect, not as a sublease, but as an *assignment* of that term (*Hallen v Spaeth* (1923)).

Not least in terms of requirements of formality, an important distinction must be maintained between:

• the rules which control the *initial creation* of a lease or sublease (**7.18–7.20**); and

• the rules which govern their *subsequent transfer* (**7.21–7.22**).

Statutory formalities for the creation (or grant) of a lease

7.18 The net effect of a hotchpotch of statutory provisions is that no deed is required for the creation of a legal lease or sublease which takes effect in possession at an open market rent without a premium for a period not exceeding *three* years (LPA 1925, ss 52(2)(d), 54(2), **2.30**). Whether relating to registered or unregistered land, such terms can be created at law by simple writing or even orally.

— *Requirement of a deed*   In all cases not covered by the statutory exemption, a legal lease can be created only by *deed* (see *R v Tower Hamlets LBC, ex parte Von Goetz* (1999)). Thus, for example, no term in excess of *three* years—nor any term which (irrespective of its duration) does not take effect *immediately*—can constitute a legal estate *unless* it is created by deed.

— *Consequence of informality*   Failure to use a deed (where one is required) usually results in the creation, not of the fixed term legal lease originally intended by the parties, but of a broadly equivalent *equitable* lease or—rather less likely—a legal periodic tenancy (**9.9**).

— *Contracting for a lease*   Parties who have in mind the creation of a lease of some duration frequently enter first into a *contract* to grant the lease envisaged. A copy of the proposed lease having been incorporated in the contract, it is not wholly unknown for parties then to leave their relationship on this purely contractual footing, thereby dispensing with the completion of their contract by formal grant. In the result, the parties are bound by an 'estate contract' (**9.8**), which confers on the prospective tenant an *equitable* term of years, which is generally, although somewhat inaccurately, supposed to be as good as a *legal* lease (**9.9**).

Registration of leases at Land Registry

7.19 Many kinds of transaction involving a leasehold estate require to be completed by registration at Land Registry if a legal estate is to vest.

— *Widening the dragnet of compulsory registration*   The LRA 2002 has dramatically reduced the length of the term which activates the requirement of registration at Land Registry. The registration threshold formerly imposed by the LRA 1925 caught only terms in excess of 21 years, but the 2002 Act recognises the increasing commercial reality that business leases are now generally short-term leases. The LRA 2002 therefore aims not only to bring a vast range of short-term leases on to the Land Register for the first time, but also, in so doing, to render them capable of electronic grant and disposition (**2.23, 12.3–12.5**). In certain special cases (relating, for instance, to the grant of a 'right to buy' lease (**7.40**) or of a reversionary lease taking effect in possession more than three months after the date of grant) a leasehold becomes registrable *irrespective* of the duration of the term (see LRA 2002, ss 4(1)(d)–(e), 27(2)(b)).

— *Possible expansions of the registration requirement*   Power has been reserved under the LRA 2002 to extend the requirement of substantive registration to any lease granted for a term of more than *three* years (LRA 2002, s 118(1)). Such a move is likely to occur when electronic conveyancing becomes fully operational, thereby ensuring that all leases which require formal grant by deed (**7.18**) also trigger compulsory registration at Land Registry (see Law Com No 271 (2001), para 3.17). Similarly, the Lord Chancellor has power to cause the mandatory first registration of a leasehold estate to be added to the statutory catalogue of 'events' which activate compulsory first registration of a previously unregistered superior estate (e.g. a freehold) out of which the registrable leasehold has been carved (LRA 2002, s 5). At present the grant of a registrable lease does not trigger any requirement to register its parent, but as yet unregistered, estate (see LRA 2002, s 6(3)(a)).

— *Multiple registrations*   The leasehold relationship can obviously produce two or more substantively registered titles in the same physical piece of land, i.e. titles to (respectively) the estates of the *freehold* owner and of any owner of a subsidiary *leasehold* granted for a term of more than seven years (**2.30–2.31**). Each of these independently registered estates will bear its own title number and have its own register of title.

Registration of newly created leasehold estates

7.20   In the case of a lease granted for a term of more than *three* years but not more than *seven* years, the use of a deed is generally sufficient to confer *legal* quality on the leasehold estate thereby created—a proposition which is true whether or not the estate out of which the leasehold is carved is itself registered. But where the term granted is more than *seven* years (and also in certain other specified cases), creation of the lease must be followed by a substantive registration of title to that leasehold estate at Land Registry (**2.30–2.31**). Only then can the term of years achieve a *lasting* legal status.

— *Lease granted out of an unregistered legal estate* Where a lease for a term of more than seven years is granted out of a legal estate which has not yet been registered at Land Registry, the lessee must apply, within two months of the date of grant, for *first registration* of his title to that leasehold estate (LRA 2002, ss 4(1)(c), (2), 6(1), (3)–(4)). Any term *not* registered within two months of grant loses its initial legal status and thereafter ranks as a mere contract for value by the lessor to grant the legal estate concerned (i.e. as an *equitable* term of years only) (LRA 2002, s 7(1), (2)(b)).

• *Classes of leasehold title on first registration* As with first registration of freeholds (**7.7**), the registrar assigns an appropriate class of title to all leasehold estates presented for first registration (LRA 2002, s 10(1)). The class awarded depends on the extent to which the registrar has been able to investigate title to the estate out of which the leasehold has been granted. There are four possible classes of title, as follows:

— *Absolute leasehold title* is the best and most frequently awarded class of title, and is awarded if the lessee can satisfy the registrar as to the reliability of the lessor's title (LRA 2002, s 10(2)). First registration with absolute title vests the relevant leasehold estate in the lessee on much the same terms as apply to a successful freehold applicant (**7.7**), but subject also to covenants contained in the lease and any burdens affecting the lessor's reversion (LRA 2002, s 12(2)–(5)).

— *Good leasehold title* is awarded when the lessor's reversionary title cannot be examined by the registrar. Registration with good leasehold title is, however, similar in effect to registration with absolute title, save that it does not preclude 'the enforcement of any estate, right or interest affecting, or in derogation of, the title of the lessor to grant the lease' (LRA 2002, s 12(6)). A good leasehold title may subsequently be upgraded to an absolute leasehold title (LRA 2002, s 62(2)).

— *Qualified leasehold title* is extremely rare.

— *Possessory leasehold title* is awarded to any lessee who cannot produce sufficient documentary evidence of his title. First registration with possessory leasehold title invests the applicant with a legal term of years, but subject to the same provisos as affect a possessory freehold registration (LRA 2002, s 12(8), **7.7**). A qualified or possessory leasehold registration can be upgraded later to good leasehold or even absolute leasehold title (LRA 2002, s 62(3), (5)).

— *Lease granted out of a registered estate* The grant of a leasehold term of more than seven years out of an estate which is already substantively registered in the lessor's name is regarded as a 'registrable disposition' of a registered estate (LRA

2002, s 27(2)(b)(i), **7.8**). Unless and until it is duly completed by registration, a dispositionary lease cannot take effect 'at law' (LRA 2002, s 27(1)) and therefore subsists only in equity (**9.9**).

- Completion by registration requires that the lessee be entered under a unique title number in the Land Register as the proprietor of the lease (LRA 2002, Sch 2, para 3(2)(a)); and a corresponding 'notice' in respect of the lease must be entered against the registered title of the lessor (LRA 2002, s 38, Sch 2, para 3(2)(b), **12.11**). Only through substantive registration of this kind can the lease achieve *legal* status.

- It was originally envisaged that all registrable leases granted out of a registered estate should be contained in, and their contents constrained by, a standard form deed of lease. A step in this direction has now been taken in respect of leases granted on or after 19 June 2006. Such leases must normally include certain prescribed clauses which detail essential information relating to the parties, the property and the leasehold terms which have been agreed (see LRR 2003, r 58A, as introduced by SI 2005/1982).

- The class of title allocated to the newly registered dispositionary lease almost inevitably reflects the class attached to the parent (or 'reversionary') title (see LRA 2002, s 29(2)(a)(iii)).

Registration of dealings with unregistered leasehold estates

7.21 A requirement of completion by registration also applies to certain dealings with any existing unregistered legal lease which, at the date of the dealing, still has more than seven years to run (LRA 2002, s 4(1)–(2)). Application for first registration of title to the leasehold estate must be made within *two months* of the date of the relevant dealing (LRA 2002, s 6(1), (3)–(4)) in the same way as described above on the grant of a new lease out of an unregistered reversion (**7.20**).

— *Events which trigger registration* The dealings which trigger compulsory first registration are:

- Any *transfer* of the unregistered legal leasehold whether by way of sale, gift, assent or court order (LRA 2002, s 4(1)(a)). The duty to apply for registration of the estate transferred rests on the transferee (LRA 2002, s 6(1), (3)(b)). Failing such an application, the transferee's term of years reverts to *equitable* status only (compare **7.7**).

• Any *protected first legal mortgage* of the unregistered legal leasehold (LRA 2002, ss 4(1)(g), 6(2)(a)). Either the mortgagor or the mortgagee may apply for registration of the leasehold estate (LRA 2002, s 6(2)(b), (6); LRR 2003, r 21, **7.7**). Failing such an application, the unregistered leasehold remains a legal estate, but the mortgage takes effect only as a contract for value to create a legal charge (i.e. as a mere *equitable* mortgage) (LRA 2002, s 7(2)(b)).

— *Effect of first registration* First registration with absolute title vests the leasehold estate in the transferee or mortgagor (as the case may be) on much the same terms as apply to a successful freehold applicant (**7.7**), but subject to covenants contained in the lease and any burdens affecting the lessor's reversion (LRA 2002, s 12(2)–(5)).

Registration of dealings with registered leasehold estates

7.22 A leasehold estate, once substantively registered at Land Registry, can be dealt with in much the same manner as a registered freehold title (**7.8**). In the absence of any 'restriction' entered in the register, the registered proprietor has, in principle, plenary powers of disposition over his leasehold estate (LRA 2002, s 23(1), **7.8**). However, a requirement of registration now applies to all 'registrable dispositions' of a registered leasehold estate (including, obviously, any transfer of that estate) (see LRA 2002, s 27(2)(a)).

— *Contract to transfer* As a matter of conveyancing practice, most dispositions of a registered leasehold are preceded by a specifically enforceable *contract* to engage in the dealing in question, with the result that the contract confers equitable rights on the disponee pending completion of the disposition (**9.7–9.9**).

— *Form of disposition* A registrable transfer of a registered leasehold estate must be made in the form prescribed by the LRR 2003 (see LRA 2002, s 25(1); LRR 2003, r 58, 206(1), Sch 1, **7.6**).

— *Completion by registration* All 'registrable dispositions' of a registered leasehold estate must be completed by the entry of the disponee in the Land Register as the proprietor of the relevant interest under the disposition (LRA 2002, s 27(2), Sch 2), failing which the disposition 'does not operate at law' (LRA 2002, s 27(1)). Thus a transfer of an existing registered leasehold passes a legal estate only on due registration (**12.5**). Pending registration of the transfer, the transferee holds only an *equitable* leasehold term (**9.9**), the *legal* title to the lease remaining vested in the transferor (see e.g. *Brown & Root Technology Ltd v Sun Alliance & London Assurance Co Ltd* (1996); *Scribes West Ltd v Relsa Anstalt (No 3)* (2005)). In such cases the failure to vest a legal title in the transferee by registration has the effect of relegating all the latter's future transactions (e.g. by way of sale or mortgage) to *equitable* effect only, since none of these transactions is, for the moment, capable of registration.

— *Electronic dispositions of registered leaseholds* At present most unregistered dispositions generate at least an *equitable* entitlement in the disponee. However, under the stricter system of electronic conveyancing envisaged by the LRA 2002, dispositions of a registered leasehold estate will have no effect at all—*either* at law *or* in equity—until communicated electronically to the registrar and simultaneously recorded in the Land Register (LRA 2002, s 93(1)–(3), Sch 2, **7.8**).

Residual categories of unregistrable lease

7.23 Irrespective of whether any superior estate has been substantively registered, leasehold terms of seven years or less are currently ineligible for substantive registration (**7.20–7.22**), thus remaining off the register as mere 'deeds bundles'. We have already seen, however, that it is quite likely that legal terms of more than *three* years will, at some future point, be drawn on to the register as substantively registrable estates (**7.19**).

— *Overriding interest protection* Even under the LRA 2002 in its present form, leasehold terms of seven years or less are declared to 'override' both first registration and subsequent dispositions of the relevant superior title (LRA 2002, ss 11(4)(b), 12(4)(c), Sch 1, para 1; s 29(1), (2)(a)(ii), Sch 3, para 1, **2.31, 12.17, 12.33**).

— *Limited protection by 'notice'* Following the commencement of the LRA 2002, it has become possible for a lease granted for a term of more than *three* years to be protected by the entry of a 'notice' on the superior registered title (LRA 2002, ss 32, 33(b), **12.11**).

Periodic tenancy

7.24 A periodic tenancy may be created as a *legal* estate without compliance with any statutory requirement of formality or registration. A periodic tenancy simply runs from week to week, or from month to month, or from quarter to quarter, or from year to year, continuing indefinitely until determined by the giving of the appropriate notice (**7.31**). In strict theory a periodic tenancy is viewed, not as an aggregate of distinct terms of years, but as comprising one single unbroken term which, unless and until duly determined, perpetually elongates itself by the superaddition of a fresh unit or period (see *Hammersmith and Fulham LBC v Monk* (1992) per Lord Bridge of Harwich).

— *Creation* Even though a periodic tenancy may actually endure for decades, it is not caught by the statutory requirement of creation by *deed* (**7.18**). Periodic tenancies may be created *at law* by merely oral means and can be granted either expressly or impliedly. The common law used to apply a strong presumption that, in the absence of express words, a periodic tenancy—often a tenancy from year to year—was impliedly created by the payment and acceptance of a periodic sum in the nature of rent. Ultimately, however, the question whether an implied tenancy has arisen and the precise periodicity of such a tenancy depend upon the 'intentions of the parties in all the circumstances' (*Cardiothoracic Institute v Shrewdcrest Ltd* (1986)). Particularly in view of the likelihood that tenancies may attract various kinds of long-term statutory protection, there is nowadays less inclination to presume the existence of a common law tenancy from the mere fact of possession and periodic payments (see e.g. *Leadenhall Residential 2 Ltd v Stirling* (2002) at [48] per Judge LJ). The onus is upon the claimant tenant to demonstrate that the payments connoted an agreement for a periodic tenancy (see *Dreamgate Properties Ltd v Arnot* (1997)). However, in the total absence of any other 'material sur-rounding circumstances', the creation of such a tenancy may represent the only inference 'sensibly and reasonably to be drawn' from the payment of periodic sums (*Javad v Mohammed Aqil* (1992) per Nicholls LJ). It is nevertheless relatively rare that the fact of periodic payment should stand isolated from other factors which may help to clarify the matter of intention; and, where a periodic tenancy is found ·to exist on the basis of monthly or weekly payments, less weight is nowadays attached to the old presumption in favour of *yearly* tenancy rather than a *monthly* or *weekly* tenancy (see *Javad v Mohammed Aqil* (1992)).

— *Transfer* Any assignment (or transfer) of a periodic tenancy must be effected by *deed* if it is to vest a legal term of years in the assignee (*Crago v Julian* (1992), **7.17**).

Tenancy by estoppel

7.25 A person who is not currently entitled to an estate in land cannot grant a term of years (**7.10**), but remains competent to create a 'lease' or 'tenancy' which, precisely because its effect rests on a principle of estoppel, is known as a *tenancy by estoppel*.

— *Estoppel and relativity of title* It is a fundamental principle of the common law that a grantor is debarred (or estopped) from disputing the validity of his own grant and may not therefore disaffirm the title of his grantee. Accordingly, a landlord is never permitted to deny that his grant of a lease has created an effective leasehold estate in his grantee; and, for his part, the grantee, so long as he continues in possession and enjoys the benefits of the lease, is debarred from questioning the validity of his landlord's title in any action which the landlord may bring against him (*Cuthbertson v Irving* (1859) per Martin B, **7.34**). Thus, provided that the subject matter of the grant conforms to the definitional characteristics of a 'lease' or 'tenancy' (**7.11**), it matters not that, in reality, the 'landlord' owned no proprietary estate in the land out of which he could carve a term of years. As Lord Hoffmann indicated in *Bruton v London & Quadrant Housing Trust* (2000), 'it is not the estoppel which creates the tenancy, but the tenancy which creates the estoppel.' At least vis-à-vis each other, both parties are regarded as having an imaginary (but undeniable) estate in the land capable both of supporting independent dealings and of qualifying for various kinds of statutory protection. In the absence of any challenge by a third party, it cannot matter to either that the assumed proprietary base of their relationship is non-existent. Even if both parties were, at the date of the leasehold grant, fully aware of the deficiency of the landlord's title, they are each credited, by force of common law doctrine, as holding an estate *by estoppel* which—in view of the basic relativity of title in English law (**6.1**)—binds all save those who can claim a superior title.

Bruton v London & Quadrant Housing Trust (2000) (**7.10**) Lambeth London Borough Council granted to a charitable housing trust a licence to use a block of flats as short-term accommodation for homeless persons, the housing trust undertaking that it would grant no occupant security of tenure. The housing trust then allocated short-term accommodation in the block to B, a homeless person, on payment of a weekly 'licence' fee. B later claimed that he qualified for the benefit of various statutorily implied repairing obligations available only under a tenancy (**14.5**). Notwithstanding the clear label of licence applied by the parties and notwithstanding that the housing trust had no proprietary estate to support the grant of a term of years, the House of Lords ruled that B, in so far as he enjoyed exclusive possession at a rent for a periodic term, had acquired a tenancy by estoppel which fell within the scope of the housing trust's repairing obligations as landlord (see also *Kay v Lambeth LBC* (2006), **7.10**)

— *Feeding the estoppel* If, after granting a lease out of a title which he did not currently own, a landlord by estoppel at some later date acquires a legal estate in the land which would have sustained his grant, the estoppel is said to be 'fed' (compare **8.19**, **15.15**). The tenant's lease, together with the landlord's reversion, 'then take[s] effect in interest and not by estoppel' (*Cuthbertson v Irving* (1859) per

Martin B). The benefit of the grantor's subsequent acquisition thus goes 'automatically to the earlier grantee', the tenant acquiring a legal term of years which is now good against the world unless and until it is brought to an end by any of the modes of termination which apply to a lease (see *Kay v Lambeth LBC* (2006) at [143]–[148]).

Tenancy at sufferance

7.26 A *tenancy at sufferance* arises where a tenant who has enjoyed a perfectly valid term of years holds over at the end of his term without the consent or dissent of the landlord. A tenant at sufferance has no 'tenancy' in any true sense; he is not liable to pay rent as such, but is liable to a money claim for use and occupation of the land.

Tenancy at will

7.27 The phenomenon of the *tenancy at will* occupies an obscurely defined no-man's land between the *periodic tenancy* (**7.24**) and the mere *licence* (**4.2**). A tenancy at will arises if, with the consent of the owner, a person enters into occupation of land for an indefinite period in circumstances where *either* party may at any time terminate the arrangement at will, i.e. on demand. (Compare the *periodic tenancy*, which is terminable only after the giving of notice to quit (**7.31**).) A tenancy at will is said to comprise a 'personal relation between the landlord and his tenant' (*Wheeler v Mercer* (1957)) and a tenant at will, having no estate in the land, cannot sublet or assign his tenancy to a stranger. The tenant at will is nevertheless accounted to be in 'possession' of the land, with the result that he may maintain an action in trespass against a stranger (although not against the owner himself). Tenancies at will are nowadays uncommon and slightly anomalous, usually serving during a transitional period to confer upon an occupier some form of intermediate status pending the arrival of a more permanent estate in the land.

Termination of leases and tenancies

7.28 A lease or tenancy may come to an end in many ways, of which the following are the most important:

- effluxion of time (**7.29**);
- activation of break clause (**7.30**);

- notice to quit (**7.31**);
- forfeiture (**7.32**);
- surrender (**7.33**);
- disclaimer (**7.34**);
- repudiatory breach (**7.35**);
- frustration (**7.36**);
- termination on statutory grounds (**7.37**);
- enlargement (**7.38**);
- merger (**7.39**); and
- leasehold enfranchisement (**7.40**).

In the context of registered land, moreover, the registrar is required to close the registered title to any leasehold estate which he is satisfied has been determined (see LRR 2003, r 79(2)).

Effluxion of time

7.29 Except in specific statutory contexts (**14.26–14.27, 14.30**), a lease or tenancy for a fixed term automatically ends, without any notice to quit, on the expiration of the term certain. It is not, however, lawful for a landlord to enforce his right to recover possession of premises let 'as a dwelling' by any means other than proceedings in court (Protection from Eviction Act 1977, s 3(1)).

Activation of 'break clause'

7.30 In the commercial context a long lease often contains a 'break clause' which allows either the landlord or the tenant to determine the lease by notice at any of a number of stipulated intervals (e.g. at seven year intervals) in advance of the final expiry date of the term certain.

Notice to quit

7.31 In terms of the currently fashionable contractual analysis of leasehold relationships (**7.10**), periodic tenancies are 'founded on the continuing will of both landlord and tenant that the tenancy shall persist' (*Hammersmith and Fulham LBC v Monk*

(1992) per Lord Browne-Wilkinson (**7.24**)). Thus either landlord or tenant may terminate a periodic tenancy by serving on the other a notice to quit, thereby indicating that the will to continue no longer exists. In effect a periodic tenancy 'comes to an end by effluxion of time, namely the expiry of the last period for which the tenant or tenants have been willing for it to continue' (*Newlon Housing Trust v Alsulaimen* (1999) per Lord Hoffmann).

— *Length of notice required by common law*   In the absence of express agreement between landlord and tenant, the minimum periods of notice required at common law are the following:

- *Yearly tenancy*: half a year's notice
- *All other periodic tenancies*: one full period (e.g. one month's notice in the case of a *monthly* tenancy, and one week's notice in the case of a *weekly* tenancy).

— *Length of notice required by statute*   In the case of most residential premises statute law superimposes an extended period of notice upon the notice already required at common law. In such cases no notice to quit, whether given by the landlord or by the tenant, is valid if given less than *four weeks* before the date on which it is to take effect (PEA 1977, s 5(1)(b)). A notice served by a landlord must, moreover, include certain statutorily prescribed information aimed at safeguarding the interests of vulnerable tenants (see PEA 1977, s 5(1)(a)).

— *Notice in cases of joint ownership*   In the case of joint ownership of either the landlord's estate or the tenant's estate, a valid notice to quit may be given by any one of the relevant estate owners acting quite unilaterally (see *Harrow LBC v Qazi* (2004) at [74] per Lord Hope of Craighead). In a periodic tenancy 'the will of all the joint parties is necessary to the continuance of the interest' (*Hammersmith and Fulham LBC v Monk* (1992) per Lord Bridge of Harwich), and the withdrawal of *any* party's assent to the continuance of the tenancy therefore has a terminal effect.

> *Hammersmith and Fulham LBC v Monk* (1992) Following a domestic dispute, one of two cohabiting joint tenants of a council flat gave the landlord authority notice to quit, thereby precipitating the homelessness of her erstwhile partner. (The party giving notice had first ascertained the willingness of the council to rehouse her on termination of the tenancy.) The House of Lords upheld the effectiveness of this notice, albeit that it was given without the knowledge or consent of the other cohabitee. Although Lord Browne-Wilkinson acknowledged an 'instinctive reaction' founded on a 'property based' perspective, which prompted a 'revulsion' against the idea that one joint tenant could unilaterally terminate her partner's property rights in the home, he and the remainder of the House of Lords ultimately endorsed the 'contract based' reaction that a cohabitee could not be 'held to a tenancy contract which is dependent for its continuance on the will of the tenant.'

• In *Harrow LBC v Qazi* (2003) the House of Lords confirmed—extremely controversially—that no escape from this rather harsh conclusion could be found in the European guarantee of respect for the 'home' (see ECHR Art 8, **2.15**). As one of the judges in the majority indicated, Article 8 is 'not ordinarily infringed by enforcing the terms on which the applicant occupies premises as his home' (*Qazi* at [100] per Lord Millett, although compare the refinement of this proposition contained in *Kay v Lambeth LBC; Leeds CC v Price* (2006), **2.15**).

• Nor can a joint tenant's unilateral notice to quit (and its devastating effects) be challenged as an improper exercise of a trustee's 'function' under the Trusts of Land and Appointment of Trustees Act 1996 (see TOLATA 1996, s 11(1), **11.27–11.28**). Since the orthodoxy flowing from *Monk*'s case insists that the service of a notice to quit is not a positive act, but rather a negative act of withdrawal of consent to the continuation of the periodic tenancy, there is here no 'function' which requires the consultation of trust beneficiaries (*Notting Hill Housing Trust v Brackley* (2002) at [23], [32]).

Forfeiture

7.32 In the event of a breach of covenant by the tenant, a lease may become determinable according to the rules governing forfeiture (**14.11–14.14**).

Surrender

7.33 A lease or tenancy may be determined by a *surrender* of the tenant's interest to his immediate landlord. If (but only if) the landlord accepts the surrender, the tenant's term of years merges forthwith in the landlord's reversion and is extinguished (see *Barrett v Morgan* (2000) per Lord Millett). A surrender of the tenant's term may be made either *expressly* or *impliedly by operation of law*.

— *Express surrender* constitutes a disposition of an estate in the land and, in order to be effective at law, must be contained in a deed (LPA 1925, s 52(1), **7.6**). Surrender must also be accompanied by some (even notional) delivery up of possession.

— *Surrender by operation of law* occurs where, with the landlord's concurrence or acquiescence, the tenant consciously does some act which is inconsistent with the continuance of the tenancy (*Mattey Securities Ltd v Ervin* (1998)). This kind of surrender requires no formality (see LPA 1925, s 52(2)(c)), but effectively involves 'a change of possession, or something that is equivalent to a change of possession', in circumstances where it would subsequently be unconscionable to plead the absence of a formal deed of surrender (*Hoggett v Hoggett* (1980)). A typical circumstance of implied surrender arises, for instance, with the return of the tenant's key, accompanied by the tenant's intentional and unequivocal removal, in so far as possible, of all evidence of his possession under the former tenancy (see e.g. *Sanctuary Housing Association v Campbell* (1999)). Even then, in the absence of the landlord's clear acceptance of a surrender, rent continues to be payable (see e.g. *Bellcourt Estates Ltd v Adesina* (2005) at [29]–[32]).

Disclaimer

7.34   A lease or tenancy may be terminated on *disclaimer* of the relationship of landlord and tenant. Any clear and unambiguous denial or repudiation of his landlord's title by a tenant entitles the landlord to re-enter the demised premises and forfeit the lease (*W G Clark (Properties) Ltd v Dupre Properties Ltd* (1992)). Another kind of disclaimer may arise on the insolvency of the tenant. It is open to a corporate tenant's liquidator (or a non-corporate tenant's trustee in bankruptcy) to disclaim any subsisting lease if that lease comprises property which is 'unsaleable or not readily saleable' or is likely to give rise to a 'liability to pay money or perform any onerous act' (Insolvency Act 1986, ss 178(2), 315(1)–(2), **7.9**). Such a disclaimer automatically extinguishes the lease and releases the insolvent tenant from all further liability in connection with it (*Hindcastle Ltd v Barbara Attenborough Associates Ltd* (1997), **14.21**), although the landlord of a corporate tenant may prove in a winding up as an unsecured creditor for loss sustained in consequence of the disclaimer (*Re Park Air Services plc* (2000)).

Repudiatory breach

7.35   One consequence of the modern 'contractualisation' of the lease (**7.10**) is the increased willingness of the courts to hold that breach by either landlord or tenant of a 'fundamental term' of the lease constitutes a *repudiation* of the lease entitling the other party, at his election, to regard the lease as *terminated* and to sue immediately for damages in respect of the loss of the lease. However, such cases represent extreme instances: in most circumstances of breach by landlord or tenant the appropriate remedy is *damages* not the termination of the lease (*Nynehead Developments Ltd v RH Fibreboard Containers Ltd* (1999)).

Hussein v Mehlman (1992) The tenants under a three-year lease vacated their rented home after only 15 months on the ground of gross and persistent breaches by their landlord of his statutory obligations of repair and maintenance under the Landlord and Tenant Act 1985 (**14.5**). Assistant Recorder Sedley QC held that the tenants were entitled to throw up the tenancy (rather than seek other remedies for non-repair) and claim immediately for damages for repudiatory breach of contract by their landlord.

Chartered Trust plc v Davies (1997) D claimed to rescind the lease of a unit in a shopping mall where the landlord had failed to prevent acts of nuisance arising from other lettings in a supposedly 'high class retail' development. (D alleged that her business had been impeded by the proximity of a pawnbroker's shop and a coffee shop whose tables littered the common parts of the mall premises.) The Court of Appeal agreed that there had been a repudiatory breach of the tenancy by the landlord and that D had been correct in declining to keep her business open and in refusing to pay further rent.

Frustration

7.36 It is now well recognised that the contractual doctrine of frustration may, in exceptional circumstances, strike down a lease *as a whole* (as distinct from the individual covenants contained within it). It must be shown that a 'supervening event' has brought about such a 'fundamental change of circumstances as to enable the court to say—"this was not the bargain which these parties made and their bargain must be treated as at an end"' (*National Carriers Ltd v Panalpina (Northern) Ltd* (1981) per Lord Roskill).

Termination on statutory grounds

7.37 Leases and tenancies may also be terminated on a number of express statutory grounds which are examined more closely elsewhere (**14.26–14.30**).

Enlargement

7.38 Section 153 of the Law of Property Act 1925 provides a little used facility for the enlargement of certain long leases into a fee simple estate. It is open to the tenant to execute a deed of enlargement in respect of a lease which was granted for a term in excess of 300 years, of which at least 200 years remain unexpired. After enlargement the tenant takes the fee simple subject to all the same covenants and provisions which governed the now extinguished lease (LPA 1925, s 153(8)), with the result that the device of enlargement provides a rare means by which the burden of positive covenants may be made to run with freehold land (**13.12**).

Merger

7.39 A lease may be determined by *merger* where the tenant acquires the landlord's reversion and holds both interests in the same name and in exercise of the same legal capacity. Under these circumstances—at least so long as there is no contrary intention—the lease merges with the reversionary title and is extinguished (see LPA 1925, s 185; LRR 2003, r 79).

Leasehold enfranchisement and extension

7.40 Modern legislation has introduced, in various forms, the possibility that a tenant may purchase the freehold reversion on his leasehold estate, thereby causing the merger of his lease in that freehold. The most important means of leasehold enfranchisement are the following:

— *Leasehold Reform Act 1967*   Controversially in the view of some, the Leasehold Reform Act 1967 confers on certain tenants holding a long lease a right of compulsory acquisition of the freehold out of which their lease was granted (or, if they prefer, an extended term of years in the premises). Although expropriatory in effect, the LRA 1967 has been held to be a measure aimed at securing 'greater social justice in the sphere of people's homes' and, therefore, to constitute no violation of the property guarantee contained in ECHR Protocol No 1, Art 1 (*James v United Kingdom* (1986)).

• The LRA 1967 applies only to a 'house' let at a low rent under a tenancy which was granted for a term certain in excess of 21 years (LRA 1967, ss 1(1)(a), 3(1)). Moreover, the benefit of the statute is confined to the tenant who has held his tenancy for a period of at least two years immediately preceding his application under the Act, although there is now no requirement that this tenant should have *occupied* or *resided in* the house during this period (LRA 1967, s 1(1)(b), as amended by Commonhold and Leasehold Reform Act 2002, ss 138(1), 139, Sch 14).

• The price payable for enfranchisement is usually fairly low and is fixed, in default of agreement, by a local residential property tribunal, with a right of appeal to the Lands Tribunal.

— *Collective enfranchisement* For tenants of blocks of flats an analogous 'right of collective enfranchisement' is conferred by the Leasehold Reform, Housing and Urban Development Act 1993, as amended by the CALRA 2002, under which the tenants may buy out their landlord's interest. Alternatively such tenants may be able to take over the management of the premises through a 'RTM company' (CALRA 2002, ss 71–113, **14.6**).

— *The council tenant's 'right to buy'* The Housing Act 1985 confers upon certain categories of public sector tenant a 'right to buy' the home in which the tenant lives (or to take a long lease over it). This 'right to buy' has dramatically opened up the opportunity of freehold home ownership for a generation of council tenants and it has been estimated that some 10 per cent of all households in Britain today have, at some time, participated in the purchase of public or quasi-public accommodation which they previously rented. The 'right to buy' relates *only* to a 'dwelling-house' and operates *only* in favour of someone who has been a 'secure tenant' (**14.29**) of a public sector landlord for a period of at least two years (HA 1985, s 119(1)). The 'right to buy' is not available to a tenant who, at any stage before the completion of his purchase, becomes the subject of a possession order (*Enfield LBC v McKeon* (1986)), but a qualifying tenant is otherwise entitled to purchase either the freehold or a long leasehold term at a discount which varies according to the duration of the pre-existing secure tenancy (HA 1985, s 126(1)(b)). The completion of a purchase under the 'right to buy' terminates any secure tenancy previously enjoyed by the purchasing tenant (HA 1985, s 139(2)), and the position of the purchaser is thereafter governed largely by the terms and covenants which are attached by the Housing Act 1985 to the conveyance of his freehold or the grant of his lease (HA 1985, s 139(1)). There is also a statutory obligation to repay (in whole or part) any discount allowed to the purchaser in the event that he makes an 'early disposal' (i.e. within the next three years) of the estate purchased by him (see HA 1985, ss 155(1)–(2), 159(1)). The 'right to buy' has become increasingly controversial in recent years, partly because its widespread exercise has gravely diminished the stock of good-quality affordable housing available to social landlords and partly because of evident profiteering by property companies which, in return for terms hugely disadvantageous to cash-strapped tenants, have financed the exercise by tenants of their statutory right. Accordingly, in respect of secure tenancies created on or after 18 January 2005, the Housing Act 2004 has tightened up the availability of the 'right to buy' by imposing a qualification period of *five* years and by extending the embargo on 'early disposal' to cover the *five* years following the exercise of the statutory right (see HA 2004, ss 180, 185–6).

Freehold ownership of commonhold land

7.41 The Commonhold and Leasehold Reform Act 2002 (and the Regulations drafted thereunder) inaugurate a long-awaited form of estate ownership which is specially designed as a new form of landholding for blocks of flats and other multi-unit properties such as office blocks and similar commercial accommodation (see *Commonhold and Leasehold Reform: Draft Bill and Consultation Paper* (Lord Chancellor's Department, Cm 4843, August 2000)). The relevant provisions of CALRA 2002 came into force on 27 September 2004.

— *Commonhold ownership as a species of freehold ownership* 'Commonhold ownership' is a species of *freehold* ownership of *registered* land which has been deliberately adapted to resolve many of the legal problems arising in respect of multiple occupation of premises (**13.11–13.12**). In essence, the commonhold regime establishes the owner of each unit in a larger development (e.g. each owner of a flat in a block) as the owner of a registered fee simple estate in his or her *individual unit*, whilst vesting the registered fee simple ownership of the *common parts* of the multi-occupied land in a collective management or 'commonhold' association. Commonhold schemes combine freehold ownership of individual units with exclusive membership of a private limited company (i.e. a 'commonhold association') which owns and assumes responsibility for the management and upkeep of the common parts of the grounds and building (including its structural walls and any garden or other communal facility). Commonholders thus enjoy 'the security of freehold ownership' coupled with a collective freedom to 'control and effectively manage their own common areas and to apply positive obligations to every successive owner of the individual units in the development' (Land Registry, *Commonhold (Land Registration) Rules: A Land Registry Consultation Paper* (September 2002), p 11).

— *An alternative to long leasehold ownership* In many respects the device of commonhold ownership provides yet another way in which existing mechanisms of leasehold ownership (which have never proved entirely satisfactory as a means of regulating multi-occupied premises) can be converted into some form of freehold title. Ownership of a lease, which is a wasting asset, is 'replaced by ownership of a freehold, which is not', commonhold thus offering a distinctively different 'alternative to long leasehold ownership of flats and other interdependent properties' (see *Commonhold Proposals for Commonhold Regulations: A Consultation Paper* (Lord Chancellor's Department, CP: 11/02 (October 2002)), p 10).

The introduction of the commonhold scheme, which is heavily derivative of 'condominium' and 'strata title' schemes practised in other parts of the common law world, represents a remarkable addition to, or variant of, the conceptual structure of estate ownership in English law.

— *Creation of a commonhold* A commonhold can only be created out of a freehold estate which is already registered at Land Registry; and the commonhold itself must be created expressly by a further act of registration at the Registry (CALRA 2002, ss 1(1)(a), 2(1)). The Chief Land Registrar is authorised to register a freehold estate in land as 'a freehold in commonhold land' (CALRA 2002, s 2(1)) if the land concerned is not already commonhold land and if certain other conditions are fulfilled. Land can be 'commonhold land' only if:

• There is in existence a 'commonhold association' (i.e. a private company limited by guarantee and registered at Companies House) whose memorandum of association specifies certain land as 'land in relation to which the association is to exercise functions' (CALRA 2002, s 1(1)(b)) and whose business it will be to own and manage the common parts of the development (see CALRA 2002, Sch 3).

• There is in existence a 'commonhold community statement' which makes provision for the rights and duties of the commonhold association and its unit-holders (CALRA 2002, s 1(1)(c)). The commonhold community statement must specify not only the 'commonhold units' comprised within the scheme (these being at least two in number), but must also, by reference to a filed plan, define the extent of each relevant commonhold unit (CALRA 2002, s 11).

Some categories of land (e.g. 'flying freeholds' and certain agricultural land) cannot comprise 'commonhold land' (CALRA 2002, s 4, Sch 2).

— *Contents of application* An application for commonhold registration may be made by any person who is (or is entitled to be) registered as the proprietor of a freehold estate in the land with absolute title (CALRA 2002, s 2(3), **7.8**). All applications must be accompanied (see CALRA 2002, s 2(2), Sch 1) by the memorandum and articles of association of the commonhold association, by the commonhold community statement, and by evidence of a number of requisite consents to the application given by:

• the registered proprietor of the freehold estate in the whole or any part of the land;

• the registered proprietor of any leasehold estate in the whole or any part of the land granted for a term of more than 21 years;

• the registered proprietor of any charge over the whole or any part of the land; and

- other prescribed classes of person (such as proprietors of a rentcharge and persons holding unregistered short leases).

— *New developments*   The developer of a site which, as yet, has no unit-holders in occupation may apply for registration of the global commonhold title in respect of that site (CALRA 2002, s 7(1)). The developer then remains registered proprietor of the freehold estate in the entire commonhold land (see CALRA 2002, s 7(2)(a)) until such time as at least one other person becomes entitled to be registered as freehold proprietor of one of the units. At this point, the Chief Land Registrar is obliged to register the commonhold association as proprietor of the freehold estate in the common parts (CALRA 2002, s 7(3)(a)–(b)), and the rights and duties contained in the commonhold community statement come into effect (CALRA 2002, s 7(3)(c)).

— *Registration with existing unit-holders*   Where an application for registration of commonhold land indicates that the relevant site has *existing* unit-holders, registration has the immediate effect of vesting the registered freehold estate in the common parts in the designated commonhold association (CALRA 2002, s 9(3)(a)). Each person specified in the application as an initial unit-holder of a commonhold unit is then entitled to be registered as the proprietor of the freehold estate in that unit (CALRA 2002, s 9(3)(b)); the commonhold community statement comes immediately into effect (CALRA 2002, s 9(3)(e)); and cross-referenced entries are made in the Land Register in order to reflect the emergence of these various freehold titles (CALRA 2002, s 9(3)(d)). The corollary of this general mutation to freehold title is that any existing lease of the whole or any part of the commonhold land is extinguished (CALRA 2002, s 9(3)(f)), although a partial system of compensation is provided for leaseholders who lose their interests and who were not persons whose consent was an essential precondition of the application for commonhold registration in the first place (CALRA 2002, s 10).

— *Effect of registration*   When a commonhold registration takes effect, the Land Register carries cross-referenced entries relating to the freehold titles taken by the individual unit-holders and by the commonhold association itself. The Chief Land Registrar is required, in respect of any commonhold land, to retain (and refer in the register to) certain prescribed details of the commonhold association, prescribed details of the registered freeholder of each commonhold unit, a copy of the commonhold community statement, and a copy of the memorandum and articles of association of the commonhold association (CALRA 2002, s 5(1)).

— *Commonhold community statement*   At the heart of the commonhold model is the idea that, in respect of his or her own commonhold unit, each unit-holder is governed by a charter of standardised rights and obligations defined by a 'commonhold community statement', which effectively operates as a binding constitutional document for the entire commonhold community (see CALRA 2002, ss 14, 31). The statement allocates the benefit and the burden of such matters as support, access, services, defects, repairs and common facilities and must also require the commonhold association to insure, repair and maintain the common parts (CALRA 2002, s 26). The directors of the commonhold association have a statutory responsibility to establish and maintain a 'reserve' fund or funds for financing repair and maintenance. For this purpose all unit-holders within the commonhold scheme may be required to pay a proportionate levy or service charge (CALRA 2002, s 39(1)–(2)). The rights and obligations contained in the commonhold community statement attach automatically by force of statute to each unit, irrespective of subsequent changes in the ownership of the unit, thus forming a comprehensive framework for the long-term governance of relationships and mutual dealings within the commonhold community.

— *Management by the commonhold association* The commonhold association is a private company limited by guarantee (see CALRA 2002, s 34(1)), which owns the common parts and is charged with a statutory duty to manage the development 'so as to permit or facilitate so far as possible' the exercise by each unit-holder (or his tenant) of his rights and the enjoyment by each unit-holder of the freehold estate in his unit (CALRA 2002, s 35(1), (4)). Every unit-holder is entitled to be entered in the register of members of the relevant commonhold association (CALRA 2002, Sch 3, Part 2, para 7) and to vote accordingly. The commonhold community thus manages its own affairs without reference to a third party landlord, although some fears have been expressed that this may lead to tyranny by the majority in the matter of decisions affecting the whole community (see e.g. P Kenny [2003] Conv 3). The directors of the community association also have certain powers to require or ensure due compliance by a unit-holder or his tenant with any duty imposed by the commonhold community statement or any relevant statutory provision (CALRA 2002, ss 35(2), 37). There is, moreover, to be provision for the reference of disputes to some form of alternative dispute resolution (e.g. by reference to an approved Ombudsman of disputes arising between the commonhold association and individual unit-holders, but not of disputes between unit-holders themselves (see CALRA 2002, s 42)).

— *Dealings with a commonhold unit* The commonhold community statement must not prevent or restrict the transfer of a freehold estate in a commonhold unit (CALRA 2002, s 15(2)), although on any transfer the new unit-holder has a statutory obligation to notify the commonhold association of the fact of transfer.

• *Automatic transmission of rights and obligations* One of the major advantages of commonhold ownership is undoubtedly the statutory provision that any right or duty conferred or imposed by the commonhold community statement will 'affect a new unit-holder in the same way as it affected the former unit-holder' (CALRA 2002, s 16(1)), thus removing at a stroke the almost intractable difficulty which, for centuries, has impeded the transmission of the burden of freehold covenants on a transfer of land (**13.12**).

• *Other dealings* The unit-holder is free to grant a mortgage charge over his or her unit (CALRA 2002, s 20(1), (3), (6)), although the creation, grant or transfer of other interests (e.g. an easement) in or over the whole or part of the unit may require the participation or written consent of the commonhold association (CALRA 2002, s 20(3)–(4)). Certain restrictions curtail the power of residential unit-holders to grant long leases in respect of their units (CALRA 2002, s 17), thus reflecting yet again the current government distaste for leasehold estates in residential premises (**7.10**).

— *Termination of a commonhold scheme* A commonhold scheme may be terminated voluntarily by a winding-up resolution passed by the commonhold association (in some cases with the necessary addition of a court order) or compulsorily by court order (CALRA 2002, ss 43–55).

FURTHER READING

Gray and Gray, *Elements of Land Law* (4th edn, OUP, 2005), ch 7.

Relevant sections of this work and other land law textbooks may be supplemented with:

Bright, Susan 'Avoiding Tenancy Legislation: Sham and Contracting Out Revisited' [2002] *CLJ* 146.

Bright, Susan 'Ending Tenancies by Notice to Quit: the Human Rights Challenge' (2004) 120 *LQR* 398.

Clarke, David 'The Enactment of Commonhold—Problems, Principles and Perspectives' [2002] *Conv* 349.

Hinojosa, John-Paul 'On Property, Leases, Licences, Horses and Carts: Revisiting *Bruton v London & Quadrant Housing Trust*' [2005] *Conv* 114.

Howell, Jean 'Land Law in an E-Conveyancing World' [2006] *Conv* 553.

Loveland, Ian 'After Qazi: 1—Sole Tenant Termination of Joint Tenancies and Article 8 ECHR' [2005] *Conv* 123.

Pawlowski, Mark 'Acceptance of Repudiatory Breach in Leases' [1995] *Conv* 379.

Pawlowski, Mark and Brown, James '*Bruton*: a new species to tenancy?' (2000) 4 *L & TR* 119.

Smith, Peter 'The Purity of Commonholds' [2004] *Conv* 194.

SELF-TEST QUESTIONS

1   Which transactions trigger registration of title at Land Registry (**7.7, 7.19–7.22**)?

2   What is the difference between a lease and a licence (**7.11–7.16**)?

3   Are leaseholds essentially proprietary estates or merely contractual phenomena (**7.10–7.16, 7.31, 7.35–7.36**)?

8

Other legal estates in land

SUMMARY

This chapter introduces a further range of interests and charges affecting land which are statutorily declared to be capable of existing *at law*. The holder of any of these entitlements is eligible under the Land Registration Act 2002 to be registered as 'proprietor' of the right in question. In view of their registrable status within the statutory scheme, these categories of entitlement must be isolated and identified with care. They include:

- easements (**8.5–8.24**);

- profits *à prendre* (**8.4, 8.25–8.26**);

- rentcharges (**8.27**);

- certain kinds of mortgage charge (**8.28–8.34**); and

- rights of entry (**8.35**).

This chapter is concerned with the definition of these potentially legal estates in land, the ways in which they may be created, transferred and extinguished, and the manner in which each is accommodated within the regimes of registered (and unregistered) title.

To the extent that any of these entitlements fails to attain the status of a legal estate—for want of due formality or registration—it ranks as merely the equitable version of the right concerned and is therefore dealt with in the more general treatment of equitable rights located in Chapter 9. The regulation (as distinct from the definition) of mortgage charges is the subject of detailed discussion in Chapter 15.

Statutory catalogue of legal interests and charges

8.1 Chapter 7 provided an analysis of the *fee simple absolute in possession* and the *term of years absolute,* the two primary estates in land demarcated by LPA 1925, s 1(1) as having the potential to exist at law. The present chapter shifts the focus to other categories of right in or over land which are likewise indicated (by LPA 1925, s 1(2)) as being 'capable of subsisting or of being conveyed or created at law.' These rights, to the extent that they actually subsist or have been conveyed or created 'at law', are also referred to as 'legal estates' (see LPA 1925, s 1(4), **2.30**). However, their distinguishing feature is that they all comprise entitlements exercisable over or in respect of someone else's land, i.e. land in which some other person is entitled to a freehold or leasehold estate. This group includes certain kinds of:

- easement (**8.3**);

- profit *à prendre* (**8.4**);

- rentcharge (**8.27**);

- mortgage charge (**8.28**); and

- right of entry (**8.35**).

The distribution of proprietary entitlement

8.2 We noted earlier (**2.5**) that it is possible for a number of people to acquire different, but essentially compatible, rights in or over the same land. The law does not positively require cooperation between neighbours, but the most efficient utilisation of land resources usually occurs only where the privileges inherent in estate ownership are parcelled out amongst a number of persons—often between neighbouring landowners—as part of a more general scheme of social or commercial interaction. It rarely makes sense, for instance, that someone should be required to purchase an entire freehold or leasehold estate in an adjacent piece of land merely in order permanently to secure some valued user facility (e.g. a right of way) connected with that land.

The present chapter is therefore concerned with the most important categories of right which may be acquired over other people's land. The rights contained in these categories comprise various forms of *proprietary* (as distinct from *personal*) entitlement, with the usual consequence in English law that they have the capacity to bind third parties (**2.12–2.14**). But, for precisely this reason, the law draws fairly stringent definitional boundaries around the species of incorporeal right which enjoy the potential of third party impact (**2.18**). This imposition of severely limiting threshold criteria is traditionally rationalised as being necessary in order to prevent the proliferation of undesirable long-term burdens or 'clogs upon title' (Gray and Gray, 'The Rhetoric of Realty', in J Getzler (ed), *Rationalizing Property, Equity and Trusts: Essays in Honour of Edward Burn* (Butterworths, 2003), pp 210–13). In the absence of restrictive rules governing the creation and distribution of land rights, it is feared that land would become encumbered by useless and anti-social rights of dubious enforceability, vested in unspecified or unidentifiable third parties (see *Keppell v Bailey* (1834)). The resulting chaos, it is said, would be inimical to the large social interest which pervades the law of property—namely, that property should be both readily alienable and capable of commercial exploitation (**2.10**).

Easements and profits *à prendre*

8.3　An *easement* comprises either a positive or a negative right of user over the land of another. The easement must be annexed—i e., its benefit must be attached—to one piece of land (the 'dominant tenement') and must be exercisable over another piece of land (the 'servient tenement'). The easement entitles the dominant owner to use the servient land in a particular way or, indeed, to prevent the owner of the servient land from using his own land in a particular way. A typical example is provided by the limited form of user comprised in a right of way over another's land. The owner of the incorporeal right of way is regarded in English law as holding some of the 'property' in the servient land in the guise of a proprietary right of easement (**2.5**). But an easement cannot extend a right of user to the point where it becomes a right to take or abstract part of another's land or its natural produce: such a right is classified not as an easement but as a profit *à prendre* (**8.4**). Likewise a claim of right to any particularly intense form of land use (measured either geographically or temporally) may indicate that the claimant is alleging an exclusiveness of possession more readily associated with ownership of a freehold or leasehold estate in the land (see e.g. *Copeland v Greenhalf* (1952), **8.14**; *Taylor v North West Water* (1995), **3.4**).

Defining characteristics of a profit *à prendre*

8.4　A profit *à prendre* is a proprietary interest in another's land which confers on the owner of the profit a right to take part of the soil, minerals or natural produce of the 'servient tenement'. Unlike an easement (**8.6**), a profit *à prendre* may exist 'in gross', i.e. the owner of the profit need not be the owner of any adjoining or neighbouring land or indeed of any land at all. The profit may comprise a right to take either some part of the servient land itself (e.g. sand or gravel) or something which grows on that land (e.g. grass, crops, fruit or timber) or fish, fowl or wild animals which are found on the servient owner's land or in his waters. The profit entitles its holder to take or sever the subject matter of the profit from the land, but this subject matter must be something which is capable of ownership. A right to take water itself cannot, for instance, comprise a profit, since water is incapable of being owned (*Alfred F Beckett Ltd v Lyons* (1967)). A profit *à prendre* may, however, confer either an exclusive right or a right enjoyed in common with others (including the grantor).

Defining characteristics of an easement

8.5 In view of the proprietary potential of the easement, the courts have applied strict qualifying conditions to the class of rights which may be asserted under this head. In *Re Ellenborough Park* (1956) Danckwerts J confirmed the classic statement of the essential qualities of an easement:

- there must be a dominant and a servient tenement (**8.6**);
- an easement must 'accommodate' the dominant tenement (**8.7**);
- the dominant and servient owners must be different persons (**8.8**);
- the right claimed must be capable of forming the subject matter of a grant (**8.9**).

Irrespective of the precise label which the right in question may have been given by the parties themselves, there is a strong tendency to accord the status of an easement to any right which satisfies these requirements. We must examine each criterion in turn.

There must be a dominant tenement and a servient tenement

8.6 Unlike the law of many other jurisdictions, English law generally requires that an easement must be appurtenant to a defined area of 'dominant' land (**2.5**): it *cannot* exist 'in gross' (i.e. unattached to dominant land). An easement is necessarily linked, therefore, with two parcels of land, its benefit being attached to the *dominant tenement* and its burden being asserted against a *servient tenement* (see *London & Blenheim Estates Ltd v Ladbroke Retail Parks Ltd* (1992) per Deputy Judge Paul Baker QC). Since an easement connotes an essentially *real* as distinct from *personal* relationship, it must be possible to point to a particular piece of land (or tenement) which is benefited or commoded by the right claimed as an easement. Thus, for instance, it could never be said that a member of a golf club has acquired an easement to play golf on the club course, since there exists no dominant tenement in the sense required (*Banstead Downs Golf Club v Customs and Excise Comrs* (1974)). As this last example clearly illustrates, such a right 'in gross' is 'personal only, and cannot be assigned' (see *Ackroyd v Smith* (1850) per Cresswell J). The requirement of dominant and servient tenements is sometimes abrogated in the case of statutory easements (**8.19**) and it would be true to say that its rationale has increasingly come into doubt in modern conditions. Nevertheless, the prohibition of easements in gross helps to prevent the distribution of burdensome user rights amongst vast numbers of mobile and (eventually) unidentifiable persons and may even serve the ecologically important purpose of protecting fragile land from excessive and damaging traffic. Moreover, the annexing of a defined burden to a servient tenement and of an equivalent benefit to a dominant tenement emphasises the proprietary character of the easement, with the consequence that burden and benefit can run with their respective tenements in such manner as to affect the successors in title of the original grantor and grantee (**8.24**).

The easement must 'accommodate' the dominant tenement

8.7 An easement must confer a significant benefit on the dominant land as distinct from merely offering some personal advantage or facility to the dominant owner. This conventional criterion of easement status is, however, somewhat elusive, not least since there is a crude sense in which all benefits are ultimately enjoyable only by people rather than by land. But the core idea is that an easement, properly so called, must make the dominant land more beneficial or commodious in a way which is capable of applying indifferently to both the current dominant owner and his successors in title. Again, the benefit must be *real* as distinct from *personal*; and the dominant land must be sufficiently closely situated to derive the practical benefit of the relevant user over the servient land. Thus, in the classic dictum, there cannot be 'a right of way over land in Kent appurtenant to an estate in Northumberland' (*Bailey v Stephens* (1862) per Byles J). Moreover, the test of an easement is not necessarily whether the market value of the dominant land is enhanced, but whether the user 'accommodates' the dominant land itself. This question is often heavily coloured by value judgements about the propriety of using the law of easements to confer long-term protection on various kinds of land use. Easements do not, in general, exist to safeguard purely personal or blatantly commercial advantage.

> *Hill v Tupper* (1863) The owner of a canal leased to H some land on the canal bank (including a landing stage), and purported to grant H a 'sole and exclusive' right to put pleasure boats on the canal. When T, the landlord of a nearby inn, later interfered with H's trade by putting rival boats on the canal, H claimed to have an exclusive easement over the waterway. The claim failed, partly because of the court's fear of proliferating burdens on land, partly because the exclusiveness of user claimed was over-broad, and partly because H was effectively seeking, under the banner of an easement, to set up a commercial monopoly which had no normal connection with the ordinary use of the land leased to him. Above all, H's right was not demonstrably appurtenant to any dominant tenement. Far from H's right over the canal 'accommodating' the landing stage, that landing stage served in reality to facilitate the efficient pursuit of a wholly independent business enterprise on the canal. Accordingly H had a mere licence (unenforceable against T), as distinct from a generally enforceable easement over the canal (**4.11**).

> *Re Ellenborough Park* (1956) A number of owners of residential properties had been given a right of common enjoyment of a park which was adjacent to their houses and which was vested in trustees. This right was held to have been validly granted as an easement. The Court of Appeal regarded the park as a communal garden for the houses and took the view that 'the use of a garden undoubtedly enhances, and is connected with, the normal enjoyment of the house to which it belongs'.

The requirement that an easement must accommodate defined land has, particularly in recent years, thrown up an additional (and difficult) question whether a right granted to X for the benefit of Greenacre may also be used by X for the benefit of X's adjacent land, Redacre. There is longstanding authority that, in effecting an unauthorised extension of the dominant tenement, such user constitutes a trespass (see *Harris v Flower* (1904), as followed in *Peacock v Custins* (2002)). It is possible that an easement for Greenacre can properly serve Redacre as well if the user vis-à-vis Redacre is merely 'ancillary' to the primary benefit which the easement confers on Greenacre (see *Massey v Boulden* (2003) at [45]). The courts are, however, extremely reluctant to expand the idea of 'ancillary' user (see e.g. the rejection in *Das v Linden Mews Ltd* (2003) that a right of way benefiting X's dwelling-house on Greenacre could also be used as a means of access to a parking area on X's adjacent land, Redacre).

Dominant and servient tenements must be owned or occupied by different persons

8.8 Since an easement is by definition a right over somebody else's land, it is impossible that the same person should both own *and occupy* the dominant and servient tenements. A person cannot meaningfully have rights against himself (see *Peckham v Ellison* (2000) per Cazalet J), but the required diversity of occupation is satisfied as between landlord and tenant. Thus a tenant may acquire an easement over his landlord's land and a landlord may likewise be entitled to an easement over land which is the subject of a lease.

The right claimed must be capable of forming the subject matter of a grant

8.9 All easements must be capable of forming the subject matter of a grant by deed (even if they are not actually so granted). This apparently innocuous requirement contains a compendious subset of important and interlinking criteria for the constitution of a valid easement, each criterion imposing strict parameters on the kinds of right admissible under the head of easement:

- there must be a capable grantor and a capable grantee (**8.10**);
- the right must be sufficiently definite (**8.11**);
- the right must be within the general nature of the rights traditionally recognised as easements (**8.12**);
- the right must not impose any positive burden on the servient owner (**8.13**);
- the right must not exclude reasonable alternative users of the servient tenement (**8.14**).

There must be a capable grantor and capable grantee

8.10 No easement may be created except by a person who is competent to subject the servient land to an easement. Thus, save in cases of easements arising by way of *estoppel* (**8.19**), an easement may be carved out of land only by a person currently entitled to a freehold or leasehold estate in the land. Likewise no easement may be claimed if the alleged dominant owner was at the time legally incompetent to receive such a grant (e.g. a company without power to acquire easements).

The right must be sufficiently definite

8.11 In order to be capable of grant by deed, all easements must have a certain quality of definitional clarity (**2.18, 8.2**). The category of easement therefore excludes user rights which are loose, over-broad or ill-defined. There can, for instance, be no easement in respect of a good view (see *Hunter v Canary Wharf Ltd* (1997)): such a right may be acquired only by way of a restrictive covenant which precludes the owner of neighbouring land from obstructing the view by erecting new buildings on his land (**9.24**). Nor can an easement be granted to protect the uninterrupted access of light or air except through defined apertures in a building. English law likewise recognises no easement of indefinite privacy. Even a claim of harmless recreational user—such as the right to wander at will over another's land (or *ius spatiandi*)—is vulnerable as an easement, in part because it probably confers a mere personal benefit (**8.7**), and in part because it lacks the discreteness of definition required by the law of easements (see e.g. the 'Stonehenge case', *Attorney-General v Antrobus* (1905)). So wide-ranging a right cannot be comprised in an easement, since it encapsulates precisely the sort of unrestricted entitlement which characterises ownership of a fee simple estate or term of years (**3.4, 8.14**).

> *Hunter v Canary Wharf Ltd* (1997) D's recently constructed building, the Canary Wharf Tower, caused extensive interference with P's television reception. Pointing in particular to the indeterminate nature of the amenity supposedly injured, the House of Lords held that English law knows no such right as an easement to receive a television signal.

The right must be within the general nature of the rights traditionally recognised as easements

8.12 In keeping with the innately conservative tradition of English property law, courts are normally reluctant to admit new kinds of right to the status of easement (see e.g. *Hill v Tupper* (1863), **8.7**). Although the list of easements is not closed, there is a general unwillingness to include within it any entitlement which lies markedly outside the range of rights which have hitherto been acknowledged as easements. There is, for instance, no such easement known to the law as a right to hit cricket balls into your neighbour's land (see *Miller v Jackson* (1977) per Lord Denning MR). The courts have evinced a particular disinclination to sanction the creation of new *negative* easements, i.e. easements which require the servient owner to refrain from certain action on his own land (see *Hunter v Canary Wharf Ltd* (1997) per Lord Hope of Craighead). Thus, for example, the Court of Appeal has rejected the claim of a supposed easement of protection from the weather, on the ground that such a right would effectively inhibit legitimate development on adjoining land (*Phipps v Pears* (1965)). Such a constraint can be enforced against a neighbouring landowner only after a process of bargain resulting in the creation of a restrictive covenant (**9.24**) (though see now *Rees v Skerrett* (2001)).

The right must not impose any positive burden on the servient owner

8.13 A true easement generally requires of the servient owner nothing more than an act of sufferance, in allowing the dominant owner to do something on the servient land or in abstaining from some action of his own on that land. Except in rather special (and possibly anomalous) circumstances, an easement must not involve the servient owner in any expenditure of money or in any positive or onerous action (see *Liverpool CC v Irwin* (1977) per Lord Wilberforce). Thus, for instance, no easement can require the servient owner to repair a particular facility or access. Likewise no easement can impose a positive obligation to maintain a supply of water or electricity, although a servient owner may validly be subjected to an easement which requires that he take no positive steps to interfere with an existing supply, e.g. by cutting it off or otherwise preventing its passage across the servient land (see *Duffy v Lamb* (1997)).

The right must not exclude reasonable alternative users of the servient tenement

8.14 English law has traditionally disapproved of 'possessory' easements, on the ground that a claim of exclusive possession or joint occupation of the supposedly servient land more closely resembles a claim of freehold or leasehold ownership (**3.4, 8.3**). The archetypal easement merely permits some form of restrained or intermittent user of the servient land (as in the case of a right of way). The greater the intensity of user claimed, the less likely the courts are to admit the existence of an easement. '[T]here is no easement known to the law which gives exclusive and unrestricted use of a piece of land' (*Reilly v Booth* (1890) per Lopes LJ). Accordingly, a claim that the alleged servient owner can visit the land only by invitation is fatal to any claim of easement (see e.g. *Hanina v Morland* (2000)).

> *Copeland v Greenhalf* (1952) For 50 years G, a wheelwright, had used a narrow strip of C's land to store motor vehicles awaiting and undergoing repair. Upjohn J held that the right claimed by G was too extensive to constitute an easement in law. G was effectively claiming 'the whole beneficial user' of one strip of C's land. A right of such 'wide and undefined nature' could not be the proper subject matter of an easement. G's claim comprised 'virtually a claim to possession of the servient tenement, if necessary to the exclusion of the owner', and was therefore more akin to an allegation of adverse possession of C's land.

— *A test of 'substantial interference'* In more recent years, however, the supposed rule against possessory easements has been slightly relaxed. It is likely nowadays that a claim of easement will be disallowed on the ground of intensity of user *only if* the right claimed is apt to 'leave the servient owner without any reasonable use of his land' (*London & Blenheim Estates Ltd v Ladbroke Retail Parks Ltd* (1992) per Deputy Judge Paul Baker QC). The user asserted must not amount to an 'invasion of the servient land', and the disinclination to accept possessory easements has probably been commuted to a recognition that the class of easements cannot include any claim which substantially interferes with the whole of the servient tract or exhausts its entire beneficial user. The question whether the servient owner is deprived of all reasonable alternative user is ultimately a test of fact and degree (see e.g. *Jackson v Mulvaney* (2003), **2.3**). Thus, while an easement cannot comprise an exclusive right to store goods in a confined cellar (see e.g. *Grigsby v Melville* (1974)), a valid claim of easement may be asserted in the form of less obstructive users of more general areas of land.

— *Parking 'easements'* Doubt still surrounds the vexed issue whether a right to park a car can constitute an easement. There has been a modern drift towards acceptance of the easement status of parking rights (see e.g. *London & Blenheim Estates Ltd v Ladbroke Retail Parks Ltd* (1992) per Deputy Judge Paul Baker QC). Nevertheless the Court of Appeal has preferred to leave the question open (see *Saeed v Plustrade Ltd* (2002) at [22]), whilst making it clear that a claim to monopolise a limited area (e.g. by parking cars on it during all useful working hours of the day) constitutes such a usurpation of the rights of the alleged servient owner as to 'make his ownership of the land illusory' (see *Batchelor v Marlow* (2003) at [18]). No easement can extend to the point where the servient estate owner is left 'without any reasonable use of his land' (see also *Montrose Court Holdings Ltd v Shamash* (2006) at [30], where the Court of Appeal doubted whether an exclusive right to park for a continuous period of 72 hours could subsist as an easement).

Creation of easements and profits *à prendre*

8.15 Easements and profits *à prendre* are created in a variety of ways. Creation may be by way of either *grant* or *reservation* (**8.17**); and the *duration* of the rights created can extend in perpetuity or for a fixed term or, indeed, for any other period of time (**8.16**). Creation may be either *express* (**8.19, 8.23**), *implied* (**8.20, 8.23**) or *presumed* (**8.22**); and the means of creation can be either *formal* or *informal* (**8.16, 9.12–9.13**). Whether an easement or profit is *legal* or *equitable* turns on the precise circumstances of its creation.

Creation of easements and profits *à prendre* at law

8.16 An easement or profit *à prendre* can be created *at law* only if certain cumulative conditions are fulfilled:

— *Capacity of grantor* The grantor of the easement or profit must himself hold a legal estate in the servient land (i.e. a legal fee simple or a legal term of years). Any right granted out of a merely equitable estate can only be *equitable*.

— *Duration* The duration of a legal easement or profit must be framed on the analogy of either a *freehold* or a *leasehold*, i.e. the entitlement must be created 'for an interest equivalent to an estate in fee simple absolute in possession or a term of years absolute' (LPA 1925, s 1(2)(a); LRA 2002, s 27(4), Sch 2, paras 6(3), 7(1)(a)). Thus legal quality attaches, at least potentially, to rights which are granted or reserved without limit of time or for a fixed period of time, but an easement or profit created for an indeterminate period other than in perpetuity (e.g. for life) can take effect only *in equity*.

— *Mode of creation* Legal easements and profits may be created in several ways.

• *Creation by deed* A legal easement or profit must be created by *deed* (see LPA 1925, s 52(1), **7.6**) or must arise by *statute* (**8.19**), by *implication* (**8.20, 8.23**), or by *prescription* (**8.21**). In the context of unregistered land, formal creation by deed is sufficient to establish the legal quality of a right, provided that the entitlement in question is inherently capable of creation at law. Thus, for example, an easement for life, even if created by deed, can give rise to no more than an equitable easement.

• *Voluntary registration of certain profits* The grantee of a profit *à prendre* in gross over unregistered land (**8.4**) may apply for voluntary first registration of title to his profit under a unique title number at Land Registry (see LRR 2003, r 2(2)(b)), provided that the profit was granted in perpetuity or for a term which still has more than seven years left to run (LRA 2002, s 3(1)(d), (2)–(3), **2.31**). In this way the grantee can opt to appear on the Land Register as the substantively registered proprietor of a legal estate in the relevant profit.

— *Completion by registration* The express creation of a legal easement or a profit *à prendre* over *registered* land ranks as a disposition of a registered estate which must itself be 'completed' by some form of registration at Land Registry (LRA 2002, s 27(2)(d), **7.8**). An 'express' grant does not, for present purposes, include any grant resulting from the operation of LPA 1925, s 62 (**8.20**) (see LRA 2002, s 27(7)).

• *Profits* à prendre *in gross* The recipient of a profit *à prendre* in gross created out of registered land is required, as a precondition of taking a legal estate in the profit, to complete the disposition by applying to be entered under a unique title number in the Land Register as proprietor of the profit (LRA 2002, Sch 2, para 6(1)–(2), **2.30**). The holder of the profit thus acquires an independently registered title to his profit (see LRR 2003, r 2(2)(b)), but only where the profit was created without limit of time or for a term of more than seven years. The profit should also be entered by 'notice' in the register of title of the land over which it is exercisable (LRA 2002, s 38, Sch 2, para 6(2)(b), **12.11**).

• *Easements and all other profits* à prendre The creation of legal easements and other legal profits (i.e. appurtenant profits) out of registered land must be completed by the entry of a 'notice' in respect of the relevant burden in the registered title of the *servient* owner (LRA 2002, s 38, Sch 2, para 7(2)(a); LRR 2003, r 9(a)) and by the registration of the correlative benefit in the register of title (if any) of the *dominant* owner (LRA 2002, ss 27(2)(d), 59(1), Sch 2, para 7(2)(b); LRR 2003, r 5(b)(ii), **1.14**, **2.31**). The dominant owner thus becomes, by non-substantive registration, the proprietor of a registered 'legal estate' in the particular easement or profit. In *leasehold* land no separate entries are necessary in respect of easements granted by the lease itself, since the lease is incorporated by reference into the property register of the dominant land and is noted in the charges register of the servient land.

— *Failure to comply with the preconditions of creation at law* All easements or profits created otherwise than in due compliance with the conditions outlined above are inevitably *equitable* only (LPA 1925, s 1(3); LRA 2002, s 27(1), **9.13**). Moreover, under the new regime of the LRA 2002, an easement or profit over registered land whose express grant is not completed by registration can never 'override' further registered dealings with the land (LRA 2002, s 29(1), (2)(a)(ii), Sch 3, para 3(1), **12.26**).

Distinction between grant and reservation

8.17 The difference between *grant* and *reservation* turns on the identity of the party in whose favour the easement or profit is created.

— *Grant* occurs where a landowner, X, creates in favour of Y an easement or profit over land held by X. Consistently with the prohibition of easements in gross (**8.6**), Y must, in the case of a grant of easement, hold some dominant land capable of deriving benefit (**2.5**). The grant of an easement often occurs on a subdivision of X's land, Y (the transferee of a part of the land) taking the benefit of an easement granted over the land retained by X.

— *Reservation* arises where a landowner, X, disposes of part of his land to Y on terms that X shall nevertheless retain an easement or profit *over the land transferred to Y*. Here the easement or profit concerned is one created in favour of X, the *transferor* of the land.

Grant of easements and profits

8.18 Grant of an easement or profit *à prendre* may be brought about by express grant (**8.19**), implied grant (**8.20**) or prescription (**8.21**).

Express grant

8.19 Express grant arises in three categories of case—by means of express words of grant, by way of estoppel, and by virtue of statute.

— *Express words of grant* Express words constitute the most common form of grant of easements and profits *à prendre*. A grant of an easement by express words is normally incorporated in a transfer of a freehold estate or a grant of a leasehold estate where it is intended that the new estate owner should enjoy certain rights of easement over the land retained by the transferor or lessor. For example, the builder of a housing development almost invariably grants the purchaser of each individual plot certain rights of way, rights of drainage and rights which facilitate the supply of mains services. The grant being contained in a deed of transfer or lease (subsequently registered where necessary (**8.16**)), the easements so created are *legal*. An expressly conferred profit *à prendre* is usually granted in conjunction with a licence to enter the servient land, in which case the licence is an incident of the grant of profit and is irrevocable during the term of the profit (**4.10**).

— *Estoppel* The doctrine of proprietary estoppel (**10.18**) provides what is really a subset of the category of express grant of easements and profits. If relied upon to the grantee's detriment, a grant of rights by informal means (i.e. otherwise than by deed) may sometimes generate an equity of estoppel to which a court will give effect by declaring that the intended grantee takes an easement or profit (see also *Valentine v Allen* (2003) at [73] per Hale LJ).

> *Crabb v Arun DC* (1976) C allowed himself to become landlocked in reliance on an 'agreement in principle' that he should have a right of access and egress over land belonging to an adjacent owner, A. C's failure to reserve a more formal right of way was regarded as sufficient detrimental reliance (**10.25**) to found an estoppel claim on the basis of which he was declared by the Court of Appeal to have the benefit of an easement (**10.25**).

Another variety of easement by estoppel arises where a person expressly grants an easement over land to which he currently has no title but to which he later acquires title (see **7.25**). Any subsequent acquisition of title by the grantor 'feeds the estoppel', so that the initial grant now operates as effectively as if the grantor had always had title to the land (*Rajapakse v Fernando* (1920)).

— *Statute* Easements and profits may be granted expressly by statute. Particularly in the case of easements, such grants are often made in favour of various public or privatised service utilities which provide and maintain supplies of gas, electricity and water. These easements represent an exception to the general principle which requires that an easement must accommodate a specific dominant tenement (**8.6–8.7**).

Implied grant

8.20 In certain kinds of circumstance the grant of an easement can be implied or inferred on behalf of a transferee of land. Since all such cases of grant are impliedly incorporated in a deed of transfer (**8.16**), the rights to which they give rise are inevitably *legal* rights. As such they become automatically enforceable (in the case of *unregistered* land) against successors in title of the servient land (**12.34**) and (in *registered* land) constitute an overriding interest (**8.24, 12.26**).

The categories of implied grant often overlap, but generally give expression to the principle that, in the absence of contrary intention, a grantor 'may not derogate from his grant' (i.e. he must not transfer land to another on terms which effectively negative the utility of the transfer). The cases of implied grant relate principally to easements (rather than to profits *à prendre*), but cannot convert into an easement any user which is intrinsically incapable of subsisting as an easement under the *Ellenborough Park* criteria (**8.5**) (see *P & S Platt Ltd v Crouch* (2004) at [43] per Peter Gibson LJ, **8.20**). These cases of implied grant fall into *four* categories:

— *Easements of necessity* An easement impliedly founded on necessity arises where a claimant can establish that, without the provision of the desired easement, his own tenement cannot be used at all. The criterion of necessity is strictly construed: it is not sufficient, for example, that a particular user of the alleged servient land is convenient or even *reasonably necessary* for the proper enjoyment of the alleged dominant tenement. The classic case of necessity is provided by the 'landlocked close'. If V transfers land to P which has no legally enforceable means of access except across land still owned by V, it is clear that the courts will imply on behalf of P an easement of access even though the conveyance or transfer to P made no express reference to such a right. In another, rather specific, case of necessity, statute now confers a judicial discretion to create temporary rights in the nature of an easement. The Access to Neighbouring Land Act 1992 authorises a court to make an 'access order' allowing unconsented entry upon adjoining or adjacent land for the purpose of certain works of preservation in respect of buildings on the entrant's own land (ANLA 1992, s 1(1)–(2)).

— *Easements of common intention* Easements may be implied in favour of the transferee of land in order to give effect to the common intention of transferor and transferee. Such easements are probably not essentially different from those implied from necessity (see *Nickerson v Barraclough* (1980) per Megarry V-C), in that a common intention to grant a particular easement will normally be found only in cases of necessity.

> *Wong v Beaumont Property Trust Ltd* (1965) W purchased leasehold premises for use as a Chinese restaurant, covenanting to comply with public health regulations and to eliminate all noxious smells and odours. Unknown to both W and BPT, his landlord, these obligations could be performed only by the installation of a new ventilation system leading through the upstairs premises retained by BPT. The Court of Appeal held that W was entitled to an easement in respect of the construction of the ventilation duct which would enable him to comply both with the terms of the lease and with public health regulations.

— *Quasi-easements (easements under the rule in Wheeldon v Burrows)* The rule in *Wheeldon v Burrows* (1879) operates to prevent derogation from grant on a subdivision of land. The rule confers on P, the transferee of a part of V's land, the benefit of any acts of user over the land retained by V, which V himself had earlier found it convenient to exercise on his own behalf during the period prior to the subdivision. (In this sense the rule goes far beyond the strict criterion imposed in respect of easements of necessity.) Prior to the transfer to P, such user could not truly have been described in terms of an easement—for the simple reason that both tenements were then within the common ownership and possession of V (**8.8, 8.26**). The rule in *Wheeldon v Burrows* operates upon these *quasi-easements* and causes them to ripen by implication into 'easements properly so called' in favour of the land now held by P (see *Peckham v Ellison* (2000)). The doctrine of quasi-easements provides a mode of implied grant applicable to rights of way, support and light, together with many other users 'enjoyed *de facto* during unity of possession [which] would, had that unity not existed, have been easements' (*Nelson v Walker* (1910) per Isaacs J). The doctrine applies not only to legal grants (e.g. of an estate in fee simple or a term of years), but also to grants which take effect only in equity (e.g. on a contract for a lease (**9.8–9.9**)) (see *Borman v Griffith* (1930)). It is generally thought, however, that the rule in *Wheeldon v Burrows* cannot apply to profits *à prendre*. In the case of easements, moreover, it applies only to acts of user which were:

- *'continuous and apparent'*—enjoyed over substantial periods of time and discoverable on careful inspection, e.g. user of a well-worn track (*Hansford v Jago* (1921); see, conversely, *Robinson Webster (Holdings) Ltd v Agombar* (2002) at [81]);

- *reasonably necessary for the enjoyment of the alleged dominant tenement*—a criterion probably synonymous with 'continuous and apparent user' (see *Wheeler v JJ Saunders Ltd* (1996)); and

- *exercised prior to and at the date of transfer*—the rule catches only those quasi-easements which had been, and at the time of the relevant transfer were still, used by the owner of the entirety for the benefit of the part now conveyed away.

> **Example**: If V, while he occupied the quasi-dominant tenement prior to subdivision (or lease of part) of his land, was accustomed to pass and re-pass along a track or driveway over land which he still retains after the disposition, this user may now be claimed by P to be annexed, as of right, to what was the quasi-dominant tenement. In effect P receives, as implied easements, such rights over the land retained by V which V had previously found to be reasonably necessary for the proper enjoyment and utilisation of the tenement now transferred to P (see e.g. *Holaw (470) Ltd v Stockton Estates Ltd* (2001)).

— *Easements under Law of Property Act 1925, s 62* Another form of implied grant of easements and profits *à prendre* is made possible by the operation of the 'word-saving provision' contained in LPA 1925, s 62 (**1.8**). Section 62 contains 'general words' which, in the absence of any contrary intention expressed in the conveyance (see LPA 1925, s 62(4)), imply into any conveyance of a legal estate in land a number of rights thenceforth to be enjoyed by the purchaser of that estate. The section passes to the purchaser of land the benefit of existing easements and profits and also those 'liberties, privileges, ... rights, and advantages' which appertain to the land conveyed, or are reputed to appertain to it, or which are at the date of the conveyance enjoyed with that land (see e.g. *Kent v Kavanagh* (2006) at [57]). This provision sometimes has the incidental—and somewhat surprising—effect of creating entirely new easements and profits out of many kinds of quasi-easement, right or even merely revocable privilege subsisting at the date of the relevant conveyance (see *Peckham v Ellison* (2000) per Cazalet J). The logic supposedly enabling section 62 to bring about such a transmutation of rights has been subjected to incisive criticism (see L Tee, 'Metamorphoses and Section 62 of the Law of Property Act 1925' [1998] *Conv* 115).

> *International Tea Stores Co v Hobbs* (1903) L owned two adjacent plots of land in fee simple, occupying one of them himself and leasing the other to a tenant, T. During the currency of the lease L permitted T, as a matter of grace and favour, to use a means of access to T's premises which ran across the plot occupied by L. L later conveyed to T the freehold reversion in the previously rented premises. Farwell J held that this conveyance caused the statutory 'general words' provision to vest in T not only a freehold estate in the land purchased but also a right *by way of easement* to continue against L the user which had previously been merely precarious. What was only a licence before the conveyance was converted into a *legal easement*. (A similar result would have followed if L had granted a new lease to T.)

Section 62 is not constrained by the same tight conditions which apply under the rule in *Wheeldon v Burrows*, but is qualified by other important restrictions.

- *Prior diversity of occupation* Section 62 normally operates only where there has been some 'diversity of ownership or occupation of the quasi-dominant and quasi-servient tenements prior to the conveyance' (*Sovmots Investments Ltd v Secretary of State for the Environment* (1979) per Lord Edmund-Davies). Without at least some element of prior separate occupation of two tenements it would be difficult to point to any 'rights' or 'liberties' or 'privileges' (strictly so-called) which might be caught by the operation of section 62 (see *Long v Gowlett* (1923)). Such 'prior diversity of occupation' is, of course, precisely what was present in the landlord-tenant situation dealt with in *International Tea Stores Co v Hobbs*, but may be destroyed by a period of common occupation of both tenements (even as short as one week) immediately before the relevant conveyance (see *Payne v Inwood* (1997)). The only exception to the requirement of 'prior diversity of occupation' arises where the existence of some advantage intrinsically associated with one tenement was already obvious, as under the rule in *Wheeldon v Burrows*, on the basis of continuous and apparent user (see e.g. *P & S Platt Ltd v Crouch* (2004)).

> *P & S Platt Ltd v Crouch* (2004) C and his wife transferred to P Ltd their hotel premises on the Norfolk Broads, retaining for themselves adjacent land on which they had previously allowed hotel patrons to moor boats, fish, or simply pass and repass. P Ltd took an option to purchase this adjacent land for an extra £200,000, but failed to exercise the option before its expiry date. The Court of Appeal nevertheless held that P Ltd, who had taken over the hotel as a going concern, had acquired the relevant mooring, fishing and other associated rights by virtue of LPA 1925, s 62. These rights comprised 'continuous and apparent' entitlements which, even in the absence of 'prior diversity of occupation' of the various tenements, 'appertain[ed] to and were reputed to appertain to and were enjoyed with the hotel.'

• *No application to temporary or excessively precarious advantages* Section 62 has been said to exclude any privilege which was contemplated by the parties as being of a 'purely temporary' nature (see *Wright v Macadam* (1949); *P & S Platt Ltd v Crouch* (2004) at [59]) or which was exercised on an excessively intermittent basis or on the footing of an extremely fragile permission (see *Green v Ashco Horticulturist Ltd* (1966)).

Prescription

8.21 A third method of acquisition of easements and profits *à prendre* is provided by the law of prescription or long user. Prescriptive acquisition is something of a hybrid, since it combines elements of *fictional* express grant with implications derived from long-term user. We have already seen (**6.4**) that the law of property tends to legitimise acts of user which have continued de facto over long periods of time (see *R v Oxfordshire CC, ex parte Sunningwell PC* (2000) per Lord Hoffmann; *Bakewell Management Ltd v Brandwood* (2004) per Lord Hope of Craighead). Thus, although there is no evidence of any actual grant, the law of prescription readily presumes a fictional grant of an easement or profit *à prendre* from the fact of prolonged enjoyment of rights over the land of another (generally for a period of at least 20 years). But, whereas the law of adverse possession operates negatively by extinguishing old titles, prescription operates positively and creatively by generating *new* rights. Prescriptive acquisition is underpinned by a strong element of deemed acquiescence by the servient owner in full knowledge of the circumstances surrounding the long user (see *Mills v Silver* (1991) per Dillon LJ). Although the precise grounds or theoretical rationales of prescriptive acquisition vary (**8.22**), their common feature is that a successful claimant must demonstrate the following:

— *User in fee simple*   Since prescriptive rights are perpetual in duration, prescription must be founded upon user by or on behalf of one fee simple owner against another fee simple owner. The common law does not, for example, attach prescriptive consequences to a user which began against a limited owner of the servient land (e.g. a tenant for years), largely on the ground that the fee simple owner should not be affected by a user of which he may have been unaware and which he was powerless to prevent (see *Pugh v Savage* (1970) per Cross LJ).

— *Continuous user*   The degree of continuity required depends obviously on the circumstances of the case and the nature of the right claimed. Infrequent user does not necessarily destroy a claim of continuity, and a prescriptive claim to a right of way may, for instance, succeed where there has been user on six to ten occasions each year for 35 years (*Diment v N H Foot Ltd* (1974)).

— *User as of right*   It is only against a background of assumed entitlement that the courts can infer the existence of some earlier grant from which the lawful exercise of an easement or profit is deemed to have derived. Obviously, therefore, no claim of right can be based on a claimant's illegal actions (unless it lay within the power of the alleged servient owner to authorise those actions and thereby counteract their essential unlawfulness: see *Bakewell Management Ltd v Brandwood* (2004)). It is not, however, fatal that the claimant mistakenly believed that he owned the disputed land anyway or that he already enjoyed rights by way of express grant (see *Bridle v Ruby* (1989)). It is commonly said that the user required for prescriptive acquisition must be *nec vi, nec clam, nec precario* (i.e. without force, without secrecy and without permission).

• *User nec vi*   Forcible user (e.g. by deliberate removal of an obstruction lawfully in situ or against a background of consistent protest by the landowner affected) vitiates any claim to entitlement *as of right* (see *R (Beresford) v Sunderland CC* (2004) at [56] per Lord Rodger of Earlsferry).

• *User nec clam*   No surreptitious or concealed user can found a prescriptive claim. Thus, for instance, underground fixings which remain long undetected cannot give rise to an easement by prescription (see *Union Lighterage Co v London Graving Dock Co* (1902)). Prescriptive user must be open and readily discoverable by an owner who is reasonably alert.

• *User nec precario*   Being premised on a claim of right, prescriptive acquisition cannot be generated by any 'precarious' user which is based on *permission* or *consent* from the landowner. Thus, for example, no prescription can normally be alleged where the claimant is required to make periodic payments to the landowner (*Mills v Silver* (1991)) or where a gate over a path is locked for substantial periods at the owner's discretion (see *Goldsmith v Burrow Construction Co Ltd* (1987)). It is not always easy, however, to distinguish between the kind of consent which negatives prescription and the element of deemed acquiescence which enables the courts to infer a grant of rights as the obvious explanation for some evident long user. Courts are naturally reluctant to uphold claims of prescription in cases where a landowner has merely tolerated a trespass out of good neighbourliness. For the purpose of prescriptive acquisition, true acquiescence by a servient owner is present (see *Dalton v Angus & Co* (1881) per Fry J) only where there is:

— a knowledge on the part of the servient owner as to the acts done;

— a power to stop the acts or to sue in respect of them; and

— an abstinence on his part from the exercise of such a power.

The user leading to prescription must be 'such as to bring home to the mind of a reasonable person that a continuous right of enjoyment is being asserted' (*Mills v Silver* (1991)). But if these circumstances are present, it will be no defence for the owner who does nothing to assert later that he merely tolerated the user in question (see *R v Oxfordshire CC, ex parte Sunningwell PC* (2000) per Lord Hoffmann).

Grounds of prescriptive acquisition

8.22 Both common law and statutory prescription depend largely on the fiction that long user is evidence of past grant, with the consequence that prescriptive rights, having been the subject matter of a presumed formal grant, are *legal* in character.

— *Common law presumption from long user* According to an almost redundant presumption of the common law, user as of right for more than 20 years is taken to indicate that the user in question must have commenced before remembered time, a date fixed somewhat arbitrarily as 1189, and that such user has now become unimpeachable. This fiction is easily frustrated, however, if a particular user could not possibly have been exercised or enjoyed at all times since 1189, e.g. if a building in respect of which an easement is claimed was clearly constructed after 1189 (see e.g. *Duke of Norfolk v Arbuthnot* (1880)).

— *Lost modern grant* The old common law presumption has nowadays been overtaken by the doctrine of 'lost modern grant'. This doctrine concedes that user dating back to 1189 cannot be proved, but treats the sheer fact of 20 years' user as providing the basis for the fiction that some incorporeal right, supportive of the user in question, was once the subject of a formal 'modern' grant which has since been misplaced and lost (see *Dalton v Angus & Co* (1881)). Thus, in a controversial juxtaposition of empirically founded and right-based notions of 'property' in land (**2.16**), English law generally presumes a prescriptive acquisition of easements and profits following continuous user as of right for a period of 20 years (see e.g. *Smith v Brudenell-Bruce* (2002) (right of way)).

— *Prescription Act 1832*   Statute law deals somewhat haphazardly with certain artificially distinguished categories of prescriptive acquisition. All such cases must, again, arise from user which is *nec vi, nec clam, nec precario.* The Prescription Act 1832, which can be invoked only in the context of litigation over an alleged incumbrance, provides that uninterrupted user as of right for 20 years cannot be defeated by evidence that such user commenced after 1189 (PA 1832, s 2). An easement (other than an easement of light) enjoyed for 40 years as of right and without interruption is deemed to be 'absolute and indefeasible' unless enjoyed by written consent or agreement (PA 1832, s 2). Special rules relate to an easement of light. Uninterrupted actual enjoyment of access to light (albeit not necessarily as of right) for a period of 20 years renders that access 'absolute and indefeasible' unless it was enjoyed merely by reason of consent or agreement in writing or by deed (PA 1832, s 3). A profit *à prendre* which has been enjoyed as of right and without interruption for a period of 60 years founds a prescriptive claim which is 'absolute and indefeasible' (PA 1832, s 1). Any period of time pleaded in support of a claim under the 1832 Act must be the period 'next before some suit or action' in which the claim is challenged (PA 1832, s 4), with the consequence that a discontinued period of long user which is isolated in the past cannot, irrespective of its duration, provide any basis of claim under the Act (see *Mills v Silver* (1991)). The confused and confusing provisions of the 1832 Act are a self-evident eyesore and are long overdue for statutory reform.

— *Possible statutory reform*   The Law Commission, whilst acknowledging the deficiencies of the Prescription Act 1832, has made the provisional proposal that, for the future, no prescription of easements or profits *à prendre* should be permissible except under the terms of the 1832 Act (Law Com No 254 (1998), paras 10.90–10.94, 10.111). The Law Commission is currently engaged in a comprehensive review of the law of easements.

Reservation of easements and profits

8.23   *Reservation* is the converse of *grant* (**8.17**) and occurs where a transferor of land reserves for himself easements or profits over the land which he transfers to another. Reservation may be either *express* or *implied.*

— *Express reservation*   If a vendor wishes to retain any right in the nature of an easement or profit *à prendre* in respect of land which he conveys to a purchaser, it is open to him to do so by means of express words contained in the document of transfer. Such a reservation is supposed to be construed strictly against the dominant owner who framed the reservation, the reservation thus operating 'at law without ... any regrant' (LPA 1925, s 65(1)). Somewhat perversely the relevant case law nevertheless seems to favour the proposition that express reservations of an easement or profit are to be construed against the servient owner and in favour of the dominant owner (see e.g. *St Edmundsbury and Ipswich Diocesan Board of Finance v Clark (No 2)* (1975)).

— *Implied reservation* The law is much more inclined to imply easements in favour of the *transferee* of land than in favour of the *transferor* (see *Peckham v Ellison* (2000) per Cazalet J). Therefore a transferor who wishes to reserve any rights over the land transferred by him must do so expressly in clear and unambiguous terms— this being the actual *decision* in, as distinct from the so-called *rule* emanating from, *Wheeldon v Burrows* (1879) (**8.20**). Implied reservation is possible in only two cases, namely those of necessity and common intention.

• *Easements of necessity* The implication of a reservation on grounds of necessity is rare, largely because a transferor must generally be out of his mind not to have reserved his entitlements expressly. But if, for instance, a transferor disposes of all the land adjacent to or surrounding the land which he retains, in circumstances where the only possible access to his 'landlocked close' lies across the transferred land, an easement of access will arise by implied reservation. Without such a reservation the transferor's retained land would be rendered completely unusable. In this context, however, necessity is strictly construed. No implied reservation is available if the retained land enjoys the benefit of a legal right of access over some other neighbour's land (*Barry v Hasseldine* (1952)) or if the transferor retains an adjoining property which permits an alternative means of access (*Ray v Hazeldine* (1904)).

• *Easements of common intention* A reservation will sometimes be implied in order to give effect to a common intention left unexpressed in a subdivision of land. A heavy onus of proof rests on the transferor who wishes to show that a reservation was mutually intended (see *Re Webb's Lease* (1951); *Peckham v Ellison* (2000)).

Transmission of the benefit and burden of legal easements

8.24 Easements are proprietary rights in the sense that, once duly created, they annex a benefit to the dominant land (and a corresponding burden to the servient land) so as to affect the successors in title of either tenement.

— *Benefit* Since they cannot exist in gross (**8.3, 8.6**), easements cannot be transferred independently of the land which they benefit (**2.5**).

• *Registered land* The benefit of an easement granted *expressly* out of a registered estate requires to be entered in the property register of the dominant title (**6.2, 8.16**). The owner of the dominant land becomes, effectively, the proprietor of two separate 'estates' (i.e. the relevant freehold/leasehold estate and also the estate of the easement) (**2.31**). His proprietorship of both estates is usually recorded within one and the same individual register of title (see LRA 2002, s 59(1), Sch 2, para 7(2)(b); LRR 2003, r 3(1)), with the result that, on any subsequent transfer of the dominant title, the benefit of the easement—now an intrinsic component of the relevant property register (LRR 2003, r 5(b)(ii))—automatically passes to the transferee (**1.14**). The benefit of *implied* and *prescriptive* easements, if established to the satisfaction of the registrar, can likewise be registered as appurtenant to the estate of the dominant land (LRR 2003, r 74).

• *Unregistered land* Where a legal easement is appurtenant to a dominant tenement, it becomes notionally affixed to that tenement in much the same way that fixtures become annexed to realty (LPA 1925, s 187(1)). In consequence the benefit of the easement passes with a subsequent conveyance by deed of the land concerned (LPA 1925, s 62(1)–(2): see *Graham v Philcox* (1984)) and will be entered as appurtenant to the dominant title at the point of first registration (LRA 2002, s 14(b); LRR 2003, r 33).

• *Benefit available for tenants* In the case of either registered or unregistered land, the benefit of an easement created between freeholders may be enjoyed by any occupier for the time being of the dominant land even if he is a mere lessee of that land (see *Thorpe v Brumfitt* (1873)). Similarly, easements created in a lease can be enjoyed by a subtenant.

— *Burden* In certain instances the successful assertion of the benefit of the easement may depend on whether the *burden* has run with the servient land so as to affect successors in title of the original servient owner. Reception of the *benefit* of an easement is, of course, futile if it cannot be shown that its *burden* has come to rest upon the party against whom enforcement is sought.

• *Registered land* The burden of any legal easement *expressly* created out of a registered estate requires, by way of fulfilment of the relevant 'registration requirement', to have been noted in the charges register of the servient estate (**8.16**). Such an entry clearly binds all subsequent transferees of the servient land (LRA 2002, s 29(1), (2)(a)(i), **12.9**). (For want of compliance with this 'registration requirement', the disposition of an expressly created easement cannot, in any event, 'operate at law' and the easement takes effect only in equity (LRA 2002, s 27(1), **9.15, 12.26**).)

The burden of any easement over registered land which arises by way of implied grant (**8.20**) or prescription (**8.21**) generally 'overrides' a registered disposition of that land. Such an easement (necessarily a legal easement) automatically binds the transferee of the servient land, provided at least that the easement was 'obvious on a reasonably careful inspection of the land' (LRA 2002, s 29(1), (2)(a)(ii), Sch 3, para 3(1), **12.26**).

• *Unregistered land* Simply by virtue of its legal quality, a legal easement over unregistered land binds all persons (including, quite clearly, all purchasers of the servient land) (**2.38, 12.34**). When the servient land is finally brought on to the Land Register, the burden of the legal easement is noted in the newly opened register of title (LRA 2002, s 14(b); LRR 2003, r 35(1), **12.33**).

Transmission of the benefit and burden of legal profits *à prendre*

8.25 Both the benefit and the burden of a legal profit *à prendre* may be transmitted to third parties.

— *Benefit* In the case of both registered and unregistered land, the benefit of a profit *à prendre* which is appurtenant to a particular dominant tenement normally passes on the transfer of the dominant land (see, in the case of registered land, LRA 2002, Sch 2, para 7(2)(b), **8.16**). A profit in gross (**8.4**) is, by contrast, transferable only as an independent 'piece of real property' (*Lovett v Fairclough* (1989)). In the case of registered land, such a profit is substantively registrable under a unique title number as a 'registered estate' which is thereafter capable of being the subject of independent disposition.

— *Burden* The burden of any legal profit *expressly* created out of a registered estate is necessarily noted in the charges register of the servient estate (**8.16**) and therefore binds all subsequent transferees of the land over which it is exercisable (LRA 2002, s 29(1), (2)(a)(i), **12.9**). The burden of any profit over registered land which arises by way of implied grant (**8.20**) or prescription (**8.21**) generally 'overrides' a registered disposition of that land (LRA 2002, s 29(1), (2)(a)(ii), Sch 3, para 3(1), **12.26**). In unregistered land the burden of a legal profit automatically binds all (including purchasers of the servient tenement) (**12.34**).

Extinguishment of easements and profits *à prendre*

8.26 Although courts are generally slow to hold that rights of easement or profit have been terminated by events subsequent to their creation, there are several ways at common law in which they may be extinguished. In registered land, moreover, the registrar is required to close the registered title to any estate which he is satisfied has been determined (LRR 2003, r 79(2)).

— *Unity of ownership and possession* Easements and appurtenant profits are extinguished automatically if at any time the dominant and servient tenements to which they relate pass into the ownership of the same person (see *Payne v Inwood* (1997), **8.20**) and are probably suspended during any period of unified possession.

— *Release* Release may be *express* or *implied.*

• *Express release* of a legal easement or profit must be contained in a deed (*Lovell v Smith* (1857)) and is usually made for valuable consideration. In the case of registered land, of course, an application should be made to cancel the relevant entries in the property register of the dominant title and the charges register of the servient title.

• *Implied release* of an easement or profit occurs where abandonment of the exercise of the right is coupled with a clear intention to release the right in question. No abandonment is established, however, by a short-lived cessation of user or by the temporary suspension of a user by agreement with the servient owner. Even in relation to relatively long periods of discontinued user, the courts have shown themselves to be disinclined to uphold claims of abandonment.

> *Benn v Hardinge* (1992) The Court of Appeal was unwilling to presume an intention to abandon a right of way even after a period of non-user of 175 years. In the view of Hirst LJ, the abandonment of such a 'valuable latent property' was not lightly to be inferred since the right might be of 'considerable value in the future'. Here the fact of non-user was met by the 'simple explanation' that throughout this period the dominant owner and his predecessors in title had enjoyed an alternative means of access to their tenement.

— *Change of circumstance* There is no statutory provision in English law for the discharge or modification of easements or profits which have become redundant or obstructive with the effluxion of time (compare, in relation to restrictive covenants, LPA 1925, s 84, **9.33, 13.20**). There is, however, some support for the view that obsolete incumbrances may be terminated by a 'change of circumstance' doctrine.

> *Huckvale v Aegean Hotels Ltd* (1989) The Court of Appeal, although declining to uphold the termination of the easement in the present case, left open the possibility that an easement may be extinguished by operation of law when it ceases to accommodate the

dominant tenement. Whilst agreeing that a court should be slow to hold that an easement has been 'extinguished by frustration', Slade LJ was prepared to contemplate precisely such an outcome if circumstances 'have changed so drastically since the date of the original grant of an easement (for example by supervening illegality) that it would offend common sense and reality for the court to hold that an easement still subsisted.'

Rentcharges

8.27 The rentcharge provides another instance of a right in land which is statutorily declared to be capable of creation *at law* (LPA 1925, s 1(2)(b)). A rentcharge is a right to a revenue, i.e. a right to a periodic payment of money charged on or issuing out of land other than under a lease or mortgage (Rentcharges Act 1977, s 1). A rentcharge arises for instance where A has charged his freehold land with a payment of £1000 per annum in favour of B. In such circumstances B is regarded as having a proprietary estate—in the form of a *rentcharge*—in A's land. B's rentcharge can be *legal* only if it is created by deed (LPA 1925, 52(1)) and is 'either perpetual or for a term of years absolute' (LPA 1925, s 1(2)(b)), being *equitable* in all other cases.

— *Substantive registration of rentcharges* A rentcharge over *unregistered* land can be the subject of a voluntary first registration of title under a unique title number at Land Registry (see LRR 2003, r 2(2)(b)), provided that the rentcharge in question was granted without limit of time or for a term which still has more than seven years left to run (LRA 2002, s 3(1)(b), (3)). The creation of a legal rentcharge over *registered* land ranks as a 'registrable disposition' (LRA 2002, s 27(1), (2)(e)) which must itself be 'completed' by the substantive registration of the grantee as proprietor of the 'registered estate' of the rentcharge and by the entry of a corresponding 'notice' in the register of the land charged (LRA 2002, Sch 2, para 6(2)). Such registration is compulsory, as the precondition of an effective grant 'at law', in respect of any rentcharge created without limit of time or for a term of more than seven years (LRA 2002, Sch 2, para 6(1)).

— *Phasing out of rentcharges* Rentcharges have become increasingly uncommon and are now being phased out of existence under the terms of the Rentcharges Act 1977. Subject to very specific exceptions, it is no longer possible to create a new rentcharge either at law or in equity (Rentcharges Act 1977, s 2(1)), and most existing rentcharges are liable to be extinguished by 2037 or 60 years after the commencement of due payment (whichever is later) (Rentcharges Act 1977, s 3(1)).

— *Estate rentcharges* The 1977 Act nevertheless preserves the 'estate rent-charge' (Rentcharges Act 1977, s 2(3)–(5)), which often plays a useful role in the enforcement of positive freehold covenants (**13.12**).

Mortgages

8.28 A *mortgage*—or more accurately a 'charge *by way of legal* mortgage'—constitutes another entitlement indicated by the Law of Property Act 1925 as being capable of creation *at law* (LPA 1925, s 1(2)(c)). Most lenders of large amounts of money, being reluctant to rely merely upon the borrower's contractual promise to repay, require some form of security in respect of the debt owed to them. The device of the mortgage provides this security precisely because, come what may, the contractual debt (plus any accrued interest thereon) is ultimately recoverable from a sale of the land which has been subjected to the mortgage charge (**15.1**). A mortgage is, therefore, a security over land which is created by the borrower (or *mortgagor*) in favour of the lender (or *mortgagee*).

— *The modern prevalence of the mortgage* Although not of course confined to residential premises, mortgage transactions have become the primary means of financing home ownership, the prospective home-owner often raising the bulk of the required purchase price by means of a loan from an institutional mortgagee such as a bank or building society. The purchaser acquires the freehold or leasehold estate in the property purchased and contemporaneously grants the lender a charge by way of legal mortgage as security for the loan. Small wonder that Lord Diplock once observed that Britain has become 'a property-owning, particularly a real-property-mortgaged-to-a-building-society-owning, democracy' (*Pettitt v Pettitt* (1970), **2.10**). The borrower retains ownership of his estate throughout the loan term (usually 20 or 25 years) and is effectively able to acquire a major capital asset by instalment purchase (**15.1**). Within the residential sector almost 60 per cent of all properties are nowadays subject to some current mortgage liability (*Social Trends 32* (2002 edn, London), p 167).

— *Acquisition mortgages and later mortgages* It should not be forgotten that borrowing on the security of land is not confined to *acquisition mortgages* (which facilitate the initial purchase of property), but often extends to *later mortgages* (which tap into the increased capital value derived from the steady inflation of land prices). Land may be mortgaged many times over (see *Downsview Nominees Ltd v First City Corpn Ltd* (1993) per Lord Templeman), the limiting factor being the difference between its open market value and the total debt currently secured. (This surplus or uncharged value, the so-called *equity of redemption* (**15.3**), may fluctuate and, if it plunges to below zero, will give rise to the infamous phenomenon of 'negative equity'). When second mortgages and commercial mortgages are taken into account, it is reckoned that there are some 10 million mortgages in force over land in the United Kingdom.

Creation of a legal mortgage over registered land

8.29   An expressly created legal mortgage of registered land (whether freehold or leasehold) must be effected by way of *registered charge*. (The cumbersome method of mortgage by demise or subdemise (**8.31**) is no longer available in relation to registered land (see LRA 2002, s 23(1)(a)).)

— *Charge by way of legal mortgage*   In the absence of any contrary entry in the register, every proprietor of registered land is statutorily empowered to charge his registered estate at law with the payment of money (LRA 2002, ss 23(1)(b), 24(1)). The proprietor may thus mortgage to a lender by declaring that the land comprised in the registered title is charged 'by way of legal mortgage as security for the payment' of the sums specified to be due under the charge (e.g. in the sum of £X,000, the capital debt, plus interest). A legal charge of registered land may now be effected, necessarily as a deed, in the standard form provided by the LRR 2003 (see LRA 2002, s 25(1); LRR 2003, r 103, Sch 1, **7.6**, **7.8**).

•   *Effectiveness 'at law'*   The grant of a charge over a registered estate ranks as a disposition which requires to be 'completed' by registration (LRA 2002, s 27(2)(f)). The charge therefore becomes effective 'at law' only when the chargee (i.e. the lender) is entered as the proprietor of the charge in the charges register of the chargor's title (LRA 2002, ss 27(1), 59(2), Sch 2, para 8, **2.30–2.31**). Such registration has definitive force: the charge takes effect, 'if it would not otherwise do so, as a charge by deed by way of legal mortgage' (LRA 2002, s 51). It is at this point that the chargee finally acquires a 'legal estate' in the mortgage (see *First National Bank plc v Thompson* (1996) per Millett LJ, **2.31**).

•   *Failure to register*   Until registration of the charge the chargee takes only rights in equity, i.e. receives merely an *equitable* charge over the registered estate (see *Mortgage Corpn Ltd v Nationwide Credit Corpn Ltd* (1994), **9.18**).

•   *Electronic mortgages*   When e-conveyancing becomes operational (**2.23**, **2.26**, **12.3–12.5**), the 'relevant registration requirements' will comprise the transmission of an electronic mortgage document to Land Registry, with the result that unless and until such transmission occurs, the charge will have effect *neither* at law *nor* in equity.

Effects of the registered charge

8.30 The registration of a legal charge at Land Registry brings about the following consequences:

— *Rights of the registered chargee* All registered chargees are statutorily invested with a general power 'to make a disposition of any kind permitted by the general law' in relation to the registered charge (LRA 2002, s 23(2)(a)). The chargee also has available, most significantly, a power of sale in respect of the estate which has been charged (see LPA 1925, ss 87–108, **15.21**).

— *Subsequent registered charges* If the borrower wishes to create another legal charge in favour of a different lender, this later charge must likewise be completed by registration. Subject to any contrary indication in the register, registered charges on the same registered estate rank as between themselves according to the order in which they are entered in the register, and not according to the order in which they are created (LRA 2002, s 48(1); LRR 2003, r 101). A person dealing with the registered proprietor of an estate in land can readily discover how many registered charges exist over the land by obtaining an official copy of the title from Land Registry (LRR 2003, r 134(1), **6.2**). A multiplicity of charges entered against the same registered estate is usually a pretty sure indication that the proprietor of the land is already in deep financial trouble (e.g. when American Express and MasterCard are entered as fifth and sixth registered chargees).

Creation of a legal mortgage over unregistered land

8.31 A legal mortgage of *unregistered* land must be created by *deed* (LPA 1925, s 52(1)). Such a mortgage may take either of two forms (one of which is now obsolete):

— *Charge by way of legal mortgage* (LPA 1925, ss 85(1), 86(1)) Albeit entitled to no estate as such in the land, the recipient of a charge by way of legal mortgage is deemed to have 'the same protection, powers and remedies (including the right to take proceedings to obtain possession)' *as if* a leasehold term of 3,000 years had been created in his favour (LPA 1925, s 87(1)).

— *Charge by way of demise or subdemise* An alternative, and nowadays archaic, means of mortgaging unregistered land lies in a special manipulation of the borrower's estate. Under the method of mortgage by demise, the security granted to a lender takes the form of a long lease in the borrower's land (usually a term of 3,000 years), although there is normally no intention that the lender should assume physical possession under the lease (LPA 1925, s 85(1)).

• *Mortgage by subdemise* Where the mortgaged estate is itself a leasehold, any mortgage by long lease must take effect by subdemise carved out of the leasehold estate for a period 'less by one day at least than the term vested in the mortgagor' (LPA 1925, s 86(1)).

• *Effect of mortgage by demise* In the case of both demise and subdemise, the mortgagee is invested, for security purposes, with an estate in the land—a term of years absolute—subject to a proviso for 'cesser on redemption' (i.e. automatic termination of the leasehold estate on full discharge of the borrower's loan liability). The leasehold estate taken as security is *never* eligible for substantive registration as a leasehold title at Land Registry (LRA 2002, s 4(5)).

— *Trigger for compulsory first registration of title* Any first charge by way of legal mortgage of a freehold (or of a leasehold with more than seven years left to run) now triggers compulsory first registration of the freehold (or leasehold) title at Land Registry. Registration is required where, as is usual in cases of first charge, the relevant mortgage is protected by the deposit of title deeds (LRA 2002, ss 4(1)(g), (8), 6(2)(a), **7.7, 7.21**). First registration of the borrower's estate is accompanied, in practice, by registration of the lender as proprietor of the relevant mortgage charge (see LRA 2002, Sch 2, para 8). In such cases a legal mortgage of unregistered land quickly turns into a *registered charge* against the newly registered freehold or leasehold title (**2.30**). Consistently with an age of increasingly electronic transactions in land, the LRA 2002 provides that any electronic creation of a mortgage charge in prescribed form which triggers a compulsory first registration at Land Registry is deemed to have complied with the statutory requirement of creation by deed (LRA 2002, s 91(2)(c), (5), **7.6**).

— *Title documents* A first legal mortgagee of an unregistered estate is entitled throughout the mortgage term to retain the title deeds pertaining to the mortgaged property (LPA 1925, s 85(1)). Any subsequent attempt by the mortgagor to deal with his land will thus be hampered by his inability to produce the original documents of title as evidence of his estate ownership (**6.2**); and any person dealing with the mortgagor will be deemed to have notice of the existence of at least one mortgage (**15.27**).

— *Protection for second and later legal mortgagees* The safeguard of deposit of title documents therefore serves to prevent subsequent adverse dealings without the knowledge of the first mortgagee, but this protection is, of course, unavailable to second and later mortgagees.

• *Land charge registration* Second and later legal mortgagees, if they are to preserve their priority over further dealings (whether by sale or mortgage) must protect their mortgage by the registration against their mortgagor's name of a *Class C(i) land charge* (Land Charges Act 1972, s 2(4), **12.36**). The legal mortgage not secured by the deposit of title deeds—the so-called 'puisne mortgage'—constitutes one of the anomalies of unregistered land. In that it requires protection by some form of registration, the puisne mortgage provides an exceedingly rare example of a *legal* interest in unregistered land which is not simply governed by the classic principle that legal rights bind the world (**2.38, 12.34**).

• *No compulsory registration* Precisely because it involves no deposit of title documents, the puisne mortgage does not trigger compulsory first registration of title at Land Registry (**2.30–2.31, 7.7**).

Statutorily created charges

8.32 Nowadays a number of statutes provide for the creation of a charge over land for the recoupment of various kinds of liability incurred by the landowner. Such charges generally arise without the necessity of any deed and tend to constitute enforceable first legal charges in respect of the land, sometimes enjoying automatic priority over securities already taken by banks and building societies. A controversial example is provided by the power enjoyed by local authorities to recover the costs of residential nursing home accommodation by imposing a charge on property retained by the elderly person concerned (Health and Social Services and Social Security Adjudications Act 1983, s 22(7)–(8): see *R v Somerset CC, ex parte Harcombe* (1997)). Likewise the Legal Services Commission takes a statutory charge in relation to any interest 'recovered or preserved' in legally aided litigation (Access to Justice Act 1999, s 10(7), **12.36**).

• *Local land charges* Local authorities also have power to impose a charge for the recovery of costs incurred in connection with street works (Highways Act 1980, ss 203(3), 212(1)–(3)) and the abatement of a statutory nuisance on a landowner's premises (Environmental Protection Act 1990, s 81A, **14.5**). Once registered as local land charges, such levies take effect as if they had been created by deed by way of legal mortgage (see Local Land Charges Act 1975, s 7); and a charge over registered land which is a local land charge may be realised only if the title to the charge is registered at Land Registry (LRA 2002, s 55; LRR 2003, r 104).

• *Duty to inform* The LRA 2002 imposes for the first time a duty on Land Registry to inform current registered chargees of the registration of any new statutory charge which displaces existing priorities (LRA 2002, s 50; LRR 2003, rr 105–6).

Transfer of mortgages

8.33 From the viewpoint of the lender a legal charge represents a valuable asset. During its life the mortgagee receives interest on the capital sum outstanding and is entitled to repayment of the capital itself either by instalments during the mortgage term (under a 'repayment mortgage') or as a lump sum at its end (under an 'endowment mortgage'). If the lender wishes to accelerate his realisation of the value represented by a mortgage charge, he is perfectly free, without any requirement of consent from the borrower, to sell the charge to a stranger (LRA 2002, s 25(2)(a)). The disponee of the mortgage charge, having paid the market price for the security in question, thereafter collects all payments due under the mortgage. In registered land the disposition is effected using the prescribed Land Registry form (LRA 2002, s 25(1); LRR 2003, r 116). In order to take a legal security the transferee must then complete the disposition by registration (LRA 2002, s 27(3)(a)), i.e. must apply to be registered in the charges register of the borrower's title as the new proprietor of the charge concerned (LRA 2002, Sch 2, para 10), failing which the transferee holds only an equitable interest in the charge (see *Paragon Finance plc v Pender* (2005)).

Discharge of mortgages

8.34 Once the borrower has met his contractual obligation to repay all sums due under the mortgage, he is entitled to call for a discharge of the mortgage secured on his land. (Discharge often occurs when the mortgagor sells his land and the mortgage debt is satisfied out of the proceeds of sale. Alternatively, discharge may occur without any sale of the property, e.g. on a remortgage of the land to another lender, or if the mortgagor applies his lottery winnings or his late aunt's legacy in payment of his outstanding liability.)

• *Discharge of registered charge* Discharge can occur where the registered chargee duly executes the statutory form of discharge (LRR 2003, r 114(1)), thereby enabling the chargor to apply to Land Registry for cancellation of the relevant entries in the charges register (LRR 2003, r 114(5)). Alternatively a discharge may be delivered to the registrar in electronic form (LRR 2003, r 115(1)).

• *Discharge of mortgage over unregistered land* Here the mortgage is usually discharged by the endorsement of a receipt on the mortgage deed in the form required by statute for all moneys due (LPA 1925, s 115(1)).

— *Other contexts of termination* In both registered and unregistered land there also exist less agreeable contexts (as viewed from the borrower's perspective) in which a mortgage charge may be terminated, e.g. on sale of the mortgaged property under the mortgagee's power of sale (**15.21**) or on foreclosure (**15.23**).

Rights of entry

8.35 One final form of interest in land which may take effect *at law* is the 'right of entry' (LPA 1925, s 1(2)(e)). A right of entry, although it *sounds* similar to a right of way or other easement, is a quite distinct kind of entitlement and performs a very different sort of function. A right of entry is a *penal* right to enforce forfeiture of an estate in land or to enter land and remove some object from it (**1.9**). Although subject to the court's jurisdiction to afford the defaulting party relief against forfeiture (**14.14**), a right of entry often provides a means 'to take his land altogether away' (*Shiloh Spinners Ltd v Harding* (1973) per Lord Wilberforce). Rights of entry are frequently attached to a lease (**14.11**) or rentcharge (**8.27**), the right effectively comprising an entitlement to 're-enter', i.e. resume possession of land, in the event of some non-compliance with the terms of the relevant lease or rentcharge (e.g. for non-payment of rent or for failure to perform any other covenanted obligation).

— *Proprietary character of a right of entry* A right of entry constitutes a free-standing proprietary right in the subject land which is distinct from the estate or rentcharge to which the right of entry is appended. A right of entry ranks as a *legal* entitlement in land if exercisable in respect of a *legal* lease or annexed to a *legal* rentcharge (LPA 1925, s 1(2)(e)) and if any further requirement of formality or registration has been satisfied. Indeed, the enforceability of a right of entry is not, in strict terms, dependent on whether the party against whom it is enforced is *bound* by the obligation for non-compliance with which the right of entry is exercised. A right of entry is, in effect, a peremptory self-help remedy often visited upon someone who is simply the wrong person in the wrong place at the wrong time. Thus, for instance, a landlord can enforce a leasehold right of re-entry against a squatter who adversely possesses against his tenant, not on any theory that the squatter is bound as an assignee of the leasehold term, but merely on the rather stark ground that the right of re-entry is triggered by sheer non-performance of that which was promised in the lease (**14.15**).

• *Registered land* Where a right of entry is expressly created by deed for the benefit of a registered estate (other than a leasehold estate), the proprietor of that estate must be entered in the register as proprietor of the right of entry and a corresponding notice must be entered against the registered estate affected by it (LRA 2002, s 27(1), (2)(e), Sch 2, para 7(1)–(2); LRR 2003, r 77). The registrar has power to record on any relevant register of title the fact that a right to determine a registered estate in land appears to have become exercisable (LRA 2002, s 64(1)).

• *Unregistered land* A right of entry created by deed automatically binds the land in the hands of all parties. A right of entry created otherwise than by deed (or exercisable merely in respect of some equitable estate) can only be *equitable* (see LPA 1925, s 1(3), **2.29**) and has binding effect, if at all, in accordance with the *bona fide purchaser* rule (see *Shiloh Spinners Ltd v Harding* (1973)).

FURTHER READING

Gray and Gray, *Elements of Land Law* (4th edn, OUP, 2005), ch 8.

Relevant sections of this work and other land law textbooks may be supplemented with:

Goymour, Amy 'Rabbits beware: residents gain rights to drive over common land' [2005] *CLJ* 39.

Lawson, Anna 'Easements', in L Tee (ed), *Land Law: Issues, Debates, Policy* (Willan, 2002), p 64.

Luther, Peter 'Easements and exclusive possession' (1996) 16 *Legal Studies* 51.

Paton, Ewan and Seabourne, Gwen 'Can't get there from here?: permissible use of easements after *Das*' [2003] *Conv* 127.

Sturley, Michael 'Easements in Gross' (1980) 96 *LQR* 557.

Tee, Louise 'Metamorphoses and Section 62 of the Law of Property Act 1925' [1998] *Conv* 115.

Ziff, Bruce and Litman, Moe 'Easements and Possession: An Elusive Limitation' [1989] *Conv* 296.

SELF-TEST QUESTIONS

1   Is it possible in English law to have an easement to walk one's dog in someone else's paddock (**8.6–8.14**)?

2   How does the grant of an easement or a profit *à prendre* differ from the reservation of such rights (**8.17–8.19, 8.23**)?

3   To what extent does long user generate rights of easement or profit *à prendre*? How does the prescriptive process differ from adverse possession (**6.4, 8.21–8.22**)?

4   How does a legal mortgage arise in (i) registered land, and (ii) unregistered land (**8.29–8.31**)?

9

Equitable rights in or over land

SUMMARY

This chapter is concerned with an extensive residue of entitlements in land which can never be the subject of any registered proprietorship under the Land Registration Act 2002, but can at best be protected by the entry of a 'notice' or 'restriction' in someone else's register of title.

Equitable rights tend to have their origins deep in the doctrines and maxims of equity. This chapter explains how modern equitable entitlements in land have evolved from equity's historic thematic concerns with substance rather than form, with the inner reality of intent rather than the external manifestations of conduct, and above all with the priority of conscience-driven obligation over strict legal entitlement. The chapter is therefore concerned with the *definitional* aspect of certain entitlements such as restrictive covenants and beneficial trust interests—which are inherently equitable—leaving the *operational* aspect of these categories of rights to be dealt with in Chapters 11–13.

The present chapter also draws attention to the equitable version of certain rights which, for want of due formality or registration, have failed to attain the status of a legal estate. These entitlements include:

- leases (**9.9**);
- equitable easements and profits *à prendre* (**9.12–9.15**); and
- certain kinds of equitable charge (**9.16–9.18**).

The statutory classification

9.1 Chapters 7 and 8 have described the principal forms of estate, interest and charge which are capable of existence *at law*. In the present chapter we turn our attention to the range of proprietary entitlements which subsist—sometimes necessarily—*in equity* (**1.24, 2.29**).

Some of these rights enjoy equitable status precisely because they are excluded from the categories of interest statutorily declared capable of legal existence (see LPA 1925, s 1(3)). Such rights have no potential to exist at law, and their inherently equitable status can usually be rationalised in terms of the maxims and historic jurisdiction of equity. Examples include:

- estate contracts (**9.8**);
- liens (**9.22–9.23**);
- restrictive covenants (**9.24**); and
- beneficial interests existing under a trust of land (**9.34**).

On the other hand, certain equitable entitlements are merely the analogue of rights which, on due compliance with some requirement of formal creation or transfer or some requirement of registration at Land Registry, would normally have ranked as *legal* rights. Examples include various kinds of:

- leases (**9.9**);
- easements and profits *à prendre* (**9.12–9.15**); and
- mortgage charges (**9.16–9.18**).

The role of equitable principle

9.2 Much of land law cannot be understood without some sense of the way in which the conscience-based jurisdiction of equity has infused various sorts of *Leitmotiv* into the formulation and recognition of rights in land. Attention was drawn in Chapter 1 to the fact that legal rights frequently give expression to the *external* or *formal* elements of proprietary entitlement, whilst equitable rights tend to acknowledge the *inner reality* of transactions in respect of land (**1.24**). If, for instance, the question arises who owns title to a particular piece of land, the common law instinct is to look either to the possessory position on the ground or to the name inscribed on the documentary title. Equity, by contrast, attempts rather more subtly to determine the inner motivations of the relevant parties and to allocate ownership accordingly. It is indeed a constant characteristic of equity to look beneath the superficial appearance of transactions in order to discover and, so far as conscience will allow, give effect to the substantive reality of the parties' actual or presumed intentions as responsible moral agents. The maxims of equity are redolent with such notions as

- equity has regard to intent rather than form (**9.9, 9.31, 9.35**);
- equity will not suffer a wrong to go without remedy (**9.2**);
- he who comes to equity must come with clean hands (**9.3, 9.6**);
- equity will not assist a volunteer (**9.2–9.3, 9.6, 10.11**);
- equality is equity (**10.13**);
- equity follows the law (**9.35, 10.3, 11.9, 11.24**);
- equity looks on that as done which ought to be done (**9.7, 9.9, 9.18**).

These maxims of equity (and there are others) are far from being binding rules of inflexible application. In fact they are not rules at all, but operate merely as background doctrines or principles—of varying vitality—which exert an almost subliminal influence on the reasoning processes of lawyers. Sometimes these maxims come to the fore only as a last resort, where there exists no clearer signpost to the resolution of a difficulty. (The idea that 'equity follows the law' falls clearly into this category of residual application (**11.9, 11.24**), but nevertheless reinforces the broad idea that equity, being merely a corrective system of justice, is needed only where the dogmatic assertion of a formal rule of law produces an unacceptably unfair or 'inequitable' outcome.) Sometimes a maxim (e.g. 'equity will not suffer a wrong to go without remedy') expresses no more than a generalised moral imperative which, if actualised in other than extreme cases, would in fact spell the disintegration of any ordered or structured system of justice. Again, the proposition that 'equality is equity' provides only an ultimate 'fall-back presumption' in the ascertainment of beneficial ownership under a trust (*Mortgage Corpn v Shaire* (2001) per Neuberger J). Another of the maxims ('equity will not assist a volunteer', i.e. one who provides no consideration) is actually and richly falsified in the primary equitable phenomenon of the express trust, where most beneficiaries are indeed volunteers (**1.26, 9.37**). Yet the maxims of equity continue to play an insidiously formative role in giving sense to many of the categories of entitlement discussed in this chapter. Indeed, it has been said that equity 'calls into existence and protects equitable rights and interests in property only where their recognition has been found to be required in order to give effect to its doctrines' (*Commissioner of Stamp Duties (Queensland) v Livingston* (1965) per Viscount Radcliffe).

Equity acts *in personam*

9.3 Of all the keynotes of equitable principle, perhaps the most influential is ultimately the idea that 'equity acts *in personam*'. In the exercise of equitable jurisdiction

(**1.24**), courts fashion their orders and remedies so as to affect the litigant much more directly and coercively than any remedy devised in the traditional regime of the common law. In civil matters the characteristic remedy of the common law is the remedy of damages. In equity, however, the range of available remedy extends much more widely, embracing forms of relief which act directly *in personam* (e.g. injunctions, decrees of specific performance and orders for rectification).

— *Remedial characteristics of equity* This procedural difference between law and equity acquires a vast significance in the context of land law. It means, for instance, that the usual remedy for breach of contract in relation to a land interest is not the mere award of money damages, but rather an order of *specific performance* which operates directly upon the party in breach by requiring him to do that which he contracted to do. In most cases, therefore, a specifically enforceable contract relating to land must be completed by the delivery of the contracted performance. The defaulting party is not permitted to buy his way out of breach by the proffering of money damages. Again, the traditional remedy for non-compliance with a restrictive covenant is not only the award of compensation to the aggrieved party, but also an order (or *injunction*) restraining further breach of the covenant on pain of liability for contempt. In these and many other ways equity, by virtue of the immediacy of its remedial impact, effectively converts contractual promises into a conferment of enforceable 'property' in the promisor's land (**2.5, 9.4, 9.7, 9.26**).

— *Discretionary nature of equitable remedies* Unlike common law remedies (which are available as of right), equitable remedies are always discretionary; and equity has laid down guidelines for the exercise of this discretion (see *Cooperative Insurance Society Ltd v Argyll Stores (Holdings) Ltd* (1998) per Lord Hoffmann). For instance, equity will not, in general, lend its assistance to a volunteer. Again, even a claimant who has proved his case may be denied equitable relief on the ground that he has not come to court 'with clean hands'. That is, he may be precluded from relief simply because he has forfeited any claim to the assistance of equity by reason of his own inequitable or unconscionable conduct (see e.g. *Wilkie v Redsell* (2003)).

Proprietary effect of contracts relating to land

9.4 Many forms of equitable right in land derive their existence from some contractual relationship affecting the land. Although it seems at first implausible, the doctrinal effect of equitable principle often elevates rights of mere *contractual* significance into rights of *proprietary* consequence. In this sense, the borderline between contract and property is much more fluid or ambivalent than initially appears (see Gray [1991] *CLJ* 252 at 302–3). Although the chain of propositional logic can be understood only against the background of historic equitable principle, the net effect is that those who enter into contracts to purchase various sorts of interest in land frequently find that the sheer fact of contract has already conferred on them some kind of *proprietary interest* in the land. Moreover, because this metamorphosis of the contractual into the proprietary has occurred under the shadow of equitable doctrine (**9.7–9.8**), the proprietary rights created by contract are properly classifiable as *equitable* rights in land. The chain of logic which produces this result turns on the significance of the remedy of specific performance.

Specifically enforceable contracts

9.5 The rationale underlying the equitable perspective on contracts relating to land is the recognition that the subject matter of a land contract is unique and that breach of such a contract cannot adequately be compensated by money (see *Hall v Warren* (1804)). Although the remedy is ultimately discretionary, it is now well settled that a contract relating to land is one in respect of which equity will generally grant *specific performance*. If a contracting party fails to grant or transfer the promised interest in land, the court will normally order him to perform the contract by completing the relevant disposition, whether the original undertaking was to convey a freehold or to grant or transfer a lease, or even to create an easement or mortgage over the land in question. Because of the availability of specific enforcement of the contractual promise, the disposition of the interest is *inevitable*. The contracting party will either perform his contract or be made to do so by a decree of specific performance. The end result is not in doubt.

Preconditions of specific performance

9.6 Although available in land transactions almost as a matter of course, the award of specific performance is always dependent on the satisfaction of certain preconditions by the contractual party who invokes the aid of equity.

— *There must be a transaction for value* Equity, being generally unwilling to assist a volunteer (**9.2**), grants specific performance only to contracting parties who provide valuable consideration.

— *There must be a contract in writing duly signed* In relation to almost all contracts for the disposition of any interest in land, the Law of Property (Miscellaneous Provisions) Act 1989 imposes a requirement that the contract be 'made in writing' and signed by or on behalf of each contracting party (LP(MP)A 1989, s 2(1), (3), **9.4**). The contract must incorporate all expressly agreed terms in one document or, where contracts are exchanged, in each document.

• The 1989 Act allows few exceptions from the scope of these provisions—although one important exception catches contracts to grant certain short leases not exceeding three years (LP(MP)A 1989, s 2(5)(a)). The Act otherwise applies to all contracts entered into on or after 27 September 1989; and failure to comply with the statutory requirements renders a contract not merely unenforceable, but entirely *ineffective*.

• The old doctrine of *part performance* (which used to save many oral contracts) is now abolished (LP(MP)A 1989, s 2(8)), although it is possible that, in certain restricted kinds of circumstance, doctrines of estoppel or constructive trust may still perform a similar function (see e.g. *Yaxley v Gotts* (2000), **10.12**; *Oates v Stimson* (2006)). Only contracts entered into prior to 27 September 1989 remain subject to the old rule on formality which, apart from cases of part performance and estoppel, required that an enforceable contract relating to land should be *evidenced in writing* signed by or on behalf of the party to be charged (LPA 1925, s 40(1)).

• For modern land contracts, the message is unmistakable: in order to be valid, contracts must be made in writing and signed by all contracting parties (see e.g. the problem exposed by the lack of one signature in *Chandler v Clark* (2003)). There is, however, a steady drift towards the electronic age. The Electronic Communications Act 2000 prepared the ground for the introduction of electronic contracting with interests in land (see ECA 2000, s 8; LP(MP)A 1989, s 2A, as proposed by Draft Law of Property (Electronic Communications) Order 2001, art 4). This innovation, not yet brought into effect, would significantly supplement the requirements of contractual formality affecting both registered and unregistered land, but is likely—in the former context—to be superseded by the advent of electronic contracting under the LRA 2002 (**12.4**).

— *The party seeking specific performance must come 'with clean hands'* The party who seeks to invoke specific performance must not have disqualified himself from equitable relief by gross or wilfully unconscionable conduct (see *Coatsworth v Johnson* (1885)). 'In a court of equity', said Lord Uthwatt, 'wrongful acts are no passport to favour' (*Winter Garden Theatre (London) Ltd v Millennium Productions Ltd* (1948)).

— *Specific performance must not prejudice third parties or cause excessive hardship* Specific performance will not be granted if, for instance, the subject matter of the contract has already been transferred to a third party or in those rare cases where the decree would cause a 'hardship amounting to injustice' (*Patel v Ali* (1984) per Goulding J).

Contract confers some form of equitable title

9.7 The general inexorability of due transfer or grant under a specifically enforceable land contract activates the equitable maxim that 'equity looks on that as done which ought to be done'. Even though no order of specific performance has yet been made, equity *anticipates* the completion of the contract and treats the contractual promisee as having *already* received some equitable version of the interest which forms the subject matter of the contract (see *Mountney v Treharne* (2003) at [76]). From the moment of specifically enforceable contractual commitment, the purchaser of a land interest thus acquires not merely a *contractual* right but also a *proprietary* right in the land—an *equitable* proprietary right. As Lord Jenkins explained in analogous circumstances in *Oughtred v IRC* (1960), the contractual purchaser is 'treated in equity as entitled … to the property'. His interest under the contract 'is … a proprietary interest of a sort, which arises … in anticipation of the execution of the transfer for which the purchaser is entitled to call'. The irresistible right to call for the legal estate has thus conferred on the contractual purchaser some significant quantum of 'property' in the land (**2.5**). Although there may be some question as to the exact nature of this proprietary entitlement, and even as to the precise moment at which it arises, there is no doubt that a specifically enforceable contract confers substantial proprietary rights on the contractual purchaser (see *Lysaght v Edwards* (1876)). In effect, contract confers an equitable title—a doctrine which accounts for many of the species of equitable proprietary entitlement discussed in this chapter.

Estate contracts

9.8 A specifically enforceable contract to create or transfer a legal estate in land is termed an 'estate contract' and has the effect of passing some species of equitable (or beneficial) ownership of the estate to the purchaser at the point of contract, subject to the payment of the purchase money (see *Lysaght v Edwards* (1876) per Jessel MR; *Jerome v Kelly (Inspector of Taxes)* (2004) at [32] per Lord Walker of Gestingthorpe). An estate contract therefore represents an equitable interest in the hands of the purchaser: ownership of the estate 'is, in equity, transferred by [the] contract' (*Rose v Watson* (1864) per Lord Westbury LC). From the exchange of contracts (**12.4**) the purchaser of a freehold estate acquires an equitable interest in the fee simple, and the grantee or assignee of a term of years correspondingly acquires an equitable interest in the land to be held on lease, the normal expectation being that these forms of beneficial ownership will in due course merge with the respective legal estates yet to be transferred in pursuance of the contract (see *Walsh v Lonsdale* (1882), **9.9**). Completion of the contract merely causes the purchaser's equitable title to be reunited with, and 'absorbed' in, the legal estate, thereby confirming in the purchaser 'the whole right of property in the land' (*DKLR Holding Co (No 2) Pty Ltd v Commissioner of Stamp Duties (NSW)* (1982) per Gibbs CJ). If the relevant contract is *not* completed by transfer or assignment (and, where appropriate, registration at Land Registry), the contractual purchaser retains the estate in equitable form and, in almost all conceivable circumstances, can call irresistibly for specific performance of the contract by court order (see *R v Tower Hamlets LBC, ex parte Von Goetz* (1999) per Mummery LJ). This proprietary dimension of the 'estate contract' produces certain important consequences.

— *The vendor becomes a trustee for the purchaser* The availability of the contractual remedy of specific performance engrafts, at least temporarily, some sort of trust upon the relationship between vendor and purchaser (see *Jerome v Kelly (Inspector of Taxes)* (2004) at [30] per Lord Walker of Gestingthorpe, **12.4**). Under an estate contract the vendor 'becomes in equity a trustee for the purchaser of the estate sold' (*Lysaght v Edwards* (1876) per Jessel MR). A fiduciary responsibility is placed on the vendor not to damage or prejudice the land during the interim between the contract and its completion by transfer (**12.2**). The vendor must, for instance, repel trespassers and prevent decay or dilapidation to the property (*Englewood Properties Ltd v Patel* (2005) at [54] per Lawrence Collins J). The vendor nevertheless continues to enjoy certain valuable rights in relation to the property. He may remain in possession until completion, is meanwhile beneficially entitled to the rents and profits of the land, and retains an 'unpaid vendor's lien' (**9.22**) over the property until the purchase money is paid in full.

— *The insurable risk in the land passes to the contractual purchaser* The anticipatory effect of equitable doctrine attaches a further implication to a specifically enforceable estate contract. In the absence of contrary contractual provision, the insurable risk in the subject matter of the contract passes concurrently with the equitable interest in the land (see *Lysaght v Edwards* (1876)), with the result that a prudent purchaser arranges insurance cover with effect from the exchange of contracts. No purchaser wishes to be contractually obligated to receive a transfer of an uninsured charred ruin.

— *Protection for the estate contract* The contractual purchaser's proprietary right, like other equitable interests, requires protection against third parties. The purchaser is vulnerable to the possibility that the vendor may dispose of the legal estate in breach of contract, not to the contractual purchaser, but to some other purchaser who offers to pay a higher price. Alternatively, the vendor may charge the estate to a lender and abstract the value of the loan money advanced.

• *Registered land* In view of the possibility of such dangers arising in the interim between contract and due completion, the purchaser's estate contract requires protection by the entry of a 'notice' in the register of the vendor's title (LRA 2002, ss 32–4, **2.32, 12.11–12.13**).

• *Unregistered land* If the vendor's title is unregistered, the estate contract must be protected by the registration of a *Class C(iv) land charge* against the name of the vendor (LCA 1972, ss 2(4), 3(1), **2.41, 12.36**).

• The effect of protection is generally to render the estate contract enforceable against any other person who takes title in defiance of that contract, the incumbrancer remaining fully entitled to call for a transfer or grant of the legal estate—in accordance with the original contract—from that person. Protection of the estate contract likewise binds any later mortgagee or chargee.

• Failure to protect the estate contract is likely to prove fatal, both in *registered land* (where the contractual purchaser is unlikely to be able to claim that his interest 'overrides' by reason of his 'actual occupation' of the land (**12.18**)) and also in *unregistered land* (see *Lloyds Bank plc v Carrick* (1996)).

> *Lloyds Bank plc v Carrick* (1996) In 1982, before the commencement of the Law of Property (Miscellaneous Provisions) Act 1989, O, the owner of a maisonette in unregistered land, contracted verbally to sell it to his sister-in-law, C. Although initially unenforceable under LPA 1925, s 40 (**9.6**), this contract became specifically enforceable by reason of part performance when C later paid the purchase price and went into possession. The legal estate was never transferred to C, and in 1986 O mortgaged his legal title to Lloyds Bank. On O's subsequent default the Court of Appeal upheld the bank's right to recover possession from C. Morritt LJ indicated that, when the contract became specifically enforceable, O was converted into a trustee for C and, with the full payment of the purchase money by C, retained no further beneficial interest in the property. O was therefore a mere 'bare trustee' of the legal title and C became 'the absolute beneficial owner of the maisonette' (**11.26**). Her equitable interest, founded on the estate contract with O, was, however, rendered statutorily void against the bank as mortgagee by reason of C's failure to register her estate contract against O as a Class C(iv) land charge (see LCA 1972, s 4(6), **2.41, 12.36**). C's equitable title was therefore defeated by the bank. The Court of Appeal held, moreover, that in the presence of the trust relationship already created by the specifically enforceable contract (and here rendered statutorily unenforceable), there was no room for the superimposition on O of

a further constructive trust (**10.6**) which might arguably affect the rights of the bank. (Significantly, the Court noted that the result would have been different if title to the maisonette had been *registered*—on the unusual facts of this case C would have had an overriding interest binding the bank (LRA 2002, s 29(1), (2)(a)(ii), Sch 3, para 2, **2.33, 12.18**).)

Equitable leases

9.9 The salutary force of equitable doctrine also catches many cases where an attempt to grant or transfer a leasehold term has failed, by reason of some informality or technical imperfection, to invest the intended lessee with a *legal* term of years. Such instances include the following:

• A *formally defective* grant or transfer (e.g. using mere writing instead of a deed) prevents the creation of any legal lease for a term in excess of three years (LPA 1925, ss 52(1), 54(2), **7.18**) and also prevents the subsequent legal assignment of any term irrespective of its duration (**7.17**).

• A *failure to apply for substantive registration* at Land Registry, where such registration is required (**7.19–7.22**), has the consequence that no legal term of years can pass or remain vested in the intended recipient (LRA 2002, ss 7(1)–(2), 27(1)).

• The relevant parties have merely entered into a *contract* to create or transfer a leasehold term (**7.18**) and this contract has never reached the stage of completion (i.e. no legal lease has actually been granted or transferred).

• The lessor holds only an *equitable* entitlement (e.g. an equitable fee simple estate) and is therefore incompetent to create a *legal* term of years of any kind.

In many such cases of abortive grant or transfer of a *legal* lease, equity is quite prepared to regard the incomplete, informal or imperfect transaction as nevertheless generating an *equitable* term of years which is the equivalent, in all but legal quality, of the term of years which was originally intended to pass. Thus, for instance, an ineffective grant of a ten-year lease *at law* is commuted, under this doctrine of broad equivalence, into a fully valid ten-year lease *in equity* (see *R v Tower Hamlets LBC, ex parte Von Goetz* (1999)). In some instances this outcome is indirectly mandated by statute (see e.g. LRA 2002, s 7(2)(b), **7.20**), but the effect merely mirrors a more general approach adopted by equity (**9.18**), under which defective grants or transfers may be rescued by reference to their underlying contractual intent.

— *Reference to underlying contractual intent* The mere fact that a transaction is ineffective to vest legal rights does not prevent the court from having recourse to the *contractual* substratum of the parties' antecedent dealings. Since many of the transactions in question are preceded by some sort of agreement (**7.18**)—a fortiori, if the parties never got beyond the stage of contract anyway—equitable doctrine gives independent effect to the contractual rights which 'lie behind or beyond' any legal estate purportedly conferred (see *Corin v Patton* (1990) per Deane J). In conformity with its maxims, equity *either* 'has regard to the intent rather than the form' of the transaction *or* 'looks on that as done which ought to be done' (**9.2**).

— *Specifically enforceable contractual rights* Provided that the antecedent contractual relationship was one of which equity would grant specific performance (**9.6**), equity will recognise the intended recipient of a term of years as holding, not a legal lease, but an *equitable* lease for the same fixed term and on the same covenants and conditions as would have obtained if the transaction had been effective at law (see *Tinsley v Milligan* (1994) per Lord Browne-Wilkinson). Once again, even in the absence of any actual order for specific performance, equity is preoccupied by intent rather than form (**1.24, 9.2**). '[T]he intention of the parties having been that there should be a lease ... the aid of equity [is] only invoked to carry that intention into effect' (*Parker v Taswell* (1858) per Lord Chelmsford LC). Thus formally defective leases and leases which have not yet been substantively registered bring about the same effect as a specifically enforceable contract to create a term of years. Under the so-called doctrine in *Walsh v Lonsdale* (infra), all such leasehold transactions give rise to an *equitable* leasehold term in the intended recipient, each recipient holding the benefit of an *estate contract* which requires protection in the appropriate manner in either registered or unregistered land (**9.8**).

— *Cases where specific performance is unavailable* If, for any reason, the antecedent dealings of the parties are *not* specifically enforceable, the anticipatory doctrine of equity is clearly inapplicable and the intended recipient of a legal lease cannot simply be regarded as holding an equivalent fixed term in equity. In the case of the grant of a leasehold term, however, the intended lessee may well enter into possession of the land and a periodic rent may begin to be paid and received. (Indeed, the intended lessee may be unaware, in many cases, that his fixed term leasehold estate is ineffective at law.) Such circumstances of entry into possession and periodic payment are, nevertheless, apt to generate an implied periodic tenancy—a tenancy which is, of course, *legal* in quality (**7.24**). This implied common law tenancy can continue only for the duration of the fixed term originally contemplated, but is deemed to incorporate all the covenants and conditions of the incomplete or abortive lease in so far as they are compatible with and transferable to a periodic tenancy (see *Martin v Smith* (1874)). In other words, the lack of specific enforceability relegates the intended lessee, by implication, to a sort of legal tenancy, but one which, unlike the fixed term equitable lease under *Walsh v*

Lonsdale, is readily terminated by the giving of appropriate notice to quit (**7.31**). Thus, although this common law periodic tenancy ranks as an overriding interest (in registered land) and is automatically binding (in unregistered land), its vulnerability to premature termination renders it distinctly less preferable to the fixed term equitable lease yielded by the application of *Walsh v Lonsdale*.

— *Resolution of the conflict between law and equity* It is ultimately the availability of specific performance which determines whether the parties' relationship falls to be analysed in terms of a *legal periodic tenancy* or in terms of an *equitable fixed term lease*. The Judicature Acts 1873–75 introduced the principle that any conflict between the rules of law and equity should be resolved by an application of the rules of equity (Supreme Court of Judicature Act 1873, s 25(11); see now Supreme Court Act 1981, s 49(1), **1.24**). In the context of specifically enforceable land contracts, the priority accorded to the equitable perspective was classically confirmed by what has now become known as the doctrine in *Walsh v Lonsdale* (1882).

> *Walsh v Lonsdale* (1882) L granted W a seven-year lease in writing under which W's rent was payable annually *in advance*. No lease by deed was executed, but W entered into possession and proceeded to pay rent *in arrear*, thereby appearing to become a yearly periodic tenant at common law (**7.24**). L then demanded a year's rent in advance and, on W's refusal to pay in advance, distrained for the rent (by seizing W's goods). W's action for damages for trespass was dismissed by the Court of Appeal, which ruled that W was holding, not a *legal* tenancy from year to year (under which rent would have been payable in arrear), but an *equitable* seven-year term (under which rent was expressly payable in advance). The distraint on W's goods had therefore been entirely lawful. Since specific performance was clearly available, Jessel MR was able to declare that 'there are not two estates as there were formerly, one estate at common law by reason of the payment of rent from year to year, and an estate in equity under the agreement. There is only one Court, and the equity rules prevail in it. The tenant holds under an agreement for a lease. He holds, therefore, under the same terms in equity as if a lease had been granted.'

The doctrine in *Walsh v Lonsdale* has come to apply to a wide range of purportedly legal transactions which are vitiated by non-compliance with some legal formality or registration requirement. The doctrine establishes a principle of general application to such transactions as the granting of easements, profits and mortgages, and brings about the effect that informal or incomplete grants in any of these cases are construed as contracts which, if capable of specific performance, are regarded as grants of equitable interests of the relevant kind (**9.13, 9.18**).

— *Is a Walsh v Lonsdale lease as good as a legal lease?* It is sometimes alleged that a *Walsh v Lonsdale* lease, which replicates in equity the effect of an incomplete or imperfect legal lease, is as good as a legal lease itself. Indeed, some parties may well not seek specific performance at all, being content to leave their respective rights and obligations to subsist purely in equity (**7.18**). There are, however, certain significant respects in which a *Walsh v Lonsdale* lease is markedly less efficacious than the grant or transfer of a valid fixed term legal leasehold estate.

• Status as an equitable tenant under *Walsh v Lonsdale* is vitally dependent on the theoretical willingness of the court to grant the discretionary remedy of specific performance.

• There is no *privity of estate* under a *Walsh v Lonsdale* lease (**14.20**), with the consequence that in certain cases the tenant's leasehold covenants may not be binding on assignees of the equitable fixed term.

• An equitable tenant cannot claim the benefit of Law of Property Act 1925, s 62 (**8.20**), with the result that no implied easements can arise in his favour under the 'general words' provision (see *Borman v Griffith* (1930)).

• An equitable tenant (in unregistered land) can never claim to be a purchaser of a *legal* estate for the purpose of gaining the immunity from equitable interests conferred by the bona fide purchaser rule (**2.43, 12.39**).

• An equitable tenant may be *insecure* against third parties who take a purchase or transfer of the landlord's estate. In registered land the *Walsh v Lonsdale* lease can 'override' subsequent dispositions of the landlord's registered estate only so long as the equitable tenant is 'in actual occupation' of the land (LRA 2002, s 29(1), (2)(a)(ii), Sch 3, para 2, **2.33, 12.20**: see *Grace Rymer Investments Ltd v Waite* (1958)). In unregistered land, an equitable lease requires to be registered under the Land Charges Act 1972 as a Class C(iv) estate contract in order to render it effective against subsequent purchasers of the legal estate (**9.8, 12.36**). Failure to achieve the protection of land charge registration is generally fatal (see e.g. *Hollington Bros Ltd v Rhodes* (1951), **12.35**).

Options

9.10 An *option* to purchase a legal estate likewise comprises a form of *estate contract*, with all the consequences for protection noted earlier (**9.8–9.9**). An option is a contractual right which entitles the option holder (or optionee) to require that the grantor of the option should, at some subsequent stage, convey or transfer a legal estate to him in accordance with the agreed terms of the option (not least concerning price). An option thus blends aspects of an irrevocable offer of sale with features of a conditional contract in favour of the optionee. Control over the exercise of the option lies wholly in the hands of the optionee.

— *Proprietary status* Since an option confers a specifically enforceable contractual right to call for a transfer of a legal estate, the option vests in the optionee, from the moment of its grant, an equitable proprietary interest in the land concerned (*London and South Western Railway Co v Gomm* (1882) per Jessel MR). Options may relate to the purchase of either a fee simple estate or a leasehold term or an easement or profit, and include a tenant's option to take a renewal of his lease or even to purchase his landlord's reversion. The proprietary status of the option is attributable to the anticipatory effect of equitable doctrine (**9.7**) and marks a recognition that, with the granting of the option, a significant part of the 'property' in the grantor's land has thereby passed to the optionee (**2.5**).

— *Protection* The actual transfer of the legal estate in question now depends upon the mere election of the optionee, but this right, like all other equitable rights, requires protection against the possibility that the grantor of the option may wrongfully deal with his legal estate in favour of somebody other than the optionee. An option to purchase an interest in *registered* land may be entered by 'notice' in the grantor's register of title (LRA 2002, ss 32–4, **12.11**), although, in special kinds of circumstance, it may automatically 'override' registered dispositions of the grantor's estate (see e.g. *Webb v Pollmount* (1966), **12.18–12.20**). In *unregistered* land the rule is rather more strict: options *must* be protected by the registration of a land charge against the name of the grantor (see e.g. *Midland Bank Trust Co Ltd v Green* (1981), **12.35**).

Rights of pre-emption

9.11 A *right of pre-emption*, although superficially similar to an option, differs in important respects. Rights of pre-emption nevertheless constitute another form of equitable entitlement in land.

— *Nature* A right of pre-emption confers upon its grantee merely a right of *first refusal* should the grantor of the right ever choose to sell the land concerned. A person who receives a right of pre-emption is not entitled to *demand* or *compel* any transfer of a legal estate. The decision when or whether to sell lies always within the discretion of the estate owner.

— *Proprietary status* It has long been debated whether, before it becomes exercisable on the estate owner's election to sell, a right of pre-emption confers sufficient 'property' in realty to qualify its recipient as the owner of any equitable entitlement capable of protection in either registered or unregistered land (see e.g. *Pritchard v Briggs* (1980)). It has been suggested that a right of pre-emption remains, until the point of exercise, a merely personal contractual right of the grantee. Now, however, the LRA 2002 has resolved the controversy for the future at least. A right of pre-emption created in registered land after 13 October 2003 is declared to have effect 'from the time of creation as an interest capable of binding successors in title' (LRA 2002, s 115(1)). Such a right is therefore protectable by the entry of a 'restriction' in the estate owner's register of title (LRA 2002, ss 40–3, **7.8**) and may, in certain circumstances, 'override' registered dispositions of that title (LRA 2002, s 29(1), (2)(a)(ii), Sch 3, para 2, **12.20**).

Equitable easements and profits *à prendre*

9.12 Unlike an estate contract (which can exist only in *equity*), an easement or profit *à prendre* can exist *either* at law *or* in equity, depending on a number of circumstances. The defining characteristics of easements and profits *à prendre* (whether legal or equitable) are set out in Chapter 8 (**8.4–8.14**). The conditions necessary for the creation of a *legal* easement or profit have also been outlined already (**8.16**), but either interest can assume an *equitable* form where these conditions are not met.

Creation of equitable easements and profits

9.13 Equitable easements and profits *à prendre* therefore arise in circumstances where *legal* creation founders on obstacles relating to the following:

— *Capacity of the grantor*   A grantor who is himself entitled merely *in equity* (e.g. to an equitable freehold or leasehold estate) is competent to create only *equitable* easements and profits.

— *Duration*   An easement or profit which is not framed on the analogy of either a *freehold* or *leasehold* (i.e. is not created in perpetuity or for a fixed period) can, again, be equitable only (see LPA 1925, s 1(2)(a), (3), **8.16**). Thus any easement or profit which is created for some other period (e.g. for life) takes effect as an equitable right.

— *Mode of creation*   Equitable status also attaches, inevitably, to any easement or profit which is not created:

- by *deed* (see LPA 1925, s 52(1), **7.6**);
- by *statute* (**8.19**);

- by *implication* (**8.20, 8.23**); or

- by *prescription* (**8.21–8.22**).

The informal grant of an easement or profit gives rise, at most, to an equitable right (see *Wood v Leadbitter* (1845)). It is certainly the case, however, that an equitable easement or profit can be created in writing otherwise than by deed, provided that the transaction is for value. This outcome represents simply another application of the doctrine of *Walsh v Lonsdale* (**9.9**) (see e.g. *ER Ives Investment Ltd v High* (1967), **12.42**). Likewise a specifically enforceable contract to grant an easement or profit gives rise to rights of an equitable character, so long as the contract is intended to create immediate rights.

(It used to be that an equitable easement or profit could be created by an *oral* agreement for value supported by part performance (see *McManus v Cooke* (1887)). Now that the doctrine of part performance no longer applies to informal agreements concerning land (LP(MP)A 1989, s 2(8), **9.6**), a merely verbal grant can create equitable rights only if there are circumstances which justify a claim of *proprietary estoppel* on behalf of the intended grantee (**8.19, 10.18–10.19**)).

— *Completion by registration* Only equitable rights can subsist where, in registered land, the express grant of a legal easement or appurtenant profit *à prendre* is not itself 'completed by registration' (see LRA 2002, s 27(1), (2)(d), **7.8, 8.16**).

Termination of equitable easements and profits

9.14 As in the case of legal easements (**8.26**), an equitable easement is terminable by a merger of dominant and servient tenements in common ownership. The dominant owner may also release equitable easements and profits either expressly or impliedly (**8.26**) and may be taken to have done so in circumstances in which it would be inequitable to revive the rights thereby abrogated (*Davies v Marshall* (1861)).

Transmission of the benefit and burden of equitable easements and profits

9.15 The *benefit* of equitable easements and appurtenant profits *à prendre* is transferable only in conjunction with the estate to which that benefit relates (**8.24–8.25**). Any transfer of the dominant land (whether registered or unregistered) is effective to pass the benefit of such rights to the transferee (LPA 1925, s 62(1)–(2)), since these equitable rights are annexed to the dominant realty no less effectively than are legal rights (see *Leech v Schweder* (1874)).

The *burden* of equitable easements and profits *à prendre* is capable of passing to third parties who later take a transfer of the servient land.

— In *registered land* equitable easements and profits are binding on a disponee who takes otherwise than for valuable consideration (LRA 2002, s 28(1)). In all other cases, however, the relevant burden is enforceable against a registered disponee of the servient land only if that burden was the subject of a 'notice', entered prior to the registered disposition in question, in the charges register relating to the servient tenement (LRA 2002, s 29(1), (2)(a)(i), **12.11**). Equitable easements and profits created *after* the commencement of the LRA 2002 no longer rank as interests which automatically 'override' registered dispositions of the servient land (in sharp contrast to the binding status controversially accorded to equivalent rights created *prior to* 13 October 2003: see *Celsteel Ltd v Alton House Holdings Ltd* (1986), **12.26**). An easement or profit which comprised an overriding interest *before* this commencement date will continue to 'override' pursuant to the LRA 2002 (see LRA 2002, Sch 12, para 9).

— In *unregistered land* equitable easements and profits (if created on or after 1 January 1926) can be rendered enforceable against subsequent purchasers of the servient land by the registration of a Class D(iii) land charge against the name of the estate owner who granted the right in question (LCA 1972, s 2(5), **12.36**). (Equitable easements and profits created prior to 1926 remain governed by the equitable doctrine of notice (**2.43, 12.42**).)

Equitable mortgages and charges

9.16 Mortgage charges are normally created at law (**8.28**)—institutional lenders tend to accept nothing less on a first mortgage of realty—but it is not impossible that various kinds of mortgage or charge may be created *in equity*. These can take various forms, including:

- a mortgage of a borrower's equitable interest in land (**9.17**);
- an informal or incomplete mortgage of a legal estate in land (**9.18**);
- a mortgage by deposit of documents of title coupled with a written and signed contract of loan (**9.19**);
- an equitable charge (**9.20**);
- a charging order under the Charging Orders Act 1979 (**9.21**);

- an unpaid vendor's lien over the subject matter of a sale (**9.22**); and
- a purchaser's lien to secure a deposit (**9.23**).

Mortgage of an equitable interest in land

9.17 A mortgage or charge may remain *equitable* precisely because it is created over a mere *equitable* interest in land, e.g. a beneficial interest under a trust of land (**9.34**) (see also *First National Bank plc v Thompson* (1996)). Such a mortgage or charge is usually effected by the assignment of the equitable interest to a lender as security for money advanced, the assignment being subject to a proviso for re-assignment on full repayment of the loan (see *Thames Guaranty Ltd v Campbell* (1985)). (A prudent assignee immediately gives notice of the assignment to the relevant land trustees in order to obtain priority over other mortgagees under the rule in *Dearle v Hall* (**15.28**).)

A mortgage or charge of an equitable interest is self-evidently *equitable* and is, in any event, effective only if the assignment is made either by will or by other signed writing (see LPA 1925, s 53(1)(c), **10.5**). Equitable mortgages of an equitable interest under a trust of land are normally overreached (**2.34, 2.42, 11.30**) on a transfer of the legal estate in that land to a third party, and are thereafter satisfied out of the proceeds of sale in the hands of the trustees (LPA 1925, s 2(1)(ii)).

Informal or incomplete mortgage of a legal estate in land

9.18 An equitable mortgage or charge also arises where the owner of a legal estate in land:

- mortgages the estate *otherwise than by deed*; or
- charges the estate by way of legal mortgage, but the chargee *fails to complete* the disposition by securing the entry of his name as registered proprietor of the charge at Land Registry; or
- *contracts* to mortgage or charge the estate, but the contract is never completed by the execution of a deed.

— *Purported legal charge over a registered estate* A mortgage of a *registered* estate which is not itself completed by registration cannot, until it is duly registered, constitute a registered charge (**8.29**). The charge therefore takes effect only in equity, a consequence which reinforces a more general approach adopted by equity in cases of defective disposition. Equity 'looks on that as done which ought to be done' and, under the doctrine in *Walsh v Lonsdale* (**9.9**), treats informal or incomplete transactions as valid *equitable* mortgages of the legal estate (see *Swiss Bank Corpn v Lloyds Bank Ltd* (1982)). The operation of this equitable doctrine presupposes, of course, that the relevant preconditions of specific enforceability have been met and, in particular, that the mortgage transaction to which equitable effect is given has its roots in a contract contained in writing and signed by all relevant parties (LP(MP)A 1989, s 2(1), **9.6**). (Transactions undertaken prior to 27 September 1989 must comply merely with the less rigorous requirement of written evidence or part performance imposed by LPA 1925, s 40, **9.9**.) The equitable charge which emerges from an informal or incomplete mortgage of a legal estate in registered land requires to be protected by the entry of a 'notice' in the borrower's register of title if it is to be enforceable against subsequent disponees of the registered estate (LRA 2002, ss 32–4, **12.11**).

— *First legal charge over an unregistered estate*   Where a charge is drawn as a first legal charge over an unregistered estate in land (and accompanied by the deposit of title deeds), the charge requires to be completed, within two months of the date of the charge, by first registration at Land Registry of the borrower's estate and of the lender's charge thereover (**8.31**). Failure to register within this time limit causes the charge to lose its legal status, rendering it a mere contract for valuable consideration to create a legal charge (i.e. an equitable charge only) (LRA 2002, s 7(1), (2)(b)). In such circumstances the equitable chargee is protected by his retention of the relevant title deeds.

— *Other equitable mortgages over an unregistered estate in land*   are protectable by registration of a 'general equitable charge' under Class C(iii) of the Land Charges Act 1972 (LCA 1972, s 2(4), **12.36**).

Equitable mortgage or lien by deposit of documents of title

9.19   Under a venerable doctrine dating back more than two centuries (see *Russel v Russel* (1783)), it used to be possible to create an equitable mortgage of land, without the necessity of writing or any other formality, through the mere deposit by a land-owner of his title deeds or land certificate. Such deposit readily gave rise to an equitable mortgage if coupled with an intention that the depositee should hold such document or documents as his security for a loan of money. Documentary deposit was generally, although probably inaccurately, construed as a sufficient act of part performance to amount to evidence of a contract to create a mortgage (see *Swiss Bank Corpn v Lloyds Bank Ltd* (1982)). The bank customer whose unsecured overdraft had reached dangerously high levels frequently found himself faced with a curt request that he drop his documents of title into the bank: such a deposit functioned, without further formality, as a highly convenient form of real security.

— *Requirement of written contract* It is now absolutely clear that an equitable mortgage can no longer be created by the mere act of documentary deposit. The Law of Property (Miscellaneous Provisions) Act 1989 invalidates almost all contracts relating to land not contained in writing signed by all parties (LP(MP)A 1989, s 2(1), **9.6**), with the consequence that, in the absence of a written contract, there subsists no agreement in respect of which the act of documentary deposit could ever be said to provide evidence. Notwithstanding the deposit of all relevant documents, an agreement to mortgage land can no longer be made orally and the convenient practice of equitable mortgage by deposit is now wholly ineffective *unless* coupled with a written contract signed by both lender and borrower (see *United Bank of Kuwait plc v Sahib* (1997)). It is significant that the LRA 2002 deliberately contains no replica of an earlier statutory provision (LRA 1925, s 66) authorising the creation of liens and charges over registered land by mere documentary deposit.

— *Protection of an equitable mortgage or charge by deposit* An equitable mortgage or charge by deposit and signed contractual writing may be protected (in the case of registered land) by the entry of a 'notice' in the charges register of the title affected (LRA 2002, ss 32–4, **12.11**). In unregistered land such mortgages are excluded from the category of registrable general equitable charges under Class C(iii) (see LCA 1972, s 2(4), **12.36**), precisely because the lender's retention of the title deeds provides him with adequate protection against adverse dealings with the legal estate.

Equitable charge

9.20 An equitable charge can be created when land or any interest in it (whether legal or equitable) is expressly made liable, or specially appropriated with immediate effect, to the discharge of a debt or some other obligation. Thus, even without any deposit of title documents, an informal arrangement under which land is declared to be security for a debt creates an equitable charge. Although such a charge brings about 'no change of legal or equitable ownership', it nevertheless generates for the chargee some sort of 'proprietary interest' or 'security interest' in the land (*Buhr v Barclays Bank plc* (2001) at [47] per Arden LJ; *Kinane v Mackie-Conteh* (2005) at [18] per Arden LJ), the chargee having a right of realisation by judicial process (usually through an order for sale or the appointment of a receiver) (see *Bland v Ingrams Estates Ltd* (2001) at [17]–[19] per Nourse LJ). An equitable charge of this kind must, at the very least, be contained in writing signed by the chargor (LPA 1925, s 53(1)(a)). The Court of Appeal has recently left open the question whether the creation of such a charge is governed by the even more onerous requirements of LP(MP)A 1989, s 2(1) (**9.6**) (see *Kinane*, supra), although, if so, some relief may be found in the doctrine of estoppel (see *Bankers Trust Co v Namdar* (1997)). A validly created equitable charge over a *legal* estate can be protected, in the case of registered land, by the entry of a notice (**12.11**) and, in the case of unregistered land, by registration of a general equitable charge (**12.36**). A charge over an *equitable* interest constitutes an overreachable interest in the case of both registered and unregistered land (**9.17**).

Charging order under the Charging Orders Act 1979

9.21 The device of the charging order now provides an increasingly important mechanism for the legal recovery of debts. Under the Charging Orders Act 1979 it is open to a creditor, on obtaining a High Court or county court judgment in respect of a debt, to apply to the court for a 'charging order' for the purpose of enforcing the judgment in his favour. The court has discretion whether or not to make a charging order (COA 1979, s 1(5): see *Harman v Glencross* (1985)).

— *Effect* A charging order, if made, converts what was at most a contractual debt into an enforceable security with proprietary attributes. The order has the effect of imposing on specified property of the debtor a 'charge for securing the payment of any money due … under the judgment or order' (COA 1979, s 1(1)). The range of property potentially affected includes any interest held by the debtor beneficially in land (COA 1979, s 2(1)(a)). The principal advantage of a charging order is that the charge imposed by the court becomes enforceable 'in the same manner as an equitable charge created by the debtor by writing under his hand' (COA 1979, s 3(4), **9.20**). Accordingly the judgment creditor ultimately has a right to invoke legal process for the purpose of realising his security together with appropriate interest (see *Ezekiel v Orakpo* (1997)), and is entitled to apply to the court either for an order for sale of the property charged or for the appointment of a receiver.

— *Protection* In the case of *registered land*, the judgment creditor can protect his charge against third parties by the entry of a 'notice' in the register of the debtor's title (LRA 2002, ss 32–4, **12.11**) or, where the charging order relates to an interest under a trust, by the entry of a 'restriction' (LRA 2002, s 42(1)(c), (4), LRR 2003, r 93(k), **7.8**). In *unregistered land* protection is available through registration of the charge under the Land Charges Act 1972 in the register of writs and orders affecting land (LCA 1972, s 6(1)(a), **12.38**).

Unpaid vendor's lien

9.22 The vendor of land retains an *equitable lien* over this land if he transfers the legal estate to the purchaser or gives him possession before the purchase money is paid in full (see e.g. *Bridges v Mees* (1957)). The *unpaid vendor's lien* thus operates as the vendor's security for full payment of the agreed purchase price and is accounted as a species of mortgage (see LPA 1925, s 205(1)(xvi)). In effect, the lien confers on the vendor an equitable charge over the land from the date of the contract of sale, with the potentially significant consequence that a lender whose advance is intended to assist the purchase can claim, to the extent that this money reaches the vendor, to be subrogated to the unpaid vendor's security (see e.g. *Halifax plc v Omar* (2002) at [84], **15.14**). In *registered land* the protection of an unpaid vendor's lien depends on the entry of a 'notice' in the *vendor's* register of title immediately following the contract of sale which generated the lien (**12.11**). In *unregistered land*, the lien is protectable against subsequent purchasers as a Class C(iii) general equitable charge under the Land Charges Act 1972 (**12.36**).

Purchaser's lien to secure deposit

9.23 A lien may arise by operation of law over a vendor's land where a contract for sale remains unperformed. This equitable lien entitles the purchaser to recover any deposit which has already been paid under the contract (**9.4**). The *purchaser's lien to secure deposit* operates as an equitable charge (**9.20**) and may be particularly significant, for instance, where land is developed as a housing estate. In such circumstances it is not uncommon for the developer to market most of the properties before they are built. Each purchaser enters into a contract to buy a house which is to be erected on a particular plot and pays over a deposit to the developer (see e.g. *Lyus v Prowsa Developments Ltd* (1982), **9.18**). If the developer goes into liquidation before completing the construction, the lien may be vital in enabling the purchaser to recover his deposit money (see e.g. *Chattey v Farndale Holdings Inc* (1998)), but the lien requires protection by the entry of a 'notice' against a vendor's registered title (**12.11**) and registration of a Class C(iii) land charge in the case of unregistered land (**12.36**).

Restrictive covenants

9.24 A *restrictive covenant* is an agreement between two estate owners limiting the use of the land of one for the benefit of the other. Restrictive covenants rank in English law as *equitable proprietary interests* in land (**2.5**). They have come to play a significant role in the preservation of environmental welfare and are almost invariably found in any residential context which involves multiple habitation in conditions of close proximity. Although not confined to the residential sphere, restrictive covenants have as their primary function the safeguarding of various kinds of amenity considered important for enlightened urban planning and civilised coexistence. A typical restrictive covenant comprises an undertaking that the covenantor's land shall not be used for any trade or business or shall be used for residential purposes only. Restrictive covenants may equally seek to control the extent, type or density of the construction permissible in certain areas or, more insidiously, to police the lifestyles of those living within an area or development by protecting the tone of the neighbourhood. Restrictive covenants often restrain various kinds of noise or nuisance, or the number or character of domestic animals which may be kept as pets, or otherwise regulate the nature and quality of a locality.

In many respects the role of the privately bargained freehold restrictive covenant has been overtaken, since the late 1940s, by various regimes of public planning law (**13.22**). There is, however, mounting evidence that restrictive covenants frequently function as the residual guarantor of a degree of environmental amenity which individual citizens can no longer count on receiving at the hands of their local planning authority (see Gray and Gray, 'The Future of Real Burdens in Scots Law' (1999) 3 *Edinburgh Law Rev* 229 at 234). Existing public planning controls, operating under conditions of increasing pressure, cannot be concerned with all the detailed matters for which private covenants make provision. The device of the restrictive covenant remains a valuable and efficient means of land use control, in that it enables land use preferences to be targeted accurately—at minimal transaction cost—by the very persons best positioned to assess the environmental utility required in given contexts (**13.5**).

The limitations of contractual regulation

9.25 Restrictive covenants are often generated by a simple bilateral agreement between two estate owners. Even more frequently, as in the case of a large building development, a network of intersecting bilateral agreements between the developer and each individual purchaser brings about a complex structure of locally enforceable regulations about land use within the area concerned. But a profound difficulty arises—irrespective of whether the contractual model involves only *two* covenanting parties or *many*. Each restrictive covenant has clear contractual force as between the *covenantor* and *covenantee* but, in accordance with the traditional rules concerning privity of contract, can never confer burdens on others who later purchase the estate of the original covenantor. Yet any purposive scheme of environmental control would be fundamentally flawed if bilateral constraints on land use, designed to produce beneficial long-term effects, were liable to be frustrated by any change in ownership of the land involved. A purely contractual scheme of land regulation, precisely because it cannot by common law impact on third parties, is doomed to failure.

The evolution of a new proprietary interest

9.26   The limitations of purely contractual regulation were quickly recognised in the burgeoning industrial and residential development which occurred in mid-19th-century England. The courts' response was the initiation of a doctrine which rested the enforcement of covenants between freeholders, not on privity of contract or even privity of estate (**14.20**), but rather on 'the equitable principle of privity of conscience' (see *Forestview Nominees Pty Ltd v Perpetual Trustees WA Ltd* (1998)). This revolutionary development effectively transformed *contractual arrangements* into a species of *proprietary right*; and because the innovation was achieved by the courts of equity (in the days before the fusion of jurisdiction), the proprietary right generated by the doctrinal change was clearly classified as *equitable*. After the landmark decision of *Tulk v Moxhay* (1848), the covenantee under a restrictive covenant came to be viewed as having, in some sense, a *proprietary* interest in the covenantor's land to the extent of the covenantee's entitlement to control activities conducted on that land (**2.5**). The covenantee's interest in the performance of the covenantor's promise was regarded as no longer a purely contractual interest. Somewhat as in the case of the estate contract (**9.8**), the covenantee's *contractual right* had enlarged into, and arrogated to itself the character of, a *proprietary interest* in the land. Most significantly, as a proprietary interest, it acquired the potential to confer both benefits and burdens on third party strangers to the original covenant.

> *Tulk v Moxhay* (1848) T sold a vacant portion of his land in Leicester Square to E, who covenanted on behalf of himself, his heirs and his assigns that he would keep and maintain that land 'in an open state, uncovered with any buildings, in neat and ornamental order'. The land was later conveyed to M, who had full knowledge of the restrictive covenant agreed between T and E. Lord Cottenham LC upheld an injunction restraining M from building on the open land in defiance of the covenant. This decision was grounded on the stern view taken by equity on matters of conscience. The Lord

Chancellor accepted that the vital question was 'whether a party shall be permitted to use the land in a manner inconsistent with the contract entered into by his vendor, and with notice of which he purchased'. Lord Cottenham thought that 'nothing could be more inequitable than that the original purchaser [i.e. the covenantor] should be able to sell the property the next day for a greater price, in consideration of the assignee being allowed to escape from the liability which he had himself undertaken'. In order to prevent such an unconscionable outcome, the Lord Chancellor concluded that 'if an equity is attached to the property by the owner, no one purchasing with notice of that equity can stand in a different situation from the party from whom he purchased'.

There is today no doubt that '[t]he benefit of a restrictive covenant … can constitute a valuable asset. It is incorporeal but it is, nonetheless, property' (*Commonwealth of Australia v State of Tasmania* (1983) per Deane J).

Defining characteristics of enforceable restrictive covenants

9.27 Precisely because of the potential impact of restrictive covenants on third parties, the courts were careful—even from the earliest period—to lay down strict criteria governing the recognition of an enforceable restrictive covenant (**2.18**). To this day certain requirements (over and above requirements of register entry (**9.32**)) must be met before a covenant can be enforced otherwise than between the original parties. The imposition of these limiting threshold conditions was thought necessary not least in order to prevent the proliferation of undesirable 'clogs upon the title' of land. The defining characteristics of the enforceable restrictive covenant include the following:

- the covenant must be *negative* or *restrictive* of the user of land (**9.28**);
- the covenant must relate to an identifiable *dominant tenement* (**9.29**);
- the covenant must *benefit* or *accommodate* the dominant tenement (**9.30**);
- the covenant must have been *intended to be made on behalf of the covenantor's successors in title* (**9.31**).

The covenant must be negative or restrictive of the user of land

9.28 Equity takes cognisance of only those covenants which are, in their nature, truly negative or restrictive of the user of land (see *Haywood v Brunswick Permanent Benefit Building Society* (1881)). The equitable principle underlying *Tulk v Moxhay* was soon declared to have no application to positive covenants and, because the purview of equity was now confined to restrictive covenants, the remedy provided by equity for the enforcement of restrictive covenants became pre-eminently the remedy of *injunction*. The question whether a covenant is *restrictive* always involves a test of substance. A covenant phrased in a restrictive manner (e.g. a covenant 'not to let the property fall into disrepair') may nevertheless conceal a positive covenant to repair. A commonly used rule of thumb holds that if the covenantor is required 'to put his hand into his pocket', the covenant cannot be negative in nature (see *Haywood v Brunswick Permanent Benefit Building Society* (1881) per Cotton LJ).

The covenant must relate to an identifiable dominant tenement

9.29 On a clear analogy with the law of easements (**8.6**), a restrictive covenant can be enforced only if it relates to a defined *servient tenement* and is appurtenant to an ascertainable *dominant tenement*: there cannot, in general, be any restrictive covenant *in gross*. Moreover, the covenantee must own an estate in the dominant tenement at the date of the making of the covenant and the covenantor must likewise own an estate in the servient tenement (see *London CC v Allen* (1914)). Dominant and servient tenements need not be immediately adjacent, but must be sufficiently close to satisfy the requirement of benefit to the dominant tenement (**9.30**). As Pollock MR once indicated, 'land at Clapham would be too remote and unable to carry a right to enforce ... covenants in respect of ... land at Hampstead' (*Kelly v Barrett* (1924)). Moreover, if the covenantee subsequently parts with all of the dominant tenement, he loses the right to enforce the covenant except against the original covenantor (and even then the only remedy available will be a nominal recovery in damages).

Only limited exceptions are made from the otherwise stringent requirement of dominant ownership (e.g. on the sale of the last plot subject to a 'scheme of development' or 'building scheme' (**13.17**)). Likewise, some public and quasi-public bodies are dispensed by statute from any requirement of dominant ownership. (Local planning authorities are allowed, for instance, to enter into restrictive planning agreements with land developers for the purpose of guaranteeing the preservation or improvement of local amenities (see Town and Country Planning Act 1990, s 106; Planning and Compulsory Purchase Act 2004, ss 46–7 (**13.23**))—a prolific modern source of restrictive covenants unattached to any definable dominant tenement.)

The covenant must benefit or accommodate the dominant tenement

9.30 No restrictive covenant can be enforced in equity unless the covenant in question was made for the *benefit and protection* of dominant land retained by the covenantee. (In the past this requirement was sometimes expressed in the form that the covenant must 'touch and concern' the land of the covenantee (see e.g. *Rogers v Hosegood* (1900)).

— *Benefit must be real rather than personal* Whether the criterion be formulated in terms of 'benefit' or 'accommodation' or 'touching and concerning' quality, the underlying idea is essentially the same. A restrictive covenant capable of enforcement against third parties must, in some way, enhance the *dominant land* rather than gratify some merely personal interest or whim which is dear to the heart of the covenantee. Nowadays, however, it tends to be presumed that a covenant confers benefit upon the alleged dominant tenement unless it can be shown that such a view cannot reasonably be held (see e.g. *Wrotham Park Estate Co Ltd v Parkside Homes Ltd* (1974)). It is a fairly rare covenant which does not involve 'something affecting either the value of the land or the method of its occupation or enjoyment' (*Re Gadd's Land Transfer* (1966) per Buckley J). For instance, most covenants restricting property to residential use or prohibiting various kinds of development pretty clearly 'benefit' the dominant land in the required sense.

— *The 'benefit' requirement filters out undesirable long-term burdens on land* By excluding commitments of a substantially personal character, the requirement of 'benefit' to land operates as a residual restraint upon eccentric, ideological or religious prejudices which it is not in the public interest to impose as long-term burdens upon any piece of land. One might, for instance, have a whimsical belief that soap operas or party political broadcasts rot the mind of the television viewer; one might even persuade one's neighbour on public health grounds to covenant that she would never watch such programmes on her servient land; but such a commitment could never be visited indefinitely on successive owners of that servient tenement. The 'benefit' criterion conveniently filters out those capricious undertakings which cannot, in any reasonable sense, be said to accommodate the allegedly dominant tenement.

The covenant must have been intended to be made on behalf of the covenantor's successors in title

9.31 Since equity looks always to matters of intention, no restrictive covenant can bind third parties unless it was intended by those who created it to have a wider than purely personal effect. Nowadays this requirement is easily satisfied, at least in relation to those covenants entered into on or after 1 January 1926. Unless a covenant is phrased in such a way that it clearly binds only the original covenantor, there is a statutory presumption that any restrictive covenant relating to land of the covenantor was intended to be made on behalf of the covenantor's successors in title, on behalf of all persons deriving title from him or them, and also on behalf of 'owners and occupiers for the time being' of the land affected (see LPA 1925, s 79(1)–(2)). The rebuttable presumption that such covenants are not intended to be purely personal operates as 'a necessary condition, but not a sufficient condition, for making the burden of the covenants run with the land' (*Morrells of Oxford Ltd v Oxford United Football Club Ltd* (2001) at [40] per Robert Walker LJ). In order that the burden should 'run with the land' so as to bind successors, other conditions (relating to register entry) also require to be fulfilled (**13.18**).

The third party impact of restrictive covenants

9.32 The scope of the ruling in *Tulk v Moxhay* (**9.26**) was soon limited to *restrictive* covenants entered into between *freeholders*. (Restrictive covenants arising in the *leasehold* context have always been the subject of a different regime of enforcement (**14.20**).) It was nevertheless clear that *Tulk v Moxhay* recognised the covenantee, by virtue of his contractual control over user, as having some form of 'property' in the covenantor's land (**2.5**). Indeed, as an *equitable* right of property the restrictive covenant was binding on all persons other than a bona fide purchaser of a legal estate for value without notice (actual or constructive) of the covenantee's rights (**12.42**). The covenantee's entitlement is today categorised as a proprietary interest within the canon of estates and interests recognised by the 1925 legislation. Not being included amongst the statutory list of entitlements which can exist *at law* (see LPA 1925, s 1(1)–(2), **8.1**), the restrictive covenant can exist only *in equity*—although this result is entirely consistent with its historic provenance. The 1925 legislation, as adapted by the LRA 2002, creates a convenient framework which enables both the benefit and the burden of freehold restrictive covenants to run with land so as to affect later estate owners.

> **Example**: A is the covenantor and B the covenantee in relation to a restrictive covenant which precludes trade or business user on A's land. A later transfers his legal fee simple estate to C, and B transfers his legal fee simple estate to D (see *Fig 6*). May D now enforce the restrictive covenant against C?

— *Transmission of the burden from A to C* In relation to restrictive covenants created between freeholders after 1925, the traditional doctrine of notice has been displaced or modified by rules which require protection by register entry.

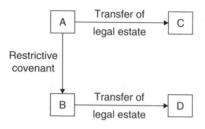

Fig 6

- In *registered land*, the burden of A's covenant passes to C only if B has entered a 'notice' in the charges register of A's title (LRA 2002, ss 29(1), (2)(a)(i), 32–4, **12.11–12.13, 13.18**). (A restrictive covenant cannot rank as any category of overriding interest.)

- In *unregistered land*, the burden of A's covenant passes to C only if registered by B against A as a Class D(ii) land charge (LCA 1972, ss 2(5), 4(6), **12.36**). (In relation to freehold restrictive covenants entered into before 1926—effectively those covenants regulating buildings on unregistered land which are now at least 80 years old—the equitable doctrine of notice still applies (**12.42**).)

— *Transmission of the benefit from B to D*   Unless the benefit of the restrictive covenant passes to D, it is irrelevant that its burden has been duly fixed on C: the covenant will be unenforceable by D against C (see e.g. *J Sainsbury plc v Enfield LBC* (1989)). In both *registered* and *unregistered* land, however, the benefit of A's covenant is normally transmitted to D as an incident of the estate transferred by B to D, the benefit having been 'annexed' (or attached) to B's land by virtue of LPA 1925, s 78(1) (*Federated Homes Ltd v Mill Lodge Properties Ltd* (1980), **13.15**) (see also Contracts (Rights of Third Parties) Act 1999, s 1(1)–(2), **13.11**).

Extinguishment, modification, and discharge of restrictive covenants

9.33 Freehold restrictive covenants are extinguished by any supervening unity of ownership and possession of the dominant and servient tenements (see *University of East London Higher Education Corpn v Barking and Dagenham LBC* (2005) at [53]–[54]). They may also be terminated by voluntary release (usually in return for a cash premium or equivalent value). There exists, moreover, a statutory jurisdiction, vested in the Lands Tribunal, to discharge or modify—with or without compensation—restrictive covenants which have become 'obsolete' or have come to 'impede some reasonable user of the land for public or private purposes' (see LPA 1925, s 84(1), **13.20**).

Beneficial interests under a trust of land

9.34 A further, and extremely important, category of equitable proprietary rights in land emerges in the range of beneficial entitlements generated by various forms of *trust* affecting land (**1.26**). These rights comprise the subject of the remainder of this chapter and will also be dealt with in Chapters 10 and 11.

The constitution of a beneficial interest in land

9.35 Fundamental to trust law is the proposition that a transfer of a legal title in land carries with it, prima facie, the *absolute* beneficial interest in the property conveyed (*Pettitt v Pettitt* (1970) per Lord Upjohn). Equity, in this respect, 'follows the law' (**9.2**) and, indeed, there is no strict need to distinguish between *legal* and *equitable* ownership whilst land is vested in one person absolutely (**1.25**). However, as soon as some *other* person asserts a competing beneficial or equitable entitlement in the land, an onus rests on that person to demonstrate that beneficial title does *not* coincide with the existing legal ownership. The claimant must be able, in effect, to 'establish a basis upon which equity would intervene on [his or] her behalf' (*Allen v Snyder* (1977) per Mahoney JA), and equity intervenes only if such action is necessary in order to give effect to one or other of its doctrines (**9.2**).

Accordingly, trusts are founded on the willingness of equity, consistently with its historic concern with conscience, to call into existence some form of *equitable* interest or ownership in opposition to the *legal* title. The recognition of such beneficial entitlement amounts to the finding of a *trust relationship*: the owner of the legal estate in land is conventionally described as holding his legal title *on trust* (in whole or part) for the claimant or *cestui que trust*. (It matters not, for present purposes, whether the legal ownership is concentrated in *one* trustee or in *several* trustees collectively. Nor is it relevant whether beneficial ownership is asserted by more than one claimant or even shared with some or all of the trustees in some independent capacity as *cestui que trust* (**1.26, 11.20**).)

Nowadays almost all claims to a *beneficial interest* in land necessarily presuppose the existence of a statutorily governed 'trust of land' under the Trusts of Land and Appointment of Trustees Act 1996. In order that such a trust of land should exist,

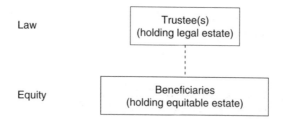

Fig 7

it must be shown that the person in whom the legal estate in land is vested 'holds it as a trustee upon trust to give effect to the beneficial interest of the claimant' (*Gissing v Gissing* (1971) per Lord Diplock). It is here that the difficulties in trust law begin, for some degree of controversy often surrounds the definition of the precise circumstances which will permit equitable rights to be impressed on pre-existing legal titles under the compelling mandate of conscience (**10.5, 10.14–10.15**).

— *The role of conscientious obligation* The point cannot be overemphasised that the trust embodies the practical realisation of equity's historic *Leitmotiv*—the idea that conscientious obligation takes priority over strict legal right. This does not mean, however, that a trust arises in *every* case where broad considerations of justice or fair play seem to demand that a trust should come into existence. Such an outcome would ultimately cause every litigant's claim 'to be consigned to the formless void of individual moral opinion' (see *Carly v Farrelly* (1975) per Mahon J). The tradition of English equity (as distinct, perhaps, from that practised elsewhere in the common law world) is that the courts do not sit 'as under a palm tree, to exercise a general discretion to do what the man in the street, on a general overview of the case, might regard as fair' (*Springette v Defoe* (1992) per Dillon LJ).

— *The role of intention* As befits a jurisdiction which is less impressed by form than by substance, equity's recognition of the trust focuses ultimately on matters of *intention*. Indeed, beneficial ownership depends fundamentally on intentions, proved or presumed, as to the equitable title in land. These intentions are often found expressed in documentary form. Sometimes they must be gathered (with greater difficulty and perhaps many years later) from parol evidence tendered by participants or bystanders (**10.14**). Failing such evidence, inferences as to intention may be drawn from the conduct of the parties (**10.15**); and, in the last resort, certain equitable presumptions as to intention may have to come into play (see *Pettitt v Pettitt* (1970) per Lord Upjohn, **10.3–10.4**). The ascertainment of relevant intention is particularly problematic in relation to the family home, since arrangements for domestic cohabitation are usually forged over the course of many years in a fairly ill-defined and inarticulate fashion.

The classification of trusts of land

9.36 'Trusts of land' under the Trusts of Land and Appointment of Trustees Act 1996 can be classified as either *express trusts* or *implied trusts*, the latter category subdividing into further categories of *resulting* and *constructive* trusts (see *Fig* 8).

Consistently with the characteristic preoccupation of equity, the primacy of intention is highlighted in each of the three cases of trust with which we shall be concerned.

- The *express trust* is the very embodiment of an intention formulated by a legal owner regarding the beneficial ownership of his property (**9.37**).
- The *resulting trust* gives effect to an intention presumed to have been formulated in the light of money contributions made in the context of a purchase of land (**10.3**).
- The *constructive trust* arises in circumstances where it would be unconscionable not to give effect to a common intention or bargain which has provided the basis of the parties' mutual expectations and dealings (**10.6**).

The terminology used to refer to these different kinds of trust sometimes lacks uniformity and consistency (see e.g. *Burns v Burns* (1984), **10.15**, where May LJ described as a resulting trust what would more usually be called a constructive trust). For the moment, however, we shall leave these confusions aside and concentrate on the *expressly created* trust of land, reserving the difficulties of *implied* trusts for explanation in Chapter 10.

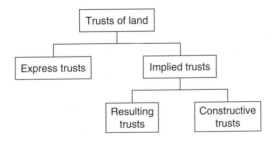

Fig 8

Express trusts of land

9.37 An *express trust of land* arises principally in two sorts of circumstance:

- *either* where A, the sole owner of a legal estate in Greenacre, expressly declares himself to be a trustee of that estate for B, whether absolutely or in respect of some limited or fractional beneficial interest (*Fig 9*)

- *or* where S, the sole owner of a legal estate in Redacre, transfers that estate to A, subject to a trust of the estate (accepted, and thus declared, by A) under which B is entitled to an absolute or limited or fractional beneficial interest (*Fig 10*).

An express trust need not be phrased in a particular formula; any words which plainly evince an intention to create a trust will be sufficient. Provided this beneficial intention is clear, it is possible that 'a person may create a trust, as Monsieur Jourdain talked prose, without knowing it' (see *Re Schebsman, decd* (1944) per Du Parcq LJ). Thus an express trust can be generated by some loosely worded conferment of a life interest or fractional share or even by the grant of some functional equivalent of a limited interest, as where A undertakes to allow B rent-free occupation for life of some of A's land (see e.g. *Bannister v Bannister* (1948), **10.9**). Likewise the person who fondly declares that he regards his spouse or

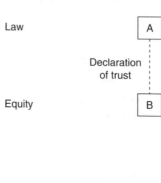

Fig 9

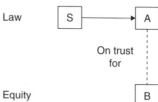

Fig 10

partner as having equal rights with him in his home may well find that he has effectively created a trust of the legal estate in her favour (see *Hammond v Mitchell* (1991) per Waite J, **10.14**).

Statutory requirement of formality

9.38 It matters not whether an express trust is declared contemporaneously with the acquisition of the legal estate or at some subsequent time. It is generally irrelevant whether an express trust nominates one beneficiary or many; it may allocate various kinds or sizes of equitable entitlement. However, irrespective of the content of the express trust, one overriding rule prevails in English law: a declaration of trust relating to land is enforceable *only* if 'manifested and proved' by some writing signed by the declarant (LPA 1925, s 53(1)(b)). The date of the writing is irrelevant—it would even be sufficient that the fondly generous domestic partner (**9.37**) subsequently recorded his generosity on the back of an envelope and signed it—but *without* such written evidence a declaration of trust relating to land is simply *unenforceable*.

— *Rationale* This venerable requirement of formality, dating back to the Statute of Frauds 1677, performs at least two related functions:

- it curtails costly controversy arising from mistaken or fraudulent allegations of beneficial ownership (perhaps many years after the events in dispute)
- it provides a classic illustration of the general disfavour shown in English land law towards informal mechanisms of rights creation.

The requirement of written evidence also severely restricts the possibility that informal language—particularly in the domestic context—may lead to the creation of unexpected trust relationships. In the absence of writing a trust 'does not come into being merely from a gratuitous intention to transfer or create a beneficial interest' (*Austin v Keele* (1987) per Lord Oliver of Aylmerton). The failure of documentary formality brings about, at least initially (**9.39, 10.14**), a 'merely voluntary declaration of trust ... unenforceable for want of writing' (*Gissing v Gissing* (1971) per Lord Diplock).

— *Electronic declarations* The LRA 2002 contains provisions for electronic dealings with interests in land (**7.6**). An electronically signed document will be deemed to be a deed (LRA 2002, s 91(5)), with the result that it will necessarily satisfy the requirements for an enforceable declaration of trust under LPA 1925, s 53(1)(b) (see Law Com No 271 (2001), para 13.19).

Exemptions from the requirement of formality

9.39 However compelling the policy motivation behind the statutory requirement of written evidence of an express trust of land, there are nevertheless certain circumstances where even this potent rationale is displaced by concerns ranking higher in the scale of values which animate equitable jurisdiction. These concerns permit an exception from the statutory formality rule in cases where insistence on compliance with the rule would occasion an even greater offence against equitable principle—usually where failure to relax the statutory requirement enables the declarant of an oral trust to profit from his own unconscionable conduct.

— *Resulting and constructive trusts* (**10.3**, **10.6**) are exempted from the requirement of written evidence by the LPA 1925 itself. If the beneficial ownership protected by such forms of trust were to be shut out by a dogmatic exclusion of all supporting evidence of a merely *parol* nature, the inequity of outcome thereby caused would outweigh the policy motivation underpinning the statutory requirement of signed writing. In consequence the 1925 Act provides that the requirement of documentary formality does not affect the 'creation or operation of resulting, implied or constructive trusts' (see LPA 1925, s 53(2)). It is therefore quite possible that an originally unenforceable oral declaration of trust may sometimes become enforceable, not as an express trust, but rather as a *resulting* or *constructive* trust. For example, an informal declaration of equal beneficial entitlement for a spouse or partner may later acquire a new vitality as a *constructive trust* if the recipient of the declaration has since acted to her detriment in reliance on the substance of the initially unenforceable representation (**10.11**).

— *Use of statute as an instrument of fraud* is abhorrent to equity. The fundamental purpose of the statutory formality rule is to prevent fraud being practised upon a trustee by those who fabricate allegations of trust. But the insistence on formality is not pursued to the insensate degree that reliance upon an absence of writing is allowed to facilitate fraud *by the trustee himself*. Thus the rule in *Rochefoucauld v Boustead* (1897) abrogates the statutory requirement of writing where A acquires a title in land from X on terms of A's express oral undertaking that he will, from the moment of acquisition, hold on trust for B. From the date of his acquisition onwards, A is affected by a fiduciary obligation towards B, and it would be fraud in equity if A were to rely on the absence of written evidence as a ground for disavowing the very trust on whose terms he was enabled to acquire title. (The rule in *Rochefoucauld v Boustead* has, incidentally, no application to oral declarations of trust made *after* the date of A's acquisition of title—since there would otherwise be no circumstances at all which came within the reach of LPA 1925, s 53(1)(b).)

Conclusive effect of a declaration of trust

9.40 An express declaration of trust, when duly supported by signed writing, is almost always definitive as to the nature and extent of the beneficial rights subsisting under a trust of land. At least as between the persons who execute (i.e. sign) the declaration, the declaration 'necessarily concludes the question of title ... for all time' (*Pettitt v Pettitt* (1970) per Lord Upjohn). Nowadays, in the case of any transfer of registered land to joint proprietors, the statutorily prescribed Land Registry form (TR1) includes a declaration of trust specifying the nature and extent of the intended beneficial entitlements (see LRA 2002, s 25(1); LRR 2003, rr 58, 206(1), Sch 1, **11.24**). All new joint proprietors are now, therefore, encouraged to execute a written declaration of trust which settles their equitable rights.

> **Example**: A legal estate is transferred into the joint names of A and B, subject to an expressly declared trust for themselves as beneficial *joint tenants* (**11.2, 11.20**). Here the equitable rights of A and B are clarified definitively as those of joint tenants (see *Pettitt v Pettitt* (1970) per Lord Upjohn). In other words, either A or B can later and quite unilaterally sever the beneficial joint tenancy (**11.10**), thereby becoming entitled to an equal share as a beneficial *tenant in common* irrespective of the precise money contributions made by A and B towards the purchase of the property. This result follows inexorably from the binding nature of the beneficial terms on which they initially agreed to hold the legal estate. Severance by A will, for instance, net a 50 per cent beneficial share for A even though all the purchase money was paid by B.

Only extremely limited exceptions are permitted from this rule of conclusive effect:

— *Rescission for fraud or mistake* The terms of an express declaration of trust can be rebutted by evidence of 'fraud or mistake at the time of the transaction' by which the legal title is vested (*Pettitt v Pettitt* (1970) per Lord Upjohn). This ground of exception is, however, construed extremely narrowly. It is, for example, entirely irrelevant that the technical significance of the declaration of trust was quite incomprehensible to a lay person (see e.g. *Pink v Lawrence* (1978)).

— *Rectification* Apart from instances of fraud or mistake, it is possible in rare cases that a court may grant rectification of a declaration of trust in order to give effect to intentions which the parties clearly had at the date of the transaction, but which were expressed only imperfectly or not at all in the declared trust (see e.g. *Wilson v Wilson* (1969)).

Dispositions of land held on trust

9.41 The legal estate in land held subject to a trust of land should (in the case of *registered* land) be registered in the name of the trustee or trustees; and the equitable interests of the trust beneficiaries may be protected—at least to some degree—by the entry of a 'restriction' in the proprietorship register of the trustees' title (LRR 2003, rr 91(1), 93(a), 94(1), 95(2)(a), **7.8**). For this purpose the registrar has a general discretion to enter a 'restriction' in order to secure that overreachable trust interests are in fact overreached (LRA 2002, s 42(1)(b)). Indeed, the registrar *must* enter such a 'restriction' in any case where two or more persons are recorded in the Land Register as joint proprietors of a registered title and hold as trustees otherwise than for themselves as beneficial joint tenants (LRA 2002, s 44(1), **11.29**).

The rationale underlying the facility of restrictions in this context is, of course, the fact that any subsequent disposition of a registered estate held on trust which results in payment of capital money to the registered proprietors (being at least *two* in number) automatically overreaches the equitable interests of the trust beneficiaries (LPA 1925, ss 2(1)(ii), 27(2))—whether or not those beneficiaries are themselves 'in actual occupation' of the land (see *City of London Building Society v Flegg* (1988), **2.34, 11.30**). The beneficiaries' rights attach thereafter to the money held by the trustees. (Exactly the same result follows in the case of *unregistered land* (**2.42**).) The consequence, in either case, is that the disponee of the legal estate takes title absolutely free of the beneficial trust interests, although these interests are preserved in an equivalent money form in the capital proceeds of the disposition.

Life interests under a trust of land

9.42 It is not impossible that the author of an express trust of land may confer on a particular beneficiary some beneficial interest other than an absolute or fractional equitable interest (**9.37**). The most obvious alternative beneficial entitlement is a *life interest* (see LPA 1925, s 1(3))—a limited right which might very well seem to make sense where it is desired to make short- to medium-term residential provision for an intended beneficiary. The creation of a life interest (followed inevitably by an interest in *remainder* or *reversion* (**1.18, 7.4**)), is nowadays severely disadvantageous for tax reasons and is therefore rather rare. Nevertheless, if created in relation to land on or after 1 January 1997, a life interest takes effect, not under the Settled Land Act 1925 (**9.43**), but under a trust of land governed by the Trusts of Land

and Appointment of Trustees Act 1996 (TOLATA 1996, s 2(1), **11.25**). The declaration of trust containing the beneficial life interest (together with any interest or interests in remainder) must be evidenced, as usual, by signed writing (LPA 1925, s 53(1)(b), **9.38**). In the event of any subsequent disposition of the legal estate, the beneficial entitlement of the holder of the life interest is normally overreached on payment to the trustees of the capital proceeds of the transaction (LPA 1925, s 2(1)(ii), **9.41, 11.30**). His rights thereafter attach to this money as held by the trustees (in effect, as rights to the annual income derived from the investment of the capital).

Life interests under the Settled Land Act 1925

9.43 Life interests which were created in land prior to 1997 (otherwise than behind an express 'trust for sale' (**9.44**)) still take effect under a 'strict settlement' governed by the Settled Land Act 1925. This legislation provided an ingenious and highly artificial mechanism for the regulation of a range of successive and limited interests in land (**7.3–7.4**). Although originally devised to facilitate dynastic patterns of landholding, it had become obvious, even by the commencement of the Settled Land Act 1925, that the institution of the strict settlement of land had outlived its social and economic purpose. Ironically the 1925 Act incorporated the very machinery required to dismantle the great settled estates of England, introducing means by which the legal title in settled land could most efficiently be sold off and the beneficial interests under the settlement afforded some degree of financial protection. The provisions of the Settled Land Act 1925 are nowadays of virtually antiquarian interest only (see Law Com No 271 (2001), para 11.45). The fiscal consequences of a strict settlement are disastrous and it came to be the case, long before 1997, that only the unwary and the misguided ever fell into the trap of Settled Land Act settlements (usually through the informal conferment of a life interest in the confused circumstances of some family arrangement) (see e.g.*Bannister v Bannister* (1948); *Ungurian v Lesnoff* (1990); *Costello v Costello* (1994), **10.28**).

— *Creation of a strict settlement* It is integral to the proper constitution of a strict settlement that two documents should be executed—a *vesting deed* (which vests the paper—i.e. legal—title in the settled land in the appropriate recipient) and a *trust instrument* (which details the beneficial entitlements intended to be held under the trusts of the settlement) (SLA 1925, ss 4(1), 6; LRA 2002, s 89(1); LRR 2003, r 186, Sch 7, para 4). The settlor usually nominates up to four persons (who may include a settlement beneficiary) to act as 'trustees of the settlement'

(SLA 1925, s 30(1)) and who play a residual role of oversight in relation to the affairs of the strict settlement.

— *Vesting of the legal estate in the 'tenant for life'* Central to the scheme of the Settled Land Act is the concept that, wherever possible, the commerciable legal estate in the settled land—the fee simple or the term of years—should be vested in the 'tenant for life' (usually the person currently entitled in possession to a beneficial life interest) (SLA 1925, s 19(1); LRA 2002, s 89(1); LRR 2003, r 186, Sch 7, paras 1, 4(3)). Thus the holder of a life interest in possession has a dual entitlement. The quantum of his beneficial enjoyment is confined to his *life interest* (in terms of either occupation of the land or receipt of rents and profits drawn from it). But he also holds (or is entitled to call for) the full *legal estate* in the settled land (SLA 1925, s 9(2); LRR 2003, r 186, Sch 7, para 9), with which he then stands invested as a fiduciary on behalf of all those holding beneficial interests under the settlement (including himself) (SLA 1925, s 107(1)). In effect, the split role of the tenant for life marks the distinction between the *managerial* or *administrative responsibilities* in respect of the entire settled estate (which attach to his function as tenant for life) and his entitlement to *personal beneficial enjoyment* (as measured by his own equitable interest under the settlement).

— *Powers of the tenant for life* The tenant for life, in addition to his competence to deal independently with his own beneficial life interest, is statutorily invested with a range of important powers in relation to the legal estate in the settled land (SLA 1925, ss 38–72). He is empowered, as a fiduciary, to *sell* the legal estate and (subject to certain restrictions) to *lease* and *mortgage* the settled land. These powers can be expanded by the express terms of the settlement (SLA 1925, s 109(1)), but any provision which purports to prohibit, restrict or inhibit the tenant for life's exercise of his statutory powers is, by statute, declared 'void' (SLA 1925, s 106(1)).

— *Sale of the settled estate* The most significant of the tenant for life's powers is, ultimately, his power to sell the legal estate in the settled land (SLA 1925, s 38(i)). Here the statutory device of overreaching (**2.34, 2.42, 11.30**) enables the land to be disposed of entirely free of the beneficial interests of the settlement, these interests surviving the disposition as beneficial entitlements in the capital money generated by the transaction (see *Fig* 11). A 'restriction' should be entered in the register in order to ensure that the necessary preconditions of overreaching are met and the trusts of the settlement overreached (LRA 2002, s 42(1)(b); LRR 2003, r 186, Sch 7, paras 2, 3, 4(2), 7(1), **7.8**). The proprietorship register (in the case of *registered land*) and the vesting deed (in the case of *unregistered land*) will thus make it obvious to any stranger that the land is subject to the trusts of a strict settlement and will, moreover, identify the trustees of that settlement (SLA 1925, s 5(1); LRR

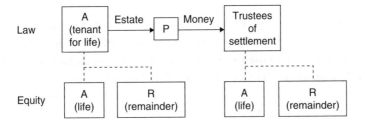

Fig 11

2003, r 186, Sch 7, para 4(1)). Provided that the disponee of the legal estate pays the capital money arising on the disposition to the *trustees of the settlement* (of whom there must be at least *two*), he takes the legal title entirely unencumbered by the beneficial interests (SLA 1925, ss 18(1)(c), 94(1); LPA 1925, s 2(1)(i)). These interests are automatically swept off the land and, precisely because this is so, the purchaser normally has no right to call for or to inspect the trust instrument (SLA 1925, s 110(2)). In the case of settled land, however, the preconditions of statutory overreaching are enforced with rigour. Any unauthorised disposition which fails to ensure that the capital proceeds are safeguarded by payment to the settlement trustees is, in a most draconian provision, declared void by statute (SLA 1925, s 18(1)(a): see e.g. *Weston v Henshaw* (1950)).

Beneficial interests under a trust for sale

9.44 Prior to 1997 virtually all *concurrent* interests in land—in effect all forms of co-ownership of a legal or equitable estate—were required to exist *either* under an express 'trust for sale' deliberately created for the purpose *or* under a 'trust for sale' arising by implication of statute (**11.22**). It was also possible that some *successive* interests (e.g. life interests) could take effect expressly under a 'trust for sale' of land. As initially conceived by the 1925 legislation, the trust for sale placed its pre-eminent focus on the exchange value, as distinct from the use value, of land (see *Mortgage Corpn v Shaire* (2001) per Neuberger J). However, the terminology of the trust *for sale*, whilst it may have made some sense in the contemporary context of 1925, later came to seem highly inappropriate—particularly in relation to land held by co-owners who had no intention or desire to *sell* their estate. TOLATA 1996 brought about radical changes.

— The *statutorily implied trust for sale* (**11.23**) has now disappeared, all existing instances being automatically converted into 'trusts of land' (TOLATA 1996, ss 1(1)–(2), 5(1), Sch 2).

— *Existing express trusts for sale* continue in existence and *new trusts for sale* can be *expressly* created, but with the important qualification—in both cases—that, notwithstanding any provision to the contrary, the trustees have an irreducible power to *postpone sale* (TOLATA 1996, s 4(1)–(2)).

FURTHER READING

Gray and Gray, *Elements of Land Law* (4th edn, OUP, 2005), ch 9.

Relevant sections of this work and other land law textbooks may be supplemented with:

Barnsley, David 'Equitable Easements—Sixty Years On' (1999) 115 *LQR* 89.

Maitland, Frederic William *Equity* (2nd edn, London, 1936).

Hopkins, Nicholas 'Acquiring Property Rights from Uncompleted Sales of Land' (1998) 61 *MLR* 486.

Wilde, David 'Formalities for Declaring Trusts of Land', in P. Jackson and D.C. Wilde (eds), *Contemporary Property Law* (Ashgate, 1999), p 204.

SELF-TEST QUESTIONS

1   What is the impact of equity's tendency to 'look on that as done which ought to be done' (**9.7, 9.9, 9.18**)?

2   In what circumstances is a mortgage charge over land *equitable* rather than *legal* (**9.16–9.20**)?

3   Can I acquire an enforceable restrictive covenant which stops my neighbours (and their successors in title) from ever watching *Coronation Street* on television (**9.30**)?

4   In what kinds of circumstance does equity fashion a trust in order to regulate proprietary entitlement (**9.35–9.36**)?

10

Informal creation of rights in land

SUMMARY

English law generally disfavours the informal creation of long-term proprietary rights in land. Yet such rights can arise by way of:

- *implied trusts* (which give effect in equity to the presumed intentions or informal bargains which underlie the acquisition of legal title);
- *proprietary estoppel* (which gives some kind of force to promises of entitlement which have been the subject of reliance);
- *informally conferred life interests* (which emerge from ill-defined arrangements for long-term occupation); and
- *donatio mortis causa* (an informal—and extremely rare—testamentary substitute).

Informal mechanisms of rights creation

10.1 As will be clear from earlier chapters, English law—and particularly the common law—is heavily influenced by a distaste for *informal* mechanisms directed towards the creation of property rights in land. Considerations of clarity and certainty argue strongly in favour of the use of *formal* means of rights creation such as those provided by a deed or other formal writing (see LPA 1925, s 52(1), **7.6**; s 53(1), **9.38**). Yet the powerful policy motivation underlying the requirement of formality sometimes comes into collision with even more significant concerns, particularly of equitable origin, which override the general preference that rights in land should be created or evidenced by documentary means alone. Equity attaches ultimate priority to the underlying intent of transactions and to the demands of conscionable dealing (**9.2**). Although the conscience of equity is far from comprising a complete system of social or commercial morality, the longstop of equity is an abhorrence of *fraud*, especially where it subverts the basic intentions or shared understandings underpinning various sorts of transaction.

English law therefore allows, in certain circumstances, for the *informal* creation of rights in land where a dogmatic insistence on documentary formality would grossly controvert the relevant intentions of the parties or unconscionably frustrate their legitimate expectations. Such cases are recognised principally, although not exclusively, by the law relating to:

- implied trusts (**10.2**);
- proprietary estoppel (**10.18**);
- informally conferred life interests (**10.28**);
- donationes mortis causa (**10.29**).

Classification of implied trusts

10.2 The generic category of *implied trusts* (**9.36**) consists of two subgroups of trust relationship:

- the resulting trust (**10.3**), and
- the constructive trust (**10.6**).

Whereas *express* trusts are founded on the expressly declared intentions of the parties (**9.37**), *implied* trusts arise by operation of law, albeit against the background of the parties' actual or presumed intentions. In relation to the latter sorts of trust the documentary requirements normally imposed by statute on the creation and operation of trusts have no application (LPA 1925, s 53(2), **9.39**). Although much recent case law has tended to conflate resulting and constructive trusts, Lord Browne-Wilkinson has pointed out that they 'are two different animals' and that failure to distinguish them has caused 'great confusion' (see 'Constructive Trusts and Unjust Enrichment' (1996) 10 *Trust Law International* 98 at 99). Claims of resulting or constructive trust feature in those cases where parties are unable to found their allegation of beneficial entitlement on any enforceable *express* trust, their hopes of success being relegated, therefore, to the contention that an *implied* trust of some variety has been generated in their favour.

— *Resulting trusts* are generally concerned with the pattern of money contributions laid out in the purchase of property. A resulting trust gives effect to the intentions which are presumed to underlie the way in which such moneys are put towards the acquisition of a legal title. In the absence of any intention of gift or loan, a money contribution towards the purchase of a legal estate in the name of another will usually generate a resulting trust on behalf of the contributor, the latter's equitable entitlement being in strict arithmetical proportion to his or her cash contribution.

— *Constructive trusts* are intimately concerned—not so much with money—but rather with expressly or implicitly bargained commitments respecting equitable entitlement. A constructive trust arises where it would be fraudulent for the owner of a legal title to assert his sole beneficial ownership in derogation of equitable rights which have already been bargained away informally to another. The existence of the prior bargain, once relied on by the claimant party, now renders it unconscionable for the legal owner to assert his beneficial title to the exclusion of that claimant. To prevent such inequitable outcomes, equity imposes or 'constructs' a trust to give effect to the parties' earlier understanding as to their respective equitable rights.

— *The avoidance of confusion* Both forms of implied trust are alike exempted from any requirement of formal writing or evidence, but the ambivalent relationship between them stems precisely from the fact that each is premised upon *intended* beneficial ownership—in one case as inferred from the pattern of money purchase, and in the other case as embodied in some antecedent bargain struck by the relevant parties. The nomenclature of trust law is 'unfortunately far from uniform' (see *Birmingham Midshires Mortgage Services Ltd v Sabherwal* (2000) per Robert Walker LJ) and further confusion flows from the fact that the constructive trust coalesces remarkably with many applications of the principle of proprietary estoppel (see *Yaxley v Gotts* (2000) per Robert Walker LJ (**10.12**); *Chan Pui Chun v Leung Kam Ho* (2003) at [91] per Jonathan Parker LJ). Despite indiscriminate references in the case law (**9.36**), it is probably best nowadays to regard the *resulting trust* as a relatively rare phenomenon applicable only where contributions of *cash* have been channelled directly towards the initial purchase of realty, thereby relegating all other forms of contributory activity (whether *before* or *after* the acquisition of title) to be dealt with under the law of *constructive trusts* (see e.g. *Mollo v Mollo* (1999)).

Resulting trusts

10.3 Resulting trusts reflect the *presumed intentions* of parties who join together in a cooperative purchase of property. Like all presumptions of intended beneficial ownership, the presumption of resulting trust is 'no more than a consensus of judicial opinion disclosed by reported cases as to the most likely inference of fact to be drawn in the absence of any evidence to the contrary' (*Pettitt v Pettitt* (1970) per Lord Diplock).

> **Example 1:** The presumption of resulting trust operates in cases where a legal estate is purchased in the name of one person (A) with the aid of money provided entirely by another (B). According to a venerable doctrine of equity, a 'trust of a legal estate … results to the man who advances the purchase-money' (*Dyer v Dyer* (1788) per Eyre CB). The *nominal* purchaser (A) is deemed to hold the legal estate on a trust which 'results' back to the *real* purchaser (B), A holding only a bare paper title in the land **(11.26)** whilst B is presumed to take the absolute beneficial ownership (see *Fig* 12).

> **Example 2:** If A and B *both* contribute money towards a purchase of a legal estate in the name of A (or even of A and B), the doctrine of resulting trust presumes the beneficial interest to be taken by them both in proportion to their respective contributions (see *Fig* 13). The principle of resulting trust is adaptable, mutatis mutandis, to any number of financial contributors: each is presumed to have intended to take beneficially in proportion to his own contribution of cash.

— *Rationale of the resulting trust* A resulting trust arises where the availability of more precise information concerning the source of purchase money displaces the prima facie inference that *equitable ownership follows legal title* **(9.2, 9.35, 11.9, 11.24)**. Equity, with its superbly realistic grasp of human motivations, 'assumes bargains, and not gifts'. In the normal run of things, people who lay out large cash

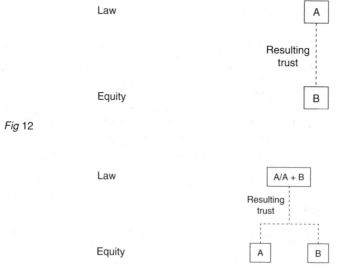

Fig 12

Fig 13

sums in the context of a purchase of land do not harbour particularly altruistic intentions, but really rather expect, regardless of the destination of the legal title purchased, to derive a beneficial return from their investment in the form of an *aliquot share* of the equity. (The legal title is, after all, a mere paper title; and equity's concern has long been with the inner substance of transactions rather than with their outer form (**1.24, 9.2**).) Thus, in responding to 'the solid tug of money' (see *Hofman v Hofman* (1965) per Woodhouse J), the presumption of resulting trust acknowledges the general inequity of allowing A to retain property purchased in his own name without acknowledging the material assistance given in its purchase by B. If B pays money *in the character of a purchaser*, equity, in second-guessing the average view of the matter, holds it to be unconscionable for A subsequently to assert an *absolute* legal and beneficial title in the subject matter of the purchase. Accordingly the doctrine of resulting trust recognises an 'equity' as inhering in B in direct proportion to his contribution—an 'equity' which is founded on the assumed intention of both parties that B should participate in the beneficial ownership. In this sense, the resulting trust simply gives 'the force of law to moral obligations' (*Sekhon v Alissa* (1989) per Hoffmann J). Nor, perhaps controversially, are these moral obligations diminished by the fact that B may have had improper motives for arranging to make money contributions towards the purchase of a title vested deliberately in A (see e.g. *Tinsley v Milligan* (1994), where a majority in the House of Lords upheld a claim of resulting trust notwithstanding that B's contributions were both motivated and facilitated by a conspiracy to defraud the Department of Social Security).

— *Time-frame of the presumed intention* According to the classic theory, resulting trusts are based on intentions presumed to exist at the date of *acquisition* of the property concerned, at which point the precise distribution of beneficial entitlement is definitively 'crystallised' (see *Bernard v Josephs* (1982)). In a very strict sense the only intentions relevant to a *resulting* trust—as distinct from a *constructive* trust (**10.10**)—are those which can be presumed to have been contemporaneous with the initial taking of legal title (see *Pettitt v Pettitt* (1970) per Lords Morris of Borth-y-Gest and Upjohn; *Gissing v Gissing* (1971) per Lords Reid and Diplock and Viscount Dilhorne). Events or circumstances *subsequent* to acquisition are thus incapable, in principle, of raising any presumption of resulting trust. Later contributions of money (towards improvement of the property or otherwise) cannot normally, in the rigorous theory of resulting trust, generate any presumed intention as of the date of acquisition (see e.g. *Curley v Parkes* (2004) at [14]–[19] per Peter Gibson LJ).

— *The problem of instalment purchase* The major difficulty with this historic concentration on the isolated moment of purchase is that it fails to take account of that relatively modern phenomenon—the mortgage-assisted purchase of land (which, in reality, elongates the process of acquisition over many years). Clearly, it is inequitable to apply resulting trust theory in total disregard of mortgage instalments paid or shared over a prolonged period by some party other than the mortgagor-owner of the legal estate. Yet it is exceedingly difficult to accommodate the practice of instalment purchase within the dogmatic confines of the resulting trust without contorting the doctrine to almost unimaginable extremes. For a while the courts attempted to suggest that, contrary to basic principle, conduct subsequent to the acquisition date might sometimes provide a ground for retrospective inference as to the actual intentions of the parties on that date. However, the inevitable artificiality of this approach had the effect of causing a gradual slippage away from resulting trust theory towards more liberating applications of constructive trust, where the timing of relevant intentions has never been so critically defined (**10.10**). It is for this reason that, although much of the debate in the case law remains inarticulate and confusing, the primary phenomenon in the area of implied trusts is fast becoming the *constructive* trust (see *Curley v Parkes* (2004) at [15] per Peter Gibson LJ, **10.5**).

Rebuttal of the presumption of resulting trust

10.4   The presumptions of equity are, indeed, only that—they are *presumptions*, based on standardised expectations of human action and reaction. Presumptions of intention are called into play only in the absence of convincing evidence of the *actual* intentions of the parties. As an American judge once said, 'presumptions may be looked on as the bats of the law, flitting in the twilight but disappearing in the sunshine of actual facts' (*Mackowik v Kansas City* (1906)). The presumption of resulting trust is therefore rebuttable by any evidence (including parol evidence) which unambiguously demonstrates that B, although providing all or part of the finance for a purchase in the name of A, did not actually *intend* to take a beneficial interest in the property (see *Pettitt v Pettitt* (1970) per Lord Upjohn). Alternatively, the precise proportions of beneficial ownership indicated by a presumed resulting trust are sometimes overturned by reference to a different pattern of intended entitlement which is inferable (by way of constructive trust) from the whole course of the parties' mutual dealings (see *Oxley v Hiscock* (2005), **10.15**). A presumed resulting trust may even be displaced by a counter-presumption of equitable origin. The categories of circumstance which throw up evidence of a countervailing intention sufficient to oust the presumption of resulting trust include the following:

—   *Gift*   The possibility of resulting trust is clearly excluded if the *nominal purchaser* (A) can show any actual evidence of *donative intent* on the part of a money contributor to his purchase (B). No resulting trust can be claimed, for instance, by the father who announces at his son's wedding reception that he proposes to give the newly married couple money to set up a house (see *Walker v Walker* (1984)). Compelling evidence of a gift relationship, particularly in the family context, pre-empts any explanation that cash provision was intended to generate either loan-based contractual rights or equity shareholding behind a resulting (or any other) trust. Statute deals, moreover, with one specific case of donative intent. The doctrine of resulting trust presupposes a purchase in the name of A of property previously owned by a stranger. No presumed resulting trust arises by strength of the mere fact that B, the current owner of a legal estate, transfers that estate voluntarily (i.e. gratuitously) into the name of A (LPA 1925, s 60(3): see *Ali v Khan* (2002) at [24] per Morritt V-C). Under these circumstances and in the absence of any evidence of contrary intention, A takes both legal and equitable title *absolutely*.

— *Counter-presumption of advancement* The presumption of resulting trust is sometimes displaced by a countervailing equitable presumption, the 'presumption of advancement'. This presumption relates to a specialised form of assumed gift. The presumption of advancement operates, in certain restricted and stylised circumstances, to supply an inference of *donative intent* in the case of money contribution to somebody else's purchase of a legal estate. In these sorts of circumstance, the presumption of resulting trust which would normally arise on the basis of a provision of cash is rebutted by a contrary presumption that the contributor in fact wished to 'advance' (or make a gift to) the nominal purchaser of the legal title. The presumption of advancement tends to arise in familial contexts where altruism, rather than cold cash calculation, may be expected to be the motivating force behind transactions of purchase. In effect, 'the presumption of gift arises from the moral obligation to give' (*Bennet v Bennet* (1879) per Jessel MR) and, unless itself rebutted by evidence of actual contrary intention, confirms that the purchaser is entitled absolutely (i.e. both at law and in equity). When it applies, the presumption of advancement simply reinforces 'the prima facie position . . . that the equitable interest is presumed to follow the legal estate and to be at home with the legal title' (*Calverley v Green* (1984) per Deane J).

> **Example:** A father provides the funds for the purchase of a legal estate in the name of his adult son. The son is presumed to take the estate both at law and in equity, on the ground that, by virtue of the bonds of familial affection, his father had some 'obligation in conscience to provide' (see *Scott v Pauly* (1917)). The father is presumed, in other words, to have intended to make a *gift* of his money contribution to the son.

• The presumption of advancement is applicable to a range of family relationships—although oddly not as between *mother* and child (see *Sekhon v Alissa*

(1989)). Nor is the presumption applicable to money contributions made by a child towards a *parent*'s acquisition of a legal estate (a phenomenon given some contemporary currency by the prevalent practice of council house purchase (**7.40**)). Here the child still takes under a resulting trust (*Binmatt v Ali* (1981)).

• The stark reality is that the concept of presumed advancement has a distinctly patriarchal resonance which causes many to question whether, under modern social conditions, it properly has any substantial role in the ascertainment of beneficial intentions. The presumption may now have dwindled to a 'judicial instrument of last resort' (see *Ali v Khan* (2002) at [30] per Morritt V-C). Its most controversial historical application—between husband and wife—has encountered devastating criticism. In *Pettitt v Pettitt* (1970) Lord Diplock considered it 'an abuse of legal technique … to apply to transactions between the post-war generation of married couples "presumptions" which are based upon inferences of fact which an earlier generation of judges drew as to the most likely intentions of earlier generations of spouses belonging to the propertied classes of a different social era' (see also *Lowson v Coombes* (1999) per Robert Walker LJ). The presumption of advancement nowadays seems unlikely to illuminate questions of equitable ownership between living spouses in anything other than the most marginal way.

— *Loan* A lender does not advance money *in the character of a purchaser* and can therefore take no beneficial interest under any presumed resulting trust. The fact of loan generally negatives any intention creative of a trust. Were it otherwise, banks and building societies would acquire a myriad of beneficial interests in the millions of properties bought on the strength of mortgage advances.

• One of the attractions of the standard mortgage device (from the borrower's viewpoint) is that the lender is *not* an equity participant in the inflating value of the realty purchased with the help of the mortgage loan. It is normally the exclusive privilege of the 'home-owning democrat' to ride up on the increasing worth of his or her 'equity of redemption' (**8.28, 15.3**). Except in the case of the 'shared appreciation' mortgage (**15.6**), the lender's rights are confined to contractually based rights to the repayment of capital plus interest, backed up by a right of possession and a power of sale should the borrower default (**15.20–15.21**).

• Exceptionally a private lender derives larger rights from a loan of money made as part of a family arrangement which contemplates, perhaps rather hazily, that the lender should be afforded, pending repayment, some form of residential privilege in the property purchased. But even here, the existence of a loan excludes the possibility of an aliquot share under a resulting trust and the lender's rights are measured in terms of some more tentative entitlement such as an irrevocable equitable licence or proprietary estoppel (**4.9, 10.27**).

> *Re Sharpe (A Bankrupt)* (1980) S acquired a leasehold interest in a shop and maisonette, much of the purchase price being contributed by S's 77-year-old aunt, J. J had sold her existing home and moved into the maisonette with S and his wife on the understanding that she would be able to stay there for as long as she wished. Acting on her solicitor's advice, J obtained from S a promissory note in respect of her financial contribution. When S later became bankrupt, Browne-Wilkinson J held that J had no interest in the maisonette by way of resulting trust, taking the view that the money paid by J had been paid by way of loan. He nevertheless thought that J had acquired a right, enforceable against S's trustee in bankruptcy, 'to stay on in the premises until the money she provided indirectly to acquire them has been repaid.' This right did not derive from any resulting trust, but was more in the nature of a 'contractual licence or an equitable licence or an interest under a constructive trust'.

— *Legally ineffective relationships* Some relationships, especially in the domestic context, provide no basis on which a resulting trust can be presumed from the mere fact that money changes hands. Here again the contributor cannot be said to have advanced the money *in the character of a purchaser*. Payments made to the owner of the legal estate may be more in the nature of contributions to current living expenses and shared outgoings (see e.g. the failure of trust claims in *Mehra v Shah* (2004)). The son who gives his mother part of his jobseeker's allowance whilst living at home does not normally acquire thereby a beneficial interest in his parents' realty.

> *Hannaford v Selby* (1976) A young couple bought a house in their own names with the aid of a mortgage loan. The wife's elderly parents moved in with them, paying £5 per week into the family kitty over a substantial period of time. When friction later erupted between the generations, Goulding J rejected the parents' claim to a beneficial interest in the home, holding that here the pattern of regular payments into a common pool resulted in no more than an occupation licence revocable on reasonable notice.

Contributions of 'purchase money' relevant to the resulting trust

10.5 The presumption of resulting trust depends on a finding that B has acted *in the character of a purchaser* by providing money for a purchase in the name of A. It has never been easy to identify the kinds of financial contribution which can be accounted as 'referable to' A's acquisition of title (see *Burns v Burns* (1984) per Fox LJ, **10.15**) and which can therefore serve as the basis of a presumed resulting trust.

In particular, it is difficult to establish the 'referable' character of a payment which was made (e.g. for improvements) some time *after* the acquisition of a particular property and full payment of its purchase price (see *Winkworth v Edward Baron Development Co Ltd* (1986)). In recent years the definition of relevant 'purchase money' has become strained to the point where it is best to reserve *resulting trust* terminology for the relatively straightforward, although unusual, case where outright contributions of money are made 'up front' at the point of purchase, leaving all other kinds of contribution to be assessed in terms of *constructive trust* (see *Curley v Parkes* (2004) at [15]–[16] per Peter Gibson LJ).

— *Direct contribution to cash price* The clearest and easiest case is that of direct cash contribution to the purchase price of property at the date of its acquisition. Regardless of the name or names in which the legal title is purchased, such a contribution raises, in the absence of contrary evidence, a presumption of resulting trust in exact proportion to the contribution.

> **Example 1:** The legal estate in Greenacre is transferred to A for £150,000. A provides £100,000 out of her own available cash resources and B provides £50,000 out of his. Here a resulting trust is presumed under which A takes a two-thirds interest and B a one-third interest (see *Cowcher v Cowcher* (1972) per Bagnall J). A and B are presumed, in effect, to have formulated a 'money consensus' that their respective beneficial interests should accord with the relative proportions of their contributions. This 'money consensus' requires no documentary formality under LPA 1925, s 53(1)(b) (see LPA 1925, s 53(2), **9.38–9.39**). Exactly the same outcome would follow if A's contribution is made possible by a mortgage advance of £100,000 from A's bank for the repayment of which A undertakes full responsibility. The loan money, once advanced to A by the bank, is regarded as the exact equivalent of A's freely available cash resources.
>
> **Example 2:** If A generously agrees, in the circumstances above, that notwithstanding the disparity in financial contributions she wishes B to have an equitable half-share, this attempt to vary the original 'money consensus' is ineffective in the absence of a written disposition of the extra one-sixth beneficial share which she is thereby purporting to give to B (see *Cowcher v Cowcher* (1972) per Bagnall J). The replacement of the original *presumed* 'money consensus' by a different and *actual* 'interest consensus' involves the 'disposition of an equitable interest or trust subsisting at the time of the disposition' and must therefore be 'in writing and signed by the person disposing of the same' (LPA 1925, s 53(1)(c)).
>
> **Note:** One possible escape route from the need for a written disposition of a larger beneficial share than strictly justified by the original resulting trust may be found in the law of *constructive trust* (**10.6**). If B were subsequently to rely to his detriment on A's offer

of increased beneficial entitlement—e.g. by applying his late Aunt Agatha's legacy to some substantial improvement of the realty—it would then seem 'unconscionable for [A] to set up the statute and repudiate the agreement' (*Re Densham (A Bankrupt)* (1975) per Goff J). A would, in effect, become a 'constructive trustee of the property so far as necessary to give effect to the agreement', so that B's eventual beneficial interest derives, as to one-third, from a *resulting* trust and, as to a further one-sixth, from a *constructive* trust.

— *Contribution to initial deposit or legal expenses* A resulting trust may also be presumed where B contributes in cash to the initial deposit or legal expenses payable on the acquisition of A's legal title (see *Gissing v Gissing* (1971) per Lord Diplock). However, there is now a tendency to subsume even these forms of payment under the heading of *constructive* trust (see e.g. *Halifax Building Society v Brown* (1996) per Balcombe LJ; *Curley v Parkes* (2004) per Peter Gibson LJ).

— *Contribution of council tenant's discount* A frequent contribution to the purchase of a legal estate nowadays takes the form of the statutory discount available to a council tenant on the purchase of the freehold reversion or long lease in his or her home (Housing Act 1985, s 126(1), **7.40**). This discount, which varies in accordance with the duration of the pre-existing secure tenancy, may well amount to many thousands of pounds. Family members often combine their efforts in the purchase, the value of the discount being contributed by the qualifying tenant and mortgage finance by another family member. In these circumstances, the availability of the statutory discount is now generally regarded as the equivalent of a contribution of money or money's worth for the purpose of generating a resulting trust of the legal estate (see *McKenzie v McKenzie* (2003) at [87]), despite the occasional judicial grumble that the discount is effectively a handout from the state and therefore 'money which is not provided by anybody' (*Evans v Hayward* (1995) per Staughton LJ).

— *Contribution of mortgage payments* It is nowadays rare for purchasers of land to finance their purchases entirely from their own freely available cash reserves. In *Gissing v Gissing* (1971), Lord Diplock pointed out that the 'economic reality' underlying the much more usual case of mortgage-assisted acquisition is 'that the freeholder is purchasing the family home upon credit and that the purchase price is represented by the instalments by which the mortgage is repaid in addition to the initial deposit in cash.' Of course, where some party other than the freeholder later contributes towards the discharge of the mortgage debt by contributing some portion of these mortgage instalments, it becomes (pace Lord Diplock) 'unreasonably legalistic' to leave out of account the shared pattern of payment. Nevertheless it has proved uncommonly difficult to accommodate such forms of collaborative purchase within the strictures of a theory of resulting trust, according to which beneficial entitlement 'crystallises' at the date of acquisition (see *Curley v Parkes* (2004) at [18]–[19] per Peter Gibson LJ). The modern trend—foreshadowed so long ago by Lord Diplock—is, instead, to treat a consistent pattern of regular and substantial contributions to the mortgage instalments as evidence from which it can be inferred, by way of *constructive trust,* that the relevant parties had a common intention to share beneficial ownership on a basis to be calculated more precisely later (**10.15**).

— *Other forms of contribution to general household welfare*   It is, again, extremely difficult to argue that other forms of contribution to the general welfare of a joint household can constitute the equivalent of money or money's worth sufficient to establish a presumed resulting trust. English land law recognises no distinct regime of family property—except, oddly, on divorce and death—and the mere sharing of family living expenses does not in itself connote a joint contribution towards the acquisition of family property (see *Gissing v Gissing* (1971) per Lord Diplock, **10.15**). Still less does the valiant devotion of household effort (by way of domestic management and child care) count as the equivalent of a cash contribution towards purchase of a jointly occupied family home. The fact that parties 'live together and do the ordinary domestic tasks is ... no indication at all that they thereby intended to alter the existing property rights of either of them' (*Burns v Burns* (1984) per Fox LJ, **10.15**). As so often, the invaluable comes to appear valueless, and the reward for generalised, and usually unquantifiable, contributions of domestic performance is to be found—if at all—only in the law of *constructive* trust.

Constructive trusts

10.6   Whilst resulting trusts focus on *contributions* towards the purchase of realty, constructive trusts are more heavily concerned with *bargains* relating to beneficial ownership (**10.2**). The starting point in the law of constructive trusts is the recognition that, consistently with its disfavour of informal mechanisms of rights creation, land law generally denies effect to mere oral gifts or bargains (LPA 1925, s 53(1)(b)–(c), **9.17, 9.38**). But once the repudiation of an informally promised beneficial entitlement crosses a certain threshold of unconscionable behaviour, equity is ultimately prepared to impose a special form of trust liability on the errant estate owner, thereby safeguarding the bargained interest notwithstanding its informality of origin. Accordingly, where the owner of a legal title has entered into an agreement, since acted upon, to share or allocate beneficial ownership in some particular way, equity will not allow him *unconscionably* to deny the beneficial interest conceded and will therefore 'construct a trust to give effect to it' (*Grant v Edwards* (1986) per Nourse LJ).

— *A formula of equitable relief* The constructive trust is, effectively, a counter-agent of equitable fraud. In Justice Cardozo's memorable phrase, it provides 'the formula through which the conscience of equity finds expression' (*Beatty v Guggenheim Exploration Co* (1919)). The constructive trust is, indeed, one of the most far-reaching of the devices used by equity in vindication of its own doctrines (see *Commissioner of Stamp Duties (Queensland) v Livingston* (1965) per Viscount Radcliffe, **1.25, 9.2**). In its more dramatic manifestations, the imposition of a constructive trust actually resembles a decree of *confiscation,* awarding to B, in whole or part, property which A had previously thought belonged to himself both at law and in equity.

— *Enforced compliance with a prior bargain* The constructive trust derives from no direct intention on the part of the legal estate owner to hold as a fiduciary—but rather because he has sought to *avoid* liability as a fiduciary. The trust is 'constructed' by the court precisely because of some prior bargain or common intention which makes the legal owner's assertion of an absolute beneficial title now appear wholly unconscionable (see e.g. *Banner Homes Group plc v Luff Developments Ltd* (2001), **10.11**).

The operation of the constructive trust

10.7 The constructive trust operates against a background in which an estate owner, A, has already bargained away some equitable entitlement in his land to B—and A then *resiles* from the bargain, possibly even pleading its ineffectiveness under the statutory rules requiring formality. (Had A granted B's entitlement under a written declaration of trust, B's equitable rights would, of course, have been absolutely secure (**9.38–9.40**).)

— *The Diplock formula* In the terms of Lord Diplock's now classic description of the constructive trust (see *Gissing v Gissing* (1971), **10.15**), equity enforces or 'constructs' a trust in circumstances where

> [A] has so conducted himself that it would be inequitable to allow him to deny to [B] a beneficial interest in his land.

Put in this way, the Diplock soundbite threatens to provide only an extremely vague—perhaps even circular—formula of general equitable relief. However, Lord Diplock instantly qualified the scope of the constructive trust by adding that the

278 | Informal creation of rights in land

inequitable outcome which the constructive trust aims to prevent will arise *only if*

[A] by his words or conduct has induced [B] to act to [her] own detriment in the reasonable belief that by so acting [she] was acquiring a beneficial interest in the land.

In such a case equity acts, if through no other means, to frustrate A's unconscionable behaviour by imposing on A's legal estate a constructive trust in favour of B. Unlike the unenforceable declaration contained in the prior informal bargain, this constructive trust is fully enforceable by B, precisely because constructive trusts are statutorily exempted from any requirement of formal writing (LPA 1925, s 53(2), **9.39**). Depending on the circumstances, the constructive trust imposed on A may confer on B either an *absolute* beneficial interest (e.g. an equitable fee simple estate) or a *limited* beneficial interest (e.g. a life interest) or a *fractional* beneficial interest (e.g. one-third or a half). The trust then takes effect as a 'trust of land' under the Trusts of Land and Appointment of Trustees Act 1996 (**9.35–9.36**).

— *The role of bargain* is central to the constructive trust. In *Gissing v Gissing* (1971), Lord Diplock observed that much previous case law on the constructive trust had passed over the first—and critical—stage in the analysis of this form of trust, i.e., 'the role of ... agreement ... in the creation of an equitable estate in real property.' The heavily formative function played by *agreement* has since been reinforced by the House of Lords in *Lloyds Bank plc v Rosset* (1991) (**10.13**). The equitable interest protected by the constructive trust results invariably from some antecedent bargain or agreement relating to the property, by which the owner of a legal title has undertaken to give effect to an equitable entitlement in someone else.

— *The role of conscience* is likewise vital in the genesis of a constructive trust. No court will impose a constructive trust 'unless it is satisfied that the conscience of the estate owner is affected' (*Ashburn Anstalt v Arnold* (1989) per Fox LJ); and the inequity which triggers the imposition of a constructive trust is established by a legal owner's disclaimer of obligations of conscience founded upon some prior agreement. In the words of Viscount Dilhorne in *Gissing v Gissing,* such a disclaimer amounts to a 'breach of faith', and equity immediately counteracts the equitable fraud by 'constructing' a trust.

Component elements of the constructive trust

10.8 Against this background, it can therefore be said that the imposition of a constructive trust requires proof of three elements:

- *bargain* (or common intention) (**10.10**);
- *change of position* (or detrimental reliance) (**10.11**); and
- *equitable fraud* (or unconscionable denial of rights) (**10.12**).

Moreover, these three elements are inevitably interlinked:

- A common intention is relevant only if one party *changes his or her position* in reliance upon the prior bargain.
- A change of position occurs only if truly *referable to a common intention* that rights of beneficial ownership should be acknowledged or shared by the legal owner.
- Equitable fraud is present only if the legal owner then *tries to deny the bargain* by asserting the absolute, exclusive or unqualified nature of his own rights.

Thus stated, the constituent elements of the constructive trust bear a remarkable similarity to the features of proprietary estoppel (**10.19**)—indeed some even refer nowadays to 'the estoppel principle enunciated by Lord Diplock in *Gissing v Gissing*' (see *Mason v Brown* (1997) per Deputy Judge Lawrence Collins QC). It is not uncommon to find that in many cases claims based on constructive trust and proprietary estoppel are pleaded in the alternative (see e.g. *Chan Pui Chun v Leung Kam Ho* (2003) at [91]–[93]).

Classic demonstration of constructive trust

10.9 The operation of constructive trust doctrine is classically demonstrated in *Bannister v Bannister* (1948).

> *Bannister v Bannister* (1948) B conveyed her freehold interest in two cottages to A, her brother-in-law, at much less than market value, upon A's oral undertaking that B would be allowed to live rent-free in one of the cottages for the remainder of her life. The conveyance made no reference to this oral promise. When, in the teeth of the agreement, A later sought to evict B from her home, the Court of Appeal ruled that A held his legal title on constructive trust to give effect to the beneficial life interest promised to B. Scott LJ held that a constructive trust is 'raised against a person who insists on the absolute character of a conveyance to himself for the purpose of defeating a beneficial interest, which, according to the true bargain, was to belong to another'. Equitable fraud of this kind could not be covered up by the plea that 'no written evidence of the real bargain is available'.

The facts of *Bannister* quite clearly disclosed:

- a *bargain* under which A acquired a legal estate at an undervalue in return for the offer of rent-free occupancy;

- a *change of position* by B in relying on the bargain to her detriment in conveying the property to A; and

- an *equitable fraud*—not necessarily at the actual date of transfer to A—but certainly as soon as A attempted, quite unconscionably, to set up an absolute entitlement for himself in derogation of the beneficial rights which he had already agreed should be taken by B.

Bargain or common intention

10.10 The role of authentic bargain (express or implied) is both central and irreducible in the context of the constructive trust. In *Oxley v Hiscock* (2005) the Court of Appeal identified, as 'the primary, or threshold, question' in co-ownership claims, the issue whether there was a common intention on the part of A and B that each 'should have a beneficial interest' in the land. Provided that there has been an agreement for *some form* of shared beneficial entitlement, this bargain can generate a constructive trust even though the agreement itself discloses no common intention as to the precise *quantum* of the parties' respective beneficial interests. Thus, for example, where the legal title is held by one party alone, quantification of entitlements raises a 'secondary, or consequential, question' which can settled later by the court with reference to what is fair in the light of the parties' 'whole course of dealing' in relation to the land. In this way the court may, on occasion, *infer* a real common intention from the parties' conduct (**10.15**), but the court—at least in the conventional view—may never *impute* to the parties a fictitious common intention for shared beneficial ownership.

— *Nature and timing of bargain* Provided that the parties' bargain is a demonstrable fact, their agreement need not expressly refer to the legal owner as a *trustee*: it is sufficient that there is a common intention to confer or share some recognisable form of proprietary interest in the land concerned (see e.g. *Bannister v Bannister* (1948)). Again, by contrast with the presumed intention which founds a resulting trust (**10.3**), the precise timing of the agreement is much less critical. The relevant common intention need not arise contemporaneously with the acquisition of the legal estate in the land concerned. It may emerge either *before* or *after* acquisition (see *Gissing v Gissing* (1971) per Viscount Dilhorne and Lord Diplock; *Grant v Edwards* (1986) per Mustill LJ), thus imparting to the constructive trust a flexibility absent from the resulting trust. Constructive trusts have given effect to such interests as:

- an equitable fee simple (*Doohan v Nelson* (1973))

- a life interest (*Bannister v Bannister* (1948))

- an aliquot share under a trust of land (*Grant v Edwards* (1986))

- a long lease (*Yaxley v Gotts* (2000)) and

- an estate contract (*Lyus v Prowsa Developments Ltd* (1982)).

— *Less well-defined bargains* More controversially, claims of constructive trust may relate to rights—such as those of the contractual licensee (**2.13, 4.6**)—which are not conventionally acknowledged as proprietary interests at all (see e.g. *Binions v Evans* (1972) per Lord Denning MR, **12.42**; *Ashburn Anstalt v Arnold* (1989) per Fox LJ, **12.25**). It seems that, in the context of the modern constructive trust, the balance of emphasis rests ultimately on the conscientiousness of the title holder rather than on the intrinsic nature of the rights which it is sought to enforce against him (see e.g. *Melbury Road Properties 1995 Ltd v Kreidi* (1999); *Banner Homes Group plc v Luff Developments Ltd* (2001), **10.11**). In all cases, however, the interest claimed must relate to specific land. A vague offer of 'financial security' cannot found a claim of constructive trust in relation to the offeror's real property (*Layton v Martin* (1986), **10.24**). Nor, for instance, does the mere fact that the parties planned to 'share the practical benefits of occupying the matrimonial home' throw 'any light on their intentions with respect to the beneficial ownership of the property' (*Lloyds Bank plc v Rosset* (1991) per Lord Bridge). The common intention or bargain which is critical is one which relates, not to the mere conduct of some joint venture between the parties, but to the acquisition or sharing of some recognisable proprietary entitlement—an approach which has done little to humanise the law of constructive trusts.

> *Buggs v Buggs* (2003) H and W provided the funds which enabled H's mother, M, to take advantage of the 'right to buy' her council flat at a discounted price (**7.40, 10.5**). H and W raised these funds by increasing the mortgage loan outstanding on their own family home. The extra financial burden imposed hardship on W and her family ('our children were in jeans with holes before that became fashionable'). H and W later divorced; and M died, leaving her flat by will to H and his brother. The High Court rejected W's claim to beneficial entitlement under a constructive trust of the flat. The Court accepted that W, an 'impressive woman', had been a 'determined, hard-working wife who made a strong contribution to the family's welfare in financial as well as personal terms', but held that the mere fact that the purchase of M's flat had been a 'joint

exercise' did not 'amount to a general agreement that all property acquired involved an intention of shared ownership'.

Change of position or detrimental reliance

10.11   Even the clearest oral agreement to confer an equitable right in land is ineffective for want of writing unless the claimant can show that she has 'altered her position in reliance on the agreement', thereby acquiring 'an enforceable interest ... by way either of a constructive trust or of a proprietary estoppel' (*Lloyds Bank plc v Rosset* (1991) per Lord Bridge). Traditionally equity will not assist a volunteer (**9.2–9.3, 9.6**) (see *Austin v Keele* (1987) per Lord Oliver of Aylmerton).

— *Material sacrifice*   A relevant *change of position* is classically and most easily demonstrated where the claimant can prove that she incurred a 'detriment' or made a 'material sacrifice' in response to some bargain for beneficial entitlement (*Gissing v Gissing* (1971) per Lord Diplock). The nature of the required change of position may vary greatly in accordance with whether the trust enforced is an '*express bargain*' constructive trust or an '*implied bargain*' constructive trust (**10.13**). In general terms a change of position can include contributions of finance and the devotion of onerous labour to a joint venture (see e.g. *Chan Pui Chun v Leung Kam Ho* (2003) at [96] per Jonathan Parker LJ), but may not extend to matters of a merely emotional character. 'Equity operates on conscience but is not influenced by sentimentality' (*Winkworth v Edward Baron Development Co Ltd* (1986) per Lord Templeman). Moreover a change of position usually involves a *net* disadvantage to the individual concerned: it *hurts*. (Compare the failure, in the analogous area of proprietary estoppel, of arguments that detriment could be established by a woman who voluntarily left an unhappy marriage in order to enjoy a new life with her lover and to give birth to and rear their child (*Coombes v Smith* (1986), **10.25**).)

> *Christian v Christian* (1981) The Court of Appeal rejected the allegation that a female claimant had suffered 'detriment' in the form of the social embarrassment caused by living with her de facto husband in a house situated close to *his* wife's current home. Brightman LJ observed that equity is 'concerned with the protection of property and proprietary interests, not with the protection of people's feelings.' In his view, 'the only contributions, detriments and sacrifices, that move the court in this field are those of a monetary or proprietary nature' (**10.25**).

— *The change of position must be 'referable to' the bargain*   It has always been said that the change of position undertaken by the constructive trust claimant must be at least broadly 'referable to' the bargain on which beneficial entitlement is premised. There must exist, in other words, a 'sufficient link between the common intention and the conduct which is relied upon to show that the claimant has acted on the common intention to [her] detriment' (*Green v Green* (2003) at [12] per Lord Hope of Craighead). This requirement of a chain of causation is deeply entrenched in the law of constructive trusts. In his classic exposition in *Gissing v Gissing* (1971), Lord Diplock indicated that the legal owner must have 'induced' the claimant to act to her own detriment 'in the reasonable belief that by so acting [she] was acquiring a beneficial interest in the land' and the claimant must so have acted 'with the intention of acquiring that beneficial interest' (**10.7**). Thus, ironically, a claim of constructive trust will fail if the claimant is 'almost wholly unmercenary' (see *Layton v Martin* (1986)) or if she merely continues to contribute the same onerous effort which she willingly gave before the alleged bargain was struck (see *Britannia Building Society v Johnston* (1994)) or if there is a history of joint venture 'without an understanding of what the property rights would be between the parties' (see *Buggs v Buggs* (2003) at [43], **10.10**).

— *The 'Pallant v Morgan equity'* Whereas earlier case law seemed to emphasise 'detriment' or 'material sacrifice' for the claimant as an essential substratum of an allegation of constructive trust, in recent years there has been a gradual, almost imperceptible, widening of the concept of 'change of position'.

- It is noticeable that, in his seminal speech in *Lloyds Bank plc v Rosset* (1991) (**10.14**), Lord Bridge viewed 'detriment' and 'change of position' as not entirely synonymous terms. For the purpose of establishing a constructive trust, said Lord Bridge, the claimant must show *either* that he or she 'has acted to his or her detriment' or that he *or* she has 'significantly altered his or her position in reliance on the agreement' (see similarly *Hammond v Mitchell* (1991) per Waite J; *Chan Pui Chun v Leung Kam Ho* (2003) at [93] per Jonathan Parker LJ). Relevant conduct on the claimant's part can therefore go beyond the mere incurring of a *detriment* and may connote the conferment of an *advantage* on the legal owner (**10.14**).

- Accordingly, the courts have begun to impose constructive trusts, in vindication of what is sometimes termed a '*Pallant v Morgan* equity', in those rare circumstances where an antecedent (and contractually unenforceable) bargain between two parties accords one party the *benefit* of acquiring land without competition from the other in return for the promise of shared rights in the land after purchase (see *Pallant v Morgan* (1953), where one party agreed not to bid against a potential rival at an auction).

Banner Homes Group plc v Luff Developments Ltd (2001) A and B, two corporate property developers, although initially rival purchasers of an area of land, reached an understanding that B would withdraw from the market in order to let A secure the purchase on behalf of C, a venture company jointly owned by A and B. When instead A bid for, and purchased, the land in the name of A's wholly owned subsidiary company, D, the Court of Appeal imposed a constructive trust, holding that the circumstances made it 'inequitable for the acquiring party to retain the property for himself in a manner inconsistent with the arrangement or understanding on which the non-acquiring party has acted.' The Court therefore ordered that the shares of D be held, as to one half, on constructive trust for B. Chadwick LJ thought that a '*Pallant v Morgan* equity' could be triggered by the presence either of advantage for the acquiring party (i.e. the absence of competition) or of detriment for the non-acquiring party (i.e. loss of the chance to acquire on equal terms).

It is not entirely clear that the recent (and slightly surprising) resurgence of the '*Pallant v Morgan* equity' departs markedly from the traditionally understood constructive trust doctrine of bargain-based detrimental reliance (see e.g. *Cox v Jones* (2004) at [46]). Even Chadwick LJ thought, in the *Banner* case, that it could be said that B 'suffered detriment from the fact that it never regarded itself as free to consider the site as a potential acquisition of its own' (see also N Hopkins, 'The *Pallant v Morgan* Equity' [2002] *Conv* 35). Furthermore, in a world of finite opportunity, any advantage for another almost inevitably represents some form of detriment for oneself.

Equitable fraud

10.12 The element of unconscionable behaviour which finally triggers the constructive trust is the component of *equitable fraud*. It is the legal owner's disclaimer of the antecedent bargain relating to beneficial entitlement which converts his actions into a fraud on the claimant. Against the background of the claimant's reliance on their bargain, his attempt to derogate from the agreed entitlement amounts to an *unconscientious* use of his legal title—a form of cheat—and is accordingly penalised by the imposition of a constructive trust.

> *Yaxley v Gotts* (2000) X, in an offer later found to have been adopted by his son, A, promised to give B the ground floor of certain premises 'for ever' in exchange for B's supply of labour, materials and services in the conversion of the premises to a block of flats. The oral agreement with B was a mere 'gentleman's agreement' and never reached the stage of a valid written contract (**9.6**). A then purchased the premises in question but, although B carried out the agreed conversion, A refused to grant B any interest in the land. The Court of Appeal ruled that, in the clear absence of any specifically enforceable contract, A must hold on a constructive trust to give B a 99-year lease of the ground floor since it would now be 'unconscionable' to allow A to resile from

the promise of entitlement. (The application of constructive trust doctrine is explicitly preserved in the context of contracts which fail to comply with the statutory requirement of writing (LP(MP)A 1989, s 2(5)).) Here the constructive trust—and, for that matter, the principle of proprietary estoppel—operated to avert 'injustice' in circumstances where it would have been 'inequitable to disregard the claimant's expectations.' (Compare *Lloyds Bank plc v Carrick* (1996) (**9.8**), where the existence of a specifically enforceable contract left no room for the court to 'superimpose a further constructive trust'.)

Two types of constructive trust

10.13 In *Lloyds Bank plc v Rosset* (1991)—slightly to the surprise of most land lawyers—the House of Lords drew a sharp distinction between *two* distinct forms of constructive trust, namely

- the *'express bargain' constructive trust* (**10.14**) and
- the *'implied bargain' constructive trust* (**10.15**).

This typology has now taken firm root in English constructive trust jurisprudence. As Lord Bridge said in *Rosset*, the difference between *express bargains* and *implied bargains* is a 'critical distinction which [the] judge ... should always have in the forefront of his mind' since it directly controls the character of the evidence required, particularly in the context of the family home, in support of a claim of constructive trust.

The 'express bargain' constructive trust

10.14 An *'express bargain' constructive trust* emerges where the legal estate owner and the beneficial claimant orally reached some 'agreement, arrangement or understanding ... that the property is to be shared beneficially' (*Lloyds Bank plc v Rosset* per Lord Bridge). For this purpose there must be clear evidence of 'express discussions between the [parties], however imperfectly remembered and however imprecise their terms may have been.' Not for the first time English land law is shown to be fairly unsympathetic to the realities of family life, placing a premium upon intentions which are rarely articulated or even contemplated in the daily round of domestic existence.

- The court is, in reality, looking for dealings between the parties of 'a consensual character falling not far short of an enforceable contract' (*Chan Pui Chun v*

Leung Kam Ho (2003) at [91] per Jonathan Parker LJ). But if the parties did genuinely reach some kind of express bargain as to their beneficial rights, the court 'will give effect to it—notwithstanding the absence of any written declaration of trust' (*Gissing v Gissing* (1971) per Lord Diplock).

- Inevitably such cases will be relatively infrequent (but see *Eves v Eves* (1975) and *Grant v Edwards* (1986)). The conception of 'a normal married couple spending the long winter evenings hammering out agreements about their possessions appears grotesque' (*Pettitt v Pettitt* (1970) per Lord Hodson). Nevertheless the House of Lords' approach in *Lloyds Bank plc v Rosset* means that 'the tenderest exchanges of a common law courtship may assume an unforeseen significance many years later when they are brought under equity's microscope' (see *Hammond v Mitchell* (1991) per Waite J).

— *The express agreement must be consciously communicated* The requirement of shared intention is stringent. The express bargain must be a demonstrable reality and must be communicated between the relevant parties. It is not sufficient, for instance, that each of the parties independently 'happened to be thinking on the same lines in his or her uncommunicated thoughts' (*Springette v Defoe* (1992) per Dillon LJ). The law must concentrate on the 'external signs of common intention' (*Mollo v Mollo* (1999)) and does not recognise communication at a subconscious level. 'Our trust law', said Steyn LJ in *Springette v Defoe*, 'does not allow property rights to be affected by telepathy'. The trend in the recent case law is, however, to accept that express agreements creative of a constructive trust may arise at any time before, at, or even after, the acquisition of title (see *Clough v Killey* (1996) per Peter Gibson LJ).

— *There must be a change of position* The express agreement must, as always, be supported by some *change of position* on the part of the beneficial claimant (**10.11**). In the absence of writing a trust 'does not come into being merely from a gratuitous intention to transfer or create a beneficial interest' (*Austin v Keele* (1987) per Lord Oliver of Aylmerton); and an agreement which fails to 'provide for anything to be done' by the beneficial claimant is 'a merely voluntary declaration of trust and unenforceable for want of writing' (*Gissing v Gissing* (1971) per Lord Diplock).

— *The change of position can take any form* The critical variant between constructive trusts based on express and implied bargains is that, in an *'express bargain'* constructive trust, a relevant 'change of position' may be established by a much wider range of acts of reliance on the part of the claimant (compare **10.15**). Since express agreement has already been found as a fact, relevant conduct extends well beyond that conduct which is explicable only on the basis of some bargain over beneficial title. All that need now be shown is that the claimant 'has acted to his or her detriment or significantly altered his or her position in reliance on the agreement' (*Lloyds Bank plc* *v Rosset* per Lord Bridge)—the *alternative* nature of this formula having an importance which we noted earlier (**10.11**). It may even be that more recent analyses of 'change of position' as inclusive of the conferment of *benefit* on the legal owner are particularly appropriate to cases of expressly negotiated bargain (see e.g. *Banner Homes Group plc v Luff Developments Ltd* (2001), **10.11**), leaving the traditional understanding of 'change of position' as connoting detriment or material sacrifice to be relevant primarily to situations of implied bargain (**10.15**).

• It follows that general contributions to the family economy—whether by way of domestic achievement, child bearing and rearing, indirect expenditure on the joint household or otherwise—comprise a sufficient change of position for the purpose of founding an 'express bargain' constructive trust. Moreover, the explicit nature of the parties' agreement obviates the need to demonstrate a positive causal connection between bargain and reliance: the causal link is readily presumed to be self-evident (see *Gissing v Gissing* (1971) per Lord Diplock).

• It has been suggested, by analogy with the law of proprietary estoppel (**10.25**), that a relevant change of position can, for instance, embrace all activities connected with the setting up of a joint home, even though such conduct may be 'referable to the mutual love and affection of the parties and not specifically referable to the claimant's belief that she has an interest in the house' (*Grant v Edwards* (1986) per Browne-Wilkinson V-C).

Eves v Eves (1975) The claimant came to live in a home owned by her partner, having been told by him explicitly that the legal title was vested in his sole name only because she was then under 21 years of age. She then effected extensive improvements to the property. Amongst other activities, she redecorated the entire house; she demolished a garden shed single-handed; she wielded a 14 lb sledgehammer to break up an area of concrete at the front of the house; and prepared the garden for turfing. The Court of Appeal awarded the claimant a one-quarter share under a constructive trust, the House of Lords in *Rosset*'s case later viewing this ruling as a classic demonstration of the 'express bargain' constructive trust. There had been clear evidence of a common intention, expressly adverted to in the parties' discussions and then acted upon by the claimant, that she would eventually be accorded some form of shared ownership.

The 'implied bargain' constructive trust

10.15 *Implied bargain* is, at one level, more straightforward and much more common: the existence of a bargain or agreement to share or confer beneficial ownership may be inferred from the conduct or mutual dealings of the relevant parties (see *Gissing v Gissing* (1971) per Lord Diplock). It is in this context that the jurisprudence of the constructive trust has recently shown the most dramatic indications of positive evolution.

— *Requirement of a 'referable' change of position* For many years the law of constructive trusts had been bedevilled by the courts' insistence that, where no *express* bargain or agreement could be shown, the claimant should at least be able to point to some *implied* agreement between the parties on the basis of which the claimant had been induced to change her position. As Lord Diplock said in *Gissing v Gissing* (1971), the claimant's 'detriment' or 'sacrifice' must be 'referable to the acquisition' of a beneficial interest in the land. This approach effectively ensured, in many cases, the denial of women's rights to participate in family assets accumulated during relationships of even substantial duration (see e.g. *Burns v Burns* (1984); *Philip Lowe (Chinese Restaurant) v Sau Man Lee* (1985)). As Simon Gardner once put it ((1996) 112 *LQR* 378 at 382), there was an inevitable 'clash of cultures' between a failing, but classical, law of trusts dominated by a longstanding commercialist ethos and the rather different mutualist ethic which underlies the property relationships of families. The strict requirement of detrimental reliance on some bargain inferable from conduct threw almost insuperable obstacles in the way of those who failed to clarify at a sufficiently conscious mental level the motivations and implications of their day-to-day actions. (In the matrimonial context some redress came eventually in the form of legislation in the early 1970s which governed the redistribution of assets after divorce, but parties outside the marital bond were still profoundly affected by the shortcomings of constructive trust doctrine.)

Gissing v Gissing (1971) During a marriage of some 25 years, the claimant wife had made indirect financial contributions towards the purchase of the family home through the use of her own money on various forms of household and other family-related expenditure. The House of Lords nevertheless denied her any beneficial entitlement in the property (which was vested at law in the sole name of her husband). The failure of the claim was not based on any perception that it was *inequitable* to grant the wife a beneficial share in the home. The decision rested simply on the fact that, in the absence of any express agreement to share the beneficial title, the House of Lords declined to infer that the wife's expenditure had been 'referable to' the acquisition of the property. The mere fact of contribution to joint expenditure did not in itself constitute a sufficient change of position without evidence of some deliberate arrangement that the wife's assumption of responsibility for more general household expenditure was intended to free her husband to pay the mortgage. Such allocations of family burden are in practice extremely difficult to prove. The *Gissing* decision indicated, once again, that the law favours only those more sophisticated claimants who are either calculating or particularly convincing in the advancement of their own self-interest.

Lloyds Bank plc v Rosset (1991) A wife had rendered substantial assistance in the renovation of the family home legally vested in her husband. In rejecting her claim of constructive trust, the House of Lords declined to accept that her labours comprised work 'upon which she could not reasonably have been expected to embark unless she was to have an interest in the house'. Her intensive efforts were explicable simply on the basis of the fact that she had been 'extremely anxious' that the home should be available for occupation as soon as possible. Indeed, Lord Bridge observed, 'it would seem the most natural thing in the world for any wife, in the absence of her husband abroad, to spend all the time she could spare and to employ any skills she might have, such as the ability to decorate a room, in doing all she could to accelerate progress of the work quite irrespective of any expectation she might have of enjoying a beneficial interest in the property'. (A direct consequence of this ruling was to destroy any claim that the wife had an overriding interest taking priority over the husband's bank-mortgagee (**12.24**).)

— *Requirement of direct money payments* The unsympathetic stance of constructive trust doctrine was underlined by the judicial insistence that, where a bargain over beneficial title is claimed to be inferable from conduct alone, much more exacting proof of 'detriment' or 'sacrifice' is required of the claimant. Here the preoccupation has been narrowly, and perhaps exclusively, with contributions of a *monetary* variety. In *Lloyds Bank plc v Rosset*, Lord Bridge accepted that a relevant change of position would include a claimant's 'direct contributions to the purchase price … whether initially or by payment of mortgage instalments', but thought it 'at least extremely doubtful whether anything less will do'. It was even conceded by Lord Bridge that the execution of substantial or arduous renovation works on property in such cases as *Eves v Eves* (**10.14**) fell 'far short' of the kind of conduct required.

• Although a constructive trust may possibly be raised by financial contributions made in unforeseen circumstances long after the acquisition of the legal estate (e.g. by using Aunt Agatha's legacy to pay off a large part of the mortgage debt), the tenor of the *Rosset* ruling is severely—and unnecessarily—restrictive. In *Mehra v Shah* (2003), for instance, the High Court, with the subsequent approval of the Court of Appeal, rejected claims of constructive trust, holding that substantial transfers of capital and income within an extended Kenyan Asian family connoted 'no direct contributions to the purchase price' of the family's various properties, but had been made 'by way of loan or gift out of family feeling'.

- It is sometimes said that even a prolonged pattern of *indirect* expenditure on the shared general outgoings of a common household raises no constructive trust (see e.g. *Mollo v Mollo* (1999); *Mehra v Shah* (2003) at [48], **10.4**), although contrary authority can be found in long-forgotten statements made by Lord Diplock in *Gissing v Gissing* (1971) (see also *Le Foe v Le Foe* (2001)).

— *A more optimistic future*   The English law of constructive trusts has not stood still during recent years. There are strong indications that the courts have become increasingly embarrassed by the historic injustices perpetrated by the classical trust doctrine and are beginning to propel the law in a more positive direction. An important breakthrough came with the decision in *Oxley v Hiscock* (2005). Here, in the absence of an *express* bargain based upon direct negotiations, the Court of Appeal made it clear that a constructive trust can be founded upon an *implied* bargain which demonstrates a common intention that the claimant should have at least *some* beneficial entitlement. Working broadly within the limitations imposed by the seminal authority of *Gissing v Gising* (1971), the Court of Appeal managed to fashion a more liberated version of the constructive trust applicable to family homes owned at law by one partner alone. However, as the Court conceded, the overall outcome is not easily reconciled with a 'traditional, property-based, approach'.

> *Oxley v Hiscock* (2005) A woman claimant, O, had contributed financially towards the purchase of a home vested at law in her partner, H, the parties having never articulated any express understanding as to their respective beneficial rights. H argued that O should be confined to a resulting trust interest commensurate with her actual financial contribution (i.e. a share possibly in the region of 20 per cent). In awarding O a share of 40 per cent, Chadwick LJ indicated (at [68]) that an affirmative answer to the 'threshold' question of intention to share beneficially will 'readily be inferred' from the fact that each party has made *some* kind of financial contribution to the purchase of the home. Thus even a minimal financial contribution can afford evidence of the implied bargain or common intention which is required in order to trigger the creation of a constructive trust. It is no bar that the parties are honest enough to admit that they never actually gave ownership a thought (see e.g. *Midland Bank plc v Cooke* (1995)); nor is it problematical that the inferred common intention involves no precise quantification of the parties' shares. Once the gateway has been opened to a finding of *some* constructive trust, the 'secondary' issue of quantum can be left to be determined later by the court against the background of the parties' 'whole course of dealing ... in relation to the property' (at [73] per Chadwick LJ). The respective shares of O and H were therefore left to be defined by reference not merely to money contributions, but to a much broader range of factors (**10.16**).

— *Recent developments* The principles outlined in *Oxley v Hiscock* have greatly eased the law in respect of family homes titled in one party alone. It will be a rare domestic partner who cannot, in such cases, point to some minimal qualifying contribution of money towards the purchase of a home, thereby engaging the court's jurisdiction to award a larger share of beneficial ownership than is strictly commensurate with their money contribution. More recently, in *Stack v Dowden* (2007), the House of Lords has gone even further in dealing with the beneficial implications of jointly owned legal titles in the domestic consumer context. Here a majority of the law lords agreed that the fact that a home is held legally in joint names not only satisfies the 'threshold' test of intention to share beneficially, but also points to an extremely weighty presumption that the inferentially intended beneficial outcome is *equal* shareholding (although this presumption was, as it happens, rebutted on the unusual facts of *Stack v Dowden* itself).

Quantification of constructive trust entitlements

10.16 It is one thing to establish the existence of a constructive trust; it may be an entirely different matter to quantify the beneficial entitlements which emerge from that finding of trust. The court does not sit 'as under a palm tree, to exercise a general discretion to do what the man in the street, on a general overview of the case, might regard as fair' (*Springette v Defoe* (1992) per Dillon LJ). Nor can the maxim 'equality is equity' be applied 'unthinkingly' (*Hammond v Mitchell* (1991) per Waite J). In all cases the extent of the claimant's interest is 'prima facie ... that which the parties intended' (*Grant v Edwards* (1986) per Browne-Wilkinson V-C). Each case 'must depend upon its own facts' (*Gissing v Gissing* (1971) per Lord Diplock).

— *'Express bargain' constructive trusts* Here the shares or interests which the parties have agreed are normally definitive unless it can be shown that there has been some 'subsequent renegotiation' or subsequent conduct 'so inconsistent with what was agreed' as to point unmistakably to a variation or cancellation of that agreement (*Mortgage Corpn v Shaire* (2001) per Neuberger J). If, however, the parties' express agreement did *not* specify the precise shares to be taken, the court must do so in their place using the yardstick of what is 'fair having regard to the whole course of dealing between them in relation to the property' (see *Oxley v Hiscock* (2005) at [69], [73] per Chadwick LJ, as applied, for example, in *Cox v Jones* (2004) at [80]).

— *'Implied bargain' constructive trusts* In 'single legal owner' cases proof of some kind of financial contribution is required in order to trigger the claim of constructive trust (**10.15**), but thereafter the respective money contributions of the parties are far from determinative of the proper inference of intention to be drawn from the parties' conduct. The court must 'do its best to discover from the conduct of the [parties] whether any inference can reasonably be drawn as to the probable common understanding about the amount of the share' to be taken by the claimant (*Gissing v Gissing* (1971) per Lord Diplock). In recent years it has become increasingly clear that the process of quantification almost inevitably collapses back into something approaching an assessment of fair outcome. The sheer unreality of spelling common intentions out of half a lifetime of inarticulate dealings is frequently so overwhelming that the courts have become 'reasonably broad-brush' in calculating the relevant proportions of beneficial entitlement behind the trust (see e.g. *Mollo v Mollo* (1999)). Modern courts have begun to express a distinct preference for 'the more holistic approach of looking at the parties' global dealings over the span of their ownership of the property' rather than the 'straitjacket' of a purely mathematical approach (*Le Foe v Le Foe* (2001) at [52]–[53]). This approach received the emphatic endorsement of the Court of Appeal in *Oxley v Hiscock* (2005) and, in the 'joint legal owner' context exemplified in *Stack v Dowden* (2007) (**10.15**), has even generated a heavy presumption in favour of intended *equality* of beneficial shareholding. The roots of the newer view are to be found in a controversial decision of 1995.

> *Midland Bank plc v Cooke* (1995) (**10.15**) Here the Court of Appeal advocated a resort to 'general equitable principles' in formulating a 'fair presumed basis for the sharing of beneficial title' between spouses. Although W had contributed less than 7 per cent of the money ploughed into the matrimonial home, Waite LJ led the Court in attributing to the parties an intention to share beneficial ownership equally, explicitly because such a conclusion was mirrored in the past pattern of their shared endeavour, their family life and their mutual commitment (see G Battersby 'How not to judge the quantum (and priority) of a share in the family home' (1996) 8 *C & FLQ* 261).

The future of the constructive trust

10.17 A powerful argument can be mounted for the proposition that social justice would be more effectively served by abandoning the search for phantoms of common intention in the law of trusts (see Gray, 'The Law of Trusts and the Quasi-Matrimonial Home' [1983] *CLJ* 30 at 33). Indeed, over the past 30 years other common law jurisdictions have moved towards much more free-ranging doctrines of trust entitlement which break away decisively from the strictures of the traditional application of constructive trust theory.

• The Supreme Court of Canada has embraced a liberal understanding of the constructive trust as an overtly remedial mechanism designed to counteract widely defined instances of 'unjust enrichment' (*Pettkus v Becker* (1980); *Sorochan v Sorochan* (1986); *Peter v Beblow* (1993); *Soulos v Korkontzilas* (1997); and see also *Nova Scotia (Attorney General) v Walsh* (2002)).

• This lead was soon followed in New Zealand (see *Gillies v Keogh* (1989); *Lankow v Rose* (1995)), an initiative now crystallised in a new statutory rule of presumptive equal entitlement for almost all domestic partners (see Property (Relationships) Act 1976 (NZ), ss 11–15, as amended with effect from February 2002).

• Australian courts in their turn have elaborated a similarly broad jurisprudence of 'unconscionability' in the application of the constructive trust (*Baumgartner v Baumgartner* (1987); and see also Property (Relationships) Act 1984 (New South Wales), s 20 (effective June 1999)).

The effect of all these adaptations of the constructive trust is dramatically to loosen up the conditions of beneficial entitlement in accordance with perceptions of a more fundamental equity in property relationships.

— *The 'new model' constructive trust* During the 1970s this liberated approach enjoyed a brief flourishing in England, predictably under the influence of Lord Denning MR (see e.g. *Cooke v Head* (1972); *Hussey v Palmer* (1972)). Lord Denning championed the recognition of virtually automatic beneficial co-ownership—'equity's latest progeny ... a constructive trust of a new model' (*Eves v Eves* (1975))—whenever such an outcome seemed 'fair' in the context of joint ventures in respect of land. Such unstructured applications of trust law are, of course, vulnerable to objection of the ground of their unpredictability of outcome. Equity begins to intervene as a sheer instrument of distributive justice in a series of one-off adjudications. Such an uncertain and unprincipled approach also appears severely prejudicial to purchasers and creditors who have relied on an apparently unqualified legal title. The 'new model' constructive trust eventually proved to be too high a price to pay for 'just resolutions' of disputed entitlement and has quietly faded from view, castigated as 'a mutant from which further breeding should be discouraged' (*Allen v Snyder* (1977) per Samuels JA).

— *Future evolution of the constructive trust* Although broad principles of restitution for unjust enrichment are beginning to be accepted by English courts in other contexts (see *Westdeutsche Landesbank Girozentrale v Islington LBC* (1996); *Kleinwort Benson Ltd v Lincoln CC* (1998)), there is still a considerable reluctance to introduce anything resembling the transatlantic remedial constructive trust. Such trusts appear, at least to the conservatively minded, to confer on the courts a discretion to reapportion property rights in a manner completely unsanctioned by parliamentary authority. In *Re Polly Peck International plc (No 2)* (1998), Nourse LJ was careful to point out that Lord Denning's 'new model' constructive trust had been rejected by the English Court of Appeal during the 1980s as being 'at variance with the principles stated in *Gissing v Gissing*'. The courts, said Nourse LJ, have no 'inherent jurisdiction to vary … beneficial interests' in property.

• Other influential voices have conceded that 'the law took a wrong turning in *Gissing v Gissing*' and that the time has come for a 'rethink' of the common intention constructive trusts 'invented' in that case (see Browne-Wilkinson, 'Constructive Trusts and Unjust Enrichment' (1996) 10 *Trust Law International* 98 at 99–100). Whilst, as Lord Browne-Wilkinson maintained, there may be 'great dangers in seeking to turn equity into one comprehensive law of unjust enrichment based on some sweeping fundamental concept', it may ultimately prove feasible to refashion trust law more flexibly on the analogy of proprietary estoppel (**10.19**).

• The Law Commission has recently returned to the task of constructing a special statutory regime for the property problems of cohabitants on relationship breakdown (see *Cohabitation: The Financial Consequences of Relationship Breakdown* (CP No 179, May 2006)) and hopes to produce a final report by August 2007.

Proprietary estoppel

10.18 The law relating to proprietary estoppel provides a further means, closely allied to the constructive trust, by which rights in land may be created informally. Whilst the law of the constructive trust places its primary emphasis on *bargains* for beneficial ownership, the principle of proprietary estoppel focuses on *representations* which generate expectations of entitlement.

— *Function* The doctrine of estoppel has its root in 'the first principle upon which all courts of equity proceed', that is, 'to prevent a person from insisting on his strict legal rights—whether arising under a contract, or on his title deeds, or by statute—when it would be inequitable for him to do so having regard to the dealings which have taken place between the parties' (*Crabb v Arun DC* (1976) per Lord Denning MR, **8.19**). Accordingly the law of proprietary estoppel confers on the courts a residual power to scrutinise the *appropriateness* of particular assertions of legal entitlement. Its essential purpose is to restrain (or 'estop') any attempt by a legal owner unconscientiously to resile from basic assumptions which were previously understood to underlie dealings in relation to his land. Although starting in this way as a principle of *inhibition*, the doctrine usually has the indirect (but more *positive*) effect of creating rights on behalf of the successful claimant of an 'equity' founded upon estoppel.

— *Flexibility* Few other doctrines of modern property law demonstrate so clearly the flexibility and potency of the courts' jurisdiction to arrive at broadly just or 'equitable' solutions of the property difficulties of opposed parties.

- Frequently in the ill-defined and chaotic circumstances of everyday life—especially in the family context—problems of entitlement arise for which the relatively orderly framework of structural property principles provides no convenient answer. It is here that proprietary estoppel has emerged as a dramatic source of rights. The notion of proprietary estoppel is increasingly invoked in order to plug the awkward gaps which exist between well established heads of claim and between various forms of accepted entitlement. In these marginal or interstitial areas the estoppel principle now plays an important, often controversial, role. The concept of estoppel enables the courts to address many difficult questions which would otherwise escape satisfactory analysis.

- The reach of estoppel doctrine extends well beyond family situations to affect wide ranges of business dealings. As Neuberger J once declared, equity is 'flexible and strong enough to ensure that any estoppel results in a sensible commercial outcome, which is not thwarted by archaic and technical rules of property law, unless those rules are based on public policy or are so fundamental as to be incapable of being overridden' (*PW & Co v Milton Gate Investments Ltd* (2004) at [207]).

- The sheer flexibility of estoppel doctrine has proved uniquely suitable for translating into comprehensible legal form the more nebulous and confused aspects of lay persons' informal arrangements in relation to land. The doctrine thus provides an essential supplement to the law of licences and trusts, enabling the courts to fashion remedial justice on the basis of extremely loose and often ill-considered patterns of informal or formally defective dealing. The precise scope of its operation is not, of course, unproblematical and it is not surprising that many uncertainties remain as to the parameters of proprietary estoppel and even as to the ultimate objectives of the doctrine.

The operation of proprietary estoppel

10.19 The law of proprietary estoppel (or equitable estoppel) operates where the owner of a legal estate in land has expressly or impliedly given some informal assurance respecting present or future rights in his land. The doctrine of estoppel restrains that person from any unconscientious withdrawal of his representation if the person to whom it was made has meanwhile *relied* upon it to his or her own *detriment*. The primary inquiry for the court is 'whether, in particular individual circumstances, it would be unconscionable for a party to be permitted to deny that which, knowingly or unknowingly, he has allowed or encouraged another to assume to his detriment' (*Taylors Fashions Ltd v Liverpool Victoria Trustees Co Ltd* (1982) per Oliver J). Estoppel doctrine finds its ultimate purpose in 'enabling the courts to do justice', and the overriding emphasis of the doctrine is that the outcome of its application must indeed be 'just' (see *Sledmore v Dalby* (1996) per Hobhouse LJ; *Jennings v Rice* (2003) at [36] per Aldous LJ).

A successful claim of proprietary estoppel therefore depends, in some form or other, on the demonstration of *three* elements:

- *representation* (or an assurance of rights) (**10.24**);
- *reliance* (or a change of position) (**10.25**); and
- *detriment* (or unconscionable disadvantage) (**10.26**).

Overarching (and unifying) these elements is the idea that it must now be *inequitable* or *unconscionable* (**10.26**) to allow the representor to overturn the assumptions reasonably created by his earlier informal assurance of entitlement in the land.

Thus stated, the elements of representation, reliance and detriment are inter-dependent and capable of definition only in terms of each other.

- *Representation* is present only if the representor intended his assurance to be relied upon.
- *Reliance* occurs only if the representee is caused to change her position to her detriment.
- *Disadvantage* results, ultimately, only if the representation, once relied upon, is unconscionably withdrawn.

The components of proprietary estoppel are overwhelmingly similar to those which underpin the constructive trust (**10.8**), and there are many today who claim that the convergence of notion is now so marked that, for some purposes, no real difference exists between these two strands of doctrine (see e.g. *Birmingham Midshires Mortgage Services Ltd v Sabherwal* (2000) per Robert Walker LJ, referring in particular to the context of the family home). To the extent that the notions are not congruent, the difference resides largely in the fact that the fields of bargain and representation may not necessarily coincide. Proprietary estoppel may therefore extend beyond the constructive trust to circumstances of passive representation of entitlement, where the representor has in no sense 'bargained' with the representee for a conferment of rights, but has simply stood back watching the representee incur disadvantage in the expectation that he has rights (see *Yaxley v Gotts* (2000) per Robert Walker and Beldam LJJ (**10.12**)).

A textbook illustration of proprietary estoppel

10.20   A classic demonstration of the estoppel principle at work can be found in *Inwards v Baker* (1965). This case illustrates the way in which vaguely expressed entitlements are often left dormant for years amidst some legal haze until disaffection, death or insolvency acts as the immediate catalyst of greater precision in the identification of land rights.

> *Inwards v Baker* (1965) An elderly man, F, encouraged his adult son, S, to build a bungalow on F's land, telling him that the bungalow, once built, would be available indefinitely for S as long as he wished to use the property as his own home. (Consistently with the messy way in which family dealings are usually conducted, no details of the arrangement were ever expressed formally or even in writing; legal title remained in F.) S nevertheless proceeded, at his own expense, to construct the bungalow and to live there for some 30 years. When F then died leaving no will in S's favour, free rein was at last given to the destructive force of sibling rivalry. S's half-brothers (acting as F's personal representatives) sought to revoke S's occupation licence and to recover possession from him. The Court of Appeal ruled, however, that they were *estopped* from evicting S. S had acquired 'a licence coupled with an equity' (**4.9**) which bound not only F while alive, but also F's successors in title and indeed any purchaser with notice (**12.42**). Accordingly the Court of Appeal awarded S a right of lifelong residence in the property.

Several features of *Inwards v Baker* deserve emphasis, for S's rights in the property, despite their undoubted strength as a moral claim, seemed initially likely to crash into a number of legal barriers. In particular, S's claim to proprietary protection ran counter to a number of hallowed doctrines of English law.

• *The law disfavours the informal creation of rights in land*   F should have used a deed of grant, or a formal declaration of trust, or—at the very least—made a testamentary disposition to S. He did absolutely none of these things and, as Sam Goldwyn famously remarked, 'a verbal promise isn't worth the paper it's written on!'

• *Gratuitous promises are unenforceable*   There is 'no equitable jurisdiction to hold a person to a promise simply because a court thinks it unfair, unconscionable or morally objectionable for him to go back on it. If there were such a jurisdiction, one might as well forget the law of contract and issue every judge with a portable palm tree' (*Taylor v Dickens* (1998)). The relationship between F and S was not, for any number of reasons, contractual in nature. Familial arrangements are seldom intended to have legal consequence (see *Balfour v Balfour* (1919)) and if F, immediately after offering the land to S, had resiled from the offer, no contractual remedy would have been available. Nor could F have alleged any breach of contract if S had subsequently refused to construct the bungalow.

• *Voluntarily rendered services are not generally compensable* English law has not, at least historically, been ready to recognise any broad principle of restitution for gratuitously rendered service. One who voluntarily improves another's land does so, in English law, 'entirely at his own risk' (*Stilwell v Simpson* (1983)). To confer an uncontracted benefit and then expect reward is a 'folly' (*Ramsden v Dyson* (1866) per Lord Cranworth LC). S's construction of a bungalow was therefore apt to be considered, in principle, as resulting merely in an uncompensated accession to F's realty (**1.8**).

• *Consensual presence cannot rank as adverse possession* Any suggestion that S might have acquired title by adverse possession was comprehensively negatived by the *permissive* character of his many years of occupancy (**6.11**).

In consequence it seemed generally unlikely in *Inwards v Baker* that S would derive assistance from conventional principles of property, contract or tort. Yet the law of proprietary estoppel came to his rescue because:

• F had *represented* that S would have an indefinite right of occupation;

• S *relied* on this clear, albeit informal, conferment of entitlement—i.e. he proceeded to build his home on F's land in preference to any other location;

• S incurred *detriment*—i.e. his money and labour generated an improvement which was inevitably and non-compensably annexed to F's land, a personal investment which stood to be snatched away by the assertion of a strict legal entitlement.

These threefold elements raised an 'equity' in favour of the volunteer improver which supplemented and crucially reinforced the bare occupation licence which had been his from the start. Lord Denning MR pointed out that it was necessary merely to show that the licensee, 'at the request or with the encouragement' of the landowner, had 'spent the money in the expectation of being allowed to stay there'. The court would not allow that expectation to be defeated 'where it would be inequitable so to do'. Danckwerts LJ likewise spoke of 'an equity created by estoppel or equitable estoppel' as arising where a person who undertakes expenditure has been 'induced by the expectation of obtaining protection'. This being so, 'equity protects him so that an injustice may not be perpetrated'.

Three further features of the doctrine of proprietary estoppel merit reference. *First,* proprietary estoppel can arise even outside the scope of contractual relationships, although in practice proprietary estoppel and contractual rights often overlap. *Second,* proprietary estoppel does not merely provide a *shield* for the vulnerable but may be relied on as a *sword,* conferring rights of action where none otherwise exist. *Third,* the equity arising in connection with proprietary estoppel may *bind* third parties and, in this sense, seems to constitute a substantive equitable proprietary right (**10.22, 12.25, 12.42**), albeit that the *benefit* flowing from the estoppel is arguably personal to the original estoppel representee (see *Jones (AE) v Jones (FW)* (1977)). It may even be that an estoppel-based equity gives rise to an enduring personal liability in the representor even after a transfer of the land to a third party (see S Bright and B McFarlane, 'Personal Liability in Proprietary Estoppel' [2005] *Conv* 14).

Estoppel doctrine applies to a wide variety of circumstance

10.21 Estoppel doctrine penalises unconscientious departure from the fundamental assumptions made by parties in several interlinked categories of circumstance. Each category of case, in its turn, gives a heightened emphasis to one or other of the constituent elements of *assurance, reliance,* and *detriment.*

— *Imperfect gift* Although it is always said that equity will not perfect an imperfect gift (see *Milroy v Lord* (1862)), the doctrine of estoppel often achieves exactly this result. Such an outcome can arise in circumstances where an abortive gift of land indicates the landowner's intention to make an *assurance* of entitlement in favour of another (see e.g. *Pascoe v Turner* (1979), **7.6, 10.24**).

> *Dillwyn v Llewelyn* (1862) F placed his son, S, in possession of land belonging to F, both parties signing an informal memorandum of gift intended to provide S with land for the construction of a dwelling-house. (For want of a grant by deed, this memorandum was, of course, ineffective to convey any legal estate in the land (**7.6**).) S proceeded at vast expense to build a residence for himself on the land. Lord Westbury LC decreed that the intention to give the fee simple estate must now be performed, even though title to the land had by this stage passed to the executors of F's estate. The executors were ordered to convey the fee simple to S.

— *Common expectation* The *reliance* element underlying estoppel comes to the fore where parties have consistently dealt with each other in such a way as reasonably to cause one to rely on a shared supposition that he or she would acquire rights of some kind in the other's land. It often becomes unconscionable to permit the landowner to frustrate the substance of the common expectation (see e.g. *Crabb v Arun DC* (1976), **8.19**, **10.25**; *Greasley v Cooke* (1980), **10.25**).

> *ER Ives Investment Ltd v High* (1967) H incurred expenditure in reliance on an informal agreement for a right of way reached with I's predecessor in title. The Court of Appeal held this agreement to be binding on I **(12.42)**. By reason of his detrimental reliance, H had acquired an 'equity' founded on the fact that I's predecessor had 'created in [H's] mind a reasonable expectation that his access over the yard would not be disturbed'.

— *Unilateral mistake* An equity of estoppel may also arise—albeit more rarely—in circumstances of unilateral mistake by one party as to the precise scope or nature of his or her rights. In this context primary importance is attached to the element of *unconscionable disadvantage*. It is unacceptable that a legal owner should wilfully stand by and watch another incurring clear disadvantage by reason of some uncorrected misapprehension of the genuine legal position. (The classic case is that of the volunteer improver who mistakenly supposes that he has rights in land and therefore ploughs uncompensated value into the realty of the true legal owner.)

> *Ramsden v Dyson* (1866) A court of equity 'will not allow me afterwards to assert my title to the land on which [the stranger] had expended money on the supposition that the land was his own. It considers that, when I saw the mistake into which he had fallen, it was my duty to be active and to state my adverse title; and that it would be dishonest in me to remain wilfully passive on such an occasion, in order afterwards to profit by the mistake which I might have prevented' (per Lord Cranworth LC).

— *The Willmott v Barber probanda* In *Willmott v Barber* (1880) Fry J laid down extremely strict *probanda* (or criteria) for the success of estoppel claims. These *probanda* required essentially that the landowner should have behaved *fraudulently* in that, although fully aware of the true legal position and of the estoppel claimant's mistaken belief in some supposed entitlement, he nevertheless encouraged her to expend money on the land or otherwise act to her detriment. For many years the courts, somewhat implausibly, applied the *Willmott v Barber probanda* indiscriminately to *all* forms of estoppel claim (i.e. well beyond the category of *unilateral mistake* to which they obviously relate), thereby dramatically curtailing the availability of estoppel-based remedies. In particular the estoppel doctrine was rendered virtually inapplicable to cases of *common expectation* in which mistaken assumptions of entitlement—if there are any—are usually *bilateral* and wholly *innocent*. It is now clear that the *Willmott v Barber probanda* are properly relevant only to cases of 'pure acquiescence' or 'mere passivity', and not to 'common expectation' estoppel (*Taylors Fashions Ltd v Liverpool Victoria Trustees Co Ltd* (1982) per Oliver J; see also *Orgee v Orgee* (1997) per Hirst LJ).

— *The essential test of unconscionability* Over the past 20 years the focus of estoppel doctrine has decisively turned towards the 'essential test' of *unconscionability*: the court must 'look at the matter in the round' as part of a 'broad inquiry as to whether the repudiation of an assurance is or is not unconscionable in all the circumstances' (*Gillett v Holt* (2001) per Robert Walker LJ, **10.24**; see also *Parker v Parker* (2003) at [241]–[246] per Lewison J). But the court must always 'take a principled approach, and cannot exercise a completely unfettered discretion according to the individual judge's notion of what is fair in any particular case' (*Jennings v Rice* (2003) at [43] per Robert Walker LJ).

Outcome of estoppel doctrine

10.22 In the law of proprietary estoppel the modification of strict legal entitlements is dependent on the ability of one of the parties to point persuasively to the existence of an 'inchoate' equity of estoppel.

— *'Inchoate' equities* The equity of estoppel arises in an 'inchoate' form as soon as the conscience of the relevant landowner is affected by the transactions of the parties, i.e. when the landowner unconscionably sets up his rights adversely to the legitimate demands of the estoppel claimant. From this point onwards the claimant has 'an equity which would attract the discretion of the Court', entitling him to bend the ear of the court of conscience to listen sympathetically to his plea for a restraint upon the landowner's exercise of his rights (see *Beaton v McDivitt* (1987) per Kirby P). It then becomes the task of the court to decide whether, and if so in what form, to vindicate or perfect the 'equity' which has been asserted. But even before the estoppel is formalised in some court-ordered remedy, the inchoate equity has a certain anticipatory or embryonic proprietary quality. Although never easily accommodated within the canon of proprietary rights recognised in the Law of Property Act 1925 (**2.29**), an inchoate equity of estoppel can possibly be claimed by a successor in title of the original representee (**10.20**) and it is nowadays even more clear that the burden of the inchoate equity is transmissible to third parties who purchase an interest in the land to which that equity relates (see e.g. *Sledmore v Dalby* (1996), **10.26**; *Lloyds Bank plc v Carrick* (1996), **9.8, 12.42**; LRA 2002, s 116(a), **4.9, 12.8, 12.20, 12.25**). It is also arguable that, notwithstanding a transfer of the land to which an inchoate equity of estoppel relates, the representor remains subject to an underlying personal liability to the representee which may give rise to a money remedy (see Susan Bright and Ben McFarlane, [2005] *Conv* 14).

— *Wide judicial discretion to concretise the inchoate equity* The mere fact that a claimant can demonstrate that an inchoate equity of estoppel has arisen in his favour does not mean that he automatically has a right to some particular court-ordered remedy. His equity finally crystallises only when it is concretised in the form of a specific interest, award or order selected by the court. The court retains an extremely wide discretion to mould relief in order to take account of all the circumstances of the case (see *Plimmer v Mayor etc of Wellington* (1884)). The remedy awarded may involve the grant of a recognised proprietary interest in land or may sometimes take the more limited form of the conferment of a long-term occupation licence or a money remedy or a lien for expenditure (**10.27**).

— *A minimalist approach* It is a recurrent theme in estoppel cases that the court must preserve some kind of *proportionality* between the detriment which has been incurred by the estoppel claimant and the remedy eventually awarded (see *Jennings v Rice* (2003) at [36] per Aldous LJ, [56] per Robert Walker LJ). As Robert Walker LJ indicated in *Gillett v Holt* (2001), it is the function of the court in each case to identify the 'maximum extent of the equity' founded on estoppel and then 'to form a view as to what is the minimum required to satisfy it and do justice between the parties'. The court may never award estoppel claimants a greater interest in law than was within their induced expectation (*Parker v Parker* (2003) at [210] per Lewison J), but may in some circumstances award rather less (see e.g. *Sledmore v Dalby* (1996), **10.26**).

> *Jennings v Rice* (2003) J worked for nearly 30 years as a gardener and odd-job man for R, a childless widow. He was initially paid a wage, but payment was discontinued when R told J that 'he would be alright' and that her house (worth over £400,000) would all be his 'one day'. R, now in her eighties, became increasingly dependent on J and his wife, who provided very substantial nursing care services for her in the belief that J would benefit under R's will. R died intestate, leaving him, of course, nothing. J claimed the entire value of the house and its furniture on the footing of proprietary estoppel. The judge at first instance awarded him a payment of £200,000 out of R's estate on the ground that any larger award would have been out of all proportion to what J might reasonably have charged for his services. The Court of Appeal upheld this award, Robert Walker LJ observing (at [56]) that '[t]he essence of the doctrine of proprietary estoppel is to do what is necessary to avoid an unconscionable result, and a disproportionate remedy cannot be the right way of going about that' (**10.23**).

Overall aim of estoppel remedies

10.23 Even today the overall aim of the law of proprietary estoppel remains unresolved in at least two fundamental respects.

— *Enforcement of expectations or compensation for unacceptable loss?* The law of estoppel still hovers between two rather different remedial perspectives. Is it the proper role of estoppel doctrine to give belated effect to the *expectations of entitlement* engendered by the parties' dealings or merely to protect against the *detrimental consequences* caused when these expectations are undermined by an unconscientious insistence upon legal rights? In other words, does estoppel effectively provide

- specific performance of expectations, or
- mere recovery of reliance loss?

Much may depend on the precise perspective adopted. The *expectation-based* approach leads to the enforced delivery of otherwise unenforceable promises of entitlement. The *compensation-based* approach aims more modestly to require the owner of land, as a condition of the insistence upon his strict rights, to eliminate or neutralise any disadvantage unconscionably caused by his frustration of the other party's assumptions. An extreme instance serves to symbolise the divergence of perspective.

> **Example**: A, who owns a block of land valued at £1,000,000, induces B to incur expenditure on the faith of a wholly gratuitous verbal representation that B is henceforth the fee simple owner of the land. B erects on the land a shed worth £100 (see *Commonwealth of Australia v Verwayen* (1990) per Deane J).
>
> • An *expectation-based* approach requires the court to validate B's initial assumption as to her rights by making good the expectation on which she relied. On this analysis the court should order A to transfer the fee simple estate to B (even though to do so is to outflank the law of contract and to whitewash the informal creation of property rights in land).
>
> • A *compensation-based* approach requires the court, by contrast, merely to restrain A from insisting upon his strict legal right to recover possession pending restitution to B of her outlay of funds. On this analysis the court should order a simple return of B's lost investment of £100 (although to do so is to discard any concern for the legitimate expectations generated by A's representation and may often reduce the estoppel remedy to the analogue of a money recovery in the law of tort or restitution).

The distinction between these two approaches effectively involves the difference between guaranteeing the claimant *what she was originally promised* and awarding her *what she has otherwise lost*. English law retains a stance of extreme flexibility in determining the extent to which one or other measure of relief should prevail

(**10.27**). There are, admittedly, some cases where the expectation and compensation-based approaches coalesce and 'the only way to prevent the promisee suffering detriment will be to enforce the promise' (*Commonwealth of Australia v Verwayen* (1990)). In *Jennings v Rice* (2003) (**10.22**), the Court of Appeal did much to clarify the issue:

• The expectation-based approach is more likely to be appropriate where the relevant parties have reached 'a mutual understanding which is in reasonably clear terms but does not amount to a contract' (e.g. the case of the live-in carer who is promised that he or she will eventually inherit the home or enjoy lifelong occupancy). Here the 'consensual element' suggests that the parties probably both regarded the expected benefit and the accepted detriment as 'being (in a general, imprecise way) equivalent, or at any rate not obviously disproportionate' (per Robert Walker LJ at [45], [50]).

• A more limited judicial response is appropriate where (as in *Jennings v Rice* itself (**10.22**)) the claimant's expectations are 'uncertain, or extravagant, or out of all proportion to the detriment which the claimant has suffered' (e.g. the case of minor expenditure on the improvement of realty). The overarching task facing the court is to satisfy the *equity* raised by 'the combination of expectations, detrimental reliance, and the unconscionableness of allowing the [representor or his/her estate] to go back on the assurances'. The task is not simply, necessarily or even in principle to satisfy the claimant's *expectations* as such ([49]–[51] per Robert Walker LJ). In difficult cases—such as those involving informal participation in speculative building or development ventures—the temptation is to reach a compromise. In *Cobbe v Yeoman's Row Management Ltd* (2006) at [95], Mummery LJ thought 'the least unsatisfactory of the various forms that relief might take' to make a monetary award which bridged the difference between mere reimbursement of expenditure ('too stingy') and the vindication of the claimant's expectation of profit ('too speculative').

— *Fair dealings or fair outcomes?* In the law of estoppel it remains unclear whether the issue of unconscionability is to be measured in terms of *conduct* or in terms of *outcome*. Does the relevant test relate to:

• the conscientiousness of the parties' mutual dealings, or
• the fairness of outcome of these dealings?

An excessive bias towards the latter concern would cause estoppel doctrine to operate blatantly as an agent of distributive justice, correcting unexplained disparities of entitlement between the parties even though such maldistributions are not attributable to unconscionable dealing by *either*. At this point property rules lose any resemblance to their characteristically clear-cut, crystalline form and dissolve into the 'mud' of discretion-laden formulas aimed at 'equitable' outcomes in isolated cases (see Carol Rose, 'Crystals and Mud in Property Law' 40 *Stanford L Rev* 577 (1987–88)). For some there is a real fear that estoppel doctrine, like the constructive trust, may wind up as a blunt instrument of social justice premised on ill-defined notions of fairness (see Browne-Wilkinson, 'Constructive Trusts and Unjust Enrichment' (1996) 10 *Trust Law International* 98). All this contrasts markedly with the historic belief of the common lawyer that hard-edged rules of property are ultimately more efficient in minimising confusion, limiting costly controversies and generally facilitating the productive processes of commerce (**2.18, 12.14**). As Carol Rose says in her racy way, 'sticking it to those who fail to protect themselves in advance ... will encourage people to plan and to act carefully, knowing that no judicial cavalry will ride to their rescue later'.

It is against the background of these uncertainties over the precise function of estoppel doctrine that we now turn, in greater detail, to the component elements underlying claims of estoppel.

Representation (or 'assurance') of entitlement

10.24 In order to raise an 'equity' of estoppel there must have been some representation or 'assurance' of entitlement given by or on behalf of the relevant landowner (see *Matharu v Matharu* (1994)). Reliance *without* representation generates no 'equity'. Proprietary estoppel cannot be founded on a mere expectation of rights, however reasonable that expectation, if the owner of the relevant land never encouraged or allowed any belief or expectation that the claimant would acquire rights (see e.g. *Parker v Parker* (2003) at [235], infra). The mere existence of a long-standing practice or course of dealings between the parties cannot suffice (*Keelwalk Properties Ltd v Waller* (2002) at [62] per Jonathan Parker LJ): detrimental reliance upon a self-induced expectation gives rise to no valid claim of estoppel.

> *Attorney-General of Hong Kong v Humphrey's Estate (Queen's Gardens) Ltd* (1987) P, an intending purchaser of land, contended that, although no formal contract had been concluded, V, his proposed vendor, was estopped from withdrawing from a transaction which had been agreed 'in principle'. The Privy Council declined to uphold this claim of estoppel. P had 'acted in the confident and not unreasonable hope' that the agreement in principle would subsequently be formalised, but could not prove that V had ever created or encouraged any expectation that he would not withdraw from the transaction. Indeed P had known at all times that V retained the right to resile from the informal agreement for sale.

— *Content of the representation* The subject matter of the representation may take the form of almost any objectively recognisable proprietary right, provided that the assurance of entitlement is 'clear and unequivocal' (*JT Developments Ltd v Quinn* (1991) per Ralph Gibson LJ). The real question is whether, as a reasonable person, the estoppel claimant was led to believe that he or she either *had* or *would acquire* rights over the land (see *Parker v Parker* (2003) at [218], where the ninth Earl of Macclesfield was unable to claim a right of life occupancy in the ancestral castle merely on the basis of a 'tradition' that the Earl would live there).

In appropriate cases courts have shown themselves willing to give effect to a wide range of expectations of entitlement:

- fee simple interest (*Pascoe v Turner* (1979), **7.6, 10.24**);
- beneficial ownership of a share in land (*Lim Teng Huan v Ang Swee Chuan* (1992));
- life interest (*Inwards v Baker* (1965) (**10.20**); *Greasley v Cooke* (1980) (**10.25**));
- lease (*Lloyd v Dugdale* (2002), **10.25, 12.14**);
- easement (*Crabb v Arun DC* (1976) (**8.19, 10.25**));
- right of pre-emption (*Stilwell v Simpson* (1983)).

> *Pascoe v Turner* (1979) On the breakdown of a de facto relationship, P left T in occupation of his house, informing her orally that the house and its contents were thenceforth entirely hers (**7.6**). T later effected repairs to the house costing about £230. When P tried to recover possession from T, the Court of Appeal ordered that the fee simple in the house should be transferred by P to T. Cumming-Bruce LJ held that the circumstances raised an 'equity' in favour of T which could be satisfied only by directing P to perfect his imperfect gift of realty.

Pascoe v Turner presents, in an extreme form, the tension between the *expectation-* and *compensation-oriented* views of estoppel (see *Jennings v Rice* (2003) at [26] per Aldous LJ, **10.23**). In *Pascoe v Turner* the Court of Appeal preferred to enforce T's expectation of title, rather than to award a mere restitution of her outlay. (The Court alleged that only the freehold title could protect T from the 'ruthless' behaviour of her former lover and provide her with an interest which she might charge in order to raise finance for future repairs and improvements to the property.)

— *Ill-defined representations* In more recent years the courts have begun to stress that estoppel cannot be claimed in defence of expectations which fall short of a 'sufficiently concrete character' (*Orgee v Orgee* (1997) per Hirst LJ). Some transactions, although involving unconscionable behaviour, may produce a detriment so uncertain in nature and extent 'that even equity may not be able to devise an appropriate remedy for it … There are parts that sometimes even equity cannot reach' (*Willis v Hoare* (1998) per Auld LJ). Thus, for instance, no estoppel is generated by a legal owner's vague assurance of 'financial security' both before and after his death, without reference to any specific asset or assets (*Layton v Martin* (1986), **10.10**). Nor can an estoppel be raised by an undertaking that a live-in lover 'did not need to worry her pretty little head about money' (*Lissimore v Downing* (2003)). Again, a promise of a tenancy may be wholly inefficacious if unaccompanied by some identification of the terms and conditions of the leasehold grant (see *Orgee v Orgee* (1997); *Parker v Parker* (2003) at [232]). It is difficult to do justice if, in such circumstances, the representee 'cannot even point in the vaguest way to what form his ultimately arguable equity might take' (*Willis v Hoare*, per Auld LJ).

— *Promises of testamentary gift*   In order to raise an estoppel, promises of future entitlement must leave no room for doubt as to the inevitability of the entitlement concerned. Thus, for example, a mere expression of opinion as to likely future entitlement cannot rank as a relevant form of assurance (see *E & L Berg Homes Ltd v Grey* (1980) per Sir David Cairns). Even more difficult is the status of an oral undertaking by a legal owner that, in consideration of either past or future services, he will dispose of his property by a will made out in favour of the provider of these services. Such promises are, of course, contractually ineffective (*Taylor v Dickens* (1998); see LP(MP)A 1989, s 2(1), **9.6**) and the courts are mindful that 'the right to decide, and change one's mind as to, the devolution of one's estate is a basic and well understood feature of English law' (*Gillett v Holt* (1998) per Carnwath J). The case law of the recent past reflects a deep ambivalence as to whether representations of testamentary impulse can ever go beyond mere unenforceable expressions of intention, but it is equally clear that testamentary promises can *sometimes* be given effect in the law of estoppel (see e.g. *Re Basham, decd* (1986); *Wayling v Jones* (1993); *Ottey v Grundy* (2003)).

> *Gillett v Holt* (2001) H, a wealthy gentleman farmer, made a series of wills over the years leaving the bulk of his estate to G, a favoured farm worker, promising G that 'all this will be yours.' After a sudden breakdown in their personal and working relationship, H made a new will which completely excluded G from benefit. H's promises were considered by the Court of Appeal to impose an 'exceptionally strong claim' on H's conscience which could not be disclaimed after 40 years of underpaid labour by G on the farm. The Court indicated that the intrinsic revocability of a will is nothing to the point where consistent and unambiguous intimations of testamentary intent, coupled with substantial acts of reliance, 'make clear that the assurance is more than a mere

statement of present (revocable) intention, and is tantamount to a promise.' Even though H was still alive, G was awarded the freehold of the farmhouse in which he had lived, together with 42 hectares of land and a sum of £100,000 to compensate him for his exclusion from the farming business.

Reliance (or 'change of position')

10.25 It is intrinsic to a claim of estoppel that the claimant has acted *in reliance upon* some assurance of entitlement given by the landowner. A number of consequences follow.

— *Causal link* There must be an effective causal link between the representation of entitlement and the change of position incurred by the estoppel claimant (*Gillett v Holt* (2001) per Robert Walker LJ). The courts have sometimes, rather harshly, disallowed claims where this causal nexus has been deemed absent (see e.g. *Philip Lowe (Chinese Restaurant) Ltd v Sau Man Lee* (1985), **10.15**). More recently, however, the courts have held that any showing of disadvantage incurred by the estoppel claimant causes the burden of proof to shift to the representor to establish that the representee did *not* rely on the assurance of entitlement given (*Wayling v Jones* (1993)). Reliance can thus be *presumed* once it is demonstrated that the relevant representation was 'calculated to influence the judgment of a reasonable [person]' (see *Greasley v Cooke* (1980) per Lord Denning MR). It is also clear that the representation relied upon need not be the *sole* inducement for the change of position undertaken by the representee (*Campbell v Griffin* (2001) at [29] per Robert Walker LJ).

— *Knowledge* No proprietary estoppel is raised unless the representor had actual or constructive knowledge that the claimant was acting in reliance on the expectation of entitlement generated by his representation (*Crabb v Arun DC* (1976) per Lord Denning MR, **8.19**; *Barclays Bank plc v Zaroovabli* (1997)).

— *Reliance must involve some relevant 'change of position'* A critical element of any successful claim of proprietary estoppel is the showing of a relevant disadvantage or *change of position* incurred by the claimant on the faith of the representation made to her. Without such evidence her claim must fail, since all that remains is a voluntary and informal declaration of entitlement by the legal owner (see LPA 1925, ss 52–4, **9.38**, **10.14**). The required change of position is 'not a narrow or technical concept' (*Gillett v Holt* (2001) per Robert Walker LJ), but may take any of a wide range of forms provided that the claimant's actions are 'distinct and substantial' (*Sledmore v Dalby* (1996) per Hobhouse LJ).

— *Improvement of the representor's realty* The classic way in which an estoppel claimant may demonstrate the required 'change of position' includes the expenditure of the claimant's money or labour on some substantial or permanent improvement of the landowner's realty (see *Dillwyn v Llewelyn* (1862), **10.21**; *Inwards v Baker* (1965), **10.20**; *Dodsworth v Dodsworth* (1973), **10.27**; *Pascoe v Turner* (1979), **7.6, 10.24**).

— *Disadvantage unrelated to improvement of land* A 'change of position' may also comprise contributions of onerous effort or the incurring of almost any personal disadvantage or sacrifice other than a self-induced change of lifestyle. The range of contribution rewarded under the law of estoppel is possibly even more extensive than that recognised in much of the law of constructive trusts (**10.15**) (see *Grant v Edwards* (1986)). The following are examples of successful claims:

- abandonment of an existing job and home in order to live with representor (*Jones (AE) v Jones (FW)* (1977); compare, however, *Christian v Christian* (1981), **10.11**);

- devoted performance of 'all the functions of a live-in carer' (*Campbell v Griffin* (2001));

- failure to reserve a formal right of way (*Crabb v Arun DC* (1976), **8.19**);

- forgoing of opportunities for alternative employment (*Gillett v Holt* (2001)).

Lloyd v Dugdale (2002) (**12.14**) I orally agreed to grant D a long lease of commercial premises for £20,000. D was the managing director and majority shareholder of a company, JAD. I, professing himself to be 'a man of his word', further agreed that the company could move into the premises in advance of the expected formal lease, at which point D ceased to look for alternative accommodation for JAD's operations. Pursuant to this 'gentleman's agreement', and with I's knowledge and approval, JAD then spent £15,000 refurbishing the premises. I later declined to proceed with the transaction, having meanwhile received a better offer for the land. The Court of Appeal conceded (at [38]) that D could have asserted a good estoppel claim against I, not on the basis of expenditure incurred by a third party (JAD), but by reason of D's own change of position in forgoing the purchase of alternative business premises. (The Court held, however, that D's equity of estoppel did not override the eventual disposition of the land to L (**12.25**).)

Greasley v Cooke (1980) C, a 16-year-old girl, started employment as a living-in maid in a house owned by A, a widower with four children. Eight years later she began to cohabit in the house with one of A's sons, K. For almost the next 30 years C looked after members of the family, receiving no financial reward for her services. C later alleged that she had been encouraged by members of the family (including G, one of the present plaintiffs) to believe that she could regard the property as her home for the rest of her life. Following the deaths of A and K, the remaining members of the family sought possession against C, but the Court of Appeal upheld C's claim of proprietary estoppel, declaring that C was entitled to occupy the house rent-free for the remainder of her life. C's services in the family home and her consequent forgoing of career opportunities outside the home were accounted as a sufficient change of position on her part.

Grant v Edwards (1986) In upholding an estoppel claim in the family home (**10.14**), Browne-Wilkinson V-C seemed prepared to have regard to 'any act done by [the claimant] to her detriment relating to the joint lives of the parties', such as '[s]etting up house together, having a baby, [and] making payments to general housekeeping expenses', even though all such activity might be more accurately referable to 'the mutual love and affection of the parties and not specifically referable to the claimant's belief that she has an interest in the house'.

Note: Compare the approach in *Grant v Edwards* with the much less sympathetic stance adopted in *Coombes v Smith* (1986). Here, in rejecting allegations of estoppel and constructive trust (**10.11**) made by C, a woman who had left her husband to move into a house legally owned by S, Deputy Judge Jonathan Parker QC observed that the claimant had done nothing more than might be expected of her 'as occupier of the property, as [S's] mistress, and as [their child's] mother, in the context of a continuing relationship with [S]'.

Unconscionable disadvantage (or 'detriment')

10.26 The preconditions for the application of proprietary estoppel are met only if and to the extent that the representee is left *unconscionably* disadvantaged by her reliance on the relevant assurance of entitlement. No disadvantage ever truly arises, in any event, until that assurance is revoked or withdrawn: only then does a change of position operate to the detriment of the representee (*Grundt v Great Boulder Pty Gold Mines Ltd* (1937) per Dixon J). But even then the claimant must show that the undermining of her expectation involves such 'prejudice ... that it would be inequitable to allow the party who made the relevant representation to go back on it' (*Watts and Ready v Storey* (1984) per Slade LJ).

— *The criterion of unconscionability* By insisting on his strict legal rights, the representor must be 'taking advantage of [the representee] in a way which is unconscionable, inequitable or unjust' (*Crabb v Arun DC* (1976) per Scarman LJ). Whether the recipient of an assurance has incurred unremedied detriment in consequence of reliance requires close consideration of the totality of circumstance.

The courts have been particularly sensitive, for instance, to the presence of counter-balancing advantages enjoyed by the relier which, by offsetting in whole or part the disadvantage which he or she has suffered, negative any *unconscionability* of outcome (see e.g. *Sledmore v Dalby* (1996); *Campbell v Griffin* (2001); *Wilkie v Redsell* (2003)).

— *The 'equity' of estoppel may fluctuate over time* In assessing whether the representee is left the victim of *unconscionable* disadvantage, the approach of equity remains extremely flexible. Estoppel doctrine inhibits the denial by the promisor of an assumed state of affairs only 'until the detriment is removed or the innocent party otherwise compensated' (*Commonwealth of Australia v Verwayen* (1990) per McHugh J). Equity requires parties to act on the basis of the assumed relationship only so long as the 'equity' raised by estoppel persists. Once the detriment has 'ceased or been paid for', there is 'nothing unconscionable in a party insisting on reverting to his or her former relationship with the other party and enforcing his or her strict legal rights' (per McHugh J).

> *Sledmore v Dalby* (1996) S and her husband purchased a house in their own names for occupation by their daughter and *her* husband, D. D carried out substantial improvements to the property in reliance on his expectation, encouraged by S's husband, that he would be allowed rent-free occupation for the remainder of his life. After the death of S's daughter, D enjoyed rent-free residence for a further 17 years. S, now a widow, finally sued for possession on the ground that she required the house for her own occupation and D now lived elsewhere with his new partner. The Court of Appeal agreed that D had initially acquired an 'equity' based on estoppel, but held that the force of this 'equity' had become spent over the intervening years. (As Roch LJ observed, D would now have 'to be content with something less than his expectations'.) In view both of D's prolonged period of rent-free residence and of the balance of the parties' respective accommodation needs, it was 'no longer inequitable' to allow D's expectation of rights to be defeated by the assertion of S's rights as legal owner. Taking account, moreover, of the need for 'proportionality between the remedy and the detriment which is its purpose to avoid', it could not be 'properly said that there was anything unconscionable' in S seeking now to recover possession of her house. (Hobhouse LJ cited, as being of 'particular value', the approach of the Australian High Court in *Commonwealth of Australia v Verwayen.*)

The decision in *Sledmore v Dalby* is significant not least because it exemplifies the operation of a *compensation-based* approach to estoppel in conjunction with an emphasis on fairness of *outcome* (**10.23**). The flexibility of the estoppel doctrine was effectively used as an instrument of housing policy, *private law* obligations being manipulated in order to secure *public law* objectives—S was living on state benefit and the mortgage interest on her existing home was being paid by the Department of Health and Social Security (compare *Baker v Baker* (1993)).

The spectrum of estoppel remedies

10.27 All estoppel remedies ultimately impose a judicial restraint on the exercise of a strict legal entitlement (**10.18**), thus operating, in one sense, as a functional equivalent of relief against forfeiture (**14.14**). The legal owner is effectively restrained from obtaining the arbitrary eviction of the estoppel claimant. But in deciding how to reinforce or concretise the estoppel claimant's 'inchoate equity', the court can go much further. The upholding of a claim of proprietary estoppel opens up the court's jurisdiction to fashion *new* rights for relevant parties. The court has a virtually unlimited discretion, in the light of individual circumstances, to select from a fairly well established spectrum of remedial possibilities. '[T]he Court must look at the circumstances in each case to decide in what way the equity can be satisfied' (*Plimmer v Mayor etc of Wellington* (1884)). Sometimes the remedial outcome is tantamount to specific enforcement of the original promise of rights; at the other end of the remedial spectrum the circumstances may call for nothing more than an order for compensatory damages (**10.23**).

— *Grant of an unqualified estate or interest in land* In some cases the detriment flowing from dislocation of a promised entitlement is such that the 'equity' of estoppel can be satisfied only by a court order that the full assumed entitlement be transferred or granted to the claimant. This larger and more radical form of relief may be particularly appropriate

- where the claimant's assumption of rights has been relied upon for an extended period (*Gillett v Holt* (2001), **10.24**) or

- where the detriment incurred by the claimant is 'substantial and irreversible' or otherwise irremediable (*Commonwealth of Australia v Verwayen* (1990) per Mason CJ) or

- where a 'clean break' is advisable in order to avoid or minimise future friction (*Gillett v Holt* (2001) per Robert Walker LJ; *Jennings v Rice* (2003) at [52] per Robert Walker LJ).

On this basis it is possible, although it happens rarely, that the court will direct the transfer to the estoppel claimant of a fee simple estate (see e.g. *Dillwyn v Llewelyn* (1862), **10.21**; *Pascoe v Turner* (1979), **7.6, 10.24**). Alternatively the 'equity' of estoppel may be met through the grant of a court-ordered beneficial interest (*Lim Teng Huan v Ang Swee Chuan* (1992)) or leasehold estate (see *Habermann v Koehler*

(No 2) (2000); *Yaxley v Gotts* (2000), **10.12**) or easement (*Crabb v Arun DC* (1976), **8.19, 10.25**).

— *Grant of a right to occupy land* In the past a more commonly granted remedy has been a court order that the estoppel claimant should enjoy an irrevocable (or 'equitable') licence (**4.9**) to occupy land rent-free either for life or for some shorter period (see e.g. *Inwards v Baker* (1965) **10.20**; *Greasley v Cooke* (1980), **10.25**; *Matharu v Matharu* (1994)). This form of order often seems to mirror the ill-defined but nevertheless very real expectations of parties under informal family arrangements. Nowadays, however, an award of an occupation right for life takes effect under a statutorily regulated 'trust of land' (**9.42**), a complication which, for reasons of administrative inconvenience and expense, tends to make this solution seem rather less attractive (see *Campbell v Griffin* (2001) at [34] per Robert Walker LJ).

— *Grant of monetary compensation* In certain circumstances it may not be appropriate to grant a remedy which involves any form of long-term occupation right, the 'equity' of estoppel calling for only an award of money compensation (see e.g. *Campbell v Griffin* (2001) at [36], where the land in dispute was charged with a fixed sum award of £35,000). Money remedies appear particularly germane where the 'equity' is founded on expenditure for improvements which are not in themselves substantial (see *Jennings v Rice* (2003) at [51] per Robert Walker LJ). Although courts are naturally reluctant to allow a landowner to use a tender of compensation as a means of buying his way out of an estoppel claim or of forcing an inequity upon the claimant, there may well be circumstances in which a simple offer of compensation negates any question of unconscionability (see e.g. *Ottey v Grundy* (2003)).

> *Dodsworth v Dodsworth* (1973) X, the owner of a bungalow, allowed D1 and D2 (her younger brother and his wife) to live with her in that property. D1 and D2 proceeded to spend some £700 on improvements in the expectation that they could live in the property during the indefinite future. The Court of Appeal considered that the appropriate remedy in the circumstances comprised merely the return of their capital outlay together with some compensation for the labour invested in making the improvements. The complaint of D1 and D2 had been essentially that it would be unfair to evict them in the light of their expenditure, but in the Court's view this objection was easily deflected by a simple reimbursement of the money expended by them.

— *Grant of occupation lien* It is even possible that the court may combine a compensation order with the grant of a limited occupation right pending payment out to the claimant. Such an order effectively recognises that the claimant enjoys some kind of lien or charge over the land to the value of the financial detriment alleged by her (see e.g. *Hussey v Palmer* (1972), as explained in *Re Sharpe (A Bankrupt)* (1980), **10.4**).

> *Hussey v Palmer* (1972) H, an elderly widow, was invited to live in a house already owned by her son-in-law, P. An extra bedroom was built for her as an extension to the existing house, and the cost of this construction was paid by H. Domestic discord brought the arrangement to a premature end, but the Court of Appeal decided, by a majority, that it would be 'entirely against conscience that [P] should retain the whole house and not allow [H] any interest in it, or any charge upon it'. The Court imposed a constructive trust on behalf of H to give effect either to some proportionate share in the beneficial ownership of the property or to a lien for the money advanced by her.

Informally conferred life interests

10.28 A further context for the informal creation of interests in land involves the casual conferment of a life interest. Problems have always been raised by the loosely worded grant—particularly in dealings between family members—of informal rights of rent-free occupation for life.

— *Pre-1997 grants* Prior to 1997 the dilemma was that the oral grant of a life interest either created nothing more than a *revocable* occupation licence (**4.2**) or caused the grantee to become enmeshed, unwittingly, within the cumbersome machinery of a *strict settlement* governed by the Settled Land Act 1925 (**9.43**). Indeed the conferment of a life interest seemed to constitute the grantee a 'tenant for life' within the meaning of the 1925 Act (see *Bannister v Bannister* (1948), **10.9**; *Ungurian v Lesnoff* (1990)), thereby consigning him to a chain of consequence never foreseen by the relevant parties. Quite apart from the technicality that strict settlements generally required the execution of at least two deeds, the grantee of a casual right of rent-free occupation appeared to be entitled, however implausibly, to call as tenant for life for a vesting of the full legal estate (together with the statutory powers of sale, lease and mortgage). Although courts often fought shy of these unintended—and absurd—implications of interests granted for life (see e.g. *Binions v Evans* (1972) per Lord Denning MR, **12.42**; *Griffiths v Williams* (1977)), the clutches of the Settled Land Act came to seem inescapable.

> *Costello v Costello* (1994) D and her husband purchased their council house in their own names, their son, P, providing the entire cash purchase price. P protected his interest in the property by means of a trust deed which permitted his parents a right of rent-free occupation for the remainder of their lives. After his father's death, P sought to have the legal title transferred into his own name, claiming that D had merely a licence to occupy.

The Court of Appeal held, however, that D was beneficially entitled as tenant for life under the SLA 1925 and therefore had the right—albeit never contemplated at the date of the trust deed—to sell the house and require the trustees of the settlement to purchase another property in which she would have a similar right of occupation for life.

— *Post-1996 grants* Any grant of a life interest on or after 1 January 1997 requires a declaration of trust in compliance with the Law of Property Act 1925 (see LPA 1925, s 53(1)(b), **9.38**), unless the informality of grant can be cured by reliance on some claim of resulting or constructive trust (LPA 1925, s 53(2), **9.39**). In either case the grant now takes effect under a 'trust of land' (**9.42**).

Donationes mortis causa

10.29 The normal rule relating to dispositions of property on death requires that the disponor (or testator) should incorporate his wishes in written form in a will which is duly signed and attested (Wills Act 1837, s 9). There has always existed, in the law of personal property, a startling exception to this requirement of formality. The formality of a will may be circumvented by a parol (or oral) gift made in contemplation of death, otherwise known as a *donatio mortis causa*. A valid *donatio mortis causa* requires that three preconditions be met.

- The gift must be made in contemplation of impending death.
- The gift must be made on the condition that it is to be absolute only on the death of the donor, being revocable until then, and entirely ineffective if death does not occur.
- The subject matter of the gift, or the essential indicia of title to it, must be delivered to the donee, thereby signifying a parting with dominion and not merely with physical possession over that subject matter.

Prior to 1991 it was generally accepted that land could never form the subject matter of a *donatio mortis causa,* partly because oral gifts of land seemed to be precluded by statute (LPA 1925, ss 52–4, **7.6**, **9.38**) and partly because a handing over of title documents relating to land would not prevent an owner from dealing with his estate (e.g. through the grant of a short tenancy, the tenant having no right to call for evidence of his landlord's title). In *Sen v Headley* (1991), however, the Court of Appeal—to the surprise of most—upheld a *donatio mortis causa* in respect of land, apparently suggesting that the exemption of such a gift from the normal rules of formality is sanctioned by the last century of developments in the law of constructive trusts and proprietary estoppel. The applicability of the *donatio mortis causa* to land is still less than clear. The best that can be said is that the dealing which comprises a *donatio mortis causa* operates upon the conscience of the deceased's personal representatives and thus generates some kind of constructive trust—or possibly constitutes some strained version of the rule in *Rochefoucauld v Boustead* (1897) (**9.39**).

> *Sen v Headley* (1991) Three days before his death from inoperable cancer, H told his long-time partner, M: 'The house is yours, Margaret. You have the keys. They are in your bag. The deeds are in the steel box'. After H's death intestate, M discovered that H had put her in possession of the only key to the deeds box. The Court of Appeal held that H's words and conduct sufficiently connoted a parting with dominion over H's house and that, all the other conditions of a *donatio mortis causa* being satisfied, H had effectively transferred the house to M.

FURTHER READING

Gray and Gray, *Elements of Land Law* (4th edn, OUP, 2005), ch 10.

Relevant sections of this work and other land law textbooks may be supplemented with:

Auchmuty, Rosemary 'Unfair shares for women', H Lim and A Bottomley (eds), *Feminist Perspectives on Land Law* (Routledge-Cavendish, 2007), p 171.

Bottomley, Anne 'Women and Trust(s): Portraying the Family in the Gallery of Law', in S Bright and JK Dewar (eds), *Land Law: Themes and Perspectives* (OUP, 1998), p 206.

Bright, Susan and McFarlane, Ben 'Proprietary Estoppel and Property Rights' [2005] *CLJ* 449.

Dewar, John 'Land, Law, and the Family Home', in Bright and Dewar, op cit. p 327.

Dixon, Martin 'Resulting and Constructive Trusts of Land: The Mist Descends and Rises' [2005] *Conv* 79.

Gardner, Simon 'Quantum in *Gissing v Gissing* Constructive Trusts' (2004) 120 *LQR* 541.

Gardner, Simon 'The Remedial Discretion in Proprietary Estoppel—Again' (2006) 122 *LQR* 492.

Hopkins, Nicholas *The Informal Acquisition of Rights in Land* (Sweet & Maxwell, 2000), chs 6 and 7.

McMurtry, Lara 'Informal Land Contracts and Estoppel' [2001] *Conv* 86.

Mee, John 'Property rights and personal relationships: reflections on reform' (2004) 24 *Legal Studies* 414.

Nield, Sarah 'Constructive trusts and estoppel' (2003) 23 *Legal Studies* 311.

Rotherham, Craig 'The Property Rights of Unmarried Cohabitees: The Case for Reform' [2004] *Conv* 268.

Thompson, Mark 'Constructive Trusts, Estoppel and the Family Home' [2004] *Conv* 496.

Thompson, Mark 'Proprietary estoppel, third parties and constructive trusts: a taste of the future?' [2002] *Conv* 584.

SELF-TEST QUESTIONS

1 To what extent does the law of informal trust and estoppel interests achieve the traditional preference of land law for certainty and efficiency over the claims of fairness or moral entitlement?

2 Lord Templeman once said that '[e]quity is not a computer' (*Winkworth v Edward Baron Developments Ltd* (1986)). How, then, does the law of trusts calculate the respective entitlements of beneficiaries under resulting and constructive trusts (**10.5, 10.13–10.16**)?

3 Are we within reach of a new dawn in the law of constructive trusts (**10.15–10.16**)?

4 What is the difference between a licence which is enforceable against a licensor because of an element of detrimental reliance (**10.19–10.21**) and a licence enforceable against a licensor because it was bought and paid for (**4.6, 4.11**)?

5 What is the proper objective of the law of proprietary estoppel (**10.23, 10.27**)?

11

Regulation of trusts and co-ownership

SUMMARY

In modern law the co-ownership of land interests takes the form of either *joint tenancy* or *tenancy in common*. This chapter examines both phenomena and describes how concurrent and successive ownership is incorporated into the structure of the *trust of land*. The chapter also outlines the respective roles of trustees and beneficiaries under a trust of land and how a disposition by trustees can overreach (or clear off) the beneficial interests which exist behind the trust.

Types of co-ownership

11.1 *Co-ownership* is the term used to describe those forms of ownership in which two or more persons are *simultaneously* entitled in possession to an interest or interests in the same property. Co-ownership thus connotes some form of concurrent (as distinct from successive) holding. Concurrent ownership of land has been given a contemporary prominence largely, although not exclusively, by the shared rights of ownership found in the modern family home. Virtually all forms of co-ownership of land nowadays operate in conjunction with a *trust of land* regulated by the Trusts of Land and Appointment of Trustees Act 1996 (TOLATA 1996) (**9.35–9.36, 11.20–11.21**).

English law has known four types of co-ownership, of which only the first two now have any real significance:

- joint tenancy (**11.2**);
- tenancy in common (**11.6**);

- tenancy by entireties (**11.19**);
- coparcenary (**11.19**).

Joint tenancy

11.2 *Joint tenancy* is a form of co-ownership in which each 'joint tenant' is said to be 'wholly entitled to the whole' of the estate or interest which is the subject of co-ownership (see *Burton v Camden LBC* (2000) per Lord Millett). A joint tenancy can subsist in either a *legal* or an *equitable* estate in land (or both). The key to understanding joint tenancy is the realisation that no joint tenant holds any distinct *share* in the co-owned estate, but is—together with the other joint tenant or tenants—invested with the *total interest* in the land (*Wright v Gibbons* (1949) per Dixon J). Thus, for instance, an entire undifferentiated estate in fee simple may be vested in joint tenants, each simultaneously holding the *whole* of the estate rather than any defined proportion or aliquot share. Indeed any reference to ownership in *shares* of any kind (e.g. 'A owns a one-quarter interest and B a three-quarters interest') is normally sufficient to establish that A and B co-own *not* as joint tenants, but rather as *tenants in common* (**11.6**). (It should be pointed out, for the avoidance of doubt, that the term 'tenant' in this context has nothing *necessarily* to do with the landlord-tenant relationship: it merely signifies 'owner'.)

Such is the comprehensive nature of joint tenancy that joint tenants comprise, in the eyes of the law, a collective entity—one composite person—together holding one and the same estate in the subject land, whether that estate be freehold or leasehold. In this way, a transfer of land to two or more persons as joint tenants 'operates so as to make them, vis-à-vis the outside world, one single owner' (*Hammersmith and Fulham LBC v Monk* (1992) per Lord Browne-Wilkinson). It must be added, however, that every joint tenancy of an equitable estate is reducible, by a process known as 'severance', into a *tenancy in common* in equal shares (**11.10**).

Distinguishing characteristics of joint tenancy

11.3 The distinguishing characteristics of joint tenancy are two in number.

- Joint tenants enjoy as between themselves a *right of survivorship* (**11.4**).
- Joint tenancy always presupposes the presence of the *four unities* (**11.5**).

Right of survivorship (*ius accrescendi*)

11.4 It is an inherent characteristic of joint tenancy that, on the death of any one joint tenant, the entire co-owned estate 'survives to' the remaining joint tenant or tenants. Ultimately, in the manner of the medieval tontine, the surviving joint tenant becomes the sole owner—the winner takes all. This right of survivorship (or *ius accrescendi*) ensures that the entitlement of each joint tenant is simply *extinguished* on his death. No *share* devolves upon those who take under the deceased's will or on his intestacy, precisely because a joint tenant never has any *share* as such which is even remotely capable of transmission on his death. Nor, although it is tempting to say otherwise, does any share or interest *pass* from the deceased to the surviving joint tenant or tenants—joint tenants just don't have *shares!*

> **Example**: Suppose that a fee simple estate in Greenacre is registered in the names of three joint tenants, A, B and C, holding for themselves as beneficial joint tenants (**11.20**). If C then dies, the legal and equitable estates remain vested in A and B as survivors. A and B are already fully entitled as joint tenants to the entire fee simple in Greenacre, and no further vesting in them as survivors is required. C simply drops out of the picture, the register of title being altered to reflect the fact that the legal estate has ceased to be vested in him (see LRR 2003, r 164). Even if C attempted by will to leave his own 'share' to X, survivorship operates immediately on C's death—before his will can take effect—with the result that there is nothing on which his testamentary disposition can bite. (Another way of expressing this is to say that a joint tenancy can *never* be severed by will (**11.11**).)
>
> Similarly, if B predeceases A, the right of survivorship operates once more: B disappears, and the entire fee simple estate in Greenacre 'survives to' A as sole legal and equitable owner. (In English law, if there is any unresolved doubt as to the precise sequence in which A, B and C died—e.g. in a late-night car crash—the deaths are presumed, rather absurdly, to have occurred in order of seniority (the *commorientes* rule), the youngest 'surviving' longest (LPA 1925, s 184).)

Under the strict theory of survivorship, the survivor's ownership never *enlarges*, although the operation of the *ius accrescendi* does, of course, bring about a distinct shift of economic interest in his favour. Furthermore, survivorship takes effect regardless of whether the survivor made much (or any) money contribution towards the initial purchase of the property. The capricious outcome of the joint tenants' gamble on longevity might well be a proper subject of complaint were it not for several significant factors which combine to make joint tenancy a sensible and convenient medium of certain kinds of co-ownership.

— *Survivorship is a testamentary substitute* In many instances joint tenancy (with its automatic rule of survivorship) operates as a crude *testamentary substitute*—the poor man's will. Particularly in the context of joint ownership of the family home, survivorship plays a valuable modern role as a simple and cost-effective estate planning device in a country where the majority of the population still make no will. On the death of one partner the co-owned estate vests without further ado in the survivor.

— *Joint tenancy is mandatory for co-ownership of any legal estate* Since 1925 co-ownership of any legal estate in land, whether freehold or leasehold, has necessarily taken the form of *joint tenancy* (**11.9, 11.11**). A legal estate is declared incapable of 'subsisting or of being created in an undivided share in land' (LPA 1925, s 1(6)), with the obvious corollary that '[n]o severance of a joint tenancy of a legal estate, so as to create a tenancy in common in land, shall be permissible' (LPA 1925, s 36(2)).

— *Joint tenancy is ideal for legal co-ownership* Because legal estates constitute a merely formal title (**1.24, 7.3**), no harm in general flows from the hazard of survivorship. In the context of co-ownership, legal title, whilst of course it binds the whole world, is otherwise relatively unimportant. It comprises a mere *paper* title to land which is necessarily held on trust (**11.20**), indicating those persons who are entrusted with nominal ownership and fiduciary powers of management and disposition. The *substance* of ownership resides in equity (**1.26**). It is *beneficial ownership* which determines such matters as rights of occupation of the land, the allocation of the rents and profits derived from it, and ultimately of course entitlement to the capital proceeds of any sale.

• Joint tenancy, albeit with the accompanying unpredictability of survivorship, is therefore uniquely adapted to the efficient management of the formal legal title. Joint ownership at law achieves distinct advantages in respect of both the internal administration of trusts of land and the conduct of transactions with strangers (**11.22**). In particular, the rule of survivorship avoids the inconvenience of fresh vestings of the trust estate on every occasion of death within the trusteeship, since the surviving trustees are *already* invested with the entire legal estate in the land and require no further vesting in their names. (New trustees of a legal estate can be appointed quite easily (TA 1925, ss 36, 40, 41(1); TOLATA 1996, s 19(2).)

• Joint tenancy becomes potentially capricious only in so far as it governs *equitable title*—although, even here, it does so only because the equitable co-owners have actively chosen joint tenancy as the vehicle of their concurrent entitlement.

The 'four unities'

11.5 It is axiomatic that the 'four unities' must be present before a joint tenancy can be said to exist (*AG Securities v Vaughan* (1990) per Fox LJ); and that where all 'four unities' are present in a multiple holding of land there is joint tenancy (*Corin v Patton* (1990) per Deane J). These four unities comprise the unities of *possession, interest, title* and *time*. (Only unity of *possession* is required as a precondition of tenancy in common (**11.8**).)

— *Unity of possession* means that each joint tenant is as much entitled to possession of every part of the co-owned land as the other joint tenant or tenants. Thus no joint tenant may ever point physically to any part of the co-owned land as being his to the exclusion of the other or others (*Meyer v Riddick* (1990)). Between joint tenants the concept of trespass has no significance except in the sense that any wrongful ouster of another joint tenant from the co-owned land indeed ranks as a trespass. A joint tenant who simply finds the presence of another joint tenant irritating or even intolerable has no remedy at common law (see *Wiseman v Simpson* (1988)). The joint tenants' jointness of possession is only rarely displaced by statutory intervention, e.g. by a court order based on circumstances of domestic violence (see *Davis v Johnson* (1979)).

— *Unity of interest* follows from the proposition that each joint tenant is 'wholly entitled to the whole'. The interest held by each joint tenant is necessarily the same in extent, nature and duration. Therefore no joint tenancy can exist between a *freeholder* and a *leaseholder*, between an owner *in possession* and an owner *in remainder*, or between an owner of a *fee simple* interest and an owner of *a life* interest.

— *Unity of title* entails that each joint tenant must derive his title to the land from the *same* act (e.g. of adverse possession) or document (e.g. of transfer or grant). In the case of a co-owned legal estate, this particular form of unity also has the implication that a purchaser from joint tenants need investigate only *one* title (**11.22**). Moreover, the legal estate in jointly owned land cannot be irreversibly disposed of in favour of a third party without the active participation of *all* the joint tenants, *each* of whom must put his signature to the document of disposition.

— *Unity of time* requires that the interest of each joint tenant must normally vest at the same time.

Tenancy in common

11.6 By contrast with joint tenancy, tenancy in common is a form of co-ownership in which the co-owners hold *distinct shares* or notional proportions of entitlement. The LPA 1925 describes tenants in common as holding land in 'undivided shares' (see LPA 1925, ss 1(6), 36(2)), this slightly confusing terminology serving to indicate merely that the co-owned land has not yet been divided up physically. The giveaway lies in the reference to the word 'shares', since it is only as *tenants in common* that co-owners can properly be said to hold specific shares at all (e.g. 'A owns a one-quarter interest and B a three-quarters interest', or even 'A and B own a half-share each').

The principal characteristics of tenancy in common are two in number.

- There is *no right of survivorship* between tenants in common (**11.7**).
- Only unity of *possession* is required between tenants in common (**11.8**).

There is no right of survivorship

11.7 No right of survivorship operates between tenants in common. The size of each tenant in common's share is a fixed quantum, unaffected by the death of any tenant in common; and the share of each tenant in common passes on his death to those entitled under his will or on his intestacy.

Only unity of possession is required

11.8 By contrast with joint tenancy, only *unity of possession* is an essential constitutive element of tenancy in common. It is, for instance, the potential *disunity* of interest between tenants in common which enables one tenant in common to own, say, a *one-third* share and another tenant in common a *two-thirds* share. But the irreducible component of tenancy in common is *unity of possession*: without it there would exist no co-ownership at all, merely separate ownership of physically distinct areas of land.

— *Occupation and enjoyment* As in the case of joint tenants, no tenant in common may physically demarcate any part of the co-owned land as his to the exclusion of any other co-owner. Each tenant in common has a right to exercise acts of ownership over the whole land, provided that he does not interfere with the like right of any other co-owner. Regardless of the quantum of his share, each tenant in common is entitled to possession—but not *exclusive* possession—of the entire property (or any part of it). Each has a right to the 'use and enjoyment of it in a proper manner' (see *Bull v Bull* (1955) per Denning LJ), the tenant in common's right to occupy now receiving statutory reinforcement from TOLATA 1996, s 12(1) (**11.28**). Again, save in cases of physical ouster of another tenant in common or gross interference with mutual rights of enjoyment, the notion of trespass between tenants in common has no meaning at common law (*Jacobs v Seward* (1872)). Modern legislation has, however, provided the courts with an armoury of statutory powers to regulate the exercise of occupation rights between equitable co-owners (see TOLATA 1996, s 14(2); FLA 1996, ss 33(3), 36(5), **11.33**).

— *Liability for occupation rent* As between tenants in common themselves, no rent liability normally arises at common law even though one co-owner may happen, as a matter of fact, to enjoy sole occupation of the entire co-owned land. In view of the unity of possession inherent in tenancy in common, the decision to cede sole occupancy to one of the co-owners is regarded as a matter of voluntary choice and not therefore as the proper basis of any relationship of landlord and tenant (*Henderson v Eason* (1851)). Trustees of land now have a statutory power to exclude one or more (but not all) of the beneficial co-owners from occupation under a trust (TOLATA 1996, s 13(1), **11.27**). In such cases it is open to the trustees to require the payment of 'compensation' to any beneficiary whose enjoyment of the land has been precluded or restricted (TOLATA 1996, s 13(6)(a)).

— *Entitlement to rent from a stranger* Any rents received from a letting of co-owned land to a stranger are divisible between the tenants in common in strict proportion to the value of their respective shares (*Job v Potton* (1875)).

— *Liability for repairs and improvements* Where one co-owner, at his own expense, effects repairs or improvements to the co-owned land, he has, in general, no right of immediate recovery of his costs from the other co-owner or co-owners (a principle equally applicable, incidentally, between joint tenants). The co-owner who is out of pocket is, however, entitled to a lien on the co-owned property (or its proceeds of sale) when the value of the land is realised and distributed between the co-owners (see *Leigh v Dickeson* (1884)). In this way the cost of any repair or improvement resulting in an enhanced sale price is effectively shared out between all the co-owners (see *Re Pavlou (A Bankrupt)* (1993) per Millett J). It is also now open to the trustees of land, in allocating a right of occupation of the co-owned land to one or more co-owners, to impose conditions relating to 'expenses in respect of the land', a power probably wide enough to cover the cost of repairs and improvements (see TOLATA 1996, s 13(5), **11.28**).

The equitable preference for tenancy in common

11.9 Whereas the common law historically preferred joint tenancy to tenancy in common (largely because of the sweeping together of interests by survivorship), equity has always preferred *tenancy in common* as the medium of co-ownership. Tenancy in common represents certainty and fairness in the property relations of co-owners (see *Kinch v Bullard* (1999) per Neuberger J, **11.13**). Each tenant in common holds a fixed beneficial interest immune from 'the gamble of the tontine' (*Corin v Patton* (1990) per Deane J). In a tenancy in common each share constitutes a distinct and indefeasible quantum of wealth which can serve as the subject of either commerce or family endowment.

— *Mandatory joint tenancy at law*   The common law presumption in favour of *joint tenancy* has now been crystallised, in an irrebuttable form, in the property legislation of 1925—co-ownership of a legal estate in land *must* take the form of joint tenancy (LPA 1925, ss 1(6), 36(2), **11.4, 11.11**).

— *Nature of equitable co-ownership*   It is undoubtedly true that, in an extremely general sense, *equity follows the law* (**9.2**). Equity's starting assumption is therefore that joint tenants of the legal estate are likewise entitled as *joint tenants* of the equitable estate (see *Pettitt v Pettitt* (1970) per Lord Upjohn; *Cowcher v Cowcher* (1972) per Bagnall J). But this assumption as to the nature of equitable co-ownership is readily displaced by any of a number of contra-indications which demonstrate that, regardless of the mandatory joint tenancy *at law*, equitable ownership is intended to take the form of *tenancy in common*. Indeed, these contra-indications have now become so prevalent that it is relatively rare that the nature of equitable co-ownership falls to be ascertained by a despairing resort to the residual proposition that equity follows the law.

In the absence of contrary agreement (as expressed for instance in a declaration of trust (**9.37–9.38**)), a variety of circumstances overrides the superficial presumption that co-ownership entails equitable joint tenancy. Notwithstanding the legal position, equity leans in favour of *tenancy in common* in the following situations— and the list is not exhaustive (see *Malayan Credit Ltd v Jack Chia-MPH Ltd* (1986) per Lord Brightman).

- *Express or implied words of severance* clearly point to equitable tenancy in common (e.g. any language in a document of transfer or conveyance indicating that the parties were intended to take distinct and identifiable shares in the land).

- *Absence of the 'four unities'* is fatal to any suggestion that joint tenancy subsists in equity (**11.5**).

- *Contributions of purchase money in unequal proportions* raise an equitable presumption that, regardless of legal title, the contributors intended to take proportionate equitable shares under a resulting trust (**10.3**). The disparity of contribution is taken to indicate, in the absence of contrary agreement (**10.5**), that the equitable entitlements of the contributors were not intended to be regulated by the crude rule of survivorship.

- *Commercial partners* are presumed to hold the equitable estate as tenants in common, on the ground that the hazards of survivorship are believed inimical to the essence of commercial partnership (see *Lake v Craddock* (1732)).

- *Business tenants* who take a joint tenancy of a legal leasehold estate 'for their several individual business purposes' are similarly presumed to have intended to hold as tenants in common in equity (*Malayan Credit Ltd v Jack Chia-MPH Ltd* (1986)).

- *Joint mortgagees*, who lend money on the security of property, are presumed to hold the equitable estate in the mortgage as tenants in common inter se, each having intended to 'lend his own and take back his own' (*Morley v Bird* (1798)).

Severance

11.10 *Severance* is the process by which *joint tenancy* is convertible into *tenancy in common*, thereby causing the undifferentiated co-ownership of joint tenancy to crystallise into co-ownership in distinct and undivided shares (**11.6**).

— *Contexts of severance* The law has generally tended to facilitate severance in order to mitigate the hazards of survivorship, with the consequence that severance emerges in the context of any dealing which

- excludes the future operation of *survivorship* or
- destroys the continued existence of the *unities of interest and title*.

(The *first* of these tests seems to be more relevant in relation to dealings between the joint tenants themselves; the *second*, in relation to dealings between a joint tenant and a stranger.)

— *General effect of severance* When it occurs, severance normally separates off an *equal* aliquot share for the severing joint tenant. In other words, irrespective of the relative proportions of the joint tenants' original contributions to the purchase of the co-owned property, the severing tenant will take 1/*n*th of the property beneficially, where *n* is the current number of the joint tenants (*Nielson-Jones v Fedden* (1975) per Walton J). Except where there are merely *two* joint tenants, severance affects the interest of only the *severing* tenant. Thus, in a joint tenancy comprising A, B and C, if A severs, he separates off for himself a one-third share as a *tenant in common*, but leaves B and C as *joint tenants* of the *whole* of the remaining two-thirds share (see *Wright v Gibbons* (1949) per Dixon J). If B then dies, C takes that two-thirds share by survivorship.

General limitations on severance

11.11 Few constraints limit the availability of severance, but two are of some importance.

— *Severance cannot be effected by will* Although severance can often be quite unilateral (i.e. requiring no consent from the other joint tenant or joint tenants), it is an inveterate rule that severance must be effected *inter vivos*. The broad principle is that there can be no severance *by will* (**11.4**) although, as we shall see later, the execution of *mutual* wills by joint tenants may sometimes bring about a severance (**11.16**).

— *Severance cannot be effected in relation to a legal estate* Following the commencement of the LPA 1925, joint tenancy has been capable of severance only in respect of an *equitable* estate in land. There can be no severance of a joint tenancy in a *legal* estate (LPA 1925, s 36(2), **11.4, 11.9**), and severance in equity has no effect on co-ownership *at law*. (The clear statutory purpose was to prevent the fragmentation of legal title between endless numbers of fractional owners, with the conveyancing complexity that such fragmentation was apt to produce (**11.22**).) The result is now that

- co-ownership *at law* automatically and unavoidably takes the form of *joint tenancy*
- co-ownership *in equity* may take the form of *either* joint tenancy *or* tenancy in common (with the possibility that equitable *joint tenancy* may be converted, by severance, into an equitable *tenancy in common*).

Severance by a co-owner who is, say, a joint tenant of the fee simple estate both at law and in equity does not affect his trusteeship of the legal estate or his status as a trustee of land (**11.4**). Although after severance he becomes a *tenant in common* of the equitable estate, he remains a *joint tenant* of the legal estate until such time as he

- 'releases' his legal estate to the other joint tenant or tenants (LPA 1925, s 36(2), **11.36**), or
- is removed from the trust (see TOLATA 1996, s 19, **11.28**), or
- dies (**11.4**).

Methods of severance of an equitable joint tenancy

11.12 Severance is a process now confined to *equitable* joint tenancy. The principal means of severance are six in number, some unilateral, some definitely not; some sanctioned by statute, some by case law, and one method fairly clearly lacking encouragement from either source:

- severance by written notice under LPA 1925, s 36(2) (**11.13**);
- severance under *Williams v Hensman* (1861), i.e. by
  - an act operating on a joint tenant's share (**11.14**);
  - mutual agreement (**11.15**);
  - mutual conduct (**11.16**);
- severance by homicide (**11.17**);
- severance by merger of interests (**11.18**).

Severance by written notice

11.13 The most convenient form of severance is provided by statute. A joint tenant may sever by giving to the other joint tenants a 'notice in writing' of his 'desire' to sever the joint tenancy (LPA 1925, s 36(2)).

— *Advantages* Severance by written notice may be quite unilateral: no consent is needed from other joint tenants (see *Harris v Goddard* (1983)). The notice need not be signed and may even take the form of an application for a judicial determination of the joint tenants' respective rights (*Re Draper's Conveyance* (1969)). Moreover, the severance is effective if there is evidence that the notice was duly posted to the other joint tenants (see LPA 1925, s 196), even though it was not actually read (or even received) by them.

> *Kinch v Bullard* (1999) H and W were beneficial joint tenants of the matrimonial home. W, who was terminally ill, commenced divorce proceedings and posted a notice of severance to H at their shared home address. Before it arrived, H suffered a serious heart attack and was hospitalised. When the notice arrived through the letter box, W, reckoning that her chances of survivorship had improved dramatically, promptly destroyed the letter. H died a week later and W argued that no valid severance had occurred and that she therefore took the entirety by survivorship. Neuberger J held that, once the process of delivery to the addressee's last-known abode or place of business had been put in train, it was no longer open to W to change her mind as to

severance. Severance had therefore occurred and H's estate was therefore entitled to a one-half share.

— *Limitations* For all its utility, the written notice has certain drawbacks. Notice must be served on *all* the existing joint tenants. The notice must express a desire to sever with *immediate* effect rather than at some time in the future (*Harris v Goddard* (1983)). Furthermore, at a very technical level, it is arguable that the notice method is inapplicable where the names on the legal title are not identical to the beneficiaries behind the trust (e.g. where A and B hold the legal estate on trust for A, B and C) (see the precise wording of LPA 1925, s 36(2)).

Severance by an act of a joint tenant 'operating upon his own share'

11.14 The 1925 legislation (see LPA 1925, s 36(2)) specifically preserves the three classic pre-1926 modes of severance as laid down by Page Wood V-C in *Williams v Hensman* (1861). The first of these comprises any 'act' by a joint tenant 'operating upon his own share'—usually an act of total or partial *alienation* of that joint tenant's 'share'. This form of severance has the advantage of being quite unilateral (see *Harris v Goddard* (1983)) and the 'act' of severance may even be concealed from the other joint tenant or tenants (see e.g. *Mortgage Corpn v Shaire* (2001)). The 'act' must, however, evince a final or irrevocable character which precludes or estops any future claim of survivorship for the severing co-owner. The range of 'act' which falls under this head includes the following:

— *Transfer inter vivos* Almost by a process of reverse engineering it can be deduced that alienation of a joint tenant's 'share' results in severance. Although joint tenants do not hold shares as such (**11.4**), any attempt by a joint tenant to transfer a share (either to a stranger or to another joint tenant) is regarded as an act of severance since, paradoxically, any valid disposition would necessarily pre-suppose that a severance had *already* occurred. The transfer of the joint tenant's share, being effective only in equity (**11.12**), must be made by written disposition or otherwise under the protection of a constructive trust (LPA 1925, ss 53(1)(c), 53(2), **10.5**). Unity of title is inevitably destroyed in equity and the transferee becomes an equitable tenant in common of the severed aliquot share.

> **Example**: Suppose that A, B and C are joint tenants of the legal and equitable fee simple in Redacre. If A transfers to P his 'share' or 'interest' in the joint tenancy, the legal ownership remains unchanged since severance operates only in equity, but the equitable ownership is transformed. Thus, although A, B and C remain as trustees of land,

they now hold the legal estate as joint tenants on a trust for P (as a tenant in common owning a one-third share in equity) and B and C (as collectively joint tenants of the remaining two-thirds share in equity) (see *Fig* 14). The jointly held interest of B and C is, of course, still subject to the rule of survivorship.

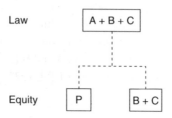

Law   A + B + C

Equity   P   B + C

Fig 14

- Exactly the same result emerges if A, instead of transferring his 'interest' to P outright, enters into a *specifically enforceable contract* to transfer it to P. Equity 'looks on that as done which ought to be done' (see *Walsh v Lonsdale* (1882), **9.9**).

- A similar result follows, moreover, if A, instead of transferring his 'share' to P, transfers it *to B*. Here B acquires a dual status in equity, as a *tenant in common* of a one-third interest in his own right and as a *joint tenant* with C of the remaining two-thirds interest (the right of survivorship still applying to the *latter* entitlement).

— *Alienation by mortgage*   If one joint tenant attempts to charge or mortgage the jointly held entitlement either at law or in equity, the effect of severance follows in precisely the same way as if there had been an outright transfer of that joint tenant's 'share' (see *First National Securities Ltd v Hegerty* (1985), **15.13**). The 'share' is severed in equity (although the legal estate remains unaffected).

— *Involuntary alienation*   Various forms of involuntary alienation constitute an 'act' operating upon a joint tenant's 'share'. For instance, the making of a *bankruptcy order* against a joint tenant has the effect of severing any beneficial joint tenancy (see *Re Pavlou (A Bankrupt)* (1993)), the bankrupt's aliquot 'share' vesting in his trustee in bankruptcy on the latter's appointment (Insolvency Act 1986, s 306(1)).

— *Insufficient 'acts' for the purpose of severance*   We have already seen that an attempted testamentary disposition of a joint tenant's interest does not normally constitute an 'act ... operating upon his own share' for the purpose of severance (**11.4, 11.11**). A will, being revocable, lacks the definitive quality required by the first limb of the rule in *Williams v Hensman*; and the *ius accrescendi* prevails over the testamentary disposition. It is equally clear that a mere unilateral declaration of intention to sever, unless incorporated in a written notice, is also ineffective (see *Corin v Patton* (1990) per Mason CJ and McHugh J).

Severance by mutual agreement

11.15 In *Williams v Hensman* (1861), Page Wood V-C recognised that severance may also be brought about by a *mutual agreement*, involving *all* the existing joint tenants, that their entitlements should henceforth be regarded as severed. The consideration for the agreement is the consent of each party to 'relinquish the beneficial interest of a joint tenant ... including the right of accretion by survivorship, in return for the share of a tenant in common' (*Corin v Patton* (1990) per Deane J). Mutual agreement provides a fairly flexible kind of severance. The agreement need not take the form of a specifically enforceable contract and need not even be in writing (see LP(MP)A 1989, s 2(1), **9.6**). However, severance is probably not achieved by a mere process of negotiation between joint tenants which reaches only an 'agreement in principle' if there is evidence that the parties reserved the right to alter their respective bargaining positions in the light of later developments (see *Gore and Snell v Carpenter* (1990)).

—*Exclusion of survivorship* In order to be effective, the mutual agreement must contemplate that the joint tenants will deal with the property in a manner which necessarily involves severance (*Burgess v Rawnsley* (1975)). The vital question is usually whether the agreement precludes further survivorship. Thus severance is achieved, for instance, by an agreement that either joint tenant's 'share' should, on death, pass to a third party. The same result emerges from an agreement that the proceeds of sale of the co-owned property should be divided between the joint tenants in specified proportions (*Crooke v De Vandes* (1805)), although (ironically) the shares which follow from such a severance are *equal* shares rather than the shares as agreed between the parties (see e.g. *Hunter v Babbage* (1994), where, amidst divorce proceedings, one spouse died before a draft consent order for unequal shares could be finalised by the court).

> *Burgess v Rawnsley* (1975) H and R, elderly lovers who met, poignantly, at a scripture rally in Trafalgar Square, purchased a dwelling-house as legal and beneficial joint tenants. Each provided half of the purchase price. On the subsequent breakdown of the relationship, R orally agreed (according to a dubious finding of fact by the trial judge) to sell her share in the house to H for a specified price. R later revoked that agreement and demanded a higher price, but H died before negotiations could proceed further. The Court of Appeal held that the beneficial joint tenancy had been effectively severed prior to H's death and that his estate was therefore entitled to a half-share of any proceeds of sale of the property. The decision remains a controversial illustration of mutual agreement construed in its broadest possible form. (Both Browne LJ and Sir John Pennycuick reluctantly based their conclusion on the trial court's finding of fact.)

Severance by mutual conduct

11.16   Severance may also result from 'any course of dealing sufficient to intimate that the interests of all were mutually treated as constituting a tenancy in common' (*Williams v Hensman* (1861) per Page Wood V-C). *Mutual conduct* requires a pattern of dealings between all of the joint tenants which, although falling short of an agreement to sever, nevertheless indicates an unambiguous common intention that the joint tenancy should be severed. In particular, severance by mutual conduct must effectively exclude the future operation of a right of survivorship. Thus mutual conduct can comprise long-term assumptions that the parties hold as tenants in common (see *Gore and Snell v Carpenter* (1990)) or even the concurrent execution by the joint tenants of mutual wills which direct the future disposition of the 'share' of each joint tenant (see *Re Wilford's Estate* (1879)). But mutual conduct is not constituted by a physical conversion of jointly owned premises into separate and self-contained units (see *Greenfield v Greenfield* (1979)), nor by the sheer fact of abortive or inconclusive negotiations between joint tenants in relation to their respective 'shares' in their property (see *Harris v Goddard* (1983)). No intention to sever can be ascribed to joint tenants 'merely because one offers to buy out the other for X and the other makes a counter-offer of Y' (*Burgess v Rawnsley* (1975) per Sir John Pennycuick, although compare Lord Denning MR, who thought that the parties' inconclusive dealings in that case disclosed mutual conduct (**11.15**)).

Severance in consequence of unlawful killing

11.17   Largely in consequence of the rule of public policy that no wrongdoer should profit from his own wrong, it seems to be accepted that some sort of severance results where one joint tenant unlawfully kills another, thereby skewing the normal lottery of survivorship (see *Re K, decd* (1985)).

> **Example**: Suppose that A and B are joint tenants of both the legal and the equitable estate in land. If A unlawfully kills B, A remains invested with the legal estate by survivorship, but holds that estate on trust for himself and B's successors as *tenants in common* in equal shares, subject only to the proviso that A may not take (directly or indirectly) as one of B's successors.

In cases other than those involving murder, the court has a limited statutory discretion (Forfeiture Act 1982, s 2(2)) to modify the operation of this forfeiture rule if, having regard to the conduct of the offender and of the deceased and other material circumstances, 'the justice of the case requires the effect of the rule to be so modified' (see, by analogy, *Dunbar v Plant* (1998)).

Severance by merger of interests

11.18 Severance may also be brought about in certain rare situations where the four unities characteristic of joint tenancy are destroyed by a 'merger' of interests, e.g. where A, B, and C are joint tenants for life, with remainder to D in fee simple, and A later acquires D's remainder. Such a transaction severs the joint life interest by destroying unity of interest between A, B and C. A becomes a tenant in common while B and C remain joint tenants for life.

Archaic forms of co-ownership

11.19 Before 1 January 1926 there existed in England a type of co-ownership known as *tenancy by entireties*. This form of co-ownership comprised an *unseverable* joint tenancy between husband and wife, supposedly symbolising the indivisible unity of matrimonial partners. The creation of new tenancies by entireties had been pro-hibited in 1882 (see Married Women's Property Act 1882, ss 1, 5), and in 1926 all remaining tenancies by entireties were transmuted automatically into joint tenancies (LPA 1925, Sch 1, Part VI). Another form of co-ownership—now archaic—is *coparcenary*.

Coordination of legal and equitable co-ownership under a trust of land

11.20 Co-ownership of land is now coordinated by the device of the 'trust of land' pursuant to the terms of the Trusts of Land and Appointment of Trustees Act 1996. The 1996 Act offers a unified model of landholding suitable for the regulation of various forms of concurrent and successive entitlement. The coord-ination of legal and equitable co-ownership under a *trust of land* becomes much easier to understand once it is realised that, in general terms, legal and equitable title are really concerned with rather different matters. Ownership *at law* pinpoints the allocation of formal title and its attendant administrative and fiduciary responsibilities; ownership *in equity* determines the distribution of beneficial enjoyment (**11.4**).

— *Co-ownership of the legal estate under a trust of land* mandatorily takes the form of joint tenancy (**11.4, 11.9, 11.11**). Unity of title and interest ensures that the legal co-owners hold one and the same estate (**11.5**) and, under the scheme of the 1996 Act, hold that legal estate as *trustees of land*.

— *Co-ownership of the equitable estate under a trust of land* may—depending on the relevant circumstances—take the form of *either* joint tenancy *or* tenancy in common (**11.9**). The difference revolves essentially around the question whether *survivorship* still operates between the co-owners or whether the co-owners have crystallised their entitlement in the form of distinct and indefeasible shareholdings.

- If the co-owners are *joint tenants* in equity, this means merely that each equitable joint tenant is still exposed to the risk that his premature death will concentrate beneficial enjoyment in the surviving joint tenants to the exclusion of the deceased's successors.

- To the extent, however, that any equitable co-owner is a *tenant in common* (whether from the outset or by subsequent severance), this co-owner is now immune from the caprice of survivorship and his quantum of beneficial ownership remains irreducibly within his own control.

— *Trustees of land may also be beneficiaries* A firm distinction between legal and equitable ownership lies at the heart of every trust of land (**1.25**), but there is nothing, in principle, to prevent (some or all of) the trustees and beneficiaries from being the *same* people. Where, however, the trustees and beneficiaries coalesce, their respective functions remain crucially different. In their capacity as *trustees of the legal estate*, these persons are concerned with fiduciary powers of management and disposition; in their capacity as *co-owners of the equitable estate*, they are concerned with beneficial enjoyment in the form of money and actual occupation (**11.4**). In the performance of their different roles they wear quite separate hats; their various headgear must never be confused.

— *Differing status at law and in equity* It is therefore quite possible that, in certain cases, two co-owners, A and B, will be joint tenants of both the legal and equitable estates in land (see *Fig* 15). But a moment's thought will also confirm that there is no

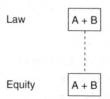

Law   A + B

Equity   A + B

Fig 15

Law

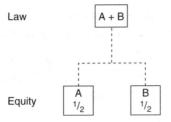

Equity

Fig 16

inherent contradiction in the idea that, in other cases, the same persons may be simultaneously *joint tenants* at law and *tenants in common* in equity (see *Fig* 16). In the latter kinds of case, all that is really being said is that A and B are jointly charged with the managerial and dispositive functions connected with the paper title and that these functions will eventually be concentrated in the survivor. In relation, however, to the fruits of beneficial enjoyment, A and B, as tenants in common, each enjoy a distinct and irreducible share free from the fateful gamble on longevity.

Coverage of the trust of land after 1996

11.21 The 'trust of land' introduced by TOLATA 1996 seeks to provide a unitary structure for the governance of a wide variety of beneficial entitlements in land which, before the commencement of the 1996 Act, were incompletely regulated by an untidy collection of legislative measures. Principal amongst the forms of beneficial entitlement covered by the 1996 Act are cases of:

- *concurrent interests* (**11.24**);
- *successive interests* (**11.25**); and
- *bare trusts* (**11.26**).

Overriding constraints on the trust of land

11.22 Few fundamental restraints curtail the potential shape of the *trust of land*, but some are significant.

— *No trusteeship for minors* The legal estate subject to the trust may be held only by persons who have attained the age of 18 (LPA 1925, ss 1(6), 20, 205(1)(v), **1.20**), although there is absolutely no prohibition on a minor holding a *beneficial* entitlement under the trust. (Any attempt to transfer a *legal estate* to a minor is clearly ineffective, operating instead as a declaration that the land is held in trust for the minor (TOLATA 1996, s 2(1), (6), Sch 1, para 1(1)(b)).)

— *Maximum of four trustees* The maximum number of trustees of the legal estate—necessarily joint tenants of that estate—is generally limited to *four* (TA 1925, s 34(2); LPA 1925, s 34(2), **1.20**).

• This cap on the number of legal co-owners is dictated by conveyancing convenience. For present purposes, *overreaching* of the equitable interests behind a trust of land can occur only on a disposition of the legal estate which is effected by 'trustees of land' (in the plural) (see LPA 1925, s 2(1)(ii), **2.34, 11.30**). But the restriction of the trusteeship to a maximum of four—with the constant possibility of further reduction by mortality and survivorship—greatly facilitates dealings with the co-owned legal estate. The compulsory unity of the title vested by way of joint tenancy in a limited number of trustees means that no purchaser faces having to investigate title to an estate which has been horribly fragmented between numerous shareholders (**11.5, 11.11**). Nor does any disposition of the legal estate ever require more than four signatures (at most) on the part of the disponors.

• The limitation to four trustees does not apply to land vested in trustees for charitable, ecclesiastical or public purposes (TA 1925, s 34(3)).

— *No limit on the number of beneficial owners* Although the number of legal owners is strictly limited, there is no corresponding restriction on the number of potential co-owners of the *equitable estate* under a trust of land (except in the ultimate sense that the numbers must not be so impossibly large as to render the trust unworkable).

— *Aberrant transfers of the legal estate* Any improper attempt to transfer a legal estate into the names of more than *four* persons (or otherwise than as *joint tenants*) results, by force of statute, in a vesting of the legal title by way of joint tenancy in the *first four* persons named in the transfer, with the other or others being arbitrarily relegated to beneficial ownership only (see LPA 1925, s 34(2)). Thus, for instance, a wholly misguided attempt to transfer a legal estate 'to A, B, C, D, E and F in equal shares' has the statutory consequence that A, B, C and D hold the legal estate as *joint tenants* on a trust of land for A, B, C, D, E and F as *tenants in common* of the equitable interest. In other words, the tenancy in common envisaged by the transfer is given effect only in the *beneficial* ownership of the land.

— *Legal ownership vested in only one trustee* Statute does not directly specify the *minimum* number of trustees who may hold the legal estate under a trust of land. It is, however, the clear policy of the 1925 property legislation (as reinforced by TOLATA 1996 and LRA 2002) that the legal estate associated with a trust of land should, at least for the purpose of dealings, be held by at least *two* trustees. No overreaching conveyance can normally be made by fewer than two trustees of land (LPA 1925, ss 2(1)(ii), 27(2), **2.34, 2.42, 11.30**). Nor, usually, can a sole trustee give a valid receipt for the proceeds of sale or other capital money arising under a trust of land (TA 1925, s 14(2)(a), **11.31**). In consequence a sole trustee who deals unilaterally with a legal estate in the trust land is acting *in breach of trust*. Yet, as we have already seen (**10.3, 10.6**), there must be numerous trusts of land which emerge by implication from circumstance and in which some kind of resulting or constructive trust has been silently engrafted upon an existing sole ownership of a legal estate. In such cases the equitable co-ownership created by the trust—usually in the form of beneficial tenancy in common—leaves no documentary trace precisely because the trust in question is *implied* (but see LRA 2002, s 42(1)(b), **11.24, 11.29**). In most instances the legal owner himself is blissfully unaware that he is a 'trustee of land' under TOLATA 1996. But under the *two trustee rule*, any purchaser who innocently deals with such a trustee, on the basis of his obviously sole legal title, will clearly be unable to overreach the beneficial interests behind the trust and may find, to his cost, that these interests remain binding on him (**11.30–11.31**).

Assimilation of existing trust forms within the 'trust of land'

11.23 Concurrent ownership arises under a trust of land in a number of cases. The concurrent ownership may be the result of an *express trust* (**9.37**) or may emerge from some *resulting trust* (**10.3**) or *constructive trust* (**10.6**). Prior to 1997 the courts strained mightily to bring all such trusts, by dubious statutory implication or otherwise, within the shelter of the legislative device of the 'trust for sale' (**9.44**), largely in order that all instances of co-ownership trusts could attract the advantageous facility of overreaching (**2.34, 2.42, 11.30**) which statute provided in the case of 'trusts for sale' (see e.g. *Bull v Bull* (1955)). Nowadays, thankfully, such ingenuity is unnecessary.

— *Broad definition of the 'trust of land'* The new device of the 'trust of land' is liberally defined as including trusts *of any kind*, 'whether express, implied, resulting or constructive', whether arising before or after 1 January 1997 (TOLATA 1996, s 1(2)).

— *Suppression of implied 'trusts for sale'* The old cases of *implied (or statutory) trusts for sale*, which were forced, in procrustean manner, within the reach of the LPA 1925, are now automatically converted into 'trusts of land' (TOLATA 1996, s 5(1), Sch 2, paras 3–4, **9.44**).

— *Express trusts for sale are subsumed* Old and new express trusts for sale can exist under TOLATA 1996 where the author of the trust has explicitly directed that land should be held on trust 'for sale', thereby demonstrating an intention that the subject land be *sold* and the proceeds divided between the designated beneficiaries. But such 'trusts for sale' are subsumed within the general machinery of the 'trust of land' and, indeed, made relatively pointless by the overriding statutory mandate that the trustees have, in all cases, an irreducible power to postpone sale indefinitely (TOLATA 1996, s 4(1)). Moreover, TOLATA 1996 explicitly abandons the old overworked doctrine of conversion, under which the equitable interests of trust for sale beneficiaries were regarded as mere interests in the prospective sale proceeds of the land (see TOLATA 1996, s 3(1)). Land held subject to a trust for sale is no longer, therefore, to be regarded as personalty.

Concurrent interests under a trust of land

11.24 The range of entitlement brought within the ambit of the *trust of land* thus includes the following permutations of concurrent entitlement by way of joint tenancy and tenancy in common. In all such cases the co-ownership in question (and the rights and obligations attached to it) are governed by the statutory regime contained in LPA 1925 and TOLATA 1996. (The prescribed Land Registry forms for transfer to joint proprietors now enable the transferees to indicate whether they hold on trust for themselves as joint tenants, as tenants in common in equal shares, or on some other specified trusts (LRA 2002, s 25(1); LRR 2003, rr 58, 206(1), Sch 1, **9.40**).)

— *Joint tenancy both at law and in equity*   The legal title subject to a trust of land may be held by two or more (but generally not more than four) joint tenants (**11.22**), holding on trust for themselves or any number of others as joint tenants of the equitable estate. Indeed joint ownership both at law and in equity is today the landholding of choice for most matrimonial homes (see *Fig* 17), largely because of the convenience conferred by the right of survivorship (**11.4**). Such an arrangement is normally brought about as an *express* trust of land contained in the document of transfer of the legal estate (thus complying with LPA 1925, s 53(1)(b), **9.38**). More rarely equitable joint tenancy has, in the past, arisen by implication from

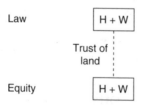

Fig 17

the sheer circumstance that a legal estate has been vested in joint names—without any specification of the equitable ownership—in which case, absent all other information, 'equity follows the law' (**11.9**). In default of any expressly created trust of land, joint legal and equitable owners hold their legal estate on a trust of land implied by statute (LPA 1925, s 36(1); TOLATA 1996, s 1(1)–(2)).

— *Joint tenancy at law coupled with tenancy in common in equity* It is possible that the legal title subject to a trust of land may be held by two or more trustees as *joint tenants* on trust for two or more beneficial *tenants in common* (see *Fig* 18). Such an outcome may, of course, emerge under a trust of land which expressly declares the existence of an equitable tenancy in common in specified proportions (**9.37–9.38**). It more commonly arises, in the absence of any express declaration of trust, where the purchase of a legal estate is funded by unequal contributions of money provided by persons who, in consequence of some resulting or constructive trust (**10.3**), take proportionate shares of the equitable ownership.

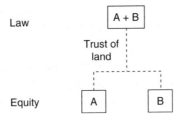

Fig 18

— *Sole trusteeship coupled with co-ownership in equity* We have already noted that some instances of implied trust (whether *resulting* or *constructive*) can cause a legal title held by one person alone to be impressed by a trust of land (see *Fig* 19) in favour of two or more beneficial owners (almost always as equitable tenants in common). The scheme of the 1925 legislation implicitly requires that the sole trusteeship be regularised by the appointment of a second trustee as co-owner of the legal estate (**11.22**). There is no direct statutory provision making such a course mandatory, but the same effect is procured indirectly by the duty now imposed on a sole trustee of a

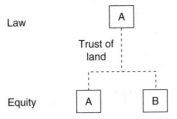

Fig 19

registered estate to apply for the entry of a *restriction* against his own title which prohibits any future disposition by a *sole* proprietor (see LRR 2003, r 94(1)–(2), **7.8, 11.29**). Precisely how many sole trustees are likely to comply with (or even know about) this obligation is unclear (**11.22**), but the purpose of entering such a 'restriction' is, quite plainly, to prevent any future dealings by a sole trustee which would fail to attract the advantageous effects of statutory overreaching (**11.30**).

Successive interests under a trust of land

11.25   Since TOLATA 1996 prohibits any further creation of strict settlements under the SLA 1925 (TOLATA 1996, s 2(1)), new successive interests can be created only under a *trust of land*. The declaration of trust containing the successive equitable interests must be evidenced by signed writing (LPA 1925, s 53(1)(b), **9.38**). Of the many possible forms of successive entitlement, the most obvious is the *equitable life interest* (**9.42**) followed by an *equitable remainder in fee simple* (**7.4**). In order to bring about such successive ownership in equity the settlor (if invested with a legal estate in the land) must

- *either* constitute *himself* a trustee of land, holding his legal estate on the terms of the trust which he has declared (see *Fig 20*)

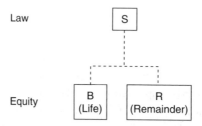

Fig 20

- *or* vest his legal estate in *nominated trustees of land* for the same purpose (see *Fig 21*).

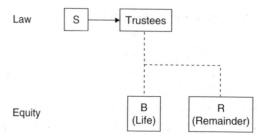

Fig 21

Bare trusts

11.26 A *bare trust* is a trust in which the trustee's control over the trust property is minimal and the beneficiary's control is paramount. The most common example of a bare trust arises where, in relation to the same estate in land, A is absolutely entitled *at law* and B is absolutely entitled *in equity* (see *Fig 22*).

The trustee of a bare trust has no active duty to perform: he is merely the repository of the naked or *bare* legal title. Although he has power to dispose of the legal estate in the trust property, he must at all times comply with the directions as to disposition given by his beneficiary. In this sense, the bare trust provides the ultimate demonstration of the idea that legal ownership is merely formal or titular, the substance of ownership residing *in equity* (**1.24, 9.2**). By an application of the rule in *Saunders v Vautier* (1841), the bare beneficiary, if *sui iuris* (i.e. of full age and sound mind), may terminate the trust and direct a transfer of the legal estate to himself or by his direction. Conversely, the bare trustee can insist that the beneficiary, if *sui iuris*, takes the legal title from him (TOLATA 1996, s 6(2)). A bare trust comes within the scope of the 'trust of land' under TOLATA 1996 (see TOLATA 1996, s 1(2)(a)) although, for the sake of conformity with the legislative scheme, the legal title associated with a bare trust should—at least for the purpose of dealings—be vested in at least *two* trustees (**11.22**).

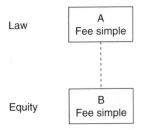

Law	A Fee simple

Equity	B Fee simple

Fig 22

Powers of the trustees of land

11.27 Irrespective of the precise nature of the beneficial entitlement involved, TOLATA 1996 confers a uniform range of powers upon those who hold the legal estate under the new unitary *trust of land*. In keeping with the broad concept of a trust, the functions of the trustees are essentially concerned with *management* and *disposition*, beneficial enjoyment being reserved for those who hold the equitable interests under the trust (**1.26, 11.4, 11.20**).

— *Powers of an absolute owner* In marked contrast to the more limited powers statutorily conferred on legal owners under the historic *strict settlement* or *trust for sale*, TOLATA 1996 declares that, in relation to the land subject to the trust, the trustees of land have 'all the powers of an absolute owner' (TOLATA 1996, s 6(1)).

- The powers of the trustees of land may be excluded or restricted by express provision in any 'disposition' creating a trust of land (see TOLATA 1996, s 8(1)) and are, in any event, available to trustees of land only for the purpose of 'exercising their functions as trustees' (TOLATA 1996, s 6(1)). The trustees' powers must not be exercised 'in contravention of ... any other enactment or any rule of law or equity' (TOLATA 1996, s 6(6)).

- The Trustee Act 2000 imposes a 'duty of care' on trustees, i.e. a duty to exercise 'such care and skill as is reasonable in the circumstances', having particular regard to any special knowledge or experience possessed or professed by any relevant trustee or which it would be 'reasonable to expect' of that trustee if acting as trustee in the course of a particular business or profession (TA 2000, s 1(1)). The statutory 'duty of care' applies to the exercise by land trustees of any of the powers conferred by TOLATA 1996, s 6, including the 'powers of an absolute owner' (TOLATA 1996, s 6(9), as inserted by TA 2000, s 40(1), Sch 2, para 45(3)).

— *Content of the trustees' powers* In general the powers enjoyed by trustees of land include powers:

- to *sell, lease or charge* the legal estate in the trust land (**11.30**)

- to *acquire freehold or leasehold land* anywhere in the United Kingdom under the power conferred by TA 2000, s 8, whether or not for occupation by a trust beneficiary (TOLATA 1996, s 6(3)). (Unless disapplied by the relevant trust instrument, the 'duty of care' applies to a trustee when exercising any power to acquire land or when exercising any power in relation to land so acquired (TA 2000, s 2, Sch 1, paras 2, 7).)

- to *partition* the trust land between absolutely entitled beneficiaries of full age (TOLATA 1996, s 7(1), **11.36**)

- to *exclude or restrict the occupation right* of one or more (but not all) of the beneficiaries (TOLATA 1996, s 13(1), **11.8, 11.28**)

- to *apply for a court order* resolving disputes over the trust land (TOLATA 1996, s 14(1), **11.32**) and

- to *delegate any of the trustees' statutory functions* to any one or more of the beneficiaries of full age entitled to an interest in possession in the trust land (TOLATA 1996, s 9(1)). (The 'duty of care' imposed by TA 2000, s 1, applies both to the trustees' decision whether to delegate at all and to their responsibility to keep the delegation under constant review (TOLATA 1996, s 9A(1)–(3), as inserted by TA 2000, s 40(1), Sch 2, para 47).)

— *Trustees' powers are fiduciary* Trustees of land are clearly fiduciaries in respect of their powers. In the exercise of the 'powers of an absolute owner', they are obliged to 'have regard to the rights of the beneficiaries' (TOLATA 1996, s 6(5)). Thus for instance, in making any disposition of the trust land, they must obtain the best price reasonably obtainable. Moreover, in the exercise of any 'function' relating to trust land, the trustees—in the absence of contrary provision—have a broad duty, so far as practicable, to 'consult the beneficiaries of full age' and, so far as consistent with the 'general interest of the trust', to give effect to 'the wishes of those beneficiaries, or (in case of dispute) of the majority (according to the value of their combined interests)' (TOLATA 1996, s 11(1)–(2), **11.28, 11.31**) (compare, however, *Notting Hill Housing Trust v Brackley* (2002), **7.31**).

Rights of beneficiaries under a trust of land

11.28 Beneficiaries under a *trust of land* have a number of rights in respect of the trust land, its management and disposition, and ultimately the application of the eventual proceeds of sale. Some of these rights are inherent in the idea of any trust; some emerged from the archaic jurisprudence of the 'trust for sale'; and some are conferred by TOLATA 1996. In particular, recent developments have seen a gradual democratisation of the trust, the beneficiaries gaining an increasing power to intercept the decision-making processes of their trustees. In a broad sense it can be said that the trust beneficiary is entitled to receive the benefits of the land held on trust and, in particular, to claim a share in any capital money arising on dispositions of the legal estate.

— *Right to occupy the trust land* In the case of the *trust for sale*, the courts came only slowly and painfully to recognise a right of beneficial occupation as an incident of equitable ownership under the trust (see *Bull v Bull* (1955); *Williams & Glyn's Bank Ltd v Boland* (1981); *City of London Building Society v Flegg* (1988)). The issue has been made much simpler in relation to the *trust of land*: here it is readily acknowledged that entitlement to the *use value* of land has nowadays become just as important as any entitlement to participate in its *exchange value* on eventual sale (see Law Com No 188 (1989), para 3.3). Accordingly TOLATA 1996 confers a general 'right to occupy' trust land on any beneficiary who is 'beneficially entitled to an interest in possession' (TOLATA 1996, s 12(1)). This 'right to occupy' under a trust of land sometimes takes on a critical importance in that it may, in certain circumstances, bind third parties who receive a disposition of a legal estate in the land (**11.31, 12.24, 12.42**). The beneficial right of occupation recognised by TOLATA 1996 is nevertheless hedged around by limitations:

- The purposes of the trust must include 'making the land available' for occupation (TOLATA 1996, s 12(1)(a)).

- A beneficiary has no 'right to occupy' land which is either 'unavailable or unsuitable' for occupation by him (TOLATA 1996, s 12(2)). Thus, for instance, a beneficiary may be unable to claim the statutory occupation right in respect of a house which is vastly disproportionate to his needs (see *Chan Pui Chun v Leung Kam Ho* (2003) at [102]); and a beneficiary of a trust of an office block will have no right to residential occupation of it.

- In relation to one or more (but not *all*) of the beneficiaries, the trustees of the land have discretion to *exclude* or *restrict* the statutory 'right to occupy'. The discretion is necessarily limited since a blanket exclusion of all beneficiaries collectively 'would make no sense' (*Rodway v Landy* (2001) at [33] per Peter Gibson LJ).

  — The trustees must not act unreasonably in the exercise of their discretion to exclude or restrict the entitlement to occupation (TOLATA 1996, s 13(1)–(2)). In allocating occupation, the trustees must have regard to a range of factors including the 'circumstances and wishes' of all of the trust beneficiaries (TOLATA 1996, s 13(4)), and may impose financial or other conditions as the price of occupation of the property (TOLATA 1996, s 13(5)–(6), **11.8**: see *Rodway v Landy* (2001)).

  — In relation to a building which lends itself to physical partition, the trustees' discretion is sufficiently wide to permit the allocation of different parts of the building for exclusive occupation by different beneficiaries (e.g. by squabbling partners in a medical practice: *Rodway v Landy* (2001) at [33], [41] per Peter Gibson LJ).

  — It is an overriding condition of the trustees' exercise of discretion in all these matters that no person already in occupation of the land should be prevented from continuing to occupy it except by that person's consent or with the approval of the court (TOLATA 1996, s 13(7)).

— *Right to appoint and remove trustees* Absolutely entitled beneficiaries under a trust of land have an important degree of control over the composition of the trusteeship where the relevant trust instrument (if there is one) fails to nominate some person as responsible for the appointment of trustees and does not otherwise exclude the beneficiaries' statutory rights (TOLATA 1996, ss 19(1), 21(5)). Acting unanimously the beneficiaries (if of full age and capacity) may give written directions that one or more of their trustees should retire from the trust or that the existing trustee or trustees should appoint a designated person as an additional or replacement trustee (TOLATA 1996, ss 19(2), 21(1)–(2)).

— *Right to be consulted* Trust beneficiaries normally have a right to be *consulted* about the exercise of the trustees' functions (TOLATA 1996, s 11(1), **11.27**), but the trustees' duty to accede to the wishes of beneficiaries is somewhat limited. Trustees may override beneficiaries' preferences in the 'general interest of the trust' and, in cases of dispute, are constrained only by the wishes of the majority (according to the value of their combined interests). There is no duty to consult a beneficiary who is also a trustee (see *Notting Hill Housing Trust v Brackley* (2002) at [25] per Peter Gibson LJ). Weak though the statutory right of consultation may be, it does entitle a trust beneficiary to apply for an injunction restraining the trustees from completing a sale of the land without having first discharged their minimal duty to consult the beneficiaries' wishes (see *Waller v Waller* (1967); though compare *Notting Hill Housing Trust v Brackley* (2002), **7.31**).

— *Right to require that consent be obtained* It is open to the author of an express trust of land to impose, by express provision in the trust instrument, a requirement that specified acts by the trustees (e.g. sale or other disposition) should be subject to a *right of consent* vested in a named person or persons (usually one or more of the trust beneficiaries). This requirement may be reinforced by the entry of a 'restriction' in the relevant registered title (see LRA 2002, s 40(2), (3)(b), **7.8, 11.29**).

— *Right to apply for a court order* All beneficiaries have the right to apply to the court under TOLATA 1996 for an order resolving various kinds of dispute in relation to the trust land (TOLATA 1996, s 14(1), **11.32**).

— *Right to an appropriate interest in capital proceeds* The ultimate beneficial entitlement relates to the capital money arising on a disposition of the legal estate in the trust land. When overreaching occurs (**11.30**), the beneficiary's rights are deflected on to that capital money, and the beneficiary is entitled to:

- an aliquot share (if a *joint tenant* or *tenant in common*);
- a life interest in the income drawn from the invested capital fund (if a *tenant for life*);
- the entire capital fund (if an *absolutely entitled beneficiary* under a bare trust).

If the disposition of the legal estate takes the form of a *mortgage charge*, the equitable interests of trust beneficiaries are deflected on to the *equity of redemption*, i.e. the legal estate as subject to the mortgage charge (**15.3**). Their rights thereafter attach to the *encumbered* legal estate (see *City of London Building Society v Flegg* (1988) per Lord Oliver of Aylmerton; *State Bank of India v Sood* (1997) per Peter Gibson LJ) but, in compensation, the beneficiaries are regarded as also having appropriate entitlements in the loan money advanced to their trustees.

The registered land dimension of the trust of land

11.29 Where a trust of land arises in *registered land*, the trustees are registered as proprietors of the legal estate (**9.41**) but, so far as possible, references to the trust are excluded from the register (see LRA 2002, s 78). This so-called *curtain principle* (**6.2**) tends to keep beneficial interests off the title, consistently with the general policy that trust interests are unobtrusively overreached on subsequent dealings by the trustees (**11.30**). Once registered as proprietors, trustees of land have generally unfettered powers of registered disposition subject to any 'restriction' entered in the proprietorship register for the purpose of curtailing their dispositive powers (LRA 2002, ss 40–4, **2.34, 7.8**).

— *No 'restriction' of the proprietors' powers is necessary*   where the trustees of land hold on trust for themselves (and for no others) as joint tenants in equity. In such cases, the overreaching of beneficial interests can never be in doubt following a disposition of the registered estate. The disponee will inevitably take free of all beneficial interests, precisely because *all* the beneficiaries have necessarily joined in executing the disposition. None can possibly claim to retain any priority over the disponee. In this context no 'restriction' is needed 'for the purpose of securing that interests which are capable of being overreached … are overreached' (LRA 2002, s 44(1)). The joint registered proprietors remain fully competent to give a valid receipt for capital money arising on any disposition of their legal estate (**11.22, 11.30**). If, however, no disposition occurs and the legal and beneficial estates later come to vest in a sole owner by reason of survivorship, the surviving registered proprietor simply ranks as the *absolute owner* at law and in equity free of any trust (**11.36**).

— *Entry of a 'restriction' is required in all other cases*   in order to protect the rights of any disponee of the registered estate in the trust land (and, indirectly, the rights of beneficial owners under the trust). However, the nature of the beneficiaries' interests is such that, even if the subject of a 'restriction' in the register, these interests will still be overreached by any disponee who pays capital money to trustees who are at least *two* in number (LPA 1925, ss 2(1)(ii), 27(2), **2.34, 11.30**). The entry of a 'restriction' in the proprietorship register of the trustees' title simply ensures that the overreaching provisions of the LPA 1925 are implemented for the mutual safeguard of disponees and beneficiaries. For this reason the entry of a 'restriction' is now *obligatory* in all cases of joint registered proprietorship except those in which the same persons hold as joint tenants at law and in equity (LRA 2002, s 44(1); LRR 2003, r 95(2)(a)).

— A *'restriction' on dispositions by a sole proprietor* directs that no disposition by a sole proprietor of the registered estate under which capital money arises (other than a disposition by a trust corporation) is to be registered by Land Registry unless authorised by an order of the court. In the terminology of LRR 2003, this is a 'restriction in Form A' (see LRR 2003, Sch 4). The entry of such a 'restriction' may be sought by:

- the *trustee of land* (on whom there now rests an obligation to apply for the entry of the 'restriction' (LRR 2003, r 94(1)–(2), **9.41, 11.24**)) or

- any person who has an *interest in the registered estate*, e.g. a trust beneficiary (LRA 2002, s 43(1)(c); LRR 2003, r 93(a)).

The relevant 'restriction' will, in practice, be entered by the registrar if he becomes aware of the existence of a trust of land (LRA 2002, s 42(1)(b), **9.41**). The 'restriction' on dispositions by a sole proprietor effectively forces the appointment of a second trustee for the purpose of any disposition involving the payment of capital money. The entry of the 'restriction' indirectly guarantees that overreaching of the beneficial trust interests *must* occur, but, having been overreached, these beneficial interests are themselves safeguarded—in the vast generality of cases—by their transmutation into equivalent entitlements in the money received by the trustees (**2.34, 11.30**).

— *Additional forms of 'restriction'* can be used to indicate that some other specific limitation has been imposed on the trustees' powers as registered proprietors (e.g. through the express requirement of a *consent*—usually on the part of a beneficiary—which needs to be given as a precondition of any disposition of a registered estate (**7.8, 11.28**)).

- It is the duty of the *trustees* to apply for the appropriate 'restriction' (usually a 'restriction in Form B') to be entered in the register (LRR 2003, r 94(4), Sch 4). In default, application may also be made by any person with an interest in the registered estate, e.g. a trust beneficiary (LRA 2002, s 43(1)(c); LRR 2003, r 93(c)).

- The protection achieved by entry of such a 'restriction' is important, not merely for the trust beneficiaries, but also for prospective disponees, who inevitably want to ensure that any relevant limitations have been complied with in advance of completion of the transaction with the trustees. A disponee's insistence on compliance with the terms of 'restrictions' thus reinforces, of course, not only his own position but also the rights of trust beneficiaries.

— *Dispute as to the existence of a trust of land* In the case of dispute as to the existence of a resulting or a constructive trust affecting a sole proprietor's registered title, it is open to the claimant beneficiary to apply for entry of a 'restriction' in the register (LRA 2002, s 43(1)(c); LRR 2003, r 93(a)).

Overreaching of beneficial interests under a trust of land

11.30 We have seen that one of the major triumphs of the property legislation of 1925 was to combine protection for the purchaser of real property with a guarantee of security for the owners of equitable interests (**2.10–2.11, 2.34**). In the context of trusts of land, this dual objective was achieved by a statutory device which clears the purchaser's title by translating certain pre-existing equitable entitlements into their equivalent value in money. In effect, the LPA 1925 conveniently facilitates the surrender (or 'overreaching') of the equitable interests of beneficial co-owners in a compulsory exchange for money rights in the capital proceeds of dispositions of land held on trust.

• A fundamental form of protection for the disponee of a legal estate in trust land thus lies in his claim to have *overreached* all subsisting trust interests, thereby taking title unencumbered by any beneficial rights behind the former trust of land.

• If this claim is made good, the disponee of land (whether *registered* or *unregistered*) has an absolute defence against any future claim founded on the equitable rights of trust beneficiaries. Provided that the preconditions of over-reaching are satisfied, the disponee need not concern himself with these equitable interests at all (LPA 1925, s 27(1)). Beneficial interests are 'kept behind the curtain and do not require to be investigated' (*City of London Building Society v Flegg* (1988) per Lord Oliver of Aylmerton).

The preconditions of overreaching are *three* in number (see LPA 1925, s 2(1)(ii), **2.34, 2.42, 9.41**):

— *The conveyance must be made by trustees of land* (in the *plural*) A 'conveyance' includes, for this purpose, a mortgage, charge and lease (LPA 1925, s 205(1)(ii), **2.10**). The conveyance must be executed by *all* the trustees (of whom there must be at least two). Thus a conveyance made by a *sole* trustee of a registered title cannot normally enjoy the overreaching effect provided by the LPA 1925 (see e.g. *Williams &*

Glyn's Bank Ltd v Boland (1981), **12.24**). An exactly similar outcome follows a dealing by a *sole* trustee of a legal estate in unregistered land (see e.g. *Kingsnorth Finance Co Ltd v Tizard* (1986), **12.42**).

— *The equitable interests must be capable of being overreached* For present purposes, the category of statutorily overreachable interests comprises principally those equitable interests which subsist under a *trust of land* (**9.34**). Such interests are readily convertible into a cash equivalent and, at least in the money-oriented perspective of the 1925 legislation, are not intrinsically diminished by the transmutation from one mode of investment into another. The thoroughly exchangeable quality of these *general* or *non-specific* burdens on land makes them peculiarly suitable candidates for a mechanism of overreaching which depends on the convenient translation of economic value in and out of money forms (**2.34**).

• Statutory overreaching operates in relation to the beneficial rights of *joint tenants, tenants in common*, holders of *life interests* and *remainders*, and *bare beneficiaries*. It has even been suggested that overreaching nowadays extends to the close relative of the trust interest in land, i.e. an entitlement based on proprietary estoppel (see *Birmingham Midshires Mortgage Services Ltd v Sabherwal* (2000) at [24], [31]; but compare *Lloyd v Dugdale* (2002) at [55], **12.14**, *Sommer v Sweet* (2005) at [26]).

• Statutory overreaching has *no* application at all to other types of equitable interest, such as equitable leases, options and other estate contracts (**9.8–9.9**), easements (**9.12**), restrictive covenants (**9.24**) and rights of entry (**8.35**). Following a transfer of title, interests of these kinds are actually intended, within the design of the 1925 legislation, to remain binding on land (as distinct from being swept off it). The continuing force of such *real* or *specific* burdens on land is usually dependent upon their protection by some appropriate register entry (**2.32, 2.41, 12.11–12.13**), although sometimes these rights (if subsisting in registered land) remain binding simply as 'overriding interests' even in the *absence* of protection in the register (**2.33, 12.18–12.20**).

— *The capital money must be paid over in the prescribed manner* Irrespective of any contrary provision in any trust instrument, the capital money arising on a disposition of trust land must not be 'paid to or applied by the direction of fewer than two persons as trustees' (LPA 1925, s 27(2)). This *two trustee rule* is a principle of stern application. Payment to fewer than two trustees precludes the purchaser from claiming that he has statutorily overreached the equitable trust interests except in *three* cases:

• where payment has been made to a *trust corporation* (e.g. a bank trust corporation) (see LPA 1925, s 27(2));

- where payment has been made to a *sole personal representative* (see LPA 1925, s 27(2));

- where *no capital money actually arises* on the disposition of the legal estate (e.g. in the case of an exchange of land or a lease granted otherwise than for a premium).

In effect, the *two trustee rule* marks a pragmatic recognition that a payment made to *two* trustees of land is much less likely to be misappropriated or misapplied than a payment made to a single individual, although admittedly in some instances the protection for beneficiaries may turn out to be 'no safeguard at all' (*State Bank of India v Sood* (1997) per Peter Gibson LJ). The third category of exception to the otherwise mandatory *two trustee rule* is beginning to gather a previously unsuspected importance. Notwithstanding failure to pay two trustees, it has been held that overreaching may still take place where the payment of capital money occurs, not *contemporaneously* with the disposition by the trustees, but rather at some other date. The requirement of actual payment to two trustees applies *only* when capital money arises at the date of *disposition* of the legal estate and not, for instance, when money has already been paid in advance of the relevant disposition or is left to be drawn down subsequently.

> *State Bank of India v Sood* (1997) S1 and S2 were registered proprietors of a freehold property, which they held on trust for themselves and five others (all in actual occupation). S1 and S2 charged the legal estate by way of legal mortgage to the bank. The charge was duly registered and was intended to secure any future borrowings on bank overdraft for business and other purposes. Money was later advanced by the bank on overdraft. The bank called in the debt when over £1 million was outstanding and sought possession of the property. The Court of Appeal held that, even though the payment of loan money was not contemporaneous with the execution of the legal charge, the equitable interests of all the beneficiaries had nevertheless been overreached and did not affect the bank as chargee. Overreaching would already have occurred, said Peter Gibson LJ, even if the overdraft moneys were subsequently paid otherwise than to two trustees. (The *Realpolitik* of the *Sood* case was, of course, that the courts could not afford to jeopardise the protection which banks assume they have under overdraft mortgages.)

Apart from these exceptional cases, however, if the three statutory preconditions for overreaching are satisfied, the disponee takes title free of the trust equities 'whether or not he has notice thereof' (LPA 1925, s 2(1)). He therefore overreaches even those beneficial entitlements of which he has *express* notice (see *City of London Building Society v Flegg* (1988) per Lord Oliver of Aylmerton) and also the rights of beneficiaries who are in 'actual occupation' of registered land (see LRA 2002, s 29(2)(a)(ii), Sch 3, para 2, **2.34, 12.24**. All such equitable interests thenceforth take effect conclusively in the capital money generated by the disposition.

> *City of London Building Society v Flegg* (1988) H and W purchased in their own names a registered title in property appropriately called 'Bleak House', the greater part of the purchase money having been provided by W's elderly parents, F1 and F2 (who therefore became beneficiaries behind a trust). F1 and F2 moved into joint occupation of the property with H and W and remained there at all material times. Without the knowledge or consent of either F1 or F2, H and W later charged their legal title to a building society, dissipated the mortgage advance and were adjudicated bankrupt. The House of Lords held that the mortgage charge overreached the equitable rights of F1 and F2 behind the trust, even though they had clearly been in 'actual occupation' at the date of the charge. The building society's payment of the mortgage money to two registered proprietors as trustees (i.e. H and W) had instantly ensured that the rights of F1 and F2 were 'shifted from the land to the capital moneys in the hands of the trustees', with the result that F1 and F2 no longer had any rights in land which could 'override' the registered disposition to the building society. In consequence F1 and F2 lost their home and their life savings, their dilemma sadly illustrating that the two trustee rule may still leave beneficiaries in occupation 'insufficiently protected' (see *State Bank of India v Sood* (1997) per Peter Gibson LJ). The *Flegg* ruling has nevertheless been declared to be undisturbed by the enactment of TOLATA 1996 (see *Birmingham Midshires Mortgage Services Ltd v Sabherwal* (2000) per Robert Walker LJ) and has also survived—at least so far—the objection that it violates the protection afforded by the European Convention on Human Rights in respect of the 'home' and 'family life' and the 'peaceful enjoyment of possessions' (see *National Westminster Bank plc v Malhan* (2004)).

Other protection for the disponee of trust land

11.31 Once the preconditions of overreaching have been satisfied, additional statutory protections are heaped upon the purchaser of a legal estate from trustees of land (usually, but not always, irrespective of whether the land is *registered* or *unregistered*).

— *Accountability* The purchaser is *not answerable* for the application of capital proceeds (TA 1925, s 14(1)).

— *Relevant consents* Where the exercise of any of the functions of the trustees is subject to the consent of *more than* two persons, the consent of *any two* of such persons is deemed sufficient in favour of the purchaser (TOLATA 1996, s 10(1)).

— *Duties owed to beneficiaries* The purchaser of *unregistered* land is unaffected by any failure by the trustees to discharge any statutory duty which they may have to consult their beneficiaries or have regard to their rights (TOLATA 1996, s 16(1), (7)).

— *Breaches of trust relating to registered land* The legal title taken by the disponee of a registered estate—whether by way of sale, lease or mortgage charge—is unaffected by any limitation on the disponor's powers which is not itself reflected by some entry in the latter's register of title or imposed by or under the LRA 2002 (LRA 2002, s 26).

• This means, for instance, that the disponee's title cannot be questioned merely on the basis that a single requisite consent to the disposition has not been obtained, a conclusion unaltered by the possibility that the person whose consent was required may have been in 'actual occupation' of the land (see Law Com No 271 (2001), para 4.10).

• The disponee's title seems likewise unimpeachable where a disposition occurs in the face of some other breach of trust by the disponor. Such a case arises, for example, where a sole trustee of land makes a disposition in circumstances which preclude his disponee from the benefits of a statutory overreaching of the beneficial interests under the trust (**11.22, 11.30**). This protection of the disponee's title at law reflects a public policy biased towards the protection of innocent purchasers, although there always remains a possibility that the disponee, whilst taking a good legal title, may be affected by *equitable* interests which rank as 'overriding' (see e.g. *Williams & Glyn's Bank Ltd v Boland* (1981), **12.24**).

• It is always possible that a disponee who consciously participates in an improper transaction in respect of trust land may render himself personally liable to the trust beneficiaries on the ground of 'knowing receipt' of trust property (see LRA 2002, s 26(3)).

— *Breaches of trust relating to unregistered land* Similar outcomes almost certainly apply to dispositions of unregistered land. TOLATA 1996 provides rather opaquely that a conveyance by trustees of unregistered land in contravention of statute or any rule of law or equity or in breach of some limitation on the trustees' dispositionary powers is not *invalidated* as against a purchaser who has 'no actual notice' of the contravention or limitation (TOLATA 1996, s 16(2)–(3)).

• This seems to mean, for instance, that a failure by trustees of land to secure a requisite consent to the conveyance, even though illicit on their part (see TOLATA 1996, s 8(2)), cannot invalidate the transaction vis-à-vis a purchaser who has no actual notice. The disposition still ranks as a 'conveyance' for the purpose of enabling the purchaser to overreach outstanding trust equities under

LPA 1925, s 2(1)(ii), provided of course that the preconditions of statutory overreaching are fulfilled (**2.42, 11.30**).

- An initially similar effect occurs in relation to a disposition made by a sole trustee of land who acts in breach of trust—his breach of trust being evidenced by his inability to give a valid receipt for the capital money arising on the disposition (see TA 1925, s 14(2)(a), **11.22**). The mere fact that the trustee's disposition violates a rule of equity does not invalidate the transaction as a 'conveyance'. But this time the conveyance cannot attract the overreaching consequences provided by LPA 1925, s 2(1)(ii), precisely because the capital money has not been paid to trustees of land (in the plural) (**2.42, 11.30**). Instead, the purchaser, although taking a good legal title, may find that he is bound by actual or constructive notice of the unoverreached *equitable* rights of trust beneficiaries (see e.g. *Caunce v Caunce* (1969); *Kingsnorth Finance Co Ltd v Tizard* (1986), **12.42**).

Judicial resolution of disputes over trust land

11.32 TOLATA 1996 provides machinery for the resolution of a number of disputes which may emerge in relation to trusts of land. Application for a court order resolving any of these disputes may be made by

- any *trustee of land* or
- any *person who 'has an interest in property subject to a trust of land'* (TOLATA 1996, s 14(1)), a phrase which is broad enough to include not merely trust beneficiaries, but also a trustee in bankruptcy, a chargee or mortgagee and a personal representative.

The court may, in general, make any order which it thinks fit in relation to the exercise by the trustees of any of their functions or for the purpose of declaring the 'nature or extent' of any person's interest in the trust land or its proceeds (TOLATA 1996, ss 14(2), 17(2)). The court has no jurisdiction, however, to vary the quantum of any beneficial entitlement under the trust (see *Mortgage Corpn v Shaire* (2001)).

— *The range of potential dispute* The issues which call for resolution under TOLATA 1996 thus include the following kinds of dispute:

- disputes as to the trustees' allocation of the 'right to occupy' (**11.28, 11.33**);
- questions whether trustees should be relieved from any obligation to consult beneficiaries (**11.27**) or obtain otherwise requisite consents to the performance of any of their functions (**11.28**);
- disagreement between the trustees whether to sell the trust land (**11.34**);

- attempts by one or more beneficiaries to prevent (or force) a sale by the trustees (**11.34**);

- applications by creditors for sale of the trust land (**11.35**).

— *Relevant criteria* In determining these questions, the court is generally directed (see TOLATA 1996, s 15(1)) to have regard to a range of considerations *including*

- the intentions of the person or persons who created the trust;

- the purposes for which the trust land is held;

- the welfare of any minor who occupies (or might reasonably be expected to occupy) the trust land as his home;

- the interests of any secured creditor of any beneficiary.

Applications relating to occupation of trust land

11.33 In determining any dispute relating to the trustees' allocation of the 'right to occupy' trust land (**11.28**), the court must have regard, not only to the criteria which generally qualify its discretion, but also to 'the circumstances and wishes of each of the beneficiaries' who would normally be entitled to occupy the land (TOLATA 1996, s 15(2)).

Disputes over sale arising between trustees and beneficiaries

11.34 It is possible that unresolved disagreement may occur—between trustee and trustee or between trustees and beneficiaries or even between beneficiaries themselves—as to whether trust land should be *retained* (for purposes of occupation or investment) or *sold* (thereby releasing the proceeds for immediate distribution between the beneficial owners under the trust). This tension between the *use value* and the *exchange value* inherent in land (**11.28**) was, in earlier times, determined by the court with reference to the extensive case law generated under LPA 1925, s 30, which conferred a broad discretion on the court to make such order as it thought fit. A similar, but rather more expansive, discretion is now enjoyed by the court pursuant to TOLATA 1996, s 14(1)–(2). (Where equivalent issues arise between divorcing spouses, they are of course dealt with as part of the specialised matrimonial regime built up around the Matrimonial Causes Act 1973.)

— *General principles* It has been accepted that the general criteria laid down by TOLATA 1996, s 15(1) (**11.32**) for the resolution of internal disputes within a trust of land are a 'consolidation and rationalisation' of the jurisprudence developed under LPA 1925, s 30 (see *A v B* (1997) per Cazalet J), and that the principles established under the earlier legislation are still broadly relevant to TOLATA applications. Against a background in which all parties are probably reacting entirely reasonably in expressing a vigorous preference for either sale or retention of the trust land, it falls to the court to decide, on the basis of what is 'right and proper', whose voice should be allowed in equity to prevail (*Re Buchanan-Wollaston's Conveyance* (1939) per Sir Wilfred Greene MR).

— *The doctrine of subsisting collateral purpose* In resolving the issue, the courts have traditionally relied upon a doctrine of *collateral purpose*, holding it to be generally wrong to order sale of the trust property if the original or 'collateral' purpose underlying the trust is still capable of substantial fulfilment (see *Jones v Challenger* (1961) per Devlin LJ). The court thus leans in favour of ordering sale of a family home if the property was initially purchased in order to house a relationship which has since broken down irretrievably, leaving no minor children who still require the home as a base. But the continuing presence of minor children (whose welfare is adverted to specifically in TOLATA 1996, s 15(1)(c), **11.32**) may well serve to prolong the collateral purpose of a trust beyond the termination of the mutual relationship of the trustees or beneficiaries (see *Williams (JW) v Williams (MA)* (1976); but compare *White v White* (2003) at [22]–[24] per Arden LJ). Likewise, the balance of the parties' respective accommodation requirements may, almost as a matter of privately ordered housing policy, point towards the solution of the problem.

> *Re Evers' Trust* (1980) A cohabiting couple purchased a home in joint names largely with the aid of a joint mortgage loan. After their separation the woman and three children (including two from an earlier union) remained in the house. The Court of Appeal refused, at least for the time being, to endorse a sale which would have allowed the male partner to evict the woman and the children from their home merely in order to extract his capital investment and apply it for other purposes. Ormrod LJ pointed out that the underlying purpose of this trust had been to provide a home for the couple and the three children 'for the indefinite future' and that this purpose was still capable of substantial fulfilment. The Court of Appeal took into account that the man now had a secure home with his own mother and had no present need to realise his investment, while the woman was prepared to accept full responsibility for the outstanding mortgage liability and would have found it extremely difficult to rehouse herself if the property had been sold.

The notion that a collateral or underlying purpose may render the sale of trust land inequitable is even more clearly demonstrated in circumstances where the participants in the trust have covenanted not to sanction any sale without the agreement of all parties.

> *Re Buchanan-Wollaston's Conveyance* (1939) Four individuals, who each owned separate but neighbouring properties overlooking the sea, took a purchase as joint tenants of an adjacent piece of land which they desired to keep as an open space in order to preserve their common sea view. The parties covenanted not to part with the co-owned land except by unanimous consent or majority vote. When one, on later selling his own property, sought a court order directing his fellow trustees to join with him in a sale of the co-owned open land, the Court of Appeal refused the order on the ground that the plaintiff 'could not ... ask the Court to act in a way inconsistent with his own contractual obligations'. Sale would not be ordered while the parties' underlying contractual purpose subsisted.

Applications for sale of trust land brought by creditors

11.35 The tension between the *use value* and the *exchange value* of trust land takes on an even more poignant dimension when the pressure towards a court-ordered sale of the property comes, not from any of the participants in the trust of land, but from some *external creditor* who requires that the land be sold in order to release funds for the satisfaction of debts incurred by one or more of the trust beneficiaries. The balance of the relevant issues is profoundly affected by the introduction of third party claims relating to the property.

— *Applications made by a trustee in bankruptcy* On an application for sale brought by a beneficiary's *trustee in bankruptcy* (effectively on behalf of the bankrupt beneficiary's creditors), the relatively liberal and humane criteria outlined in TOLATA 1996, s 15(1) (**11.32**) are expressly declared inapplicable (see TOLATA 1996, s 15(4)). Although the trustee in bankruptcy applies for an order for sale under TOLATA 1996, s 14(1), the application is heard by the bankruptcy court, which is directed to make such order as it thinks 'just and reasonable' having regard to the interests of the bankrupt's creditors and (in cases involving a family home) such factors as:

- the conduct of the bankrupt's spouse or former spouse, so far as contributing to the bankruptcy;
- the needs and financial resources of the spouse or former spouse;
- the needs of any children; and

- all the circumstances of the case other than the needs of the bankrupt.

(Insolvency Act 1986, s 335A(2), as added by TOLATA 1996, s 15(4), Sch 3, para 23.)

As if it were not already clear, the bias of the legislation is readily apparent in the controlling injunction that, in any application made more than one year after the trustee in bankruptcy is invested with the bankrupt's estate, the court must assume, unless the circumstances of the case are 'exceptional', that 'the interests of the bankrupt's creditors outweigh all other considerations' (IA 1986, s 335A(3)). In other words, after the bankrupt and his family have been allowed a breathing space of one year to retrieve their situation or make alternative residential arrangements, the needs of the bankrupt's creditors are normally regarded as *paramount* (see also IA 1986, s 313A(2)). This statutory direction closely mirrors the historic pattern of the case law which, even before the introduction of the Insolvency Act 1986, almost invariably accorded priority to the claims of the trustee in bankruptcy by ordering the sale of trust property and the consequent release of capital for the satisfaction of the bankrupt's debts (see e.g. *Re Bailey (A Bankrupt)* (1977); *Re Citro (A Bankrupt)* (1991)). The stance adopted in the application of the post–1996 statutory code displays just as solicitous a concern on behalf of commercial creditors, many of whom (it sometimes has to be emphasised) have mortgages, spouses and children too. 'Exceptional' circumstances capable of averting a court order for sale must involve truly extreme circumstances such as severe ill-health or terminal illness affecting the bankrupt or a member of his family (see e.g. *Claughton v Charalambous* (1999); *Re Bremner* (1999)). Recent case law has, however, raised a tentative query whether so restrictive an approach is ultimately consistent with the principle of respect for 'private and family life' and for the 'home' enshrined in ECHR Art 8 (**2.15**) (see *Barca v Mears* (2005) at [39]–[43]). One concession in favour of the domestic residence now appears in the rule that a trustee in bankruptcy must normally apply for an order for sale of a home within *three* years of the date of the bankruptcy (IA 1986, s 283A, inserted by Enterprise Act 2002, s 261(1)).

— *Claims by other creditors*   Where indebtedness has not yet been pressed to the point of bankruptcy (i.e. where creditors' claims are *not* represented by a trustee in bankruptcy), contested applications for sale of trust land fall to be dealt with in accordance with the general criteria enunciated in TOLATA 1996, s 15(1) (**11.32**).

- It was initially believed that this provision might facilitate a substantially more liberal approach to applications for sale brought outside the context of bankruptcy, not least because the interests of secured creditors are specified by statute as ranking alongside, and having no automatic priority over, such factors as 'the welfare of any minor' (TOLATA 1996, s 15(1)(c)–(d)). In *Mortgage Corpn v*

Shaire (2001) Neuberger J thought that the 'new code' of the 1996 Act, in abandoning the bias towards sale implicit in the now 'obsolete' trust for sale (**9.44**), had probably been intended 'to tip the balance somewhat more in favour of families and against banks and other chargees.'

• Subsequent experience has, however, demonstrated that, although the 1996 Act 'may have given the court somewhat greater flexibility' in non-bankruptcy cases, the new statutory provision 'has hardly revolutionised things' (*Re A; A v A* (2002) at [115] per Munby J). Recent case law has indicated that the courts remain strongly influenced by the argument that, unless an order for sale is made, 'the bank will be kept waiting indefinitely for any payment out of what is, for all practical purposes, its own share of the property' (*First National Bank plc v Achampong* (2004) at [65] per Blackburne J). Nor have the courts allowed this concern for the lender's commercial interests to be deflected by reference to ECHR Art 8 (**2.15**). Indeed, the major thrust of the House of Lords' majority ruling in *Harrow LBC v Qazi* (2004) was the insistence that ECHR Art 8 is not violated by the simple enforcement of entitlements which have been determined to belong to parties as a matter of private domestic law (**11.12, 15.21**)—an approach substantially endorsed by the House of Lords in subsequent litigation (see *Kay v Lambeth LBC; Leeds CC v Price* (2006), **2.15**).

• In particular, the original purpose of a family home trust (see TOLATA 1996, s 15(1)(b)) is widely regarded as spent and therefore no longer operative where, as is so often the case, the family relationship has now broken up (see e.g. *Bank of Ireland Home Mortgages plc v Bell* (2001) at [28]; *First National Bank plc v Achampong* (2004) at [61], [65]). Likewise, compassionate factors weighing against sale—such as ill-health or disability within the family or the presence of minor children—are frequently taken as pointing, at most, towards a mere postponement (rather than refusal) of the sale order sought by the lender (see e.g. *Bell* at [29]; *Edwards v Lloyds TSB Bank plc* (2005) at [3], [33]). Moreover, the hardship caused by forced sale is regularly treated as offset by the fact that the evicted family has already effectively enjoyed a prolonged period of rent-and mortgage-free accommodation (see *Bell* at [32]; *Achampong* at [62]). Indeed, the decision of the Court of Appeal in *Bell*'s case is now commonly regarded as epitomising the tone of the jurisprudence emerging from the courts' application of the 1996 Act (see *Re A; A v A* (2002) at [127]–[130], [171]; *Achampong* at [61]; [2003] Conv 314 (MP Thompson)).

> *Bank of Ireland Home Mortgages Ltd v Bell* (2001) W owned a 10 per cent beneficial share in the family home which was owned at law by H and W. H forged W's signature on a mortgage of his legal estate to the claimant bank, with the result that the bank ranked as only an equitable chargee of H's interest in the home. H then abandoned W to live and work abroad, but for most of a decade after H ceased making mortgage

payments W, together with the son of the family, continued to live in the home. When the question of sale finally reached the Court of Appeal, H's debt to the bank was well over £300,000 'and increasing daily'. The Court thought it 'plainly wrong' not to order a sale of the house, emphasising that 'a powerful consideration is and ought to be whether the creditor is receiving proper recompense for being kept out of his money.' Here, regardless of the needs of the son and W's ill-health, it was 'very unfair to the bank' that it should be 'condemned ... to go on waiting for its money ... and with the debt increasing all the time, that debt already exceeding what could be realised on a sale' ([31] per Peter Gibson LJ). The bank after all, said Sir Christopher Staughton at [38], 'is a beneficiary of the trust referred to in s 15 as much as Mrs Bell' (see also [2002] *Conv* 61 (R Probert)).

Termination of a trust of land

11.36 A trust of land may be terminated in a variety of ways, of which the most obvious involves a transfer of the legal estate to some person who takes free of the trust. Compliance with the preconditions of statutory overreaching (**11.30**) ensures precisely this result, the transferee of the legal estate thereafter enjoying immunity from the trust beneficial interests (whether *concurrent* or *successive*). Likewise the ultimate performance of duty by a bare trustee—conveyance at the direction of his beneficiary *to the beneficiary himself* (**11.26**)—terminates any trust of land since the former beneficiary is now entitled absolutely both at law and in equity. Other means of terminating or extinguishing trusts of land include the following.

— *Partition of co-owned land* The unity of possession which is essential to both joint tenancy and tenancy in common is destroyed if, with the consent of the beneficiaries, the trustees physically divide up or partition co-owned land amongst the individual co-owners (TOLATA 1996, s 7(1), **11.27**). Partition effectively involves the transfer to each co-owner of an appropriate portion of the trust land.

— *Union of the property in one joint tenant* Co-ownership clearly ends if a co-owned estate comes into the sole ownership of one joint tenant.

• *Release inter vivos* A joint tenant may 'release' his interest inter vivos to the other joint tenant or joint tenants (LPA 1925, s 36(2), **11.11**). Where, at the date of release, there remains only one other joint tenant, a release which operates both at law and in equity destroys any trust of land.

• *Operation of survivorship* On the death of one of two remaining joint tenants of the legal and equitable estate, the entire interest both at law and in equity survives to the remaining tenant, thereby terminating the trust of land (see *Re Cook* (1948)). In registered land the sole surviving registered proprietor may deal with the land as the absolute owner (see LRR 2003, r 164, **11.4**). In unregistered land, in the absence of any memorandum of severance endorsed on the conveyance to the joint tenants (see *Grindal v Hooper* (2000)), a purchaser can safely assume that the deceased joint tenant *never* severed the equitable joint tenancy and that the survivor is therefore competent to convey the absolute estate (see Law of Property (Joint Tenants) Act 1964, s 1(1)).

FURTHER READING

Gray and Gray, *Elements of Land Law* (4th edn, OUP, 2005), ch 11.

Relevant sections of this work and other land law textbooks may be supplemented with:

Clements, Linda 'The Changing Face of Trusts: The Trusts of Land and Appointment of Trustees Act 1996' (1998) 61 *MLR* 56.

Dixon, Martin 'Trusts of Land, Bankruptcy and Human Rights' [2005] *Conv* 161.

Ferris, Graham and Battersby, Graham 'The General Principles of Overreaching and the Modern Legislative Reforms, 1996–2002' (2003) 119 *LQR* 94.

Fox, Lorna 'Creditors and the concept of "family home": a functional analysis', (2005) 25 *Legal Studies* 201.

Harpum, Charles 'Overreaching, Trustees' Powers and the Reform of the 1925 Legislation' [1990] *CLJ* 277.

Jackson, Nicola 'Overreaching In Registered Land Law' (2006) 69(2) *MLR* 214.

Pascoe, Susan 'Right to Occupy Under a Trust of Land: Muddled Legislative Logic' [2006] *Conv* 54.

Tee, Louise 'Co-ownership and trusts', in L Tee (ed.), *Land Law: Issues, Debates, Policy* (Willan, 2002), p 132.

SELF-TEST QUESTIONS

1 What factors might influence legal co-owners when deciding *how* to hold their land in equity (**11.2, 11.4, 11.6, 11.9**)?

2 Romeo (aged 20) and Juliet (aged 18) were joint tenants at law and in equity of Villa Verona. In a fit of shared melancholia, they administered a lethal poison to each other, each having made a will leaving a half-share to the other's family. They are discovered together, dead, next day. Who now owns Villa Verona (**11.4, 11.10–11.11, 11.16–11.17**)?

3 What is meant by *overreaching* and whom is it intended to benefit (**11.29–11.30**)?

4 A rambling mansion was owned in equal shares by its registered proprietors, Agatha and Bertha, who were elderly spinster sisters. Bertha recently died leaving her share to her favourite great-nephew, Kev. An unemployed lout with a keen eye for designer labels, Kev argues that Agatha (at 75) would be much better off in an exclusive private nursing home. He is now pressing for a sale of the property, but Agatha, still possessed of all her faculties, is unwilling to leave the house in which she has lived for 50 years. What factors will bear on the resolution of this problem (**11.20, 11.27, 11.32, 11.34**)?

5 How does the law seek to hold a balance between family members and external creditors in relation to claims that a family home should be sold in order to recoup money owed to the latter by its owner (**11.35**)?

12

Dealings with title

SUMMARY

We return in this chapter to the central problem of conveyancing and examine both the process of dealing with title and the principles which govern the priority of pre-existing interests in relation to disponees of estates in *registered* and *unregistered* land. This chapter also analyses the major changes likely to be brought about by the scheme of electronic conveyancing envisaged by the Land Registration Act 2002.

An integrated account of dealings with title

12.1 We have now reached the point in this book where we can integrate the information contained in previous chapters to form a composite account of the central problem of conveyancing (**2.11**)—the way in which dealings with title affect the various categories of legal and equitable right already outlined. We had a preliminary glimpse of the overall effect of land dealings when, in Chapter 2, we mapped out a bird's eye view of the terrain of land law (**2.21**). As always, the primary distinction lies between estates whose title has been *registered* at Land Registry and estates whose title has *not yet* been brought on to the Land Register (**2.22**). In keeping with the theme of this book, we shall continue to recognise *registered* title as the dominant regime of modern land law, but we shall also provide a parallel account of the process and effect of dealings with *unregistered* titles (**12.33**).

The process of contract and registered transfer

12.2 Land transfer in England and Wales is essentially a two-step process: first *contract*, then *transfer of title* (i.e. 'completion' of the contract by registered disposition). It is irrelevant for this purpose whether the subject matter of the transfer is a freehold estate or a long leasehold estate. In either case the relationship between vendor and purchaser (i.e. between 'seller' and 'buyer', as modern conveyancing terminology increasingly expresses it) normally develops through three sharply defined phases:

- pre-contractual negotiations and enquiries (**12.3**);
- exchange of contracts (**12.4**); and
- disposition of the legal estate accompanied by registration of the disposition at Land Registry (**12.5**).

As we move irreversibly towards an era of paperless transactions it becomes clear that entry in the digital record of the Land Register will relatively soon provide the essential constitutive source of entitlement to realty. In other words, entry in the register will be integral to the very process of dealing with most kinds of interest in land. Transfer of land and the creation of rights over land will become inseparably linked with a simultaneous act of registration.

Negotiations and enquiries prior to exchange of contracts

12.3 During the period preceding exchange of contracts, the parties inch towards agreement on such matters as price and the timing of the sale. The purchaser arranges any necessary mortgage finance and he or his prospective mortgagee obtains a survey or valuation of the property. Nowadays much domestic conveyancing is conducted in voluntary compliance with the National Conveyancing Protocol, which was introduced by the Law Society in 1990 with the general aim of providing purchasers with convenient and speedy access to all relevant information in respect of the property. Thus the vendor's solicitor commonly supplies, along with the draft contract for sale, an official copy of the vendor's register of title (**6.2**), a duly completed property information form, and the result of a recent local land charges search conducted by the relevant local authority (**12.27**).

— *Absence of contractual commitment* It used to be invariable practice at this stage for vendor and purchaser to mark all correspondence as being 'subject to contract' so that no binding contractual commitment could emerge in the absence of a formal contract for sale signed and exchanged by the parties. In view of the almost universal modern requirement that binding contracts be *contained in signed writing* (see LP(MP)A 1989, s 2(1), **9.6**), the necessity for such caution has now probably disappeared. In advance of a formal contract in signed writing, all the parties have is a 'gentleman's agreement', which in reality incorporates little more than a mutual hope that 'the other will act like a gentleman' in circumstances where neither 'intends so to act if it is against his material interests' (*Goding v Frazer* (1967) per Sachs J). It is a recurring question whether a binding contractual commitment should, as in Scotland, arise much earlier in the process of dealing with land.

— *Chain transactions* It is important to realise, particularly in the context of domestic conveyancing, that a transaction of sale and purchase rarely occurs in isolation. As homeowners move up (or down) the property ladder, transactions tend to involve highly complex chains of transfer. Each individual transaction is dependent upon the successful and simultaneous completion of a number of interlinked dealings. It is this interdependence of dealings which makes the pre-contractual phase of land transactions a particularly fraught affair, since an entire chain of sales and purchases may be frustrated if all parties concerned are not ready (and equipped, where necessary, with offers of mortgage finance) to exchange contracts on the same day.

— *'Gazumping'* The delay in contractual commitment opens up the possibility of 'gazumping' (the unattractive practice by which a potential vendor disregards an existing 'gentleman's agreement' for sale if it transpires that a more favourable price can be extracted from a different potential purchaser). A gazumped purchaser has no remedy in the absence of a 'lock-out agreement', i.e. a prior collateral contract that during a short stipulated period the vendor will not negotiate with other prospective purchasers (see *Pitt v PHH Asset Management Ltd* (1994)), breach of which entitles the disappointed purchaser to money damages.

— *Electronic conveyancing* The 'single most important function' of the Land Registration Act 2002 is to set in place the necessary legal framework for the introduction of electronic conveyancing (see Law Com No 271 (2001), paras 2.41, 13.1, **2.23, 2.26**). It is now anticipated that a system of electronic conveyancing will be piloted from October 2007 (Land Registry Press Notice 08/06). The move from paper-based to electronic dealing is, however, already underway and, in the joint view of the Law Commission and Land Registry, e-conveyancing 'seems certain to become the only form of dealing with registered land within a comparatively short time' (Law Com No 271, para 13.45). It is envisaged that the system of e-conveyancing will be operated through a secure electronic communications network (or 'intranet') accessible on a contractual basis by professionals (e.g. solicitors, licensed conveyancers, estate agents and mortgage lenders) who are authorised for this purpose by Land Registry (see LRA 2002, s 92, Sch 5). The network will be employed to conduct all stages of a transaction in electronic form and will have three particular functions during the pre-contractual phase.

- The network will be used for the *dissemination of information* about properties being sold, thereby dispensing with many of the routine enquiries and surveys which make the conveyancing process repetitive and costly. This communicative function is likely to dovetail with the statutory requirement (scheduled to be introduced in 2007) that all vendors of residential premises should provide prospective purchasers with a 'home information pack' including replies to standard preliminary enquiries and an up-to-date 'home condition report' on the physical state and energy efficiency of the home concerned (Housing Act 2004, ss 154–159; Home Information Pack Regulations 2006 (SI 2006/1503)).

- It is probable that a 'chain manager'—almost certainly an official of Land Registry—will *oversee and coordinate the linked transactions* within a chain of sales and purchases (at least within the area of domestic conveyancing) (see Law Com No 271 (2001), paras 2.52, 13.63). The expedited flow of information via the secure intranet to all chain members about the achievement of successive stages in the pre-contractual phase will relieve much of the uncertainty and tension currently experienced in conveyancing transactions and will enable the chain manager to monitor the progress of a chain and identify any party in that chain who is delaying the process of eventual transfer (see LRA 2002, s 92, Sch 5, para 9). Toward this end a prototype 'chain matrix' service was introduced by Land Registry in 2006, to be followed by a full working version in 2007 (Land Registry, *Annual Report and Accounts 2005/6*, pp 4–6, 66).

- Land Registry's involvement in the conveyancing process *will begin much earlier* than is currently the case (see Law Com No 271 (2001), paras 2.49–2.53). For instance, the draft terms of any proposed contract will require to be transmitted to the Registry in electronic form for checking by electronic means in order to eradicate, even at this stage, discrepancies or other difficulties which might impede the transaction later.

Exchange of contracts

12.4 When vendor and purchaser have finally reached a state of preparedness for contractual commitment, they enter into a formal contract—usually on the basis of the Law Society's Standard Conditions of Sale—for the disposition of the vendor's legal estate in the land (whether freehold or leasehold).

— *Form and effect* The contract must be made in writing, must incorporate all expressly agreed terms in each of the parts to be exchanged by the parties, and must be signed by or on behalf of each contracting party (LP(MP)A 1989, s 2(1), **9.6**). In extremely unusual cases, non-compliance with these requirements may be white-washed by resort to doctrines of constructive trust or proprietary estoppel (see e.g. *Yaxley v Gotts* (2000), **10.12**). The contract of sale normally provides for the payment, on exchange, of a deposit of 10 per cent of the purchase price, the balance to be paid on 'completion' of the contract by transfer. The contract can be—but in normal domestic conveyancing rarely is—protected as an 'estate contract' (**9.8, 12.11, 12.36**).

— *Electronic contracts* The LRA 2002 envisages that, under the regime of e-conveyancing soon to be inaugurated, contracts will be made in electronic form and signed electronically by the parties or their agents (see LRA 2002, s 93(1)–(2)).

• Under the LRA 2002 estate contracts will require, as a condition of their validity, to be protected by the entry of a pre-agreed form of 'notice' in the register of the vendor's title (LRA 2002, ss 32–4, **12.11**). There will thus be no 'exchange' of contracts in the traditional sense, but rather a consensual transmission of the agreement to Land Registry; and the making of the contract (i.e. the moment of contractual commitment) will be synchronous with the entry of the parties' pre-agreed 'notice' in the register of the vendor's title (see Law Com No 271 (2001), para 2.54). In this way the contractual purchaser will acquire clear (and immediate) priority protection for his contract (see LRA 2002, s 72).

• There are already moves in the direction of a more general facility of electronic contracting—applicable to both registered and unregistered land (see Draft Law of Property (Electronic Communications) Order 2001, **9.6**)—but this initiative appears likely to be overtaken in the context of registered land by the provisions of the LRA 2002.

Transfer of the legal estate

12.5 The contracted disposition of the relevant legal estate (whether freehold or lease-hold) follows on the 'completion date' specified in the contract for sale—usually, but by no means necessarily, 28 days (i.e. 20 business days) from the date of contractual commitment.

— *Completion by registration* The contract for sale is 'completed' by the signed and attested deed of disposition of the vendor's estate (**7.6, 7.17–7.18, 7.22**), but in *registered* land the transfer itself is 'completed' only when the instrument of disposition (i.e. the transfer document) is lodged at Land Registry for amendment of the relevant proprietorship register (**6.2**). A 'registration gap'—possibly a matter of several weeks—thus opens up between the dates of disposition and registration (**12.10**); and no legal estate passes until the disponee is entered in the relevant proprietorship register as the new owner of the registered estate (LRA 2002, s 27(1), (2)(a), Sch 2, para 2(1), **7.8, 7.22**). In *unregistered* land, by contrast, the formal conveyance of a legal estate is effective to vest that estate *immediately* in the purchaser, but most conveyances must be presented within two months at Land Registry for first registration of title if the legal estate is to *remain* vested in the purchaser (LRA 2002, ss 6(4), 7(1)–(2), **7.7, 7.21**).

— *Searches with priority* Before taking a transfer of a registered title, the purchaser must ensure that the register has not been altered since the date of issue of the official copy of the register supplied by his vendor (**12.3**). Shortly before the proposed completion date the prudent purchaser procures an *official search with priority* of his vendor's registered title (LRR 2003, r 147(1)). The result of this search details any entries made in the register since the issue of the official copy (and, if any adverse entries have been made, the purchaser is entitled to withdraw from the transaction). The search with priority also provides the purchaser with a priority period of 30 business days within which to lodge his dealing for registration at Land Registry. Any entry made in the register during this period is normally postponed to the title taken by the purchaser pursuant to his 'priority protection' (LRA 2002, s 72; LRR 2003, r 131).

— *Electronic dispositions* The LRA 2002 envisages the eventual elimination of the 'registration gap' which currently intervenes between the dates of disposition and registration at Land Registry (see Law Com No 271 (2001), para 2.56). The essence of e-conveyancing is the idea that the disposition of any estate in or interest out of registered land should be *synchronous* with the registration of the disponee as the new proprietor (**2.26, 7.8**). Accordingly the final stage in an electronic conveyance will involve the execution of a pre-agreed form of electronic transfer (together with any related mortgage charge) and its electronic transmission to Land Registry. This release to the Registry will result, with instantaneous effect, in a *simultaneous* registration of these various dispositions and the electronic movement of purchase and mortgage moneys, stamp duty and Land Registry fees (see LRA 2002, ss 91–4, Sch 5). All will happen in less than the twinkling of an eye; the moment of disposition and registration will exactly coincide; and the register of title will then accurately and definitively record the resulting priority of all relevant rights.

Classification of interests in registered land

12.6 The LRA 2002 confirms the existence in registered land of certain classifications of proprietary interest unknown to the common law. These classifications comprise the following:

- *registered estates* and *registered charges* (**2.30–2.31**);
- *registrable interests* (sometimes known as *minor interests*) which can be protected by the entry of a 'notice' in the register (**2.32, 12.11**); and
- unregistered interests which *override* registered dispositions of a registered estate or charge (sometimes known as *overriding interests*) (**2.33, 12.15**).

— *Terminology* It may be appropriate here to add an explanatory note about terminology. Unlike the LRA 1925, the LRA 2002 does not refer expressly to 'minor interests' within the registered land scheme, but it is still useful, from time to time, to harness this compact phrase to indicate certain categories of subsidiary right which can be 'entered in the register' (see LRA 2002, s 132(1)). Likewise the LRA 2002 does not explicitly retain the reference in the LRA 1925 to various groups of 'overriding interest' (see LRA 1925, ss 3(xvi), 70(1)). Instead, the 2002 Act refers to 'unregistered interests' which 'override' first registrations of title and subsequent registered dispositions of a registered estate (LRA 2002, Sch 1, Sch 3). The Act nevertheless speaks also of the 'overriding status' of such entitlements (see LRA 2002, s 133, Sch 11, para 26(4)) and, for clarity of exposition, it therefore seems both convenient and justifiable to revert occasionally to the familiar shorthand of the 'overriding interest'.

— *Focus on minor and overriding interests* Registered estates and registered charges—principally the fee simple absolute, the term of years absolute and various kinds of legal mortgage—have already provided the focus of much discussion in this book (**7.7–7.8, 7.19–7.22, 8.28–8.34**). We shall therefore turn now to the way in which other categories of interest affecting a registered estate are dealt with on the disposition of the registered title.

Effect of registered dispositions of a registered estate

12.7 A principal objective of the LRA 2002 is to define, with maximum certainty and accuracy, the consequences of any dealings which occur in respect of estates registered at Land Registry (**2.11**).

— *Minimising potential threats to title* Rational, clear-sighted transacting with land requires a heightened degree of transparency in relation to the benefits and burdens associated with title. The overall drive of the LRA 2002 is therefore towards cleaning up the titles taken by registered transferees and chargees. It is a primary aim of the statute to minimise or clarify the range of matters which potentially trammel the estate taken by a newly registered proprietor, thereby safeguarding the disponee from adventitious, unforeseen or effectively undiscoverable derogations from his title. The effect is undoubtedly to sharpen up the outcome of one-off dealings between strangers, to strip away many of the obstacles to the reception of a clear title, and ultimately to equip the registered proprietor with a robust and highly protected form of state-guaranteed ownership (see Gray and Gray, 'The Rhetoric of Realty', in J. Getzler (ed.), *Rationalizing Property, Equity and Trusts: Essays in Honour of Edward Burn* (Butterworths, 2003), pp 243–53).

— *The statutory language of 'priority' and 'postponement'* The central provisions of the LRA 2002 are therefore concerned with the dynamic of land dealings and with the impact that dispositions of registered land have on various sorts of interest pre-existing in or over that land. For this purpose it becomes imperative to ascertain whether, following the disposition of a registered estate in a parcel of land (say, 'Greenacre'), some pre-existing interest affecting Greenacre (i.e. *entitlement A*) remains binding on and effective against the interest (i.e. *entitlement B*) which is taken by the disponee of that registered estate (see *Fig* 23). The technical termin-ology used by the LRA 2002 to express this problem of continuing enforceability revolves around the question whether *entitlement A* enjoys 'priority' over *entitlement B*. In this context the word 'priority' has nothing necessarily to do with temporal order or sequence, but merely expresses the idea of dominance or superiority (i.e. which of the two entitlements, *A* or *B* ranks above the other in terms of jural potency). Using the correlative statutory language of 'postponement' (**12.9**), a conclusion that *entitlement A* enjoys 'priority' over *entitlement B* can just as easily be expressed in terms that *entitlement B* is 'postponed' to *entitlement A*. Here, again,

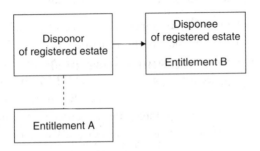

Fig 23

the concept of 'postponement' has nothing necessarily to do with temporal order or sequence, but merely articulates a notion of subjugation or relegation.

— *Extra dimensions of 'priority'* The issue of 'priority' is often given an extra complexity in land law precisely because, as we have already seen (**2.10**), the range of 'registered dispositions' (i.e. of dealings which can throw up a question of disputed 'priority') includes not merely transfers of a registered freehold or leasehold estate (**7.8, 7.22**), but also certain grants of lease (**7.8**) and mortgage charge (**8.29**) made out of a registered estate. In terms of our hypothetical disposition, *entitlement B* may therefore comprise a term of years or legal charge taken by a disponee of the registered estate in Greenacre.

The 'basic rule': priority is not affected by a disposition

12.8 In order to resolve problems of contested 'priority', the LRA 2002 announces a new, surprisingly stark (and somewhat inelegantly expressed) 'basic rule' (see LRA 2002, s 28(1)):

> Except as provided by sections 29 and 30, the priority of an interest affecting a registered estate ... is not affected by a disposition of the estate ...

— *A simple ordering of 'priority'* In the context of our hypothetical disposition of Greenacre (**12.7**), the 'basic rule' seems, in effect, to arrange priority as between *entitlement A* and *entitlement B* simply as a matter of temporal order of creation. *Entitlement A*, if already effective against a registered estate in Greenacre, cannot be disturbed by any later disposition of that estate which gives rise to *entitlement B*. In other words, *entitlement A* enjoys, on a 'first in time' basis, an automatic and unassailable priority over *entitlement B* and, in a strictly accurate explication of this rule, it is statutorily declared to make 'no difference' whether the pre-existing interest or the disposition is registered (LRA 2002, s 28(2)).

— *The key to the 'basic rule'* An important key to understanding the 'basic rule' of priority under the LRA 2002 is the realisation that its ulterior purpose is essentially the governance of registered land interests *after* the introduction of the forthcoming regime of electronic conveyancing (**2.25–2.26**). It is at this point that the 'basic rule' will really come into its own (see LRA 2002, ss 27(1), 93(2)–(4)). With the advent of electronic dealings, the intention is that most interests in registered land will have no existence at all (either at law or in equity) *unless and until* they actually appear in the Land Register (**7.8**). Since all disponees of a registered estate will plainly be bound by existing entries in the register, it will then become self-evident, in the words of LRA 2002, s 28(1), that 'the priority of an interest affecting a registered estate ... is not affected by a disposition of the estate'. The validity of most interests will depend, by definition, on register entry; and register entries will be automatically enforceable against all subsequent disponees.

— *Exceptions to the 'basic rule'* Meanwhile—largely for want of any presently available scheme of electronic dealings with registered land—the 'basic rule' of priority is rendered expressly subject to certain exceptions contained in a *special priority rule* set out in LRA 2002, ss 29–30. Although the 'basic rule' still plays, even now, a residual role in determining some issues of priority (**12.10**), the statutory exceptions from its scope exert, for the moment, a quite devastating impact on the apparent import of the rule. Indeed, it is likely that, during the immediately foreseeable future, many more transactions in registered land will be governed by these exceptions than by the 'basic rule' itself.

— *Extended coverage of the priority rules of the LRA 2002* The priority rules of the LRA 2002 are declared, for the avoidance of doubt, to extend to certain cases where *entitlement A* consists of one or other of several rights whose proprietary status was previously a matter of some controversy. These rights comprise a right of pre-emption (**9.11**), an 'equity by estoppel' (**10.18**) and a 'mere equity' (e.g. a right to have a document rectified on the ground of mistake (**12.20**) or to have a deed set aside on the ground of fraud or undue influence (**15.10**)). Rights of pre-emption created on or after 13 October 2003 are now declared to have effect 'from the time of creation as an interest capable of binding successors in title' (LRA 2002, s 115); and all equities by estoppel and mere equities are accorded a similar effect 'from the time the equity arises' (LRA 2002, s 116, **12.20**).

A special priority rule for registered dispositions: priority is reversed

12.9 Pending the arrival of a fully electronic regime of land dealings, the 'basic rule' of priority propounded by the LRA 2002 is subjected to the gravest of qualifications in the event of any 'registrable disposition of a registered estate ... for valuable consideration' (LRA 2002, s 29(1)). When such a disposition is completed by registration at Land Registry, such registration has the statutory effect of reversing the thrust of the 'basic rule'. This has radical consequences for our determination of priority in Greenacre (**12.7–12.8**) as between a hypothetical pre-existing *entitlement A* and the *entitlement B* taken by a disponee of the relevant registered estate.

In effect, the occurrence of a registered disposition for value dramatically limits the circumstances in which the recipient of *entitlement B* necessarily takes subject to any *entitlement A* previously enforceable over Greenacre. The trigger of the transaction *for value* thus activates a rather stricter rule system for the ordering of priority.

— *Reversal of priority for unprotected interests* In the context of a registered disposition for value, the priority which the 'basic rule' normally accords to a pre-existing interest (i.e. *entitlement A*) over the estate taken by the disponee (i.e. *entitlement B*) is now overturned by force of statute *unless* it can be shown that *entitlement A* enjoyed a 'protected' priority at the time of registration of *entitlement B*. For this purpose, the priority of an interest is taken to be 'protected' only in certain tightly regulated circumstances (see LRA 2002, s 29(2)), which we shortly must examine. (An equivalent effect follows a registrable disposition of a registered charge (LRA 2002, s 30(1)–(2), **8.33**).)

— *Consequence of unprotected priority* In the absence of 'protected' priority for *entitlement A*, the completed disposition of *entitlement B* is said, in the convoluted terms of the LRA 2002, to have 'the effect of postponing to the interest under the disposition [i.e. *entitlement B*] any interest affecting the estate immediately before the disposition [i.e. *entitlement A*]' (LRA 2002, s 29(1)). In plainer language— and by way of exception to the 'basic rule' enunciated in the LRA 2002—it is *entitlement B* which now enjoys priority over *entitlement A*. The registered disponee of an estate in Greenacre thus takes free of the pre-existing interest; *entitlement A* is no longer enforceable against Greenacre. Although *entitlement A* may still generate a personal remedy as against the individual who originally granted the right in question, the land lawyer's inquiry is now resolved: the registered estate in Greenacre is no longer bound by *entitlement A*.

— *Instances of 'protected' status* When translated out of the needlessly opaque language of the statute, the net effect is as follows. Under the LRA 2002, the disponee of a registered estate receives a significant immunity from pre-existing interests affecting the land, provided that the disposition is made 'for valuable consideration' and is itself completed by due registration. In this combination of circumstances, the disponee *takes free* of 'any interest affecting the estate imme-diately before the disposition' *unless* such interest enjoys 'protected' priority at the time of registration (see LRA 2002, s 29(2)). For this purpose, the priority of an interest is 'protected' if the interest is:

- a *registered charge* (**2.31, 8.29**) or
- an interest safeguarded by the entry of a *notice* in the register (**12.11**) or

- an unregistered interest which is statutorily declared to *override* registered dispositions (**12.15**) or

- an interest *excepted from the effect of first registration* (e.g. in the case of registration with less than absolute title) (**12.28**) or

- (in the case of a leasehold disposition) an interest whose *burden is incident to the leasehold estate* (e.g. a restrictive covenant) (**14.25**).

We have already referred to the binding impact of registered charges and will, in due course, examine leasehold burdens. In this chapter, however, our primary concern revolves around those interests which attain 'protected' priority (i) by reason of the entry of a 'notice' (**12.11–12.14**) or (ii) by reason of their overriding status (**12.15–12.27**).

— *Effect of non-registrable leasehold grant*   The special priority rule for registered dispositions is obviously inapplicable, in its terms, to dispositions out of registered land which do not require completion by registration (e.g. leases granted for a period not exceeding seven years, **7.23**). However, the LRA 2002 extends the special priority rule, by fiction of statute, to unregistrable dispositions of precisely this kind (see LRA 2002, s 29(4)). Thus the lessee of a term granted for no more than seven years takes free of all interests affecting the parent registered estate immediately before the disposition which did not enjoy 'protected' priority at the time of the grant.

Cases not covered by the special priority rule

12.10   Certain dispositions of a registered estate are *not* covered by the special priority rule and, in these cases, the disponee is disabled from claiming that, by virtue of this rule, he takes an automatic priority over interests which pre-existed the relevant disposition. In such circumstances the 'basic rule' of priority promulgated by the LRA 2002 comes back into play to resolve the issue.

— *Dispositions other than for value*   The special priority rule adumbrated by the LRA 2002 has no application to registered dispositions made otherwise than for valuable consideration (see LRA 2002, s 29(1)). 'Valuable consideration' is defined, for this purpose, as exclusive of marriage consideration or any nominal consideration in money (LRA 2002, s 132(1)). It follows that the disponee who provides no value enjoys *no* priority over pre-existing interests affecting the land (see Law Com No 271 (2001), para 5.9). Instead, we fall back on the 'basic rule' for the proposition that the priority of any interest affecting a registered estate is *unchanged* by the disposition of that estate (see LRA 2002, s 28(1), **12.8**). Indeed, the Act goes so far as to declare it irrelevant, for the purpose of the 'basic rule', whether the interest or disposition in question is registered (LRA 2002, s 28(2)). In consequence, the *donee* of a registered estate takes inevitably subject to all interests which pre-date the disposition to him.

— *Priority in relation to interests created during the 'registration gap'* Under the scheme of the LRA 2002, registrable dispositions are still imperfect at the date of disposition (i.e. the date of execution of the relevant document), and require to be completed by registration at Land Registry (**12.5**). Such dispositions take effect meanwhile only in equity (**7.8, 7.22**). It also follows that a period of time—the so-called 'registration gap'—elapses between the date of *disposition* and the deemed date of *registration* (see LRA 2002, s 74, **7.8**). Pending registration of the disponee as the new proprietor, the disponor obviously remains registered proprietor of the relevant registered estate and is thus technically competent to create interests in the land adverse to the disponee (although to do so is usually a clear breach of both contract and trust (**9.8**)). In rare cases it is possible that, during the 'registration gap', the disponor may create interests (e.g. leases or easements) which could not have been detected, or even predicted, on any inspection of the land by the intending disponee prior to the date of disposition (see e.g. *Barclays Bank plc v Zaroovabli* (1997)). The question is whether the disponee of the registered estate can claim priority over such a lease or easement.

• In these circumstances the disponee cannot derive any comfort from the special priority rule applicable to registered dispositions, for this rule allows him to take free only of certain interests which affected the estate 'immediately before the disposition' (LRA 2002, s 29(1), **12.9**). Instead, the case is governed by the 'basic rule' of priority (see LRA 2002, s 28(1)). In consequence, any interest which supervenes during the 'registration gap' is, in fact, *postponed* to the interest already taken by the (as yet) unregistered disponee, precisely because the 'basic rule' sets in place a principle of 'first in time' (**12.8**). The supervening interest is thus postponed to the equitable entitlement already held by the disponee of the registered title.

• The eventual introduction of electronic conveyancing pursuant to the LRA 2002 (**12.3–12.5**) will remove the possibility that interests may supervene during a 'registration gap'. Electronic dealing with land interests is premised on the *synchronous* nature of the creation and registration of expressly conferred rights, with the consequence that the 'registration gap' will completely disappear and the resulting record of the register will become, on its very face, conclusive as to the priority of all expressly created interests (Law Com No 271 (2001), paras 2.1(2), 2.56).

Interests whose priority is 'protected' by entry of a 'notice' in the register

12.11 A 'notice' is an 'entry in the register in respect of the burden of an interest affecting a registered estate or charge' (LRA 2002, s 32(1)). The LRA 2002 recognises the existence of a range of entitlements in registered land whose priority, in the context of a registered disposition, can be 'protected' by such an entry (LRA 2002, s 29(1), (2)(a)(i), **12.6**, **12.9**). These entitlements are sometimes called *registrable interests* (in order to distinguish them from 'registered estates' and 'registered charges' (**2.32**)). Alternatively, in a loose evocation of the terminology employed under the LRA 1925, this diverse class of protectable entitlements is also described as a category of *minor interests* in registered land. Whatever the terminology, the unifying feature of this group of interests is that each casts a burden on some registered estate and is therefore, in some sense, subsidiary to that estate. The interests involved here fall into several broad sub-categories.

— *Burdens entered on the initiative of the registrar*   Subject to LRA 2002, s 33 (infra), it is the task of the Chief Land Registrar, at the point of first registration of an estate, to enter in the relevant register a 'notice' in respect of the burden of any interest which appears from his examination of title to affect the newly registered estate (LRR 2003, r 35, **2.23**, **12.33**). The registrar also has a general power to enter 'notices' in respect of potentially overriding interests (LRA 2002, s 37(1); LRR 2003, r 89, **12.15**) and interests which have been omitted from the register by mistake (LRA 2002, Sch 4, para 5, **12.28–12.29**).

— *Interests which require protection under LRA 2002, s 27*   It is essential to the strategy of the LRA 2002 that most dispositions out of a registered estate require, as a precondition of their effectiveness 'at law', to be completed by registration (LRA 2002, s 27(1)–(4)). This mandate applies to the creation of various kinds of lease, easement, profit *à prendre*, rentcharge and right of entry affecting a registered freehold or leasehold estate. The 'relevant registration requirements' necessitate not only that the benefits conferred by such dispositions be appropriately recorded in the Land Register, but also that the burdens thereby created should be noted against the registered title to the encumbered estate. This cross-referencing process ensures not only that the recipient takes a good legal title to the interest concerned (whether it be a lease, easement or so forth), but also that subsequent disponees of the registered estate out of which these rights have been carved inevitably take subject to the burden of the protected interest (**12.13**).

- A 'notice' in respect of certain categories of lease granted out of registered land must be entered in the register of the landlord's title (LRA 2002, s 27(2)(b), Sch 2, para 3(2)(b), **7.8, 7.20**).

- A 'notice' in respect of certain categories of easement, profit *à prendre*, rent-charge and right of entry granted or reserved out of registered land must likewise be entered in the register of title to the 'servient' estate (LRA 2002, s 27(2)(d)–(e), Sch 2, paras 6(2)(b), 7(2)(a), **8.16, 8.27, 8.35**).

— *Other minor interests in registered land* Entry by 'notice' also provides an appropriate form of protection for a number of entitlements created out of a registered estate which have not been (and often cannot be) recorded in the Land Register in any other way. The entry of a 'notice' in the register of the relevant burdened title guarantees that the minor interests in question take priority over subsequent disponees of the registered title. Such interests include principally:

- leases granted for a term of more than *three* years (LRA 2002, ss 32, 33(b), **2.31, 7.23**);

- leases created out of a registered estate which remain equitable for want of due formality or due registration at Land Registry (**7.18–7.20, 9.9**);

- contracts to grant a lease (**7.18, 9.9**);

- other estate contracts (**9.8, 9.10**);

- equitable easements and profits *à prendre* (**9.12**);

- equitable mortgages and charges created out of a registered estate (**9.18–9.20**);

- unpaid vendors' liens (**9.22**);

- purchasers' liens to secure deposits (**9.23**);

- freehold restrictive covenants (**9.24**); and

- home rights under the Family Law Act 1996 (which confer upon qualifying spouses or civil partners certain rights of occupation in, or non-exclusion from, a dwelling-house (FLA 1996, s 30(2), **12.21**).

— *Interests ineligible for protection by 'notice'* Some interests are statutorily excluded from the facility of protection by 'notice' (see LRA 2002, s 33), and these include principally:

- beneficial interests under a trust of land (**9.34–9.42**) and any charging order affecting such interests (**7.8, 9.21**);

- beneficial interests under a Settled Land Act settlement (**9.43**) and any charging order affecting such interests (**9.21**);

- leasehold terms of three years or less (which are not otherwise required to be registered) (**7.23**); and

- restrictive covenants made between lessor and lessee (so far as relating to the demised premises) (**14.25**).

— *Priority inter se of competing minor interests* As between themselves (as distinct from vis-à-vis disponees of title), the priority of minor interests is generally governed, not by the order of their entry in the register, but by their respective dates of creation (see *Barclays Bank Ltd v Taylor* (1974)). However, when the creation/ transfer and registration of land interests become synchronous events in the brave new world of electronic dealing (**2.26, 12.3–12.5**), it will be entry in the register which is conclusive as to the priority of such interests, precisely because the interests in question will have no existence at all *unless registered* (see Law Com No 271 (2001), paras 5.3, 7.17).

Entry of a 'notice' in the register

12.12 The LRA 2002 provides for a substantial simplification and rationalisation of the ways in which minor interests affecting registered land can be protected on the register. With prospective effect, the 2002 Act abolishes some of the old forms of protection available under the LRA 1925 (e.g. the 'caution against dealings' and the 'inhibition'), thus reserving entry by 'notice' as the only means by which a minor interest can be caused to impact on a disponee's title subsequent to the registration of his proprietorship. Many 'notices' (e.g. those relating to restrictive covenants) stay on the title indefinitely and bind all subsequent disponees (**12.13**). Other 'notices' which serve a short-term purpose (e.g. those relating to estate contracts) may, when that purpose is spent, be cancelled on application to Land Registry.

— *Mode of entry* Any person who claims to be entitled to a protectable minor interest may apply for the entry of a 'notice' in respect of that claim in the *charges register* of the title affected (LRA 2002, ss 32(2), 34(1); LRR 2003, r 84(1), **6.2**). The application may be for either an 'agreed notice' or a 'unilateral notice' (LRA 2002, s 34(2)).

- *'Agreed notice'* The entry of an 'agreed notice'—essentially relating to non-contentious matters—requires the consent of the registered proprietor or proof of the validity of the applicant's claim. Alternatively, the registered proprietor himself may apply for the entry of an 'agreed notice' (LRA 2002, s 34(3)). 'Agreed notice' is the only appropriate form of entry in respect of certain kinds of entitlement, e.g. home rights (**12.11**) and orders under the Access to Neighbouring Land Act 1992

(8.20) (LRR 2003, rr 80, 82). 'Agreed notices' are not subject to the statutory cancellation procedure which applies to 'unilateral notices', with the consequence that this form of entry offers greater security to the beneficiary of the notice. An 'agreed notice' can, of course, be cancelled where the interest protected by it has come to an end (LRR 2003, r 87).

• *'Unilateral notice'* By contrast, an application for entry of a 'unilateral notice'—essentially relating to hostile or contested claims of entitlement—initiates a process of notification of and possible objection by the registered proprietor (LRA 2002, s 35; LRR 2003, r 83). The entry of a 'unilateral notice' does not require the cooperation of the registered proprietor, but the proprietor is entitled to apply at any time for the cancellation of the notice (in which case the beneficiary of the notice has certain rights of objection to the proposed cancellation) (LRA 2002, s 36; LRR 2003, r 86). Equally, the beneficiary of the notice may apply to the registrar for removal of a notice which has become spent or redundant (LRA 2002, s 35(3); LRR 2003, r 85).

— *Responsibility of applicant for entry of a notice* The LRA 2002 imposes a duty not to apply for the entry of a notice 'without reasonable cause' (LRA 2002, s 77(1)). This statutory duty is owed to any person who suffers damage in consequence of its breach (LRA 2002, s 77(2)).

Consequence of entry by 'notice'

12.13 The fact that an interest is the subject of a 'notice' does not necessarily mean that the interest itself is valid, but merely that the priority of the interest, if valid, is protected in the event of subsequent registered dispositions of the relevant registered estate or charge (LRA 2002, s 32(3)). In this way the entry of a notice helps to advance the ultimate objectives of any rational registration system.

— *Aims of registration* One of the fundamental objectives of any system of registered title must be to ensure that the register remains an accurate record—or 'mirror' **(2.23)**—of the interests affecting the registered estate. Ultimately therefore, in common with most registration schemes, the protection of minor interests under the LRA 2002 operates on the basis of two simple rules:

• A minor interest, if the subject of a notice entered in the register, acquires 'protected' priority, i.e. becomes binding on any subsequent disponee of the registered estate, regardless of whether he inspected the register (LRA 2002, s 29(2)(a)(i)). A prudent disponee will, of course, apply for an official copy of the relevant register before committing himself to the disposition **(6.2)**. Moreover, most disponees, shortly before taking their disposition, will procure a priority search of the register, thereby acquiring a 30-day priority period during which to apply for registration of that disposition (**12.5**).

- A protectable interest, if *not* the subject of a notice in the register, is postponed to the interest which passes under any registered disposition made for valuable consideration (LRA 2002, s 29(1)), although remaining enforceable against a disponee otherwise than for value, i.e. a donee or trustee in bankruptcy (**12.10**).

The LRA 2002 accordingly denies effect to unprotected minor interests in the context of most dispositions of the relevant registered estate—whether freehold or leasehold—unless the entitlement in question also happens to qualify for 'protected' priority as an unregistered interest which statutorily 'overrides' registered dispositions of that estate (LRA 2002, s 29(2)(a)(ii), **2.33, 12.15**).

— *Rationale* The motive underlying these priority rules in the LRA 2002 is readily understandable—the rules are clear-cut and relatively easily applied. Efficiency is bought at the expense of moral exactitude, in that the rules obviate any general inquiry into the state of mind or moral standing of the individual disponee in every transaction. The medium of the register serves as an effective notification of entitlement to the world; and the statutory sanction of ineffectiveness in the case of non-protection provides a healthy incentive for all interested parties to keep the register appropriately updated.

Relevance of fraud

12.14 It is a standard feature of land registration systems the world over that mere knowledge of protectable, but unprotected, interests does not normally affect the title derived from registration. There is, in the words of the Court of Appeal, 'no general principle which renders it unconscionable for a purchaser of land to rely on a want of registration of a claim against registered land, even though he took with express notice of it ... A decision to the contrary would defeat the purpose of the legislature in introducing the system of registration' (*Lloyd v Dugdale* (2002) at [50]). As one of the great Chancery judges of the last century observed, it is 'vital to the working of the land registration system that notice of something which is not on the register should not affect a transferee unless it is an overriding interest' (*Strand Securities Ltd v Caswell* (1965) per Cross J). But alongside this concern for certainty in the ascertainment of land rights there runs a clear abhorrence of *fraud* (**10.1**).

— *The longstop of fraud* It is an enduring principle of English law that 'fraud unravels everything' and that no court in the land 'will allow a person to keep an advantage which he has obtained by fraud' (*Lazarus Estates Ltd v Beasley* (1956) per Denning LJ). All legal rules come with a sort of implied 'anti-fraud proviso': no party guilty of 'fraud' can ever hope to win. In the present context, a disponee for value of a registered estate who is guilty of *fraud* may well find that, in consequence of his wrongdoing, the long arm of equity intervenes on behalf of the owners of minor interests who have not protected their entitlements by entry in the register (see, for instance, the approach adopted, pursuant to the LRA 1925, in *Peffer v Rigg* (1977)). Thus, although title registration is 'designed to provide simplicity and certitude in transfers of land', equity retains 'the ability to exercise its juris-diction *in personam* on grounds of conscience' (*Oh Hiam v Tham Kong* (1980) per Lord Russell of Killowen). The threshold of fraud or unconscionable dealing remains, however, somewhat uncertain in English law, as are the precise con-sequences of a finding that a disponee has acted unconscientiously.

— *Variant interpretations of 'fraud'* The primary difficulty is that the term 'fraud' bears no clearly defined statutory or other meaning, and the expansiveness of the term has been left to be determined on an ad hoc basis. Judges differ in the liberality with which they are prepared to discern fraud in any given situation (see e.g. the parallel of *Midland Bank Trust Co Ltd v Green* (1981), **12.35**, where a majority in the Court of Appeal found 'fraud' to be present in circumstances which caused the House of Lords to be adamant that 'fraud' was not in issue). The critical question is how to identify the borderline between 'fair game' and 'foul play', i.e. whether the relevant parties are still playing, albeit robustly, within the four corners of the game or have instead strayed so far outside its rules that the referee must now blow his whistle. Significant differences of philosophy separate two approaches to this question.

• A *restrictive* definition of 'fraud' tends towards clarity, certainty, and systemic efficiency in the operation of the Land Register. A limited definition of fraud preserves the clear-cut, hard-edged, crystalline aspect of the underlying rules and encourages people to 'plan and to act carefully, knowing that no judicial cavalry will ride to their rescue later' (see Carol Rose, 'Crystals and Mud in Property Law' 40 *Stanford L Rev* 577 (1987–8)). On this view, there is no 'fraud' in merely exploiting the legal consequences which flow from the incautious or negligent failure of others to protect their own rights. '[I]t is not fraud to take advantage of legal rights, the existence of which may be taken to be known to both parties' (*Re Monolithic Building Co* (1915) per Lord Cozens-Hardy MR). As Lord Rodger of Earlsferry recently announced with brutal candour, '[n]ice guys finish last' (*Burnett's Trustee v Grainger* (2004) at [141]).

- An *expansive* definition of 'fraud' tends, on the other hand, towards greater fairness, flexibility, and sensitivity to the unique facts of individual cases. On this view, rule systems more properly resemble open-textured 'standards' which can take account of moral relativities (see Duncan Kennedy, 'Form and Substance in Private Law Adjudication' 89 *Harv L Rev* 1685 (1975–6)). Some depict this wider approach as the disintegration of the *crystals* of a clear-cut rule system into the *mud* of multiple one-off adjudications based on the merits (see Rose, supra). But others contend that judicial tolerances should nowadays adjust in order to compensate for the demise of traditional cultural and religious constraints on unfair dealing (see e.g. Paul Finn, 'Commerce, The Common Law and Morality' (1989) 17 *Melbourne U L Rev* 87). Some have positively called for the reintroduction of an 'ethical element' into the system of registered land (see e.g. G Battersby, 'Informal Transactions in Land, Estoppel and Registration' (1995) 58 *MLR* 637 at 655).

— *Consequences of fraud* The LRA 2002 reflects an overall policy concern to ensure that, isolated exceptions apart, the system of registration of rights wholly displaces the historic doctrine of notice. The thinking preceding the enactment was underpinned by a belief that issues as to whether a disponee had knowledge or notice of a pre-existing interest, or even whether a disponee acted in good faith, should be irrelevant (see Law Com No 254 (1998), paras 3.40–3.50; Law Com No 271 (2001), para 5.16). The immunity from pre-existing and unprotected interests which is conferred by the LRA accordingly imposes no explicit requirement that the disponee be 'in good faith' (see LRA 2002, s 29(1), **12.9**). It was always inconceivable, however, that the courts would abandon their age-old concern to combat 'fraud' in its more blatant manifestations. The Law Commission and Land Registry therefore contemplated (see Law Com No 254, para 3.49) that, under the LRA 2002, the courts would retain a jurisdiction in appropriate circumstances:

- either to *set a disposition aside* on the ground of fraud
- or to subject a fraudulent disponee to *personal liability* for any loss suffered by the owners of unprotected interests.

There remains also a strong possibility—albeit not expressly envisaged by the Law Commission and Land Registry—that the courts will take the view (as under the LRA 1925) that any statutory immunity from unprotected minor interests is simply inapplicable to a disponee who *in bad faith* seeks to take advantage of a failure to enter such interests in the register. On this analysis, the unconscientious disclaimer of unprotected minor interests constitutes a form of 'postponing conduct' which displaces or reverses the special priority rule of LRA 2002, s 29(1). The dishonest disponee therefore takes his title subject—by way of constructive trust— to the unprotected interests in question (see the continuing vitality of this approach in the thinking of the Court of Appeal in *Lloyd v Dugdale* (2002) at [50]–[52], infra).

Ultimately, with the introduction of routine electronic conveyancing (**12.3**), the making of an entry in the register will become integral to the very process of *creating* interests in registered land. When this happens, the concept of an unprotected minor interest will become, in most instances, a sheer contradiction in terms.

— *Recognised cases of fraud* Fraud, for all present purposes, requires some element of *personal dishonesty* in a disponee, based on an awareness of the existence of unprotected minor interests. Although the peripheral content of the notion of fraud is inherently debatable, equity has shown itself willing to intervene in at least the following circumstances of unconscientious dealing:

• a *deliberate ploy* to defeat unprotected rights: see e.g. *Jones v Lipman* (1962) (transfer of title to transferor's limited company for the purpose of defeating a pre-existing and now inconvenient estate contract);

• a *positive stipulation* by a transferee to take *expressly 'subject to'* unprotected rights: see e.g. *Lyus v Prowsa Developments Ltd* (1982) (transferee of uncompleted housing development reneged on his agreement to honour the contractual rights of a purchaser who had already paid his deposit) (see also Contracts (Rights of Third Parties) Act 1999, s 1(1)–(2)). In this sense, it can be said, in the words of Brennan J in the High Court of Australia, that the registration system is 'designed to protect a transferee from defects in the title of the transferor, not to free him from interests with which he has burdened his own title' (*Bahr v Nicolay (No 2)* (1988)). English courts, although responsive to this idea of self-imposed conscientious obligation, have insisted—sometimes quite unreasonably—on a high threshold for the intervention of equity.

Lloyd v Dugdale (2002) The Court of Appeal conceded that, in consequence of detrimental reliance on an oral agreement made with I (**10.25**), D would have had an equity based on proprietary estoppel to require I's executors to grant D a lease of commercial premises. D's company (JAD) had already moved into occupation of the premises, but following I's death his executors transferred the registered title to L, albeit expressly subject to D's claim. The Court of Appeal held that D's equity of estoppel was not overriding against L (**12.23**), since at the relevant time the occupier of the premises had been JAD (rather than D himself). D's final hope of justice lay in the argument that L was nevertheless bound by a constructive trust to give effect to D's estoppel-based rights. Sir Christopher Slade (at [52]) led the Court of Appeal in rejecting this contention. In determining 'whether or not the conscience of the new estate owner is affected ... the crucially important question is whether he has undertaken a new obligation, not otherwise existing, to give effect to the relevant encumbrance or prior interest.' The existence of a 'new' level or dimension of self-imposed obligation could be demonstrated by proof that the disponee had paid a reduced price 'upon the footing that he would give effect to' the otherwise unprotected interest. Here, however, L had not obviously paid a reduced price and the Court, although expressing sympathy for D (who had been let down 'badly'), was unwilling to impose a constructive trust on L 'on the basis of very slender materials'.

Interests whose priority is 'protected' by virtue of 'overriding status'

12.15 As a matter of logical and linguistic necessity, all registered dispositions of a registered estate take effect subject to those unregistered interests which are specified by the LRA 2002 to 'override' such dispositions (LRA 2002, s 29(1), (2)(a)(ii), **2.33**, **12.9**). The disponee is bound automatically by such overriding interests even though, by definition, they never appear on any register of title (LRA 2002, ss 29(3), 30(3)). The categories of interest which enjoy this overriding status are now set out in Sch 3 of the LRA 2002.

— *Historic function of overriding interests* Disponees of registered land have long been subject to the potential burden of an extensive range of rights which, although never apparent from the relevant register of title, are statutorily declared to be binding (see e.g. LRA 1925, s 70(1)). These kinds of entitlement include many interests which would not normally be disclosed by an unregistered documentary title. Their discovery generally depends on physical inspection of the land (possibly coupled with inquiry of persons present on that land) or on resort to other customary sources of information (e.g. the registers of local land charges maintained by local authority bodies). Thus, in general, overriding interests have tended to comprise rights (e.g. short legal leases) which have no other means of protection within the registered land scheme of things and whose automatically binding status is often merely a replication of the unregistered land rule that legal rights bind the world (**2.38**, **12.34**). But certainly, in the case of at least one sub-category of overriding interest (see LRA 2002, Sch 3, para 2, **12.18**), overriding status is accorded to some rights which could have been—but have not been—protected by entry in the register.

— *Modern curtailment of the scope of overriding interests* The range and effect of overriding interests, existing in a binding form *outside* registers of title, has come in recent years to be seen as a 'major obstacle' to the achievement of the 'ultimate goal of total registration' of land rights (Law Com No 271 (2001), paras 2.24, 3.16, 3.58, 8.1). Such overriding interests inevitably derogate from the comprehensive record of the Land Register and, in practical terms, are plainly incompatible with the on-line investigation of title which is envisaged as the principal benefit of electronic conveyancing (**2.23, 12.3–12.5**). It was therefore a major objective of the LRA 2002 to cut back the scope of overriding interests 'so far as possible' (Law Com No 271, para 2.25).

— *The guiding principle* The 'guiding principle' underlying this aspect of the LRA 2002 is the proposition that interests should have overriding status *only* 'where protection against buyers is needed, but where it is neither reasonable to expect nor sensible to require any entry on the register' (Law Com No 271 (2001), paras 2.25, 8.6, 8.87). This conscious desire to restrict the role of overriding interests has been furthered in the LRA 2002 by the following means:

- *Abolition or phasing out* of certain former sub-categories of overriding entitlement, including:

  — equitable easements and profits *à prendre* (**9.15, 12.26**)

  — rights of persons in adverse possession (formerly protected by LRA 1925, s 70(1)(f), **6.4**)

  — rights of non-resident landlords (formerly protected by LRA 1925, s 70(1)(g), **12.23**)

  — rights to enforce a chancel repair liability (formerly protected by LRA 1925, s 70(1)(c) and then mistakenly believed to be unenforceable under the Human Rights Act 1998—see now *Aston Cantlow and Wilmcote with Billesley PCC v Wallbank* (2003))

  — franchises, manorial rights, certain crown rents, non-statutory rights relating to embankments or sea or river walls, and rights to payment in lieu of tithe (10-year sunset clause now imposed by LRA 2002, s 117(1), Sch 3, paras 10–14).

- *Incorporation of unregistered interests in the register* (wherever possible) The LRA 2002 provides alternative mechanisms for ensuring that existing overriding interests are brought on to the register, at which point, of course, they cease to have 'overriding' status (see LRA 2002, ss 29(3), 30(3)) and are instead binding by virtue of their entry in the register.

  — The registrar has power to enter potentially overriding interests on the register by 'notice' (LRA 2002, s 37(1); LRR 2003, r 89, **12.33**).

— Applicants for registration of a registrable estate are statutorily required to disclose known unregistered interests (LRA 2002, s 71(b); LRR 2003, r 57).

• *Curtailment* of the circumstances in which new overriding interests can arise (**12.23, 12.26**).

• *E-conveyancing* will substantially reduce the impact of overriding interests, simply because it will become impossible, in most cases, to create rights expressly except by simultaneously entering such rights in the register (**2.26, 12.5, 12.10–12.11**). In this way the potential for the existence of land interests 'off the register' will be dramatically limited.

Principal sub-categories of overriding interest

12.16 As indicated by LRA 2002, Sch 3, the principal sub-categories of unregistered interest which 'override' registered dispositions of a registered estate are the following:

• legal leases granted for a term of not more than seven years (**12.17**);

• proprietary interests of persons in actual occupation of the land (**12.18**);

• legal easements and profits *à prendre* (**12.26**); and

• local land charges (**12.27**).

— *Preconditions of priority* Two elementary preconditions must be met before any entitlement falling within LRA 2002, Sch 3 can 'override' a registered disposition (see LRA 2002, s 29(1)):

• *An overriding interest must affect the registered estate immediately before the disposition* No interest can claim overriding status under the LRA 2002 unless it subsisted immediately prior to the relevant date of disposition and affected the estate which is the subject of that disposition. Thus, for instance, no interest created during the 'registration gap' *between* the dates of disposition and registration can possibly be said to 'override' (**12.10**).

• *An overriding interest must remain in existence at the date of registration* No interest can 'override' a registered disposition unless it is still in existence, and its priority is therefore capable of being 'protected' (and is 'protected'), at the time of registration of the disposition.

— *Duties to disclose overriding interests* The disponor has a general duty to disclose subsisting overriding interests to the disponee and, in default of such disclosure, the latter may have valuable contractual rights of recovery (see *Ferrishurst Ltd v Wallcite Ltd* (1999) per Robert Walker LJ). The disponee is also subject to a duty of disclosure to the registrar at the point of registration (LRA 2002, s 71, **12.15**).

We must examine the principal sub-categories of overriding interest in turn.

Legal leases for a term not exceeding seven years

12.17   Overriding protection is given by the LRA 2002 to most leasehold estates granted for a term which does not exceed seven years from the date of grant (LRA 2002, Sch 3, para 1).

— *The seven-year threshold*   The protection conferred on short leases of this kind is the corollary of the new statutory requirement that most leasehold estates with an unexpired term of *more than* seven years should be substantively registered at Land Registry (**7.19–7.22**). It also reflects the fact that short leases are otherwise unprotectable under the regime of the LRA 2002, except in so far as a lease granted for a term of more than *three* years may be safeguarded by the entry of a 'notice' in a superior registered title (LRA 2002, ss 32, 33(b), **2.31, 7.23**). However, any lease of seven years or less which is actually *required* to be registered under the LRA 2002 (**7.19**) is specifically excluded from this category of overriding interest (LRA 2002, Sch 3, para 1(a)–(b)).

— *Protection for legal leases only*   One important limitation on overriding status pursuant to LRA 2002, Sch 3, para 1 has been said to emerge from the technical connotation of the term 'grant'. Overriding status attaches only to *legal* leases (see *City Permanent Building Society v Miller* (1952)). *Equitable* terms of years are not covered, but may still be protected against disponees if the tenant is in 'actual occupation' of the land (LRA 2002, Sch 3, para 2, **7.23, 12.20**).

Unregistered interests of persons in actual occupation

12.18   Without doubt the most difficult and controversial of the categories of unregistered interest which 'override' registered dispositions is that which comprises the rights of occupiers of land (**2.33**). Subject to certain exceptions (**12.21**), LRA 2002, Sch 3, para 2 confirms the overriding status of

> an interest belonging at the time of the disposition to a person in actual occupation, so
> far as relating to land of which he is in actual occupation …

— *Rationale of overriding protection*   Consistently with the historic aim of much of our land law, LRA 2002, Sch 3, para 2 reflects the primacy traditionally accorded to factual possession of land: it contains an important recognition of the entitlements of those who happen to have a physical presence on the ground at the date of disposition of a registered estate (**3.3**). The class of overriding interests confirmed in Sch 3, para 2 replicates, in large part, the protection given earlier—by the famous LRA 1925, s 70(1)(g)—to 'the rights of every person in actual occupation of the land … '. This venerable statutory formula was quite clearly intended to benefit lay persons who hold unprotected interests in registered land (perhaps of limited scope and duration or created under informal trusts or estoppels), where the sheer fact of actual occupation by such persons would normally signal to prudent purchasers both the possible existence of unrecorded interests affecting the land and the necessity of further inquiry (see *Strand Securities Ltd v Caswell* (1965) per Lord Denning MR, **2.33**). In other words, the phenomenon of the overriding interest safeguards the rights of those who pardonably neglect to obtain more formal protection in the register in circumstances where potential disponees of the land should, in any event, be alerted to their entitlement.

— *Reaction against overriding protection*   In recent decades it came to be accepted that the overriding interests then protected by LRA 1925, s 70(1)(g) comprised an 'intermediate, or hybrid, class' of interest in registered land (see *Williams & Glyn's Bank Ltd v Boland* (1981) per Lord Wilberforce). Quite often minor interests which could and should have been entered in the register were still, in default of such protection, preserved as overriding interests—an outcome which some found 'disquieting' (see e.g. *Kling v Keston Properties Ltd* (1983) per Vinelott J). Concern was intensified partly because some overriding interests seemed in practice to be scarcely detectable, partly because they detracted from the reliability of the 'mirror image' of the register, and partly because overriding interests notoriously generated no right to any statutory indemnity for a disponee who was trapped by their existence (see *Re Chowood's Registered Land* (1933), **12.29**). In short, the overriding status accorded to the rights of actual occupiers appeared to confer an unmerited reward upon the negligent and to inflict an uncompensable hazard upon disponees of title. Pressure accordingly developed for a drastic curtailment of such over-solicitous and one-sided protection.

— *The compromise of the LRA 2002*   In the years immediately preceding the enactment of the LRA 2002, the Law Commission eventually suppressed its initial impulse—as expressed during the 1980s—to recommend the abolition of all sub-categories of overriding interest. Instead, a certain fluidity or possible overlap between the classes of registered land interest remains a feature of the 2002 Act. The Act retains the phenomenon of the overriding interest, even though this may sometimes duplicate the protection otherwise available to actual occupiers of land. The LRA 2002 nevertheless strives, in important respects, to cut back the parameters within which the rights of such occupiers can now impinge on disponees of registered land. There is an underlying expectation that, in time, potentially overriding entitlements will be increasingly drawn on to the Land Register by positive entry (**12.15**) and that the synchronicity of disposition and registration promised by e-conveyancing will finally eliminate the possibility that unregistered rights can exist at all in registered land (**12.5, 12.10–12.11**).

The formula of LRA 2002, Sch 3, para 2

12.19 At its most basic, the operation of LRA 2002, Sch 3, para 2 collapses into a virtually mathematical formula:

'Interest' + 'actual occupation' − 'inquiry' = Interest which 'overrides'

In other words, an interest in land, if coupled with actual occupation on the part of its owner, becomes an interest which (minus inquiry) 'overrides' registered dispositions of the land.

— *The constituent elements of the formula* On closer examination, Sch 3, para 2 reveals itself to be a complex verbal structure, which consists of a lead proposition (i.e. overriding status attaches to 'an interest belonging ... to a person in actual occupation'), qualified by a number of exceptional circumstances in which this overriding protection becomes lost or unavailable. Thus the interest of an actual occupier is declared to 'override' a registered disposition of a registered estate *except* in cases where:

- the actual occupier has unreasonably failed, on inquiry, to disclose his own entitlement (Sch 3, para 2(b), **12.22**); or
- the relevant occupation was *neither* reasonably discoverable by *nor* actually known to the disponee (Sch 3, para 2(c), **12.23**).

— *Occupation is merely a trigger* It is important to note that what 'overrides', in terms of Sch 3, para 2, is not necessarily any occupancy on the part of the claimant, but rather the *interest* which the occupier claims (see *Ferrishurst Ltd v Wallcite Ltd* (1999) per Robert Walker LJ). Actual occupation is merely the trigger which activates the statutory protection of *any* proprietary interest belonging to the occupier—whatever this interest may comprise. The rights which thus become overriding may sometimes be entirely unrelated to *occupation* of the land, e.g. an option to purchase land (see *Webb v Pollmount* (1966)).

— *Protection is confined to the area occupied* Schedule 3, para 2 makes it clear that overriding protection is accorded to an occupier's interest only in so far as it relates to 'land of which he is in actual occupation'. Thus an occupier of one flat in a block who holds an option to purchase the entire block can claim his option as an overriding interest only in respect of the flat actually occupied by him (thereby reversing the rule applied under the LRA 1925 in *Ferrishurst Ltd v Wallcite Ltd* (1999)).

We must analyse more carefully the three elements which are vital to the formula in Sch 3, para 2: the nature of the 'interest' protected; the role of 'inquiry'; and the meaning of 'actual occupation'.

The range of 'interests' protected by Sch 3, para 2

12.20 Despite its apparently wide ambit, LRA 2002, Sch 3, para 2 applies only to *proprietary* rights in land as already defined under the general law (see *National Provincial Bank Ltd v Ainsworth* (1965) per Lord Wilberforce, **2.10**). This qualification flows from the statutory requirement that the 'interest' which overrides a registered disposition must be one 'affecting the estate' of the disponor (LRA 2002, s 29(1)). It is generally assumed that Sch 3, para 2 is therefore confined to interests of a recognisably proprietary character, of which the following are examples:

- equitable leases and tenancies (**7.20–7.22**) (*Grace Rymer Investments Ltd v Waite* (1958));

- beneficial interests under a bare trust (**11.26**) (*Hodgson v Marks* (1971) (**12.23**; *Collings v Lee* (2001));

- beneficial interests under other trusts of land (**9.34**) (see *Williams & Glyn's Bank Ltd v Boland* (1981), **12.24**)—unless such interests are overreached by payment of capital money to no fewer than two persons as trustees (*City of London Building Society v Flegg* (1988) (**2.34, 11.30, 12.24**));

- estate contracts (**9.8**) (*Bridges v Mees* (1957)), including options to purchase a legal estate (**9.10**) (*Ferrishurst Ltd v Wallcite Ltd* (1999));

- rights of pre-emption (**9.11**) (*Kling v Keston Properties Ltd* (1983): see now LRA 2002, s 115(1));

- Rent Act entitlements of tenants (**14.27**) (*National Provincial Bank Ltd v Hastings Car Mart Ltd* (1964) per Lord Denning MR);

- tenants' rights to recoup repair costs from the landlord (*Lee-Parker v Izzett* (1971) (**14.6**));

- rights to rectification of a disposition on the ground of mistake (**9.40**) (*Blacklocks v JB Developments (Godalming) Ltd* (1982)).

— *Statutory clarification* The LRA 2002 takes the opportunity to declare, 'for the avoidance of doubt', that in relation to registered land two other kinds of right will henceforth be regarded as sufficiently proprietary to rank as potential overriding interests. This statutory clarification refers to an 'equity by estoppel' (**12.25**) and a 'mere equity' (e.g. to have a deed set aside on grounds of fraud or undue influence, **15.10**), both of which are now said to have effect 'from the time the equity arises as an interest capable of binding successors in title' (LRA 2002, s 116).

— *Overriding interests must be intrinsically enforceable* It is an unspoken precondition of overriding status that, at the date of the registrable disposition, the interest which is alleged to 'override' should be fully enforceable and undiminished by any estoppel or waiver (express or implied). The operation of Sch 3, para 2 cannot *enhance* or *alter* the intrinsic quality of the rights which comprise the overriding interest.

> *Paddington Building Society v Mendelsohn* (1985) S purchased a registered title in his own name, the purchase money being provided partly by S's mother, M, and partly through a mortgage loan advanced by PBS. M later claimed that her beneficial interest behind the implied trust, coupled with her actual occupation of the property, gave her an interest which overrode the charge executed by S in favour of PBS. The Court of Appeal held, however, that since M had both known and intended at the date of purchase that there was to be a charge in favour of PBS, the 'only possible intention to impute to the parties' was an intention that M's rights were to be subject to the rights of PBS. It followed that M, having impliedly conceded priority to PBS, no longer retained any interest adverse to PBS which was capable of overriding the legal charge. Under the general law, M was effectively estopped (**10.18**)—by virtue of her silent representation to PBS—from later advancing any claim to priority over PBS's security. (For the adoption of exactly the same approach in unregistered land, see *Bristol and West Building Society v Henning* (1985).) M's claim to 'override' would also now be disallowed on the grounds that PBS's charge was an *acquisition* mortgage (**12.24, 15.13**) and that M was not in 'actual occupation' *in advance of* the disposition of that charge (**12.23**).

— *Personal rights cannot 'override'* Schedule 3, para 2 provides no protection for merely personal rights such as those of a bare licensee (see *Strand Securities Ltd v Caswell* (1965)), since such rights can never, in the conventional view, bind third parties.

Occupiers' interests which cannot 'override'

12.21 Certain species of interest, even though belonging to persons in 'actual occupation' of land, are specifically excluded by statute from having overriding status (see, in the main, the amendments made by LRA 2002, s 133, Sch 11). In consequence, if such rights are to bind a disponee under a registered disposition, they must be protected by the entry of a 'notice' or (in one case) a 'restriction' in the disponor's register of title (**12.11, 7.8**). The rights which cannot 'override' include:

- home rights under the Family Law Act 1996 (FLA 1996, s 31(10)(b), **12.11–12.12**);
- equitable rights of beneficiaries under a strict settlement governed by the Settled Land Act 1925 (see LRA 2002, Sch 3, para 2(a), **9.43**);
- rights conferred by an access order made under the Access to Neighbouring Land Act 1992 (ANLA 1992, s 5(5), **8.20**);
- tenant's notice of purchase under the Leasehold Reform Act 1967 (LRA 1967, s 5(5), **7.40**);
- rights of collective enfranchisement under the Leasehold Reform, Housing and Urban Development Act 1993 (LRH & UDA 1993, s 97(1), **7.40**);
- secure tenant's 'preserved right to buy' under the Housing Act 1985 (HA 1985, Sch 9A, para 6(1), **7.40**);
- tenant's right to call for an 'overriding lease' under the Landlord and Tenant (Covenants) Act 1995 (L & T(C)A 1995, s 20(6), **14.21**).

No protection for undisclosed rights

12.22 The LRA 2002 also excludes from overriding protection the interest of any actual occupier 'of whom inquiry was made before the disposition and who failed to disclose the right when he could reasonably have been expected to do so' (LRA 2002, Sch 3, para 2(b)). In this respect, the statute strikes some sort of balance between the respective responsibilities of an intending disponee of a registered estate and any actual occupier of the land concerned (other than the disponor himself).

— *Onus on disponee* A burden is clearly placed on any intending disponee of registered land to ask any person in actual occupation 'what rights he or she has in the land' (*Winkworth v Edward Baron Development Co Ltd* (1986) per Nourse LJ).

This duty of inquiry is not satisfied by mere interrogation of the disponor himself; the question requires to be addressed to all other persons who happen to be in actual occupation of the land. As Russell LJ once observed, 'reliance on the untrue ipse dixit of the [disponor] will not suffice' (*Hodgson v Marks* (1971)). If an actual occupier (other than the disponor) discloses some existing entitlement, the intending disponee is then well placed to demand a waiver of that entitlement as a precondition of going ahead with the transaction. If, however, the disponee completes the disposition without such a waiver, the occupier's interest continues to 'override' in terms of the Act.

— *Onus on actual occupier* An occupier's failure to make reasonable disclosure operates, in effect, as a form of estoppel (see Law Com No 271 (2001), para 8.60). The priority accorded to an overriding interest is obviously unavailable to any person who, upon due inquiry, fails to reveal the existence of his rights (see e.g. *Holaw (470) Ltd v Stockton Estates Ltd* (2001)).

Meaning of 'actual occupation'

12.23 The term 'actual occupation' has a long history in the context of land registration statutes.

— *A plain factual situation* In the absence of any statutory definition, it was once thought that 'actual occupation' stood to be construed as a matter of sheer physical fact (see e.g. *Williams & Glyn's Bank Ltd v Boland* (1979) per Lord Denning MR, **3.3**). In the House of Lords in *Boland* (1981) Lord Wilberforce observed that the phrase comprised 'ordinary words of plain English' and Lord Scarman noted that this variety of overriding interest protection had 'substituted a plain factual situation for the uncertainties of notice, actual or constructive, as the determinant of an overriding interest'.

> *Hodgson v Marks* (1971) H, an elderly fee simple owner of a registered title, was persuaded by her lodger, E, to effect a voluntary transfer of the title into his name on the verbal understanding that H would remain the real owner. H and E continued to live together in the house at all material times—both before and after the transfer. E later dishonestly transferred the legal estate to M, without the knowledge or concurrence of H, and then promptly died. The Court of Appeal held that, before his transfer to M, E had held the registered estate on an implied (or bare) trust for H. The beneficial interest of H, as a person in 'actual occupation', therefore overrode the disposition to M (and also M's disposition of a legal charge to a building society). Neither M nor the chargee had addressed any sort of inquiry to H herself. In fact, it was not at all clear how *apparent* H's

actual presence on the land had been from the viewpoint of either M or his chargee—there was some evidence that H had been seen on one occasion walking up the garden path. Nevertheless the Court ruled that 'actual occupation' did not necessarily connote *apparent* or *obvious* occupation of the land—merely a physical presence on the part of persons other than the disponor.

— *Reasonably discoverable occupation*   More recent years saw a gathering tendency in the case law to construe 'actual occupation' as requiring to be not only 'actual' but also 'apparent' or 'patent', i.e. such as to 'put a person inspecting the land on notice that there was some person in occupation' (*Malory Enterprises Ltd v Cheshire Homes Ltd* (2002) at [81] per Arden LJ). Indeed, in *Ferrishurst Ltd v Wallcite Ltd* (1999) Robert Walker LJ indicated that the function of overriding interests in registered conveyancing is 'comparable to that of notice, actual, constructive or imputed, in unregistered conveyancing'.

• It became increasingly obvious that the internal logic of overriding interests demanded that relevant occupation be *reasonably discoverable*, since otherwise the process of inquiry and disclosure envisaged by the statute threatened to become futile, if not altogether impossible. The LRA 2002 reflects this more restrictive and more purposive understanding of the role played by 'actual occupation' in the ordering of registered land priorities. Accordingly, the 2002 Act provides that an actual occupier cannot claim that his interest 'overrides' in any circumstances where his occupation 'would not have been obvious on a reasonably careful inspection of the land at the time of the disposition' (LRA 2002, Sch 3, para 2(c)(i)). The only exception to this requirement of reasonable discoverability arises where the disponee of the land had 'actual knowledge' of the occupier's interest at the time of the disposition (LRA 2002, Sch 3, para 2(c)(ii)). The legislative intention is quite clearly to protect disponees for value where the fact of occupation is neither subjectively known to them nor readily ascertainable.

• The LRA 2002 also confirms a point which had been disputed in the earlier case law. Relevant occupation, for the purpose of any claim to overriding status, must exist both before and at the date of the registrable disposition (thus mirroring the conclusions reached by the House of Lords in *Abbey National Building Society v Cann* (1991), **12.24**). Again, this limitation (inherent in the wording of LRA 2002, s 29(1)–(2), Sch 3, para 2) is essential to the feasibility of meaningful or 'fruitful' inquiry in advance of the transaction in hand (see *Abbey National Building Society v Cann* (1991) per Lord Oliver of Aylmerton).

• The logic of reasonably detectable occupation as the trigger of overriding interest protection is reinforced by the provision that a reversionary lease granted to take effect in possession more than three months after the date of grant cannot 'override' if it has not yet taken effect in possession by the time of the registrable disposition to which it is adverse (LRA 2002, Sch 3, para 2(d)).

— *Intermittent or symbolic occupation* Pre-2002 case law indicated, for relevant purposes, that 'actual occupation' did not necessarily comprise continuous personal occupation. It is inevitable that a similar approach will be adopted under the LRA 2002. Obviously a pattern of substantial absence will prove fatal to any claim of 'actual occupation' (see e.g. *Stockholm Finance Ltd v Garden Holdings Inc* (1995), where a Saudi princess was deemed insufficiently resident in Hampstead Garden Suburb). 'Actual occupation' can, however, be regarded as subsisting so long as a *temporarily* absent occupier can point to some physical evidence or symbol of continued residence coupled with an intention to return to the property (see e.g. *Kling v Keston Properties Ltd* (1983) (parked car)).

> *Chhokar v Chhokar* (1984) H held the registered title in the matrimonial home on an implied trust for himself and W in equal shares. H secretly agreed to transfer that title at an undervalue to an acquaintance, P, H intending to rid himself of W whilst extracting for himself in cash much of the outstanding equity in the matrimonial home. H and P deliberately arranged that the transfer should occur while W was in hospital having a baby. Immediately after the transfer of title, H disappeared with the proceeds of the sale and W found herself and her young family locked out. Ewbank J and the Court of Appeal nevertheless regarded the continuing presence in the house of W's furniture and belongings as a notional or token occupation which was quite sufficient to constitute 'actual occupation'. W was, accordingly, held to have an overriding interest binding on P. (Ironically, W had managed to break back into her home and later become reconciled with H, with the consequence that P ended up owning a house which he could neither occupy nor sell and from which he could derive no rental income—although, as Cumming-Bruce LJ observed, this in itself provided no reason for the shedding of 'crocodile tears' on behalf of P).

— *Some persons cannot be said to be in 'actual occupation'* Not every individual human being who is present on relevant premises at a relevant time can automatically be described as 'a person in actual occupation' for purposes of Sch 3, para 2. Although the view is now discredited (see *Williams & Glyn's Bank Ltd v Boland* (1981), **12.24**), it used to be said that a wife's residence in the family home was submerged within—was a mere 'shadow' of—the occupation asserted by her husband (*Bird v Syme-Thomson* (1979) per Templeman J). This anachronism has faded away, but it remains clear, for instance, that a child of tender years—even if a trust beneficiary in possession—cannot nowadays claim to be a 'person in actual occupation', if only because such a child is almost certainly incapable of making any adequate response to inquiry by a disponee as contemplated by Sch 3, para 2. In *Hypo-Mortgage Services Ltd v Robinson* (1997), Nourse LJ regarded it as 'axiomatic that minor children of the legal owner are not in actual occupation . . . they are only there as shadows of occupation of their parent'. Any other view would leave lenders potentially defenceless, for their security 'could always be frustrated by simple devices' (i.e. the strategic conferment of a miniscule or token beneficial entitlement on a minor). In a variant of this 'shadow' theory in the corporate context, it has even been held that 'actual occupation' cannot be claimed by a company's managing director, since his presence on company premises is as an agent of the company and 'not on his own account' (see *Lloyd v Dugdale* (2002) at [49], **10.25, 12.14**).

— *Rights of non-resident landlords*   Under the LRA 1925 overriding status was also accorded to the rights of persons who were not in actual occupation, but were 'in receipt of the rents and profits' derived from the land (LRA 1925, s 70(1)(g), **12.15**). The receipt of rents and profits by a non-resident landlord was viewed as the symbolic equivalent of actual occupation. This over-generous protection has now been abandoned, with prospective effect, by the LRA 2002 (see, however, LRA 2002, s 134(2), Sch 3, para 2A as inserted by Sch 12, para 8).

Trust interests as overriding interests

12.24   Following the rationalisation of trust law brought about by TOLATA 1996, it is clear that the equitable interests (whether absolute, concurrent or successive) held by beneficiaries under a trust of land (**9.34–9.42**) come within the field of rights which, pursuant to the LRA 2002, can 'override' a disposition of a registered estate. The major qualification on this proposition arises in the context of a disposition of a registered title by two or more trustees in circumstances where the preconditions of statutory overreaching are satisfied (LPA 1925, ss 2(1)(ii), 27(2), **11.30**). Here, as the House of Lords made clear in *City of London Building Society v Flegg* (1988) (**2.34, 11.30**), the interests of trust beneficiaries are inescapably overreached by the disponee of the registered title, notwithstanding that the beneficiaries were, at the time of the disposition, persons 'in actual occupation' of the land.

— *The prevalence of latent trust interests*   In other contexts the status of trust interests as potentially overriding interests has taken on a highly controversial aspect precisely because such interests provide the focal point for a longstanding tension between claims to residential security in the family home and conflicting claims to commercial security for institutional lenders (**15.4**). With the conversion of Britain into a home-owning democracy and the 'diffusion of property and earning capacity' which facilitates cooperative purchases of the family home (see *Williams & Glyn's Bank Ltd v Boland* (1981) per Lord Wilberforce), there is nowadays a distinct possibility that the average family home is held on some implied trust for two or more family members (**9.36, 10.2**). Frequently the participants in informal family arrangements are unaware of their precise entitlements and even less conscious of their need for formal protection against third parties (e.g. chargees) who take dispositions for value of the family home. Sole ownership of the legal title by an unwitting trustee of land often conceals, quite innocently, the reality of an underlying beneficial co-ownership—especially, but not exclusively, where cultural traditions cause deference to, and therefore a vesting of title in, a male head of household.

— *The tension between family integrity and commercial security* It is in relation to such trusts of land that a tension, and indeed an ideological struggle, have emerged at the heart of land law doctrine—the conflict between the claims of residential protection and commercial security. Social concern to preserve the integrity of the family home does not always accord easily with the bank manager's understandable concern to recover moneys advanced on the security of this home. The friendly bank manager who magically provided large sums for the purchase of a family residence—or for the business purposes of one of the family members—may suddenly turn ogre at the first sign of financial adversity. The lender who had seemed at first so anxious to further Thatcher's home-owning democracy will adopt a quite different character when pursuing the hapless borrower on default. There is a clear conflict of interest between the need to streamline banking and building society practice and the need to ensure residential security and some degree of social justice for vulnerable family members. In this context it thus becomes critically important to determine whether beneficial rights behind a trust—almost inevitably unprotected by entry in the relevant register—take priority over those who lend money on the security of the family home. In the case of legal ownership by a sole trustee, the lender is *unable* to claim that he has statutorily overreached the latent equities (because capital money will have been paid to only *one* trustee (**11.30**)). Given that the trustee himself is utterly defenceless against the lender's claim for possession of the family home, much turns on whether other trust beneficiaries can assert an overriding interest which turns back the claim to possession or at least salvages some of the family's assets from the hands of the secured creditor.

— *The Boland ruling* Before the 1980s the courts simply used to deny that beneficial trust rights could *ever* constitute an overriding interest in land, thereby collapsing any claim for family protection against creditors (see now TOLATA 1996, s 3(1), **11.23**). An historic change of course was signalled by the Court of

Appeal and the House of Lords in *Williams & Glyn's Bank Ltd v Boland* (1981), but the courts have now spent much of the past two decades reversing the liberal effects of the *Boland* decision. This particular phase in the law of overriding interests has proved something of a rollercoaster ride.

> *Williams & Glyn's Bank Ltd v Boland* (1981) H was sole registered proprietor of a family home in which W asserted an equitable interest on the basis of her contribution towards the purchase. Some years after acquisition H charged his title to the bank by way of legal mortgage as security for a business loan. The bank made no inquiry of W before advancing the loan money; and W later claimed that she had had no contemporary knowledge of the creation of the mortgage charge. Although W had two protectable interests—her beneficial share under an implied trust (**10.5**) and her statutory rights of occupation in the matrimonial home (**12.11–12.12**)—neither had been protected on the register of H's title. When the bank, as chargee, asserted its right to possession against the defaulting H, Lord Denning MR led the Court of Appeal in holding that the courts 'should not give monied might priority over social justice'. This policy preference in favour of the integrity of the family home was affirmed on appeal. The House of Lords held that W's beneficial interest under the implied trust—but not her *statutory* rights of occupation (**12.21**)—constituted an overriding interest which had priority over the bank. Since W's beneficial entitlement included an equitable right to occupy, the bank's claim for possession was defeated.

— *The rhetoric of social justice* The *Boland* ruling was widely greeted as both a resounding victory for women's rights and a timely blow in the eye for overweening institutional lenders. At its roots, the decision was a statement of social ethics about the importance of providing security for the family—and in particular for the married woman—in occupation of the family home. In reallocating the risk of defects in the titles offered by borrowers, the courts effectively traded off protection for banks and other lenders against what was then perceived to be a higher social interest. Banks, said Lord Denning MR, were 'not entitled to throw ... families out into the street—simply to get the last penny of the husband's debt'. Long before the phrase became fashionable, the *Boland* ruling was, in its context, *politically correct*.

— *The retreat from Boland* Recent years have seen the submergence of the *Boland* perspective on property priorities under the overwhelmingly commercialist ethos which has prevailed since the late 1980s (see Gray and Gray, 'The Rhetoric of Realty', in J Getzler (ed.), *Rationalizing Property, Equity and Trusts: Essays in Honour of Edward Burn* (Butterworths, 2003), pp 250–3). The balance which shifted so dramatically with the *Boland* ruling has been readjusted in a relentless retreat from the high-point of judicial activism evident in that decision. The *Boland* approach has since been emasculated by a series of decisions in which the courts have sought to minimise the hazards for conveyancers and lenders posed by undisclosed co-ownership interests under a trust of land. Silently but surely the original *Boland* principle has now been eroded almost to the point of extinction, the courts gratefully seizing every opportunity to stress the inherent limits of the *Boland* decision.

Boland cannot now protect the residential interests of families in the context of any registered disposition where:

- a beneficial co-owner had contemporary knowledge of the relevant disposition (*Paddington Building Society v Mendelsohn* (1985) (estoppel by deemed consent, **12.20**));

- the disposition is executed by two or more joint legal owners (*City of London Building Society v Flegg* (1988) (comprehensive overreaching, **11.30**));

- the relevant disposition is an 'acquisition' mortgage (*Abbey National Building Society v Cann* (1991) (abolition of *scintilla temporis*, **15.13**));

- the family home is re-mortgaged (*Equity & Law Home Loans Ltd v Prestidge* (1992) (extended effect of deemed consent));

- the beneficial owner is a minor (*Hypo-Mortgage Services Ltd v Robinson* (1997) (**12.23**));

- the lender sues not for possession but for sale of the family home (*Bank of Baroda v Dhillon* (1998));

- the lender does not assert the mortgagee's power of sale (**15.21**), but instead seeks a court order for sale in order to enforce the borrower's personal covenant to repay, thereby recovering the loan money as a contractual debt from the borrower's share of the equity (see *Alliance and Leicester plc v Slayford* (2001), **11.35**).

In effect, in the context of dispositions by way of mortgage charge, the *Boland* principle now catches only *post-acquisition* mortgages of a registered estate held by a *sole* trustee of land, and then only where latent equities belong to *adult* persons who had *no contemporary knowledge* of the charge and are not otherwise estopped from asserting their rights against the mortgagee. Even if, notwithstanding all these qualifications, a beneficial trust interest is found to have overriding status under the LRA 2002, this may mean no more than that, on a sale of the land ordered at the discretion of the court, the value of that interest is paid out to the relevant beneficiary in advance of any payment to the secured lender (see *Bank of Baroda v Dhillon* (1998); *Alliance and Leicester plc v Slayford* (2001)).

Licences and estoppels as overriding interests

12.25 Although bare licences are clearly excluded from overriding status under the LRA 2002 (**4.2, 12.20**), predictable difficulty has always been generated by the question whether equitable licences, estoppel-based rights and contractual licences belonging to actual occupiers of land can 'override' a registered disposition. Partly because these sorts of entitlement hover uncertainly around the threshold of proprietary character (**4.11**), the law in this area has tended to find itself in a state of constant evolution. Some of the difficulties are now relieved by the LRA 2002.

— *Equitable licences and estoppel rights* When a court perfects or formalises an 'inchoate equity' of estoppel by the award of some conventional property right (e.g. the conferment of a fee simple or leasehold estate or easement or life interest, **10.27**), the subsequent binding impact of the court-ordered interest turns on wholly orthodox principles of land law (see G Battersby, 'Contractual and Estoppel Licences as Proprietary Interests in Land' [1991] *Conv* 36). More difficult has always been the question whether, in advance of any intervention by the court, the *inchoate* rights of an estoppel claimant or the *rights of irremovability* enjoyed by an equitable licensee already constitute, if coupled with 'actual occupation', an overriding interest pursuant to the LRA.

> **Problem**: If in *Pascoe v Turner* (1979) (**7.6, 10.24**) P had sold or charged his legal estate before the dispute over possession arose, would the disponee (by way of sale or mortgage) have taken subject to T's inchoate equity and thus become liable to have his title qualified by the grant of some court-ordered property interest to T?

Although the point was never free of controversy, the case law immediately preceding the enactment of the LRA 2002 reflected a gradual drift towards the view that estoppel rights and equitable licences have a sufficient proprietary content to cross the threshold of the potentially overriding interest (see e.g. *Habermann v Koehler (No 2)* (2000); *Lloyd v Dugdale* (2002), **10.25, 12.14**). A comparable trend was detectable in relation to unregistered land (see *Lloyds Bank plc v Carrick* (1996) per Morritt LJ; *Sledmore v Dalby* (1996) per Roch LJ, **12.42**). Moreover, Land Registry appeared increasingly willing to accept that inchoate rights based on estoppel could be protected by entry in the register.

• The LRA 2002 now puts the matter beyond all doubt by declaring that, in relation to registered land, an 'equity by estoppel' has effect 'from the time the equity arises as an interest capable of binding successors in title' (LRA 2002, s 116(a), **12.20**). It seems that an unperfected equity of estoppel, if coupled with actual occupation on the part of the claimant, can now 'override' by virtue of LRA 2002, s 29(1), (2)(a)(ii), Sch 3, para 2. (There is even a possibility that such an equity, albeit unaccompanied by actual occupation, may impose a constructive trust on a disponee who undertakes a 'new obligation, not otherwise existing, to give effect to the relevant incumbrance or prior interest' (*Lloyd v Dugdale* (2002) at [52(3)] per Sir Christopher Slade, **10.25, 12.14**).)

• There are also increasingly frequent suggestions, although the point remains open, that estoppel-based rights, by virtue of their close similarity to beneficial interests behind a constructive trust (**10.19**), are likewise overreachable where the capital money arising on a disposition of title is paid to *joint* proprietors of that title (see e.g. *Birmingham Midshires Mortgage Services Ltd v Sabherwal* (2000) per Robert Walker LJ; *Lloyd v Dugdale* (2002) at [55] per Sir Christopher Slade).

— *Contractual licences* Greater difficulty attaches to the contractual licence. There is longstanding House of Lords authority for the proposition that a con-tractual licence, being a personal right only, can never affect third parties (see *King v David Allen and Sons, Billposting, Ltd* (1916)). More recent decades have wit-nessed a remarkable movement aimed at the elevation to proprietary status of at least those forms of contractual licence which most closely replicate the function of recognised proprietary estates in land. Particularly in relation to long-term resi-dential licences, it has seemed not entirely bizarre to advocate that the rights of the contractual licensee should enjoy an extended impact upon disponees of the registered estate (**4.7, 12.25**). The most vigorous proponent of this view, Lord Denning MR, was quick to suggest that contractual occupation licences could 'override' transactions in registered land (see *National Provincial Bank Ltd v Hastings Car Mart Ltd* (1964)). Although the House of Lords did not, at the time, wholly rule out this possibility (see *National Provincial Bank Ltd v Ainsworth* (1965) per Lords Upjohn and Wilberforce), the tide of opinion has now turned resolutely against such a proposition. In *Ashburn Anstalt v Arnold* (1989), the Court of Appeal expressed an overwhelming preference for the dogma that the confer-ment of a contractual licence creates no *proprietary* interest (**4.11**). On the balance of authority it is extremely doubtful today that the rights of a contractual licensee can properly be described as an interest 'affecting the estate' within the terms of LRA 2002, s 29(1), so as to 'override' registered dispositions of land (see also *Habermann v Koehler* (1996) per Evans LJ; *Lloyd v Dugdale* (2002) at [52(4)] per Sir Christopher Slade).

• This conclusion, although consistent with widely accepted authority, exposes an awkward divergence of outcome when compared with the parallel context of estoppel-based licences. It is not easy to differentiate convincingly between a promise of rights based on consideration and a similar promise which induces detrimental reliance on the part of the promisee.

• There remains a possibility that, in very special circumstances, a disponee of land may be bound by a constructive trust to give effect to a contractual licence (**10.7, 10.10**). Such cases could arise where, for example, a third party has 'burdened his own title' with an independent conscientious obligation towards the contractual licensee (see *Bahr v Nicolay (No 2)* (1988) per Brennan J). Thus a contractual licence may well bind the transferee of a title if the transfer was induced, at lower than market value, by the transferee's agreement to take title expressly subject to the licence (see *Ashburn Anstalt v Arnold* (1989) per Fox LJ). Here—completely outside the sphere of operation of any overriding interest—a constructive trust would arise in consequence of the court's exercise of an *in personam* jurisdiction to counteract unconscionable conduct (see also *Binions v Evans* (1972), **12.42**). In this rather different context, more emphasis is placed on the conscientiousness of the third party than on the intrinsic nature of the rights which it is sought to enforce against him (see *Melbury Road Properties 1995 Ltd v Kreidi* (1999), **10.10**).

Legal easements and profits *à prendre*

12.26 In the years preceding the enactment of the LRA 2002 it came to be widely believed that disponees of registered land were unacceptably disadvantaged by the wide range of easements and profits deemed capable of overriding status pursuant to the LRA 1925. Such rights included, for instance, a highly controversial category of *equitable* easements which were 'openly exercised and enjoyed' over registered land (see LRR 1925, r 258; *Celsteel Ltd v Alton House Holdings Ltd* (1986)). Such rights, although they could have been the subject of an entry in the register of the servient land, remained overriding, for want of such protection, as against unwitting purchasers of that land. The LRA 2002 therefore cuts back quite severely the kinds of easement or profit which can henceforth 'override' registered dispositions under the Act.

— *No overriding status for equitable easements and profits* Overriding interest protection for newly created easements and profits is strictly confined by the LRA 2002 to *legal* rights alone (LRA 2002, Sch 3, para 3(1)). The objective of the 2002 Act is to ensure that, following the statutory commencement, the express disposition of *any* new easement or profit out of registered land must, if the disposition is to 'operate at law', be completed by registration (LRA 2002, s 27(1), (2)(d), **8.16**). If duly completed by registration, the relevant disposition creates rights which appear quite visibly on the register and cannot therefore be overriding.

If not so completed, the disposition creates merely *equitable* rights for the disponee which, under the altered regime of the LRA 2002, are explicitly excluded from the category of easements and profits which can 'override' later dispositions of the servient land.

— *Overriding status for legal easements and profits created by implication or prescription* The net effect of the LRA 2002 is, at least prospectively, to confine the overriding interest category to rights which arise by prescription (**8.21**) or by implied grant or reservation (**8.20, 8.23**). Even in relation to these kinds of entitlement, a disponee of a registered estate for value is bound (see LRA 2002, Sch 3, para 3) *only if*, at the time of the disposition, the right in question:

- was patent, i.e. 'obvious on a reasonably careful inspection of the land'; or
- was 'within the actual knowledge' of the disponee; or
- had been exercised within the period of one year immediately preceding the disposition; or
- was registered under the Commons Registration Act 1965 (in which case, the right was readily discoverable by the disponee).

— *Existing easements and profits* Any easement or profit which was an overriding interest immediately before the commencement of LRA 2002, Sch 3, automatically retains its overriding status under the new Act (LRA 2002, s 134(2), Sch 12, para 9(1)–(2)). Furthermore, for a transitional period of three years until 13 October 2006, *all* legal easements and profits were declared to 'override' registered dispositions irrespective of whether they were reasonable discoverable or actually known to the relevant disponee (LRA 2002, s 134(2), Sch 12, para 9(3)).

Local land charges

12.27 Local land charges relate to such matters as local government impositions and restrictions in respect of listed buildings, planning and environmental controls, tree preservation orders, and the abatement of statutory nuisances (**8.32**). Such charges 'override' registered dispositions of title (LRA 2002, Sch 3, para 6).

Alterations of the register

12.28 The Land Register requires constant updating in order to reflect new transactions in land and to ensure the removal of redundant entries. It is also the case that, regardless of the class of title awarded, no register of title is ever bullet-proof (**7.7, 7.20**). Indeed, one of the merits of land registration is that technical defects in an unregistered title can be cleared off either at the point of first registration or at some later date. Registered titles are examined and classified by the Chief Land Registrar at the time of first registration (**2.23, 12.33**). Applicants with a good holding title are normally awarded an *absolute title* (**7.7, 7.20**). Errors are nevertheless bound to occur in view of the sheer volume of titles being registered (**2.11**), although Land Registry currently prides itself on processing 98.8 per cent of all registrations free of any error (Land Registry, *Annual Report and Accounts 2005/6* (July 2006), pp 13, 23). Title plans may be ever so slightly awry; pre-registration deeds and subsequent dispositionary documents may themselves contain inaccuracies; undisclosed interests may suddenly emerge as affecting the land; initial assessments of the reliability of the title offered for first registration may turn out, in the event, to have been misjudged. It follows that, whilst an absolute title is the most secure form of title available, even a proprietor with absolute title is liable to have his register or title plan altered to his prejudice in certain kinds of circumstance. All forms of alteration of the register are now governed by LRA 2002, s 65, Sch 4.

— *Powers of alteration* Wide powers are conferred on both the court and the registrar to bring about the 'alteration' of any register of title in order to correct a 'mistake', to bring the register 'up to date', and to give effect to any estate, right or interest excepted from the effect of registration (**12.9**) (LRA 2002, Sch 4, paras 2(1), 5). The registrar has an additional power to remove superfluous entries (LRA 2002, Sch 4, para 5(d)).

— *Remote electronic alteration of the register* It is also envisaged that, within the foreseeable future, a power to initiate alterations of the register (e.g. to remove discharged mortgages or other spent entries) will also be enjoyed by practitioners who are so authorised under the sorts of 'network access agreement' which will underpin the process of electronic conveyancing (see LRA 2002, Sch 5, para 1(2)(b); Law Com No 271 (2001), para 10.23, **12.3**).

'Rectification' as a sub-species of 'alteration'

12.29 The LRA 2002 uses the generic term 'alteration' to describe *any* change which is made to a register of title, thus reserving the narrower term 'rectification' for those alterations of a register which involve 'the correction of a mistake' and which 'prejudicially affect' the title of a registered proprietor (LRA 2002, Sch 4, para 1).

Rectification and *overriding interests* are therefore, in one sense, rather similar in that they both represent ways in which reliance on a register of title may ultimately prove to be misplaced (see Law Com No 158 (1987), paras 1.4, 2.10).

— *Link between rectification and indemnity* Registered titles are backed by a state guarantee that an indemnity will be paid from Land Registry funds to any person who suffers loss by reason of 'rectification' of the register (**12.30**). The availability of such an indemnity represents the practical realisation of the *insurance principle* which classically underlies all schemes of state-regulated registration of title (**6.2**). It remains the case, however, that an 'alteration' of the register which causes no genuine loss does not rank as a 'rectification' of the register and cannot give rise to any indemnity. Thus, for example, an alteration which gives visible effect to an overriding interest merely confirms a subsisting, albeit previously unrecorded, entitlement. Such alteration inflicts no true derogation from the rights of the registered proprietor and does not qualify him for any indemnity (see *Re Chowood's Registered Land* (1933), **12.18**).

— *Restriction on rectification against registered proprietors in possession* In the face of the ever present possibility of rectification, the LRA 2002 confirms one significant protection for certain kinds of registered proprietor. Save in cases of consent, no rectification may normally be made 'affecting the title of the proprietor of a registered estate in land ... in relation to land in his possession' (see LRA 2002, Sch 4, paras 3(2), 6(2)). This important restriction on rectification helps to preserve the accuracy and reliability of the Land Register. It also recognises that a third party's loss of a land interest by reason of the withholding of rectification is likely to be much less grievous (particularly if compensated by payment of an indemnity) than the loss otherwise suffered by the proprietor who has been in possession of a unique piece of land (see *Kingsalton Ltd v Thames Water Developments Ltd* (2002) at [40] per Arden LJ, [53] per Sir Christopher Slade). Pursuant to this principle of 'qualified indefeasibility', the protection of the proprietor in possession against the prejudicial correction of mistakes in the register gives way in only two instances, i.e. where:

- he has by fraud or lack of proper care caused or substantially contributed to the mistake in question, or
- it would for any other reason be unjust for the alteration not to be made.

For present purposes, land is taken to be 'in the possession of the proprietor' if it is 'physically in his possession' or in the possession of his tenant, mortgagee or licensee or of a beneficiary of a trust of which he is trustee (LRA 2002, s 131(1)–(2)). Where a registered proprietor is *not* in possession in any relevant sense, the existence of grounds for rectification must, in other than 'exceptional circumstances', lead to rectification (LRA 2002, Sch 4, paras 3(3), 6(3)).

— *Rectification has prospective effect only* The impact of rectification on a registered proprietor may be to divest him of some or all of the land comprised within his title or to subject his estate to burdens which were not previously entered on the register, although he may sometimes qualify for an indemnity in respect of loss suffered thereby. Rectification of the register may also affect derivative interests such as leases, easements and covenants which have already been created out of a registered estate. Rectification can, however, change the priority of such interests only 'for the future', i.e. prospectively from the date of the rectification (LRA 2002, Sch 4, para 8).

Indemnity

12.30   It is integral to the insurance principle underlying title registration that any person who innocently suffers loss by reason of the operation of the Land Register should receive compensation. Land Registry acts, in effect, as a statutory insurer of titles in England and Wales and is currently estimated to guarantee land assets worth in the order of £2.5 trillion (Land Registry Press Notice LRP03/03, issued 4 February 2003). The payment of indemnity is regulated by LRA 2002, s 103, Sch 8.

— *Entitlement to indemnity* An entitlement to indemnity arises in all cases of 'rectification' (as more narrowly defined by LRA 2002, Sch 4, para 1, Sch 8, para 11(2), **12.29**) and also in various cases of 'mistake' or failure by Land Registry. 'Rectification' necessarily connotes a prejudicial alteration of the register, with the result that any person who 'suffers loss' by reason of the rectification has a statutory right to be indemnified (LRA 2002, Sch 8, para 1(1)(a)). The notion of 'loss' is, in this context, accorded an extended definition. For instance, the 2002 Act provides that the proprietor of a registered estate or charge who, in good faith, claims under a disposition which was in fact *forged* is to be regarded, when the register is rectified against him, as having suffered a relevant loss and as therefore deserving of indemnity (see LRA 2002, Sch 8, para 1(2)(b)). This is so even though, in strict terms, a rectification which merely confirms the outcome of a null disposition inflicts no technical loss.

— *Restrictions on indemnity* Indemnity is not, however, payable (see LRA 2002, Sch 8, para 5) on account of any loss suffered by a claimant

- wholly or partly as a result of his own fraud, or
- wholly as a result of his own lack of proper care.

The 2002 Act nevertheless recognises a principle of contributory negligence, in that any indemnity paid may be reduced 'to such extent as is fair having regard to [the claimant's] share in the responsibility for the loss' (LRA 2002, Sch 8, para

5(2)). The registrar also has powers to recover amounts paid by way of indemnity from any person who turns out to have caused or substantially contributed to the loss by his fraud (LRA 2002, Sch 8, para 10).

Dealings with unregistered estates

12.31 Even when (as is today increasingly the case) a dealing with title to an unregistered estate triggers a requirement of *substantive registration* of that estate at Land Registry (**7.7, 12.5**), the pre-registration rights and liabilities of the purchaser under the dealing must be determined largely by reference to the principles which regulate *unregistered land*. It is the operation of these principles which settles the priority of the estates, interests and rights which have accumulated around the unregistered title and which need to be recorded on a first registration of title in the Land Register. The importance of the rules governing unregistered titles is nowadays heavily diminished by the steadily continuing translation of titles on to the Land Register, but the law of unregistered land retains a significance which we must explore more fully. (Once again, a bird's eye view of unregistered land was provided in Chapter 2 (**2.36–2.44**).)

The historic priority rules governing unregistered estates

12.32 The law of unregistered title derives, of course, from much earlier origins than the regime of registered title and operates, accordingly, on the basis of certain axioms which lie deeply embedded in the sedimentary layers of English land law. These axioms still remain exposed to view at some vantage-points across the terrain of modern property law, thus continuing to provide a solution for a few contemporary problems of land law priority. In other places, however, the historic axioms of unregistered land have been overlaid by different strata deposited by the later action of legislative change, although even here the erosive activity of judge-made law has occasionally stripped back the more recent strata to reveal the bed-rock of original principle.

The *fundamental axioms* which underlie the law of unregistered land turn on the all-important distinction between *legal* and *equitable* rights. As we have seen in earlier chapters, this distinction is fixed by statute (**2.28**) coupled with the rider that the *legal* quality of many rights depends upon their creation or conveyance by the formal means of *deed* (**2.30, 7.6**).

The historic axioms at the base of unregistered land law are the following:

- *legal* rights bind *all persons* in the world (irrespective of notice);
- *equitable* rights bind all persons except a *bona fide purchaser of a legal estate for value who has no notice* of such equitable rights.

Whilst the first of these axioms still determines the outcome of many priority problems in unregistered land, the second axiom has been largely superseded by limited systems of *registration* of rights (**12.35**) and by the statutory device of *overreaching*, which transmutes certain equitable rights in land into an equivalent money form (**11.30**). In consequence the '*bona fide purchaser* rule' now plays only a residual and highly marginal role in determining questions of priority when other methods have failed or are inapplicable (**12.42**).

Effect of dispositions of an unregistered estate

12.33 The principles which regulate unregistered land priorities have the cumulative effect that a purchaser (including a mortgagee) of a legal estate in unregistered land takes title *subject to*:

- any other *pre-existing legal estates* (**12.34**);
- any registered *land charges* (**12.35**) or *local land charges* (**12.27**);
- any *unoverreached equitable interests* of which he has *notice* (actual, constructive or imputed) (**12.40–12.42**); and
- (in the case of leasehold land) certain *covenants and obligations* arising under the lease (**14.20–14.24**).

— *First registration at Land Registry*   Most forms of dealing with an unregistered estate (whether freehold or leasehold) nowadays trigger a requirement of first registration of that estate at Land Registry (**7.7, 12.5**). At this point the Chief Land Registrar collates, in the newly opened register of title, as complete a list as possible of those interests which appear, from his examination of the unregistered title, to benefit or burden the estate in question (see LRR 2003, rr 29–30).

- *Entry of benefits and burdens* The registrar enters in the register the benefit of any appurtenant rights enjoyed over other land (including other land which is as yet unregistered) (LRA 2002, ss 13–14; LRR 2003, r 33). Likewise the registrar enters charges which burden the newly registered estate, together with a 'notice' in respect of any registrable lease, easement, profit *à prendre* or other burden which appears to affect the registered estate (LRR 2003, rr 22, 35, 37). The first registered proprietor takes his title with the benefits and burdens thus entered in the register (LRA 2002, ss 11–12, **7.7, 7.20**).

• *Unregistered interests which 'override' first registration* The first registered proprietor also takes his title subject to certain interests which are specified by statute to 'override' first registration and which, for one reason or another, have escaped the dragnet of entry in the register (see LRA 2002, ss 11(4)(b), 12(4)(c)). These interests, listed in LRA 2002, Sch 1, resemble fairly closely the interests which 'override' subsequent registered dispositions of the registered estate (see LRA 2002, Sch 3, **12.15**), and thus include various categories of short leases, occupiers' rights and legal easements and profits *à prendre*. However, the list of overriding interests contained in Sch 1 is more broadly defined than that in Sch 3, in that the first registered proprietor takes subject to Sch 1 overriding interests *without* reference to any question of prior 'inquiry' made by him as to such rights. The first registered proprietor is, at the date of his registration, already bound by the interests which 'override' and cannot be saved therefrom by *any* amount of inquiry (see Law Com No 271 (2001), paras 8.3–8.4). The number of interests which 'override' first registration will, of course, be minimised by the fact that the registrar has power, of his own motion, to enter potentially overriding interests on the register by 'notice' (LRA 2002, s 37(1); LRR 2003, r 89, **12.15**). For this purpose, moreover, applicants for first registration now have a statutory obligation to disclose known unregistered interests which could 'override' and which are capable of entry by 'notice' (LRA 2002, s 71(a); LRR 2003, r 28). In these ways, it is hoped, most interests which pre-exist at first registration will be disclosed to the registrar and thus find their way on to the register (see Law Com No 271 (2001), para 8.25).

• *Equitable easements and profits* existing before the disposition which gives rise to first registration still require to have been protected against the disponee by registration of a Class D(iii) land charge (**12.36**) and will not be elevated to overriding interests on first registration. If the registrar finds them so protected, he will enter them in the first registered proprietor's newly opened register.

Legal rights bind the world

12.34 The force of the rule which governs legal rights in unregistered land is straightforward. As a matter of fundamental principle, if B owns a *legal* right in or over land belonging to A, B's right binds all persons *irrespective* of their knowledge or notice (**2.38**). In consequence B's legal entitlement binds:

• P, a subsequent purchaser of an estate in A's land;

- S, a squatter on that land (see *Re Nisbet and Potts' Contract* (1906), **6.6**); and

- X, any other person.

It matters not whether B's right is that of legal lease (**7.18**), easement (**8.24**), mortgage (**8.31**), or rentcharge (**8.35**). His right automatically binds all comers (except in certain tightly limited cases of mortgage or charge (**8.31–8.32**)). The axiomatic nature of this result works for both efficiency and clarity. The owner of legal rights knows that his position is secure notwithstanding future transfers of the land; likewise the purchaser is made aware in general that he takes his disposition subject to any legal rights which belong to others.

Registration of land charges

12.35 Prior to 1926 the binding force of equitable rights turned very largely on the hazardous operation of the *equitable doctrine of notice* (**2.43**). This *bona fide purchaser rule*, whilst motivated by a principle of fairness or equity, created some uncertainty for both the equitable owner and any later purchaser of the land. In particular, neither party could confidently predict the scope of *constructive notice* (**1.26, 12.40**), which, depending on its presence or absence, would determine whether a purchaser was bound by, or took free of, pre-existing equitable interests. In consequence the 1925 legislation introduced a limited regime of registration of rights—even in the context of 'unregistered' land—whose objective is to harness the publicity inherent in registration as an inescapable medium of notice to the world of the existence of certain kinds of entitlement.

— *The subject matter of registration* The Land Charges Act 1925 (now consolidated in the Land Charges Act 1972) provided a scheme of public registration not merely for certain categories of interest (as *land charges*), but also for other matters, actions and documents relating to land (**12.38**). The matters eligible for registration under the LCA 1925/1972 are generally the kinds of interest which are appropriate for long-term enforcement as real or specific burdens on the land concerned, irrespective of the identity of the current estate owner (see *Birmingham Midshires Mortgage Services Ltd v Sabherwal* (2000) per Robert Walker LJ, **2.34, 11.30**). In the main, therefore, registered land charges comprise entitlements suitable for enduring through changes of ownership of the land. This registration of isolated kinds of interest under the Land Charges Act must, however, be firmly distinguished from the much more comprehensive scheme of *registration of title to estates* which occurs pursuant to the Land Registration Act 2002 (**2.31, 6.2**). Land charges affecting unregistered land are recorded in the *Register of Land Charges*; registrations of title are recorded in the *Land Register*.

— *The process of registration of land charges* At the heart of the LCA 1972 is the idea that owners of statutorily designated categories of interest (almost always *equitable* in quality) should be afforded the facility of registering their rights against the *name* of the estate owner whose estate is intended to be affected (LCA 1972, s 3(1)). Thus, whereas registration of title under the LRA 2002 involves the substantive registration of an estate identified by *title number* (**2.31, 6.2**), it is the *names* of estate owners which provide the 'fixed point of reference' in the scheme of land charge registration (see *Standard Property Investment plc v British Plastics Federation* (1985) per Walton J). Registrations are effected against *names* and searches of the register are likewise conducted against *names* (LCA 1972, ss 3(1), 10(1)). The definitive version of the estate owner's name is deemed to be that contained in his title deeds, with the result that a careless registration against some informal or inaccurate version of this name may be ineffective to bind purchasers (see e.g. *Diligent Finance Co Ltd v Alleyne* (1971)).

— *Effect of registration* Registration of a land charge is 'deemed to constitute actual notice ... of the fact of such registration, to all persons and for all purposes connected with the land affected' (LPA 1925, s 198(1)). Thus, for the kinds of interest specified by the LCA 1972, registration as a land charge adapts the pre-1926 doctrine of notice by rendering notice of registered rights utterly *inescapable*. As Richard Epstein once observed, a registration system is 'routine and ministerial—a notable social triumph of the humdrum ... the problem of notice disappears in all but the most unusual case' (73 *Cornell L Rev* 906 at 909 (1987–8)).

— *Effect of non-registration* The consequence of non-registration of a land charge depends on the precise category of land charge concerned, but the general result of failure to register is the draconian outcome that the registrable interest becomes *void* against most kinds of purchaser. In this context a 'purchaser' is defined as some person (including a mortgagee or lessee) who gives 'valuable consideration' (LCA 1972, s 17(1)).

- Land charges of Classes A, B, C(i), (ii) and (iii), and F become void as against a purchaser of *any* interest in the land, whether legal or equitable (LCA 1972, s 4(2), (5), (8)).

- Land charges of Classes C(iv) and D become void as against *only* a purchaser of a *legal estate for money or money's worth* (LCA 1972, s 4(6): see e.g. *Lloyds Bank plc v Carrick* (1996), **9.8**).

— *The general irrelevance of traditional notice* The consequence of non-registration of rights is strict. It is generally irrelevant that the purchaser has knowledge, from some other source, of the unprotected land charge: he still takes free (LPA 1925, s 199(1)(i)). In this sense the LCA marks a 'shift from a moral to an a-moral basis' for the determination of land law priorities (see HWR Wade [1956] *CLJ* 216 at 227). Only in rare circumstances does the purchaser for value lose his immunity, although precisely this may occur in cases where the purchaser is liable to some constructive trust or estoppel (see e.g. *Old & Campbell Ltd v Liverpool Victoria Friendly Society* (1982); *ER Ives Investment Ltd v High* (1967), **10.21, 12.42**).

> *Hollington Bros Ltd v Rhodes* (1951) L contracted to grant a lease to T, who failed to register his estate contract against L as a land charge of Class C(iv). L later conveyed his legal estate to P, expressly 'subject to' T's contractual lease. Despite his actual express knowledge of T's rights, P gave T notice to quit the premises, thereby effectively forcing T to negotiate a new lease for a higher sum. Harman J nevertheless held that T's estate contract was void as against P for non-registration and ruled moreover that it was quite irrelevant that P had actual knowledge of the existence of T's tenancy. (It is arguable that today P would be subjected to a *constructive trust* to give effect to T's unprotected rights: compare e.g. *Lyus v Prowsa Developments Ltd* (1982), **12.14**.)

— *The exception for fraud* The mechanical principle of registration still recognises the overarching nature of the general prohibition of *fraud* (**10.1, 12.14**), but the notion of fraud is fairly restrictively construed.

> *Midland Bank Trust Co Ltd v Green* (1981) W, a fee simple owner of unregistered land, granted his son, G, an option to purchase the land for £22,500. G failed to register this estate contract as a Class C(iv) land charge. Six years later, in consequence of some family discord, W sought to avoid G's option. Discovering that it had never been registered, W speedily conveyed the legal estate to his wife, E, for a consideration of £500. The House of Lords held that G's option over the land (now worth £400,000) was void against E as a 'purchaser for money or money's worth ... of a legal estate in the land' (see LCA 1972, s 4(6), **2.41**). In the Court of Appeal, Lord Denning MR had regarded the conspiratorial actions of W and E as a form of fraud sufficient to vitiate the transfer to E ('Fraud unravels everything'). The House of Lords held, however, that a requirement of good faith purchase under the LCA would introduce 'the necessity of enquiring into the purchaser's motives and state of mind'—a re-emergence of the very doctrine of notice which the 1925 legislation had sought to avoid. Accordingly, Lord Wilberforce took the view that 'it is not fraud to take advantage of legal rights, the existence of which may be taken to be known to both parties' (see *Re Monolithic Building Co* (1915)). The LCA provided 'a simple and effective protection for persons in [G's] position, viz by registration'. Since the payment of £500 was not merely nominal consideration, G's option became unenforceable against E.

The outcome in *Midland Bank Trust Co Ltd v Green* was later described by the Law Commission as not an 'acceptable' resolution of the problem in hand (Law Com No 158 (1987), para 4.15). Interestingly, the result would have been different in registered land since G, being 'in actual occupation' of the land, would have had an overriding interest binding upon his mother's estate (LRA 2002, s 29(1), (2)(a)(ii), Sch 3, para 2, **2.33**, **12.18**). It is also noteworthy that the asperity of the House of Lords' decision was mitigated by the fact that G's estate was held, in different proceedings, to be entitled to damages in respect of the negligence of G's solicitor in failing to register G's land charge (see *Midland Bank Trust Co Ltd v Hett, Stubbs and Kemp (A Firm)* (1979)).

Categories of registrable land charge

12.36 The categories of land charges registrable under the LCA 1972 fall into six Classes (A–F) (see LCA 1972, s 2), of which the most important are Classes C, D, and F.

— *Class A* comprises various kinds of land charge which derive ultimately from statute and which arise only on the making of some statutory application (e.g. a landlord's right to compensation under Agricultural Holdings Act 1986, s 86).

— *Class B* comprises various charges directly imposed by statute (e.g. the Legal Services Commission's charge on land recovered or preserved for a legally assisted client (Access to Justice Act 1999, s 10(7), **8.32**)).

— *Class C* charges fall under four heads:

- *Class C(i)* puisne mortgages (**8.31**);
- *Class C(ii)* limited owner's charges under a strict settlement;
- *Class C(iii)* general equitable charges (**9.18**, **9.20**); and
- *Class C(iv)* estate contracts (**9.8**, **12.4**), including options to purchase (**9.10**), contracts to grant a lease and equitable leases (**9.9**).

— *Class D* charges comprise:

- *Class D(i)* Inland Revenue charges for unpaid tax;
- *Class D(ii)* restrictive covenants entered into on or after 1 January 1926 and arising otherwise than between a lessor and a lessee (**9.24**); and
- *Class D(iii)* equitable easements created or arising on or after 1 January 1926 (**9.15**) (but see *ER Ives Investment Ltd v High* (1967), **10.21**, **12.42**).

— *Class E* comprises rare pre-1926 annuities.

— *Class F* includes statutory rights of occupation in the matrimonial home (under the Matrimonial Homes Acts 1967 and 1983) or 'home rights' conferred by the Family Law Act 1996 (**12.11–12.12**).

Search of the Register of Land Charges

12.37 It is usual for the purchaser of unregistered land to search the Register of Land Charges during the interim between *contract* and *conveyance*. The purchaser may request an official search of the computerised register against any estate owners whose names appear in the vendor's title deeds (LCA 1972, s 10(1)), the purchaser being entitled to require that the vendor deduce title from a 'good root of title' at least 15 years old (LPA 1969, s 23, **2.24**).

— *Conclusive effect of official search* The official certificate of search is statutorily deemed to be conclusive in favour of the purchaser (LCA 1972, s 10(4)), with the consequence that a mistakenly issued *clear* certificate of search *destroys* any subsisting but undisclosed entry on the register, leaving the relevant incumbrancer to a negligence remedy against the registry (cf. *Ministry of Housing and Local Government v Sharp* (1970)). In the extremely rare case that the purchaser is affected by a charge registered behind a 'good root of title' (i.e. registered against an estate owner whose name he could not have discovered), the purchaser is bound by the charge (see LPA 1925, s 198(1), **12.35**), but entitled to compensation from public funds (LPA 1925, s 25(1)).

— *Consequence of discovering a registered charge* A purchaser who, after exchange of contracts but before completion, discovers on the issued search result the existence of a registered charge not revealed by the contract of sale is entitled to have the contract *rescinded* (LPA 1969, s 24(1)–(2)).

Other registers maintained under the LCA 1972

12.38 The LCA 1972 provides a number of additional registers, which include the following (LCA 1972, ss 5–7).

— *The register of pending actions* records the existence of certain kinds of litigation or disputed claim affecting a title to unregistered land. The register of pending actions may be used for the registration of bankruptcy petitions and for the entry of any pending land action (or *lis pendens*) covering any of a range of matters from disputes over rights based on trust or estoppel to a claim of entitlement to an easement.

— *The register of writs and orders affecting land* provides a means of recording the existence of such matters as charging orders (**9.21**), orders appointing a receiver (**15.19**), and any bankruptcy order.

The 'bona fide purchaser rule' (or equitable doctrine of notice)

12.39 As noted already, the second major axiom of pre-1926 land law, the equitable doctrine of notice, has been substantially displaced by the device of overreaching and by mechanisms of registration (**12.32**). It was indeed a large part of the strategy of the property legislation of 1925 to eliminate the uncertainty generated by the notice doctrine (**12.35**). The notice doctrine applies today only to unregistered land (see *Holaw (470) Ltd v Stockton Estates Ltd* (2001) per Neuberger J) and its role is severely limited. There are nevertheless circumstances in which the impact of equitable interests upon a purchaser of unregistered land can be determined only by a residual application of the 'bona fide purchaser rule' (**2.43**).

Content of the bona fide purchaser rule

12.40 Under the equitable doctrine of notice, equitable rights bind all persons *other than* a bona fide purchaser of a legal estate for value without notice (actual, constructive or imputed). The doctrine effectively hammers out the circumstances in which equity is prepared to fasten upon the conscience of the purchaser. In order to establish his immunity from unoverreached and non-registrable equitable interests, the purchaser must demonstrate the following:

— *Bona fides* The purchaser must show that his absence of notice was 'genuine and honest' (*Midland Bank Trust Co Ltd v Green* (1981) per Lord Wilberforce). Little ever turns upon this element.

— *Purchase of a legal estate* The purchaser must take a *legal* estate in the land concerned, although a lender who takes a charge 'by way of legal mortgage' is regarded, for this purpose, as having 'the same protection' as if a legal estate had been created in his favour (LPA 1925, s 87(1), **8.31**). A purchaser who takes only an equitable interest in the land is, in principle, subject to all pre-existing equitable interests irrespective of notice: where the equities are equal, the first in time prevails.

— *Purchase for value* In its strictest common law sense the term 'purchaser' merely signifies one who takes property by reason of the *act* of another (as distinct from one whose title arises by *operation of law*). In this sense the term 'purchaser' includes a *donee* (who takes by an act of gift), but not a *squatter* (whose title derives from the effluxion of time). The equitable doctrine of notice therefore operates only in favour of a purchaser *for value*.

— *Absence of notice*　At the heart of the doctrine of notice is the idea that only in the absence of notice can it truly be said that the conscience of the purchaser is unaffected by adverse pre-existing rights. Notice may be actual, constructive or imputed.

• *Actual notice* refers to matters of which the purchaser was consciously aware at the date of his purchase, i.e. matters which were 'within his own knowledge' (LPA 1925, s 199(1)(ii)(a)).

• *Constructive notice* relates to matters of which the purchaser would have been consciously aware if he had taken reasonable care to inspect both land and title (LPA 1925, s 199(1)(ii)(a)). The courts are generally reluctant to extend the ambit of constructive notice to any large degree (see the classic observation of Farwell J in *Hunt v Luck* (1901)). An inspection of the land may, however, disclose the presence of persons other than the vendor, in which case the purchaser may be fixed with constructive notice of such rights as these persons may have in the property.

> **Example 1**: The presence of a tenant provides constructive notice of the tenant's lease-hold interest and of the terms of his lease, but not necessarily of the rights of any person to whom the tenant may be paying rent (*Hunt v Luck* (1901)).
>
> **Example 2**: A purchaser is likely to be bound by the equitable rights of members of the vendor's family (and perhaps even of others) who are in joint occupation of the property with the vendor.

• *Imputed notice is* attributed to a purchaser in virtue of knowledge possessed actually or constructively by some agent (e.g. his solicitor) (see LPA 1925, s 199(1)(ii)(b)).

Destructive effect of purchase for value without notice

12.41　Purchase for value without notice not only frees the purchaser from adverse equitable interests; it defeats *for ever* the equitable rights involved. These rights cannot revive even as against a subsequent purchaser who *does* have notice of the fact that equitable rights once existed (*Wilkes v Spooner* (1911)).

Surviving applications of the bona fide purchaser rule

12.42 Only relatively few examples remain of equitable rights in unregistered land which are neither *overreached* (**11.30**) nor *capable of registration as land charges* (**12.35**), but that some instances persist was confirmed by the House of Lords in *Shiloh Spinners Ltd v Harding* (1973) (**2.43**) (see also *Birmingham Midshires Mortgage Services Ltd v Sabherwal* (2000) per Robert Walker LJ). In these circumstances, problems of priority over a purchaser must be resolved by reference to the traditional doctrine of notice. The bona fide purchaser rule thus applies to the following cases:

— *Equitable interests of beneficiaries under a trust of land* where legal title has been conveyed by a sole land trustee.

> *Kingsnorth Finance Co Ltd v Tizard* (1986) H held an unregistered legal title on an implied trust for himself and his estranged wife, W. H and two children of the family lived in the house and W visited the home twice a day in order to cook meals for the children. H secretly charged the legal title to KF, a finance company, and then disappeared to America with one of the children. (H had arranged the usual mortgagee's inspection and valuation for a Sunday afternoon for the purpose of suppressing all signs of W's intermittent occupation.) Not having paid the mortgage moneys to at least two trustees, KF could not claim to have overreached W's beneficial interest; nor did W's interest constitute a registrable land charge pursuant to the LCA 1972 (**12.36**). The doctrine of notice was therefore applicable to W's beneficial entitlement. In rejecting KF's action for possession, Judge Finlay QC held that the obvious presence of children in the house should have alerted KF, as mortgagee, to the need to make further inquiry as to the possible rights of a wife. Failure to make such inquiry, coupled with the unsatisfactory form of inspection, fixed KF with constructive notice of W's equitable interest under the trust.

— *Inchoate rights founded on proprietary estoppel*, certainly where the purchaser has actual notice of the circumstances giving rise to the equity (see e.g. *ER Ives Investment Ltd v High* (1967) (**10.21**); *Lloyds Bank plc v Carrick* (1996) (**9.8**)) and probably also where the purchaser has merely constructive notice (see *Bristol & West Building Society v Henning* (1985)).

> *ER Ives Investment Ltd v High* (1967) H and X were neighbouring freehold owners of unregistered land. X began to construct on his property a block of flats the foundations of which marginally encroached upon H's land. H waived his right to complain of

trespass on being granted, in writing (but not by deed), a right of way for his car across X's yard. H never registered his equitable easement against X as a Class D(iii) land charge (**12.36**), but subsequently built a garage on his own land which was accessible only across X's yard. H also contributed part of the cost of resurfacing this yard. X later sold and conveyed the servient estate to Y (who had full knowledge of the facts), and Y in turn conveyed that land to I, expressly subject to H's right of way. The Court of Appeal held H's rights (notwithstanding their non-registration) to be enforceable against I. The majority (Danckwerts and Winn LJJ) agreed that H's equitable easement was statutorily void for non-registration, but ruled that I was *estopped* from pleading non-registration in view of the known history of acquiescence in H's expenditure on the land (**10.21**). Whilst H's rights as derived from the original informal grant had been rendered ineffective by reason of their non-registration, his rights as generated by subsequent circumstances of estoppel were not registrable at all under the Land Charges Act, but comprised an 'equity' binding all subsequent purchasers who took the land with actual notice.

— *Restrictive covenants* between freeholders created *prior to 1926* (**9.32**).

— *Equitable easements* created *prior to 1926* (**9.15**).

— *Restrictive covenants* between lessor and lessee which relate, not to the user of the land demised, but to the user of other adjoining land retained by the lessor (see *Dartstone v Cleveland Petroleum Co Ltd* (1969)).

— *Equitable rights of entry* (e.g. under an equitable lease) (*Shiloh Spinners Ltd v Harding* (1973), **14.11**).

For reasons discussed earlier in the parallel context of registered title (**12.25**), it seems unlikely that the equitable doctrine of notice can ever apply to make *contractual licences* binding on third parties. Such licences are neither overreachable nor registrable as land charges. Despite suggestions that contractual licences are subject to the bona fide purchaser rule, it is probable that third parties are affected by such licences only in circumstances which generate liability to a constructive trust (see *Ashburn Anstalt v Arnold* (1989), **10.7, 10.10, 12.25**).

Binions v Evans (1972) In a written agreement E was allowed by T, the trustees of the estate for which her late husband had worked, to reside rent-free for the remainder of her life in a cottage on that estate (in which she had already lived for some 50 years). T later conveyed the property to B expressly subject to the rights enjoyed by E and at a reduced price in view of E's occupation. The Court of Appeal rejected a possession action brought by B against E (then 79 years of age). Lord Denning MR somewhat tenuously construed E's rights as based on a contractual licence. He took the view that B, having purchased expressly 'subject to' E's contractual rights, were bound by a constructive trust to give effect to E's licence for life. The constructive trust arose 'for the simple reason that it would be utterly inequitable for [B] to turn [E] out contrary to the stipulation subject to which [B] took the premises'. (Megaw and Stephenson LJJ preferred, albeit with no great conviction, to analyse E's rights in terms of the Settled Land Act 1925 (**9.43**).)

FURTHER READING

Gray and Gray, *Elements of Land Law* (4th edn, OUP, 2005), ch 12.

Relevant sections of this work and other land law textbooks may be supplemented with:

Battersby, Graham 'Contractual and Estoppel Licences as Proprietary Interests in Land' [1991] *Conv* 36.

Battersby, Graham 'Informal Transactions in Land, Estoppel and Registration' (1995) 58 *MLR* 637.

Conaglen, Matthew 'Mortgagee Powers Rhetoric' (2006) 69(4) *MLR* 583.

Dixon, Martin 'The Reform of Property Law and the Land Registration Act 2002: A Risk Assessment' [2003] *Conv* 136.

Howell, Jean 'Land Law in an E-Conveyancing World' [2006] *Conv* 553.

McFarlane, Ben 'Constructive Trusts Arising on a Receipt of Property *Sub Conditione*' (2004) 120 *LQR* 667.

Perry, Raymond 'E-Conveyancing: Problems Ahead?' [2003] *Conv* 215.

SELF-TEST QUESTIONS

1 Does the scheme for the protection of rights in *registered* land achieve a better balance between the owner of those rights and the purchaser of land than the corresponding *unregistered* land scheme?

2 Arthur, who owned Bleak House in fee simple, used to live there with his sister Brenda. A year ago he agreed in writing to let part of Bleak House to Clarissa for five years at a rent of £3,000 per annum. He also executed a deed of trust giving Brenda a half-share in the property. Clarissa moved in and has paid rent ever since. Arthur has just sold the house to Patrick with vacant possession. When Patrick inspected the house before his purchase, he assumed that Brenda and Clarissa were relatives staying temporarily with Arthur. Arthur has now disappeared with the proceeds of sale, but Brenda and Clarissa both refuse to vacate the property. Advise Patrick on the assumption that title to Bleak House is (i) *registered*, and (ii) *unregistered*.

13

Freehold covenants and environmental regulation

SUMMARY

The beneficial regulation of the landowner's local environment is achieved through an interplay of privately bargained covenants between freeholders and state-imposed controls on land use. This chapter examines the balance between the regimes of private and public regulation and describes the way in which private covenants relating to land use can be made to affect future owners.

An obligational view of landholding

13.1 Much of this book has analysed 'property' in land from the perspective of either *socially constituted fact* or *abstractly defined entitlement*. Yet, in terms of the future facing our readers, perhaps the most significant and durable image of 'property' will emerge as the perception that all 'property' in land involves some form of *delegated responsibility* for land as *a community resource* (**2.19**). Land may, of course, be turned to advantage in many overlapping ways: it can be occupied or exploited commercially; it can be a vehicle of investment, consumption, endowment or exchange; it can simply be an object of aesthetic or recreational appreciation. These elements of utility all require to be held in balance. An *obligational* analysis of 'property' in land focuses on the way in which the precise mix of utilities in land is ultimately governed by socially conditioned restraints which seek to maximise the efficient utilisation, in the general public interest, of even privately owned land resources. One of the controversial, yet vital, challenges for the future is the question whether, in some radical sense, all land resources are held on trust for the public good (see Gray, 'Equitable Property' (1994) 47(2) *Current Legal Problems* 157).

The historic view

13.2 The view that modern estate ownership is permeated by community- or even neighbour-oriented expectations of responsible land use stands in stark contrast to the historic analysis of 'property' in land. With their ringing assertions of 'property absolutism' (**2.1**), the great judges of the Victorian era acknowledged no overriding duty on the part of the private landowner to safeguard wider interests in the exploitation of his land. The estate owner remained free to utilise 'his' land selfishly with little or no regard for community concerns or environmental sensitivities. 'Every man', declared Lord Cranworth amidst an age of unrestrained industrial expansion, '[has] a right to use his own land by building on it as he thinks most to his interest' (*Tapling v Jones* (1865)). The common law mandated no duty of cooperation between neighbours. The common law recognised, for instance, no such right as a prescriptive (or any other) easement to preserve a good view (see *Hunter v Canary Wharf Ltd* (1997)). Beauty of prospect could be secured only by means of some bargained restriction under which the owner of neighbouring land covenanted not to develop his land so as to obstruct the vista (**2.5, 8.11**). Equally clearly, concerns of personal privacy conceded priority to the competing merits of economic development (see Gray, 'Property in Thin Air' [1991] *CLJ* 252 at 261–3). The householder could no more complain about being overlooked by the factory next door (*Tapling v Jones* (1865)) than he could object to the loss of amenity inflicted by the recently constructed road or railway which ran past his house (*Duke of Buccleuch v Metropolitan Board of Works* (1870); *Re Penny and the South Eastern Railway Co* (1857)). In the competition of life, each estate owner took no prisoners; his autonomy was almost unqualified; the 'bundle of rights' inherent in ownership remained virtually intact.

> *Bradford Corpn v Pickles* (1895) P abstracted underground water on his own land which would otherwise have fed the water supply needed to support the rapidly developing domestic and industrial requirements of the city of Bradford. Bradford Corporation alleged that P was motivated simply by a malicious desire to inflict injury upon the city and its inhabitants. Lord Macnaghten expressed, with admirable clarity, the viewpoint of the property absolutist, holding P entitled 'to force the corporation to buy him out at a price satisfactory to himself ... Why should he, he may think, without fee or reward, keep his land as a storeroom for a commodity which the corporation dispense, probably not gratuitously, to the inhabitants of Bradford?' Lord Macnaghten noted that P

'prefers his own interests to the public good. He may be churlish, selfish, and grasping. His conduct may seem shocking to a moral philosopher.' The House of Lords nevertheless refused to restrain P's conduct by injunction.

The modern perspective

13.3 It is significant that virtually every single exercise of the landowner's prerogative described in the last paragraph would today be rendered impossible by the pervasive impact of public and private regimes directed towards the socially beneficial use of land resources (see *South Bucks DC v Porter* [2003] at [10] per Lord Bingham of Cornhill). Planning control (if not also privately bargained covenants) would prohibit the construction of factories in residential areas (see Town and Country Planning Act 1990, Part III, **13.23**), control the location of roads and railways (see Town and Country Planning (General Development Procedure) Order 1995, art 15) and secure the preservation of scenic landscape views (see *Gilbert v Spoor* (1983)). The right to abstract water is nowadays strictly controlled by a statutory licensing scheme (see Water Resources Act 1991, s 24(1); Environment Act 1995, s 2(1)(a)(i); Water Act 2003, s 1(1)). Whether or not we realise it, the 'property absolutism' of a bygone era has been largely replaced by a 'property relativism' which holds that the estate owner's 'bundle of rights' contains no entitlement ruthlessly to exploit land resources regardless of the communal good. Indeed, at the heart of contemporary environmental law lies the proposition that the estate owner's 'bundle of rights' is intrinsically delimited by social or community-oriented obligations of a *positive* nature (**2.4**). According to this line of argument, the owner's 'bundle of rights' is inherently restricted by various sorts of communitarian concern for environmental integrity (**13.22–13.24**).

The reallocation of 'sticks' in the 'property' bundle

13.4 This relativist view of 'property' is entirely consistent with the major theme of modern property theory. We saw long ago that 'property' in land correlates with varying degrees of socially approved power exercisable over the resource of realty and that distinct quantums of 'property' in the same land can be distributed simultaneously amongst a number of persons and entities (including the state) (**2.3–2.5**). The amount of 'property' which we can assert either in relation to our own land or in relation to somebody else's is determined by a range of factors, some of which stem from the law of torts (and particularly the law of nuisance and negligence) and some from within land law itself. We noted, for instance, the way in which the law of easements (**2.5, 8.3**) can effect a marginal shift in the 'property' implicit in a landholding (as where one estate owner grants a right of way or drainage or support to his neighbour). In the present chapter, however, we shall analyse the means by which the quantum of 'property' enjoyed in land may be varied either through *privately negotiated covenant* or by *direct state intervention*. In effect, modern environmental regulation involves the voluntary reallocation of various 'sticks' within the 'property' bundle (as in the case of private covenants relating to land use) or even the more profound recognition that the state has always held a 'retained stick in the bundle of rights' (see J.E. Cribbet, 'Concepts in Transition: The Search for a New Definition of Property' (1986) *U Ill L Rev* 1 at 26).

The balance between private and public regulation of land use

13.5 It is clear that regimes of private ordering may substantially alter the balance of advantage associated with landholding—one theory being that private contracting enables land use preferences to be targeted accurately by the very persons best positioned to assess the environmental utility required in specific contexts. Thus one neighbour may covenant with another to safeguard a quiet residential enclave from intrusive or disruptive development; groups of neighbours may covenant with each other to preserve the civilised ambience or aesthetic character of their surrounding area. Increasingly, however, the *private* regulation of land use has been supplemented or superseded by *public* regulation imposed by agencies of the state. These agencies exercise a vast range of controls relating to urban planning, the built environment, the conservation of natural resources and the preservation of the local and national heritage. The local authority planning officer can make or break your aspirations for a garage or 'granny annexe' in your back garden; he or she will tell you exactly how you can and cannot renovate your listed building. A local authority official can demand that you maintain your house and garden to a certain standard and ultimately force its sale if you do not (see HA 1985, ss 193(3), 300(3), Sch 10, para 7(3); EPA 1990, ss 81(4), 81A(4); T& CPA 1990, ss 215–19, **8.32**). In the most dramatic manifestation of state power, your land can be compulsorily purchased by the state in order to further some supervening community purpose such as the construction of a new highway or the regeneration of an urban area or, rather more controversially perhaps, the profitable operation of a privatised utility company (**13.24**).

The residual quality of modern estate ownership

13.6 So pervasive is the intervention of the state that, in many ways, the 'property' of estate ownership has been stripped back to a bare residue of socially permissible power. 'Property' in land can be seen, quite realistically, as the distribution of state-approved usufructs (or mere rights of user), each exercisable subject to an overarching criterion of publicly defined responsibility (**2.19**). (As we move slowly in the direction of European harmonisation, it is interesting to compare the prescription in Article 14(2) of the German *Grundgesetz* that 'property imposes duties. Its use should also serve the welfare of the community'.) In effect, 'property' in land is constituted simply by those publicly endorsed user-forms which the state, at its discretion, allows individuals to enjoy consistently with large strategies of community policy and social design. 'Property' in land means no more and no less than what the state actually allows you to do with 'your' land (**2.1**). Although European Union law purports in no way to 'prejudice the rules in Member States governing the system of property ownership' (Treaty of Rome, Article 222), it is inevitable that our understanding of property will be increasingly coloured by the emphatic insistence of the European Court of Justice that the right to property is not 'an absolute prerogative in Community law' (*O'Dwyer v Council of the European Union* (1995)). In common with all fundamental rights recognised by the Court, rights of property, far from being 'absolute', must be 'considered in relation to their social function' (*Wachauf v Federal Republic of Germany* (1989)).

This analysis is far removed from the classic liberal perception of 'property' as a self-interested claim of unfettered power: 'property' in land has become little more than a highly qualified, ultimately defeasible privilege for the citizen. The modern state retains an eminent domain or overriding 'property' in all land—perhaps the most significant present-day emanation of the crown's radical title (**1.22**)—thus providing the state with a dominating stake in the determination of all land use priorities. Eminent domain has been aptly described as 'the proprietary aspect of sovereignty' (*Minister of State for the Army v Dalziel* (1944) per Rich J), and even the regulation of land use by privately bargained covenant is, in truth, only a *delegated* form of an overriding social control exercisable by, and adjudicated through, courts and tribunals acting as guardians of the public interest (**13.20**).

The contextual nature of 'property'

13.7 It follows, on this view, that the deep structure of 'property' is not absolute, autonomous and oppositional. It is, instead, delimited by a strong sense of community-directed obligation, and is rooted in a contextual network of mutual constraint and social accommodation mediated by the agencies of the state. One American scholar, Eric Freyfogle, has spoken of 'a new property jurisprudence of human interdependence ... Autonomous, secure property rights have largely given way to use entitlements that are interconnected and relative' (E.T. Freyfogle, 'Context and Accommodation in Modern Property Law' 41 *Stan L Rev* 1529 at 1530–1 (1988–9)). 'Property' becomes not a summation of individualised power over scarce resources, but an allocative mechanism for promoting the efficient or ecologically prudent utilisation of such resources. So analysed, this community-oriented approach to 'property' in land plays a quite obviously pivotal role in the advancement of our overall environmental welfare, although in the process it raises peculiar tensions of its own.

> *Tesco Stores Ltd v Secretary of State for the Environment* (1995) Tesco applied for planning permission (**13.23**) to construct a food superstore outside Oxford. The House of Lords, although upholding the refusal of permission in the instant case, indicated that the considerations properly regarded as 'material' to the outcome of this application nevertheless included the fact that Tesco had offered £6.6 million to fund communal off-site benefits (such as a new link road which would help to relieve the local traffic congestion likely to be exacerbated by the proposed development). Thus a willingness on the part of a developer to defray the external costs imposed on the community by a proposed development of land (or even to offer a positive 'planning gain' to the local planning authority) can properly be one of the conditions on which that authority may grant permission for the development. Yet the House of Lords was keenly alert to the possibility that the offer of an unrelated planning gain is tantamount to 'an attempt to buy planning permission' (per Lord Keith of Kinkel) and that the coupling of such offers with planning applications might lead to the 'auction' of planning permissions to the highest bidder (per Lord Hoffmann).

Although public planning processes have now taken over much of the function of privately contracted arrangements, there still remains an important role for private and quasi-private governance of land use. It is increasingly recognised that existing planning control cannot always concern itself with the detailed issues dealt with in private covenants. Private covenants can be particularly significant in regulating the immediately local environment of neighbours as, for instance, where parties contract for the maintenance and repair of a boundary fence or agree to adhere to a vernacular style of construction or specific pattern of density in any future development. More generally, however, it is painfully apparent nowadays that privately bargained covenants frequently operate as the longstop guardian of wider, community-spirited, conservationist concerns, protecting a range of environmental amenities which the individual citizen can no longer rely on to be provided by his or her local planning authority (see Gray and Gray (1999) 3 *Edinburgh Law Rev*

229 at 232–5). We are even beginning to observe the invocation of other private law devices—such as the trust—for the purpose of ensuring the conservation of areas of special character (see e.g. the creation of the Covent Garden Area Trust described in R. Cooper and T. O'Donovan, 'Covent Garden: A Model for Protection of Special Character?' [1998] *JPL* 1110). The modern protection of environmental quality indeed involves a combination of private and public law controls which it is the purpose of this chapter to explore.

The function of private covenants relating to land

13.8 Our first concern is with private covenants relating to *freehold land* and the way in which the rights and obligations generated by such covenants can be made to 'run with' that land. (Covenants arising between *landlord* and *tenant* are governed by different principles which are the subject of discussion in the next chapter of this book (**14.20–14.25**).)

In the context of real property a 'covenant' is an undertaking contained in a deed (**7.6**) in which one party (the 'covenantor') promises another party (the 'covenantee') that he *will* or *will not* engage in some specified activity in relation to a defined area of land. Such covenants play an enormously important role in facilitating the efficient use of land resources: it rarely makes sense for the estate owner of Redacre to buy out the entire freehold or leasehold estate in the adjoining land, Greenacre, simply in order to secure, on behalf of Redacre, some future advantage over that land (see, however, *Re Buchanan-Wollaston's Conveyance* (1939), **11.34**). Covenants thus provide a means of binding adjacent landowners to a common plan for the user of their respective lands and often operate effectively as a form of private legislation affecting successive generations of owners. Schemes of enforceable covenants tend, moreover, to enhance the value of land on the open market, increasing the commercial attraction of particular sites or areas through the guarantee that certain advantages or local amenities or desirable neighbourhood characteristics will be preserved indefinitely.

Covenants may be either *positive* or *negative* in quality, and different rules apply to each.

— *Positive* covenants impose on the covenantor an obligation to perform some specified act or activity (e.g. an obligation to maintain a boundary fence or wall in good repair).

— *Negative* covenants prohibit specified kinds of activity or development on the covenantor's land for the benefit of land retained by the covenantee (e.g. by precluding the covenantor from using his own land for trade or business or by restricting the nature or density of any future development of that land).

The boundary between contract and property

13.9 The essential historic limitation on the utility of the freehold covenant has always been the fact that, by virtue of the rule of privity, contracts confer enforceable benefits and burdens upon only the initially contracting parties, the covenantor and the covenantee. In this respect the law of covenants has simply given effect to a profound common law principle governing the impact of contractual commitments (see *Rhone v Stephens* (1994) per Lord Templeman, **13.12**). Yet the function of covenants as devices for the long-term regulation of land use would be severely impeded if covenants *never* affected successors in title of the original covenantor and covenantee (**9.25**). Accordingly, although the approach of the law has always been cautious lest durable burdens sterilise land titles (**2.18, 9.27**), developments in English law over the centuries have conferred certain long-term consequences upon the ordering of land use by private covenant. An inevitable by-product of this evolution of principle has been to blur the boundary between contract and property, by conceding the conventional attributes of *proprietary* character (**2.12, 9.26**) to obligations of purely *contractual* derivation.

The transmission to third parties of covenanted benefits and burdens is simultaneously governed in English law by rules of *common law* and *equitable* origin. These must be examined in turn.

Covenants at law

13.10 The common law rules relating to covenants are of extremely ancient origin. It has been clear from early times (see *The Prior's Case* (1368)) that a covenant relating to land may be enforced at law even though the *covenantor* owns no estate of any kind in land. (This principle underpins the modern liability of the surety who, without owning any estate in land, guarantees the due performance of the leasehold obligations of a tenant (**14.21**).) In practice, however, most covenantors do own an estate in neighbouring land, and the common law requires, in any event, that the *covenantee* must hold some estate in land to which the benefit of an enforceable covenant may accrue. Difficulty inevitably attaches to the question whether the benefit and burden of the covenant can be transmitted to *third parties*.

Transmission at law of the benefit of a freehold covenant

13.11 The benefit of a covenant which is not exclusively personal may always be assigned in writing as a chose in action (LPA 1925, s 136), but doubt or complexity has affected other methods of transmission. It used to be thought, for instance, that the famously elusive wording of LPA 1925, s 56(1) might circumvent the rule of contractual privity in the context of freehold covenants relating to land (see e.g. *Smith and Snipes Hall Farm Ltd v River Douglas Catchment Board* (1949) per Denning LJ). Section 56(1) appears to provide that a person 'may take ... the benefit of any ... covenant or agreement over or respecting land or other property, although he may not be named as a party to the conveyance or other instrument'. It is now clearly established, however, that this provision merely enables the benefit of a covenant to be claimed by a party who is designated as a covenantee, not by specific *name*, but under some *generic description* (e.g. as one of the 'owners for the time being' of adjoining land) (see *Beswick v Beswick* (1968); *Amsprop Trading Ltd v Harris Distribution Ltd* (1997)). The transmission of the unassigned benefit of a freehold covenant is therefore left, at common law, to be governed by the more exacting conditions confirmed by the House of Lords in *P & A Swift Investments v Combined English Stores Group plc* (1989) (**14.22**):

- The covenant must *touch and concern* the land of the covenantee (i.e. must have been entered into for the benefit of the covenantee's *land* and not merely for his personal benefit).
- The covenantee must have held a *legal* estate in the land benefited.
- The transferee of the land must also take a *legal* estate in the land benefited, although this need not be the *same* legal estate as that of the original covenantee.
- It must have been *intended* that the benefit should *run with* the land owned by the covenantee at the date of the covenant. (This is, in reality, the *most* important of all the conditions controlling the transmission of the benefit.)

> *Smith and Snipes Hall Farm Ltd v River Douglas Catchment Board* (1949) D covenanted with X to repair and maintain the floodbanks of a river. X later sold his dominant tenement to P1, who in turn leased the land to P2. The Court of Appeal allowed an action for damages for breach of covenant on the suit of both P1 (the owner in fee simple) and P2 (who held a mere term of years). The Court held the covenant enforceable on behalf of not only the original covenantee but all successors in title and all persons deriving a legal title from such successors. Here, for the purpose of enforcement, it was sufficient

merely that subsequent claimants of the covenanted benefit held *some* legal estate in the relevant land, it being clear that the covenant *touched and concerned* X's land and had been *intended* to run with that land.

— *Statutory reinforcement* This common law basis for the transmissibility of the benefit of covenants is reinforced by the little cited provision contained in LPA 1925, s 78(1) (**13.15**) and has been taken even further by the novel terms of the Contracts (Rights of Third Parties) Act 1999. In relation to contracts (including, by implication, covenants) entered into on or after 11 May 2000, the 1999 Act provides that a person who is not a party to a contract may 'in his own right' enforce a term of that contract if *either* the contract expressly provides that he may *or* the term in question 'purports to confer a benefit upon him' (unless, on a proper construction of the contract, it 'appears that the parties did not intend the term to be enforceable by the third party') (C(ROTP)A 1999, s 1(1)–(2)). The 1999 Act appears to allow the benefit of a covenant to be claimed by wide categories of non-party to the covenant even if such persons are included in the covenant merely by way of generic description as 'successors in title' of the covenantee (C(ROTP)A 1999, s 1(3)). There is, moreover, no requirement under the 1999 Act that enforceable covenants should relate to or 'touch and concern' the covenantee's land or even that the non-party enforcing the covenant should be entitled to any sort of estate in land at all.

— *Rights under a 'commonhold' scheme* As will shortly be seen (**13.12**), one of the essential features of the regime of freehold ownership of 'commonhold land' is the idea that rights or burdens which are attached to the freehold proprietorship of a commonhold unit (by a 'commonhold community statement' (**7.41**)) are automatically transmitted to the new unit-holder on any transfer of the registered freehold estate in that commonhold unit (Commonhold and Leasehold Reform Act 2002, s 16(1)). To this extent, the device of commonhold ownership introduces a new and important means by which the benefit of certain obligations undertaken by freeholders can run with the fee simple estate into the hands of successors in title.

Transmission at law of the burden of a freehold covenant

13.12 One of the scarcely credible features of the modern law of freehold covenants is that there exists no relatively straightforward means by which the burden of a *positive* covenant can be transmitted to third parties. (As we have already seen **(9.26)**, it was left to the jurisdiction of equity in the mid-19th century to devise a means by which the burden of *negative* covenants could be enforced against successors of the original covenantor.) It is an inveterate principle of English law that only the *benefit*, and not the *burden*, of a positive covenant may run with the land. As Lord Templeman observed in *Rhone v Stephens* (1994), it is a truth 'imparted at an elementary stage to every student of the law of real property that positive covenants affecting freehold land are not directly enforceable except against the original covenantor', a principle recognised classically in *Austerberry v Oldham Corpn* (1885). And, of course, it is futile to establish that a particular claimant is fully entitled to the *benefit* of a freehold covenant if the intended target of his enforcement action is someone who is not subject to the *burden* of the covenant concerned. This general incapacity to affect a covenantor's successors in title has proved remarkably inconvenient in a crowded urban world where many features of orderly co-existence depend upon the ready enforceability of positive burdens of maintenance, repair and support undertaken by one's neighbours (see e.g. *Xpress Print Pte Ltd v Monocrafts Pte Ltd* (2000)). It is simply a bizarre fact that, outside the original contractual nexus, most positive freehold covenants are today unenforceable at common law—a conclusion 'whose discovery has shocked more than one eminent judge unversed in the subtleties of English real property law' (see *Rhone v Stephens* (1993) per Nourse LJ).

— *Pressure for reform* Although originally motivated by a policy that land should remain substantially unfettered for future generations, the rule in *Austerberry v Oldham Corpn* now retains few fervent supporters. Commentators and law reformers have frequently urged that the law be amended to allow positive burdens to run with the land (see e.g. Law Com No 127 (1984), paras 4.21–4.22, 5.2), but the challenge has certainly not been taken up by the judiciary.

> *Rhone v Stephens* (1994) S's predecessor covenanted with R's predecessor to keep in repair a roof which projected from S's house over the cottage now owned by R. The House of Lords held this covenant to be *unenforceable* by R against S when later a lack of repair caused water leakage into R's cottage. Lord Templeman held that to enforce a positive covenant in these circumstances 'would be to enforce a personal obligation against a person who has not covenanted', a conclusion contrary to more than a century of 'clear and accepted law'. The House of Lords accordingly declined the invitation to indulge in judicial legislation aimed at overturning a now widely criticised legal rule.

— *Indirect mechanisms of enforcement* In the absence of any judicial relaxation of the rule of contractual privity, there exist several indirect (and not wholly successful) means by which it may be sought to render the burdens of positive freehold covenants binding on successors of the covenantor:

- A covenantee may require that the covenantor should compel his own successor, *first*, to enter into a *direct covenant* with the covenantee (or *his* successors) in the same terms as the initial positive covenant and, *second*, to promise to impose the same obligation of direct covenant in turn on his successor. This method of transmitting the burden is unwieldy and hazardous.

- Positive covenants in certain long leases may be rendered enforceable against the covenantor's successors where the *leasehold is statutorily enlarged into a freehold* (see LPA 1925, s 153(8) (**7.38**); LRA 1967, s 8(3) (**7.40**)).

- The doctrine of *'mutual benefit and burden'* sometimes fastens the *burden* of positive covenants upon a successor who wishes to assert the benefit of a covenanted obligation (see *Halsall v Brizell* (1957)), but the courts tend to construe this rule of reciprocity extremely narrowly (see e.g. *Rhone v Stephens* (1994); *Thamesmead Town Ltd v Allotey* (1998)).

- It is possible to reserve a *right of entry* in respect of land (usually annexed to an 'estate rentcharge' (Rentcharges Act 1977, s 2(4), **8.27**), on terms that the right of entry becomes exercisable on events which amount to a violation of a positive covenant. Such a right of entry, if duly created, becomes a legal interest in the land and thus runs with the burdened land so as to affect the successors in title of the covenantor (**8.35**).

— *A partial statutory solution in the area of commonhold schemes* A remedy for some of the more grievous deficiencies of the common law rule relating to covenanted burdens is now to be found in the Commonhold and Leasehold Reform Act 2002. This statute, which provides for interlocking freehold ownership of individual commonhold units and collectively managed common parts of developments (**7.41**), offers a means by which both the benefit and the burden of positive (and, for that matter, negative) obligations arising within the context of a 'commonhold' scheme can be attached permanently to each unit incorporated within the scheme.

- The rules governing any registered commonhold scheme and its various participants are contained in a 'commonhold community statement' (CALRA 2002, ss 14, 31). Each unit-holder takes a registered freehold estate in his or her unit and it is explicitly provided that, on the transfer of that estate by the unit-holder, any right or duty conferred or imposed by the commonhold community statement 'shall affect a new unit-holder in the same way as it affected the former unit-holder' (CALRA 2002, s 16(1)). Not only do the rights and obligations comprised within the commonhold community shift immediately to the transferee of the commonhold unit. The former unit-holder, having transferred his or her estate, is freed from any new liability (and correspondingly disabled from taking any new benefit) under or by virtue of the commonhold community statement (CALRA 2002, s 16(2)). This clean cut is reinforced by the stern prohibition of any attempted disapplication or variation of the statutory principle by contrary agreement (CALRA 2002, s 16(3)(a)), although a former unit-holder always remains subject to any liability incurred (and correspondingly entitled to any right which had already accrued) before the transfer took effect (CALRA 2002, s 16(3)(b)).

• The device of commonhold ownership thus offers a 'framework in which freehold ownership of a part of a multi-occupied development will be combined with the ability to enforce positive covenants against other owners' (*Commonhold Proposals for Commonhold Regulations: A Consultation Paper* (Lord Chancellor's Department, CP: 11/02 (October 2002)), p 12). This far-reaching effect, previously attainable in relation to interdependent properties only by resort to complex structures of leasehold ownership (or even less satisfactory mechanisms such as the rentcharge), marks an important step forward in the rationalisation of the law which regulates purposive developments of land.

Covenants in equity

13.13 It was largely the inability of the common law to ensure straightforward enforcement of positive covenants against successors in title which stimulated a series of revolutionary *equitable* developments in the 19th century aimed at facilitating the transmission of both the benefit and the burden of at least *negative* covenants (**2.12, 9.26**). These developments coincided with—indeed were necessitated by—an age of unprecedented urban and industrial expansion which gave an urgent significance to the rudimentary environmental protection afforded by negative covenants. The major innovations achieved by the courts of equity—mainly during the period prior to the fusion of the administration of law and equity (**1.24**)—have since been modified and refined by legislation. But it can generally be said that whereas enforcement of a positive covenant 'lies in contract'—whence the common law's fundamental difficulty with the transmission of burdens—the enforcement of a negative covenant 'lies in property' (see *Rhone v Stephens* (1994) per Lord Templeman).

— *Reallocations of 'property' in land* The changes initiated by mid-19th century equitable doctrine had a remarkable impact on proprietary relations between covenantor and covenantee. From the moment when the courts began to enforce freehold restrictive covenants more widely, there was no doubt that both covenantor and covenantee could truthfully assert that each held some form of 'property' in the servient land, albeit that their proprietary allocations were distinguished by differing degrees of intensity (**2.5**). It is clear that the restrictive covenant deprives the covenantor (and his successors) 'of some of the rights inherent in the ownership of unrestricted land' (*Rhone v Stephens* (1994) per Lord Templeman). The covenantor thus retains 'property' in his own land although burdened by the qualified power of veto vested in the covenantee. And in so far as the covenantee enjoys a significant control over the user of the covenantor's land, the utility thereby allocated to him *also* comprises a form of 'property' in the servient land. The subtraction of a limited quantum of 'property' from the totality of the *covenantor's* rights corresponds exactly with the accretion of a quantum of 'property' to the *covenantee's* rights—which is, of course, why the restrictive covenant came to be classified, in the latter's hands, as an *equitable proprietary right* (**9.26, 13.18**).

— *Definitional precision* Exactly because equitable intervention in the area of covenants was attended by such extensive proprietary significance, it was inevitable that the 'property' of the restrictive covenant should require to be demarcated with care (**2.18, 9.27**). In order that a restrictive covenant affect parties other than the original covenantor and covenantee, it is necessary to show that the covenant in question conforms to the special characteristics which equity came to demand of any restrictive covenant falling within its purview. These defining characteristics of the enforceable negative covenant were discussed earlier in this book when we introduced the restrictive covenant as a species of equitable proprietary interest (**9.27–9.31**).

— *The character of equitable intervention* The range of equitable intervention in the law of covenants is firmly limited to covenants of a negative or restrictive variety, but, as might perhaps be expected (**9.2**), the keynote of equitable involvement in this area has tended, with some historic exceptions, to comprise a characteristic concentration on matters of *knowledge* or *intention* rather than on matters of formality or technicality. If anything, recent decades have seen the courts adopt an even more sympathetic stance in relation to restrictive covenants. This relaxation of approach may in part reflect a general change in community attitudes towards the importance of preserving the integrity and attractiveness of local environments, but may also owe something to the residual availability of a statutory jurisdiction to modify or discharge unnecessary or outdated covenants (**9.33, 13.20**).

— *Necessary correlation of benefit and burden* The proprietary analysis of negative covenants also explains why an even sharper edge has been given to the need for the party seeking to enforce a restrictive covenant to establish both that he is entitled to the *benefit* of the covenant and that the person against whom he seeks enforcement is subject to the *burden* of the covenant. If he can prove only *one* of these requirements, his action must fail (see e.g. *J Sainsbury plc v Enfield LBC* (1989), **9.32**). If he is not himself the original covenantee, the onus rests on the enforcer to demonstrate that the 'property' inherent in the restrictive covenant has been engrafted on to his own estate in land (**13.14**) and that the subtraction of 'property' from the estate of the original covenantor still affects the current owner of the servient land (**13.18**).

Transmission of the benefit of a restrictive covenant

13.14 The benefit of a restrictive covenant may be transmitted in equity to a successor in title of the covenantee by any one or more of three means:

- annexation (**13.15**);
- assignment (**13.16**);
- scheme of development or building scheme (**13.17**);

(See also the impact, in relation to restrictive covenants entered into on or after 11 May 2000, of the Contracts (Rights of Third Parties) Act 1999 (**13.11**).)

It is sometimes said that these *equitable* modes of transmission of benefit—and particularly the rules relating to annexation—are merely a replication in equity of the *common law* rules governing the passing of the benefit of covenants (see *Rogers v Hosegood* (1900)); and it is not impossible that the benefit of a restrictive covenant may sometimes pass both *at law* and *in equity*. It is nevertheless clear that the transmission of the burden of a restrictive covenant depends vitally on *equitable* principles, as now supplemented by legislation (**13.18**), with the result that the enforcement of restrictive covenants is generally viewed as a matter allocated to the realm of equity, whereas the enforcement of positive covenants—if enforcement is feasible at all—is a matter for the common law.

Annexation

13.15 Annexation is the process by which the benefit of a restrictive covenant is meta-phorically 'nailed' or attached to a clearly defined area of land belonging to the covenantee, in such a way that the benefit subsequently passes with any transfer of that land. Annexation mirrors the importance attached to the element of *intention* by the common law rules for the passing of covenanted benefits (**13.11**), for annexation traditionally comprises a formal recognition that both covenantor and covenantee intend that the benefit should run with the dominant land so as to avail future owners of that land. Once that intention has been manifested in the express terms of the covenant, the benefit is notionally fastened upon, or annexed to, the covenantee's land and passes automatically to all later estate owners and occupiers of the land, without any specific assignment and entirely irrespective of their knowledge or notice (see *Rogers v Hosegood* (1900) per Collins LJ). Annexation may take any of *three* forms.

— *Express annexation* occurs where some clear verbal formula embedded in the wording of a covenant crystallises the intention of the parties that a covenanted benefit should run with the land of the covenantee. Annexation is essentially a conferment of benefit upon *land*, not upon *persons*, and it is imperative that the formula of annexation should incorporate some reference to the covenantee's land (e.g. that the covenant is made 'for the benefit of' identified or identifiable land held by the covenantee). Such annexation is assumed, in the absence of any contrary indication, to attach the covenanted benefit to *each and every part* of the covenantee's land (*Federated Homes Ltd v Mill Lodge Properties Ltd* (1980) per Brightman LJ). Even a subsequent fragmentation of the dominant tenement between a number of successors in title will not therefore prevent each of these owners from claiming the benefit in relation to his or her own parcel of land.

— *Implied annexation* may possibly arise where an intention to attach a covenanted benefit to land, although not expressed in the deed of covenant, is so clearly implicit in the circumstances that to ignore it would be 'not only an injustice but a departure from common sense' (see *Marten v Flight Refuelling Ltd* (1962) per Wilberforce J).

— *Statutory annexation* may be brought about by the wording of LPA 1925, s 78(1), which provides, in broad terms, that a 'covenant relating to any land of the covenantee shall be deemed to be made with the covenantee and his successors in title . . . and shall have effect as if such successors . . . were expressed' (see also now Commonhold and Leasehold Reform Act 2002, s 16(1), **13.11**).

• *A liberating formula* For decades courts were reluctant to credit the plain message conveyed by this statutory language. It is now clear, however, that section 78(1) supplies a statutory formula of annexation which effectively attaches covenanted benefits to the land of the covenantee provided that these covenants can genuinely be described as *relating to* the covenantee's *land* and provided that the land to be benefited is *identifiable* from the express words of the covenant or by necessary implication (see *Crest Nicholson Ltd v McAllister* (2004)). This is the net effect of the benevolent construction accorded to s 78(1) in the decision of the Court of Appeal in *Federated Homes Ltd v Mill Lodge Properties Ltd* (1980)).

Federated Homes Ltd v Mill Lodge Properties Ltd (1980) Here a restrictive covenant referred to 'any adjoining or adjacent property retained by' the covenantee. One parcel of the covenantee's adjoining lands was subsequently transferred to FH, and the Court of Appeal held that FH could claim the benefit of the original covenant on the basis of a valid annexation. Brightman LJ liberated the law of restrictive covenants from generations of needless technicality by recognising that 'if the condition precedent of s 78 is satisfied—that is to say, there exists a covenant which touches and concerns the land of the covenantee—that covenant runs with the land for the benefit of his successors in title, persons deriving title under him or them and other owners and occupiers'. On the facts, the actual wording of the restrictive covenant had been sufficient to intimate that the covenant was one 'relating to ... land of the covenantee', with the consequence that, pursuant to section 78(1), the benefit ran with the land.

- *Automatic annexation* The decision in *Federated Homes Ltd v Mill Lodge Properties Ltd* has simplified the law, rendering largely otiose the device of *express assignment* as an alternative means of transmitting the benefit of restrictive covenants. The annexation of 'touching and concerning' covenants to identifiable land would seem to be automatic, except where the original covenant manifests a contrary intention (see *Crest Nicholson Ltd v McAllister* (2004) at [41]–[44]). Such a case arises, for example, where the covenanting parties have clearly stipulated that their covenant is intended to be *personal* to the covenantee or that its benefit is to be transmissible only by express assignment (see *Roake v Chadha* (1984)).

- *Pre-1926 covenants* The only major limitation on the impact of *Federated Homes* is that restrictive covenants entered into prior to 1926 are still governed by the significantly narrower wording of the Conveyancing Act 1881, s 58, which does *not* automatically annex the benefit to the covenantee's land (see *J Sainsbury plc v Enfield LBC* (1989)). In such cases annexation of the benefit of a 'touching and concerning' covenant can be held to have occurred only if it can be shown that the instrument creating the relevant restriction expressly or impliedly discloses an intention that the covenant should benefit identifiable land in which the covenantee had an interest (see *Re MCA East Ltd* (2003) at [20]–[21]).

Assignment

13.16 Express assignment provides a further means by which the benefit of a restrictive covenant may pass to a successor in title of the covenantee; and it is not impossible that such a successor may claim the benefit of a covenant on the basis of *both* assignment *and* annexation. Whereas annexation involves the attachment of benefit to *land*, assignment involves the conferment of benefit upon a *person*; and whilst annexation is effected at the date of the making of a restrictive covenant, assignment is effected, perhaps many years later, on subsequent transfers of the covenantee's estate to purchasers of the dominant land. Although there has been some doubt on the issue, the benefit of a restrictive covenant probably requires to be assigned afresh with every subsequent transfer of the dominant land (see *Re Pinewood Estate, Farnborough* (1958)). In order that assignment of a covenanted benefit should be effective, several preconditions must be met:

- The covenant must have been taken for the *protection or benefit* of land owned by the covenantee at the date of the covenant.
- The assignment must be *contemporaneous* with the transfer of the dominant land.
- The dominant tenement must be *ascertainable*.

Scheme of development

13.17 A third method of transmitting the benefit of restrictive covenants in equity is provided by the 'scheme of development' or 'building scheme'. It is not unusual for a property developer to subdivide a large area of land into plots and sell these plots to individual purchasers, extracting certain restrictive covenants from each in turn. The object of the exercise is plainly to institute a scheme of mutually enforceable restrictive covenants which will be valid not only for the initial purchasers vis-à-vis each other but also as between all successors in title of the original covenantors. This aim, if duly realised, has the consequence of creating a 'local law' for maintaining the character of the neighbourhood for the indefinite future. The strategy threatens, however, to be undermined by technical difficulties rooted in the law of restrictive covenants and, in particular, in the chronology of the sales effected by the developer.

— *Problems of timing* As the developer extracts restrictive covenants from each initial purchaser, the dominant tenement to which each covenant appertains is of course the area constituted by the currently unsold plots of land: this area inevitably shrinks with each successive sale. The dominant tenement in respect of any one covenant plainly cannot include the plots which have already been sold away, and neither annexation nor assignment can enable the developer/covenantee to distribute the benefits of later covenants to earlier purchasers. Given the irreversible chronology of the transfers on sale, the enforcement of the original restrictive covenants must fairly quickly break down in the absence of some other more general mechanism for transmitting the covenanted benefits to all purchasers and their successors in title.

— *The scheme of development*   The solution for the problem outlined above lies in the distinctly equitable rules which have evolved for the governance of 'schemes of development'. If a *scheme of development* is present in any given circumstances, equity takes the view that the restrictive covenants appurtenant to each and every plot of land comprised within the scheme can be directly enforced by *all* who currently own any land covered by the scheme (provided, of course, that the relevant covenants have been protected by appropriate entry in the Land Register or Register of Land Charges (**13.18**)). It matters not whether the party seeking to enforce a covenant is the original covenantee or a successor in title. Restrictive covenants within the scheme are enforceable regardless of the relative timing of the original covenants or of the date of purchase by either of the parties in any enforcement action. Thus even prior purchasers can take the benefit of covenants entered into by later purchasers. The chronology of covenant and purchase becomes utterly irrelevant, both conceding priority to the overwhelming force of an equitable principle of conscience founded upon *reciprocity of obligation*.

— *Equitable origin of the scheme of development*   The authentic basis for the enforcement of schemes of development is the idea that 'community of interest necessarily ... requires and imports reciprocity of obligation' (*Spicer v Martin* (1888) per Lord Macnaghten). The intended mutuality of the covenants created within a scheme of development attracts the protection of a jurisdiction of conscience, for it gives rise to 'an equity which is created by circumstances and is independent of contractual obligation' (*Lawrence v South County Freeholds Ltd* (1939)). The scheme of development simply has a special equitable character which makes it quite immune from many of the normal rules governing the enforcement of restrictive covenants. Thus, for example, it is irrelevant that, on the final sale under a scheme of development, the covenantee (logically) retains no dominant tenement to which the last purchaser's covenant could be said to appertain—here the requirement of benefit to dominant land is simply dispensed with (**9.29**). Equity steps over the trip-wires of technicality in order to give effect to a generally shared intention to 'lay down what has been referred to as a local law for the estate for the common benefit of all the several purchasers of it' (*Re Dolphin's Conveyance* (1970) per Stamp J).

— *Preconditions for an enforceable scheme of development*   The preconditions underlying the constitution of a scheme of development or building scheme used to be applied by the courts in a ferociously technical manner (see *Elliston v Reacher* (1908)), with the result that few such schemes were ever upheld as valid. During the last 40 years, however, the preconditions which require to be met have been substantially relaxed. In reality only two essential components must now be established (see e.g. *Williams v Kiley t/a CK Supermarkets Ltd* (2003) per Carnwath LJ).

• *There must be an identifiable 'scheme'*, which necessarily presupposes that it is possible to identify a defined area of land over which reciprocal obligations were intended to be enforceable (*Jamaica Mutual Life Assurance Society v Hillsborough Ltd* (1989)). It must also be shown that each purchaser knew the extent of the area covered by the scheme (*Emile Elias & Co Ltd v Pine Groves Ltd* (1993) per Lord Browne-Wilkinson). If the original outline or perimeter of the intended scheme can be demonstrated from filed plans or documents of transfer, there is no need to show that the area covered by the scheme was already subdivided into plots of uniform or predetermined size (see *Baxter v Four Oaks Properties Ltd* (1965)).

• *There must be a mutually perceived common intention* It must be shown that the participants in an alleged scheme of development purchased on the common footing that all would be mutually bound by, and mutually entitled to enforce, a defined set of restrictions (see *Re Dolphin's Conveyance* (1970) per Stamp J). Absent proof of such common awareness, there can be no binding scheme of development (see e.g. *Small v Oliver & Saunders (Developments) Ltd* (2006) at [46]–[47]).

— *Letting schemes* The mechanism of 'horizontal' enforcement has been held to be applicable not only to freehold building schemes, but also to 'letting schemes' where tenants from a common landlord enter into interlocking restrictive covenants governing the user of their respective premises (see e.g. *Williams v Kiley t/a CK Supermarkets Ltd* (2003)).

Transmission of the burden of a restrictive covenant

13.18 The idea that the burden of a restrictive covenant may be imposed upon a non-party is a concept alien to the common law. Yet we have already seen the way in which, in *Tulk v Moxhay* (1848) (**9.26**), the courts of equity began to enforce freehold restrictive covenants, on a par with other equitable interests in land, against all persons except a bona fide purchaser for value of a legal estate without notice (**12.39**). The precise rationale underlying the doctrine of *Tulk v Moxhay* is susceptible to a number of interacting, but slightly variant, interpretations.

— *The conscience-based analysis* At one level the covenantor's entry into a restrictive covenant can be seen as generating an equity in favour of the covenantee which binds the conscience of any successor of the covenantor who, with notice of the outstanding covenant, 'sets up the legal estate' (*Re Nisbet and Potts' Contract* (1905) per Farwell J). As Lord Cottenham LC emphasised in *Tulk v Moxhay*, 'no one purchasing with notice of that equity can stand in a different situation from the party from whom he purchased'. Equity thus intervenes, on the basis of some concept of 'privity of conscience', in order to enforce obligations of conscience against those who can fairly be regarded as 'privy' to the undertaking given by the covenantor (*Forestview Nominees Pty Ltd v Perpetual Trustees WA Ltd* (1998)).

— *The unjust enrichment analysis* The approach adopted in *Tulk v Moxhay* effectively averts the unjust enrichment which would otherwise be reaped by a covenantor who knew that he could always sell the land, even to a purchaser with actual notice of the covenant, at a higher price than he himself had paid to the covenantee (see *Tulk v Moxhay* (1848) per Lord Cottenham LC, **9.26**).

— *The proprietary analysis* When, in *Tulk v Moxhay*, the covenantor's successor was restrained from developing his land in contravention of a restriction of which he was aware on purchase, equity simply prevented him 'from exercising a right which he never acquired' (see *Rhone v Stephens* (1994) per Lord Templeman). In terms of the original covenant, the right to build on that land without the cove-nantee's consent had *never* been vested in the original covenantor and could *not* therefore pass to any of his successors who knew of this limitation on their rights. Instead the right to control development on the servient land had at all times been reserved for the *covenantee* (and his successors), who consequently could claim, with justification, that they held 'property' in the servient land to the extent of the right of control conferred by their restrictive covenant. To enforce negative covenants, said Lord Templeman in *Rhone v Stephens*, 'is only to treat the land as subject to a restriction'.

— *The doctrine of notice* Following *Tulk v Moxhay* and until the commence-ment of the 1925 property legislation, the transmission of the burden of freehold restrictive covenants was governed by the equitable doctrine of notice. Such covenants bound all third parties *other than*

- a purchaser for value of a legal estate in the covenantor's land who had no notice of the covenant, and

- any successor in title of such a person even if such successor *did* have notice of the covenant (see *Wilkes v Spooner* (1911), **12.41**).

— *The impact of the 1925 legislation* The restrictive covenantee's entitlement now ranks as an equitable proprietary interest within the categories of estates and interests recognised by the 1925 legislation (LPA 1925, s 1(3)). But this legislation effected major changes in the way in which the burden of a post-1925 freehold restrictive covenant is transmitted to later owners of the servient land. The notice principle incorporated in the bona fide purchaser rule has been replaced by the indirect statutory notification of rights achieved through the entry of covenanted burdens in various sorts of register (**9.32**).

- In *registered land* the transmission of burden now depends on the entry of a 'notice' in the charges register of the covenantor's title (LRA 2002, ss 29(1), (2)(a)(i), 32–34, **9.32, 12.11**; see also Commonhold and Leasehold Reform Act 2002, s 16(1), **13.12**).

- In *unregistered land* the transmission of burden now depends on the registration of the covenant against the name of the covenantor as a Class D(ii) land charge (LCA 1972, ss 2(5), 4(6), **12.36**). (Pre-1926 freehold restrictive covenants are still governed by the equitable doctrine of notice (**12.42**).)

Remedies for breach of a restrictive covenant

13.19 A range of remedies may be available to a claimant who successfully asserts both that he is entitled to the benefit of a restrictive covenant and that the defendant is subject to its burden and in breach of its terms. The remedy available *as of right* is that of money damages, but the real issue is often whether the court should vindicate the rights of the covenantee (or his successor) by exercising its discretion to grant more far-reaching remedies such as an injunction to restrain further breach or even a mandatory injunction requiring, for instance, that a construction in breach of the covenant should be demolished. What is at stake is whether the court should require specific compliance with the terms of the covenant or should effectively sanction the relevant wrong by allowing the party in breach to buy his or her way out of further liability.

— *A good working rule* In addressing this question the courts have generally adopted the approach that damages may be awarded in lieu of an injunction (see Supreme Court Act 1981, s 50), if the injury to the claimant's rights is small, if the damage can be estimated in money and would be adequately compensated by a small money payment, and if it would be 'oppressive' to the defendant to grant an injunction (*Shelfer v City of London Electric Lighting Co* (1895) per AL Smith LJ). In many recent cases the courts have stressed that injunctive relief is not an automatic response to breaches of restrictive covenants and that damages may sometimes represent the more appropriate remedy even though the withholding of injunctive relief causes the court, in effect, to 'license future wrongs' (see *Jaggard v Sawyer* (1995) per Millett LJ).

> *Jaggard v Sawyer* (1995) The Court of Appeal declined to award an injunction to enforce a restrictive covenant against building development. Millett LJ pointed out that in many cases 'proprietary rights cannot be protected at all by the common law', with the result that the aggrieved owner 'must submit to unlawful interference with his rights and be content with damages'. The award of injunctive relief is ultimately discretionary and even though 'the defendant may have no right to act in the manner complained of … he cannot be prevented from doing so'. Here the Court of Appeal awarded damages measured on the basis of the amount which the covenantee might reasonably have expected to receive for the *release* of the covenant in question. The Court rejected the suggestion that such a solution was effectively an 'expropriation' of the covenantee, taking the view that a 'once and for all' award of damages for future wrongs and continuing breaches of covenant could fairly reflect the value of the rights which had been lost. (Not every judge agrees with this approach: compare the objection in *Anchor Brewhouse Developments Ltd v Berkley House (Docklands Developments) Ltd* (1987) per Scott J **(1.7)** that 'once and for all' payments are tantamount to the compulsory purchase of some sort of easement or licence to do wrong.)

Damages are increasingly awarded as an approximation of likely release settlements (see e.g. *Gafford v Graham* (1998); *Small v Oliver & Saunders (Developments) Ltd* (2006)), but awards of damages have not yet been allowed overtly to serve the *restitutionary* purpose of stripping the party in breach of any illicit gains which may have been made by means of that breach (see *Surrey CC v Bredero Homes Ltd* (1993)).

— *A new ethos of 'reasonableness between neighbours'* The contemporary prevalence of monetary pre-estimates of the damage caused by breaches of restrictive covenants is associated with a highly relativist view of relationships between neighbours (**13.3–13.4**).

• There is a growing sense that the dealings of neighbours require to be regulated by a large measure of 'give and take' (see e.g. *Hunter v Canary Wharf Ltd* (1997) per Lord Cooke of Thorndon; *Southwark LBC v Mills* (2001) per Lords Hoffmann and Millett). Some have even pointed to the emergence of a 'law of neighbourhood' which is 'closely linked with the law of property' (see *Hunter v Canary Wharf Ltd* per Lord Hope of Craighead). The outcome has been the fresh articulation of an ethos of 'good neighbourliness' (see *Southwark LBC v Mills* per Lord Millett; *Hughes v Riley* (2005) at [29] per Chadwick LJ) or 'reasonableness between neighbours' (see *Delaware Mansions Ltd v Westminster CC* (2002) at [29], [34] per Lord Cooke of Thorndon; *Abbahall Ltd v Smee* (2003) at [36]–[38] per Munby J).

• This new emphasis on social cooperation between neighbours points away from the absolutist remedy of the injunction. Instead, the courts are increasingly exercising the power to license, on payment of compensation, broadly acceptable compromises of conflicting neighbourhood interests. In the interdependency of neighbourhood, 'property rules' are often commuted into 'liability rules' (see G. Calabresi and A.D. Melamed, 'Property Rules, Liability Rules, and Inalienability: One View of the Cathedral' 85 *Harv L Rev* 1089 (1971–2)). In effect—quite outside the normal market process—the courts are able to engineer socially optimal redistributions of various sorts of utility in land between parties who need to continue living in some kind of cooperative proximity (see Gray and Gray, 'The Rhetoric of Realty', in J. Getzler (ed.), *Rationalizing Property, Equity and Trusts: Essays in Honour of Edward Burn* (Butterworths, 2003), pp. 257–9).

— *Mandatory injunctions* There remain, of course, some cases which call inexorably for the award of a mandatory injunction. Thus, where a defendant has acted in 'flagrant disregard' of the claimant's rights (e.g. by constructing, in breach of covenant, a building obstructing a sea view), the courts will not enable the defendant to 'buy his way out of his wrong' but will grant a mandatory order requiring the demolition of the obstruction (see *Wakeham v Wood* (1982)). As against a defendant who has cynically or recklessly gambled that a covenant against development would not be enforced, mere delay in seeking an injunction may not be enough to disentitle the claimant from this more far-reaching remedy (see e.g. *Mortimer v Bailey* (2004)).

— *Modification or discharge* It is always open to the defendant in proceedings brought for the enforcement of a restrictive covenant to request leave to apply to the Lands Tribunal for discharge or modification of the covenant (LPA 1925, s 84(9), **13.20**).

Discharge or modification of restrictive covenants

13.20 Like all 'property' in land (**2.3**), the restrictive covenant cannot be regarded as 'absolute and inviolable for all time' (*Jaggard v Sawyer* (1995) per Sir Thomas Bingham MR). There may arise changes of circumstance where it becomes desirable, in the interests of general social utility, that the long-term constraints on land use imposed by a particular covenant should be abrogated or otherwise modified. Narrowly conceived private interests cannot be allowed to frustrate proposed developments which promise a clear benefit to the entire community or to some significant section of it. The problem of obsolescence is therefore addressed by section 84 of the Law of Property Act 1925, which vests in the Lands Tribunal a discretionary power to discharge or modify restrictive covenants (with or without compensation) on any of the following grounds, i.e. that:

- the restrictive covenant ought to be deemed 'obsolete' (s 84(1)(a));

- the continued existence of the restriction impedes 'some reasonable user of the land for public or private purposes' (s 84(1)(aa)) and the restrictive covenant no longer secures 'any practical benefits of substantial value or advantage' to the relevant dominant owners or has become 'contrary to the public interest' (s 84(1A));

- the persons entitled to the benefit of the restrictive covenant have agreed to its discharge or modification (s 84(1)(b));

- the proposed discharge or modification 'will not injure' the persons entitled to the benefit of the restriction (s 84(1)(c)).

Re Quaffers Ltd's Application (1988) The Lands Tribunal discharged a restrictive covenant (prohibiting the sale of alcohol and other trade or business user) on the ground that, during the interim since the creation of the covenant, the immediate environment—once an area of open land—had been devastated through being enveloped by dual carriageway roads including the M62. The restriction was deemed obsolete (see LPA 1925, s 84(1)(a)).

— *The relevance of planning permission* The Lands Tribunal's discretion is generally exercised with caution. The mere fact that planning permission has already been granted in respect of a proposed development does not necessarily indicate that the Lands Tribunal *must* discharge or modify a particular restrictive covenant (see *Re Martin's Application* (1989)). Indeed, there is evidence that the narrowly conceived private interests which today merit careful scrutiny are those of large property development corporations which, armed with relatively easily obtainable planning permissions, seek to use section 84 to overturn covenanted arrangements designed to secure the environmental quality of urban areas. Section 84 applications are therefore frequently resisted by covenantees (or their successors) who fear, quite rightly, that a proposed development will degrade their neighbourhood. It is not unknown for a council planning department to grant permission for a local development which nonchalantly cuts through a conservation area or an area of green belt or special character, only for the Lands Tribunal ultimately to come to the rescue by refusing to relax private covenants originally created in order to safeguard the threatened amenity (see e.g. *Re Page's Application* (1996); *Re Azfar's Application* (2002)). Such discrepancies of approach are sometimes said to illustrate 'the differences in the criteria to be applied on the one hand in the context of a planning appeal and on the other in the context of the statutory regime under section 84' (*Re Hunt's Application* (1997)). However, the increasing vigilance of the Lands Tribunal may simply underscore the point that, despite authoritative exhortations to the contrary (see e.g. *Re Sheehy's Application* (1992)), the Lands Tribunal is slowly beginning, in reality, to 'act as a substitute for the planning authority'.

— *The balance between private and public planning* The beneficial conservationist potential of conventional public planning processes can be grossly over-estimated. Many significant changes of land use (**13.23**) do not even require planning permission, with the result that only local regulation by covenant can avert disadvantageous development. Research has revealed, moreover, that half of the cases during the 1990s in which the Lands Tribunal *declined* to modify or discharge a restrictive covenant involved developments already sanctioned, for planning purposes, by the Secretary of State for the Environment (see Gray and Gray (1999) 3 *Edinburgh Law Rev* 229 at 233–4). Nowadays even local authorities themselves recognise the utility of privately covenanted restrictions on land use. As a condition of granting planning permission, they have frequently imposed 'planning obligations' or required 'planning contributions' (see Town and Country Planning Act 1990, s 106; Planning and Compulsory Purchase Act 2004, ss 46–7, **9.29**) for the specific purpose of retaining a control over relevant developments which is 'untrammelled by interference by the Secretary of State' when he hears appeals from a carefully limited planning permission (*Re Jones' and White's Application* (1989); see also *Re Bewick's Application* (1997)).

Reform of the law of covenants

13.21   It has long been recognised that the law of freehold covenants is in need of radical reform. Its principal defect centres around the disastrously limited enforceability of positive burdens (**13.12**), and as long ago as 1965 the Wilberforce Committee acknowledged that many positive covenants in respect of property in this country are, in practice, wholly unenforceable (see *Report of the Committee on Positive Covenants Affecting Land* (Cmnd. 2719, 1965)).

— *Insufficiency of the commonhold regime* Notwithstanding the statutory introduction of a 'commonhold' regime (**7.41, 13.11–13.12**), which ensures that both the benefit and the burden of a number of standardised rights and obligations are attached indefinitely to each unit within any particular commonhold scheme, there remain many situations where it would be inappropriate to adopt the communal management machinery of the commonhold scheme. One example is provided by the case of suburban property owners who covenant inter se to make periodic contributions towards the upkeep of a private road. In these circumstances it would be excessively burdensome to require the creation of a complex commonhold simply in order to provide a legal mechanism for the transmission of the positive burden from one individual property owner to his or her successor (see Law Commission, *Commonhold: Freehold flats and freehold ownership of other interdependent buildings* (Cm. 179, July 1987), para 17.2). In practice the commonhold scheme is principally aimed at facilitating the cooperative multi-ownership of premises such as residential or office blocks.

— *The land obligation* There clearly remains a more general need to enable owners to create inter se 'land obligations' of a fully and permanently enforceable character. The need for rationalisation was endorsed in 1984 by the Law Commission, which declared that reform should weld positive and restrictive freehold covenants into 'a system which is both unified and more satisfactory' (Law Com No 127 (January 1984), para 4.20). Although its proposals have never been implemented, the Commission recommended a reformulation on the analogy of the law of easements. The Commission envisaged the creation of a new interest in land (the 'land obligation'), which could impose either positive or negative burdens on 'servient land' for the benefit of 'dominant land' (Law Com No 127, paras 4.21, 5.2). 'Land obligations' would comprise two types of obligation, 'neighbour obligations' (entered into between individual owners) and 'development obligations' (entered into as part of a scheme of reciprocal obligations regulating areas of multiple occupation). The extremely technical rules currently relating to the transmission of benefits and burdens would be replaced by a simple principle that, once protected by entry on the register of the titles of both dominant and servient tenements, the benefit and burden of all land obligations would thereafter attach to the relevant tenement and be enforceable by and against the current owner.

— *A possible 'sunset' rule* The Law Commission has also recommended that most restrictive covenants between freeholders should cease to have effect 80 years after their creation (Law Com No 201 (July 1991), para 3.1). Any person aggrieved by the lapse would have a right to apply to the Lands Tribunal for the conversion of the relevant covenant into a 'land obligation'.

Planning and compulsory purchase law

13.22 Modern planning control in England and Wales dates from the enactment of the Town and Country Planning Act 1947 and is currently governed by the Town and

Country Planning Act 1990 (as most recently amended by the Planning and Compulsory Purchase Act 2004). In many ways this legislation constitutes a socialised replica, on a general scale and in the public domain, of the planning regimes envisaged by networks of privately bargained covenants relating to land use. Nor is it mere metaphor to allege that, through the medium of today's planning legislation, all citizens can now indirectly claim, in some sense, a quantum of 'property' in everyone else's land. Indeed the Planning and Compulsory Purchase Act 2004 requires that every local planning authority should prepare, and comply with, a 'statement of community involvement' in the planning process (PACPA 2004, ss 17–18).

The development and use of land are subject to a degree of surveillance in the public interest which has effectively rendered ownership heavily qualified by pervasive notions of civic responsibility (**2.4, 2.19, 13.1**). Certain commentators even say that 'some (if not most) sticks' in the estate owner's 'bundle of sticks' are intrinsically 'reserved for communal control and use' and that a 'social welfare orientation' of land use rights 'comports with a community-based sense of justice' (see Eric T. Freyfogle, 'Context and Accommodation in Modern Property Law' 41 *Stan L Rev* 1529 at 1545–6 (1988–89)). According to such an analysis, the notion of *property* has much more to do with ideas of *propriety* than of *right* (**2.2**); and private titles ultimately subserve the wider public interest. Ownership is converted into *stewardship*; rights and duties are inseparably fused; and the social responsibility of caring for land becomes a fundamental and inescapable component of real entitlement (see Gray, 'Equitable Property' (1994) 47(2) *Current Legal Problems* 157 at 188–214).

State or community directed control of land takes a myriad of forms of which the most important are:

- planning control (**13.23**); and
- compulsory acquisition and limitation of land use (**13.24**).

Planning control

13.23 Planning law is concerned with 'the orderly management of land in society so as to protect at once the interests of individuals, the community and the environment' (*Hillpalm Pty Ltd v Heaven's Door Pty Ltd* (2004) at [71] per Kirby J). Accordingly the underlying principle of the T&CPA 1990 is that planning permission (granted by the relevant local authority or, on appeal from an adverse decision, by the Secretary of State for the Environment) is required for any 'development' of land. For this purpose the concept of 'development' includes (see T& CPA 1990, s 55(1)):

- the carrying out of building, engineering, mining or other operations in, over or under land and
- the making of any material change in the use of any buildings or other land.

Planning permission for certain kinds of development which have potentially harmful environmental effects must be accompanied by an 'environmental statement' detailing the context and likely impact of the proposed development on environmental amenity (Town and Country Planning (Environmental Impact Assessment) (England and Wales) Regulations 1999 (SI 1999/293), regs 3–9, Schs 1 and 2; *R (Barker) v Bromley LBC* (2006)).

— *Operational development* Most types of building work on land, other than marginal works of internal alteration, require the grant of planning permission (and usually, also, of building regulation consent, which effectively monitors the technical quality of the construction and the materials used in it). It is specifically provided, however, that 'development' does *not* include the use of any building or land within the curtilage of a dwelling-house for any purpose incidental to the enjoyment of the dwelling-house (T&CPA 1990, s 55(2)(d)) or the use of any land for agriculture or forestry (T&CPA 1990, s 55(2)(e)). In other cases planning permission must normally be obtained, the legislation now making clear that even demolition comes within the scope of the 'building operations' covered by the requirement of permission (see T&CPA 1990, s 55(1A)).

Planning permission is sometimes granted impliedly in a blanket form where a proposed development falls within one of the standard classes of *permitted development* under the Town and Country Planning (General Permitted Development) Order 1995 (SI 1995/418). In the domestic context such exemptions cover minor works of extension or improvement.

— *Material changes of use* Change in the use of land likewise requires planning permission unless the change is non-material. The 1990 Act expressly indicates, moreover, that the conversion of a single dwelling-house for use as two or more dwelling-houses involves a material change of use (T&CPA 1990, s 55(3)(a)). However, no relevant change of use arises where the altered use falls within the same 'class' of use as the existing use under a tightly defined canon of residential and business use classes (T&CPA 1990, s 55(2)(f); Town and Country Planning (Use Classes) Order 1987 (SI 1987/764)). Thus a bookshop can become a hairdresser's (since both uses fall within Class A1), but not a coffee shop (since this use falls within Class A3). Likewise a family may decide to share its home with Aunt Agatha and her poodle (since this change of use is covered by Class C3), but may not convert the house into a hotel (since such a use falls within Class C1).

— *Procedure* Planning permission may be granted either as *outline* planning permission or as *full* planning permission, and may be subjected to *conditions* (which regulate the nature or timing of the development) or the requirement of a *planning contribution* (PACPA 2004, s 46, **9.29, 13.20**) (which causes the developer to guarantee the preservation or improvement of local amenities or to proffer payment of a sum of money). The grant of planning permission for a development provides no automatic ground for the discharge of any restrictive covenant which stands in the way of the development (**13.20**); nor does it authorise the commission of any nuisance (see *Wheeler v J J Saunders Ltd* (1996)). There may, however, be substantial difficulty in arguing that a permitted development, by diminishing the residential amenity enjoyed by neighbours, necessarily violates their right to respect for their home under ECHR Art 8 (see *Lough v First Secretary of State* (2004)). Development in breach of planning control can be penalised by *enforcement proceedings* (see *R v Wicks* (1998)), but operational developments are immune from enforcement once four years have expired since the substantial completion of the operation (T& CPA 1990, s 171B: although see also *Sage v Secretary of State for the Environment, Transport and the Regions* (2003)). The limitation period for enforcement is otherwise normally a period of ten years.

— *Other forms of environmental control* A vast range of other statutory controls regulate development and change in conservation areas, green belt areas, sites of special scientific interest, areas of outstanding natural beauty, national parks, enterprise zones and urban development areas. Yet more regulation affects such matters as the preservation of trees and hedgerows, the alteration of listed buildings and the control of hazardous waste and environmental pollution.

— *Reform* The Planning and Compulsory Purchase Act 2004 has been enacted to ensure that certain aspects of strategic planning are removed from the purview of democratically elected organs of local government and, in the supposed interests of more efficient and better coordinated planning, determined instead by centrally appointed regional planning bodies (PACPA 2004, ss 2–3). The underlying aim of the Act is to speed up a planning process which is perceived to have become over-heavy with bureaucratic regulation at a time when the country imperatively requires the rapid provision of affordable housing and associated infrastructure.

Compulsory acquisition and limitation of land use

13.24 The exercise of eminent domain for supervening community purposes constitutes, without doubt, the most far-reaching form of social intervention in the property relations of individual citizens (**13.6**). The state reserves the power, in the name of all citizens, to call on the individual, in extreme circumstances and generally in return for compensation, to yield up some private good for the greater good of the whole community. (Compensation is paid in order that the economic cost of communally beneficial policies should not be disproportionately concentrated on a few citizens but diffused instead amongst the public at large.) On these terms the state may therefore be seen as having the right to requisition, for civic purposes, some or all of the 'sticks' in the estate owner's 'bundle'. It might even be more accurate to say that the state has *always* retained for itself a strategic quota of these 'sticks' and that compelling community needs constantly operate as a tacit quali-fication upon all land ownership. Either way, it is clear that many bodies today enjoy extensive statutory powers of compulsory acquisition which enable the purchase of privately owned land for designated public purposes (ranging from the construction or improvement of highways to the renovation of housing stock). It is, of course, an altogether more controversial question whether the authority of the state may be invoked in support of compulsory acquisition for purely private purposes (see the majority decision of the United States Supreme Court in *Kelo v City of New London* (2005)).

— The process of compulsory purchase is tightly regulated by statute (see the Compulsory Purchase Act 1965) but involves, in essence, the making of a com-pulsory purchase order (pursuant to the Acquisition of Land Act 1981), leading ultimately to a transfer of title subject to compensation for actual loss suffered by the landowner as assessed under the Land Compensation Act 1961 (see *Director of Buildings and Lands v Shun Fung Ironworks Ltd* (1995)). The Planning and Compulsory Purchase Act 2004 significantly extends the power of local authorities to engage in strategic planning of developments in their respective areas and also speeds up the statutory procedure of compulsory purchase (PACPA 2004, ss 100–2).

— *Privatised utilities* Potentially more controversial nowadays is the fact that many privatised utility companies, which formerly functioned within the public sector, retain indirectly the substantial economic advantage of the compulsory purchase powers once vested in their predecessors. These companies operate typically in the water, power, transport and communications industries (see e.g. Water Resources Act 1991, s 154(1); Environment Act 1995, s 2(1)(a)(iv)). It is deeply questionable whether powers to expropriate private citizens should be available to such companies for the substantial benefit of their own equity shareholders, but the recent drive towards privatisation rather obscures the fact that the rationale of compulsory acquisition of land has now been fundamentally skewed (see Gray and Gray, 'Private Property and Public Propriety', in J. McLean (ed.), *Property and the Constitution* (1999), pp 36–7). With the advent of the privatised utility corporation, it is no longer the case that compulsory acquisition is directed towards exclusively public purposes or that every citizen is equally the beneficiary of the process. The complacency of English law in this regard has greatly intensified the risk that powers of compulsory purchase may effect a mandatory transfer from one private actor for the benefit of another, thus compelling the sale to a commercial corporate entity of that which it could not acquire through arm's length negotiations.

— *Environmental regulation*   Much modern environmental regulation involves not the direct acquisition of property by the state, but rather the imposition of substantial restrictions upon the free enjoyment of estate ownership. One of the large questions for the future relates to whether *mere limitations* of land use merit compensation from public funds. It can be argued that, at some point, regulation shades into confiscation and comprises a compensable 'taking' by the state of the substance of the estate owner's 'bundle of sticks'. On this view, uncompensated regulation is ultimately a form of environmental fascism, in that it dumps the cost of communal environmental benefits arbitrarily on isolated groups of citizens. Equally, however, it can be argued that the estate owner never actually had any *right* to exploit his land in an environmentally harmful fashion and that regulatory control merely renders more explicit those limitations on user which were always latent qualifications on his title. Thus analysed, state regulation has not really deprived him of *any* of the 'sticks' in his bundle of rights and has therefore caused him no net loss. The community was already entitled—had always been entitled—to the benefit of a public-interest forbearance on his part (see Gray and Gray, 'The Idea of Property in Land', in S. Bright and J.K. Dewar (eds), *Land Law: Themes and Perspectives* (1998), pp 43–51).

— *Defining the scope of the landowner's property*   In this context the vital question is not about the statutory competence of environmental regulation, but rather about who should *bear the cost* of the environmental protection which we all profess to desire. Across the common law world the environmental debate is being transformed into a major struggle about the definition of 'property' (see e.g. the epic confrontation of philosophies evident in the United States Supreme Court in *Lucas v South Carolina Coastal Council* (1992)). As another American decision puts it, 'the question is simply one of basic property ownership rights: within the bundle of rights which property lawyers understand to constitute property, is the right or interest at issue, as a matter of law, owned by the property owner or reserved to the state?' (*Loveladies Harbor, Inc v United States* (1994)).

• The *Lucas* case itself involved a statutory prohibition of building construction on an ecologically fragile coastal area. In a highly symbolic decision the Supreme Court signalled that, as a matter of inherent obligation, owners of environmentally sensitive areas bear only an extremely attenuated duty to promote the integrity or amenity of their land. The majority in the Court ruled that the potential for profitable (albeit damaging) development of such areas was intrinsically limited merely by 'background principles' of property and nuisance. On this basis compensation for regulatory control could be denied to the landowner *only if* the control in question merely made explicit some restriction which 'inhere[s] in the title itself', with the result that the 'proscribed use interests' were therefore 'not part of [the owner's] title to begin with'. Otherwise, regulatory legislation which wholly prohibited economically productive or beneficial land use automatically gave rise to a claim for public compensation. Significantly, the Supreme Court majority indicated that compensation could not be withheld simply on the basis that a landowner's proposed exploitation of his land was 'inconsistent with the public interest'. This outcome reflected little sense that community-directed obligations in respect of environmental amenity might tacitly comprise a pre-existing and constant qualification on a landowner's title.

• The *Lucas* decision has been widely understood as evincing a strong judicial inclination to stem a tide of uncompensated taking from American citizens under the cover of a mere exercise of regulatory power. The ruling has, however, proved controversial. A more recent dissent in the United States Supreme Court has pointed to the way in which *Lucas* raises 'the spectre of a tremendous—and tremendously capricious—one-time transfer of wealth from society at large to those individuals who happen to hold title to large tracts of land' in environmentally sensitive locations (see *Palazzolo v Rhode Island* (2001) per Justice Stevens). Even American courts have now realised that to regard all regulatory impositions as compensable 'takings' threatens to 'transform government regulation into a luxury few governments could afford' (see *Tahoe-Sierra Preservation Council, Inc v Tahoe Regional Planning Agency* (2002)). The costs of social and economic organisation would become wholly prohibitive. The approach embraced by the majority in *Lucas* has not been adopted in Ireland (see *O'Callaghan v Commissioners of Public Works in Ireland and the Attorney General* (1985)) or Canada (see *Mariner Real Estate Ltd v Nova Scotia (Attorney General)* (1999)), where concern for environmental integrity has been more readily perceived as inherently delimiting the intrinsic scope of the landowner's 'property'.

— *The European perspective* English law does not generally provide public compensation for the economic impact of land use regulations (see Planning and Compensation Act 1991, s 31). As Lord Hoffmann put it in *Grape Bay Ltd v Attorney-General of Bermuda* (2001), '[t]he give and take of civil society frequently requires that the exercise of private rights should be restricted in the general public interest' (see also *R (Alconbury Developments Ltd) v Secretary of State for the Environment, Transport and the Regions* (2003) at [71]–[72] per Lord Hoffmann). This stance is broadly consistent with the characteristically European perception that all land use is necessarily constrained by a socialised sense of community-oriented duty on the part of the landowner (**2.7 13.6**).

• This duty-based perspective is typified by the way in which the European Convention on Human Rights specifically preserves, without any presumptive right to compensation, the claim of the state 'to enforce such laws as it deems necessary to control the use of property in accordance with the general interest' (ECHR Protocol No 1, Art 1 (**2.7**), as construed in *Banér v Sweden* (1989)). Uncompensated exercises of regulatory intervention—such as that flowing from the designation of a site of special scientific interest—may therefore involve no violation of the Convention (see *R (Trailer and Marina (Leven) Ltd) v Secretary of State for the Environment, Food and Rural Affairs* (2005)).

• The idea that environmental regulation is non-compensable may require revision in the light of recent developments in European jurisprudence (see e.g. *Booker Aquaculture Ltd v Secretary of State for Scotland* (1998)). The European Court of Human Rights has clarified that even a regulatory 'control' of land use (e.g. for purposes of urban planning or other measures of environmental protection) may require compensation from public funds if it otherwise fails to meet the overarching standard of 'peaceful enjoyment of . . . possessions' guaranteed by the European Convention. There are already signs of an increased willingness to hold that the 'peaceful enjoyment' clause is breached by certain kinds of land use control which, even though directed towards perfectly rational regulatory aims, fail to balance fairly the interests of the individual owner and the wider community, thus leaving the landowner uncompensated for his involuntary contribution to public welfare goals (see e.g. *Chassagnou v France* (2000)).

• *Matos e Silva, LDA v Portugal* (1997) The European Court of Human Rights found that the applicants' use of their land was 'incontestably' restricted by a prolonged ban on both new construction and new farming activities. The ban had been imposed in connection with the creation of an aquacultural research station and national nature reserve for migrant birds to be sited on the applicants' portion of the Algarve coast. The Court held that, although the intended environmental strategy 'did not lack a reasonable basis', the substantial (and uncompensated) interference with the landowners' rights had contravened the 'peaceful enjoyment' guarantee of Article 1.

Gone are the days when environmental issues intersected importantly with the law of tort and only barely with the law of land. The primacy of environmental concern seems likely to convert the definition of 'property' into one of the most pressing questions of 21st century land law.

FURTHER READING

Gray and Gray, *Elements of Land Law* (4th edn, OUP, 2005), ch 13.

Relevant sections of this work and other land law textbooks may be supplemented with:

George, Susan '*Tulk v Moxhay* Restored—To its Historical Context' (1990) 12 *Liverpool L Rev* 173.

Gray, Kevin 'Land Law and Human Rights', in L Tee (ed.), *Land Law: Issues and Debates* (Willan, 2001), p 211.

Howell, Jean 'The Annexation of the Benefit of Covenants to Land' [2004] *Conv* 507.

Lucy, William and Mitchell, Catherine 'Replacing Private Property: The Case for Stewardship' [1996] *CLJ* 566.

Martin, Jill 'Remedies for Breach of Restrictive Covenants' [1996] *Conv* 329.

Millichap, Denzil 'Real Property and its Regulation: The Community-Rights Rationale for Town Planning', in S. Bright and J.K. Dewar (eds), *Land Law: Themes and Perspectives* (OUP, 1998), p 428.

Tee, Louise 'A Roof Too Far' [1994] *CLJ* 446.

Wade, H.W.R. 'Covenants—"A Broad and Reasonable View"' [1972B] *CLJ* 157.

SELF-TEST QUESTIONS

1 How does the enforcement of covenants at law differ from enforcement in equity (**13.10–13.18**)?

2 To what extent do the purposes of private regulation of land use coincide with the motivations of public planning control (**13.5–13.8, 13.20–13.24**)?

3 How extensive is the landowner's duty to preserve the environmental quality of the nation's land base? Who should bear the cost of promoting and safeguarding environmental welfare (**13.22–13.24**)?

14

Regulation of leases and tenancies

SUMMARY

The average lease or tenancy confers on the landlord and the tenant a substantial range of rights and obligations (express, implied and statutory). This chapter indicates:

- the principal obligations which arise in the leasehold context;
- the ways in which those entitled to the benefit of these obligations may enforce their rights; and
- the corpus of protective and regulatory legislation which governs the relations of landlord and tenant.

The leasehold relationship as a framework of rights and duties

14.1 We noted earlier (**7.10**) that the term of years has an inherent duality of character as both a *proprietary* and a *contractual* phenomenon (see *PW & Co v Milton Gate Investments Ltd* (2004) at [73] per Neuberger J). The leasehold relationship normally involves not merely the conveyance of an estate in land but also the creation of an intricate network of contractual obligations. Even after grant a lease is 'partly executory: rights and obligations remain outstanding on both sides throughout its currency' (*National Carriers Ltd v Panalpina (Northern) Ltd* (1981) per Lord Simon of Glaisdale). It is certainly true that a lease or tenancy must, by definition, confer upon the lessee or tenant a right to exclusive possession and a guarantee of immunity from detailed supervision of his activities on the land (**7.13–7.14**). But this does not mean that the relationship between landlord and tenant is *not* usually controlled fairly closely by a range of obligations (express and implied), the due performance of which requires to be policed throughout the term. It is the governance of these aspects of the leasehold nexus which forms the subject matter of this chapter, a task of regulation made more complex by a number of factors.

— *The explosion of protective legislation*   Particularly in the residential sector, the modern tenancy is commonly a vehicle for the delivery of a sophisticated amalgam of consumer utilities of shelter, safety, security and convenience—a role reinforced by a vast body of contemporary statute law (**14.5, 14.27–14.31**). This corpus of legislation has grown both unwieldy and convoluted and there now exists an overwhelming case for the replacement of all landlord and tenant rules by the enactment of a more simple consolidated code of landlord-tenant relations (**14.32**). Moreover, it remains the case that, despite the plethora of legislation, the allocation of burdens in many landlord-tenant relationships is somewhat one-sided. Legal provisions aimed at the protection of vulnerable occupiers have not, in general, been accorded a particularly liberal application and one judge has even been moved to refer to 'what many might consider to be the harsh way in which tenants are treated by the common law' (*Baxter v Camden LBC (No 2)* (2001) per Tuckey LJ). Accordingly in 2006 the Law Commission proposed a major rationalisation of housing law in order to create a new 'single social tenure' which would incorporate a strong ethos of 'consumer protection' (**14.32**).

— *The European dimension*   Recent experience has demonstrated the way in which European Community standards and policing mechanisms are beginning quite markedly to infiltrate the English law of landlord and tenant.

• The European-derived Unfair Terms in Consumer Contracts Regulations 1999 (SI 1999/2083) (**15.8**) have introduced the possibility that certain residential tenancy obligations which operate harshly or oppressively in favour of the landlord may be invalidated as 'unfair' in so far as, 'contrary to the requirement of good faith', they cause a 'significant imbalance in the parties' rights and obligations' (see S. Bright, 'Winning the battle against unfair contract terms' (2000) 20 *Legal Studies* 331).

• Some leasehold provisions (e.g. tied-house covenants obliging a tenant publican to purchase beer supplies only from his landlord, **14.22**) may turn out to comprise an anti-competitive practice prohibited by Article 81 of the EC Treaty (see, for instance, the controversy culminating in the House of Lords' decision in *Crehan v Inntrepreneur Pub Co (CPC)* (2006), **15.9**).

• It is also becoming increasingly clear that the European Convention on Human Rights can impinge quite heavily on landlord and tenant legislation, even to the extent of causing such legislation to be reformulated by the courts in order to ensure conformity with Convention guarantees (see e.g. *Ghaidan v Godin-Mendoza* (2004), **14.27**). It is also possible that, in certain circumstances, restrictive rules regulating the enforceability of leasehold covenants may now require modification in the light of the landlord's right to 'peaceful enjoyment of his possessions' (**2.7**) (see *PW & Co v Milton Gate Investments Ltd* (2004) at [134] per Neuberger J, **14.25**).

— *The public and quasi-public impact of private law enforcement*   The increasing 'contractualisation' of the lease (**7.10**) has tended to suggest the imposition, on behalf of tenants, of something approaching an implied warranty of habitability or fitness for use. There is certainly greater room for such an approach in view of the courts' willingness in recent years to have recourse to general doctrines of contract law in the resolution of leasehold problems. Yet it is also often the case that an expansive interpretation of contractual and other liability, particularly as it bears upon hard-pressed public sector landlords (e.g. local authorities) and other social landlords (e.g. housing charities), imposes financial burdens which threaten the provision of much needed publicly accessible low-cost accommodation (**14.3–14.5**).

— *The dimension of transferability*   The greater the duration of a tenancy, the more likely it is that the original parties to the leasehold grant will assign their respective entitlements to others, thereby enormously complicating the business of enforcing leasehold covenants against persons not privy to the initial grant (**14.20**).

Express obligations of the landlord

14.2   Although most express leasehold burdens tend to fall on the shoulders of the tenant, formal leases commonly contain a range of express covenants entered into by the landlord stipulating responsibilities in respect of such matters as repair, insurance, and maintenance of the common parts of premises.

Implied obligations of the landlord

14.3   In the absence of express contrary agreement, the landlord–tenant relationship impliedly imposes certain traditionally defined obligations on the landlord. The tenant's remedy for breach of covenant by his landlord is generally a remedy in damages, but there is nowadays an increased willingness to allow the tenant to repudiate the lease in its entirety for any breach of a fundamental covenant (see e.g.

Hussein v Mehlman (1992); *Chartered Trust plc v Davies* (1997), **7.35**). The landlord's implied obligations under a legal lease include the following.

— *Covenant for quiet enjoyment* The landlord impliedly covenants that neither he nor anyone claiming under him will do anything which 'substantially interferes with the tenant's title to or possession of the demised premises or with his ordinary and lawful enjoyment of the demised premises' (*Southwark LBC v Mills* (2001) per Lord Millett). It is this guarantee of immunity from interference during the currency of the lease which ultimately gives meaning to the tenant's right to exclusive possession (**7.13**). The covenant for quiet enjoyment is not intrinsically concerned with acoustic interference but more generally prohibits such conduct as the harassment or unlawful eviction of the tenant (**14.12**), the unauthorised removal of the tenant's belongings, and the cutting off of mains services or central heating in the tenant's home (see *Perera v Vandiyar* (1953)). Conversely, no breach of the covenant for quiet enjoyment is committed by a landlord who takes all reasonable precautions to avoid disturbance flowing from the carrying out of covenanted repairs on the demised premises (*Goldmile Properties Ltd v Lechouritis* (2003)). The obligation to provide the tenant with quiet enjoyment is, however, narrowly construed and has been said—rather unsympathetically—to impose on the landlord no previously uncovenanted duty to repair or improve premises which were already defective at the commencement of the lease.

> *Southwark LBC v Mills* (2001) Southwark London Borough Council granted lettings of council flats in a jerry-built block where inadequate sound insulation between the flats caused horrendous daily transmission of noise. The House of Lords held unanimously that there had been no breach of the covenant for quiet enjoyment. The House viewed the absence of sound-proofing at the date of grant of the tenancies as an 'inherent structural defect for which the landlord assumed no responsibility'. The noise generated by neighbours was the consequence of perfectly ordinary, reasonable and proper user of neighbouring flats and, in the context of a building constructed or adapted for multiple occupation, it 'must have been within the contemplation of the prospective tenants that the adjoining flats would be let to residential tenants, and that the occupiers would live normally in them'. In the absence of any existing covenant by the council to install sound-proofing, the House of Lords declined to construe the landlord's implied covenant so as to extend the operation of the grant. 'The council granted and the tenant took a tenancy of that flat. She cannot . . . require the council to give her a different flat' (per Lord Hoffmann). As Schiemann LJ had observed in the Court of Appeal, the situation had not 'changed one whit for the worse since the demise'. (Installation of the necessary soundproofing in the claimant's block would have cost the council some £60,000.)

— *Covenant against derogation from grant* The landlord may not grant land to the tenant on terms which effectively or substantially negative the utility of the grant. Thus neither the landlord nor any person claiming under him may engage in conduct which is inconsistent with the purpose for which the lease was granted or which renders the demised land materially less fit for that purpose (see e.g. *Chartered Trust plc v Davies* (1997), **7.35**).

• In the classic illustration of derogation from grant, a landlord leased land for the storage of explosives and then allowed adjoining land to be used for mining operations (*Harmer v Jumbil (Nigeria) Tin Areas Ltd* (1921)). Most—but not all—breaches of the landlord's duty to afford quiet enjoyment also constitute a derogation from grant.

• Under an equitable lease or a contract for a lease (**9.9**) there is an implied term, which may be displaced by contrary agreement, that the formal lease when executed should contain 'the usual covenants'. These covenants include the traditional qualified covenant by the landlord to permit quiet enjoyment to the contractual tenant.

Implied common law obligations of the landlord in respect of repair, maintenance and general amenity

14.4 The historic analysis of a lease as a proprietary conveyance has generated the bleak view that the common law implies no covenant on behalf of the landlord that premises should be reasonably fit for habitation or occupation throughout the tenancy. The thoroughly 19th-century emanation of this view was the infamous proposition that, 'fraud apart, there is no law against letting a tumble-down house' (*Robbins v Jones* (1863) per Erle CJ). The starting point for the common law has therefore been the principle—voiced even in modern times—that if the prospective tenant 'wants more he should bargain for it and be prepared to pay the extra rent' (*Southwark LBC v Mills* (2001) per Schiemann LJ, **14.3**). The dogma of contractual autonomy means that, in the absence of statutory intervention, the parties are 'free to let and take a lease of poorly constructed premises and to allocate the cost of putting them in order between themselves as they see fit' (*Southwark LBC v Mills* (2001) per Lord Millett). The courts have shown themselves profoundly unwilling to imply at common law any term that a landlord should keep a dwelling in good condition or even in such condition as enables the tenant to perform *his* obligations under the tenancy (see *Lee v Leeds CC* (2002) at [62]–[68] per Chadwick LJ). Particularly in relation to cash-strapped social landlords, the courts have felt that the 'limits of permissible judicial creativity' do not permit the fashioning of extra obligations not expressly agreed by the parties (see *Southwark LBC v Mills* (2001) per Lord Hoffmann, **14.1**).

— *Moderation of the laissez-faire approach*   Such abstentionism on the part of the law has been subjected, over the last century, to numerous piecemeal exceptions with the result that the law in this area is now complex, untidy and deeply unsatisfactory. Indeed the Law Commission has recommended that the thrust of the law should be reversed by a new statutory principle that all repairing liability should fall upon the landlord in default of an express contractual term allocating that responsibility to the tenant (Law Com No 238 (1996), paras 1.5, 7.10). In advance of the achievement of this legislative goal, it is beginning to be realised that the European Convention on Human Rights has already reshaped, in some degree, the obligations owed by certain landlords towards their tenants. In *Lee v Leeds CC* (2002) at [48], the Court of Appeal indicated that local authority landlords are obliged to 'take steps to ensure that the condition of a dwelling house which it has let for social housing is such that the tenant's Convention right under article 8 [respect for "private and family life" and the "home" (**2.15**)] is not infringed'. This duty involves, however, no 'general and unqualified' guarantee of the quality of a local authority's housing stock. The decision whether a tenant's right has been 'infringed' depends, as always in Convention jurisprudence, on the maintenance of a 'fair balance' between the competing needs and resources of the community and of individuals in the light of straitened public finances and the democratic determination of budgetary priorities (see *Lee v Leeds CC* at [49] per Chadwick LJ).

Amongst the *common law* inroads upon the general immunity of the landlord in matters of repair and amenity are the following.

— *Implied condition of fitness for human habitation*   It is an implied condition in the letting of any *furnished dwelling-house* that the premises should be reasonably fit for habitation at the commencement of the term (see *Smith v Marrable* (1843), where premises were infested by bugs). Breach of this condition entitles the tenant to quit the letting immediately and without notice, but the condition applies only to a *residential* tenancy and has no relevance to *unfurnished* premises or to defects which emerge *after* the commencement of the tenancy. In these respects English common law falls far short of the more wide-ranging 'warranty of habitability' implied in recent decades by American courts (see e.g. *Javins v First National Realty Corporation* (1970)).

— *Implied contractual duty of care*   A landlord may sometimes have an implied contractual duty to take reasonable care to keep in repair certain facilities enjoyed by the tenant (e.g. the lifts in a high-rise block of flats), where, in the absence of such an implied duty, 'the whole transaction becomes inefficacious, futile and absurd' (see e.g. *Liverpool CC v Irwin* (1977) per Lord Salmon). This duty is owed, however, only to the contracting tenant (and not, for example, to members of his family) and covers only the maintenance of truly essential facilities.

— *The landlord's liability in negligence* Although a landlord cannot normally be liable to a tenant in negligence for defects existing in premises at the *commencement* of a tenancy (see the much criticised ruling of the House of Lords in *Cavalier v Pope* (1906)), liability in negligence can be generated by defects which arise *after* the commencement date (see e.g. *Sharpe v Manchester CC* (1977), where the tenant's premises were invaded by cockroaches from service ducts supposedly maintained by his landlord).

— *The landlord's liability for nuisance* A tenant may have some redress in respect of disrepair or lack of amenity suffered in the tenanted premises where acts or omissions of *the landlord* on his own land unduly interfere with the tenant's comfortable and convenient enjoyment of his premises (see again *Sharpe v Manchester CC* (1977), supra). A landlord is not, however, liable in nuisance to one tenant for acts committed by *other tenants* of the same landlord unless the landlord has specifically authorised, adopted or consented to these acts (see *Chartered Trust plc v Davies* (1997), **7.35**). Nor is a landlord necessarily liable in nuisance merely because he grants a letting to a tenant whom he knows to be nuisance-prone (*Smith v Scott* (1973)). However, failure to halt an offending tenant's nuisance may now, in certain restricted categories of case, constitute an infringement of the right to respect for 'private and family life' and the 'home' guaranteed by ECHR Article 8 (see *Lee v Leeds CC* (2002) at [50] per Chadwick LJ). Further protection is afforded by the Anti-social Behaviour Act 2003, which authorises the issue of injunctions against anti-social conduct, unlawful use of rented premises and certain other breaches of a tenancy agreement (see Housing Act 1996, ss 153A–E, as inserted by ASBA 2003, s 13(3)).

> *Hussain v Lancaster CC* (2000) H, the owners of a shop and residential property on a council housing estate, were subjected to horrifying racial and other harassment by council tenants and other persons living on the estate. The Court of Appeal declined to hold the council liable in nuisance for failing to exercise its statutory powers as a housing or highway authority to prevent the commission of crime on the estate. In the Court's view, the appalling abuse suffered by H, whilst interfering with H's enjoyment of their own premises, did not involve the use by the wrongdoing tenants of *their own land* and therefore fell strictly outside the scope of the tort of nuisance. Moreover, the council could be liable only for conduct which it had itself authorised or adopted—clearly not the case here. The wrongs inflicted on H must be fought by 'multidisciplinary co-operation and not by civil suit against one of the relevant agencies' (per Thorpe LJ).

The circumstances of *Hussain* are exactly those addressed by the extended powers now conferred by the Anti-social Behaviour Act 2003.

Statutorily implied obligations of the landlord in respect of repair, maintenance and general amenity

14.5 The landlord's duties at common law, restricted as they may be, are supplemented by a series of statutory interventions, including the following.

— *Implied terms as to fitness for human habitation* Two implied contractual terms in the letting of a dwelling-house are imposed by the Landlord and Tenant Act 1985 (see L&TA 1985, s 8(1)):

- that the house is 'fit for human habitation at the commencement of the tenancy'

 and

- that the house 'will be kept by the landlord fit for human habitation during the tenancy'.

Although these statutory terms cannot be excluded even by express contractual provision, they apply only in respect of properties whose annual rental falls below prescribed levels so low that few, if any, tenancies can nowadays qualify for this form of protection.

— *Implied covenant for repair and maintenance* In leases of a dwelling-house for a term of *less than* seven years, the landlord impliedly covenants by force of statute (see L&TA 1985, s 11(1)):

- to keep in repair the structure and exterior of the dwelling-house

 and

- to keep in repair and 'proper working order' installations for the supply of water, gas and electricity, facilities for sanitation, and installations for space heating and heating water.

It has been said, in one of the more remarkable asides of landlord and tenant jurisprudence, that the standard of repair required by the statute 'may depend on whether the house is in a South Wales valley or in Grosvenor Square' (*Quick v Taff Ely BC* (1986) per Lawton LJ)! No liability arises for the landlord under section 11(1) unless and until he is notified of the relevant defect (*O'Brien v Robinson* (1973))—a rule which effectively immunises the landlord from liability for *latent* defects. Furthermore, the statutory provision imposes on the landlord no duty to *improve* the tenanted premises beyond their condition at the commence-ment date of the tenancy, although the landlord may be obligated to make certain *modifications* to the premises, e.g. by altering the size of water pipes in order to accommodate a later drop in the pressure of the water supply (see *O'Connor v Old Etonian Housing Association Ltd* (2002)). In general, however, the concept of relevant disrepair is construed extremely narrowly (see e.g. *Lee v Leeds CC* (2002) at [50]).

> *Quick v Taff Ely BC* (1986) The Court of Appeal held the implied statutory covenants substantially inapplicable to a council house where 'very severe condensation' had rendered the living conditions of the tenant and his family 'appalling'. In the absence of evidence of physical damage to the walls or the windows, the landlord authority was not in breach. Here there was no *damage* to the tenant's walls, merely lots of mould on them; and relevant disrepair does not include mere loss of amenity. (The horrifying reality appeared to be that the cost of remedying this kind of complaint across the entire range of the defendant local authority's housing stock would have been in the region of £9 million. The tenant in *Quick* was subsequently rehoused by the local authority.)

— *Intervention in the case of 'statutory nuisance'* A 'statutory nuisance' arises where any premises are 'in such a state as to be prejudicial to health or a nuisance' (Environmental Protection Act 1990, s 79(1)). In a needlessly restrictive way, the courts have refused to allow the 'statutory nuisance' jurisdiction to be used as a forum for complaints which are more closely related to design defects in housing than to 'public health' complaints arising from housing conditions (see e.g. *R v Bristol CC, ex parte Everett* (1999), where a dangerously steep internal staircase was held not to come within the concept of 'statutory nuisance'). Where established, a statutory nuisance may lead either to the service by the local authority of an abatement notice (EPA 1990, s 80(1)) or to an order by a magistrates' court that the nuisance be abated and remedial works executed (EPA 1990, s 82(2)). The local authority may itself take steps to remove the nuisance at the owner's expense (EPA 1990, s 81(3)–(4)). A proven statutory nuisance does not, however, confer upon the aggrieved tenant any cause of action for damages (see *Issa v Hackney LBC* (1997)).

Other forms of potential landlord liability arise pursuant to:

- Defective Premises Act 1972, s 4 (see e.g. *Sykes v Harry* (2001));
- Health and Safety at Work etc Act 1974, s 4(2) (see e.g. *Westminster CC v Select Management Ltd* (1984));
- Housing Act 2004, ss 1–7, 28–35.

The tenant's remedies for breach of the landlord's repairing covenants

14.6 In the context of the landlord-tenant relationship the performance of the parties' respective obligations is not interdependent (*Bluestorm Ltd v Portvale Holdings Ltd* (2004) at [33]–[37]). Thus the tenant is not generally entitled to withhold payment of rent or service charges on the ground that his landlord has patently failed to discharge a duty to repair (though see now L&TA 1985, s 21A(1), as substituted by CALRA 2002, s 152; L&TA 1987, s 42A(9), as inserted by CALRA 2002, s 156). Instead the aggrieved tenant must pursue one or more of the following remedies:

— *Damages for breach of covenant* The object of which is 'not to punish the landlord but . . . to restore the tenant to the position he would have been in had there been no breach' (see *Calabar Properties Ltd v Stitcher* (1984), but compare *Earle v Charalambous* (2006) at [30]–[32]).

— *Order for specific performance* (See L&TA 1985, s 17(1), in the case of residential premises).

— *Self-help and set-off* Under which a tenant has a *common law* right to recoup the reasonable cost of necessary repairs by withholding future payments of rent (see *Lee-Parker v Izzet* (1971), **12.20**) or otherwise an *equitable* right to set off any unliquidated claim for damages for non-repair against his landlord's claim for non-payment of rent (see *Smith v Muscat* (2003)). Equitable rights of set-off are not, however, enforceable against a transferee of the landlord's reversion (*Edlington Properties Ltd v JH Fenner & Co Ltd* (2006)).

— *Secure tenant's 'right to repair'* Under which a 'secure tenant' (e.g. a council tenant (**14.29**)) is entitled, on application to the landlord, to have certain 'qualifying' repairs to his dwelling effected within a prescribed period at the landlord's expense and, in cases of default by the landlord, to receive compensation (see HA 1985, s 96(1), as substituted by LRH & UDA 1993, s 121; Secure Tenants of Local Housing Authorities (Right to Repair) Regulations 1994 (SI 1994/133)).

— *Appointment of a receiver* In the case of continuing default by a corporate landlord, to receive the rents from tenants and to manage the entire property in accordance with the landlord's obligations.

— *Appointment of a manager* In the case of a block containing two or more flats, to take over the management of the premises or the functions of a receiver or both (L&TA 1987, ss 21–4, as amended by HA 1996, ss 85–6, CALRA 2002, ss 158, 160, Sch 11). The Commonhold and Leasehold Reform Act 2002 confers a more general right (a 'right to manage' or 'RTM') on the tenants of such premises—even in the absence of any breach of obligation by the landlord—to take over the management of the block through a private company limited by guarantee (a 'RTM company') of which all participating tenants, together with the landlord, are members (see CALRA 2002, ss 71–113, **7.40**).

— *Rejection of the entire tenancy* In the event of a landlord's repudiatory breach of a *fundamental* covenant of the lease, entitling the tenant both to throw up the tenancy without notice and to sue for breach of the landlord's repairing obligation (*Hussein v Mehlman* (1992), **7.35**).

Other statutory obligations of the landlord

14.7 Statute law also imposes a number of duties on landlords, including obligations:

- to disclose certain information as to the identity of the landlord (L&TA 1985, s 1(1)) or of any new landlord to whom the landlord's reversionary interest has been assigned (L&TA 1985, ss 3(1), 3A, as added by HA 1996, s 93);

- to provide a rent book for weekly tenants (L&TA 1985, s 4(1));

- to provide the tenant with a written statement of the terms of certain kinds of orally granted assured shorthold tenancy (**14.28**) (HA 1988, s 20A);

- to provide tenants in a block of flats with regular certified statements of account relating to charges for services, repairs, maintenance, improvements, insurance and management costs (L&TA 1985, ss 21–1A, as substituted by CALRA 2002, s 152) and to facilitate the tenants' right effectively to audit the management of the premises (L&TA 1985, s 22, as substituted by CALRA 2002, s 154; LRH & UDA 1993, ss 76–9);

- to demand only such service or administration charges as are reasonable and to submit such charges to the determination of a leasehold valuation tribunal in cases where their propriety or reasonableness is challenged by a residential tenant (L&TA 1985, ss 19, 20–20ZA, 27A, as amended by CALRA 2002, ss 151, 155; CALRA 2002, s 158, Sch 11, paras 2–3).

Express obligations of the tenant

14.8 The express terms of leases both formal and informal tend to impose extensive liabilities and disabilities on the tenant, ranging from the obligation to pay rent to restrictions upon the tenant's freedom to assign or sublet the premises. It is almost invariable, in a written lease, for the landlord to retain control over future assignment or subletting by his tenant. In the case of tenancies granted before 1996, any requirement of prior consent by the landlord to such dealing by the tenant is subject to the statutory proviso that the landlord's consent must not be *unreasonably* withheld (L&TA 1927, s 19(1); L&TA 1988, s 1; see *Ashworth Fraser Ltd v Gloucester CC* (2001)). However, in the case of most non-residential tenancies granted after 1995 it is now possible for the landlord and the tenant by agreement to specify the conditions which shall control future assignments, *whether or not* these conditions are objectively 'reasonable' (see L&TA 1927, s 19(1A), as added by L&T(C)A 1995, s 22). In relation to post-1995 leases it is almost always a condition of consent to assignment that the assignor-tenant should enter into an 'authorised guarantee agreement' (**14.21, 14.24**).

Implied obligations of the tenant

14.9 In the absence of contrary stipulation in the lease, the tenant undertakes, by implication of law, certain obligations to pay rent, not to commit waste, and (in the case of periodic tenancies other than yearly tenancies) to use the premises in a 'husbandlike' or 'tenantlike' manner, i.e. to 'do the little jobs about the place which a reasonable tenant would do' (*Warren v Keen* (1954) per Denning LJ). The law in this area is lamentably vague and much in need of coherent restatement.

Landlord's remedies for breach of covenant by the tenant

14.10 The landlord has a number of remedies in respect of the tenant's breach of the covenants contained (either expressly or impliedly) in a lease. These remedies include the following:

- forfeiture of the lease (**14.11**);
- distress for unpaid rent (**14.16**);
- action for arrears of rent (**14.17**);
- damages for breach of covenant (**14.18**);
- injunction and specific performance (**14.19**).

Forfeiture of the lease

14.11 The right to 're-enter' the demised premises and forfeit the lease or tenancy is the most draconian weapon in the armoury of the landlord whose tenant has committed a breach of covenant. Most written leases contain an ample forfeiture clause, whose primary purpose is to provide the landlord with a lever to enforce compliance with the covenants of the lease.

- The right of re-entry constitutes for the landlord both his ultimate security against the non-payment of rent and his ultimate insurance in respect of the commercial investment represented by the lease (see *Inntrepreneur Pub Co (CPC) Ltd v Langton* (2000) per Arden J). The right of re-entry ranks, moreover, as an independent proprietary interest vested in the landlord over the land demised to the tenant (LPA 1925, s 1(2)(e), **8.35**).

- In a *legal* term of years the landlord's right to re-enter and forfeit the lease must be reserved *expressly* (unless the performance of the tenant's obligations is stipulated as a 'condition' on which the future subsistence of the lease depends). In other words, a right of re-entry cannot be *implied* in a legal lease, although precisely such a right is normally implied in every *equitable* lease (*Chester v Buckingham Travel Ltd* (1981)), clearly ranking in such cases as an *equitable* right of re-entry (see *Shiloh Spinners Ltd v Harding* (1973), **8.35**). Where a right of re-entry is available to the landlord, it gives him the right, in the event of breach, to elect either to *waive* forfeiture or to *enforce* it, enforcement comprising an actual physical entry upon the demised premises or the service of possession proceedings against the tenant (see *Billson v Residential Apartments Ltd* (1992)).

Restrictions upon exercise of the right of re-entry

14.12 The exercise of a landlord's right of re-entry is subject to certain important restrictions.

— *Residential leases* There is in English law a 'basic rule' that it is unlawful for an owner, otherwise than by court proceedings, to enforce his right to recover possession of premises which have been let wholly or partly as a dwelling (Protection from Eviction Act 1977, ss 2, 3(1) (**7.29**): see *Harrow LBC v Qazi* (2004) at [36] per Lord Hope of Craighead). This requirement of curial process accords vital recognition to the tenant's right to respect for his private life and home in compliance with ECHR Art 8 (see *Patel v Pirabakaran* (2006) at [44] per

Wilson LJ). It also ensures that, for purposes of ECHR Art 6, the tenant's civil rights and obligations are determined only after a 'fair and public hearing' (see *Southwark LBC v St Brice* (2002) at [16] per Kennedy LJ, [34] per Chadwick LJ).

• No matter how heinous the breach committed by the tenant, the landlord who re-enters against a residential tenant *without* a court order for possession commits a serious criminal offence (PEA 1977, ss 1(2), 2). The availability of this criminal sanction demonstrates yet again the age-old common law concern to protect actual, even if errant, occupiers of land (**3.3**). (In the case of tenancies protected under the Rent Act 1977 or the Housing Acts 1985 and 1988, this protection against arbitrary eviction is reinforced by a series of further restrictions which curtail the landlord's right to recover possession even against tenants in substantial default, **14.27–14.29**.)

• Criminal liability also attaches, in general, to any form of harassment or constructive eviction of a residential tenant (see PEA 1977, s 1(3)). The victim of unlawful eviction may sue both in contract and in tort and is nowadays afforded a significant statutory remedy in civil damages against his landlord (Housing Act 1988, s 27(1)–(3): see e.g. the award of £31,000 in *Tagro v Cafane* (1991)). Despite the apparent breadth of the standard leasehold forfeiture clause, extra-curial eviction of a residential tenant is likely to prove an extremely expensive activity.

• It seems clear that the removal of a residential tenant from his premises 'is bound to interfere with his enjoyment' of the right to respect for his 'home' pursuant to ECHR Art 8(1) (see *Harrow LBC v Qazi* (2004) at [70] per Lord Hope). However, the balance of 'proportionality' which, under ECHR Art 8(2), requires to be maintained between the individual's right to such respect and wider public or other interests is, in practice, addressed in the terms on which various statutory schemes empower the court to make a possession order against the tenant (see *Qazi* at [73] per Lord Hope, [109] per Lord Millett; *Kay v Lambeth LBC, Leeds CC v Price* (2006) at [39] per Lord Bingham of Cornhill). Indeed, a majority in the House of Lords in both *Qazi* and *Kay/Price* (**2.15**) went to some pains to reinforce its view that a landlord's entitlement to possession against his tenant cannot, by reference to ECHR Art 8, be deflected by some additional exercise of discretionary judgment based on the degree of impact on the tenant's home life of the eviction. Furthermore, the majority in *Qazi* was anxious to counter the suggestion that Convention guarantees can apply with 'horizontal effect' to the relations of *private* landlords and *private* tenants (see e.g. *Qazi* at [108] per Lord Millett, [142]–[143] per Lord Scott). Nevertheless the rulings in *Qazi* and *Kay/Price* are controversial. The principal instinct of the majority judges in the House of Lords was to prevent regimes of *mandatory* repossession from being diluted into regimes of merely *discretionary* repossession, but the question remains whether the approach evidenced in *Qazi* and *Kay/Price* is truly reconcilable with the more open-textured proprietary morality displayed by the European Court of Human Rights in its ruling in *Connors v United Kingdom* (2004) (**2.15**).

— *Non-residential leases* The requirement of a court order for possession does not generally apply to re-entry under non-residential leases except in the case of re-entry for breach of a repairing covenant (see Leasehold Property (Repairs) Act 1938, s 1). Provided that the landlord first serves any statutory notice which the tenant may be entitled to receive (**14.13**), forfeiture by peaceable re-entry remains a perfectly viable—indeed sometimes highly attractive—option in response to breaches of covenant under a business lease (see e.g. *Kataria v Safeland plc* (1997)). The risk of criminal liability (see Criminal Law Act 1977, s 6(1), **3.8, 15.16**) can normally be averted by the simple expedient of ensuring that re-entry upon commercial premises is effected outside business hours or at weekends. Forfeiture by physical re-entry nevertheless displays a certain surreptitious and lawless aspect, leading the courts in recent years to voice distaste for this 'hole-in-the-corner, self-help route' to the recovery of possession (*Billson v Residential Apartments Ltd* (1992) per Nicholls LJ).

> *Billson v Residential Apartments Ltd* (1992) T, the tenants of unoccupied premises, undertook major works of reconstruction in blatant contravention of the terms of their lease. Doubtless incensed by this flagrant breach, L carried out a 'dawn raid', peaceably re-entering the vacant premises at 6 a.m. and changing the locks. Four hours later T's workmen broke back into the premises and regained occupation. The House of Lords, whilst affirming the continuing legality of forfeiture by actual re-entry, nevertheless expressed a strong preference for 'the civilised method of determining the lease by issuing and serving a writ' rather than 'the dubious and dangerous method of determining the lease by re-entering the premises' (**14.14**).

— *Leases generally* A new factor has emerged to qualify a landlord's right to seek possession against his tenant. The broadly drafted terms of the Disability Discrimination Act 1995 have opened up the possibility that the courts may be confronted by 'a deluge of cases in which disabled tenants are resisting possession proceedings' on the ground of improper discrimination (see *Manchester CC v Romano and Samari* (2004) at [68] per Brooke LJ).

Preliminaries to forfeiture

14.13 Certain preliminaries require to be observed in advance of any attempt to forfeit a lease for breach of covenant. The legislation of recent years has been particularly concerned to bolster the protection of residential tenants against oppressive threats or acts of forfeiture by a landlord.

— *Formal and other demands for rent* Where breach comprises the non-payment of rent, re-entry must be preceded by the making of a 'formal demand' for rent unless the requirement of formal demand is obviated either by the express terms of the lease or by statute (see Common Law Procedure Act 1852, s 210). (Today almost all professionally drafted leases exempt the landlord from making any formal demand for rent.) Where the tenant holds under a 'long lease' of a dwelling (generally a lease granted for a term exceeding 21 years), the tenant is not liable to make any payment of rent unless the landlord first serves on him a notice specifying a date for payment between 30 and 60 days following the notice (CALRA 2002, ss 76–7, 166). Furthermore, under a long residential lease of this kind the landlord is not even entitled to exercise a right of re-entry or forfeiture unless the unpaid amounts of rent (or service or administration charges) exceed a prescribed sum or have been due for more than a prescribed period (CALRA 2002, s 167(1)–(2)).

— *Section 146 notices* Forfeiture for breach of covenants *other than* the covenant to pay rent is governed by the special notice procedure laid down by LPA 1925, s 146. The landlord may not enforce any right of re-entry or forfeiture, either by court action or by peaceable re-entry, unless he has first served a valid statutory notice on the tenant and the tenant has failed within a reasonable time to comply with its terms. In order to protect *residential* tenants holding under a 'long lease' from trigger-happy complaints of breach, the Commonhold and Leasehold Reform Act 2002 introduces a requirement that, prior to service of the statutory notice, the fact of breach must have been established on the landlord's application to a leasehold valuation tribunal, by the tenant's admission or otherwise by some final determination of a court (CALRA 2002, s 168). The interposition of this requirement merely reinforces the point that, in terms of ECHR Art 6, the tenant's civil rights and obligations have been determined only after a 'fair and public hearing' (see also *Southwark LBC v St Brice* (2002))—an issue which might otherwise have remained highly debatable in cases involving forfeiture by peaceable re-entry.

• The overall impact of the 'section 146 notice' regime (and of the jurisdiction to provide relief against forfeiture which is activated by the service of a notice (**14.14**)) is to superimpose certain rudimentary requirements of due process and proportionality upon the compulsory divesting of a substantial proprietary asset. The 'section 146 notice' must:
  — specify the particular breach of which complaint is made;
  — require that the tenant remedy the breach 'if the breach is capable of remedy'; and

— normally require that the tenant make compensation in money for the breach.

• The purpose of the section 146 procedure is 'to give even tenants who have hitherto lacked the will or the means to comply with their obligations one last chance to summon up that will or find the necessary means before the landlord re-enters' (*Expert Clothing Service & Sales Ltd v Hillgate House Ltd* (1986) per Slade LJ). Where a breach is 'capable of remedy', the section 146 notice gives the tenant the opportunity to remedy his breach 'within a reasonable time' after the service of the notice and then, if necessary, to apply to the court under section 146 for relief against forfeiture. Where, however, the tenant's breach is *not* 'capable of remedy', the object of the notice procedure is simply to enable the tenant to throw himself immediately upon the court's discretion to grant relief (although such relief is unlikely to be forthcoming, **14.14**).

— *Forfeiture for breach of the tenant's repairing covenants* Any section 146 notice which relates to a breach of the tenant's repairing covenants must make visible reference to the tenant's rights under the Leasehold Property (Repairs) Act 1938. The 1938 Act applies to leases for a term of seven years or more, of which at the relevant time at least three years remain unexpired (LP(R)A 1938, ss 1(1), 7(1)). The Act requires that the landlord obtain the sanction of the court before pursuing any remedy of forfeiture or damages on the basis of non-repair (LP(R)A 1938, s 1(3)).

— *Forfeiture for failure to pay a service or administration charge* Any section 146 notice which relates to a tenant's alleged failure to pay a service or administration charge in respect of residential property must, if it is to be effective, inform the tenant that the landlord is not entitled to exercise any right of re-entry or forfeiture on this ground unless the tenant's liability to pay the charge in question has been admitted by the tenant or has been established by some final determination of a leasehold valuation tribunal or other court (HA 1996, ss 81(1)–(2), 82(2)–(4), as amended by CALRA 2002, s 170).

— *Remediable breaches of covenant* In recent years the test of the remediability of a *breach*—for the purposes of LPA 1925, s 146—has tended to be construed as a test of the remediability of the *damage* caused by that breach. As Slade LJ indicated in *Expert Clothing Service & Sales Ltd v Hillgate House Ltd* (1986), the 'ultimate question' is whether the 'harm' suffered by the landlord would be 'effectively remedied' if the tenant were to comply within a reasonable time with a section 146 notice demanding both remedy and compensation. A breach is therefore 'capable of remedy' if, but only if, the landlord can be restored within a reasonable time to the position he would have been in if no breach had occurred. In the relatively rare case where he cannot be so restored, the way is opened for the landlord to enforce the forfeiture.

- Breaches of *positive covenants* (e.g. to repair) are almost always capable of remedy, since such a breach can usually be cured by belated performance of the covenanted action.

> *Expert Clothing Service & Sales Ltd v Hillgate House Ltd* (1986) The Court of Appeal held that T's breach of a covenant to reconstruct premises within a specified time was 'capable of remedy' by performance *out of time,* since L would not suffer irretrievable prejudice if T tendered late performance of his covenant and made adequate money compensation for his breach.

- Breaches of *negative covenants* are also now regarded as normally capable of remedy, provided that 'the mischief caused by the breach can be removed' by belated compliance with the tenant's covenants (see *Savva and Savva v Hussein* (1996) per Staughton LJ). It is possible that certain 'once and for all' breaches of a negative covenant (e.g. not to assign without consent) can *never* be remedied, leaving the tenant entirely dependent on the court's discretion to grant relief against forfeiture (see *Scala House and District Property Co Ltd v Forbes* (1974), although compare *Akici v LR Butlin Ltd* (2005) at [66] per Neuberger LJ). However, the modern approach is set firmly in favour of treating the breach of most negative covenants as remediable if the harm inflicted on the landlord can be effectively removed by due compliance coupled with appropriate money compensation (see *Bass Holdings Ltd v Morton Music Ltd* (1988) per Bingham LJ; *Savva and Savva v Hussein* per Aldous LJ). In rare cases the tenant's breach is of such a nature that it cannot be remedied by mere cesser of the prohibited activity (even if coupled with compensation). Here 'the taint lingers on and will not dissipate within a reasonable time' (*Expert Clothing Service & Sales Ltd v Hillgate House Ltd* (1986) per O'Connor LJ), and forfeiture is thus virtually inevitable.

> *Rugby School (Governors) v Tannahill* (1935) The Court of Appeal held that the use of the demised premises in breach of covenant as a brothel was *irremediable* because even a complete cesser could not remove the 'stigma' which the tenant's wrongful activities had caused to attach to the premises.

> *Van Haarlam v Kasner* (1992) A tenant's conviction for offences committed under the Official Secrets Acts was held to be an *irremediable breach* of a leasehold covenant against user of the premises for illegal purposes. (There was evidence that much of the tenant's illegal activity as a spy had been conducted from within his flat.)

The tenant's access to relief against forfeiture

14.14 The most important general limitation on the successful exercise of a landlord's right of re-entry lies in the possibility that the tenant may in appropriate circumstances obtain *relief against forfeiture*. From the earliest times courts of equity have asserted the right to relieve against the forfeiture of rights on the ground that such a penalty is disproportional to the breach upon which the forfeiture is premised. For instance, the tenant who spends £150,000 on the purchase of a 99-year lease of a flat may well have placed herself in breach of her leasehold covenants by keeping a cat or a budgerigar on the premises, but it seems wrong in principle that the entire lease should be rendered forfeitable in the event of trivial misconduct which activates the landlord's right to re-enter.

— *Non-payment of rent* The courts have traditionally restrained the exercise of the landlord's right to re-enter for non-payment of rent. Since the entitlement to re-enter is essentially a security to ensure due compliance with the covenant to pay rent (see *Bland v Ingrams Estates Ltd* (2001) at [70] per Chadwick LJ, **14.11**), re-entry seems improper where the tenant, albeit belatedly, pays all rent owed to and costs incurred by the landlord (*Howard v Fanshawe* (1895)).

• The tenant therefore has certain rights to the automatic termination of possession proceedings brought against him in either the High Court or the county court if he pays all rent arrears and costs before the trial date (Common Law Procedure Act 1852, s 212; County Courts Act 1984, s 138(2)). The courts even retain a discretion to grant relief in certain cases where arrears and costs are tendered either *after* a court order for possession but *before* the premises have been re-let to a stranger (CLPA 1852, s 210; CCA 1984, s 138(3)–(5), (9A)) or within six months of a peaceable re-entry by the landlord (CCA 1984, s 139(2)).

• In cases not covered by any statutory jurisdiction to relieve against forfeiture, the courts have a residual *equitable* jurisdiction to grant relief, with the consequence that, even following a fairly appalling history of rent default, relief against forfeiture for non-payment tends to be withheld only in the most exceptional circumstances (see e.g. *Public Trustee v Westbrook* (1965), where no rent was paid for 22 years). However, in a lacuna uncovered only relatively recently, no jurisdiction to relieve against forfeiture applies to assured tenancies (**14.28**) granted under the Housing Act 1988 (effectively most modern private lettings of residential property). Here the Housing Act provides a self-contained and definitive code for the termination of such tenancies and leaves no room for the range of protection afforded the defaulting tenant by the CCA 1984 (see *Artesian Residential Developments Ltd v Beck* (2000)).

— *Breaches other than non-payment of rent*   The court also has a broad statutory discretion to relieve against forfeiture for breaches other than non-payment of rent (LPA 1925, s 146(2)). Access to the court's merciful discretion becomes available immediately from the point when the landlord serves a section 146 notice on the tenant. The House of Lords made it clear in *Billson v Residential Apartments Ltd* (1992) that the section 146 jurisdiction may therefore be invoked:

- where the landlord has not yet instituted possession proceedings against the tenant; or

- where the landlord has obtained a court judgment for possession against the tenant, but has not yet executed this judgment by physical re-entry; or

- where the landlord elects to forfeit the lease, not by obtaining and executing a court order for possession but instead by exercising his simple right of peaceable re-entry upon the demised premises (i.e. the factual situation in the *Billson* case itself, **14.12**).

Billson v Residential Apartments Ltd (1992) The House of Lords ruled that the section 146 jurisdiction to relieve against forfeiture remained available to T even after actual re-entry by L without a court order. The decision goes some distance towards ensuring that the self-help remedy of forfeiture by actual re-entry (**14.12**) is not rendered visibly *more* advantageous for landlords than the alternative remedy of forfeiture by due legal process. Both Nicholls LJ (dissenting in the Court of Appeal) and the House of Lords were anxious to avoid any construction of section 146 which would amount to 'a charter for forcible entry', thereby encouraging the landlord 'to keep away from court and to pounce on the property, in the evening or at the weekend, and change the locks and then sit back secure in the knowledge that forfeiture is complete'.

The tenant's access to the exercise of discretion under section 146 is finally cut off *only*:

- where the landlord has forfeited the lease by initiating a claim for possession and has *both* recovered judgment *and* already entered into possession pursuant to this judgment; or

- where the landlord has made a peaceable re-entry, but the tenant has failed, within a reasonable time thereafter, to seek relief against forfeiture, at which point his delay debars him from relief altogether.

Where the section 146 jurisdiction is still available, the court obviously has substantial regard to the gravity of the breach and the disparity between the value of the property of which forfeiture is claimed and the extent of the damage caused by the breach. Relevance may be attached to an evasive and aggressive demeanour on the part of the tenant (*Akici v LR Butlin Ltd* (2005)). Relief will be available, however, only if the landlord's position has *not* been 'irrevocably damaged' by the breach (*WG Clark (Properties) Ltd v Dupre Properties Ltd* (1992) per Deputy Judge Thomas Morison QC). Whilst relief is normally granted in cases of relatively minor or unintentional breach or where a breach has been effectively remedied, *irremediable* breaches are almost always beyond the scope of the discretion to relieve against forfeiture (see e.g. *Dunraven Securities Ltd v Holloway* (1982) (use of premises as a sex shop)).

Effect of forfeiture

14.15 The exercise of the landlord's right of re-entry has a number of important consequences (both actual and potential) for the tenant and for other persons.

— *Effect on tenant* Once the landlord's right to immediate possession has been converted into actual possession by means of re-entry, the tenant becomes a trespasser and the landlord may use such force as is reasonably necessary to expel him.

— *Effect on subtenant* Forfeiture of a head lease necessarily and automatically destroys any sublease created out of the head lease (*Great Western Railway Co v Smith* (1876); *Kay v Lambeth LBC* (2006) at [147])—a common law principle which flows logically from the derivative nature of the sublease (see *PW & Co v Milton Gate Investments Ltd* (2004) at [73], [136] per Neuberger J, **14.25**). The subtenant nevertheless has an independent right to seek relief against forfeiture on such terms as the court thinks fit (LPA 1925, s 146(4)). The court may even invest the subtenant with an entirely new estate in the demised premises, although this new estate cannot last for any longer term than he had under his original sublease (see also CCA 1984, s 138(9)).

— *Effect on mortgagee* Forfeiture has a potentially devastating effect on any security held by a lender whose loan money has helped to finance the purchase of a lease by a tenant who has since committed breaches of his leasehold covenants.

• The termination of the tenant's estate in the land will, of course, destroy the mortgage, but a legal mortgagee or chargee is generally eligible to seek independent relief against forfeiture (see LPA 1925, s 146(4); CCA 1984, ss 138(9C), 139(2)–(3), 140). The High Court also retains an equitable jurisdiction to grant relief to a legal mortgagee or chargee who knew nothing of the tenant's breaches and from whom the landlord deliberately concealed the existence of his forfeiture proceedings (see *Abbey National Building Society v Maybeech Ltd* (1985) per Nicholls J).

• Equitable chargees have no direct access to this inherent equitable jurisdiction, but may nevertheless seek relief against forfeiture for non-payment of rent either by joining the defaulting tenant as a defendant in any forfeiture action and claiming relief in the tenant's shoes (see *Bland v Ingrams Estates Ltd* (2001) at [34] per Nourse LJ) or simply by virtue of CCA 1984, ss 138(9C), 139(2)–(3) (see *Bland v Ingrams Estates Ltd* at [64], [69] per Chadwick LJ, [83] per Hale LJ).

— *Effect on squatter* A squatter who has acquired a title by adverse possession against a leaseholder (**6.8**) has no sufficient interest in the lease to enable him to apply for relief against its forfeiture (*Tickner v Buzzacott* (1965)).

— *Proposals for reform* The Law Commission has long expressed the view that the existing law of forfeiture is 'unnecessarily complicated, is no longer coherent and may give rise to injustice' (see Law Com No 142 (1985), para 1.3). Accordingly the Commission has recommended the statutory introduction of a new 'termination action' scheme (see Law Com No 303 (2006)) under which no distinction would be made between termination for non-payment of rent and termination for other reasons. Every tenancy would remain in full force until the court made a 'termination order' fixing the date on which the tenancy should end (Law Com No 303, paras 5.19, 5.30–5.31). The landlord (but *not* the tenant) could seek such a termination order on the basis of statutorily indicated events, the court having discretion either to grant the termination requested (together with compensation) or to make a 'remedial order' requiring specified remedial action (including payment of rent arrears) within a certain time scale. The landlord would also have, as an alternative to a termination claim, the right to invoke a 'summary termination procedure' under which, without the necessity of a court order, he could recover possession from a defaulting tenant who has no reasonable prospect of defending any termination claim (ibid, paras 7.61–7.114). The 'summary termination procedure' would, however, be available only in respect of commercial premises and residential premises which have been abandoned (ibid, paras 7.81–7.82). The procedure would never apply to any tenancy whose unexpired term exceeds 25 years (ibid, para 7.83).

Distress for unpaid rent

14.16 Distress is an ancient common law remedy which entitles the landlord, in appropriate circumstances, summarily to seize goods found on the demised premises, sell them up and recoup from the proceeds of sale any arrears of rent owed by the tenant. Although sometimes described as an obsolete remedy, distress is not infrequently used, especially by local authority landlords, as a means of recovering arrears of rent from a defaulting tenant. Distress can generally be levied without the necessity of any prior court process, but is subject to certain important restrictions relating to the time and manner of its execution and the nature of the goods which may be seized. The Law Commission has proposed that distress for rent should be abolished (Law Com No 194 (1991), para 3.1). In view of its extra-curial nature, distress is now particularly vulnerable to challenge as infringing guarantees under the ECHR of the right to a 'fair and public hearing' (ECHR Art 6) and of protection for the tenant's 'peaceful enjoyment' of his possessions (ECHR Protocol No 1, Art 1). It seems likely that the government will soon introduce legislation to end the availability of distress in at least the residential sector (see Law Com No 288 (2004), para 3.36).

Action for arrears of rent

14.17 A maximum of six years' arrears of rent may be recovered in an action brought by the landlord in respect of a tenant's non-payment of rent (Limitation Act 1980, s 19). It is traditionally said that, in English law, the landlord has no duty to mitigate loss by re-letting premises which have been abandoned mid-term by a tenant who fails to pay his rent (see *Boyer v Warbey* (1953) per Denning LJ). The landlord need not re-enter, but may simply sue for the unpaid rent as it continues to accrue. It is increasingly debatable whether this approach can survive the gradual contractualisation of the leasehold relationship (**7.10**). (The Law Commission has proposed that the limitation period for the recovery of rent be reduced to three years from the landlord's actual or constructive knowledge of the rent default or 10 years from the date of that default, whichever period first expires (Law Com No 270 (2001), paras 4.154–4.157).)

Damages for breach of covenant

14.18 Damages may be awarded in respect of breach by the tenant of any covenant other than a covenant respecting payment of rent. Except where the breach is of a repairing covenant, damages are assessed on the usual contractual basis, i.e. for the purpose of placing the landlord in the position—in so far as this can be done by means of a monetary award—in which he would have been if there had been no breach by the tenant. Damages for breach of a tenant's covenant to keep or put premises in repair cannot exceed the amount by which the value of the reversion has been diminished through the breach (L&TA 1927, s 18(1)).

Injunction and specific performance

14.19 It is possible in appropriate circumstances for the landlord to seek the discretionary remedy of the injunction for the purpose of restraining breaches of certain covenants in the lease. In recent years the courts have even set aside venerable authority in order to enable the landlord, through an order for specific performance, to compel the tenant's compliance with repairing covenants. Such enforcement may be particularly appropriate where a lease contains no provision for forfeiture or re-entry or for any right of access by the landlord for the purpose of effecting necessary repairs (see e.g. *Rainbow Estates Ltd v Tokenhold Ltd* (1999)). Generally, however, the courts have withheld the award of mandatory injunctions and orders of specific performance where compensatory damages constitute an adequate remedy (**13.19**).

> *Co-operative Insurance Society Ltd v Argyll Stores (Holdings) Ltd* (1998) 15 years after the commencement of a 35-year lease of supermarket premises in a shopping centre, T closed its supermarket because it was losing money. The closure, in clear breach of T's obligation under the lease to keep the premises open for retail trade during the usual hours of business, threatened the commercial vitality of much of the remainder of the shopping centre. The House of Lords declined to issue a mandatory injunction requiring that T continue to trade on the premises, citing a settled (although not invariable) practice *not* to require a defendant positively to carry on a business. (The decision has been fiercely criticised as allowing a thoroughly cynical tenant to buy its way out of covenanted obligations undertaken pursuant to an arm's-length bargain: see e.g. A.M. Tettenborn, 'Absolving the Undeserving: Shopping Centres, Specific Performance and the Law of Contract' [1998] *Conv* 23.)

Privity of contract and privity of estate

14.20 The enforceability of leasehold covenants presents little difficulty as between the original landlord and tenant, but grows more awkward as successive assignees and subtenants become increasingly remote from the initial contractual relationship of the lease (**7.17**). As Lord Templeman pointed out in *City of London Corpn v Fell* (1994), the common law was faced centuries ago with the 'problem of rendering effective the obligations under a lease which might endure for a period of 999 years or more beyond the control of any covenantor.' It simply could not be that the essential covenants of a lease fell away with the disappearance of the original contracting parties, leaving the residue of the leasehold term ungoverned by clear or durable ground rules. It was therefore vital that the law should provide a framework of liability which would ensure the policing of the covenants of the lease in the more distant reaches of the leasehold relationship well beyond the nexus of original lessor and original lessee. This objective came to be achieved largely by means of a distinction drawn between *privity of contract* and *privity of estate*, although in some cases the operation of these concepts has now been dramatically modified by the complex and ungainly provisions of the Landlord and Tenant (Covenants) Act 1995 and, more recently, by the Contracts (Rights of Third Parties) Act 1999.

Let us now examine the framework of enforcement relationships which can gather around the leasehold term, using for this purpose a model of a head lease which has given rise to a number of assignments and subleases (see *Fig* 24, adapting a model used earlier in this book, **7.17**).

The framework of legal rules governing the enforcement of leasehold liabilities is premised upon the duality of character implicit in the leasehold device (**7.10, 14.1**). A term of years 'originates in contract' (*City of London Corpn v Fell* (1993) per Nourse LJ), but it also confers on the tenant a proprietary estate in the land which, like the correlative reversionary estate held by the landlord, is assignable to third parties (**7.17**).

— *Privity of contract* obtains between the original contracting parties in the leasehold relationship, L1 and T1, and is replicated on every fresh grant of an inferior leasehold estate. Thus, in *Fig* 24, privity of contract also obtains, on the grant of the five-year sublease, between T2 and ST1, and on the subsequent grant

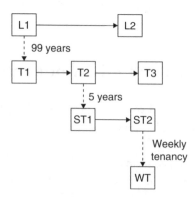

Fig 24

of a weekly tenancy, between ST2 and WT. At common law these relationships of contractual privity endure unaffected by any subsequent assignment of any estate.

—   *Privity of estate*   obtains between any two persons who, in respect of the same leasehold estate, currently stand vis-à-vis each other in the position of landlord and tenant. As the title or status of each person 'privy' to a particular leasehold estate is shuffled on by assignments of the superior or inferior interest, each successive assignee can describe himself, both functionally and technically, as holding as either *landlord* or *tenant* in relation to some other identified person. Thus, in *Fig* 24, L1 and T1 are initially conjoined in a privity of both *contract* and *estate,* but as soon as, say, T1 assigns his term to T2, a *new* privity of estate arises, this time between L1 and T2. T1 'cannot properly be described as the tenant. He no longer holds the land. It is the assignee who now holds the land. It is he who has the tenancy' (*City of London Corpn v Fell* (1993) per Nourse LJ). Equally when L1 assigns the superior reversionary estate to L2, it is L2 who thereafter ranks as the 'landlord' (see *Hua Chiao Commercial Bank Ltd v Chiaphua Industries Ltd* (1987) per Lord Oliver of Aylmerton) and *privity of estate* now obtains between L2 and T2. When later T2 assigns to T3, it is L2 and T3 who, at this point, stand in a relationship of privity of estate.

—   *Different privities of estate*   In effect *privity of contract* denotes the ambit of contractual liability within the leasehold framework, whilst *privity of estate* indicates at any given time the precise allocation of the tenancy of the land. At any one moment privity of estate obtains only as between those who currently hold in possession the interests of landlord and tenant. Thus privity of estate in relation to the 99-year head lease in *Fig* 24 is enjoyed at some time or other by L1, L2, T1, T2, and T3. Privity of estate in relation to the five-year sublease is enjoyed—again at some time or other—by T2, T3, ST1, and ST2. But it is important to realise that ST1 can *never* be said to be 'privy' to the estate of the head lease granted by L1 to T1, nor WT 'privy' to the estate of the five-year sublease—each is 'privy' to a different estate (**14.25**).

Liability as between L1 and T1

14.21   In *Fig* 24, prior to any assignment by either, the relationship of L1 and T1 is at common law straighforwardly *contractual*. Each is contractually liable to the other on *all* the covenants of the lease (other than those which are illegal or contrary to public policy) irrespective of whether these covenants 'touch and concern' the demised land (**14.22**). Indeed, so dominant was the contractual analysis of the relationship between L1 and T1 that, in the absence of some expressly agreed release, both used to remain fully liable on all the covenants of the lease throughout the entire duration of the term of the lease (e.g. for a full term of 99 years)—quite irrespective of subsequent assignment by either (see e.g. *Warnford Investments Ltd v Duckworth* (1979)).

— *The old rule of contract-based liability* The principle of continuing *contract-based* liability often produced harsh consequences in that it could mean that T1, although he had long ago assigned the residue of his term, was suddenly confronted with an enforceable demand for arrears of rent unpaid by T2 or T3 or for damages in respect of some other default committed by T2 or T3 (see Lord Nicholls's reference in *Hindcastle Ltd v Barbara Attenborough Associates Ltd* (1997) to the sense of shock experienced by the 'person of modest means' who 'out of the blue receives a rent demand from the landlord of the property he once leased'). With the spate of corporate insolvencies which emerged during the 1980s and early 1990s, this wholly unanticipated source of liability began to come home, with alarming frequency, to persons in the position of T1. If L1 (or, in his turn, L2) discovered that a subsequent assignee of the leasehold term was bankrupt or insolvent, it was obviously tempting and sometimes relatively easy to enforce a money liability against an attractively solvent T1.

— *The pressure for change* The principle of enduring contractual liability nevertheless came to be regarded as conferring an unfairly generous protection on L1 (see Law Com No 174 (1988), paras 4.3–4.8). Following mounting public concern the implications of contractual privity were severely curtailed by the Landlord and Tenant (Covenants) Act 1995. For present purposes the 1995 Act draws a sharp distinction between *new* tenancies (i.e. those granted on or after 1 January 1996) and *old* (i.e. pre-1996) tenancies.

— *New tenancies* A pivotal provision of the L&T(C)A 1995 is the principle that T1, on assigning the whole of the premises demised to him, is thereafter released from the 'tenant covenants' contained in the original lease and is correspondingly disabled from any further enjoyment of its 'landlord covenants' (L&T(C)A 1995, s 5(2)). T1's guarantor (if any) is simultaneously freed from further liability under his surety covenant (L&T(C)A 1995, s 24(2)). These novel principles have mandatory force: a statutory penalty of voidness attaches if and to the extent that any agreement relating to a tenancy purports to have the effect of excluding, modifying or otherwise frustrating the operation of the 1995 Act (see L&T(C)A 1995, s 25(1), but note *London Diocesan Fund v Phithwa (Avonridge Property Co Ltd, Part 20 Defendant)* (2005), infra). The statutory release of T1 does not, however, apply in *three* special cases:

- where T1's assignment to T2 is *in breach of covenant* (L&T(C)A 1995, s 11(1)–(2));

- where T1's assignment to T2 occurs *by operation of law* (L&T(C)A 1995, s 11(1)–(2));

- where L1, as a condition of consenting to the assignment to T2, causes T1 to enter into an *authorised guarantee agreement* (see L&T(C)A 1995, s 16(2)–(3)), under which T1 guarantees the due performance by T2—but only by T2—of the covenants of the lease.

  — Most leases expressly require that any assignment of the leasehold term must have the consent of the landlord (**14.8**). The imposition of an 'authorised guarantee agreement' as a precondition of such consent allows the old principle of continuing tenant liability to retain a strictly limited effect: T1 is made to bear an on-going liability for the defaults of his immediate assignee (T2), but not, for instance, for those of T3. T1's exposure to any 'fixed charge' liability of T2 is, however, restricted to such liability as is incurred during the *six months* immediately preceding the service of a statutory notice warning him of impending recovery by L1 (see L&T(C)A 1995, s 17(1)(a), (2), (4), infra).

  — Likewise T2, on a further assignment of the term to T3, can be made to enter into another 'authorised guarantee agreement', which effectively causes T2 to warrant T3's performance of the leasehold covenants. (Any former tenant compelled, pursuant to an authorised guarantee agreement, to meet another tenant's liability may be able to call for the grant to himself of an 'overriding lease' (L&T(C)A 1995, s 19(1), infra).)

L1, on assignment of *his* reversionary estate to L2, is *not* afforded the same automatic release from liability for the performance of the 'landlord covenants' of the lease. Instead, L1 has the opportunity, within certain time limits, to *apply* to T1 for a release from these covenants (L&T(C)A 1995, s 6(2)) and will be so released (see L&T(C)A 1995, s 8(2)) if:

- T1 fails to serve a written notice of objection within four weeks; or
- T1 serves a notice of consent to L1's release; or
- the court declares that L1's release is 'reasonable'.

The 'landlord covenants' from which L1 may be released do not include any covenant which was expressed to be personal to L1 (see *BHP Petroleum Great Britain Ltd v Chesterfield Properties Ltd* (2002)). Nor, in any event, can the statutory release from post-assignment liability absolve either L1 or T1 from liability for any breach of covenant occurring *prior to* their release (L&T(C)A 1995, s 24(1)). It seems, however, that it is open to L1 to stipulate from the outset by express covenant that his liability shall terminate on the transfer to L2. Such a covenant has been held merely to define the ambit of the obligations which are regulated by the 1995 Act and not to comprise an illicit attempt to frustrate the statutory operation (see the controversial view of s 25(1) taken by the majority of the House of Lords in *London Diocesan Fund v Phithwa (Avonridge Property Co Ltd, Part 20 Defendant)* (2005)).

— *Old tenancies* The L&T(C)A 1995 operates rather differently in relation to the assignment of pre-1996 tenancies. Here, T1 does *not* enjoy the benefit of any automatic statutory release from his liabilities, but remains responsible, in principle, for the defaults of assignees of his term. The principle of continuing tenant liability is, however, modified by the introduction of a requirement that L1 (if he is still the landlord) should give warning to T1 that he is about to be visited with liability for the defaults of T2 (or, for that matter, of T3).

- Within six months of any 'fixed charge' becoming due, L1 must serve on T1 (and, where relevant, any guarantor of T1) a notice bearing information that the charge is now due and that L1 intends to recover the amount specified in the notice (including appropriate interest). In the absence of a duly served notice, neither T1 nor his guarantor can be made liable for any 'fixed charge' (see L&T(C)A 1995, s 17(1)(b), (2)–(3)). For this purpose a 'fixed charge' includes rent, service charges and any other liquidated sum by way of tenant liability (L&T(C)A 1995, s 17(6)), but *not* unliquidated damages claims for breach of the covenants of the lease (see e.g. *Bloomfield v Williams* (1999)). In effect, the requirement of the statutory warning notice restricts the exposure of T1 (or his guarantor) in respect of 'fixed charge' liability incurred by later assignees to such liability as is incurred during the *six months* immediately preceding the service of the notice.

- The only crumb of comfort for T1, if he is forced to discharge a 'fixed charge' liability, lies in the statutory provision that, on full payment of the amount specified, T1 is entitled to call for the grant to himself of an 'overriding lease' carved out of L1's reversionary estate in the demised premises (L&T(C)A 1995, s 19(1)). In effect, T1 may recover, notwithstanding his earlier assignment, a statutory leasehold term which is interposed between L1 and the defaulting assignee. This term represents in T1's hands a commerciable asset, thus compensating him—at least in part—for the unwelcome imposition of liability for somebody else's default. T1 now has the opportunity to claim rent, or even to forfeit, on the basis of his 'overriding lease'.

- The L&T(C)A 1995 substantially abrogates the old common law rule of unlimited liability, but it must not be overlooked that the old rule still applies, in its full force, to *unliquidated* liabilities incurred by T2 or T3 (e.g. for previously unquantifiable damage flowing from, say, a failure to repair). In such circumstances, even though T1 has a right to be indemnified by the actual defaulter (*Moule v Garrett* (1872)), in practice such a right is almost always rendered futile by this party's insolvency. The whole reason why T1 is being sued by L1 in the first place is generally because the actual defaulter is *unable* to provide any remedy.

— *Liability of a surety for T1* It is extremely common, particularly in commercial leases, for L1 to require that the due performance of T1's covenants be guaranteed by a surety, S, who for this purpose undertakes a contractual liability directly in favour of L1. S is effectively rendered a 'quasi tenant who volunteers to be a substitute or twelfth man for the tenant's team', with the result that S is 'subject to the same rules and regulations as the player he replaces' (see *P &A Swift Investments v Combined English Stores Group plc* (1989) per Lord Templeman). Several consequences follow.

• If, following the insolvency or bankruptcy of T1, the lease is disclaimed by a company liquidator or trustee in bankruptcy (**7.34**), such disclaimer extinguishes the lease and terminates T1's rights and obligations in their entirety, but leaves it open for L1 to enforce the contractual guarantee provided by S (see *Hindcastle Ltd v Barbara Attenborough Associates Ltd* (1997) per Lord Nicholls of Birkenhead). S may even have covenanted to take over the unexpired term of T1 in the event of any disclaimer by a liquidator, in which case T1 retires 'mortally wounded' and S comes in to play as 'the substitute' (see *Coronation Street Industrial Properties Ltd v Ingall Industries plc* (1989) per Lord Templeman).

• If, however, the relevant insolvency or bankruptcy is not that of T1, but instead that of a later assignee in possession (e.g. T3), the disclaimer of the lease by T3's liquidator or trustee does not terminate *either* the enduring contractual liability of the original covenantor, T1, *or* the contractual liability of S, who guaranteed the performance of T1's covenants. This rather sobering conclusion constitutes the actual ruling of the House of Lords in *Hindcastle Ltd v Barbara Attenborough Associates Ltd* (1997). Since the ameliorating impact of the L&T(C)A 1995 affects only leases granted after 1995, the alarming implications of this ruling (for T1 and S) may continue to affect pre-1996 leases for some time to come.

Rights and liabilities of assignees

14.22 Whereas the liability inter se of L1 and T1 has rested historically on *privity of contract*, the same principle could never provide a basis of leasehold enforcement between those who took an estate from either party by assignment. By way of exception from the rules of contractual privity, the assignment of the estate held by either L1 or T1 brings into operation a series of principles based ultimately on the notion of *privity of estate*. The essential thrust of this form of privity is to confer a third-party impact upon initially contractual arrangements, but once issues of enforcement arise outside the original contractual nexus it is rare, if not impossible, for obligations of a purely *personal* character to affect strangers.

— *Privity of estate*   Under the doctrine of privity of estate, the *contractual* rights and obligations of L1 and T1 are viewed as having been *annexed to* the proprietary estates held by L1 and T1 (i.e. to the reversion and the term of years respectively). In consequence, these rights and obligations become 'imprinted' on each relevant estate and are rendered enforceable between all subsequent owners for the time being of either estate 'as conditions of the enjoyment' of that estate (*City of London Corpn v Fell* (1993) per Nourse LJ). In this way privity of estate effectively creates rights and obligations which are 'independent of the parallel rights and obligations' of the original covenantors and can therefore travel with all future assignments of the estates concerned to bind these estates in the hands of third parties (see *City of London Corpn v Fell* (1994) per Lord Templeman). It is this doctrinal mechanism of notional attachment to the *estate* which ultimately underpins the extended policing of the original leasehold covenants as between all who subsequently become 'privy' to the estate in question. Thus, in *Fig* 24 (**14.20**), the covenants entered into by L1 and T1 'run with the land' so as to affect L2 and, in turn, T2 and T3. Likewise the covenants entered into by T2 and ST1 (which ought, for practical purposes, to reflect the covenants of the head lease) will 'run' so as to affect T3 and ST2.

— *The rule in Spencer's Case*   In laying down the implications of privity of estate in *Spencer's Case* (1583), the Court of King's Bench superimposed only two conditions for the transmission to assignees of leasehold rights and liabilities:

- the assignees must take a *legal* estate in the land; and
- the covenants which 'run with the land' must *touch and concern* the demised premises.

These two conditions have been modified by subsequent statutory developments, some of which, again, distinguish between 'new' (i.e. post-1995) tenancies and 'old' (i.e. pre-1996) tenancies.

— *New tenancies*   Many of the essential features of the historic device of privity of estate have been incorporated, in a simplified form, in the rules which govern tenancies granted on or after 1 January 1996.

- The benefit and burden of *all* 'landlord' and 'tenant' covenants are statutorily transmitted to assignees, provided that the covenants concerned are not 'expressed to be personal to any person' (L&T(C)A 1995, s 3(1), (6)(a)). This exception for covenants 'expressed to be personal' was intended to avoid the potential complexity of the criterion of 'touching and concerning' quality (infra) and to place an onus on those who draft leasehold covenants to specify expressly those covenants which are *not* intended to run with the land. There is some evidence, however, that the courts may allow the personal quality of a covenant to be established implicitly by deduction 'from the language used, read in its proper context' (*First Penthouse Ltd v Channel Hotels and Properties (UK) Ltd* (2004) at [49] per Lightman J).

• Furthermore, the enduring statutory force given, on assignment, to landlord and tenant covenants makes no distinction between *legal* and *equitable* leases or between *legal* and *equitable* assignments of any estate (L&T(C)A 1995, s 28(1)).

— *Old tenancies* Tenancies granted before 1 January 1996 are still governed by *Spencer's Case* (1583), as amended by statutes enacted prior to 1995. Thus privity of estate causes the original leasehold covenants to affect subsequent assignees of the reversion and the term in so far as these covenants 'touch and concern' the land demised.

• The 'touch and concern' requirement is intended to exclude from long-term enforcement those covenants of a lease which are not integral to the leasehold relationship and which do not therefore deserve a durable impact as between future assignees. Although the test of 'touching and concerning' quality has a certain circularity, it is best understood as an intuitive formula which reserves binding leasehold effect for those covenants which intrinsically affect 'the landlord in his normal capacity as landlord or the tenant in his normal capacity as tenant' (see *Hua Chiao Commercial Bank Ltd v Chiaphua Industries Ltd* (1987) per Lord Oliver of Aylmerton). In effect, the 'touch and concern' criterion concedes long-term leasehold impact to those covenants in whose due performance the respective estate owners have a peculiar economic interest *qua estate owner*. Correspondingly the 'touch and concern' criterion withholds such impact from those other covenants, of substantially personal or private significance, in whose due performance the covenantee has no higher or more distinctive economic interest than he would if he were not a party to the lease (see also *P & A Swift Investments v Combined English Stores Group plc* (1989) per Lord Oliver). Thus, for example, a tenant's covenant to pay rent clearly 'touches and concerns', whereas a covenant to cut the landlord's hair every six weeks does not.

• 'Touching and concerning' covenants include most standard leasehold covenants (relating, for example, to rent, repair, insurance, quiet enjoyment, assignment and mode of user), but the 'touch and concern' test has sometimes led to arbitrary or inconsistent outcomes (*Harbour Estates Ltd v HSBC Bank plc* (2005) at [40] per Lindsay J). 'Touching and concerning' quality has been attributed to a tenant's covenant to retail only the landlord's brand of product on the demised premises (*Caerns Motor Services Ltd v Texaco Ltd* (1994)) but not to the correlative covenant by a landlord to avoid competition with the tenant's business (*Thomas v Hayward* (1869)); to a lessee's option to renew a leasehold term, but not to his option to purchase the freehold reversion (*Woodall v Clifton* (1905)). Perhaps most surprisingly, it has been held that the obligation to return a security deposit paid by a tenant at the commencement of the lease does *not* 'touch and concern' and cannot therefore bind the assignee of the landlord's reversion (*Hua Chiao Commercial Bank Ltd v Chiaphua Industries Ltd* (1987)).

Liability as between L2 and T1

14.23 If, during the currency of T1's possession under the term of years (see *Fig* 24, **14.20**), L1 assigns his reversionary estate to L2, the precise effects vary slightly depending on the date of grant of the tenancy.

— *New (i.e. post-1995) tenancies* The effect of the L&T(C)A 1995 is normally to ensure that:

- the *benefit* of T1's 'tenant covenants' (unless expressed to be 'personal') will pass to L2 (L&T(C)A 1995, s 3(3)(b)), together with the benefit of:
  — any right of re-entry contained in the lease (L&T(C)A 1995, s 4(b)) and, in the absence of waiver or release, the right to exercise such right of re-entry in relation to breaches of covenant whether occurring *before* or *after* the date of the relevant assignment (L&T(C)A 1995, s 23(3)), and

  — any surety covenant entered into by a guarantor of T1's obligations under the tenancy (see *P & A Swift Investments v Combined English Stores Group plc* (1989), **13.10, 14.21**).
- the *burden* of L1's 'landlord covenants' (unless expressed to be 'personal') will pass to L2 (L&T(C)A 1995, s 3(3)(a)), *unless* such covenants:
  — were not binding on L1 immediately before the assignment, or

  — relate to premises other than those subject to the assignment, or

  — (as in the case of *options* to renew a lease or to purchase a reversionary estate) require protection by register entry and have not been so registered (L&T(C)A 1995, s 3(6)(b)). In registered land, an option enjoyed by T1 is protectable by the entry of a 'notice' in the register of L1's reversionary title (**12.11**) but, failing this, may sometimes be enforceable against L2 as an *overriding interest* (**12.20**). In unregistered land T1's option is protectable by the entry of a land charge of Class C(iv) in the

Register of Land Charges (**12.36**) and, if not so protected, is void against L2 (see *Beesly v Hallwood Estates Ltd* (1960)).

— *Old (i.e. pre-1996) tenancies*   The doctrine of privity of estate ensures that all 'touching and concerning' covenants of the lease remain fully enforceable between L2 and T1, a liability which is reinforced by statute whether the relevant lease is *legal* or *equitable* (see LPA 1925, ss 141(1), 142(1)). This statutory authority does not remove any need for additional protection by registration against L1 of certain kinds of entitlement such as options (see *Beesly v Hallwood Estates Ltd* (1960)). Nor does it obviate the penumbral doubt as to the categories of covenant which truly 'touch and concern' or, to use the equivalent terminology of LPA 1925, ss 141(1), 142(1), 'have reference to the subject-matter of the lease'. L2 acquires, however, the exclusive right to sue for rent arrears arising, or in respect of other breaches occurring, prior to the date of assignment (*Arlesford Trading Co Ltd v Servansingh* (1971); *Re King, decd* (1963)) and may even exercise a right of re-entry in respect of earlier rent arrears (*Kataria v Safeland plc* (1997); *Scribes West Ltd v Relsa Anstalt (No 3)* (2005)).

Liability as between L2 and T2/T3

14.24   As between L2 and T1, at least *one* party was an original contracting party in the leasehold relationship. But if we take *Fig 24* (**14.20**) one stage further, the question arises whether the covenants of the lease are enforceable between L2 and T2, *neither* of whom was an original covenantor.

— *New (i.e. post-1995) tenancies*   We have already seen that the benefit and burden of the original leasehold covenants normally pass to L2, except in so far as these covenants are 'expressed to be personal' (L&T(C)A 1995, s 3(3), (6)(a), **14.23**). The correlative burden and benefit pass to T2 (and, in his turn, to T3) in just the same way. Thus the effect of L&T(C)A 1995 is to ensure that:

- the *benefit* of L1's 'landlord covenants' will pass to T2 and T3 (L&T(C)A 1995, s 3(2)), except in so far as such covenants relate to premises other than those subject to the assignment;
- the *burden* of T1's 'tenant covenants' will pass to T2 and T3 (L&T(C)A 1995, s 3(2)), except where such covenants were not binding on T1 immediately before the assignment or relate to premises outside the scope of the assignment.

The only other substantial qualification on the liability of T2 (or T3, as the case may be) is that each successive assignee is normally liable only in respect of breaches committed whilst he is in possession. Thus T2 cannot be rendered liable either for defaults committed by T1 (L&T(C)A 1995, s 23(1)) or for those of T3 following an assignment of T2's term (L&T(C)A 1995, s 5(2)(a), (3)(a))) unless, in the latter case, T2 has entered into an authorised guarantee agreement (**14.21**).

— *Old (i.e. pre-1996) tenancies*   Privity of estate carries the implication that all legal assignees of the reversion or the term are entitled to enforce 'touching and concerning' covenants against the current owner of the tenant's or landlord's estate (*Spencer's Case* (1583)).

• The liability of each successive assignee relates only to breaches committed whilst he is in possession of the land (see *Duncliffe v Caerfelin Properties Ltd* (1989); *City of London Corpn v Fell* (1994) per Lord Templeman).

• Anomalously, whilst *Spencer's Case* seems to allow the running of the land-lord's covenants under an equitable lease (*Manchester Brewery Co v Coombs* (1901)), there has always been some niggling doubt as to whether the burden of an equitable tenant's leasehold obligations strictly passes with the assignment of his term to a third party (see e.g. *Purchase v Lichfield Brewery Co* (1915)). In reality the avail-ability of an equitable right of re-entry (**14.11**) in such leases tends to operate as a potent stimulus toward compliance with the covenants of the lease, whether or not these covenants are technically binding on the assignee.

Liability as between L1/L2 and ST1/ST2/WT

14.25   The point has already been made (**14.20**) that, with regard to the framework of leasehold relationships depicted in *Fig* 24, ST1 (and for that matter ST2 and WT) cannot be described as 'privy' to the estate of the *head lease* (see *Amsprop Trading Ltd v Harris Distribution Ltd* (1997) per Neuberger J). ST1 enjoys privity of estate in relation to the five-year sublease (as does ST2); and ST2 and WT are, of course, privy to the estate of the weekly tenancy. It follows, therefore, that neither L1 nor L2 can normally enforce the covenants of the head lease *directly* against ST1, ST2 or WT—the absence of a vital privity of estate renders *Spencer's Case* (1583) quite inapplicable for this purpose (**14.22**). Neither L1 nor L2 may obtain a money remedy *directly* against any of these under-tenants, the appropriate remedy lying in an action against the currently entitled assignee of the term of the head lease (i.e. either T2 or T3). (We have already seen that forfeiture of a head lease auto-matically destroys any sublease, **14.15**.)

— *Statutory intervention*   The L&T(C)A 1995 does nothing to loosen up the transmissibility to subtenants of the benefit and burden of covenants contained in a head lease, but other statutes may, in part, have achieved such an effect.

• It is possible that LPA 1925, s 78(1) **(13.15)** enables a subtenant of a pre-1996 lease to claim at least the benefit of such covenants (see *Caerns Motor Services Ltd v Texaco Ltd* (1994)).

• In relation to leases arising on or after 11 May 2000, the Contracts (Rights of Third Parties) Act 1999 provides that non-contracting parties may, in their own right, enforce contractual terms if *either* the contract expressly provides that they may *or* the term in question 'purports to confer a benefit' upon them (C(ROTP)A 1999, s 1(1)–(3)).

• The Human Rights Act 1998 may indirectly require the modification of certain rules regulating the enforceability of leasehold covenants. It is at least arguable that the limitations on enforcement traditionally imposed by the doctrine of privity of estate infringe the landlord's right under ECHR Protocol No 1, Art 1 **(2.7)** to 'peaceful enjoyment of his possessions'.

> *PW & Co v Milton Gate Investments Ltd* (2004) **(14.1)** A 25-year lease of an office building gave T1 the right to terminate the lease after 12 years on service of a 'break notice' **(4.30)**, an event which at common law would also terminate any sublease carved out of the head lease **(14.15)**. The head lease also required that T1, on serving the break notice, should pay L1 a penalty of some £5 million unless 75 per cent of the building were at that time tenanted by subtenants holding on unexpired terms of at least five years. ST1 acquired substantial long-term subleases of the building. L1 later transferred the freehold reversion to L2, but T1, on activating the break clause, refused to pay L2 the penalty sum on the ground that L1 and T1 had contractually averted the normal rule that the break would collapse ST1's subleases. Neuberger J held (at [76], [279]) that, as a matter of law, it was impossible for L1 and T1 to contract out of the general rule. He indicated, however, that if (on a contrary view) the subleases had survived the termination of the head lease, L2 and ST1 would have been liable to each other—well outside the scope of privity of estate—on the covenants of the head lease. Any other approach, concluded Neuberger J (at [133]–[134], [279]), would leave the land encumbered for many years by a subtenant from whom no rent was legally recoverable—an outcome which would be 'scarcely "peaceful enjoyment of [L2's] possessions"' for the purpose of ECHR Protocol No 1, Art 1 ([126]). (T1 was held liable to the £5 million penalty.)

— *Non-monetary remedies* It should not be overlooked that certain *non-monetary* remedies may be pursued against under-tenants albeit outside the ambit of privity of estate in relation to the head lease.

• *Enforcement of restrictive covenants* A superior landlord (i.e. L1 or, in his turn, L2) may always enforce restrictive covenants contained in the head lease by way of injunction directed at some defaulting under-tenant (*Hall v Ewin* (1888), a derivative of the principle in *Tulk v Moxhay* (1848), **2.5**, **9.26**, **13.18**; and see also L&T(C)A 1995, s 3(5))).

— In registered land such covenants, in so far as they relate to the demised premises, are not capable of protection by the entry of a notice in the register (LRA 2002, s 33(c)), but are automatically binding on a transferee or underlessee by virtue of LRA 2002, ss 12(4)(a), 29(1), (2)(b).

— In unregistered land the equitable doctrine of notice still governs the effect on a sublessee of restrictive covenants contained in a head lease (**12.39**). Restrictive covenants between lessor and lessee are *never* registrable as a Class D(ii) land charge (see LCA 1972, s 2(5), **12.36**), but a sublessee inevitably has at least constructive notice of the covenants of the head lease.

• *Remedy of forfeiture* An under-tenant is also vulnerable to the exercise of any right of re-entry which was expressly reserved by L1 in the head lease (**8.35**).

Statutory regimes of protection

14.26 Part of the extraordinary complexity of the modern law of landlord and tenant is attributable to the statutory superimposition of special regimes of protection for designated categories of tenant. The following sections contain only the barest of summaries of these important legislative supplements to the basic law of tenancies:

• Rent Act 1977 (protected and statutory tenancies) (**14.27**);

• Housing Act 1988 (assured and shorthold tenancies) (**14.28**);

• Housing Acts 1985 and 1996 (secure tenancies) (**14.29**);

• Landlord and Tenant Act 1954, Part II (business tenancies) (**14.30**);

• Agricultural Holdings Act 1986 and Agricultural Tenancies Act 1995 (agricultural holdings) (**14.31**).

Rent Act 1977 (protected and statutory tenancies)

14.27 The Rent Act 1977, the successor enactment of a corpus of legislation dating back to 1915, provides substantial protection for what are now diminishing categories of residential tenant in the private rented sector.

— *A 'status of irremovability'* Although no new Rent Act tenancies have been capable of creation since January 1989 (see HA 1988, s 34(1)), the Rent Act confers upon the 'regulated' tenant a long-term security of tenure—a 'status of irremovability' (see *Keeves v Dean* (1924) per Lush J)—together with the guarantee that only a 'fair rent' is chargeable as the price of this security. The regulated tenant's security is evidenced in various ways. Irrespective of the agreed duration of the tenancy, a *protected tenancy* (i.e. the initial contractual tenancy, whether periodic or fixed term), if brought to an end by notice to quit or by the effluxion of time, automatically becomes a *statutory tenancy* on effectively the same terms and conditions (RA 1977, s 2(1)(a)). This statutory tenancy cannot be terminated except by the tenant's voluntary delivery up of possession or by a court possession order granted only on the showing of various tightly defined grounds (RA 1977, s 98, Sch 15).

— *Rights of survivors* During any period when the landlord is disabled from recovering possession, the Rent Act tenancy is usually capable of transmission, on the tenant's death, to that tenant's surviving 'spouse' or 'civil partner' (RA 1977, Sch 1, para 2, as amended by Civil Partnership Act 2004, s 81, Sch 8, para 13). Largely in response to the prohibition of gender-based discrimination contained in the ECHR (see *Ghaidan v Godin-Mendoza* (2004), **14.1**), the terms 'spouse' and 'civil partner' here include not merely formally recognised relationships but also informal liaisons which functionally resemble marriage or civil partnership. In the absence of any person qualifying under these heads, a less beneficial form of tenancy (an 'assured tenancy', **14.28**) is conferred on any person who can claim to be a 'member of the original tenant's family' (RA 1977, Sch 1, para 3). The emanations of the original Rent Act tenancy are thus capable of long-term survival—well beyond the contractually stipulated duration of that tenancy—although nowadays the 'fair rents' fixed by rent officers (RA 1977, s 70(1)) tend towards true market values (see *R v Secretary of State for the Environment, Transport and the Regions, ex parte Spath Holme Ltd* (2001)). The recent history of the Rent Act is, however, one of creeping obsolescence. Relatively few regulated tenants are now left; the private rented sector has been overtaken by the device of the 'shorthold tenancy' (**14.28**); and we are witnessing the terminal stages of an idealistic 20th-century social experiment in the rented housing market.

Housing Act 1988 (assured and shorthold tenancies)

14.28 Most private sector residential tenancies granted since January 1989 have constituted an 'assured tenancy' governed by the Housing Act 1988. The 1988 Act facilitated the creation of 'assured shorthold' tenancies, where, after service of a prescribed notice to the tenant prior to commencement, the landlord could be guaranteed quick and easy recovery of possession of the premises on the expiration of the agreed term (HA 1988, s 20(1)–(2)). In effect, the assured shorthold sought to avoid the non-consensual long-term 'status of irremovability' associated with Rent Act tenancies (**14.27**). The clear aim of the HA 1988 was to regenerate the private rented housing market with the promise of promptly recoverable possession after a contractually defined period (see *R v Secretary of State for the Environment, Transport and the Regions, ex parte Spath Holme Ltd* (2001) per Lord Bingham of Cornhill).

— *The new-style shorthold* The conditions attaching to the shorthold tenancy have now been relaxed even further in relation to tenancies granted since the end of February 1997 (see HA 1988, s 19A, as inserted by HA 1996, s 96(1)). The new-style shorthold may comprise any fixed or periodic tenancy, automatically applying to all new private residential tenancies other than those which are the subject of a specific opt-out by notice. There need no longer be any prior written notice warning the tenant that he holds under the terms of a recoverable short-hold. There is an extremely limited and little used form of rent control (see HA 1988, s 22, as amended by HA 1996, s 100(1)), which in practice relegates the shorthold tenant to the mercy of market forces prevailing in the private rental sector.

— *Termination* The shorthold tenancy cannot normally be terminated within the first six months (HA 1988, s 21(5), as inserted by HA 1996, s 99) and any fixed-term shorthold is immediately converted, on its expiry, into a statutory periodic assured tenancy (HA 1988, s 5). The tenant's rights of tenure can, however, be terminated speedily under an accelerated procedure for the recovery of possession, provided that the shorthold tenancy is in writing and a notice demanding possession has been duly served and has expired (CPR 55.11–55.19). The court also has jurisdiction to award possession to the landlord, at any time, on various grounds of statutorily specified default or termination event (HA 1988, s 7, Sch 2) (see also *Artesian Residential Developments Ltd v Beck* (2000), **14.14**).

Housing Act 1985 (secure tenancies)

14.29 The Housing Act 1985 provides for the regulation of 'secure tenancies' granted by one or other of a number of public or quasi-public bodies (principally local authority landlords). The residential housing sector covered by the 'secure tenancy' is vast, accounting for almost one-fifth of all households in Britain (*Social Trends 34* (2004 edn, London), p 153). The statutory definition of the 'secure tenancy' is wide enough to embrace not only a *tenancy* in the strict sense but also an *exclusive licence* to occupy a dwelling-house (HA 1985, s 79(3), **4.6**).

— *Terms of tenure* The secure tenant enjoys a relative permanence of tenure terminable only by court order on specified grounds (HA 1985, s 82, Sch 2). His tenancy may devolve on his death to his surviving spouse, surviving civil partner or another member of his family (HA 1985, ss 87, 113, as amended by Civil Partnership Act 2004, s 81, Sch 8, paras 20, 27; though see *Wandsworth LBC v Michalak* (2003)). The secure tenant also has a statutory 'right to buy' the house or flat in which he lives for a generously discounted price (**7.40**). There is no formal mechanism for the control of rent levels (see HA 1985, s 24(1)), but the secure tenant is given a statutory 'right to repair' in respect of certain kinds of defect in the condition of his accommodation (HA 1985, s 96(1), **14.6**). The secure tenant may not, however, assign or release his tenancy except in certain specially designated circumstances (see HA 1985, s 91; *Burton v Camden LBC* (2000)), and any subletting or parting with possession of the whole of the dwelling-house immediately causes the tenancy to cease to be a secure tenancy (HA 1985, s 93(2)).

— *Variant forms of tenancy* Under an innovation contained in the Housing Act 1996, a local housing authority or housing action trust may now elect to grant an 'introductory tenancy' for a probationary period as a prelude to the grant of a secure tenancy (HA 1996, ss 124(1), 125(1)). Furthermore, the Anti-social Behaviour Act 2003 empowers the landlord authority, in cases of alleged anti-social behaviour or unlawful user of the premises by the tenant, to apply to the county court for a 'demotion order', pursuant to which the tenant will no longer hold a secure tenancy, but will occupy on the less favourable terms of a 'demoted tenancy' (HA 1985, s 82A, as inserted by ASBA 2003, s 14(2)).

Landlord and Tenant Act 1954, Part II (business tenancies)

14.30 A certain degree of statutory protection is conferred on business tenants by Part II of the Landlord and Tenant Act 1954, as most recently amended by the Regulatory Reform (Business Tenancies) (England and Wales) Order 2003 (SI 2003/3096, effective 1 June 2004). Any agreement to exclude the operation of this Act is void unless the landlord serves a prescribed notice on the tenant prior to the agreement and the tenant declares that he has received and accepted the consequences of the notice (L&TA 1954, s 38A). The security of tenure offered to the business tenant by the 1954 Act operates through the statutory prohibition of any termination of an eligible tenancy except in strict accordance with the provisions of the Act (see L&TA 1954, s 24(1)).

— *Application to court* The landlord may seek to terminate the tenancy by serving notice on the tenant (L&TA 1954, s 25). However, if the landlord is unwilling to grant a new tenancy, the tenant is then entitled to apply to the court for a new tenancy (L&TA 1954, ss 24(1), 29A(1)) and remain meanwhile in occupation of the premises (see *Surrey CC v Single Horse Properties Ltd* (2002)). Alternatively, in the absence of a 'section 25 notice' from his landlord, the tenant may seize the initiative himself by making a request for a new tenancy (L&TA 1954, s 26) and, if the landlord fails to agree, following up his request with an application to court for the grant of a new tenancy (L&TA 1954, s 24(1)(b)).

— *Grant of a new tenancy* If and when the matter reaches the court (by either route), the court must grant a new tenancy, on such terms as it thinks fit, unless the landlord successfully opposes the grant on at least one of seven statutorily defined grounds (L&TA 1954, s 30(1)), which relate partly to default by the tenant and partly to needs or circumstances established by the landlord. If no ground of objection is made out, the court may grant the tenant a new fixed term not exceeding 15 years at an open market rent (L&TA 1954, ss 33, 34(1)). In some circumstances the tenant may be entitled to compensation from the landlord if the court fails to order a new tenancy (L&TA 1954, s 37(1)).

Agricultural Holdings Act 1986 and Agricultural Tenancies Act 1995 (agricultural holdings)

14.31 The Agricultural Holdings Act 1986 confers a limited security of tenure on certain categories of agricultural occupier and the Agricultural Tenancies Act 1995 confers broadly equivalent protection on the holder of a 'farm business tenancy' created on or after 1 September 1995. A notice to quit is normally invalid if it purports to terminate the tenancy with less than 12 months' notice (AHA 1986, s 25(1); ATA 1995, s 6(1)). A fixed-term tenancy for more than two years does not determine automatically with the effluxion of time, but continues in the form of a yearly tenancy unless either party has served written notice of termination between one and two years before the expiration of the fixed term (AHA 1986, ss 3, 4; ATA 1995, s 5(1)). Disputes over the tenant's rights and obligations may be resolved by recourse to the Agricultural Land Tribunal (see AHA 1986, ss 26, 27, Sch 3) or to arbitration (ATA 1995, s 28(1)).

Future reform

14.32 It should be fairly obvious that the law of residential tenancies incorporates a miasma of statutory regulations which seek, in different ways, to ameliorate the imbalance of power implicit in the contractual relationship of landlord and tenant. The area is now an almost impenetrable forest of legal rules little adapted to the needs of those who require accommodation in the rented sector (**14.1**). The Law Commission has therefore undertaken a monumental reformulation and rational-isation of the law of housing tenure (see Law Commission, *Renting Homes: The Final Report* (Law Com No 297, May 2006)). The product is a draft Rented Homes Bill which would bring about simplified and standardised forms of tenure for the residential rented sector. In the *Final Report* and draft Bill the Law Commission has proposed the introduction of two basic types of consumer-oriented 'occupation contract' (the 'secure contract' and the 'standard contract', offering different levels of security of tenure and incorporating with clarity and specificity a written description of the rights and obligations of landlords and tenants. These two forms of contract would merge the existing multiplicity of tenancy and licence types within a 'single social tenure' which is 'landlord-neutral' (Law Com No 297, paras 1.4, 1.21).

— *A 'consumer protection' approach to occupation contracts* The aim of the Law Commission is to integrate consumer law as a component of modern housing law. The intended strategy involves the extension of 'consumer protection principles of fairness and transparency' to almost all contexts of residential renting (Law Com No 297, paras 1.5, 1.14, 1.25). In this way it is hoped to ensure that 'the terms of agreements are fairly balanced, rather than having unfairly balanced contracts which have to be overridden by other statutory rules' (*Renting Homes 1: Status and Security* (Consultation Paper No 162, April 2002), paras 6.1–6.2). Key features of the pro-posed scheme involve the exposure of housing arrangements to the full force of the Unfair Terms in Consumer Contracts Regulations 1999 (SI 1999/2083) (**14.1**), the prescription of the structural components of all 'occupation contracts', and the comprehensive application of the scheme to any contract for rent which confers a right to occupy premises as a home (whether by way of tenancy or licence, **7.14**).

— *Requirements of due process* It is integral to the Law Commission's proposed scheme that the principle of due process be retained as a precondition of the recovery of possession from a residential occupier (Law Com No 297, paras 2.39, 4.49). The Commission therefore envisages a statutory clarification of the proced-ure of repossession and, furthermore, that even in cases of serious default no possession order should be made in respect of a 'secure contract' (providing long-term security of tenure) without the interposition of a 'statutorily structured' discretion exercised by the court (Law Com No 297, paras 2.49, 4.47). Mandatory orders for possession would be largely confined to 'standard contracts' (modelled on the current assured shorthold tenancy) (Law Com No 297, paras 2.42, 4.48).

FURTHER READING

Gray and Gray, *Elements of Land Law* (4th edn, OUP, 2005), ch 14.

Relevant sections of this work and other land law textbooks may be supplemented with:

Bridge, Stuart 'Former Tenants, Future Liabilities and the Privity of Contract Principle: The Landlord and Tenant (Covenants) Act 1995' [1996] *CLJ* 313.

Bright, Susan and Bakalis, Chara, 'Anti-Social Behaviour: Local Authority Responsibility and the Voice of the Victim' [2003] *CLJ* 305.

Clarke, Alison 'Property Law' (1992) 45(1) *Current Legal Problems* 81.

Davey, Martin 'Neighbours in Law' [2001] *Conv* 31.

Howell, Jean 'Notices to Quit and Human Rights' [2004] *Conv* 406.

Partington, Martin 'Renting Homes—New Opportunities: A Personal View' (2004) 8 *L&T Rev* 26.

Pawlowski, Mark and Brown, James 'Specific performance of repairing obligations' [1998] *Conv* 495.

Smith, Peter 'Termination of Tenancies by Tenants: A Just Cause?', in P. Jackson and D.C. Wilde (eds), *The Reform of Property Law* (Ashgate, 1997), p 91.

Smith, Peter 'A Case for Abrogation: The No-Liability for Unfitness Principle' [1998] *Conv* 189.

SELF-TEST QUESTIONS

1 What law is there today against letting a tumble-down house (**14.3–14.6**)?

2 In 1995 Len leased Grubland, an amusement arcade, to Trevor for 14 years. Under the lease, which was by deed, Trevor covenanted:

   (a) to pay a quarterly rent of £25,000;

   (b) to keep the premises in repair;

   (c) not to assign or sublet the premises without the written consent of Len; and

   (d) not to use the premises for any unlawful or immoral purpose.

In 1999 Trevor assigned the lease (with Len's consent) to Alan. In 2002 Alan (again with Len's consent) sublet part of Grubland to Steve for a term of seven years at an annual rent of £10,000. Last year Alan assigned the head lease (*without* Len's consent) to Brad. Len has just transferred the freehold reversion to Roberta, who is horrified to discover that the rent payable under the head lease is now two years in arrears, that Grubland is (on closer inspection) in a disastrous state of disrepair, and that Steve has been using his premises for the sale of pornographic materials and illegal video nasties. Advise Roberta as to her remedies (**14.10–14.25**).

3. How, in question 2 above, would your answer differ if the head lease had been granted in 1998 (**14.20–14.24**)?

15

Regulation of mortgages

SUMMARY

A mortgage of land initiates one of the most significant kinds of credit relationship in the modern world. The potential for exploitation within this relationship is
enormous, and the law of mortgage must maintain a difficult balance between
the need to protect vulnerable borrowers and the equally compelling need to
ensure that land remains an efficient and commercially productive form of
security for lenders. The *definitional* aspect of the subject of mortgage was
discussed extensively in Chapters 8 and 9 (**8.28–8.32; 9.16–9.23**). The present
chapter therefore concentrates on the *operational* dimension of this important
topic.

The significance of the mortgage transaction

15.1 As we saw earlier (**8.28**), the mortgage (or charge) over land provides a device by
which a loan of money may be secured upon an estate or interest in the borrower's
land. If the loan is not repaid in accordance with the contract of loan, the lender's
security may be realised through a forced sale of the land, the loan money being
recouped from the proceeds. Thus, like so many phenomena of land law (**2.12,
7.10, 9.7, 13.9, 14.1**), the mortgage transaction represents a conjunction of the
contractual and the *proprietary*. The mortgage arises from a contract of loan and
creates for the lender (or *mortgagee*) some form of proprietary entitlement in the
land of the borrower (or *mortgagor*). Probably more than any other land law concept
discussed so far, the mortgage will come to have a dominant meaning for the
readers of this book, for the mortgage transaction (and the liabilities which it
generates) can underpin almost every feature of the way in which we live our lives.
The mortgage provides a method of instalment purchase of the homes of millions,

thus combining 'the economic function of a tenancy ... with the ideological function of property' (Otto Kahn-Freund, 'Introduction', in K. Renner, *The Institutions of Private Law and Their Social Functions* (London and Boston, 1949), p 36). The mortgage can also play an important demographic role in shaping family size and pattern, an equally significant fiscal role in coordinating lifetime savings and the inter-generational transfer of wealth, and even a less readily recognised role as a silent disciplinary force within the workplace. Outside the strictly domestic context, the device of the mortgage operates, moreover, as a vital means of injecting capital investment into commercial enterprise. The mortgage of realty provides, in short, one of the most remarkable engines of wealth creation in the modern world.

The historic dynamic of the mortgage relationship

15.2 For over three centuries the English law of mortgage has practised a cautious regulation of credit transactions relating to land. Particularly against the background of the medieval prohibition of usury, it was inevitable that the historical development of the law of mortgage should be influenced by two truisms about human experience. *First*, those who lend money commercially are generally less concerned to render useful service to their community than they are motivated by the hope of personal gain. *Second*, the mortgage was widely perceived, in the historic stereotype, as a last desperate resort for those in financial need. Borrowers tended to be seen as persons lacking in bargaining power who were therefore especially vulnerable to harsh or unconscionable dealing. As Lord Henley LC declared, 'necessitous men are not, truly speaking, free men, but, to answer a present exigency, will submit to any terms that the crafty may impose upon them' (*Vernon v Bethell* (1762)). Not surprisingly, the jurisdiction of equity assumed, on behalf of such persons, a role of solicitous vigilance, being prepared to intervene on grounds of conscience in order to prevent exploitation of the mortgagor by the mortgagee. Equity's protective influence still overshadows the law of mortgage, although it could hardly be claimed that the average mortgage of today replicates the historic stereotype. Nowadays the borrower is, in no real sense, someone who has fallen upon hard times but is rather the securely employed and upwardly mobile person whose use of mortgage finance is motivated by a consciously acquisitive desire to join the 'property-owning democracy'.

The equity of redemption

15.3 The protective impulse of equity was—and still is—concerned with the safeguarding of the rights retained by the borrower in relation to his land. At common law the mortgagor's failure to repay the mortgage loan by the *exact* date stipulated in the mortgage deed used to trigger a permanent forfeiture of the entire mortgaged estate to the mortgagee—the ultimate 'crystalline' rule of property (see Carol Rose, 'Crystals and Mud in Property Law' 40 *Stanford L Rev* 577 (1987–8), **10.23, 12.14**). Given that the mortgage debt might be only a fraction of the market value of the land concerned, the imposition of such a drastic penalty for late repayment attracted the predictable censure of equity. From the 17th century onwards the courts of equity came to regard the mortgagor as being entitled to tender repayment and thus to redeem the mortgage *long after* the common law date for repayment had passed: the legal (or contractual) repayment date no longer provided the definitive cut-off point. This continuing right to redeem in equity was a vital component of the borrower's entitlement during the mortgage, the totality of his rights coming to be known as the mortgagor's 'equity of redemption'. The mortgagor could effectively ignore the legal date for repayment, confident that equity would uphold his right to redeem even at a much later date. Indeed equity went to great lengths to protect the borrower's right, by the simple act of repayment of the loan money, to restore himself to the state of unencumbered liberty from which he had fallen with the advent of the mortgage debt. The mortgagor's equity of redemption was itself recognised as a proprietary interest in the land (*Casborne v Scarfe* (1738)), thereby symbolising the view of equity that, irrespective of the strict legal and contractual position, the mortgagor remained *in substance* the owner of the mortgaged land—albeit subject to the mortgage created in favour of his creditor.

— *The modern equity of redemption* Although the 1925 legislation dramatically reformed the mechanics of mortgage creation (**8.29–8.31**), the *equity of redemption* remains as the inviolable and irreducible entitlement of the mortgagor. Under a post-1925 legal mortgage the mortgagor retains his full legal title in the land (subject to the mortgage charge), and the phrase 'equity of redemption' is commonly used as a term synonymous with the mortgagor's estate as burdened by the relevant mortgage or charge.

• The mortgagor's equity of redemption can even be accorded a money value (**8.28**)—effectively the difference, at any given point in time, between the market value of the land and the sum of the mortgage debt currently outstanding (for an interesting illustration, see *R v Walls* (2003)). Thus, if a property has a market value of £200,000 and is currently subject to a mortgage debt of £160,000, the value of the mortgagor's equity of redemption is £40,000. The value of this equity will tend to increase both in consequence of the steady inflation of land values and by reason of any gradual discharge of the mortgage debt. If, however, property values slump and the market value of the property declines to, say, £150,000, the equity of redemption is inevitably converted into a minus sum or 'negative equity' of £10,000.

- In general, increasing value 'appears to be a long-term characteristic of all real property' (*Palk v Mortgage Services Funding plc* (1993) per Sir Michael Kerr). The equity of redemption thus embodies the mortgagor's right to capture for himself the entire capital appreciation in his land. However, some sectors of the mortgage market are now beginning to see the introduction of 'shared appreciation' or 'equity participation' mortgages under which, in return for lower interest rates for the mortgagor, the mortgagee contracts to take some proportion of the ultimate uplift in the capital value represented by the land.

— *Short redemption dates* Since, in the view of equity, the legal or contractual date for repayment of the mortgage loan is rendered entirely academic, most modern mortgage deeds contain a clause—which strikes terror into the heart of only the uninformed lay person—apparently requiring repayment of the entire capital sum within a very short period (e.g. three or six months) of the granting of the loan. This 'short date' for redemption is for most purposes meaningless, neither mortgagor nor mortgagee having any intention that repayment should actually be made on this date. Such a clause does, however, serve the important function of accelerating the point at which the mortgagor becomes entitled to redeem or remortgage (**15.6**) and the point at which the mortgagee's power of sale becomes available (**15.21**).

— *The inescapable vigilance of equity* The significance attached to the mortgagor's equity of redemption is such that, irrespective of the superficial labels conferred on transactions, the courts accord the vigilant protection of equity (as nowadays reinforced by statute) to all transactions which *in substance* secure a loan of money upon the borrower's real property. The enduring principle, as stated memorably by Harman LJ, is 'once a mortgage, always a mortgage and nothing but a mortgage' (*Grangeside Properties Ltd v Collingwoods Securities Ltd* (1964)).

Tensions in the modern law of mortgage

15.4 While the law remains alert to strike down inequitable or unconscionable dealing in the area of credit transactions, the modern law of mortgage reflects a greater degree of realism about the inner dynamic of the relationship between lenders and borrowers.

— *The demise of the necessitous homeowner* The standard mortgage products sold by the large institutional lenders no longer resonate with the same oppressive potential as the pawnbroking or moneylending transaction—an apprehension which once shaped much of the law of mortgage. Most borrowers are aggressive consumerists avidly working their way up the ladder of property ownership; most high street lenders tumble over each other in the competition to attract potential mortgagors with the offer of tempting interest rates, fixed-rate deals, lucrative cash-backs and the like. There certainly remains a pressing need for effective consumer protection, particularly within the secondary or 'fringe' lending sector (i.e. in transactions with finance companies). But, for a number of reasons, today's institutional lenders are not, in general, the 'hard-hearted mortgagees of the 19th century . . . turning out the innocent and grinding the faces of the poor' (*Hanlon v Law Society* (1981) per Lord Denning MR). The stereotype of the destitute borrower is an image of the past: banks and building societies take good care to lend only to people with a relatively sound financial base (i.e. a reliable income and stable career prospects).

— *The productive use of private wealth* The 20th century saw a vast social diffusion of wealth and earning capacity (see *Williams & Glyn's Bank Ltd v Boland* (1981) per Lord Wilberforce, **12.24**). In consequence, as Lord Browne-Wilkinson once acknowledged, nowadays 'a high proportion of privately owned wealth is invested in the matrimonial home' (*Barclays Bank plc v O'Brien* (1994)). Even more to the point is the fact that finance released by second mortgages of family homes has become a significant source of start-up capital for the small business sector, which in this country accounts for some 95 per cent of all businesses and nearly one-third of all employment. A potent motivation underlying the recent development of the law of mortgage has therefore been the realisation that '[i]f the freedom of homeowners to make economic use of their homes is not to be frustrated, a bank must be able to have confidence that a wife's signature of the necessary guarantee and charge will be as binding on her as is the signature of anyone else on documents which he or she may sign' (*Royal Bank of Scotland plc v Etridge (No 2)* (2002) at [34]–[35] per Lord Nicholls of Birkenhead).

> *Barclays Bank plc v O'Brien* (1994) H and W, joint owners of their matrimonial home, together executed a second mortgage of that property in order to secure a bank overdraft facility of £135,000 for H's business. When the business got into difficulties, the bank sought, unsuccessfully, to enforce the mortgage and take possession of the matrimonial home (**15.10–15.11**). Significantly, however, Lord Browne-Wilkinson pointed to the need to 'keep a sense of balance' in weighing up the policy implications which bear on questions of priority between borrowers and lenders. It is all too easy 'to allow sympathy for the wife who is threatened with the loss of her home at the suit of a rich bank to obscure an important public interest viz, the need to ensure that the wealth currently tied up in the matrimonial home does not become economically sterile' (**2.10**).

As Lord Browne-Wilkinson indicated, if the law 'renders vulnerable loans granted on the security of matrimonial homes, institutions will be unwilling to accept such security, thereby reducing the flow of loan capital to business enterprises'.

Thus, for Lord Browne-Wilkinson, it was essential that a 'law designed to protect the vulnerable' should not choke the availability of loan finance, as in the circumstances of the *O'Brien* case, by rendering the matrimonial home 'unacceptable as security to financial institutions'. In the words of Lord Bingham of Cornhill, the law 'must afford both parties a measure of protection' (*Royal Bank of Scotland plc v Etridge (No 2)* (2002) at [2]). We shall therefore examine the way in which the modern law of mortgage holds a balance between the legitimate interests of lenders and the need to safeguard the rights of borrowers.

Protection for the mortgagor

15.5 Equity has always jealously supervised the mortgage relationship in order to prevent the lender of money from abusing his superior bargaining strength by imposing on the borrower *oppressive* or *unconscionable* terms. The history of the law of mortgage thus reveals a fascinating confrontation between the irresistible force of equity and the immovable object of traditional contract doctrine. In the ultimate analysis equity insisted upon the priority of conscientious obligation over even the hallowed principle of sanctity of contract. Formally agreed contractual terms may be struck down as null and void if they operate unconscionably between mortgagor and mortgagee. But the threshold of equitable concern is high. Equity does not reform mortgage transactions merely 'because they are unreasonable' (*Knightsbridge Estates Trust Ltd v Byrne* (1939) per Sir Wilfred Greene MR) or because the bargain is 'hard'. The precondition of equitable intervention involves a perception that a challenged mortgage term is 'oppressive or unconscionable' or is 'unfair' or 'morally reprehensible'. Terms of this kind necessarily comprise some stipulation 'which in the traditional phrase "shocks the conscience of the court", and makes it against equity and good conscience of the stronger party to retain the benefit of a transaction he has unfairly obtained' (*Alec Lobb (Garages) Ltd v Total Oil Great Britain Ltd* (1983) per Deputy Judge Peter Millett QC). It may be vital, for instance, to demonstrate that 'advantage has been taken of a young, inexperienced or ignorant person to introduce . . . a term which no sensible well-advised person or party would have accepted' (*Multiservice Bookbinding Ltd v Marden* (1979) per Browne-Wilkinson J).

By and large equity has protected mortgagors from grossly unfair contractual terms in the deed of mortgage but, as we shall see later (**15.16, 15.20–15.22**), has not been nearly so successful in safeguarding mortgagors from the oppressive exercise of mortgagees' remedies in the event of default. Some kinds of mortgage term which have attracted the protective attention of equity have involved matters *integral* to the mortgage relationship, e.g.:

- curtailment of the right to redeem (**15.6**);
- oppressive interest rates (**15.7**);
- extortionate credit bargains (**15.8**).

Other terms which have drawn the scrutiny of equity relate to matters *collateral* to the mortgage relationship such as unfair advantages or solus ties (**15.9**) which the mortgagee may attempt to secure for his own benefit.

Curtailment of the right to redeem

15.6 It is a cardinal principle of the law of mortgage that the mortgagor has a *legal* right to redeem the mortgage on the redemption date fixed by the mortgage deed. Once that date has passed (**15.3**), the mortgagor enjoys an *equitable* right to redeem at any time until his equity of redemption is finally extinguished by sale (**15.21**) or foreclosure (**15.23**). Any mortgage term which unduly postpones the mortgagor's right to redeem at law or excludes his right to redeem in equity is highly suspect. Thus, for instance, the courts will not allow the mortgagee to exclude redemption by taking an option of purchase which effectively precludes the mortgagor from ever recovering his security by the act of repayment of the loan (see *Samuel v Jarrah Timber and Wood Paving Corpn Ltd* (1904)).

— *Postponement of redemption* More common are cases in which the mortgagee, in the hope of prolonging a rate of interest favourable to himself, seeks to *defer* the earliest date for redemption at law. Such postponement may be struck down if it renders redemption illusory or valueless.

> *Fairclough v Swan Brewery Co Ltd* (1912) The mortgagor of a dwindling leasehold estate was supposedly denied the right to redeem until six weeks before the expiration of the lease. Redemption in these circumstances would have left the mortgagor with a worthless leasehold residue and the Judicial Committee of the Privy Council held the long redemption date to be invalid.

As always the criterion for equitable intervention is whether the contractual postponement of a repayment date is, in all the circumstances, unconscionable or oppressive (**15.5**). Although most mortgages fix a relatively early or 'short' date for repayment (**15.3**), it may not be unfair that a lender, having taken the trouble to put out his money at an agreed rate of interest, should hold his borrower to a long redemption date.

Knightsbridge Estates Trust Ltd v Byrne (1939) The Court of Appeal declined to disturb a mortgage term which postponed redemption for 40 years, where the parties had bargained at arm's length for a long-term loan of £310,000 on the best terms available at the time. The mortgage agreement had been 'a commercial agreement between two important corporations experienced in such matters' and had 'none of the features of an oppressive bargain where the borrower is at the mercy of an unscrupulous lender'. Here the mortgagor wanted release from the deal simply because there had been a general fall in interest rates and the money could now be borrowed more cheaply elsewhere.

— *Penalties for redemption* The issue of permissible curtailment of redemption is beginning to assume a new, and very contemporary, relevance. Many modern mortgage agreements offer initial periods of attractively low fixed-rate interest payments, but then purport to lock the borrower into the lender's uncompetitive standard variable interest rate for several years thereafter. Such mortgages typically allow early redemption only on the payment of a substantial 'redemption fee'. These penalties for premature redemption—the downside of the allurements offered at the point of sale of the mortgage product—are increasingly vulnerable to attack on grounds of unfairness. Yet it could be argued, in many cases, that mortgage customers quite deliberately play the market, mortgaging or remortgaging with eyes wide open to both the advantageous and the less favourable aspects of the deal. In such circumstances it may be difficult to say that the mortgage terms, even if biased towards the interests of the lender, are intrinsically 'unfair', 'oppressive' or 'unconscionable'. Much may depend on the generosity of the original fixed rate of interest, the duration of the lock-in and the scale or proportionality of the penalty for early redemption. (In relation to 'regulated mortgage contracts' entered into on or after 31 October 2004 (**15.8**) the Financial Services and Markets Act 2000 requires that all early repayment charges levied on mortgagors should comprise a reasonable pre-estimate of the cost incurred by the mortgagee by reason of the premature redemption (see FSA Handbook (2007): MCOB 12.3.1R).)

Control of oppressive interest rates

15.7 The courts' overriding equitable jurisdiction to strike down oppressive or unconscionable mortgage terms extends to the rate of interest levied on mortgage loans. Many mortgage agreements involve a wholly astonishing commitment by the mortgagor to pay an interest rate which is variable at the sole and arbitrary discretion of the mortgagee. (There is also current controversy over whether institutional lenders are always astute to pass on to their customers cuts in base lending rates determined by the Bank of England's Monetary Policy Committee.)

— *An inherent regulatory power* In extreme instances the courts may overturn or reduce any rate of interest which is deemed excessive and unconscionable (see e.g. the capitalised interest rate of 57 per cent struck down in *Cityland and Property (Holdings) Ltd v Dabrah* (1968)). The index-linking of mortgage repayments is not, however, inherently objectionable since such practices—particularly as between independently advised commercial parties—simply tend to ensure that the lender is repaid the real value of his original advance uneroded by intervening inflation (see *Multiservice Bookbinding Ltd v Marden* (1979), **15.5**).

— *Other fetters on the discretion to vary interest rates* It has recently been emphasised, for rather different reasons, that a mortgagee's power to set interest rates from time to time is not *completely* unfettered (see *Paragon Finance plc v Pender* (2005) at [118]). In an interesting transfusion of public law principles into the supposedly private law area of loan finance, the Court of Appeal has held that there is an implied term in every mortgage that the discretion to vary interest rates should not be exercised 'dishonestly, for an improper purpose, capriciously or arbitrarily' (see *Paragon Finance Ltd v Nash* (2002) at [36] per Dyson LJ). Moreover, although the average lender is 'not a charitable institution', the Court expressly imported the analogy of *Wednesbury* reasonableness in confirming that lenders are subject to an implied term that they should 'not set rates of interest unreasonably', i.e. should not exercise discretion 'in the way that no reasonable lender, acting reasonably, would do' (*Paragon Finance plc v Nash* at [41]). Thus, for instance, it would be improper if a lender's decision to raise an interest rate were 'motivated by other than purely commercial considerations', e.g. if a bank manager 'did not like the colour of the borrower's hair' or saw a borrower as a 'nuisance' and therefore raised the relevant interest rate in a desire to get rid of him (*Paragon Finance plc v Nash* at [31], [47] per Dyson LJ).

Regulation of credit bargains

15.8 Much of the equitable concern with excessive interest rates has now been for-malised in legislation, although mortgages themselves are not governed by the Unfair Contract Terms Act 1977 (see UCTA 1977, Sch 1, para 1(b); *Cheltenham and Gloucester Building Society v Ebbage* (1994)).

— *Unfair credit relationships* The Consumer Credit Act 1974 (as amended by the Consumer Credit Act 2006) empowers the court to intervene in respect of any 'unfair relationship' which an individual debtor has entered into with a creditor (CCA 1974, ss 140A–140B). The court has no jurisdiction, however, in respect of consumer credit agreements secured on land which are regulated by the Financial Services Authority under the Financial Services and Markets Act 2000 (CCA 1974, s 16(6C), infra). In practice, therefore, the main focus of this portion of the consumer credit legislation falls on second mortgages within the 'fringe' or 'sub-prime' area involving non-institutional lenders and poorer risk borrowers. Under CCA 1974, s 140A a credit relationship may be adjudged 'unfair' to the debtor in the light of any one or more of the following factors:

- *Any of the terms of the agreement (or related agreement).* Under this head the court may clearly have regard to any interest rate which is deemed exorbitant. It is, however, necessary to record that, under the unamended CCA 1974, the court always acted cautiously in exercising its power to reopen 'extortionate' credit bargains (see e.g. *A Ketley Ltd v Scott* (1980)). Even relatively high rates of interest could turn out to be defensible precisely because the borrower was already an exceedingly poor credit risk or was in the incipient throes of terminal financial difficulty (see e.g. *Woodstead Finance Ltd v Petrou* (1986)). It remains to be seen whether the replacement of the language of 'extortionate' credit bargains by reference to 'unfair' credit relationships signals a revitalised concern to subject high interest rates to particular scrutiny.

- *The way in which the creditor has exercised or enforced any of his rights under the agreement* The newly amended version of the CCA 1974 thereby sidesteps a problem which previously threatened to limit the utility of the entire statutory regime. In *Paragon Finance Ltd v Nash* (2002) the Court of Appeal held that the credit bargain which was vulnerable to statutory challenge comprised only the terms originally agreed by the parties, with the result that the court had no jurisdiction to scrutinise subsequent (and possibly crippling) variations of interest rate imposed by the creditor pursuant to the agreement. The more expansive language of the CCA 1974, as amended, ensures that this lacuna has now been closed.

- Any other thing done (or not done) by, or on behalf of, the creditor.

In deciding whether to intervene under CCA 1974, ss 140A-140B, the court must also have regard to 'all matters it thinks relevant (including matters relating to the creditor and matters relating to the debtor)' (CCA 1974, s 140A(2)). Just as under the old version of the CCA 1974, the court will therefore be concerned to examine such factors as the level of interest rates prevailing at the date of the credit agreement, the debtor's age, experience, business capacity and state of health, and the degree to which, at the time of entering into the agreement, he was under financial pressure.

— *Enforcement of irregular agreements* So serious is the potential for oppression of borrowers under credit agreements that the CCA 1974 used to bar the enforcement by the lender of any agreement which fails to comply with strict statutory rules relating to the form, content and execution of credit agreements. Thus even a relatively trivial error on the face of the agreement in the recording of the amount of the credit provided by the lender was held to render the entire debt irrecoverable (see e.g. *Wilson v First County Trust Ltd* (2001)). Having particular regard to the 'social mischief' implicit in the exploitation of vulnerable or unsophisticated borrowers, the House of Lords declined to find such a drastic penalty for the lender to be incompatible with the fair trial and property guarantees of the European Convention on Human Rights (see *Wilson v First County Trust Ltd (No 2)* (2004)). The reformulated version of the CCA 1974 now relaxes the rigour of this approach by giving the court a discretion whether to enforce credit agreements which are tainted by some irregularity (CCA 1974, s 127, as amended by CCA 2006, s 15).

— *Unfair terms in consumer contracts* Further—albeit limited—protection for many borrowers is provided by the Unfair Terms in Consumer Contracts Regulations 1999 (SI 1999/2083), which implement the European Unfair Terms Directive of 1993 (Directive 93/13) (see *R (Khatun) v Newham LBC* (2005) at [83]). These Regulations withdraw binding effect from any 'unfair term', i.e. any term 'which contrary to the requirement of good faith causes a significant imbalance in the parties' rights and obligations arising under the contract, to the detriment of the consumer' (r 5(1)). Although not directly applicable in determining the 'fairness' of the interest rate fixed by a credit agreement (see r 6(2)), these Regulations provide for a regime of administrative enforcement, principally through the Director General of Fair Trading, in respect of contract terms which prescribe harsh consequences in the event of loan default or otherwise impose unduly preferential terms for the lender (see *Director General of Fair Trading v First National Bank plc* (2002) at [12] per Lord Bingham of Cornhill).

— *Financial Services and Markets Act 2000* With effect from 31 October 2004 a large part of the mortgage industry became subject to an extensive regulatory regime imposed under the Financial Services and Markets Act 2000 and administered with reference to rules and guidance promulgated in the form of the *Financial Services Authority Handbook* (see the module in this Handbook entitled 'Mortgages: Conduct of Business' (MCOB)).

• *Mandatory authorisation* Pursuant to the FSAMA 2000 there is now, subject to certain exemptions, a 'general prohibition' on any person carrying on an activity regulated by the Act without appropriate authorisation from the Financial Services

Authority (FSAMA 2000, ss 19, 31). In effect, authorisation will be required by most mortgage lenders and mortgage administrators who deal with a 'regulated mortgage contract', i.e. a contract which provides for a loan to be secured by first legal mortgage on land substantially intended for residential occupation (FSAMA 2000, s 22(1); FSAMA 2000 (Regulated Activities) Order 2001 (SI 2001/544) (as amended), art 61). Agreements entered into in breach of the 'general prohibition' are normally unenforceable against the mortgage customer (FSAMA 2000, ss 26(1), 28(3)) and may give rise to criminal liability on the part of the unauthorised mortgage lender (FSAMA 2000, s 23).

• *Required standards of business conduct* The regulatory regime inaugurated by the FSAMA 2000 imposes on mortgage lenders and administrators certain standards of conduct which relate, inter alia, to the importance of clear communication of applicable financial terms, principles of 'responsible lending', and the transparent disclosure of all charges levied on the mortgagor (see MCOB (2007), 5–7, 11.3.4R). A firm engaged in mortgage lending or administration must always 'pay due regard to the interests of its customers and treat them fairly' (MCOB (2007), 12.2.1G(1)). The FSAMA 2000 also provides for a general rule that mortgage lenders must ensure that regulated mortgage contracts do not impose charges which are 'excessive and contrary to the customer's interests' (MCOB (2007), 12.2.1(2)(c)G, 12.5.1R). The duties imposed under the FSAMA 2000 are not usually capable of contractual variation, and the sanctions for breach range from compulsory reference to in-house complaints procedures, to compulsory reference therefrom to the Financial Services Ombudsman, and finally an action in the courts for damages for contravention of FSA rules by an authorised person (see FSAMA 2000, s 150(1)).

Unfair collateral advantages

15.9 Equity has always prohibited any attempt by the mortgagee to stipulate *unfairly* for any 'collateral advantage' which might impose 'clogs and fetters' upon the effective exercise of the mortgagor's equity of redemption. The right to redeem is an inseparable incident of the transaction of mortgage and the 'one matter that the mortgagor can insist upon is that, on redemption by payment, he gets back his security' (*Cheah v Equiticorp Finance Group Ltd* (1992) per Lord Browne-Wilkinson). The starting point here is that the sum total of the mortgagee's entitlement comprises, quite simply, the return of the loan principal together with interest and costs, and that any attempt to extract from the mortgagor some superadded obligation is inherently dubious. Thus any term smuggled into a contract of mortgage which tends to impede or devalue the mortgagor's equity of redemption becomes suspect in the eyes of equity itself: the mortgagor must always be able, by the mere act of full repayment, to free himself from the totality of the burden imposed by the mortgage. There has even been a re-emergence of the historic terminology of the 'clogs and fetters' doctrine.

> *Jones v Morgan* (2001) M procured a loan from J, secured on land in which M was interested and which he wished to develop as residential accommodation. As part of a subsequent variation of the loan agreement, M undertook to transfer to J a one-half interest in the subject land. The Court of Appeal declined, by a majority, to order specific performance of the latter undertaking. Chadwick LJ pointed (at [65]) to the inveterate principle that, upon cesser of the mortgage term by redemption, the mortgagor's estate in the land must be 'unencumbered by any interest created as a term of the mortgage.' A stipulation, agreed as a term of the mortgage, that the mortgagee 'should have a share or interest in the mortgaged property' was therefore an impermissible clog on the mortgagor's equity of redemption and could not be enforced. Here the agreement to transfer a share to J, although made three years after the mortgage, was considered (by the majority) to have been in substance and in fact 'an integral part of the mortgage transaction' rather than a separate conferment of rights.

— *A more flexible rule*   It used to be that all collateral advantages bargained for by a mortgagee were *automatically* struck down by the courts. However, this distaste for the self-serving preferences of the grasping mortgagee—once considered more a feature of Victorian mortgage deeds than of today's standard form high street mortgage transaction—has long ago relaxed into a simple prohibition of those collateral advantages which are 'unfair or unconscionable' (*G & C Kreglinger v New Patagonia Meat and Cold Storage Co Ltd* (1914) per Lord Parker of Waddington). In recent decades few cases have turned on the propriety of collateral advantages, but this may be about to change. Some mortgage agreements nowadays require that the borrower undertake onerous obligations outside the strict scope of the mortgage as a precondition of the grant of the mortgage loan (e.g. the purchase of expensive home insurance from a commercial associate of the lender). Such collateral advantages are today beginning to come under challenge as unfair collateral bargains.

— *Solus ties*   An extreme kind of collateral advantage takes the form of a 'solus tie' under which a mortgagee, such as a petrol company or a brewery, imposes on the mortgagor a condition that the latter shall deal only in the products manufactured or distributed by the mortgagee. Such a condition is generally invalid, as repugnant to the mortgagor's equity to redeem, if it purports to remain in force *after* the redemption of the mortgage (see e.g. *Noakes & Co Ltd v Rice* (1902)).

Were it otherwise, the redemption of the mortgage would leave the borrower still encumbered by some obligation towards the lender. Today, however, solus ties are much more likely to be challenged on the basis that they operate unreasonably in restraint of trade and are therefore void on the ground of public policy. Such ties may be valid if limited to relatively short periods (e.g. five years), but would not be upheld over longer periods in the absence of some very clear case of economic necessity (see *Esso Petroleum Co Ltd v Harper's Garage (Stourport) Ltd* (1968)). It is also quite clear nowadays that at least some solus ties can constitute a form of anti-competitive practice prohibited by Article 81 of the EC Treaty (see *Courage Ltd v Crehan* (2002) at [36], an issue finally resolved by the House of Lords in *Crehan v Inntrepreneur Pub Co (CPC)* (2006), **14.1**).

Undue influence

15.10 Much recent controversy in the law of credit transactions has concerned the degree to which the courts should protect the mortgagor's guarantor or surety from circumstances of exploitation or unfair advantage. The classic problem arises where one family member persuades another to stand surety for the debts of the former (or of the former's company) by means of some *coercion* or *misrepresentation* as to the nature or scale of the surety's liability (see e.g. *Barclays Bank plc v O'Brien* (1994), **15.4, 15.11**). For present purposes it matters not whether the surety who signs the contract of guarantee and charges her interest in the family home is a joint owner of the legal title or merely a beneficial co-owner. (Nor is the issue essentially different if a beneficial co-owner merely gives a written consent to the postponement of her interest to the rights of the lender: see e.g. *Alliance and Leicester plc v Slayford* (2001), **12.24, 15.18**.) In all cases the problem is the same, i.e. whether the individual concerned can be said to have participated in the transaction 'with her eyes open so far as the basic elements of the transaction are concerned' (see *Royal Bank of Scotland plc v Etridge (No 2)* (2002) at [54] per Lord Nicholls of Birkenhead).

— *Effect on the lender*   There remains the nagging possibility that the participation of the surety was procured by some impropriety on the part of the primary debtor. This problem assumes an extra dimension with the question whether the lender (who takes a mortgage over, say, the family home) should then be affected by any such impropriety (to which, of course, he was not a party). An even more alarming possibility is that, however innocent, a lender who takes a replacement mortgage over land may be inescapably implicated in some impropriety surrounding the first (and now substituted) mortgage charge (see e.g. *Yorkshire Bank plc v Tinsley* (2004)). The relevant issues, which were recently and comprehensively canvassed by the House of Lords in *Royal Bank of Scotland plc v Etridge (No 2)* (2002), are really two in number:

• First, does the wrongdoing entitle the surety to set aside the transaction as against *the wrongdoer*?

• Second, does the wrongdoing entitle the surety to set aside the mortgage or guarantee as against *the lender* (in which case the entire transaction falls to the ground, **15.11**)? It is quite feasible, however, that the offending transaction may be set aside as against the wrongdoer, but *not* as against the lender (see e.g. *CIBC Mortgages plc v Pitt* (1994)).

— *Relevant wrongdoing* In the present context, wrongdoing comprises any conduct which has 'misled' the surety as to the facts of a proposed transaction or has caused her will to be 'overborne or coerced' (see *Etridge (No 2)* at [3] per Lord Bingham of Cornhill). It is readily recognised today that there is a 'significant overlap' between the concepts of undue influence and misrepresentation (see *UCB Corporate Services Ltd v Williams* (2003) at [87] per Jonathan Parker LJ). Both kinds of equitable wrong are now dealt with by the courts under the broad heading of 'undue influence' (see *Etridge (No 2)* at [33] per Lord Nicholls), i.e. that form of unacceptable conduct which 'arises out of a relationship between two persons where one has acquired over another a measure of influence, or ascendancy, of which the ascendant person then takes unfair advantage' (*Etridge (No 2)* at [8] per Lord Nicholls). There has long been a general equitable doctrine that the court may set aside, or decline to enforce, any transaction which has been induced by such impropriety. Although there is no automatic presumption of undue influence between husband and wife (see *Etridge (No 2)* at [19] per Lord Nicholls), it may not be difficult for a wife to establish her title to relief where there is evidence that her husband has taken unfair advantage of his influence over her.

> *Barclays Bank plc v O'Brien* (1994) W joined with H in executing a second mortgage of their jointly owned matrimonial home as security for the bank overdraft of H's company. W was not made aware by the bank of the nature of the relevant documents, but signed without reading them, acting throughout in reliance on H's false representation to her that the security was limited to £60,000 (rather than a total debt of £135,000) and covered merely a short-term borrowing for three weeks while the house was remortgaged. When the overdraft exceeded £154,000, the bank sought possession of the home, but its claim to enforce its security was rejected by the House of Lords (**15.4, 15.11**).

— *Burden of proof of undue influence* The initial evidential onus falls on any surety who wishes to challenge a transaction on the ground of undue influence (see *Etridge (No 2)* at [14], [21] per Lord Nicholls). In the absence of a showing of *actual* undue influence (e.g. brought about by threats or violence), the surety may be able to establish a case of *presumed* undue influence if she can demonstrate:

- that she had placed *trust and confidence* in the primary borrower in relation to the management of her financial affairs, so that the latter party 'acquired ascendancy over the complainant'; and

- that the impugned transaction was one which *calls for explanation*, i.e. is 'not readily explicable by the relationship of the parties'.

This second evidential element has sometimes been labelled, perhaps unhelpfully, as a requirement that 'manifest disadvantage' has been inflicted on the surety (see *National Westminster Bank plc v Morgan* (1985) per Lord Scarman), in the sense that the advantage taken of the surety is explicable only on the basis that undue influence was exercised to procure it. It is clear, however, that the mere fact that a surety guarantees the payment of her husband's business debts is not, 'in the ordinary course', a transaction which, as a class, 'calls for explanation' or which in itself constitutes undue influence (*Etridge (No 2)* at [28]–[30] per Lord Nicholls). The fortunes of spouses being inseparably interlinked, nothing could be more normal than that a wife should join in charging the family home for the husband's business purposes: a 'wife's affection and self-interest run hand-in-hand'.

— *Shift of evidential burden*   If the complainant surety can establish the two probanda outlined above, the onus of proof in respect of undue influence shifts to the other party, who must now counter the inference—otherwise to be drawn— that undue influence has indeed been employed (see *Etridge (No 2)* at [14] per Lord Nicholls, [107] per Lord Hobhouse of Woodborough). The greater the disadvantage incurred by the vulnerable surety, the 'more cogent must be the explanation before the presumption will be regarded as rebutted' (*Etridge (No 2)* at [24] per Lord Nicholls). It is nevertheless eminently likely that the primary debtor will be able to discharge the evidential burden which has fallen upon him, thereby dispelling any question of undue influence as an operative factor in procuring the surety's cooperation. If, however, the primary debtor cannot discharge this burden, the surety is entitled to have the transaction set aside as against him.

Effect of undue influence on third parties

15.11   Even if the primary debtor is the source of undue influence and is the party who has committed the equitable wrong against the surety, the problem remains that the surety has contracted directly with, and undertaken obligations directly towards, a third party lender. Difficult issues arise with the question whether the lender is to be restrained from enforcing his legal rights in the light of any improper conduct by the primary debtor in relation to the surety. In what precise circumstances can the relevant impropriety be held to have reached the conscience of the lender and disabled him from enforcing the security? The case law of the past has expressed this crux, not entirely satisfactorily, in terms of the lender being 'put on inquiry' or being fixed by 'constructive notice' of the wrongdoing (see *Barclays Bank plc v O'Brien* (1994) per Lord Browne-Wilkinson).

> *Barclays Bank plc v O'Brien* (1994) The House of Lords held that W was entitled as against the bank to set aside, in its entirety, the legal charge taken over the matrimonial home (**15.4, 15.10**). The charge was disadvantageous to W in that it secured the debts of a company in which H (but not W) had an interest. The bank had failed, moreover, to take reasonable steps to satisfy itself that W had entered into the surety obligation freely and in knowledge of the true facts. The bank was therefore fixed with constructive notice of her 'equity' to set the charge aside.

— *A low threshold for 'inquiry'* Partly for the ease of banking bureaucracy, the courts have set an admittedly low threshold at which lenders are deemed to be aware of the risk of possible undue influence in surety transactions handled by them (*Etridge (No 2)* at [108] per Lord Hobhouse). In *Etridge (No 2)* the House of Lords confirmed the brightline rule that a bank or other lender is 'put on inquiry' wherever one person offers to stand surety:

- for the debts of his or her spouse (*Etridge (No 2)* at [44] per Lord Nicholls);

- for the debts of any other person involved in any non-commercial relationship with the surety (whether heterosexual or homosexual or platonic, whether or not involving cohabitation) of which the lender is aware (*Etridge (No 2)* at [47], [87] per Lord Nicholls). (Such relationships—e.g. familial liaisons such as that of son and elderly parents (see *Avon Finance Co Ltd v Bridger* (1985))—become relevant simply because of their potential to inject a distorting or exploitative pressure of an emotional or other variety into the rational decision of financial issues); or

- for the debts of a company in which any of the foregoing persons hold shares (even if the surety is *also* a shareholder) (*Etridge (No 2)* at [49] per Lord Nicholls, [110] per Lord Hobhouse).

NB: A lender is not, however, put on inquiry where money is advanced to two persons jointly, e.g. where a joint legal charge over a matrimonial home secures an indebtedness incurred for the *joint* benefit of husband and wife (see e.g. *CIBC Mortgages plc v Pitt* (1994)). In such a case the transaction is not patently 'disadvantageous' to the wife and there is nothing therefore to put the creditor on enquiry as to the circumstances in which the wife's signature was obtained—even if those circumstances involved (as in the *Pitt* case) actual undue influence (see also *Chater v Mortgage Agency Services Number Two Ltd* (2004) at [63]–[68]).

— *The duty of the lender* Where a lender is 'put on inquiry'—and the bare fact of the lender's knowledge of a relevant relationship between primary debtor and surety is enough—the lender must take 'reasonable steps' to bring home to the surety the risks involved in the transaction of guarantee (*Etridge (No 2)* at [84] per Lord Nicholls). The central concern of the House of Lords in *Etridge (No 2)* was to indicate a 'modest burden for banks and other lenders', necessitating compliance with certain minimum requirements which are 'clear, simple and practically operable' and which will 'reduce the risk of error, misunderstanding or mishap to an acceptable level' ([2] per Lord Bingham of Cornhill).

— *The Etridge protocol* The approach adopted by the House of Lords in *Etridge (No 2)* ultimately does no more than establish a protocol which, if faithfully observed in future surety transactions, will conclusively ensure that a vulnerable surety is unable to 'dispute she is legally bound by the documents once she has signed them' (*Etridge (No 2)* at [79] per Lord Nicholls) but is relegated instead to a fairly grim battle against the solicitor who advised her (see *Etridge (No 2)* at [122] per Lord Hobhouse). The vital technique which lies at the heart of this protocol is the interposition of 'some independent person, free from any taint of the relationship, or of the consideration of interest which would affect the act' who can put clearly before the surety 'what are the nature and the consequences of the act' (see *Re Coomber* (1911) per Fletcher Moulton LJ, quoted in *Etridge (No 2)* at [60] per Lord Nicholls). For present purposes, this independent person is the solicitor specifically nominated by the surety to provide her with advice in relation to the surety transaction. This solicitor's principal function is not to comment on the overall commercial wisdom of the transaction, but rather to explain to the surety that 'should it ever become necessary, the bank will rely upon his involvement to counter any suggestion that the [surety] was overborne by [the principal debtor] or that she did not properly understand the implications of the transaction' (*Etridge (No 2)* at [64] per Lord Nicholls). Only if it is 'glaringly obvious' that the surety is being 'grievously wronged' should the solicitor veto the transaction or decline to act further (*Etridge (No 2)* at [61]–[62] per Lord Nicholls).

The steps entailed by the *Etridge* protocol for the protection of lenders are as follows (see *Etridge (No 2)* at [65]–[68], [79] per Lord Nicholls), this protection breaking down in the event of non-compliance with any of the successive stages:

- *Direct approach by lender to surety* The lender must first contact the surety directly, requesting her nomination of a solicitor and informing her that the function of this solicitor will be to ensure that any resulting consent to the transaction cannot later be disputed.

- *Response from surety* The lender cannot safely proceed unless the surety responds with the nomination of a solicitor (who may, in appropriate cases, also act for the principal debtor and/or the lender).

- *Disclosure* The lender must then, with the principal debtor's consent, disclose to the nominated solicitor all relevant information in respect of the principal debtor's current financial position and the extent, purpose and terms of the requested loan facility.

- *Face-to-face meeting between surety and solicitor* The nominated solicitor must give advice to the surety 'in suitably non-technical language' at a face-to-face meeting at which the principal debtor is not present. The 'core minimum' contents of this advice must:

  — comprise an explanation of relevant documentation and its practical consequences for the surety, i.e. that she could lose her home or be made bankrupt if the loan goes sour;

  — focus on the 'seriousness of the risks involved', the nature and terms of the proposed loan facility, the amount of her liability under the guarantee and its implications for the finances of both the surety and the principal debtor;

  — emphasise the optional nature of the surety's participation—the decision is 'hers and hers alone'—in the light of the current indebtedness of the principal debtor;

  — check whether the surety wishes to proceed and is prepared for the nominated solicitor to send written confirmation to the lender that the solicitor has explained the nature of the documents and their practical implications for the surety.

Full compliance with the *Etridge* protocol, as certified in writing by the nominated solicitor, enables the lender to complete the surety transaction, freed from any possible taint of involvement in any undue influence which may have operated between the principal debtor and the surety. For all relevant purposes, the solicitor does not act in any sense as an agent for the lender and the lender is not responsible for the content or quality of the advice given to the surety (*Etridge (No 2)* at [77]–[78] per Lord Nicholls). The net result of *Etridge (No 2)* is effectively to shift the heat from the banks to the solicitors who may or may not have given accurate advice to the surety (see e.g. the surety's attempt to sue the relevant firm of solicitors in *Etridge v Pritchard Englefield* (1999)—a claim which failed only on a matter of causation). It remains to be seen how many high street solicitors are nowadays willing to become involved in tendering, inevitably in circumstances of some hazard, advice of the kind envisaged by the House of Lords.

Protection for the mortgagee

15.12 Although English law, and particularly the jurisdiction of equity, have always demonstrated a concern for the vulnerability of mortgagors, equally important policy considerations underlie the counter-balancing protection conferred on *mortgagees*. We have already seen that there is a substantial public interest in safeguarding the flow of mortgage finance (see *Multiservice Bookbinding Ltd v Marden* (1979) per Browne-Wilkinson J; *Barclays Bank plc v O'Brien* (1994) per Lord Browne-Wilkinson, **15.4**). Accordingly the mortgagee enjoys the benefit of significant measures of protection in relation to a number of matters including the following:

- substantial immunity from pre-existing equitable interests affecting the land (**15.13**);
- rights of subrogation (**15.14**);
- immunity from leases created by the mortgagor (**15.15**);
- right to immediate possession (**15.16**).

Substantial immunity from pre-existing equitable interests

15.13 The law confers important kinds of immunity on the mortgagee in respect of equitable interests affecting the land over which a security is taken. Many of these forms of immunity have already been discussed in this book (**12.24**).

— *Loan money advanced to a sole trustee of land* In *Williams & Glyn's Bank Ltd v Boland* (1981) the House of Lords highlighted the danger that a mortgagee of *registered land* vested in a sole trustee might be vulnerable to the pre-existing interests of beneficiaries under an implied trust of that land (**12.24**). The equivalent risk in *unregistered land* was that the mortgagee might find that he took his security subject to beneficial rights of which he was deemed to have constructive notice (see e.g. *Kingsnorth Finance Co Ltd v Tizard* (1986), **12.42**). Whilst these hazards have not been entirely removed, more recent case law has done much to curtail the possibility that the mortgagee may lose priority to latent trust interests.

- It is now clear that any contemporary knowledge of the mortgage charge on the part of a trust beneficiary will effectively estop a claim to priority over the mortgagee (see *Paddington Building Society v Mendelsohn* (1985) (registered land); *Bristol and West Building Society v Henning* (1985) (unregistered land), **12.20**).

• Overriding interest protection may be asserted against the chargee of registered land only if the claimant was in 'actual occupation' at the date of disposition (see *Abbey National Building Society v Cann* (1991), **12.23**). Any other approach would produce a 'conveyancing absurdity', said Lord Oliver of Aylmerton, since routine enquiries as to occupation at the disposition date would be rendered entirely futile if it were possible for a binding adverse occupation still to arise at any time prior to registration.

• The most devastating erosion of protection for beneficial trust interests in both *registered* and *unregistered* land has occurred with the denial in *Cann*'s case of the theory of the *scintilla temporis* in the law of mortgage (**12.24**). It had previously been thought that, on a mortgage-assisted acquisition of a legal estate in land, a fragment of time (or *scintilla temporis*) intervened between the arrival of the legal estate in the purchaser and the creation of the legal charge in favour of the mortgagee (see *Church of England Building Society v Piskor* (1954)). During this split second, so ran the theory, trust interests arising by way of contribution to the purchase price could engraft themselves upon the legal estate, thereby taking a marginal (but vital) priority over the mortgagee's legal charge.

> *Abbey National Building Society v Cann* (1991) D1 had purchased in his own name a dwelling-house (for occupation by his mother and step-father, D2 and D3) with the aid of a building society loan secured by a contemporaneous charge (or *acquisition mortgage*, **8.28**) of his legal title. D2 later claimed that, by virtue of the *scintilla temporis*, her beneficial interest in the house (based on financial contributions towards an earlier home) had intervened to take priority over the building society's charge. Her claim to override the lender's security failed. The House of Lords definitively rejected the interposition of any *scintilla temporis* in the process of acquisition mortgage. In the vast majority of cases of acquisition mortgage, declared Lord Oliver of Aylmerton, the acquisition of the legal title and the creation of the relevant mortgage charge are 'not only precisely simultaneous but indissolubly bound together'. One could not occur without the other, not least in the sense that mortgage finance was a necessary pre-condition of the purchase. No purchaser dependent on mortgage finance could therefore assert that he held, even momentarily, an *unencumbered* estate in the land, with the result here that the beneficial interest which D2 had sought to oppose against the mortgagee 'could only be carved out of [D1's] equity of redemption' (per Lord Jauncey of Tullichettle). The trust took effect against an already encumbered title and the building society therefore enjoyed an inevitable priority over all beneficial interests behind the trust.

The only kind of legal mortgagee now vulnerable to latent trust equities is therefore the lender who takes a *non-acquisition* mortgage of registered or unregistered land from a *sole* trustee in circumstances where the trust beneficiaries are in *evident occupation* but are genuinely *unaware* of the transaction in hand (see also LRA 2002, s 29(1), (2)(a)(ii), Sch 3, para 2(c)(i), **12.23**).

— *Loan money advanced to two or more trustees of land* A mortgagee or chargee who takes a security jointly executed by *two or more* trustees of land unfailingly overreaches all trust equities irrespective of whether he knows of their existence and even though, in other circumstances, these beneficial interests might have constituted overriding interests in registered land (*City of London Building Society v Flegg* (1988); *Birmingham Midshires Mortgage Services Ltd v Sabherwal* (2000), **11.30, 12.24**). Moreover, a mortgagee who in good faith advances money to two trustees is statutorily exonerated from any further concern with the propriety or purpose of the mortgage or with the application of the mortgage money (TA 1925, s 17; LPA 1925, s 27(1)).

— *Loan money advanced to a fraudulent trustee of land* Mortgagees also receive substantial protection in the rare, but not unknown, case where a fraudulent trustee of land obtains a mortgage advance by causing the forgery of a joint owner's signature on the document of charge (see e.g. *Mortgage Corporation Ltd v Shaire* (2001), **11.35**).

> *First National Securities Ltd v Hegerty* (1985) H and W were joint owners of the legal and equitable estate in their matrimonial home. H dishonestly obtained a loan from FNS by forging W's signature on an instrument which purported to charge the legal estate as security. H promptly left the country with the loan money. It was clear that the forged charge had no effect upon the jointly owned legal title (because it was not executed by the two legal owners). Equally FNS could not claim to have overreached the equitable interests of H and W (since FNS had not paid the loan money to two trustees). Nor could the forged charge touch W's equitable interest (since she was wholly uninvolved in the dishonest transaction). The Court of Appeal nevertheless held that the abortive legal charge had severed the joint tenancy of H and W in equity (**11.14**) and created a valid equitable charge over H's severed beneficial half-share (see similarly *Edwards v Lloyds TSB Bank plc* (2005) at [16]). FNS therefore had locus standi to apply for a sale of the jointly owned property (**11.35**) and recover its loan money from the cash value of H's share of the proceeds.

Rights of subrogation

15.14 An increasingly important protection for mortgagees is beginning to appear in the law relating to subrogation. It has long been recognised that where A advances money to a borrower with the intention of taking a security over the borrower's land and these funds are used to discharge an existing charge over that land held by B, A is normally presumed to have intended that the mortgage should, at least metaphorically, be 'kept alive' for his own benefit (*Ghana Commercial Bank v Chandiram* (1960) per Lord Jenkins). The payer, A, is in effect subrogated to the rights of the original mortgagee, B, and, subrogation being a remedial mechanism, is entitled to an equivalent charge over the property covered by the initial security.

> *Boscawen v Bajwa* (1996) The Abbey National agreed to advance money to P for his purchase of V's house. For this purpose, the Abbey National paid over the loan money to P's solicitor, S1, intending S1 on the completion date to pay the money to V's solicitor, S2. P was likewise meant, on completion, to execute a legal charge over the house in favour of the Abbey National. Instead, before the completion date, S1 paid the money to S2, who used it (wrongly and in advance of completion) to discharge V's existing mortgage to the Halifax. Completion never did take place; no legal charge was executed in favour of the Abbey National; and S1 became bankrupt. X, judgment creditors of V, then attempted to enforce their charging order (**9.21**) against the apparently unencumbered estate now held by V. The Court of Appeal held, however, that the Abbey National could trace its loan money into the payment used to discharge the Halifax mortgage and that S2, in paying off the Halifax, must be taken to have intended to keep the mortgage alive for the benefit of the Abbey National. Accordingly, the Abbey National was entitled, by way of subrogation, to a charge on the eventual proceeds of sale of V's house in priority to the claims of X.

The House of Lords has since confirmed that subrogation also provides a restitutionary remedy by which the court can regulate legal relationships in order to prevent unjust enrichment (see *Banque Financière de la Cité v Parc (Battersea) Ltd* (1999) per Lord Hoffmann). In cases such as *Boscawen v Bajwa*, where one party's funds discharge an existing charge over land, his relations with the original mortgagor who would otherwise be unjustly enriched are 'regulated *as if* the benefit of the charge had been assigned to him'. Thus, in *Halifax plc v Omar* (2002), the Court of Appeal was able to hold that the Halifax, having advanced mortgage money to a fraudulent mortgagor, was subrogated to the equitable charge held by a vendor who had received the bulk of the Halifax money and who had, until that point, enjoyed an 'unpaid vendor's lien' in respect of the land (**9.22**).

Immunity from leases created by the mortgagor

15.15 Although a mortgagee is bound by any lease created *before* the mortgage by either the mortgagor or his predecessor, he is wholly unaffected by any unauthorised lease granted by the mortgagor *after* the execution of the mortgage charge. (By statute mortgagors normally have substantial leasing powers (see LPA 1925, s 99(1)–(3)), but most mortgages expressly exclude any right to grant leases without the consent of the mortgagee.)

— *Unauthorised leases* An unauthorised lease created after the date of the mortgage is necessarily granted in its shadow, the mortgagor being entitled to transact only with his equity of redemption. In this context the classic dilemma concerns the mortgagor who, in order to help finance his loan repayments, grants multiple lettings of the mortgaged premises (e.g. to students). When the mortgagor defaults, the first indication of difficulty received by his unfortunate tenants is usually the notification of possession proceedings which drops on to their door mat. Although previously unaware that their landlord had let the property without authority, such tenants are utterly defenceless against the assertion of the paramount title of the mortgagee. The mortgagee simply has an unqualified right to take possession (see e.g. *Britannia Building Society v Earl* (1990)), leaving the tenants to an almost inevitably futile contractual action against their landlord.

— *Tenancies by estoppel* The ruling of the House of Lords in *Abbey National Building Society v Cann* (1991) (**15.13**) has effectively terminated any possibility that a mortgagee may be confronted by claims arising from a tenancy by estoppel, created by the mortgagor in advance of his taking title to the land and fed by that subsequent acquisition of title (**7.25**). The rejection of the theory of the *scintilla temporis* prevents any metamorphosis of the tenant's rights between the purchaser/landlord's acquisition of his legal estate and the creation of the mortgage charge (contrast the old law as applied in *Church of England Building Society v Piskor* (1954), **15.13**).

Mortgagee's right to immediate possession

15.16 Of all the protections afforded the legal mortgagee, perhaps the most striking and ultimately the most crucial is the right, in the absence of any contractual or statutory limitation, to take immediate possession of the mortgaged land. Irrespective of default on the part of the mortgagor, the mortgagee 'may go into possession before the ink is dry on the mortgage' (*Four-Maids Ltd v Dudley Marshall (Properties) Ltd* (1957) per Harman J).

— *An inherent incident* It is clear that many mortgagors 'would be astonished to find that a bank which had lent them money to buy a property for them to live in could take possession of it the next day' (see *Ropaigealach v Barclays Bank plc* (2000) per Clarke LJ). Nevertheless the right to possession is an inherent incident of the estate in land which the mortgagee holds either by long demise or (more usually) by statutory analogy in the case of a charge by way of legal mortgage (**8.31, 12.40**). The right may be (and quite commonly is) restricted by the express terms of a mortgage agreement, thus limiting the mortgagee's exercise of the right to cases of *actual default* by the mortgagor. But in the absence of contractual or statutory restraint and even in advance of the date fixed for redemption, the mortgagee is strictly entitled in English law to use reasonable force, without the benefit of any court order, to remove a wholly blameless mortgagor and there is, amazingly, 'nothing the mortgagor can do about it' (*Ropaigealach v Barclays Bank plc* per Clarke LJ).

—— *Inhibitions on exercise* The mortgagee's paramount right to possession has survived in this unqualified form only because a number of factors combine to make it unattractive for a mortgagee to go into possession except in cases of mortgage default (where the recovery of possession is invariably a precursor to the exercise of the mortgagee's power of sale (**15.20–15.21**)). It is doubtful whether a right of such draconian rigour can be sustained much longer as a cornerstone of the modern law of mortgage. (It is not a right automatically accorded to the equitable mortgagee: see *Ashley Guarantee plc v Zacaria* (1993).) Moreover, it is possible that the mortgagee's entitlement to arbitrary possession of residential premises contravenes the mortgagor's right to respect for his 'private and family life' and his 'home' under ECHR Art 8. The Financial Services and Markets Act 2000 additionally imposes on mortgage lenders and administrators a duty to formulate a clear statement of 'policy and procedures' regarding repossession under regulated mortgage contracts (MCOB (2007), 13.3), making it clear that repossession is a last resort in cases of default (see MCOB (2007), 13.3.2E(1)(f)). Failure to draw up such a statement provides presumptive evidence that the mortgagor has not been dealt with 'fairly' (MCOB (2007), 13.3.2E(2)).

In normal circumstances several considerations tend to inhibit mortgagees from exercising their technical right to enter into possession.

• Large institutional lenders have no interest in physical occupation of mortgaged premises; their real concern is that their *borrowers* should occupy these premises and faithfully discharge their financial obligations to the lenders (and indirectly to the millions of investors who deposit money with such lenders).

• A mortgagee who goes into possession of mortgaged property becomes subject to the particularly stringent control of equity. The mortgagee cannot simply leave the property empty, but must let the property at a 'proper market rent' (see *Palk v Mortgage Services Funding plc* (1993) per Nicholls V-C). The mortgagee in possession becomes responsible for the physical state of the premises and is liable for 'wilful default', i.e. must account to the mortgagor for all rents and profits which would have been received if the property had been managed with due diligence (*White v City of London Brewery Co* (1889)). A mortgagee concerned with deriving an income from the mortgaged land is generally much better served by the appointment of a *receiver*, whose handling of rents and profits is not subject to quite the same rigorous surveillance of equity (**15.19**).

• The mortgagee who exercises a right of physical entry upon mortgaged property may well run the risk of criminal liability under the Criminal Law Act 1977. It is an offence for any person without lawful authority to use or to threaten violence for the purpose of securing entry into any premises if, to his knowledge, there is someone present on those premises who is opposed to his entry (CLA 1977, s 6(1)).

— *Tacit agreement*   It is therefore extremely rare in practice for a mortgagee to exercise his right to go into possession while the mortgagor is acting in full compliance with the mortgage terms. There is usually a tacit agreement between mortgagor and mortgagee that possession should be enjoyed de facto by the *mortgagor* in all cases except those of actual default. But it should never be forgotten that, although it generally lies dormant, the mortgagee's right to possession is a virtually unqualified right which ultimately provides the platform for a mortgagee's sale with vacant possession (**15.20–15.21**) or otherwise ensures that the mortgaged property is correctly managed and the value of the security preserved throughout the loan term (see e.g. *Western Bank Ltd v Schindler* (1977)).

Remedies available to the legal mortgagee

15.17   In the event of default under a legal mortgage the mortgagee has available a number of remedies which operate directly against the mortgagor or the land offered as security. These remedies may, in general, be pursued either concurrently or successively, and it is no abuse of process if a mortgagee, when met with a defence in respect of one kind of remedy, has recourse to a different form of remedy (see e.g. *Alliance and Leicester plc v Slayford* (2001) at [20]–[28] per Peter Gibson LJ, **15.18**). Modern courts have nevertheless attempted, with varying degrees of success, to restrain the cavalier exercise of these remedies, not least since many mortgagees carry indemnity insurance against the possibility that the mortgagor may prove unable to discharge his debt in full. In consequence there exists nowadays something in the nature of 'a legal framework which imposes constraints of fairness on a mortgagee who is exercising his remedies over his security' (*Palk v*

Mortgage Services Funding plc (1993) per Nicholls V-C). Accordingly, it is doubtful whether a mortgagee 'is, in law or equity, at liberty to exercise his rights in a way that in all likelihood will substantially increase the burden on a borrower or guarantor beyond what otherwise would be the case' (*Lloyds Bank plc v Cassidy* (2002) at [42] per Mance LJ). Moreover, in the case of regulated mortgage contracts there is now a statutorily imposed requirement that mortgage lenders and administrators should deal 'fairly' with any customer who is in arrears or has a sale shortfall (MCOB (2007), 13.3.1R).

The principal remedies open to the mortgagee include the following:

- action on the mortgagor's personal covenant to repay (**15.18**);
- appointment of a receiver (**15.19**);
- assertion of the mortgagee's right to possession (**15.20**);
- exercise of the mortgagee's power of sale (**15.21**); and
- foreclosure (**15.23**).

Action on the mortgagor's personal covenant to repay

15.18 The mortgagee has a clear contractual right to sue the mortgagor on his personal covenant to repay the mortgage loan and interest, although in cases of serious default the mortgagee may lean more naturally towards repossession of the land and recovery of the mortgage debt from the proceeds of a forced sale (**15.21**). Contrary to popular mythology, the mortgagor's personal liability is not automatically terminated by a voluntary surrender of possession to the mortgagee. The mere fact that a mortgagor in difficulties 'throws his keys' back at his bank or building society in no way prevents his indebtedness from continuing to grow apace unless and until the money owed is fully repaid. Even after a sale pursuant to the mortgagee's power of sale, the mortgagee may still sue on the mortgagor's personal covenant to repay, e.g. if the sale does not cover the total mortgage debt and a shortfall remains outstanding (see *Bristol and West plc v Bartlett* (2003)). Equally, the fact that a mortgagee's possession claim has been defeated—e.g. by reliance on an *O'Brien/Etridge* defence (**15.11**)—in no way precludes the mortgagee from bankrupting the mortgagor on his personal covenant to repay and then seeking to force a sale of the land (see *Alliance and Leicester plc v Slayford* (2001), **11.35, 12.24**). Normally, however, the recovery of arrears of interest is statute-barred six years after becoming due (LA 1980, s 20(5)). The recovery of the mortgage principal is statute-barred after the expiration of twelve years from the date when the right to receive that money accrued (LA 1980, s 20(1): *West Bromwich Building Society v Wilkinson* (2005)), but see now MCOB (2007), 13.6.4R(1)–(2) in relation to regulated mortgage contracts.

Appointment of a receiver

15.19 In circumstances of mortgage default the mortgagee has a statutory power to appoint a *receiver* to handle the income of the mortgaged property (LPA 1925, ss 101(1)(iii), 109(1)). This power may be particularly useful if the mortgagee does not presently wish to realise his security or otherwise undertake the responsibility of going into possession himself (**15.16**). A receiver is not governed by the same strict liability for wilful default which attaches to a mortgagee who enters into possession (see *Refuge Assurance Co Ltd v Pearlberg* (1938)). The receiver's duty is to collect all the income derived from the mortgaged land, to pay all sums due including payments owed under the mortgage, and finally to pass on any surplus income to the mortgagor. In effect, the receiver's primary duty is to try to bring about a situation in which interest on the secured debt (and ultimately the debt itself) can be paid. Subject to this primary duty, the receiver owes a duty to manage the property with due diligence and if, for instance, he carries on a business previously conducted by the mortgagor, he must take reasonable steps to run the business profitably (see *Medforth v Blake* (2000)).

Assertion of the mortgagee's right to possession

15.20 We have seen that the mortgagee's right to possession, although strictly exercisable even in the absence of default, is effectively an adjunct of the mortgagee's power to sell the mortgaged land in the event of default by the mortgagor (**15.16**). Possession is therefore sought almost invariably as a preliminary to realisation of the security through a sale with vacant possession (**15.21**). Particularly in the residential context, however, the repossession of mortgaged premises necessarily involves highly traumatic consequences. The process runs counter to the instinctive impulse of English land law to protect persons in actual occupation of land (**3.3**). In general, therefore, the law has attempted to impose controls on the exercise of the mortgagee's right to possession, but recent developments have exposed a central weakness in the defences supposedly raised around the beleaguered mortgagor. One of the venerable dogmas of mortgage law upholds the mortgagee's paramount right to possession as inherent from the date of mortgage (**15.16**). It had long been assumed, however, that no responsible mortgagee would ever assume possession *without* a court order except where the mortgaged property had already been vacated by the mortgagor and, correspondingly, that repossession *without* a court order would never be enforced while a mortgagor and his family were still living in the premises. These assumptions were tested to the limit in the fortuitous circumstances of *Ropaigealach v Barclays Bank plc* (2000).

> *Ropaigealach v Barclays Bank plc* (2000) H and W jointly charged their home to the bank and subsequently fell into financial difficulties. The bank notified them at their home address that the house would be sold at auction three weeks later, but since the property was, at that time, undergoing repair or refurbishment H and W were temporarily absent and did not receive the notification. The Court of Appeal held that the bank was entitled to take possession of the house without first obtaining a court order for possession. The Court rejected, with obvious reluctance, the argument that s 36 of the Administration of Justice Act 1970 (infra) impliedly imposes a requirement of prior court order. The Court ruled that the 1970 Act in no way abrogates the mortgagee's unqualified common law power to take possession simply by virtue of his actual or deemed estate in the land. Since the Act had not inhibited the mortgagee's right to take possession by self-help, H and W were precluded from access to the potentially benign exercise of the court's discretion, pursuant to AJA 1970, s 36, to stay or suspend orders for possession of a mortgaged dwelling-house.

The ruling in *Ropaigealach* suddenly confers distinct advantages on the mortgagee who enforces his security by the self-help route of peaceable repossession—as distinct from curial process—although similar conclusions have been sternly resisted in other areas of modern land law (see e.g. *Billson v Residential Apartments Ltd* (1992), **14.12, 14.14**). In *Ropaigealach* the Court of Appeal even contemplated that, on default by a mortgagor, a mortgagee may be able to exercise his power of sale without taking possession at all, the sale serving to extinguish the mortgagor's equity of redemption (see *National and Provincial Building Society v Ahmed* (1995), **15.21**) and effectively leaving the *purchaser* to evict the mortgagor as a trespasser. If such an outcome truly represents the law of mortgage, it is highly likely that Parliament will be required to legislate more forthrightly to protect the interests of residential mortgagors.

The outcome in *Ropaigealach v Barclays Bank plc* seems particularly strange because it means that various significant forms of protection intended for hard-pressed mortgagors (and, where relevant, their families) can be circumvented by a mortgagee who chooses to evict a borrower without first obtaining a court order for possession. Where, however, the mortgagee's right to possession is asserted through court proceedings (see CPR 55.1–55.10), the protection normally available to the mortgagor includes the following.

— *The court's inherent jurisdiction to grant relief to the mortgagor* The court has long had an inherent discretion to stay a mortgagee's possession proceedings for a short time (i.e. a matter of weeks) in order to 'afford the mortgagor a limited opportunity to find means to pay off the mortgagee or otherwise satisfy him' (*Birmingham Citizens Permanent Building Society v Caunt* (1962)). This jurisdiction provides, however, only temporary relief for the resolution of financial difficulties or to enable the mortgagor to organise his own sale of the property. The court's inherent discretion may be exercised, for example, where a sale by the mortgagor himself is imminent and is likely to discharge the full debt owed to the mortgagee (see *Cheltenham and Gloucester Building Society v Booker* (1997)). In the last analysis this outcome may be preferable to a forced sale conducted pursuant to the mortgagee's power of sale.

— *Statutory discretion to stay possession proceedings* Much more significant is the statutory discretion which enables the court, in the context of possession proceedings, to grant relief to *residential* mortgagors in much the same way in which relief is granted against forfeiture in the landlord-tenant relationship (**14.14**). Section 36 of the Administration of Justice Act 1970 confers on the court a far-reaching power, in certain circumstances, 'to stop the mortgagee from taking possession' (see *Ropaigealach v Barclays Bank plc* (2000) per Clarke LJ). In cases involving repossession of a dwelling-house, the court is authorised to adjourn possession actions or to postpone the giving of possession for such period or periods 'as the court thinks reasonable' if it appears that the mortgagor is 'likely to be able within a reasonable period to pay any sums due under the mortgage or to remedy a default consisting of a breach of any other obligation arising under or by virtue of the mortgage' (AJA 1970, s 36(1)–(2)). In recent years—and particularly against the background of the depressed property market and relatively high interest rates prevailing during the 1990s—this statutory discretion began to assume a pivotal importance in relieving the financial crisis otherwise engulfing thousands of mortgagors. Indeed it is fair to say that the scale of the economic recession affecting innocent homeowners during the early 1990s generated a rather more liberal judicial construction of AJA 1970, s 36. Amongst the ground rules governing the exercise of the court's discretion are the following.

• The statutory discretion is exercisable even though the mortgagor has no realistic prospect of repaying immediately the *entire* mortgage debt which may have fallen due by virtue of some default clause in his instalment mortgage (see AJA 1970, s 36(1), as amended by AJA 1973, s 8(1)).

- The court has no discretion to adjourn possession proceedings *indefinitely*, but only for such period as is *reasonable* (see *Royal Trust Co of Canada v Markham* (1975)). It may, however, be reasonable to adjourn proceedings in order to determine at a later date whether there has emerged in the interim any prospect of the mortgagor being able, within a reasonable period, to pay sums due under the mortgage (see *Skandia Financial Services Ltd v Greenfield* (1997), where the court decided to 'wait and see' whether the mortgagor, although currently a student working for qualifications, could obtain employment which would enable her to pay off the mortgage arrears).

- It may be reasonable to *suspend* a warrant for possession against a mortgagor who has already negotiated a private sale of the mortgaged property—in order to enable him to apply to the High Court for an order for sale under LPA 1925, s 91 (**15.22**)—but *only* if the proposed sale is likely, perhaps in conjunction with independent funding, to produce a sum sufficient to discharge the entire mortgage debt (see *Cheltenham and Gloucester Building Society v Krausz* (1996)).

- It is not enough under AJA 1970, s 36, for the mortgagor simply to ask for time to pay: there must be realistic evidence of at least some ability to pay off all the current arrears of mortgage money (see *Williams & Glyn's Bank Ltd v Boland* (1981)). But the courts are nowadays prepared, in principle, to reschedule the payment of mortgage arrears using the full remaining term of the mortgage as 'the starting point for calculating a "reasonable period"' for such payment (*Cheltenham and Gloucester Building Society v Norgan* (1996) per Waite LJ). In effect the courts have shown a new willingness to rewrite the repayment terms of a mortgage provided that, in all the circumstances, it is reasonable to expect the mortgagee to recoup the arrears over the whole term of the mortgage and the mortgagor appears reasonably able to cope with such a repayment schedule (see e.g. *Household Mortgage Corpn plc v Pringle* (1998) (17 years outstanding)). The enormously beneficial relaxation of statutory discretion which was inaugurated by the *Norgan* ruling is now reflected expressly in the written 'policy and procedures' which mortgage lenders and administrators should follow in dealing 'fairly' with mortgage customers in arrears under a regulated mortgage contract (MCOB (2007), 13.3.2E(1), 13.3.6G).

- Where the mortgagor's default lies not in non-payment of money due but in some other form of breach, it is plain that the court's discretion under AJA 1970, s 36 can be exercised only where the breach is capable of remedy (see e.g. *Britannia Building Society v Earl* (1990), where the unauthorised lettings (**15.15**) were held to be irremediable).

— *Procedural rights for the mortgagor's spouse or cohabitant* Where a mortgagee seeks possession through court proceedings, the mortgagor's spouse or cohabitant has a range of procedural rights which may enable her to take advantage of the court's discretion under AJA 1970, s 36. Although such a person has no right to be informed of the *fact* of mortgage arrears (see *Hastings and Thanet Building Society v Goddard* (1970)), she has a statutory right to apply to the court to be joined as a party in any possession proceedings (MHA 1983, s 8(2); FLA 1996, s 55(2)). Furthermore, a spouse has a right to be served with notice of these proceedings if she has protected her right to occupy the mortgaged property by appropriate register entry (MHA 1983, s 8(3); FLA 1996, s 56(1)–(2), **12.11**).

Exercise of the power of sale

15.21 The most usual remedy invoked by the mortgagee in the event of serious default by his mortgagor is the exercise of the mortgagee's *power of sale*. A power of sale is sometimes conferred expressly by the terms of the mortgage deed, but a similar power is now supplied in any event by statute.

— *When the statutory power arises* The mortgagee's statutory power of sale *arises* if three conditions are satisfied (LPA 1925, s 101(1), (4)):

- the mortgage in question must have been effected *by deed*;
- the mortgage money must have become *due* (i.e. the legal date for redemption must have passed (**15.3**) or some instalment of the mortgage money must have become due); and
- the mortgage must contain *no expression of contrary intention* precluding a power of sale in the foregoing circumstances.

If these conditions are met, the next question is whether the power of sale has become *exercisable*.

— *When the power of sale becomes exercisable* The mortgagee's statutory power of sale becomes *exercisable* if any *one* of three further conditions is met (LPA 1925, s 103):

- the mortgagor has been in default for three months following the service of a notice requiring payment of the mortgage money; *or*
- some interest under the mortgage has remained unpaid for two months after becoming due; *or*
- there has been a breach of some mortgage term 'other than and besides a covenant for the payment of mortgage money or interest thereon'.

If any one of these conditions is satisfied, the mortgagee has statutory authority to proceed with a sale of part or all of the mortgaged property (LPA 1925, s 101(1)(i)).

- The sale requires no sanction or leave of any court, the mortgagee being statutorily clothed with full power to give a conveyance of an estate which does not belong to him at law. In a rather brutal way the exercise of this ultimate power involves a compulsory divesting of the mortgagor's title at the direction of the mortgagee.

- The result, in the domestic context, is almost always the eviction of a family and the destruction of a way of life. Yet it is clear that no protection against this fate can be claimed by displaced family members on the basis of the guarantees of respect for 'private and family life' and the 'home' enshrined in ECHR Art 8 (**2.15**). The House of Lords has emphasised that a mortgagor cannot invoke Art 8 'in order to diminish the contractual and proprietary rights of the mortgagee under the mortgage' (see *Harrow LBC v Qazi* (2003) at [135], [149] per Lord Scott of Foscote, citing the decision of the European Human Rights Commission in *Wood v United Kingdom* (1997)). It is unlikely that the mortgagor's legal position in this regard has been improved by the view taken more recently by the majority of the House of Lords in *Kay v Lambeth LBC; Leeds CC v Price* (2006) (**2.15**).

— *Effect of sale by the mortgagee*   Where a mortgagee sells under his statutory or express power of sale, his conveyance is effective to vest in the purchaser the mortgagor's full legal estate (whether freehold or leasehold), subject to any rights which themselves rank prior to the mortgage (LPA 1925, s 104(1)). The conveyance enables the purchaser to overreach all interests which are capable of being overreached (see LPA 1925, ss 2(1)(iii), 88(1)(b), 89(1)). The transferee even takes free of any duly protected estate contracts which have been entered into by the mortgagor, since such contracts inevitably take effect only against the mortgagor's equity of redemption (see *Duke v Robson* (1973); *Lyus v Prowsa Developments Ltd* (1982)). The mortgagor's equity of redemption has already been extinguished by the mortgagee's contract for sale (*National and Provincial Building Society v Ahmed* (1995), **15.20**), and the mortgagor can raise no complaint against the mortgagee except where it can be shown that the power of sale was exercised in an improper, harsh or oppressive manner. Furthermore, the mortgagor cannot impeach the title of the purchaser on the ground that the mortgagee's power of sale was improperly exercised unless the purchaser had actual knowledge or 'shut eye' (or 'blind eye') knowledge of the irregularity (see LPA s 104(2), as applied in *Meretz Investments NV v ACP Ltd (No 3)* (2006) at [320]-[322] per Lewison J).

Following sale the mortgagee becomes a trustee of the resulting proceeds of sale, which he must apply (see LPA 1925, s 105):

- *first*, in payment of all costs, charges and expenses properly incurred by him in connection with the sale;

- *second*, in discharge of the mortgage money and interest due under his mortgage; and
- *third*, in payment of the residue to the subsequent mortgagee or chargee (if any) and otherwise to the mortgagor. (For this purpose the selling mortgagee is fixed with deemed notice of any other mortgage or charge entered in the register (LRA 2002, s 54).)

The duty of the selling mortgagee

15.22   Perhaps the most controversial feature of the law of mortgage relates to the precise nature of the duty incumbent on the mortgagee who sells the security pursuant to an express or statutory power of sale. The selling mortgagee is commonly said not to be a *trustee* for the mortgagor in respect of the power of sale itself (*Cuckmere Brick Co Ltd v Mutual Finance Ltd* (1971)). The mortgagee, unlike a true fiduciary, is clearly entitled to have regard to his *own* interests in the matter of sale and is even entitled to give these interests priority over those of the mortgagor (*Meretz Investments NV v ACP Ltd (No 3)* (2006) at [299] per Lewison J). However, common law and equity alike have 'set bounds to the extent to which he can look after himself and ignore the mortgagor's interests' (*Palk v Mortgage Services Funding plc* (1993) per Nicholls V-C), limitations which are now reinforced in certain respects by the Financial Services and Markets Act 2000.

— *Debatable level of protection*   Although the mortgagee is plainly entitled to protect his own interests, he is 'not entitled to conduct himself in a way which unfairly prejudices the mortgagor' (*Palk v Mortgage Services Funding plc* (1993) per Nicholls V-C). Despite this rhetoric, the past decade of mortgagee sales provides no real ground for optimism about human nature or the vitality of the altruistic spirit. Mortgagee sales have tended to demonstrate the most appalling unconcern for the interests of hapless borrowers, an indifference which the courts have done relatively little to curb. Time and again mortgagee sales have been motivated by a desire merely to achieve a sufficient price to cover the mortgagee's outstanding loan and incidental costs, even if little or no surplus is left for the mortgagor. Some index of this apathy is provided by the fact that, in recent times, it has been possible, in certain parts of this country, to purchase a house for no more than £4,000 or £5,000—an astonishing testament to man's commercial inhumanity to fellow man.

— *A fusion of subjective and objective duties*   On paper, at least, the conduct of the selling mortgagee stands to be judged with reference to two criteria, one *subjective* in nature and the other *objective* (see *Freeguard v Royal Bank of Scotland plc* (2002) at [11]).

• *Subjective criterion* The mortgagee must always act in good faith: he must not deal 'wilfully and recklessly ... with the property in such a manner that the interests of the mortgagor are sacrificed' (*Kennedy v De Trafford* (1897) per Lord Herschell). This subjective requirement of *good faith* relates essentially to the avoidance of conflicts of interest which might lead the court to set aside improperly transacted sales. The demands of good faith also necessitate that a desire to recover the debt secured must be at least some part of the motivation of the selling mortgagee, but 'purity of purpose' on his part is not essential (see *Meretz Investments NV v ACP Ltd (No 3)* (2006) at [314] per Lewison J).

• *Objective criterion* The mortgagee also owes a duty of reasonable care or diligence both to the mortgagor (*Palk v Mortgage Services Funding plc* (1993) per Nicholls V-C) and to any subsequent mortgagee or relevant surety (*Raja v Lloyds TSB Bank plc* (2001) at [25] per Judge LJ). This objective requirement of *reasonable care* is an equitable incident 'arising out of the particular relationship between mortgagee and mortgagor' (*AIB Finance Ltd v Debtors* (1998) per Nourse LJ). Its breach usually generates a mere monetary liability in respect of any financial loss which is caused, e.g. by careless or imprudent exercise of the mortgagee's power of sale (see LPA 1925, s 104(2)). Thus, for instance, a sale at an undervalue gives the mortgagor only a money remedy (see e.g. *Mortgage Express v Mardner* (2004)): the mortgagee is required to account for the proceeds of sale as if the full proper price had been received (*Bishop v Blake* (2006) at [109]). The undervalue will lead to the transaction of sale being *set aside* only where the purchaser 'has knowledge of, or participates in, an impropriety in the exercise of the power' (*Corbett v Halifax Building Society* (2003) at [26], [33] per Pumfrey J).

It is likely that the subjective and objective tests of the conduct expected of the selling mortgagee often coalesce in practice, in that to 'take reasonable precautions to obtain a proper price is but part of the duty to act in good faith' (*Forsyth v Blundell* (1973) per Menzies J).

— *Duty in respect of sale price* Building society mortgagees were long subject to a statutory duty to take 'reasonable care to ensure' that the price achieved on the exercise of their power of sale was 'the best price that can reasonably be obtained' (Building Societies Act 1986, s 13(7), Sch 4, para 1(1)(a), (2)). This obligation has now been subsumed (see Building Societies Act 1997, s 12(2)) within the general duty imposed by the courts on all categories of mortgagee.

• *Duty of reasonable care* All selling mortgagees nowadays have a responsibility to 'take reasonable precautions to obtain the true market value of the mortgaged property' (*Cuckmere Brick Co Ltd v Mutual Finance Ltd* (1971) per Salmon LJ). This duty is non-delegable: the mortgagee is not relieved from responsibility merely because he entrusts the sale to an apparently competent or experienced agent. The mortgagee's duty is, moreover, owed to any guarantor of the mortgage and to others interested in the equity of redemption. (A similar duty is imposed on those who lend under mortgage contracts regulated by the Financial Services and Markets Act 2000 (see MCOB (2007), 13.6.1R(2)).)

- *A limited standard*   It is clear that perfection is not required of the mortgagee, but merely that he should invest reasonable care in the exercise of his power of sale (see *Michael v Miller* (2004) at [138]–[144] per Jonathan Parker LJ). The mortgagee must ensure that the premises are 'fairly and properly exposed to the market', but is not required to incur expense in seeking to boost their market value by making improvements or by initiating applications for planning permission or by granting profitable leases (*Silven Properties Ltd v Royal Bank of Scotland plc* (2004) at [16]–[20] per Lightman J). Again, where a mortgagee sells up business premises, there may be a limited duty to pursue a sale of the land together with the business as a going concern, but this duty cannot apply where the mortgagor had already ceased trading before the mortgagee obtained possession (see *AIB Finance Ltd v Debtors* (1998)).

- *Modalities of sale*   It is readily recognised that a forced sale by a mortgagee seldom achieves the 'highest', 'best possible' or even 'market' price, but the mortgagee is not simply entitled to adopt *any* arrangement or accept *any* price merely because it will see him paid out. The mortgagee must, for example, take reasonable steps to ascertain the value of the property before sale and must make a reasonable effort (by advertisement or otherwise) to bring the proposed sale and the property's most advantageous features to the attention of all persons likely to be interested. It is nearly always improper for the mortgagee simply to accept the first offer received (see e.g. *Bishop v Blake* (2006)). Where the mortgaged property is sold at auction, the mortgagee's duty of care is almost certainly breached if the auctioneer is instructed to do no more than 'put the property under the hammer'. Such a procedure 'may be appropriate to the sale of second hand furniture but is not necessarily conducive to the attainment of the best price for freehold or leasehold property' (*Tse Kwong Lam v Wong Chit Sen* (1983) per Lord Templeman).

> *Cuckmere Brick Co Ltd v Mutual Finance Ltd* (1971) A mortgagee realised the mortgaged property through sale by auction. Although informed expressly of a relevant (but fairly complex) planning permission relating to the property, the mortgagee failed to make adequate reference in the auction advertisements to the full extent of the permission. In consequence the land was sold at an undervalue. The Court of Appeal held the mortgagee liable in damages to the mortgagor for breach of the duty of care which it owed to the latter.

— *Timing of the sale* Once his power of sale has accrued, the mortgagee is prima facie entitled to exercise it for his own purposes at any time of his own choice (*Parker-Tweedale v Dunbar Bank plc* (1991) per Nourse LJ). The mortgagee is under no general duty to wait for an upturn in the property market and, save in circumstances of proven bad faith, is not liable for any increased sale price which the property might have commanded at a later and more propitious moment (see *Downsview Nominees Ltd v First City Corpn Ltd* (1993)). Recent case law has indicated, however, that a mortgagee may not entirely 'ignore the consequence that a short delay might result in a higher price' (*Meftah v Lloyds TSB Bank plc* (2001) at [9(h)] per Lawrence Collins J). There is, moreover, one further (and potentially crucial) limitation on the mortgagee's arbitrary power to determine the date of sale. It is open to a defaulting mortgagor to accelerate the sale of the mortgaged property by invoking the court's discretion, pursuant to LPA 1925, s 91(2), to order sale at the request of either the mortgagor or the mortgagee, notwithstanding that 'any other person dissents'.

> *Palk v Mortgage Services Funding plc* (1993) H and W defaulted on their mortgage, but managed to negotiate a private sale for £283,000. Their mortgagee declined to agree to the sale (since the total mortgage debt amounted to £358,000), and proposed instead to let the property on short-term leases until such time as the housing market improved. This strategy would have caused the mortgagors' overall debt to increase by some £30,000 each year and in desperation W sought a court-directed sale of the property in order to stem the financial haemorrhage. The Court of Appeal ordered a sale under LPA 1925, s 91(2), notwithstanding that H and W could currently show only a negative equity in the property and that £75,000 of the mortgagee's debt was left unsecured and outstanding. There was, said Nicholls V-C a 'manifest unfairness' in allowing the mortgagee to gamble on a rising market while saddling the mortgagor with a personal and open-ended liability for the ever-increasing mortgage deficit.

The discretion available under LPA 1925, s 91(2) thus provides, in appropriate cases, a valuable avenue to relief for certain categories of mortgagor caught in the trap of negative equity and escalating mortgage costs. The *Palk* decision throws the mortgagor a lifeline which may enable him or her to escape a calamitous situation in which debts increase exponentially beyond any hope of repayment from the proceeds of an eventual sale. The accelerated sale by court order in *Palk*, although not extinguishing all liability under the mortgage (**15.18**), at least substantially reduced the capital debt on which ongoing interest was chargeable to the mortgagor.

— *Conflicts of interest* The impact of the mortgagee's duty of good faith is nowadays most obviously apparent in the courts' response to cases where there is a potential conflict between the interest of the mortgagee as *vendor* in obtaining the highest price and some collateral interest of the mortgagee in achieving a lower price for the *purchaser*. In such circumstances the appropriate remedy for the mortgagor is normally rescission of the sale and return of the security. The closer the association between mortgagee and purchaser, the less likely is the court to allow the transaction of sale to stand.

- A sale by the mortgagee to *himself* (or to his solicitor or other agent) is 'no sale at all' and is hopelessly invalid, even though the sale price is the full value of the mortgaged property (*Farrar v Farrars Ltd* (1888)). (The only escape route from such an impasse lies in an application pursuant to LPA 1925, s 91(2) for a court-ordered sale (see *Palk v Mortgage Services Funding plc* (1993) per Nicholls V-C): there are some circumstances where the only potential purchaser is the *mortgagee*).

- A sale by the mortgagee to *less closely associated persons* (e.g. a business acquaintance or a company in which the mortgagee is himself a shareholder) is not *automatically* ineffective. Instead, the normal onus of proof is reversed and the burden rests on the mortgagee to 'show that the sale was in good faith and that the mortgagee took reasonable precautions to obtain the best price reasonably obtainable at the time' (*Tse Kwong Lam v Wong Chit Sen* (1983) per Lord Templeman).

> *Tse Kwong Lam v Wong Chit Sen* (1983) H, a mortgagee, exercised his power of sale by means of a public auction at which the only bidder was his wife, W, acting as the representative of the family company of which both were directors and shareholders. In the absence of competitive bidding, the property was purchased at the reserve price, fixed by H, which was of course clearly known to the purchaser. The purchase was financed from funds provided by H himself. The Judicial Committee of the Privy Council held that H had failed to show that 'in all respects he acted fairly to the borrower and used his best endeavours to obtain the best price reasonably obtainable for the mortgaged property'. The Privy Council indicated, however, that although rescission of the sale would normally have been the appropriate remedy, this remedy was rendered inequitable here by reason of the mortgagor's 'inexcusable delay' (nine years) in prosecuting his counterclaim. The mortgagor was thus relegated to damages, which were measured as the difference between the actual sale price and the best price reasonably obtainable at the date of sale.

Foreclosure

15.23 Foreclosure is the most draconian remedy open to the mortgagee in the event of default by his mortgagor. Foreclosure abrogates the mortgagor's equity of redemption and leaves the *entire* value of the mortgaged land in the hands of the mortgagee—irrespective of the amount of the mortgage debt. In view of its drastic nature, the remedy of foreclosure is available only on application to the court (see LPA 1925, ss 88(2), 89(2); LRR 2003, r 112) and, for the same reason, foreclosure actions 'are almost unheard of today and have been so for many years' (*Palk v Mortgage Services Funding plc* (1993) per Nicholls V-C).

Remedies available to the equitable mortgagee or chargee

15.24　The remedies available to an equitable mortgagee or chargee differ from those which are open to a legal mortgagee in that most owners of an equitable security have no automatic power of sale, but must apply to the court for an order permitting sale of the property charged (see LPA 1925, ss 90(1), 91(2). **9.20**). The statutory power to appoint a receiver is available only in respect of mortgages created by deed (LPA 1925, s 101(1)(iii)), but in the absence of such creation the court may be asked to appoint a receiver (Supreme Court Act 1981, s 37(1)–(2)).

Priority of mortgages over a legal estate

15.25　There is, of course, nothing inherently improper in multiple mortgages of realty, the only limiting factor usually being the capacity for further commercial exploitation of the remaining 'equity' in the property (**8.28**). Sometimes, however, difficult questions of priority arise where the same land has been mortgaged several times over to different mortgagees and the security eventually proves inadequate to satisfy all due claims.

> **Problem:** Suppose that two mortgagees, M1 and M2, take mortgages over a legal estate in Greenacre. The rules of priority which determine the order in which their claims are met out of the proceeds of sale of the security depend on:
>
> - whether title to Greenacre is *registered* or *unregistered*
> - whether the mortgages are *legal* or *equitable*.

Mortgages of a legal estate in registered land

15.26　If M1 takes a charge over a legal estate in registered land, issues of priority turn on whether his charge is itself *legal* (**8.29**) or *equitable* (**9.18**).

— *Legal charge over legal estate*   If M1 holds a *legal* charge over a registered (and therefore legal) estate in Greenacre (i.e. where M1's charge has been completed by his registration as proprietor of the charge), M1's charge takes priority over:

- any legal charge of M2 registered subsequently against the title to Greenacre, even if M2's charge was actually created *before* that of M1 (LRA 2002, ss 29(1), (2)(a)(i), 48(1), **8.30**); and

- any equitable charge created in favour of M2 *after* the date of registration of M1's charge; and

- any *earlier* equitable charge created in favour of M2 which was not protected by the entry of a 'notice' prior to the registration of M1's charge or, in unusual circumstances, protected by virtue of its status as an *overriding interest* at the date of creation of M1's charge (LRA 2002, s 29(1)–(2)).

— *Equitable charge over legal estate*   If, however, M1 holds merely an *equitable* charge over the registered estate in Greenacre, this charge requires protection by the entry of a 'notice' in the register of title to Greenacre (LRA 2002, ss 32–4).

- M1's charge, if protected by 'notice', takes priority over any legal (ie registered) charge later taken by M2, since all subsequent dispositions for value relating to Greenacre inevitably take effect subject to existing entries in the register (LRA 2002, s 29(1), (2)(a)(i), **2.32, 12.9**).

- M1's charge, if *not* protected by 'notice', loses priority to any *legal* charge subsequently registered in the name of M2 (LRA 2002, s 29(1), (2)(a)(i)), unless, unusually, M1's charge is an overriding interest (**2.33, 12.15**).

- M1's charge, whether protected or not, normally retains priority over any merely *equitable* charge created for M2 subsequent to the date of creation of M1's charge (LRA 2002, s 28(1), **12.8**). This order of priority remains generally unaffected by the possibility that M2's equitable charge (although *created* later) may at some future date be the first to be protected by an entry in the register (see *Mortgage Corpn Ltd v Nationwide Credit Corpn Ltd* (1994)). This priority rule will, of course, be reversed with the advent of electronic conveyancing. Under the electronic regime the creation and registration of such charges will become inseparable (**2.26**), with the consequence that the order of entry in the register will be definitive and conclusive as to priority.

Mortgages of a legal estate in unregistered land

15.27   If M1 takes a mortgage over a legal estate in unregistered land, issues of priority again turn on whether his mortgage is itself *legal* (**8.31**) or *equitable* (**9.18**).

— *Legal mortgage over legal estate* The rules of priority depend on whether M1's security is reinforced by custody of the title deeds relating to Greenacre (**8.31**).

• If M1 holds *both* a legal mortgage *and* the title deeds, M1's mortgage is good against the world (**2.38, 12.34**). Such a mortgage will have triggered a compulsory registration of the mortgaged estate and the consequent entry of M1's proprietorship of a registered charge (**8.31**). M1's mortgage therefore enjoys priority over any mortgage, legal or equitable, subsequently taken by M2.

• If M1 *does not* have control of the title deeds, his charge cannot constitute a 'protected first legal charge' (**7.7**) and triggers no compulsory registration of either the mortgagor's estate or M1's charge. M1's charge remains a legal charge over an unregistered estate and takes priority over any later mortgage (legal or equitable) taken by M2 *only* if M1 has registered his charge as a *puisne mortgage* under Class C(i) of the Land Charges Act 1972 (see LCA 1972, ss 2(4), 4(5), **8.31, 12.36**).

— *Equitable mortgage over legal estate* Again something depends on whether M1 has protected his security by taking custody of the title deeds relating to Greenacre.

• If M1 holds the title deeds (**9.19**), his equitable mortgage enjoys priority over any subsequent mortgage in favour of M2, unless M2 takes a *legal* mortgage over Greenacre without notice, actual or constructive, of M1's prior charge. Although the issue has been confused by old authorities (see e.g. *Oliver v Hinton* (1899)), it is almost certain that the mortgagor's inability to hand over the title deeds to M2 fixes M2 with notice of the existence of the earlier mortgage.

• If M1 does not hold the title deeds, his equitable mortgage takes priority over any later mortgage (legal or equitable) taken by M2 *only* if M1's equitable mortgage has been registered as a *general equitable charge* under Class C(iii) of the Land Charges Act 1972 (see LCA 1972, ss 2(4), 4(5), **9.18, 12.36**).

Priority of mortgages over an equitable interest in land

15.28   A mortgage of an equitable interest in land can itself be *equitable* only. Equitable interests generally presuppose the existence of a trust of land (**9.35**). Where default by the beneficial owner of a mortgaged equitable interest leads to a sale of the trust land (**11.35**), competing mortgagees of that equitable interest must look to the trustees for repayment of their respective loans out of the proceeds of the sale. It is not therefore unnatural that priority between such mortgagees should turn, in both *registered* and *unregistered* land, on a rule which stipulates that the trustees are normally obliged to pay off the mortgagees in the same order as that in which the trustees received *written notification* of the mortgages (LPA 1925, s 137(1)–(2)). This is the so-called rule in *Dearle v Hall* (1823) (**9.17**), to which there is only one basic exception. No mortgagee can ever claim priority if, at the time of making his loan, he knew (or should have known) of the existence of an earlier mortgage created in favour of another creditor (see *Re Holmes* (1885)). It would clearly be inequitable that, by the mere device of serving notice first, the later mortgagee should steal priority over an earlier mortgage of which he was (or ought to have been) fully aware. In effect, therefore, the rule in *Dearle v Hall* accords priority only to mortgagees who have no actual or constructive knowledge of existing incumbrances.

FURTHER READING

Gray and Gray, *Elements of Land Law* (4th edn, OUP, 2005), ch 15.

Relevant sections of this work and other land law textbooks may be supplemented with:

Gravells, Nigel 'Undue Influence and Substitute Mortgages' [2005] *CLJ* 42.

Haley, Michael 'Mortgage default: possession, relief and judicial discretion' (1997) 17 *Legal Studies* 483.

McMurtry, Lara 'The Section 36 Discretion: Policy and Practicality' [2002] *Conv* 594.

McMurtry, Lara 'Unconscionability and Undue Influence: An Interaction' [2000] *Conv* 573.

Omar, Paul 'Equitable Interests and the Secured Creditor: Determining Priorities' [2006] *Conv* 509.

Pawlowski, Mark and Brown, James *Undue Influence and the Family Home* (Cavendish, 2002).

Thompson, Mark 'Wives, Sureties and Banks' [2002] *Conv* 174.

Whitehouse, Lisa 'The Home-owner: Citizen or Consumer?', in S. Bright and J.K. Dewar (eds), *Land Law: Themes and Perspectives* (OUP, 1998), p 183.

SELF-TEST QUESTIONS

1 How does the protection offered to defaulting mortgagors compare with that available to tenants facing forfeiture of their leases (**14.11–14.14, 15.20**)?

2 Have the developments of the law brought about by the decisions in *Boland* (1981), *O'Brien* (1994) and *Etridge (No 2)* (2002) promoted or impeded the cause of sexual equality (**12.24, 15.4, 15.10–15.11**)?

3 What duty of care does the mortgagee owe to the defaulting borrower whose home he proposes to sell (**15.22**)?

Index